THE CAMBRIDGE HISTORY OF SOUTH AFRICA

VOLUME I

From Early Times to 1885

Written in light of South Africa's achievement of majority rule, this book takes a critical and searching look at the country's past. It presents South Africa's past in an objective, clear, and refreshing manner. With chapters contributed by ten of the best historians of the country, the book pulls together four decades of revisionist scholarship to present a detailed overview of the South African past, from the Early Iron Age to the eve of the mineral revolution on the Rand. Its findings incorporate new sources, methods, and concepts, for example, providing new data on the relations between Africans and colonial invaders and rethinking crucial issues of identity and consciousness. This book represents an important reassessment of all the major historical events, developments, and records of South Africa – written, oral, and archaeological – and will be an important new tool for students and professors of African history worldwide.

Carolyn Hamilton obtained her Ph.D. from The Johns Hopkins University in 1993. Formerly Director of South Africa's first Graduate School for the Humanities at the University of the Witwatersrand, she led the Constitution of Public Intellectual Life Research Project at Wits and is now NRF Research Professor in Archive and Public Culture, University of Cape Town. An authority on South Africa's precolonial history, she is internationally recognized for her book *Terrific Majesty: The Powers of Shaka Zulu and the Limits of Historical Invention* (1998), and for her work interrogating the concept of the archive and elucidating its political effects.

Bernard K. Mbenga holds his doctorate in history from the University of South Africa and, since 1987, has been a lecturer at the Mafikeng Campus of North-West University in South Africa (formerly the University of Bophuthatswana in Mmabatho). He has published papers in the *South African Historical Journal, Teaching History,* and the *Journal of Southern African Studies*. Professor Mbenga is the co-editor and co-author (with Hermann Giliomee) of the highly acclaimed *New History of South Africa* (2007).

Robert Ross received a Ph.D. from Cambridge in 1974 and has worked since then at Leiden University, the Netherlands. He has written seven books, including *A Concise History of South Africa* and *Status and Respectability in the Cape Colony: A Tragedy of Manners*, both published by Cambridge University Press in 1999.

THE CAMBRIDGE HISTORY OF SOUTH AFRICA

VOLUME I

From Early Times to 1885

Edited by

CAROLYN HAMILTON

University of Cape Town, Republic of South Africa

BERNARD K. MBENGA

North-West University, Mafikeng Campus, Republic of South Africa

ROBERT ROSS

Leiden University, Netherlands

CAMBRIDGE
UNIVERSITY PRESS

CAMBRIDGE
UNIVERSITY PRESS

University Printing House, Cambridge CB2 8BS, United Kingdom

One Liberty Plaza, 20th Floor, New York, NY 10006, USA

477 Williamstown Road, Port Melbourne, VIC 3207, Australia

4843/24, 2nd Floor, Ansari Road, Daryaganj, Delhi - 110002, India

79 Anson Road, #06-04/06, Singapore 079906

Cambridge University Press is part of the University of Cambridge.

It furthers the University's mission by disseminating knowledge in the pursuit of education, learning and research at the highest international levels of excellence.

www.cambridge.org
Information on this title: www.cambridge.org/9780521517942

© Cambridge University Press 2010

First published 2010

A catalogue record for this publication is available from the British Library

Library of Congress Cataloging in Publication data
The Cambridge history of South Africa / edited by Carolyn Hamilton, Bernard Mbenga, Robert Ross.
    p.   cm.
Includes bibliographical references and index.
ISBN 978-0-521-51794-2 (hardback)
1. South Africa – History.   I. Hamilton, Carolyn.   II. Mbenga, Bernard.
III. Ross, Robert, 1949 July 26–   IV. Title: History of South Africa.
DT1787.C36   2009
968–dc22   2009028976

ISBN 978-0-521-51794-2 Hardback

For Jessica Kuper

CONTENTS

ACKNOWLEDGEMENTS

The initial commissioning of these volumes was done by Jessica Kuper at Cambridge University Press. Since then, tragically, she has been struck down by sickness, so she has not been able to see these volumes through to their conclusion. We would like to dedicate this volume to her.

In addition to the support of our own institutions, and from Cambridge University Press, we specifically want to thank the National Research Foundation of South Africa for their funding of a workshop in Cape Town at which drafts of some of these chapters were discussed. The comments of the various contributors to the two volumes, at this workshop and on other occasions, and of the Press's reviewers, also, we hope, strengthened the work, and for this we are very grateful.

NOTE ON TERMINOLOGY

With regard to the orthography of words, primarily ethnonyms, deriving from Bantu languages, we have followed what is becoming the standard South African practice. When the words are used adjectivally, they do not have prefixes; in words from Nguni languages the root is capitalised, but not the prefix; and in words from Sotho-Tswana languages the prefix, but not the root, is capitalised. Thus "amaZulu", but "Basotho" and "Zulu and Sotho households".

EDITORS' INTRODUCTION

This volume is the first of two, covering the history of South Africa from about 2,000 years ago until the first democratic elections in 1994. Volume I is concerned with that history until the mid-1880s; volume II continues the story in the subsequent eleven decades.

During the period covered in this, the first, volume, South Africa was what is conventionally known as a "geographical expression" and had no status as a unit of government. For this reason, we do not limit ourselves to the modern boundaries of the Republic of South Africa. There are good reasons to consider the region of which South Africa forms the core to be a useful category for analysis. However, in dealing with the period covered in this volume, it is necessary to expand the coverage to include Lesotho, Swaziland, parts of southern Mozambique and eastern Botswana. In other words, we are dealing largely with the area to the south of the Limpopo, plus, to a certain degree, that to the west of its upper reaches and in the west of the continent to the south of the Gariep (Orange) river. Even this cannot be a hard line. There were moments during which the Limpopo valley itself was the center of political and social developments, so any division between the north and the south banks would be totally artificial. There were other times when the polities centered on the Zimbabwe plateau exercised power to the south of the river. Equally, certainly in the twentieth century, but also earlier, the political and economic sway of what was becoming South Africa was exercised far to the north of the Limpopo and certainly of the Gariep. We have attempted to be cognizant of such matters. On the other hand, this volume does not provide any systematic coverage of the history of Namibia nor of Botswana.

The question of time is a trickier matter. People have lived in the region for as long as there have been people on Earth. Exactly how long that has been depends on which of the various primates should be considered to have been genuinely human. However, no matter what decision is made on this matter, South Africa can be considered part of the cradle of humankind.

The criterion used to decide when these volumes should start was, in fact, not biological but economic. Approximately 2,000 years ago a major shift occurred, as for the first time in the history of South Africa men and women began producing food, both by growing crops and by tending animals, rather than, or in addition to, hunting game, gathering plant food and, where possible, shellfish, and fishing. From a global perspective, this was relatively late. In most other parts of the world where it was possible, this transition had long been made. As elsewhere, though, the transition entailed a major shift not merely in economic but also in social and political relations.

The division between the two volumes has been made on the basis of political and economic criteria. By the mid-1880s, virtually all of what was to become a quarter of a century later the Union of South Africa had been brought under the control of either British colonial government or of one of the Afrikaner republics. In other words, by then the last African polities had lost their independence, and nearly all the inhabitants of the region had become subject to one of these powers. At about the same time, not coincidentally, the industrialization of South Africa was beginning. The term "preindustrial" thus demarcates clearly the period the volume covers. However, we are alert to the possibility that such a term can be read as suggesting a teleological approach or as a signal of an evolutionary view, in terms of which "preindustrial" might be read as connoting "not yet" industrial. To signal our awareness of these possible meanings of the term we have elected to use the term without its customary hyphenation. We do the same with regard to the term "precolonial" for the same reason. The essays in this volume, we hope, demonstrate how both colonial conquest and industrialization emerged out of historical processes and were thus not the inevitabilities that a teleological view of South African history would assume.

This is not the first attempt to write a synthetic history of South Africa. In 1936, Eric Walker, at that time King George V Professor of History at the University of Cape Town and subsequently professor of imperial history at Cambridge University, worked as one of the editors of volume VIII of *The Cambridge History of the British Empire: South Africa, Rhodesia and the High Commission Territories.*[1] Valuable though this was in its way, and important as South Africa's imperial and colonial connections have been, as we stress in these volumes, the perspective that necessarily derived from such a project could not place in the foreground the developments going on within the country, except as part of the empire. In these volumes, we have attempted,

---

[1] E. A. Benians, A. P. Newton, J. Holland Rose (Eds.), *The Cambridge History of the British Empire*, 8 vols. (Cambridge: Cambridge University Press, 1929–1959). Volume VIII, on South Africa, was originally published in 1936 and reprinted, in a new edition, in 1963.

in so far as the available scholarship allows, to see the connections within the region that was to become South Africa not only as being imperial, though we would not deny the importance of those relationships, but also as transcending oceans and land borders in a much more diverse way than was possible in 1936. We also stress the connections across time between what went before and what came after colonial conquest, in a way of which Walker and his fellow editors could not conceive. Even more clearly, as was typical of the time, the original *Cambridge History* scarcely mentioned the actions and the agency of black South Africans. By 2009 such omissions are, thankfully, something of the past.

In the late 1960s Leonard Thompson and Monica Wilson edited the *Oxford History of South Africa*.[2] This work programmatically stressed the importance of the interaction between "peoples of diverse origins, languages, technologies, ideologies and social systems, meeting on South African soil." The volumes came at the beginning of a florescence of South African history, much of which defined itself in opposition to the *Oxford History*. The major weaknesses of the *Oxford History* were a tendency not to recognize the fluidity of identities in Southern African history, thus making the interaction of "peoples" the core of its analysis, and also, certainly in Volume II, not providing a clear narrative of events. The attempts at synthetic narratives, on the other hand, of which there have been several,[3] were, and are, implicitly or explicitly primarily concerned with the long-term establishment of apartheid and its effects. There was also the sense that these syntheses and much of the historical work on South Africa done between 1970, if not earlier, and the 1990s in its way attempted to fulfill Barrington Moore's injunction that "if the men [sic] of the future are ever to break the chains of the present, they will have to understand the forces that forged them."[4] These works do not emphasize the period before colonial conquest, which we believe to be of particular consequence for the development of a history that addresses the needs and desires of post-apartheid South Africa.

The present volumes, then, conceived and written well after 1994, can take advantage of the post-apartheid moment of South African history. Nevertheless, there is a great paradox in doing so. How can the history

---

[2] Two vols. (Oxford: Clarendon Press, 1968 and 1971).

[3] E.g., L. M. Thompson, *A History of South Africa* (New Haven and London: Yale University Press, 1990); N. Worden, *The Making of Modern South Africa: Conquest, Segregation and Apartheid* (Oxford: Blackwells, 1994); W. Beinart, *Twentieth Century South Africa* (Oxford: Oxford University Press, 1994); R. Ross, *A Concise History of South Africa* (Cambridge: Cambridge University Press, 1999); T. R. H. Davenport, *South Africa: A Modern History* (London: Macmillan, 1978. In subsequent editions together with C.C. Saunders).

[4] B. Moore, *Social Origins of Dictatorship and Democracy: Lord and Peasant in the Making of the Modern World* (London: Allen Lane, 1966), p. 50.

of the new South Africa be represented in what might be described as an imperialist, even a settler, format? A *Cambridge History* almost by definition emanates from the center of the British establishment and, in this case, is based on scholarship, although revisionist, radical, and drawing on African oral history, that developed primarily in the historically white, Anglophone South African universities and their British and American equivalents. Unavoidably, the political and social concerns, the linguistic abilities, and the European intellectual heritage of many scholars in these departments drove them in particular directions and closed off other avenues of approach.

These volumes are based to a great degree on scholarship that preceded the fall of apartheid, and as yet there have been limited signs of a blooming of new historiographies. This is especially the case in relation to Volume I. It is a paradox that cannot be denied; it has to be embraced. As Judge Albie Sachs of the South African Constitutional Court put it during a colloquium on a draft of Chapter 1 of this volume, "such a paradox is typical of our times and of post-apartheid South Africa." We – the editors and authors of these volumes – can only try to be thoroughly conscious of what is involved.

The further consequence of the times in which these volumes are being produced is that all involved realize that what they have written cannot be seen as a master narrative to determine the course of historical writing for the foreseeable future. We are neither under the illusion nor do we pretend that what we have written will endure free from criticism. Indeed, we are certain that the changing composition of the South African historical profession and the inclusion in it of many people from backgrounds or orientations that were previously marginalized or excluded will lead to a whole variety of new emphases and approaches. South African scholarship is discarding its exclusive intellectual dependence on Europe and America, and the development of dynamic new south–south intellectual links are leading us to a variety of new emphases and approaches.

We are, however, confident that we are able to provide a reasonable summation of the current state of knowledge and that, at least in a number of places, we present fresh insights. We hope that what we have written has, above all, two main virtues. First, we expect it to provide an entry into South African history for those who come from the outside, that is to say, historians specialized in other areas of the globe, those with backgrounds in other disciplines who need a basis of historical understanding and those who are coming fresh into historical studies. Also, of course, we expect that those who are specialized in one period of South African history may use these volumes to illuminate those areas in which they are not specialists. Second, these volumes will, we hope, allow scholars to see where the hiatuses in the historiography of South Africa lie. They are thus intended to be both a summation of the current state of research and facilitative in the creation of new agendas for moving that research into places that, as yet, we cannot imagine.

At the moment at which the period covered by this volume begins, then, society in the region was homogenous in the sense that all its members acquired their livelihood as hunters and gatherers. The most crucial change away from this homogeneity came early, with the introduction of agriculture and stockbreeding, and then, in the last few centuries of the period, colonial conquest. Between them, as this volume shows, the shifting economic base of African society and the imposition of colonialism led, each in its own way, to the reorganization of the ways in which access to land and labor was organized. Thus, by the end, that society – a very different one, of course, in a variety of ways – was highly heterogeneous. Admittedly, conquest by the British or descendants of European immigrants had been more or less completed, but social or economic, let alone ideological, homogeneity had not been imposed, nor had all inhabitants been incorporated into a single economic or social system and hierarchy. There were hardly any dedicated hunters and gatherers still living within the borders of what was to become South Africa. Almost all the inhabitants of the region south of the Limpopo and the Gariep lived off agriculture, animal husbandry, or, increasingly, commerce and industry. The urbanization and later industrialization, which came with the discovery of great mineral wealth in the South African interior, were also under way.

The processes of settlement, of conquest, and of social transformation were not in any way uniform. In some areas, agriculture developed early; in others, very late. In some areas, colonial conquest occurred relatively early, from the mid-seventeenth century in the southwestern corner of the country; in others it was very late, and, in what is now Limpopo province and northern KwaZulu-Natal, conquest had scarcely been completed by the mid-1880s. Equally, certain material and immaterial elements of colonialism – for instance, the use of guns and, where they could be kept, horses – were taken on board well in advance of colonial conquest and indeed often delayed it, whereas others – monogamy, wage labor, and rectangular housing, for instance – were only accepted very much later. For this reason, even without its teleological implications, the description of periods of South African history as "precolonial" is fairly meaningless. This naturally has consequences for the organization of this volume, which must necessarily reflect this diversity across space and time. Although we have attempted to maintain a loose chronological order both within and between the various chapters, it is not feasible to be too strict in such matters. The processes of history are rarely as tidy as the analysts would make them appear.

Nevertheless, a number of constant themes recur throughout these chapters, and we can only signal them at this point. First, and fundamentally,

until the very end of the period covered in this volume, South Africa was
predominantly a rural region and, at least in the last thousand years, an
agricultural and pastoral one. This had clear consequences for a variety
of other spheres, most notably gender relations. The development of the
homestead structure of the agro-pastoralists, and later of the farms of the
colonists, froze the relations between men and women and ensured the subordination of the latter. The relations of production and reproduction were
henceforth organized around the distinction between the sexes, and social
ideology, and many institutions, developed accordingly. It is perhaps in the
story of its domestic arrangements that South African history has been most
conservative. What has changed is the visibility of women, and indeed of
other subaltern groups, within the historical record, and the readiness of
historians to look for them there.

The relative fixity of gender relations in Southern Africa contrasted
with the considerable fluidity of other forms of hierarchy and the associated ideologies. Thus, second, throughout the last two millennia of the
region's history, to the extent that this can be reconstructed, there have
been attempts by the rulers to set the social and political relations between
the various groups of society as firmly as possible. This was the case in the
kingdom centered on Mapungubwe at about the turn of the millennium;
in the large Tswana, Zulu, and other African states of the eighteenth and
nineteenth century; and in the colonial society that emanated from the
Cape from the mid-seventeenth century.

Successive regimes of widely differing backgrounds struggled to impose
a level of domination over their subjects and to develop a fully hegemonic
relationship over them, that is to say, to persuade them that the current
order of things, whatever it may have been at any given time, was natural
and unchanging. In this, they were invariably unsuccessful. No group from
among the excluded would, in the long term, tolerate its total exclusion
from the structures of power and certainly would not regard such exclusion
as in some way inevitable and natural. Because political allegiances were
always fragile and conditional upon the success of the rulers in bringing
peace, prosperity, and, often, rain, this meant that the history of South
African identities, in the long term, has been characterized by enormous
fluidity.

Third, part of the project of colonial rule was to attempt to change this.
British colonial rule, and less evidently the rule of the Afrikaner republics,
required control over the population that the new regimes were attempting
to administer and exploit and, in order to acquire such control, they had
to categorize their subjects. "Modernity," as it was envisaged and imposed,
could not cope with a fluidity of identities and attempted radically to
simplify and freeze them. The designation of various tracts of South Africa

as reserved for Africans, with the corollary that the rest of the country was for the rest of the population, was part of this process.

On the other hand, the very advance of the frontier of colonialism, defined in the loosest way, provided opportunities for those who, in the long term, it was to suppress. As a result, various of the identities South Africans adopted were fragmenting and new ones were being produced, whereas others were in the process of coagulation. Within this matrix, however, the colonists were attempting to harden the line between themselves and those under their rule. In other words, South Africa was well on the way to becoming a racist society.

The fourth theme relates to the third. Part of the reason for the development of this racist society was that it made impossible the forms of inclusive citizenship that prevailed in African societies. Because, in general, African rulers gained their power from the numbers of their followers, they were prepared to admit all who accepted their rule, although certainly not necessarily as equals. European traditions of rule, in contrast, saw incomers and subjects as laborers, or potentially as threats to property, and thus rejected strategies of incorporation. Europeans and their descendants were often more concerned about controlling material resources than people, in the belief that to do so would provide them with the necessary dominance over the population. The result was the commodification of land, which followed the imposition of colonial rule and which was one of the most salient processes in the period covered in this volume. Even within the colonial group, however, there was never unanimity about the categorization and treatment of the subject population, whether African or of slave descent. The line of unadulterated authoritarianism, although not at all uncommon, both among the military and among the settlers, could be tempered, both for reasons of humanitarian principle and of cost, by the acceptance of either African structures of rule or those Africans who were beginning to take on the education, and the religion, of the conquerors.

Fifth, what is clear and argued in the various chapters of this volume is that none of the objectives of colonialism were completely attained. Politically and economically, a degree of independence, and thus of agency, even within the colonial structures, was maintained by most South Africans. In terms of the ways in which families were organized, or the ways in which people tried to understand the world in which they lived and argued about why things were as they were, the processes of interaction between Africans and Europeans, and the influence they exerted on one another, only developed slowly. What was happening, as this volume shows, is that men and women were continually finding ways to adapt the old to the new worlds in which they found themselves, and to adopt, selectively and partially, what they found attractive in what was available. A variety of individuals – missionaries perhaps above all, but also colonial officials – saw themselves called upon to impose their own value systems on the Africans. The interaction this entailed forced them to confront African ways of thought and led some of them to accept rather more from this source than they had expected or at times were prepared to admit.

Settlers were concerned to instill their specific ideas of labor discipline and of a distinct ethos of private property. As against this, African chiefs found it necessary continually to rearrange their concepts of chiefdom in the light of the new circumstances. In particular, moreover, a whole variety of interstitial individuals, at home both in the colonial world and in that of the Africans, began to come to prominence. Some of them used their skills at straddling the two worlds to further their position within African societies; others attempted to claim acceptance into colonial society, often on the basis of their literacy, Christianity, and general "respectability." It was from this group, first most clearly developed in those areas of the country that had been in longest contact, and, indeed, conflict, with the Europeans, namely, the Cape Colony, both western and eastern, that the colored and African elites, whose nationalisms were eventually to challenge European hegemony, first began to achieve prominence.

A further change from what has been written before, whether in the *Cambridge History of the British Empire* or the *Oxford History*, is that the current generation of scholars is much more explicitly aware of its own relative ignorance. Part of the advantage of knowing more is that we see what we do not know more clearly. This has affected the way in which this volume is structured. The first chapter, written by the editors in more speculative mode than is perhaps common for such a venture, discusses the ways in which the pre-twentieth-century history of what was to become South Africa has been produced, both at the time itself and subsequently. This does not merely reflect upon but also attempts to explain how these volumes have taken on the structure that they have, as, in their own way, the product of that history of developing and changing historical consciousness.

CONTRIBUTORS

NORMAN ETHERINGTON
History Department
35 Stirling Highway
    Crawley WA 6009
Perth, Australia
nether@arts.uwa.edu.au

SIMON HALL
Department of Archaeology
University of Cape Town
Private Bag, Rondebosch, 7701
South Africa
Simon.Hall@uct.ac.za

CAROLYN HAMILTON
Department of Social
    Anthropology
University of Cape Town
Private Bag, Rondebosch 7701
    South Africa
carolyn.hamilton@uct.ac.za

PATRICK HARRIES
Historisches Seminar
Hirschgässlein, 21
4051, Basel, Switzerland
Patrick.Harries@unibas.ch

PAUL S. LANDAU
Department of History

University of Maryland
College Park, MD 20742
USA
PLandau@umd.edu

MARTIN LEGASSICK
Department of History
University of the Western Cape
Private Bag X17 Bellville 7535
South Africa
mlegassi@iafrica.com

BERNARD K. MBENGA
Department of History,
    Peace Studies and
    International Relations
North-West University
Mafikeng Campus
Private Bag 2046
Mmabatho 2735 South Africa
Bernard.Mbenga@nwu.ac.za

JOHN PARKINGTON
Department of Archaeology
University of Cape Town
Private Bag, Rondebosch, 7701
South Africa
john.parkington@uct.ac.za

ROBERT ROSS
Talen en Culturen van Afrika
Postbus 9515,
2300 RA Leiden Netherlands
r.j.ross@hum.leidenuniv.nl

JOHN WRIGHT
Department of History
University of KwaZulu-Natal
Private Bag X01 Scottsville 3209
South Africa
wright@ukzn.ac.za.

THE PRODUCTION OF PREINDUSTRIAL
SOUTH AFRICAN HISTORY

CAROLYN HAMILTON, BERNARD K. MBENGA, AND ROBERT ROSS

INTRODUCTION

A new and distinctively post-apartheid historiography has yet to find its feet in relation to the period covered by this volume. Since 1994, when the first democratic elections were held in South Africa, there have been significant changes in the nature of public discourses about South Africa's past. Settlerist and narrow nationalist (notably Afrikaner and Zulu) historical projects have, unsurprisingly, largely lost their impetus. Government efforts led by the African National Congress to invoke a new national past rooted in the black struggle against oppression have focused primarily on the twentieth century. The effort to achieve reconciliation and unity initially moved to deflect public discourse away from attending to the past except as it was manifested in the proceedings of, and the texts that flowed from the Truth and Reconciliation Commission set up in 1995, and in a handful of legacy projects undertaken by the Department of Arts, Culture, Science and Technology. Concomitantly, the 1990s saw the rapid growth of the particular genre of history commonly known as heritage – celebrating, commemorating, and often commodifying selected aspects of the past. Although heritage and public history courses and research have flourished, universities have experienced a sharp decline in the numbers of students enrolled in mainstream history courses, and the substantial cohorts of graduate students undertaking primary historical research, a feature of the radical history movement of the 1980s, have evaporated.

Our thanks to colleagues (especially our discussant, Natasha Erlank), who attended the 2005 Wits Institute for Social and Economic Research colloquium where we first presented a draft of this chapter, for their comments offered at the seminar and in some instances provided in writing. We also thank Peter Delius, Martin Hall, and Clive Kirkwood for their assistance.

Small but encouraging signs of things to come are discernible in a variety of areas. Significant challenges lie in how to approach, or augment, the available archive for the period covered by this volume – an archive for the most part powerfully shaped by the colonial and later apartheid eras in which it was established – to facilitate new kinds of research. Key secondary texts that have given definition to how this period is understood themselves require critical review. Likewise, the exclusion of other texts from the historical canon may warrant reassessment. In the chapter that follows we draw attention to the signs of new developments and attempt to provide an account of the production of history in South Africa that contextualizes the methodological challenges contemporary students of South African history face.

The chapter first draws attention to how little we know about the way understandings of the past were produced in precolonial times. We go on to identify key arenas of the production of history in the colonial period, from the earliest accounts produced in the Cape Colony to the emergence of a fully fledged settler historiography. The chapter teases out the contributions of missionaries' administrators and their local interlocutors to the archiving and interpretation of the early history of the region, as well as the contributions and challenges offered by an emerging black intelligentsia. It situates the development of professional history in South Africa in the context of segregation and apartheid and tracks the initial consignment of precolonial history to the disciplines of "Bantu Studies," ethnology, and anthropology. The formal establishment of professional history based in the universities did not, of course, bring history production in other settings to a halt. This production continued, and indeed flourished, in a variety of forms. In the second half of the chapter, in which we track the development of the disciplines concerned with the preindustrial past, we give attention to those initiatives outside the disciplines that either shaped professional history in important ways or presented professional history with significant political or intellectual challenges.

The chapter further draws attention to how some accounts of the past came to be acknowledged as histories whereas others were designated sources and how certain texts were selected for preservation and accorded the space and expensive apparatus of conservation, as well as the way in which certain documents of the archive were chosen for publication and thus made to stand for the archives in the public domain. The chapter looks at what was excluded from the archive and dispatched to museums or oblivion, and how, in some cases, that material has been recovered.

The history of preindustrial South Africa – its key events, issues, processes, and drivers, as much as their interpretation – was powerfully shaped by the imperatives of colonial power, its engagement with conflicting settler and missionary agendas, and with increasingly subjugated African polities.

The written history that emerged was steadily concentrated in the hands of designated experts, backed up by authoritative archival evidence and a veritable panoply of devices for containing the expression of, and establishing control over, preindustrial, often oral, forms of knowledge.

This chapter, and those that follow in this volume, attempt to grapple with the double legacy of historical scholarship in South Africa. The first part of that legacy, dealt with primarily in this chapter, is the role played by the discipline of history and certain of its precursor forms in the making of colonial and apartheid subjects. The second part, manifest in the chapters that follow, is the outstanding scholarship of a generation of radical historians and their archæologist colleagues in the provision of accounts of the preconquest societies of Southern Africa, based largely on excavations and on recouping oral sources. Their analyses of the far-reaching reorganization of relations of production that accompanied and drove conquest, and of attendant developments in the transformation of consciousness and the construction of identities that occurred in the period covered by this volume, provide an essential foundation for understanding the shape of modern South Africa and for future programs of historical work. Only by appreciating the effects of these two legacies are we able to understand the complex processes that have resulted in the current state of historical knowledge about the preindustrial past and the almost complete exile of black historians from the academic production of accounts of that past.

Originally conceptualized as a short preface to this volume, our pursuit of these lines of inquiry opens up numerous new horizons of research concerning the production of historical knowledge, horizons to which the chapter in its current form is only able to point. We hope that for all its limitations, and its inevitably uneven coverage, it provides sufficient material to stimulate future generations of work by historians.

HISTORICAL PRODUCTION IN THE ERAS BEFORE
THE ADVENT OF WRITTEN TEXTS

The concept of history is often taken for granted and thought of as a universal phenomenon, although like many universal phenomena it is in fact specific to time and place. Introduced into southern Africa in the colonial era, this concept was first denied to the precolonial societies of the region and then written for them. Ideas about history, or related concepts concerning knowledge of the past, which may have existed before colonialism, have been little explored. We begin our discussion of how histories of preindustrial South Africa have been produced with an exploration of precolonial ideas about, and productions of, the past. We do this for two reasons: One is that we believe it to be an important step in highlighting the almost complete absence of work on the intellectual history of South Africa in precolonial times (we discuss the few exceptions below), the second is that it is an essential foundation for understanding which precolonial ideas were taken up in the colonial production of history, which were neglected, ignored, or unrecognized, and how all this gave shape to colonial, and later apartheid, resistance and postcolonial understandings of the preindustrial past, and the meaning and significance of its history.

None of the exceptions discussed below reflects a precolonial view of the past unmediated by colonialism in some form or another. Most are situated temporally on the cusp of precolonial and colonial times, and rely, to varying degrees, on a combination of along-the-grain readings of colonial texts for the logic, conventions, and consistencies of information/ misinformation that characterize those texts and against-the-grain readings for their sutures, gaps, and silences. Even where texts (oral, material, or visual) exist that are squarely precolonial in their genesis, their analysis is frequently mediated in one way or another by colonial texts or recording practices themselves demanding sensitive examination. Colonial authorities and missionaries were often acutely interested in the history of the colonized, for they sought in that history information and materials capable of facilitating their respective projects. To that end they frequently undertook substantial investigations into the history of precolonial South Africa, laying down selected information in colonial and missionary archives and early historical accounts.

The ways in which indigenous societies *themselves* produced history, or related forms of knowledge, before the advent of the first literate recorders, is a topic little treated in its own right by historians and historiographers. Until the mid-twentieth century this was a consequence of the view held by most western scholars that sub-Saharan Africa had no history prior to the coming of Europeans, never mind accounts of such history.[1] This perspective was underpinned by a series of developments across the nineteenth and first half of the twentieth century, which not only assumed that an intellectual practice like that of history production was beyond the ability of what were regarded as primitive societies, but which also classified potential historical source material, which might confound the claim that the colonized had no history for western historians to reconstruct, as cultural (read "timeless"), artifacts, or myth (read "fantastical" or "spiritual"), and saw to its exclusion from the historical archive, which was defined as factual and documentary.

The idea that Africa had no history prior to the advent of colonialism was robustly challenged in the course of the struggle for political independence on the continent. By the late 1950s a demand for decolonized African

---

[1] J. D. Fage, "The development of African historiography," in J. Ki-Zerbo (Ed.), *General History of Africa*, vol. I (London: Heinemann, 1981), p. 31.

history written from African perspectives emerged in new African universities. The campaign was accomplished through the collaborative efforts of both African nationalist and white liberal historians.[2] This historiography was characterized by what was viewed as the critical and scientific use of oral evidence for historical reconstruction, drawing on Jan Vansina's seminal methodological work, which proposed rigorous procedures for its utilization. The result was that once historians had worked on the oral traditions, rehabilitating them as viable sources, they mined them for nuggets of information that they attempted to corroborate with material from other sources, notably archaeology, latter-day ethnography, climatology, ecological analysis, and linguistics.

The characterization of oral traditions as oral sources was thus regarded as a revolutionary move that facilitated new academic research and ensured that the history of the subcontinent before contact with Europeans could be reconstructed by professional historians with the necessary methodological expertise.[3] In the act of reclaiming oral traditions as viable historical *sources*, however, this methodological breakthrough effectively denied the oral texts the status of historical *accounts* and intellectual projects in their own right that negotiated contemporary understandings of the past. The production of history was claimed as the output of the professionally trained academic historian, whereas oral texts were deemed "traditions," that is, sources fraught with subjectivity and bias and denuded by their oral transmission over time, requiring careful, professional interpretation. The possibility that precolonial intellectuals were themselves busy producing histories, or epistemological equivalents thereof, was not entertained.

The legacy of the Vansina intervention has been so influential that there have been very few attempts to look at oral texts as complex intellectual productions in their own right. In the 1970s and 1980s in South Africa this was compounded by the emphasis on the political–economy approaches of the Marxist historians on relations of production and reproduction, and the operation of power, in precolonial societies, often at the expense of an interest in intellectual, philosophical, religious, literary, and cultural developments. It has also been inhibited by the persistent interpretation of certain oral texts as myths that are understood not to aspire to be factual and that are then subjected to structuralist analyses or treated as literary genres without significant historiographical impulses.

Scattered exceptions to this trend, although not centrally focused on establishing historiographical traditions that may have existed prior to

---

[2] Among the torchbearers in this broad effort were the Nigerians Kenneth Dike and Jacob Ajayi, who helped to establish the Ibadan History Series and the *Journal of the Historical Society of Nigeria*, important fora for the publication of this new historiography.

[3] This can be seen most vividly in the first three decades of publication of the journal *History in Africa*.

the advent of literacy, provide pointers to alternative ways of probing the dynamics and imperatives that gave shape to inherited oral historical narratives.[4] In some instances this has led to the detailed reconstruction of the histories of key oral texts showing how historical accounts that played important roles in local political struggles were often contested and repeatedly reworked in light of historical argumentation from opposing parties that reflected the biases and backgrounds of both their composers and subsequent chroniclers; the intellectual currents of their times, demonstrating significant debts to one another; and adherence to well-established limits of credibility. Political and social struggles were key determinants in the making of these texts. The studies offer the beginnings of a periodisation of such historical accounts and identify moments of intense or elaborate historiographical contestation, notably concentrated around succession disputes and political crises.[5]

Any reconstruction of the intellectual history of precolonial times demands the existence of substantial archives of oral texts originally framed in terms of precolonial epistemologies and recorded in ways that keep intact something of that framing. The now almost fully published *James Stuart Archive of Recorded Oral Evidence Relating to the History of the Zulu and Neighbouring Peoples* is one such corpus, comprising almost 200 individual testimonies. Named after its compiler, the colonial official James Stuart, the archive has generated considerable debate about the extent and nature of Stuart's intervention in the texts, and researchers using the archive attend closely to Stuart's agenda in doing the collecting, his shaping of interviews, his methods of collection, interviewing, transcription, translation and annotation, augmentation, and excision. Nonetheless, the sheer extent of the archive opens up the possibility of discerning beyond Stuart's interventions the cognitive procedures, genre choices, narrative strategies, and rhetorical tactics that characterized the original spoken accounts. Archives of materials that purport to be verbatim transcripts of early African oral texts are rare and are seldom sufficiently extensive to offer insights into precolonial epistemologies.[6]

---

[4] See, for example, I. Hofmeyr, *"We Spend Our Years as a Tale That is Told:" Oral Historical Narrative in a South African Chiefdom* (Johannesburg: Witwatersrand University Press, 1993).

[5] See, for example, C. Hamilton, *Terrific Majesty: The Powers of Shaka Zulu and the Limits of Historical Invention* (Cambridge, MA: Harvard University Press, 1998); S. Ndlovu, "The Changing African Perceptions of King Dingane in Historical Literature: A Case Study in the Construction of Historical Knowledge in 19th and 20th Century South African History," unpublished Ph.D. thesis, University of the Witwatersrand (2001).

[6] The archive of Tswana chiefly praise poems, of which Isaac Schapera's published collection is the centerpiece, while much smaller in scale, warrants noting in this regard

Material considered by missionaries and other recorders to refer to pre-colonial religious ideas, and typically labeled "belief," "myth," "ritual," or "custom," offers another entry point into precolonial epistemologies, albeit one as yet little explored explicitly as a source for the reconstruction of the intellectual history of precolonial times. Acknowledgment of the potential of such materials requires recognition of the absence in precolonial cognition of a distinction between sacred and secular knowledge. Many early African intellectuals, starting with Robert Balfour Noyi in his 1848 "Ama-Xhosa history," and including Tiyo Soga, writing twenty years later, and the historian William Gqoba, writing in 1885, in their accounts of precolonial history worked explicitly across the sacred/secular knowledge divide.[7]

These studies begin to illuminate the processes by which knowledge was produced in precolonial times, drawing attention to how a case was constructed, what protocols and conventions of argument were observed, what was regarded as historically persuasive, as well as how historical materials were conceptualized, marshaled, and interpreted. They begin to suggest an epistemological status for such accounts that may well be different from that of contemporary academic histories, a difference far from the unthinking assertions of a lack by earlier generations of historians.

Some of the same terrain is traversed, though by very different means, in the work of Jean and John Comaroff in their explorations of Tswana historical consciousness, contained in genres they describe as "distinctly non-Eurocentric."[8] They find evidence of these genres in the symbolic actions and cultural practices of everyday life, which, drawing on accounts of nineteenth-century, mostly white, literate observers, earlier twentieth-century anthropological work in the area, and the historical writings of early twentieth-century black chroniclers, they consciously instate as their archive. The Comaroffs' work has been criticized for failing to recognize that, along with these genres of everyday cultural practices, Batswana also expressed their historical consciousness in narrative forms. At the core of this debate is the question of whether Batswana were exceptional in Southern

---

(I. Schapera, *Praise Poems of Tswana Chiefs* – Oxford: Clarendon Press, 1965). The testimonies reproduced in various Native Affairs Department publications, such as N. J. van Warmelo (Ed.), *History of Matiwane and the Amangwane Tribe as told by Msebenzi to his Kinsman Albert Hlongwane* (Department of Native Affairs Ethnological Publications, Pretoria: Government Printer, 1935), may yet come to be seen to fulfill these conditions.

[7] See J. Hodgson, *The God of the Xhosa: A Study of the Origins and Development of the Traditional Concepts of the Supreme Being* (Cape Town: Oxford University Press, 1982), Chapter 3.

[8] J. Comaroff and J. Comaroff, *Of Revelation and Revolution: The Dialectics of Modernity on a South African Frontier* (Chicago and London: The University of Chicago Press, 1997), vol. 2, p. 43.

Africa in not having elaborated historical annals and narratives of descent and accession.[9] By not acknowledging Tswana narrativity, John Peel and Terence Ranger imply, the Comaroffs repeat the act of denying that Africans produced precolonial histories of their own. Although the Comaroffs' work on the other genres undoubtedly expands our understanding of historical consciousness, the matter of whether precolonial Batswana made use of historical narratives turns on the extant documentary archive and its careful analysis as archive, a task yet worthy of attention.

Although these advances begin to tell us something about how precolonial farmers produced something akin to the modern idea of history, and about other forms of their historical consciousness, a far greater silence surrounds the history-producing activities of early hunter–gatherers and pastoralists.[10] The lacuna in the case of hunter–gatherers is exacerbated by the perception that they had no need for history because they supposedly did not need to lay claim to ownership of land, nor did they need histories to support the monopolization of power by leaders, because their societies were represented as egalitarian. The result was the establishment of the view among historians and anthropologists that the foragers, collectively termed San and identified as a homogenous cultural grouping, had "myths" or "folklore" rather than "histories." The substantial Bleek/Lloyd archive of recorded oral accounts by San informants (discussed below) has typically been read as a collection of such myths. The silence is also the consequence of grave difficulties in establishing a nuanced chronology for the other primary source of cognitive material pertinent to a foraging way of life – the rock art – and, flowing from that, a strong structuralist emphasis in the work of the leading rock art scholars, despite their commitment to materialist approaches.

In the case of pastoralists similarly culturally classified, in this case as Khoe or Khoekhoe, the absence of extant cognitive archives like the Bleek/Lloyd collection or the rock art is still more telling; a situation compounded by the almost total obliteration of established pastoralist communities by 1810. Indeed, when the first Europeans encountered the Khoekhoen in the Cape, they denied them the capacity for language itself, never mind "knowledge" of any kind. Khoekhoe activities, expressed in ritual or dance, were interpreted as religious, or in the numerous instances where any form of consciousness was considered skeptically, as merely

---

[9] See the Comaroffs' responses to their critics in the introduction to vol. 2, *Of Revelation and Revolution.*

[10] E. Gellner, *Plough, Sword and Book: The Structure of Human History* (London: Collins Harvill, 1988), chapters 2 and 3 on cognitive transformations. Our chapter explicitly leaves open for further deliberation the limits of the extension of the term "history," the issue of its form (Is history by definition narrative in form?), and the possible notions of time it may encompass.

expressions of pleasure. Regarded as being without reason, the inhabitants of the Cape were deemed to have neither rights to land nor, in extreme instances, any religion. The work of David Chidester shows how in the 300 years that followed the first contacts, European discussions of Khoekhoe religion – the only area in which the possibility of some form of Khoekhoe knowledge was entertained – fluctuated between denials and discoveries; shifts that can be correlated with growing or diminishing pressures to control land and people in a frontier situation. European commentators denied the existence of Khoekhoe religion when resources were directly contested, but in intervening periods religion was the object of their discovery and intensive investigation, and the information was taken up and made part of the establishment of effective colonial administration.[11]

In general, when Khoekhoen spoke and were recorded, they did not provide extensive descriptions of their societies' past as they saw it. Even in Peter Kolb's massive ethnography of the Cape Khoekhoen in the early eighteenth century there is only one short paragraph in which Khoekhoe reflections on their past are given – to the effect that they had once known how to sow and reap but had forgotten how.[12] Neither such traditions as there may have been nor Khoekhoe mythology and folklore were of interest to the literate until the nineteenth century. Even then, such descriptions were few. This was in part because it was among the Khoekhoen who had converted to Christianity and come to live on the mission stations that it was possible for such texts to be collected. These people had consciously rejected "the Devil and all his works," which were thought to include their preconversion life and experiences, which may, in any case, have been too painful for them to want to remember. In 1821, the leading missionary at the Moravian mission station of Genadendal, the Rev. H. P. Hallbeck, wrote that he was attempting "to collect their traditions respecting their origins and early history. Our Missionaries here always thought that they knew nothing about it, but the fact is, that they were ashamed and afraid to tell their tales, as on their conversion to Christianity they were led to despise their old sayings and customs."[13]

---

[11] D. Chidester, "Bushman Religion: Open, Closed and New Frontiers," in P. Skotnes (Ed.), *Miscast: Negotiating the Presence of the Bushmen* (Cape Town: UCT Press, 1996), pp. 51–59. Also see his essay "Mutilated Meaning: European Interpretations of Khoisan Languages of the Body," also in *Miscast*, pp. 24–38, even pages only.

[12] P. Kolb, *Caput bonae spei hodiernum, das ist Vollständige Beschreibung des Africanischen Vorgebürges der Guten Hoffnung*, 2 vols., Nürnberg (Peter Conrad Monrath, 1719), vol. I, pp. 353–4.

[13] Letter from H. P. Hallbeck, August 6, 1821, *Periodical Accounts relating to the Missions of the Church of the United Brethren, established among the Heathen*, VIII, London, pp. 197–8 (The "Bushmen" were described as "run-away Hottentots").

Hallbeck convinced various old men that they could talk to him of such matters without fear and managed to provide some description of what the Genadendal Khoekhoen thought of their past; notably their ideas as to the origin of the "Bushmen." What survived, both on the Moravian stations and elsewhere, were personal testimonies. They were, in the first instance, spiritual autobiographies, which every Moravian was required to produce and which other converts generally had to enunciate to demonstrate their acceptance of Christianity. As was so often the case, though, the distance between public confession and the description of the evils suffered in the past was short. Khoekhoe politics from about 1800 to the early 1850s was thus based on what was to be a typically South African combination of the personal histories of oppression and the political demand for the rectification of abuses.[14]

The idea of Khoesan inhabiting a self-contained universe in which there was no relevance for historical material is rendered questionable by the now substantial studies – focused primarily on the San rather than the Khoekhoen – that show that, rather than constituting culturally separate communities, the activities of hunting and gathering were frequently the resort of the most marginal groups in a society, specifically of those excluded from patron–client pastoral relationships, from access to land and other forms of accumulating wealth and power. Over a decade of revisionist scholarship has shown that even when practicing a foraging mode of existence, such communities interacted extensively with their neighbors (see Chapter 2). In practicing a hunting and gathering way of life, such groups laid claim to the resources of particular territories, inhabited regular settlement nodes, and followed established, flexible, annual migration routes, over which they sometimes fought to assert rights. Kinship relations, as well as gift-exchange networks that cut across kinship ties, were critically important subsistence strategies that were often long delayed. The recall of and commitment to them required maintenance in memory.

The idea of San having no need for history also rests on primordial assumptions about the nature of San identity. These persist even in recent

[14] In general, on this process see E. Elbourne, *Blood Ground: Colonialism, Missions and the Contest for Christianity in the Cape Colony and Britain, 1799–1853* (Montreal & Kingston, Ithaca & London: McGill University Press, 2002); S. Trapido, "The Emergence of Liberalism and the making of 'Hottentot Nationalism,' 1815–1834," *Collected Seminar Papers of the Institute of Commonwealth Studies, London: The Societies of Southern Africa in the Nineteenth and Twentieth Centuries*, 17 (1992); R. Ross, "The Kat River, Rebellion and Khoikhoi nationalism: the fate of an ethnic identification," *Kronos: a Journal of Cape History*, 24 (1997), pp. 91–105; the clearest expression of these views is to be found in the *South African Commercial Advertiser* September 3, 1834.

revisionist studies, which, in their emphasis on political economy, typically reduce the interaction between San and their neighbors to the subordination of one group to another. The question of the ways in which San may have contributed to the production of hybridized cultures and to processes of creolization has only recently been tackled.[15] Where this involved interaction with neighbors actively involved in the production of history in the service not only of land and status claims but also of identity politics, the claim that history production was absent requires reassessment.

Cognitive archaeologists David Lewis-Williams and David Pearce interpret rock art as a site of San spirituality and argue that the control of spiritual knowledge was central to the operation of social distinctions in San communities.[16] In that respect San spiritual knowledge would seem to operate in ways similar to certain knowledge designated historical. Geoff Blundell's highly specific study of the Nomansland San, living below the Drakensberg escarpment in the northeastern Cape in the period c.1500–1900, offers an interesting opportunity to pursue that proposition.

Blundell's purpose is to reconstruct the history of this grouping through a reading of the available sources in a manner sensitive to their subaltern status. In so doing, he probes both the documented oral accounts of the San of Nomansland, the people who lived with them, and their descendants, and analyzes the rich corpus of rock art they produced. Although he does not seek to uncover processes of history production *by* the San groups and their transient adherents (an objective advanced in this chapter), he sets himself the express task of analyzing the mechanisms they used for reflection on and the expression of complex social and political positions. He also explicitly attempts to develop a theoretical position to allow those mechanisms to speak for themselves rather than force them into European knowledge frameworks.[17] Blundell argues that "more so than any other indigenous archive, the densely communicative nature of rock art holds the potential for interpreting the perspectives of the colonised."[18]

In a detailed historical account Blundell shows that, in this one region at least, the foragers were embedded in a centuries-long history of social, political, and economic interaction and inhabited a complexly hybrid and creolized world that was often unstable. This argument resonates with Chidester's presentation of earlier situations of such interaction, and its

---

[15] G. Blundell, *Nqabayo's Nomansland: San Rock Art and the Somatic Past*, Studies in Global Archaeology, 2 (Uppsala: Uppsala Universitiet, 2004), see Introduction. Also see precursor work by T. Dowson, notably "Reading Rock Art, Writing History: Rock Art and Social Change in Southern Africa," *World Archaeology*, 25 (1996), pp. 332–45.

[16] D. Lewis-Williams and D. Pearce, *San Spirituality: Roots, Expressions and Social Consequences* (Cape Town: Double Storey, 2004).

[17] Blundell, *Nqabayo's Nomansland*, p. 176.   [18] *Ibid.*, p. 53.

main points may be true for a much greater historical period.[19] Through a process of careful argument and the use of theories of body and embodiment, Blundell goes on to make the case for the rock art of the region as a practice for the negotiation of that interaction and the attendant hybridity of identity. It was, moreover, a practice that was an important resource carefully controlled by certain shamans. Central to his approach is the idea that these negotiations of interaction and of identity were not argued out discursively but were a form of knowledge production and consumption experienced through becoming "art as a space for the experience of transference."[20] Utilizing the notion of a somatic society, where the major moral, personal, and political concerns are problematized in and expressed through the conduit of the body, Blundell posits that rock art was "bodily experienced rather than simply intellectualised."[21] The study suggests that the rock art was itself a complex, carefully worked production about the nature of identity in increasingly unstable contexts, the creation and consumption of which involved transformation through body activity – notably touching and seeing – involving altered states of consciousness and a blurring of image, body, and identity and thereby constituting reality rather than merely reflecting it.

In the argument that the production and consumption of rock art was a process of hybrid identity construction and negotiation actively manipulated in the rock art; that it entailed the restriction of expertise and the maintenance of status and social differentiation; that it involved increasing limitations – of access to the spirit world and to rainmaking skills (read "resources") – we can discern suggestive echoes of the way in which, in other settings, historical narratives work. Such investigations thus offer rare glimpses of San activities in a domain at once both strongly resonant with and very different from history in a manner helpful to the project of considering the precolonial production of history and its possible equivalents.

The massive effort invested in grasping the intellectual content of the rock art associated with hunter–gatherers has been extended by the scholars to analysis of associated myths or folklore. Lewis-Williams discusses the way in which in the 1870s a prisoner in Cape Town, //Kabbo, a man identified as "Bushman" previously living in poverty on land occupied by farmers, spoke movingly of *kukummi* that "float from afar," glossed as stories, news, talk, information, history, and myths and folklore, passed from generation to generation.[22] A vast number of such *kukummi* were recorded

---

[19] Chidester, "Bushman Religion"; also see P. Jolly, "Strangers to Brothers: Interaction between South-eastern San and South Nguni/Sotho Communities," unpublished M.A. thesis, University of Cape Town (1994); further see following, Chapter 3.

[20] Blundell, *Nqabayo's Nomansland*, p. 174.   [21] *Ibid.*, p. 81.

[22] J. D. Lewis-Williams (Ed.), *Stories that Float from Afar: Ancestral Folklore of the San of Southern Africa* (Cape Town: David Philip, 2000), Introduction, p. 11; the archive is

between 1870 and 1884 by Lucy Lloyd[23] from San including //Kabbo.
An active desire on the part of the interviewees for the *kukummi* to be
recorded in books apparently animated the recording project, showing that
"[t]hey knew beyond a shadow of doubt that they were the last repositories of these *kukummi*, and they did not want the stories to die with those
into whose ears they had for so long floated in /Xam-ka !au but whose
way of life was being rapidly destroyed."[24] The *kukummi*, which survive
today in the Bleek and Lloyd archival collection, appear to be verbatim
texts recorded from various San informants. The creation of the texts was
driven by linguistic concerns, which placed a premium on the transcrip-
tions reflecting as closely as possible the narrators' words. However, it is
not clear to what extent the tortuous process of dictation led to digres-
sions, omissions, and embellishments, notably the loss of performative
aspects, nor to what extent the telling was shaped by the questions and
prompts of the interviewers.[25] However, as with the *James Stuart Archive*,
the Bleek/Lloyd archive is sufficiently extensive to permit exploration of
the cultural and cognitive logic of the world of the hunter–gatherers. For
Lewis-Williams, the *kukummi* are stories about "daily life" or "myth, ritual and belief" in which the distinctions between daily life and spiritual
experiences are blurred. On the face of it, such stories do not immediately
resonate with the concept of "history," although the archive has also been
used as oral testimony to reconstruct the history of the /Xam during the
nineteenth century and to describe their relations with the Korana and the
Boers.[26]

In their investigation of San spirituality in myth, ritual, and rock art,
Lewis-Williams and Pearce discuss the role of shamans at length. Through
a variety of portals – rock crevices, water holes, and so on – shamans visited
the realm of the spirits, at once the realm of myth and very probably
the primal time of the "Early Race" referred to in San *kukummi*. They
argue that this form of transcosmological travel brought together disparate
entities: animals and people, the real world and the spirit world, and, most
significantly for our discussion, the past and the present.[27] As images came,

currently available in Pippa Skotnes (Ed.), *Claim to the Country: the Archive of Lucy Lloyd
and Wilhelm Bleek* (Johannesburg, Cape Town, and Athens: Jacana and Ohio University
Press, 2007), with an accompanying DVD.

[23] Lucy Lloyd was one of the very few women who contributed to the laying down of the
archive of the preindustrial past.

[24] Lewis-Williams (Ed.), *Stories that Float*, Introduction, p. 26.

[25] See the discussion in Lewis-Williams (Ed.), *Stories that Float*, Introduction, pp. 30–2.

[26] Andrew Bank, *Bushmen in a Victorian World: the remarkable story of the Bleek-Lloyd collection
of Bushman folklore* (Cape Town: Double Storey, 2006).

[27] Lewis-Williams and Pearce, *San Spirituality*, see especially p. 175. On the convergence
of present, linear time, and mythic time also see M. Guenther, *Tricksters and Trances:
Bushman Religion and Society* (Bloomington: Indiana University Press, 1999), pp. 70, 88.

over time, to overlay one another, facilitating the accretion of power on a single rock surface, the rock art began to offer a summative rather than chronologically ordered, narrative form of history.[28]

It is perhaps the difficulties presented by the attempt to decide whether *kukummi*, or at least some of them, or aspects of them, and likewise rock paintings, can be understood to be forms of history production that highlight most sharply the problem of the idea of history itself not as a universal practice but as the product of a particular, western epistemological system. The rock art scholarship in particular draws attention to the extent to which certain San practices were fundamentally visual, experiential, and performed, rather than logocentric. This is a point echoed in the attention paid by the Comaroffs to the symbolic actions and cultural practices of everyday life among the Batswana.[29]

Ideas of history, or cognate concepts, which prevailed among precolonial farmers, hunter–gatherers, and the various hybridized communities, influenced each other but did not coincide fully, and they were substantially different from the colonial concept that followed. Once the oral texts of the farmers, the *kukummi*, and the rock art intersected with European ideas of history they were judged by the extent to which they fitted the European concept and were accordingly designated oral traditions, folklore, and rock art, that is, not history or knowledge but sources. The work accomplished so far that provides insight into how such knowledge was produced in precolonial times points both to its vigor and its complexity but is also suggestive of its differences from western equivalents. Such epistemological differences warrant investigation in their own right.

THE EARLIEST COLONIAL PRODUCTIONS OF HISTORY

The first written accounts of the history of South Africa appeared at different times across Southern Africa, linked to the spread of literate European commentators in the early 1700s in the southern Cape and late in the nineteenth century in the far north of what is today Limpopo province.

Before the nineteenth century, the surviving expressions of colonial concern with the past are limited to a sermon that Ds. Le Sueur gave to celebrate the centenary of the Cape Colony's foundation. As might be expected, it

---

[28] The notion of time operating in, or absent from, various ways of conceptualizing the past merits further attention. There are pointers to this subject in work, such as K. E. Atkins, "'Kafir time': preindustrial temporal concepts and labour discipline in nineteenth-century colonial Natal," *Journal of African History*, 29(2) (1988), pp. 229–44, which looks at the imposition of colonial time regimes, and ways in which these were resisted or taken up.

[29] See also Lewis-Williams and Pearce, *San Spirituality*, notably p. 99.

is a panegyric on the glories of the Dutch imperial project, and the Dutch East India Company (Vereenigde Oostindische Compagnie or VOC) itself ordered that it be printed. The past, however, was not a major matter of debate in the Cape Colony in the mid-eighteenth century. It is difficult to imagine what arguments could have been bolstered by a recourse to history, and indeed even the first colonial political movement, the Cape Patriots of the 1780s, only made comments about the so-called golden age under the first governor, Jan van Riebeeck, as part of their criticism of the current company officials.[30] After the demise of the VOC the possibilities of identity politics emerged. Under the Patriot rule of the Batavians, a cult of van Riebeeck began. A great ceremony in 1804 sought to introduce his coat of arms to the "Town-house" in Cape Town.[31]

The British conquest of the Cape in 1806 focused the discussion. Throughout the first half of the nineteenth century a thoroughly acrimonious debate was conducted in the Cape Colony about its past. There were a number of reasons for this. First, the general intellectual life of the colony began to develop (primarily among educated men) in a variety of ways made possible by the introduction to South Africa of printing presses, leading to the establishment of newspapers and a number of literary journals.[32] Second, a major British commission of inquiry into the affairs of the colony included investigations of the records held in the colony's government offices – there were, of course, as yet no official archives. To some extent the commission based its conclusions on the results of the study carried out by P. B. Borcherds, a member of the Court of Justice who was also the son of the Dutch Reformed minister in Stellenbosch and a member of the circle surrounding *Het Nederduitsch Zuid-Afrikaansch Tydschrift* (The Dutch South African Magazine), the first organ of intellectual debate to be published in the country. As a result, various of Borcherds's findings, notably the diary kept on van Riebeeck's orders in the early years of the colony, were published in that journal,[33] which fueled an ethnic

---

[30] G. J. Schutte, *De Nederlandse Patriotten en de koloniën; Een onderzoek naar hun denkbeelden en optreden, 1770–1800* (Groningen: Tjeenk Willink, 1974), pp. 81–2.

[31] P. B. Borcherds, *An Autobiographical Memoir* (reprinted, Cape Town: Africana Connoisseur Press, 1963), pp. 279–80. For the Patriots and the rule of the Batavian republic, see Chapter 4 in this volume.

[32] A. M. Lewin Robinson, *None Daring to Make Us Afraid* (Cape Town: Maskew Miller, 1962).

[33] On Borcherds's work, see D. B. Bosman and H. B. Thom (Eds.), *Daghregister gehouden by den Oppercoopman Jan Anthonisz van Riebeeck*, Deel I, 1651–1655 (Cape Town: A. A. Balkema, 1921), pp. xxvi–xxx; see also papers relating to the condition and treatment of the "Native Inhabitants of Southern Africa, within the Colony of the Cape of Good Hope, or beyond the Frontiers of the that Colony." Part I, "Hottentots and Bosjesmen; Caffres; Griquas" (British Parliamentary Paper 50 of 1835).

consciousness among the Dutch elite of the Western Cape, a third motor of the historical controversies.[34]

The fourth and most important impulse in the debate about the past was Dr. John Philip's *Researches in South Africa*, which was published in 1828.[35] In this work, Philip, the director of the London Missionary Society in South Africa, attacked the treatment of Khoekhoen, primarily at the time at which he was writing, but also historically. His researches were aided by access to the documents Borcherds unearthed and by a number of published records of travelers to the Cape in previous centuries. What he produced was a narrative of destruction and redemption. Precolonial Khoekhoe society in the Cape, which was presented as relatively idyllic, if ignorant of the "True God," had been destroyed by the effects of colonialism, and many Khoekhoen had been forced to become "Bushmen," thus giving rise to the argument whether a sharp distinction should be made between Khoekhoen and San, which continues today. The British maintained and honed the system of oppression, and only through the work of the missionaries could freedom, and thus progress, be achieved in both religious and secular spheres (though Philip in his arguments did not really distinguish between the two). In the years after the publication of the *Researches*, this argument was written into colonial law by the enactment and entrenchment of Ordinance 50 by which legal discrimination on the basis of race was outlawed from Cape Colony.[36]

The evangelical version of Khoekhoe historical experience was developed in concert with Khoekhoe converts and expressed by them in colonial contexts and, when they had the opportunity, before a British public. It was one that offered benefits. That minority of Khoekhoen who had escaped de facto bondage on the farms made good use of their new freedoms, which they justified in personal terms and histories of dispossession. It was a line of argument employed until the early 1850s when, in the aftermath of the Kat River Rebellion, it was too closely associated with the rebel cause to have remained opportune.[37]

For a brief period, from about 1827 to the mid-1830s, however, the evangelical narrative acquired such influence with the British government

---

[34] R. Ross, *Status and Respectability in the Cape Colony, 1750–1870: A tragedy of manners* (Cambridge: Cambridge University Press, 1999), pp. 47–51; A. Bank, "Liberals and their Enemies: Racial Ideology at the Cape of Good Hope, 1820–1850," unpublished Ph.D. thesis, University of Cambridge (1995), Chapter 3.

[35] John Philip, *Researches in South Africa, illustrating the civil, moral, and religious condition of the Native Tribes*, 2 vols. (London: James Ducan, 1828).

[36] See Chapter 6 in this volume.

[37] Elbourne, *Blood Ground*; Trapido, "The emergence of Liberalism"; Ross, "The Kat River Rebellion."

in London that it could significantly alter the course of Cape history. It was most cogently expressed in the report of the Select Committee (of the British Parliament) on Aborigines, where indeed it was expanded to cover the interaction between colonizers and what would now be called indigenous peoples throughout the globe.[38] It was also used by the colonial secretary, Lord Glenelg, to order the retrocession to the amaXhosa of Queen Adelaide Province, more or less the Ciskei, which had been annexed after Mlanjeni's War of 1850 (see Chapter VI). It was, Glenelg wrote, the examination of the history of the relations between the colony and the amaXhosa, and the reasons for the beginnings of the 1835 war, that led him to take this step, although there were those in South Africa who were convinced that it was what they saw to be the malign influence of John Philip, and also of Andries Stockenström, who was examined by the Select Committee, that persuaded Glenelg.[39]

The evangelical narrative, which, in time, merged into that of Cape Liberalism, was seen as an affront to the honor of the colony and as a threat to political developments that would entrench the dominance of the colonial elite and thus their control over slave and Khoekhoe laborers. Thus, Ds. Meent Borcherds wrote a long (and probably unfinished[40]) poem on the "Volksplanting van de Kaap de Goede Hoop," almost certainly in reaction to the *Researches*, in which he repeated old stereotypes of Khoekhoe society, rejected any ideas about the nobility of their "savagery" as un-Christian, and lauded the establishment of the colony by a Christian people.[41]

Rather than criticism of its version of history, the *Researches* was met with a major libel suit. Once the Glenelg dispatch had led to a potential diminution of the colonists' wealth through restrictions on territorial expansion and the requirement that farms already staked out be vacated, the main attack on the evangelical narrative began. The governor, Sir Benjamin

[38] Z. Laidlaw, "Aunt Anna's Report: the Buxton Women and the Aborigines Select Committee, 1835–37," *Journal of Imperial and Commonwealth History, 32*(2) (2004, pp. 1–28) and "Integrating metropolitan, colonial and imperial history: the Aborigines Select Committee of 1835–1837," in T. Banivanua Mar and J. Evans (Eds.), *Writing Colonial Histories: Comparative Perspectives* (Melbourne: RMIT, 2002); Elbourne, *Blood Ground*.

[39] On Stockenström, a long-serving official in the Eastern Cape see below Chapter VI and A. du Toit, "Experiments with Truth and Justice in South Africa: Stockenström, Gandhi and the TRC," *Journal of Southern African Studies, 31*(2) (2005), pp. 422–30; in general, on the Glenelg dispatch, see J. G. Pretorius, "The British Humanitarians and the Cape Eastern Frontier, 1834–1836," *Archives Year Book for South African History*, 51, 1988.

[40] It ends with the arrival of van Riebeeck.

[41] In general, see Marjolijn Engelsman, "Een Nieuwe Uitgave van 'Gedicht over de Volksplanting van de Kaap de Goede Hoop,' Meent Borcherds, Kaapstad 1832," unpublished M.A. thesis, Leiden University (2002). The poem was originally published in two issues of *Het Nederduitsch Zuid-Afrikaansch Tydschrift* July–August and September–October 1832.

D'Urban, whose career was effectively ended by Glenelg's actions, appointed an official, Donald Moodie, at the substantial salary of £400 a year, to systematize the archives and vindicate his position, essentially by showing that Glenelg had not had all the available information at his disposal and thus had made poor decisions. Moodie used his position to pursue a vendetta against Philip, publishing at government expense substantial extracts, at times slightly but significantly sanitized, from the Dutch records of the eighteenth century. On the basis of these, Moodie accused Philip of fabricating sources. In fact he had merely been careless about a date.[42]

In opposition, an alternative history of relations between the amaXhosa and the colony to that adumbrated by Glenelg was created, notably by Robert Godlonton. Godlonton was the intellectual, and eventually the political, leader of the Eastern Cape conservatives, who generally came from among those British who had come to South Africa as settlers in 1820. Many had flourished and had, between them, laid the basis for English South African nationalism.[43] Godlonton, and with him the settler elite, assigned responsibility for the repeated breakdown in relations between the amaXhosa and the colony squarely and totally to the amaXhosa. This began a tradition of settler historical self-justification and of the demonization of the amaXhosa that lasted well into the twentieth century.

Godlonton's journalistic opponent, John Fairbairn of the *South African Commercial Advertiser*, had, together with his companion, Thomas Pringle, started with a more nuanced view of repeated conflicts on the Eastern Frontier, but even he tended to blame the amaXhosa for the collapses in relations between them and the colony, certainly by the later 1840s.[44] Thus, although the settler historical accounts of the time were far from uniform, many manifested a strongly articulated trope of "civilisation"[45] versus "barbarism" as a key rationale for colonial domination; a trope that also surfaced in certain missionary and official accounts and that drove an agenda of recording "barbarous practices."[46] The question at the heart of the contemporary

---

[42] On this controversy in general, see Ross, "Donald Moodie and the Origins of South African historiography," in R. Ross, *Beyond the Pale: Essays in the History of Colonial South Africa* (Hanover & London: Wesleyan University Press, 1993), pp. 192–212; A. Bank, "The Great Debate and the Origins of South African Historiography," *Journal of African History, 38* (1997), pp. 261–81.

[43] Ross, *Status and Respectability*, pp. 60–6.

[44] Godlonton, *Introductory Remarks*; on Fairbairn, see Pretorius, "British Humanitarians" and H. C. Botha, *John Fairbairn in South Africa* (Cape Town: Historical Publication Society, 1984).

[45] In this chapter, "civilization" is always used to refer to the bundle of traits that, mainly, western thinkers used as a contrast to "barbarism," and thus not as a concept having any meaning outside of this contrast and discourse.

[46] L. de Kock, *Civilising Barbarians: Missionary Narrative and African Textual Response in Nineteenth-Century South Africa* (Johannesburg: Witwatersrand University Press, 1996).

argument, though, was the extent to which the "barbarians" could be reclaimed through missionary work or whether their "savagery" was irredeemable.[47]

Both arguments played into metropolitan and empirewide debates, the former through the Select Committee on Aborigines in particular, the latter through the development in South Africa of biological racism. This was initiated by Robert Knox, sometime surgeon of the British army in the Eastern Cape and leading racist anatomist in Britain. It became one of South Africa's major contributions to the world of science in the nineteenth century.[48] There was, of course, a fusion between the sociocultural and the biological in white views of black South Africans, one of which was made easier by the emergence of ideas of evolution, which became general in European social science from the 1850s onward and reached their apogee with Lewis Henry Morgan, whose *Ancient Society: Or Researches in the Lines of Human Progress. From Savagery, Through Barbarism to Civilization*, was first published in 1877. The progression from "primitive" society to "civilization" mirrored the progression from "Bushman" to European. The argument could then concentrate on the speed of that progress and not on its necessity.[49]

At the same time, and as part of the same wide debate, an argument was developed that would reverberate through the country's history for close to 200 years. This was the idea that the land of South Africa had been empty before European colonization. In part, this was achieved by asserting that Khoesan occupation of the Cape was not sufficient to allow a legal claim to the territory under the precepts of (European-derived) international law.[50] This argument was taken up as the century progressed. Xhosa chiefdoms in the Eastern Cape, it was claimed, had taken such parts of the region as they occupied by "right of [recent] conquest" and might be ejected by the same right.[51]

---

[47] On this theme, see in particular, Leonard Thompson, *The Political Mythology of Apartheid* (New Haven and London: Yale University Press, 1985), pp. 69–104.

[48] A. Bank, "Of 'Native skulls' and 'Noble Caucasians': Phrenology in Colonial South Africa," *Journal of Southern African Studies*, 22 (1996), pp. 387–404; C. L. Taylor, "Knox, Robert (1791–1862)," *Oxford Dictionary of National Biography* (Oxford: Oxford University Press, 2006), who comments that Knox was run out of the colony, apparently for insulting the settlers; Saul Dubow, *Scientific Racism in modern South Africa* (Cambridge, Cambridge University Press, 1995), pp. 20–33.

[49] A. Bank, "Evolution and Racial Theory: The Hidden Side of Wilhelm Bleek," *South African Historical Journal*, 43 (2000), pp. 163–78.

[50] Bank, "Great Debate," pp. 269–70.

[51] Harry Smith, letter of August 17, 1836, cited in C. Crais, "The Vacant Land: The Political Mythology of British Expansion in the Eastern Cape, South Africa," *Journal of Social History*, 25 (1992), p. 266.

Other narratives concerning the colonial history of the Cape were being developed at the time. Some were relatively trivial, although they were to have a long life. Thus, events surrounding the hanging below Slachtersnek of five colonists for rebellion were resuscitated by Godlonton as a means to attack the new lieutenant-governor of the Eastern Province and the local representative of the Glenelg dispensation, Sir Andries Stockenström, who, twenty years earlier, as magistrate of Graaff-Reinet, had been one who suppressed the rebellion. Godlonton would repeat this attack in the early 1850s, and it would be taken up from then on, initially in one of the first histories of the Great Trek and, on the basis of oral evidence from one of the rebels' widows, as part of the mythology of Afrikaner nationalism.[52] Though the families of those who were hung at Slachtersnek maintained their animosity to the British government, this event does not seem to have formed part of the ideological justification of the Great Trek.[53] Indeed, although Retief and his fellows left the colony in protest against social, political, and ecclesiastical developments as much as for economic reasons, they did not justify their departure with historically rooted nationalist arguments.[54]

There were, however, two ethno-nationalist histories being developed in the Cape in the early nineteenth century. One was the historiography of Cape Dutch conservatism, set out in *Het Nederduitsch Zuid-Afrikaansch Tydscrift* and developed in particular by Ds. G. W. A. van der Lingen, a learned and wealthy Dutch Reformed minister at the Paarl. Although van der Lingen's main concerns were theological, and in this context antimodernist and antiliberal, his approach entailed a continued glorification of the Dutch Golden Age and of the colonists of the Cape as the true heirs of that time. It was a history that was temporarily unattractive even to most of its potential constituents because the Western Cape Dutch elite had made a conscious decision to trade its incipient ethnicity for participation in (and eventually domination of) representative Cape politics, but the possibility remained.[55] The other was, as detailed previously, the history produced by

[52] Ross, "Donald Moodie," p. 254 n. 56; Thompson, *Political Mythology of Apartheid*, pp. 105–43.

[53] C. F. J. Muller, *Die Britse Owerheid en die Groot Trek*. Johannesburg (Simondium, 1963), p. 60.

[54] This last comment is of course a corollary of Ernest Renan's famous comment that "Getting its history wrong is part of being a nation." E. Renan, *Qu'est que c'est une nation?*, pp. 7–8, cited in E. Hobsbawm, *Nations and Nationalism since 1780: Programme, Myth, Reality* (Cambridge: Cambridge University Press, 1990), p. 12; for the empirical basis of these statements see C. F. J. Muller, *Die Oorsprong van die Groot Trek* (Cape Town and Johannesburg: Tafelberg, 1974), Chapter 6.

[55] Bank, "Great Debate," pp. 265–74; Ross, *Status and Respectability*, pp. 65–9; J. du Plessis, "Colonial Progress and Countryside Conservatism: An Essay on the Legacy of van der

the British settlers in the Eastern Cape, not merely virulently anti-Philipian and anti-Xhosa but also enormously self-congratulatory. Godlonton was to claim that "the British race was selected by God himself to colonise Kaffraria,"[56] and the Eastern Cape was presented as an empty land, ready for British usage.[57] It was as if Godlonton and van der Lingen were debating the question of who had brought Western civilization to South Africa. The answer would, it was assumed, determine who was to rule the country, and on what basis.

In the event, a political compromise was reached in the aftermath of the inauguration of the Cape Parliament in 1854, by which the ethnic distinctions between English and Dutch were downplayed. The result was that the argument about who really brought Western civilization to South Africa was no longer so crucial. A white conservative consensus developed, expressed in the Cape by such writers as Alexander Wilmot, John Cantilevers Chase, and John Noble.[58] It reached its apotheosis with the work of George McCall Theal toward the end of the century.[59] It was Theal, for instance, who popularized the ideas about the recent migration of Africans into South Africa.[60] His work formed the basis for the initial syntheses of South African history in which the domination of the country by its colonizers was justified and lauded.

These syntheses inaugurated a view of South African history as commencing with the Portuguese voyages of discovery. They were backed up by the creation of an extensive archive, through the publication in English of accounts of those voyages, as early "Records." In the preface to volume one of *Records of South-Eastern Africa*, Theal noted that the creation of this archive was an explicit project to gain "as much authentic knowledge as it

Lingen of Paarl, 1831–1875," unpublished M.A. thesis, University of Stellenbosch (1988).

[56] Cited in A. Kirk, "Self-government and Self-defence in South Africa: the Inter-relations between British and Cape Politics, 1846–1854," unpublished Ph.D. thesis, University of Oxford (1972), pp. 76–7; see also Ross, *Status and Respectability*, pp. 61–4; A. Lester, "Reformulating Identities: British Settlers in Early Nineteenth-century South Africa," *Transactions of the Institute of British Geographers*, New Series, 23 (1998).

[57] Crais, "Vacant Land."

[58] A. Wilmot and J. C. Chase, *History of the Colony of the Cape of Good Hope* (Cape Town: J. C. Juta, 1869); J. Noble, *South Africa, Past and Present: a Short History of the European Settlements at the Cape* (Cape Town: J. C. Juta, 1877).

[59] Theal's major work was the eleven-volume *History of South Africa*, a revised and collected edition published by George Allen & Unwin in London in 1910; further, see D. Schreuder, "The Imperial Historian as Colonial Nationalist: George McCall Theal and the Making of South African History," in G. Martel (Ed.), *Studies in British Imperial History: Essays in Honour of A. P. Thornton* (Houndmills: Macmillan, 1986), pp. 95–158.

[60] C. Saunders, *The Making of the South African Past: Major Historians on Race and Class* (Cape Town: David Philip, 1988), pp. 38–9.

is possible to gather upon the past condition of the Bantu tribes south of the Zambesi."[61] In the digest of the knowledge "of the South African coast and of the native tribes along it acquired by the Portuguese" in volume two, Theal summarized the findings that the South African coast south of Natal was populated by "little insignificant clans too feeble to attract notice," with four named chiefdoms between Natal and Delagoa Bay, and north of that communities that "never did anything to merit a place in history."[62] The prefatory digest positioned readers to adopt that frame for reading the documents. The *Records*, particularly the accounts of the castaways, painted a general picture of the edges of a savage, untamed land, rarely prospering and illogical, and in need of Western civilization. It authenticated the views then set in place by Theal across a range of syntheses that, as in North America and Australia, justified the colonization of the region as enabling the civilization of barbarous societies and, in some instances, as occurring in depopulated regions.[63] The *Records* provided the foundation for a core narrative of the preindustrial past that was endlessly recounted though subject to continuous refashioning.

By the late nineteenth century the colonial concept of history that was becoming entrenched was one that established as its central subject matter the activities of white men and increasingly regarded historical validity as dependent on archival substantiation. Historical accounts about and by white women were excluded from this domain and typically published without archival references as memoirs, diaries, and letters.[64] "History" was, moreover, text written in English and was a part of a much wider

---

[61] G. M. Theal, *Records of South-Eastern Africa*, 9 vols. (Cape Town: Government of the Cape Colony, 1898–1903), vol. I, Preface.

[62] Theal, *Records*, II. p. xxxi.

[63] These views survived for most of the twentieth century. The revisionist historians, who sought to recover the socio-political and economic organization and logic of the early African societies whom the castaways encountered, mined the *Records* for small nuggets of information, largely about the economic practices and the extent and scope of the political power of the various chiefs encountered. They rarely gave any attention to the processes by which these accounts were generated, fixed in written form in Portuguese and later Dutch, collated, translated, edited, and represented as archival records by Theal, and subsequently by C. R. Boxer, in *The Tragic History of the Sea*, two vols., originally published in 1959 and 1968, respectively. Literary scholars have approached the texts more critically, offering insights into, amongst other things, the generic uncertainty of these texts, their tendency to disrupt the master historiographic narrative of imperialism as they reflect the liminal situation of castaways, and the impact on the record of the destruction of the royal archives in the Lisbon earthquake of 1755. (For a recent attempt to grapple with the complexity of these kinds of texts, see J. Blackmoor, *Manifest Perdition: Shipwreck Narratives and the Disruption of Empire* – Minneapolis: University of Minnesota Press, 2002.)

[64] E.g., N. Erlank, "Letters Home: the Experiences and Perceptions of Middle Class British Women at the Cape 1820–1850," M.A. dissertation, University of Cape Town (1995).

effort to establish and institutionalize the cultural firmament of the colonial order.[65]

Although the activities of white men were the central subject of history, the history of the increasingly subjugated African kingdoms was featured in both the historical accounts of the time written by white men and occupied an increasingly large space in the colonial archives. In part, this importance was the result of the value of information about these societies for traders, travelers, missionaries, and administrators.

Recent scholarship has had much to say about the extent to which these accounts reflected the fantasies and prejudices of their writers. There were, however, also powerful imperatives at stake, which ensured that much information gleaned from local sources was recorded, with considerable attention given to the achievement of accuracy in that recording. In the 1820s, for example, early traders in Natal became embroiled in the affairs of the Zulu kingdom under Shaka. Their trading initiatives depended on their ability to act as interlocutors between merchant capital interests in the Cape and the Zulu court. In pursuit of this agenda the traders relayed to their backers in the Cape and to the Cape public through the colony's newspapers, accounts of the emergence of the Zulu kingdom, and its recent political and social history. Not surprisingly, the emphases in the traders' accounts shifted in response to changes in their own situation relative to the Zulu court. Their operations in Natal were directly affected by their ability to exploit historical local tensions and loyalties, placing a premium on their mastery of salient historical and political information. Thus, whether acclaiming or decrying the Zulu kingdom, their accounts were based not only on their personal experiences but on information gleaned from a wide variety of local sources, ranging from the Zulu court to the most disaffected elements within the kingdom, as well as from neighboring communities, each with its own version of that history.[66] Much of that history is recorded in their texts, often freely mixed with their fantasies and prejudices.[67] Early traders may have been among the first to capture in writing African ideas about the past, but they were, of course, far from the only writers to do so.

COLONIAL HEGEMONY, EARLY NATIONALISMS, AND THE PRODUCTION OF HISTORY

In the course of the nineteenth century there was an outpouring of scholarly and more popular texts on the precolonial history of South Africa and on

---

[65] de Kock, *Civilising Barbarians*, Afterword.

[66] See Hamilton, *Terrific Majesty*, Chapter II.

[67] D. Wylie, *Savage Delight: White Myths of Shaka* (Pietermaritzburg: University of Natal Press, 2000).

emerging colonial conditions produced by missionaries, colonial authorities, settlers, travelers, and scholars. They provided histories, descriptions of manners and customs, grammars and dictionaries of the local languages, elaborations of systems of classification, maps, and visual representations, in some instances capturing local ideas and knowledge and in other instances erasing them.

Although often characterized as the chief agents of empire, of European modernity, and the advance of Western civilization through a campaign for the construction of colonial subjects, the missionaries nonetheless generated a detailed record of the societies among whom they pursued their missions. Events beyond the mission station, including local political developments, were sometimes recorded fully and sometimes only incidentally in their communications, often depending on how closely the missionaries participated in politics. Other kinds of material were, however, the object of systematic investigation. Many religious orders encouraged missionaries to master the local language, to investigate and become familiar with key cultural concepts, especially those relevant to cosmology and spirituality, and to collect oral histories of individuals and communities. An evangelical concern with conversion led the missionaries to take a deep interest in belief systems and matters of culture and consciousness. They were thus possessed of an imperative to undertake detailed and intensive investigation, even as it was refracted through the ideas and values of Christian cosmology as well as through the images of Africa they brought with them into the field.[68] The role of the often small groups of converts or key individuals used as informants and interpreters on whom the missionaries depended further shaped the material collected.

When in the field, missionaries were typically required to keep diaries, to write detailed reports, and to send regular letters home. The archives of the mission societies thus constitute a rich record of the missionary encounter, although written from a particular perspective. In the case of the Berlin Missionary Society, for example, this material was published in the mission newsletter, the *Berliner Missions-berichte*, and various mission societies engaged in active public discourse on the nature of the mission and of African society, as "mission testimony became a veritable industry."[69] John Philip's public campaigns and the political interventions of the London Missionary Society are perhaps the best known of these interventions. In many instances missionaries also published books based on their researches, such as Rev. Callaway's *The Religious System of the AmaZulu*. Mission activity in this area was so intensive that Kirsten Rüther identifies the emergence

---

[68] Comaroff and Comaroff, *Of Revelation and Revolution*, vol. 1, Chapter 3.
[69] *Ibid.*, p. 37.

of individual historiographic traditions in the Hermannsburg and Berlin Missionary Societies, marked by distinctive narrative forms aimed at justifying evangelical policies and stimulating donors.[70] Indeed, the various denominations had different and sometimes contradictory aims and ideological motives, which led them to engage differently with the African societies they sought to convert as well as with administrators and settlers. All these factors shaped the records they laid down and the interpretations of African society and the colonial encounter they promoted.

Missionary hostility to traditional authority and institutions and rituals that bolstered that authority, and commitment to the eradication of what they regarded as heathen superstition, typically marked their project even as they researched those topics. Then, through the promotion of literacy and learning, they began systematically to reject that body of knowledge, replacing it with a radical division of church and state and the promotion of hegemonic forms of European culture, introducing new arguments about the nature of humanity, civilization, and history in an effort the Comaroffs have termed the colonization of consciousness.[71]

Where the missionary record was primarily concerned with matters of culture and consciousness, and more incidentally the wider political context, the record created by colonial administrators focused on the nature of power and politics. The colonial historiography of the Zulu kingdom, for example, inaugurated by the traders, continued in dialogue with the local African historiography for much of the rest of the century, with the early distinctions between the written and oral forms becoming increasingly blurred as the century progressed. In sharp distinction to much of the missionary endeavor, the research of administrators was geared toward the

---

[70] K. Rüther, *The Power Beyond: Mission strategies, African conversiton and the development of a Christian culture in the Transvaal* (Hamburg, Berlin and London: Lit-Verlag, 2001), esp. pp. 8–13; also see U. van der Heyden, "The Archives and Library of the Berlin Missionary Society," *History in Africa,* 23 (1996), pp. 411–27. Also see Comaroff and Comaroff, *Of Revelation and Revolution,* vol. 1, pp. 32–9.

[71] Comaroff and Comaroff, *Of Revelation and Revolution,* vol. 1, Conclusion. Peter Delius periodizes this for the Berlin Missionary Society, noting that an initial period of generalized discovery and comment was followed by the development of an orthodoxy of concern with and understanding of society marked by a hostility to traditional authority as conflicts between the Pedi paramount, Sekhukhune, and the missionaries deepened, and a focus in on polygyny and initiation, two key institutions of traditional authority. (P. Delius, "The Pedi Polity under Sekwati and Sekhukhune, 1828–1880," unpublished Ph.D. thesis, University of London [1980], appendix A). Also see his comments on the BMS records in "Witches and Missionaries in Nineteenth-century Transvaal," *Journal of Southern African Studies,* 27(3) (2001), pp. 429–43. See Comaroff and Comaroff, *Of Revelation and Revolution,* vol. 1, Chapter 7, on the way in which the British Nonconformist southern Tswana mission attempted to drive a wedge between the realm of the spirit and sacred authority which flowed from it and secular power.

take up, or appropriation, of ideas of traditional authority. This trend was elaborated in Natal, where the Secretary for Native Affairs, Theophilus Shepstone, crafted a form of indirect rule based on intensive historical research, inaugurating what was to become a long administrative interest in African history linked to the maintenance of control over African communities.[72] Shepstone's vision found early support within his administration, notably from the compiler of the major written historical record of the time, the Natal magistrate John Bird, as well as, at least initially from another analyst of Zulu society, the outspoken bishop of Natal, John William Colenso.[73] It was the Shepstonian insistence on forms of native administration based on a thorough knowledge of local history and customs that informed and drove the enormous archival project of another colonial official, James Stuart, mentioned previously. The Shepstonian system was widely imitated as British colonization spread north to Kenya and laid the groundwork for the twentieth-century policy known as indirect rule.

A core of other officials and scholars in the wider region also believed that fluency in local language and intensive research into local history and local institutions were essential to effective governance. They included, among others, the philologist Wilhelm Bleek and his patron, Cape governor Sir George Grey. Together Bleek and Grey asserted the need for in-depth local research within colonial administration. This kind of research had massive implications, not least in that it defined peoples. The work reflected the attitudes of recorders and was drawn into the service of the colonial project. At the same time it was also the conduit by which the ideas of the colonized were filtered into colonial practices. Shepstone's receptivity to the power of the logic of African communities around him was at odds with the larger settler population of Natal, which produced its own accounts of the history of the region that decried what it portrayed as Zulu "savagery"; an interpretation that bolstered another set of archival interpolations, those of Chase, was published in Grahamstown by Godlonton.[74]

Local epistemology, and sometimes local history, also received attention from the Natal missionaries, notably Reverends Callaway[75] and Holden and

---

[72] Hamilton, *Terrific Majesty*, Chapter 3. On Shepstone's historical research, also see J. B. Wright, "The Dynamics of Power and Conflict in the Thukela-Mzimkhulu Region in the Late Eighteenth and Early Nineteenth Centuries: A Critical Reconstruction," unpublished Ph.D. thesis, University of the Witwatersrand (1989), p. 107.

[73] J. Bird (Ed.), *Annals of Natal*.

[74] J. C. Chase, *The Natal Papers: A Reprint of All Notices and Public Documents connected with that territory including a description of the country and a History of Events from 1498–1843*, 2 parts (Grahamstown: R. Godlonton and Cape Town: J. H. Collard, 1843).

[75] H. Callaway, *Nursery Tales, Traditions and Histories of the Zulu* (Pietermaritzburg: Davis and Springvale, 1868); *The Religious System of the AmaZulu* (Pietermaritzburg: Davis and Springvale, 1870).

Bishop Colenso, who largely pursued information about religious ideas. Holden and Colenso both produced historical texts seeking to persuade settlers of their common humanity with their Zulu neighbors.[76] In 1859, the year of Colenso's first exploratory trip to the Zulu kingdom in the company of Shepstone, Colenso's Bishopstowe Press published *Izindatyana zabantu*,[77] a collection of stories and myths involving historical figures and events as well as eyewitness historical accounts, oral traditions, praise poems, and songs. Colenso, unusual for a missionary, shared (though for different reasons) Shepstone's commitment to the protection and preservation of African institutions and ideas, a position that brought him into conflict with fellow missionaries in Natal and, indeed, ultimately with the highly pragmatic and increasingly tyrannical Shepstone.

Sifiso Ndlovu argues that although Colenso certainly had a hand in the making of *Izindatyana zabantu*, William Ngidi, an educated convert and Colenso's close advisor and translator, was probably the primary author, playing a central role in eliciting the various contributions. The texts are complex engagements with the then-recent past that explore crucial aspects of the operation of power in precolonial and early colonial times. Ndlovu discerns in them an incipient black nationalist discourse, which he finds echoed in certain texts recorded by James Stuart. Such texts provide a window on the intellectual efforts of Africans across the nineteenth century to grapple with the implications and effects of expanding colonialism and settlerism and a collapsing precolonial order. We see in the texts recorded by Stuart discussions of African disaffection with colonial government, critiques of current and earlier systems of native administration, protests about the colonial government's lack of knowledge of African matters, commentary on the breakdown of chiefly and patriarchal authority, and protests about the silencing of Africans, many of which were expressed by means of powerful references to the past. These discourses emerged against a background of active African protest, led by *amakholwa* (Christian, educated Africans) against the policies of the Natal native administration, notably in the pages of the early African newspaper, *Inkanyiso*, and through the activities of the Funamalungelo Society and later the Natal Native Congress, founded in 1900 to promote African rights and liberties. By the turn of the century African writers were also offering perspectives on the missionary contribution to the history of the region. Two of William Ngidi's original classmates at Colenso's Ekukhanyeni mission school, Mubi Nondenisa and Magema Fuze, sought "to engrave" for posterity the history

---

[76] See W. C. Holden, *The Past and Future of the Kaffir Races* (published for the author in London, and by Richards. Glanville and Co., SA, and G. C. Cato, Port Natal).

[77] Church of England Mission, *Izindatyana zabantu: kanye nezindaba zaseNatal* (Bishopstowe, 1858).

of the Ekukhanyeni mission by publishing a series of articles in the news-paper *Ipepa lo Hlanga* and actively used that history to challenge prevailing colonial government attitudes and race policies.[78] It was also at Bish-opstowe that one of the most vivid challenges to the operation of the barbarism–civilization trope was enacted when William Ngidi's question-ing of Colenso on religious matters converted the bishop and led him to question the literal veracity of the Bible. It was at the time, as Jeff Guy put it, a "disturbing reversal of the idea of the coloniser and colonised which switched dominated for dominant, unlearned for learned, heathen for christian, savage for civilised, the self and the other."[79]

Administrators in neighboring territories were not, at least at the time, as permeable as the Natal native administration to the absorption of African practices. In the Eastern Cape both the missionaries and most local adminis-trators, propagating a creed of progress, sought to break the power of chiefs (an agenda often shared by Shepstone, even if his methods were different) and suppress African custom, but, it should be noted, in a manner firmly rooted in personal contact and with a knowledge of African languages and traditions. That information was used to constrain chiefly authority and to entrench arguments about the "barbarism of Africans" as opposed to the "civilisation of the colonists."[80]

Notwithstanding early Christianization in this region, local African soci-eties proved remarkably resilient in the face of these pressures, and precolo-nial institutions and practices persisted in many instances. The recording of the historical traditions of the amaXhosa goes back to the beginning of the nineteenth century, making them the oldest in Southern Africa.[81] The first historical writing in isiXhosa was published in 1844–5, the earliest such work in an indigenous South African language.[82]

---

[78] V. Khumalo, "The Class of 1856 and the Politics of Cultural Production(s) in the Emergence of Ekukhanyeni, 1855–1910," in J. Draper (Ed.), *Eye of the Storm: Bishop John William Colenso and the Crisis of Biblical Inspiration* (Pietermaritzburg: Cluster, 2003), pp. 207–41.

[79] J. Guy, "Class, Imperialism and Literary Criticism: William Ngidi, John Colenso and Mathew Arnold," *Journal of Southern African Studies*, 23(2) (1997), p. 221.

[80] C. Crais, *The Politics of Evil: Magic, State Power and the Political Imagination in South Africa* (Cambridge: Cambridge University Press, 2002), Chapters 2 and 3.

[81] J. T. van der Kemp, "Religion, Customs, Population, Language, History and Natural Pro-ductions of the Country," *Transactions of the Missionary Society* I (1800), pp. 433–68; L. Alberti, *Account of the Tribal Life and Customs of the Xhosa in 1807*, translated by W. Fehr (Cape Town: A. A. Balkema, 1968; first published in Dutch in 1807, and in the German original in 1815); H. Lichtenstein, *Travels in Southern Africa in the years 1803, 1804, 1805 and 1806*, 2 vols. (reprinted Cape Town: van Riebeeck Society, 1928–9), vol. I, pp. 357–70.

[82] It was in the newspaper *Ikhwezi*. See J. Peires, *House of Phalo: History of the Xhosa people in the Days of their Independence* (Johannesburg, Ravan Press, 1981), p. 175.

These primacies obviously derive from the unfortunate circumstance of early amaXhosa contact with the Cape Colony, which resulted both in the long history of war and in the early development of a relatively large educated male elite. Although a number of the founding myths of the Xhosa monarchy remained part of the general education of every Xhosa man, the history of the amaXhosa came to be particularly dominated by the long wars with the Cape Colony. This did not lead to a lack of interest in that history among the new elite. On the contrary, for instance, the first Xhosa person to be ordained as a Christian minister, Tiyo Soga, was known for collecting "fables, legends and proverbs, fragments of . . . history, rugged utterances of native bards, the ancient habits and customs of his countrymen, and the genealogy of chiefs with striking incidents of their lives."[83] It is an irony of the mission project in South Africa that literacy and learning, the two tools in which the missionaries placed such faith to effect the transition to civilization, were increasingly mobilized by the emerging black intelligentsia not only to express their criticism of colonialism and to exchange ideas with colonial subjects elsewhere but also to preserve and discuss precolonial ideas and information. Missionary responses to the black intelligentsia's forays into publication varied across time and place. Whereas Bishopstowe facilitated such publications, refrained from intervening in their form, and published in the vernacular, Lovedale in the Eastern Cape monitored publication closely and actively sought to suppress alternative black writing in the vernacular.[84]

During the third quarter of the nineteenth century, with the tensions between English- and Dutch-speakers in the Cape in abeyance and the conflict on the Eastern frontier of the Cape Colony resolved in favor of the colonists at the expense of the amaXhosa, the Khoekhoen and their liberal protagonists, the most fervent arguments on the recent past of South Africa shifted to the borderlands between the Sotho kingdom under Moshoeshoe and the Orange Free State. This was also, not coincidentally, the area over which the struggle for land was perhaps the most intense and, furthermore, that in which an African ruler, Moshoeshoe, had long seen the advantage of employing European advocates, in particular the French Protestant missionaries, to plead his case with the colonial authorities. The result was a complicated historiography. There were certainly colonialist explications, particularly in the early histories of the Free State, but there were also works in which whites wrote defending the Sotho position.

---

[83] J. A. Chalmers, *Tiyo Soga: a page of South African mission work* (Edinburgh; Andrew Eliot, 1878), p. 343, cited in D. Williams, *Umfundisi: a biography of Tiyo Soga, 1829–1871* (Lovedale: Lovedale Press, 1978), pp. 112–13.

[84] de Kock, *Civilising Barbarians*, Chapter 3.

The early historiography of the Sotho kingdom was based on two intertwined but separate endeavors. On the one hand, there was the material produced in European languages, particularly English. The first major work was the *History of the Basutus of South Africa*, published anonymously in 1857. It soon became clear that the nominal author was J. M. Orpen, but in fact his brothers, various French missionaries, and J. P. Hoffmann, the first president of the Orange Free State, seem to have had a role in it, whereas Moshoeshoe himself persuaded Orpen to present his case in this way and provided a couple of sacks full of documents to help him.[85] Later, Theal was employed by the Cape government to collect the historical documents relating to the country while it was, temporarily, part of the colony. Perhaps surprisingly, given Theal's subsequent status as the iconic writer of South African history from the settlers' point of view, what was produced was not appreciated by the colonial government, being regarded as too supportive of Sotho land claims, and the final three volumes of the *Basutoland Records* languished unpublished in the archives until 2002. As Theal commented, his researches "show both sides of a question, while some people would have only one side seen."[86]

There was, from the later nineteenth century at least, an extensive historiography in Sesotho. It centered on the journal *Leselinyana la Lesotho*, published by the Huguenot missionaries who were so important in the country during that century. Its first editor, the Rev. Adolphe Mabille, who founded the journal in 1864, was described as understanding "better perhaps than any other South African missionary, how greatly the development of a literature in the vernacular could advance the service of God."[87] What effects this Protestant missionary monopoly had on the production of history in the Sotho kingdom is a question that awaits research into the intellectual history of the country. What is certain, however, is that between 1886 and 1925 *Leselinyana* published "several hundred" articles by Azariele Sekese, largely based on oral sources. There were also a number of others who published reminiscences and, perhaps, the results of oral research in the same journal. These fed into the works by the missionary D. F. Ellenberger, who wrote in both Sesotho and French, and his son-in-law, J. C. Macgregor, a colonial official, who apparently collected testimony in the course of his

---

[85] E. A. Eldredge, "Land, Politics, and Censorship: The Historiography of Nineteenth-century Lesotho," *History in Africa*, 15 (1988), pp. 192–7.

[86] Eldredge, "Land, Politics, and Censorship," p. 199, citing Theal to H. M. Dyke, August 16, 1883 (Morija: P.E.M.S. archives).

[87] E. Jacottet, *The Morija Printing Office and Book Depot: A Historical Survey* (Morija: Sesuto Book Depot, 1912), p. 9. (Our thanks to both Isabel Hofmeyr and Paul Germond for guiding us to relevant sources concerning early publishing in Sesotho.)

work as a magistrate and published in Sesotho. He also translated Ellenberger's *History* into English and emended it.[88] Clearly, there are enormous
problems of source criticism and intertextuality involved in this collection
of works, but it provides important possibilities for the writing of a history
of Sotho views of the country's past.[89]

The historiography of the Sotho kingdom overlapped with that of the
Great Trek, certainly with regard to the anti-Sotho arguments. Whereas
the participants in the Great Trek did not justify their actions with historical arguments, those very actions formed the basis of the myths by
which Afrikaner nationalism, as it developed, came to be justified. It is
thus not surprising that the first work published in Afrikaans was entitled *Di Geskidenis van ons Land in di Taal van Ons Volk* (The History of
our Country in the Language of our People), by S. J. du Toit, a Dutch
Reformed minister.[90] It was the aim of the First Language Movement to
turn Afrikaans into a respectable and official language.[91] In much the same
vein, but with a different ethno-political message, were the reevaluation
of Cape Dutch architecture, South Africa's first "heritage" movement, in
which Cecil Rhodes played a major part, the establishment of the Cape
archives in 1879, and the first major investigation of "white" South African
genealogy.[92] The second strand of Afrikaner nationalism derived from the
political struggles necessary to maintain the independence of the northern
republics in the face of British imperial pressure. In this context it was
easy for the Trek to be seen as the founding charter of a new people. The
initial use of the Trek as a central metaphor came in the Orange Free State
in the years after the disputes on the diamond fields. It was at this stage,
for instance, that Sarel Cilliers was interviewed on his deathbed, and the

---

[88] D. F. Ellenberger, *History of the Basuto: Ancient and Modern*, edited and translated by J. C.
Macgregor (London: Caxton, 1912).

[89] For what there is, see P. Sanders, *Moshoeshoe: Chief of the Sotho* (London (etc): Heinemann,
1975), notably pp. 321–5, 331–4; D. P. Kunene, "*Leselinyana la Lesotho* and Sotho
Historiography," *History in Africa,* 4 (1977) 149–61; Eldredge, "Land, Politics and
Censorship."

[90] Cape Town: Smuts & Hofmeyr, 1877.

[91] H. Giliomee, *The Afrikaners: Biography of a People* (Cape Town: Tafelberg, 2003), pp.
217–23.

[92] C. de Bosdari, *Cape Dutch houses and farms, their architecture and history together with a
note on the role of Cecil John Rhodes in their preservation* (Cape Town: Balkema, 1953);
lemma on H. C. V. Leibbrandt and G. M. Theal, in W. J. de Kock (Ed.), *Dictionary of
South African Biography*, 5 vols., Capetown: Tafelberg for the Human Sciences Research
Council, 1968–1987) II & IV; G. Botha, *A Brief Guide to the Various Classes of Documents
in the Cape Archives for the period 1652–1806* (Cape Town: Cape Times, 1918), pp. 1–8; R.
Ross, "The 'white' population of the Cape Colony in the Eighteenth Century," in *Beyond
the Pale*, p. 240; for the context see M. Tamarkin, *Cecil Rhodes and the Cape Afrikaners:
The Imperial Colossus and The Colonial Parish Pump* (London: Frank Cass, 1996).

transcript of the interview produced as his "Journal." Accounts of the Trek together with the records of the various republics – for the most part departmental records of government where departments existed, and including documents concerning land rights, the records of land commissions, and settlement treaties – constituted a largely ad hoc archival base underpinning Boer land settlement. The most active recordkeeping occurred in the department of the South African Republic (Transvaal) state secretary, who in 1887 appointed a commission to put the archives of his department in order and in 1896 appointed a keeper of archives.[93]

However, it was particularly after the first British occupation of the Transvaal that the Trek began to take on seriously mythical proportions. Although the major concerns had to do with battles between the Trekkers and the Zulu and the rediscovery of the covenant, the former are supposed to have made before the battle of Ncome River, the same episodes could be used as a way to strengthen republican resolve in the conflict with British imperialism. Thus it was that the first great celebrations of the victory over the Zulu at Ncome, or Blood River as the Europeans had come to call it, were held in Pretoria in 1891.[94]

Through the 1890s the production of anti-British historiography increased in step with British pressure on the South African Republic, culminating in the brilliant invective of *Een Eeuw van Onrecht*, also put out in English as *A Century of Wrong*. Jan Smuts was involved in the writing of this book which set out the Transvaal and Afrikaner historical claims in the first months of the Second Anglo-Boer War.[95]

This process was accentuated in the aftermath of the Second Anglo-Boer War as part of the creation of Afrikaner ethnicity.[96] The work of Gustav Preller constituted a particularly important element of this process. Preller, a journalist who had fought for the South African Republic in the war, collected oral testimony and private documents, both from soldiers who had fought in the war and from the few aged survivors of the Trek. He wrote a biography of Piet Retief and played a major role in organizing the celebration of what was first known as Dingaan's Day and later came to be the Day of the Covenant, turning Afrikaner nationalism into a religious act. In 1916, Preller wrote the script for a film on the Trek and was the advisor who made sure that the visual details were historically accurate.

[93] C. G. Botha, *The Public Archives of South Africa 1652–1910* (Cape Town: Cape Times Limited, 1928).

[94] Thompson, *Political Mythology*, Chapter 5.

[95] J. C. Smuts, F. W. Reitz, and J. de V. Roos, *Een Eeuw van Onrecht* (no publisher cited, 1899).

[96] See S. Marks, "Class, culture and consciousness in South Africa, 1880–1910," in vol. II of this publication.

He himself remained faithful to Louis Botha as a leader and only moved from the South African Party to the National Party in 1923, but nevertheless his work provided the basis for an Afrikaner nationalist view of history – with the Trek as its central event – which was to become dominant as Afrikaner nationalist politics came to rule South Africa.[97]

Perpetuating tactics inaugurated by Shepstone, the colonial authorities regularly countered emerging settler historiographies with reference to African historical claims, but in a manner tightly mediated by one or another colonial apparatus of government, most notably colonial commissions. Thus the British hold over the most valuable portion of South Africa in 1872 was justified, in their own eyes, on the basis of African testimony given before "a commission appointed to investigate the claims of the South African Republic, Chief Nicholas Waterboer, chief of West Griqualand, and certain other native chiefs, to portions of territory on the Vaal River, now known as the Diamond Fields." In the course of the evidence given to this commission, which sat at Bloemhof, the nineteenth-century history of much of what is today the Northern Cape province, and adjacent parts of the Free State and Northwest provinces, was discussed, though not perhaps in the terms, or with the priorities, the witnesses would themselves have used.[98] Again, in the aftermath of the South African War, British officers conducted interviews in both the Transvaal and Orange River Colony, which were to provide the grounds for the dispossession of the Boers until the decision was made to conciliate them.[99] Black history was powerfully mobilized in white quarrels.

NATIVE ADMINISTRATION AND THE PRODUCTION OF HISTORY, 1903–1928

As the Boer defeat in the South African War of 1899–1903 appeared imminent, the British authorities, as if to show who was now in charge in South Africa, replaced local administrations with *landdrosts* in the Transvaal and with British magistrates, justices of the peace, and public prosecutors in the Orange Free State. One of the immediate concerns of the Milner

---

[97] I. Hofmeyr, "Popularizing History: The Case of Gustav Preller," *Journal of African History*, 29 (1988), pp. 21–36.

[98] The evidence to the commission was printed, though never published, and is known as the "Bloemhof Blue Book"; the archival copy can be found in the Cape Archives, HA 89.

[99] See T. Keegan, "The Restructuring of Agrarian Class Relations in a Colonial Economy: The Orange River Colony, 1902–1910," *Journal of Southern African Studies*, 5 (1979), pp. 234–54; J. Krikler, *Revolution from Above, Rebellion from Below: the Agrarian Transvaal at the Turn of the Century* (Oxford: Clarendon Press, 1990), p. 7.

government was to establish an administrative framework that would govern Africans, together with a "native" policy to drive it. To achieve these objectives, the government embarked upon the production of histories of the various African communities in these areas. But first, an official bureaucracy that would realize these objectives had to be set up.

Following the annexation of the Transvaal in 1900, a Native Affairs Department was formed, headed by a commissioner for Native Affairs who was appointed in August 1901. Below him was the secretary for Native Affairs, a permanent head of the department. From about 1903, the native and subnative commissioners stationed in each district of the Transvaal conducted detailed oral research into the history of every grouping in the territory. The results of this exercise were the *Short History of the Native Tribes of the Transvaal* and the *Report by the Commissioner for Native Affairs Relative to the Acquisition and Tenure of Land by Natives in the Transvaal*, both published in 1905. In the same year, the general staff of the War Office in London published *The Native Tribes of the Transvaal*, which was rather less detailed than the other two.

The historical enquiries of commissions also provided justification for the specific forms of power and authority exerted by the colonial authorities over the African population of South Africa, building on arguments first developed in Natal for forms of control rooted in African custom and tradition. Adam Ashforth suggestively describes commissions as sites of dialogue and the published reports of such commissions as the materialization of the act of hearing, thereby pointing to their work in developing a hegemonic understanding of the past through overtly public processes.[100]

The South African Native Affairs Commission of 1903–05 was convened to address the need for a steady supply of low cost labor for the gold mines. It addressed itself to the matter of how to release more labor from rural production relations. The necessary interventions were understood to require detailed knowledge of and intervention in what was conceived as a relatively homogenous precolonial system. The interpretation chosen of that system, thought of in the singular, had to be both cost effective and acceptable to prevailing liberal sentiments. What followed was an effort at conceptualizing precolonial forms of sovereignty and an account of the extension of colonial sovereignty over "natives" through peaceful annexation of lands and appropriation of that chiefly sovereignty. The commission was charged with gathering "accurate information on certain matters relating to Natives and Native administration."[101] Although the

[100] A. Ashforth, *The Politics of Official Discourse in Twentieth-century South Africa* (Oxford: Clarendon Press, 1990), p. 7.
[101] Cited in Ashforth, *Official Discourse*, p. 29.

commission relied heavily on the information of so-called native experts and other Europeans, African testimony was recorded and, as Shula Marks has pointed out, the "still pulsating remains of powerful African kingdoms" influenced the policies that emerged.[102]

The commission used the historical information it had accumulated from a range of sources as the basis for defining different forms of citizenship for "natives" and "Europeans."[103] The former were deemed to be "tribal" and historically accustomed to an authoritarian system under which they were given rights to ancestral lands, traditionally held by the chief under communal administration in trust for the people. After annexation the chiefs were regarded as having transferred their sovereign rights to the Crown, which was then obliged to administer Africans along so-called traditional lines in terms of what came to be known as Native Law. The claim to recognize and work in terms of a historical African system became the justification for the denial of franchise rights to the bulk of the African population, a justification for limiting access to land, for the control of black women, and for the utilization of arbitrary forms of governance.

The commission's historical investigations were expressly oriented to enable it to regulate sexuality, health, education, and leisure as much as political power and access to property, and thereby to impose fundamental subjection and subjectivity. Its thinking in dividing the population into "natives" and "Europeans," "savages" and "civilized," nonetheless recognized the existence of the so-called educated natives and allowed for their advancement and evolution toward full citizenship. Despite this evolutionist aspect, the commission opened the way for subsequent developments of segregation and apartheid to be justified in terms of African tradition and historical tribalism. From this point onward, all attempts to document or reconstruct the preindustrial African past, however liberal in sentiment and aims, were profoundly implicated in racial domination.

The commission set in place the basis for a unified system of native administration for South Africa based on tribalism. However, the new Native Affairs Department was a politically weak and fragmented arm of state, which, though often directly coercive, was regarded as sympathetic to the situation of Africans, notably where it sought to keep a balance between their needs and the increasing demand for cheap labor. This took the form of a protective paternalism expressed in the 1927 Native Administration

[102] S. Marks, *The Ambiguities of Dependence in South Africa: Class, Nationalism and the State in Twentieth-Century Natal* (Johannesburg: Ravan Press, 1986), p. 5.

[103] Although primarily concerned with the legacy of these early segregationist moves, M. Mamdani's *Citizen and Subject: Contemporary Africa and the Legacy of Late Colonialism* (Cape Town: David Philip, 1996) provides a useful conceptualization of the bifurcated state and its two forms of power under one hegemonic authority.

Act, which designated the governor general as supreme chief for all of South Africa outside of the Cape.[104] Indeed, the embalming of tribal authority was part of the administrative strategy throughout the 1920s. By the time the 1932 Native Economic Commission, which focused on the need for development, recommended a revamped tribal system, it did so based on a new scientific understanding of the differences between "natives" and "Europeans," derived from anthropology and, more specifically, the newly established ethnology section of the Native Affairs Department. The divided population conceived of by the South African Native Affairs Commission was now underpinned by a structure of separate knowledge, with anthropology for "natives" and history reserved for "Europeans."

In the 1920s, specialized research on so-called natives was actively taken up in South African universities with the establishment of departments of Bantu Studies, Anthropology, and Ethnology. The research conducted in these departments laid down a vast archive of material relevant to precolonial times, some garnered with the express aim of bolstering power and traditional practices, whereas others, framed by notions of the dynamism of culture, expressly challenged such ideas.[105] The Bantu Studies Department provided diploma courses for Native Affairs Department officials, who were given bonus incentives to take them. In 1925 G. P. Lestrade was appointed to the Native Affairs Department as head of the new ethnological section concerned with investigating a "true native" identity prior to "contact."[106] This panoply of academically rooted scholarship, developed by experts and backed by elaborate verification procedures, worked to disqualify and render unscientific alternative views of the past raised by contemporary black intellectuals.[107] This division of knowledge was a development on the somewhat earlier emergence in Europe of anthropology as the science of the study of "primitive tribes." For much of the nineteenth century, information about native societies gleaned in the colonies had been fed back to the metropoles, where it was processed and analyzed by a

---

[104] S. Dubow, *Racial segregation and the origins of Apartheid in South Africa, 1919–36* (Basingstoke: Macmillan, 1989), p. 11.

[105] See for example, A. T. Bryant's, *Olden Times in Zululand and Natal* (London: Longmans, 1929). On Bryant, see J. Wright, "The dynamics of power"; *idem*, "A.T. Bryant and the wars of Shaka" *History in Africa, 18* (1991), pp. 409–25; See also, J. Sharp, "The Roots and Development of Volkekunde," *Journal of Southern African Studies, 8* (1981), pp. 16–36; R. Gordon, "Apartheid's Anthropologists: The Genealogy of Afrikaner Anthropology," *American Ethnologist, 15* (1988), pp. 535–53.

[106] Ashforth, *Official Discourse*, p. 78.

[107] See S. Dubow, *Scientific racism in modern South Africa* (Cambridge: Cambridge University Press, 1995), for a wider discussion of the various efforts to systematize study of the African population and of the links between local efforts and a broader imperial project linked to the metropolitan centers.

generation of so-called armchair anthropologists like E. B. Tylor and Henry Lewis Morgan. The new departments in South African universities signaled a departure from this approach and infused anthropology and its cognate disciplines with a politically charged local agenda.

BLACK INTELLECTUALS AND THE PRODUCTION OF HISTORY IN THE EARLY DECADES OF THE TWENTIETH CENTURY

If the intellectuals of the segregationist state researched materials pertinent to the precolonial past to support their political vision, so too did contemporary black intellectuals turn to history and print culture as they sought to negotiate their own identity in relation to the twin pressures of segregation and modernity.[108] From the late 1910s, and following the ruthless suppression of the Bhambatha rebellion (1906–8) by the colonial authorities, the embryonic sense of Zulu ethnic identity and nationalism, enunciated by William Ngidi and other members of the Zulu intelligentsia in the mid- and later nineteenth century, took hold and spread, increasingly cutting across sharpening class divisions.[109]

The royal house and the chiefs looked to a historic Zulu identity to shore up their status and power and invested in a range of cultural activities that appealed not only to rural traditionalists but also to the increasingly frustrated *kholwa* elite and the emerging Zulu-speaking working class. A growing preoccupation with history, often embedded in the key intellectual debates of the time, was reflected in the pages of John Dube's newspaper, *Ilanga laseNatal* (which on occasion expressly rejected the involvement of administrators and missionaries in the production of Zulu history and called for "natives" to write their own histories). It also characterized the formation of the Inkatha kaZulu organization of 1924 and was evident in the work of literate Zulu-speakers on the Rand in the Zulu Institute, established in 1917 (reincarnated in 1919 as the Zulu National Association), and of the

---

[108] On black intellectuals' use of print culture in establishing themselves as modern subjects in direct opposition to the identities ascribed to them by colonial and segregationist ideologies, see D. Attwell, *Rewriting Modernity: Studies in Black South African Literary History* (Pietermaritzburg: University of KwaZulu – Natal Press, 2005).

[109] See P. Maylam, "The changing political economy of the region, 1920–1950," in R. Morrell (Ed.), *Political Economy and Identities in KwaZulu Natal* (Durban: Indicator, 1996), Chapter 4; S. Marks, *The Ambiguities of Dependence in South Africa: Class, Nationalism and the State in 20th-century Natal* (Johannesburg: Ravan Press, 1986); N. Cope, *To Bind a Nation: Solomon kaDinuzulu and Zulu Nationalism:1913–1933* (Pietermaritzburg: University of Natal Press, 1993); P. la Hausse de Lalouvière, *Restless Identities: Signatures of Nationalism, Zulu Ethnicity and History in the Lives of Petros Lamula (c. 1881–1948) and Lymon Maling (1889–c.1936)* (Pietermaritzburg: University of Natal Press, 2000), Introduction.

Zulu Society, formed in 1936 to preserve and promote Zulu culture and customs.

In 1922, Magema Fuze's *Abantu Abamnyama* was published (almost two decades after it had been written). It comprised a collection of personal recollections, eyewitness historical accounts, and oral traditions, as well as a section engaging historical accounts of key events in Zulu history by European writers.[110] In 1924, Petros Lamula, self-proclaimed "Professor of the Hidden Sciences" and one of the first Zulu-speaking writers who was consciously a historian, published *uZulukaMalandela*, a strongly cultural nationalist narrative that emphasized racial pride. Paul La Hausse argues that Lamula's text reveals that he was deeply aware of the contested nature of history and of the importance of evidence and explanation.[111] Lymon Maling, the other subject of La Hausse's biographical study, was active by the mid-1920s in interpreting the history of Zulu dispossession, seeking archival documents to support claims made through oral traditions and using the conventions of professional history. In his attempts to lodge Zulu land claims he engaged the ambiguities involved in the appeal to both written historical records and oral traditions. He was also a key figure in the formulation of the historical arguments that came to underpin the African National Congress (ANC)'s response to the 1927 Native Administration Act, explicitly contesting the historical claim in the act to the secretary of Native Affairs' powers over Africans.[112]

Increasingly politically constrained, challenged by white domination of the terrain of interpretation of the African past and its consignment to anthropology and Bantu studies, and skeptical of the official versions of the history of the country, prominent members of the Zulu intelligentsia began using fictional genres – novels, plays, and poetry – to discuss the past, to present African agency, and to critique colonialism. By not claiming to be providing historical texts and thus evading the limitations of the recognized colonial archive, they were able to tell the historical truth as they saw it. In 1930, John Dube produced *Insila kaShaka*, the first Zulu novel, and in 1935 Rolfes Dhlomo produced his novel, *uDingane*.[113] B. W. Vilakazi produced

---

[110] M. M. Fuze, *Abantu Abamnyama Lapa Bavela Ngakona* (Pietermaritzburg: private publication, 1922). Also see his articles on various aspects of Zulu history, published in *Ilanga* from 1915–1922.

[111] P. Lamula, *uZulukaMalandela: A Most Practical and Concise Compendium of African History Combined with Genealogy, Chronology, Geography and Biography* (Durban: Josiah Jones, 1924). La Hausse, *Restless Identities*, Chapter 3.

[112] La Hausse, *Restless Identities*, Chapters 6 and 7.

[113] R. Dhlomo, *uDingane* (Pietermaritzburg: Shuter and Shooter, 1936), also *Izikhali Zanamuhla* (Pietermaritzburg: Shuter and Shooter, 1935); J. Dube, *Insila kaShaka* (Marianhill: Marianhill Mission Press, 1930); see also the three plays on Dingane by H. I. E. Dhlomo

historical novels and nationalist poetry deeply preoccupied with the past, often expressing disenchantment with the claims of "Western civilization," whereas H. I. E. Dhlomo's four plays about the Zulu kings, known as the Black Bulls, were written between 1935 and 1937. In these texts we see a struggle between ideas of modernity and tradition and the utilization of oral and written, African, and European sources.

These works all manifested markedly historical and nationalist aspects seeking to present the African past in textured ways that explored the past in the light of present struggles and hopes for the future. One of the sharpest historical critiques came from Dhlomo, who recognized the exclusion of Africans from institutions of cultural practice and social discourse and insisted on the importance of history written from an African point of view. Literary scholar Bhekisizwe Peterson speculates that Dhlomo chose dramatic form rather than historical biography partly because he privileged the genius involved in creative work but also because of the difficulties experienced by Africans in getting into archives and libraries, the exclusion from those repositories of precisely the materials needed for an account challenging the official historiography, as well as the accessibility of the final product.[114] Because many of the texts were written in isiZulu, their audiences were mostly Zulu-speakers and they were long ignored by white historians and literary scholars. Although historical concerns were especially concentrated in Zulu literature,[115] such interventions were by no means confined to the Zulu-speaking intelligentsia. Nor were they uniform in their treatment of the preindustrial past.

John Henderson Soga continued the work of his father, Tiyo Soga, both as a minister and as a historian, producing the first synthetic history of Xhosa-speakers, written in isiXhosa but published in English in 1930. By then, the younger Soga could build on a long written historiography in isiXhosa, mainly published in a variety of competing newspapers and magazines but in part at least anthologized by the Rev. W. B. Rubusana.[116] To a

(Dhlomo papers, JSA, KCM 8281/2, file 4); S. Skikna, "Son of the Sun and Son of the World: The Life and Works of R. R. R. Dhlomo," MA dissertation, University of the Witwatersrand (1984) and B. W. Vilakazi, "The oral and written literature in Nguni," Ph.D. thesis, University of the Witwatersrand (1945), sections 3 and 4.

[114] B. Peterson, *Monarchs, Missionaries and African Intellectuals: African Theatre and the Unmaking of Colonial Marginality* (Johannesburg: Wits University Press, 2000), pp. 187–8.

[115] Petersen, *Monarchs*, p. 8; A. S. Gerard, *Four African Literatures* (Berkeley: University of California Press, 1971); H. Scheub, "Zulu Oral Tradition and Literature," in B. W. Andrzejewski and T. Tyloch (Eds.), *Literature in African Languages: Theoretical Issues and Sample Surveys* (Cambridge: Cambridge University Press, 1985); C. L. S. Nyembezi, *A Review of Zulu Literature* (Pietermaritzburg: University of Natal Press, 1961).

[116] See J. H. Soga, *The South-Eastern Bantu* (Johannesburg: Witwatersrand University Press, 1930); W. B. Rubusana, *Zemkínkomo Magwalandini* (London: Butler & Tanner, 1906).

significant degree intellectual debates in the Eastern Cape were conducted through the medium of history writing. Elsewhere, much of the analysis of the past was expressed in the form of fiction.[117] Nevertheless, the vigorous debate about the value of Xhosa custom was, of course, largely historical,[118] whereas various official commissions generated a wide range of historical information emanating from African sources.[119]

For a while, historical debate flourished among the Xhosa-speakers of the Eastern Cape because there were a number of contesting journals. In the course of the early twentieth century, however, the Lovedale Press came virtually to monopolize vernacular publishing in the region. The result was a sharp decline in the diversity of views. The mission press used its monopoly to exercise censorship over historical and other literary productions. Criticism of missionary activity, and indeed of colonialism in general, and overt discussions of the conflict between the amaMfengu and the amaXhosa were taboo.[120] A variety of works, including at least two by S. E. K. Mqhayi, were lost as a consequence, and even J. H. Soga's massive work was only published because the Bantu Studies Department of the University of the Witwatersrand came to hear of it and rescued the manuscript from Lovedale. The debate lost its vitality. Apartheid exacerbated the process. Although historical debate continued within oral media, and in English publications only available to and only written by the very apex of the Xhosa-speaking elite, the vigor that had once characterized Xhosa historiography was suppressed.

A wider remit characterized the historical efforts of certain members of the African intelligentsia. The South African Native National Congress (SANNC), established in 1912 to resist racial subjection, simultaneously recognized the dangers of ethnic conflict and the power of historical imagination as well as the particular potency of emerging Zulu nationalism, and

See also, for example, the writings of W. W. Gqoba in *Isigidima samaXosa* (April 2, 1888), which was an explicit attempt to challenge the "Chiefs' Plot" theories of the Cattle Killing then prevalent in missionary circles.

[117] See, for example, S. E. K. Mqhayi, *Ityala lamaWele* (Lovedale: Lovedale Press, 1914).

[118] J. Opland, "Fighting with the Pen: The Appropriation of the Press by Early Xhosa Writers," in J. A. Draper (Ed.), *Orality, Literacy, and Colonialism in Southern Africa* (Leiden & Boston: Brill, 2004), pp. 9–40; see more generally W. G. Mills, "Missionaries, Xhosa Clergy and the Suppression of Custom," in H. Bredekamp & R. Ross (Eds.), *Missions and Christianity in South African History* (Johannesburg: Witwatersrand University Press, 1995), pp. 153–71.

[119] See, for example, N. Erlank, "Gendering Commonality: African Men and the 1883 Commission on Native Law and Customs," *Journal of Southern African Studies,* 19(4) (2003), pp. 937–55.

[120] J. B. Peires, "The Lovedale Press: Literature for the Bantu Revisited," *History in Africa,* 6 (1979), pp. 155–75.

sought, with varying degrees of success, to negotiate a path across these forces, as did its successor, the ANC.

Whereas Sol. T. Plaatje, the first secretary of the SANNC, nurtured a lifelong interest in the language, history, and cultural traditions of the Batswana, his published writings on these subjects were not driven by a narrow Tswana nationalist agenda. Assertively proud of aspects of Tswana tradition and keen to promote them, he was openly critical of what he called "the despicable relics of past barbarism" like circumcision rites. Politically, he was committed to an ideal of black unity, and his writings were primarily those of a political commentator speaking about unfolding political developments. His thinking was influenced by a network of international contacts and informed by international debates on race. His early campaign was "equal rights for all civilised men," and, countering a left critique of the missionary role in the dispossession of African land, he looked at episodes of missionary history to demonstrate the missionary contribution to the making of the "civilised" African. However, as the effects of the 1913 Land Act bit deep into the social and economic life of rural communities, he began to look to the past, as his biographer Brian Willan puts it, "for the means to resist the consequences of the social and economic changes taking place around him."[121] Concerned about the weakening bonds of communal life in the rural areas, he turned to history as a source of succor and for the roots of the crisis. This is reflected in his historical novel, *Mhudi*, written in the late 1910s and finally published in 1930.[122]

Novelist Bessie Head remarked, "The wonder of *Mhudi* is the ease with which new patterns are assimilated by the people and the chiefs with no great show of excitement as though that was the natural thing to do."[123] *Mhudi* explored the origins of segregation and the events that preceded the 1913 Land Act, including the complex processes of the nineteenth-century encounter between colonizers and local peoples. Its central themes were those of continuity and change. Plaatje was actively concerned to counter distortions in the historical record and to resist the cultural domination of colonialism. He used the novel both to challenge ideas about precolonial "savagery" used to justify conquest and to draw attention to the support given to the early Europeans by local inhabitants. Combining the novel form with the epic of African oral tradition, Plaatje produced a genre as hybrid as the changing communities he described. Tim Couzens has argued

---

[121] B. Willan, *Sol Plaatje: A Biography* (Johannesburg: Ravan Press, 2001, first published 1984), p. 327. Quotes above from p. 314.

[122] S. T. Plaatje, *Mhudi* (Lovedale Press, 1930).

[123] Cited in S. Gray, "Two Sources of Plaatje's *Mhudi*," in *Munger Africana Library Notes*, 37 (1976), p. 6.

that *Mhudi* was, moreover, the first South African national epic; a vision of the advantages of an alliance of all the peoples of the country, based on equality.[124] It was a vision underpinned by the lessons of history: the possibilities of a common humanity shared by divided peoples, and a warning that unless tyranny and oppression end peaceably, violence becomes the only option.

The novel was further remarkable for its recognition that conquest was not the preserve of white imperialism and for its central focus on a woman, the Mhudi of the title. The historiographical import of the woman-centeredness of this account awaits assessment, alongside historiographical evaluation of the treatment of other female figures in historical novels and plays by black writers.[125] Although women occasionally were featured in these historical accounts, the activity of historical deliberation in published form was conducted almost exclusively by men and focused on the issues central to a male-dominated political sphere.

S. M. Molema, an intellectual contemporary of Plaatje, a member of the Barolong-bo-Ratshidi royal family and, in the 1910s, a medical student studying in Edinburgh, read Plaatje's *Mhudi* avidly and was inspired to turn his hand to history. *The Bantu Past and Present*[126] was written in Edinburgh, and based heavily on Theal's published works, which he also critiqued. Molema drew its detailed historical content largely from the memories he carried with him, many of which were shaped by his family's close involvement with the major historical events in Tshidi–Rolong history. Deeply involved in the politics of church and chiefship in the course of his life, Molema was, like his mentor, Plaatje, strongly in favor of the "civilising mission." He was, likewise, deeply concerned to save Tswana history and cultural forms from extinction and actively engaged in the work of cultural translation. *The Bantu Past and Present* was rooted in wide reading about the key political issues of the day and current philosophical, intellectual, and academic developments. In two much later biographies, one on Moroka[127] published in 1951 and another on Montshiwa published after his death, Molema commented on the disrepair in which historical information about precolonial times was transported across the generations.

---

[124] Editorial commentary by T. Couzens in the 1996 edition of *Mhudi* (Cape Town: Francolin Publishers).

[125] See L. Chrisman, *Rereading the Imperial Romance: British Imperialism and South African Resistance in Haggard, Schreiner and Plaatje* (Oxford: Clarendon Press, 2000); *idem*, "Fathering the Black Nation of South Africa: Gender and Generation in Sol Plaatje's *Native Life in South Africa* and *Mhudi*," *Social Dynamics*, 23(2) (1997), pp. 59–73.

[126] S. M. Molema, *The Bantu Past and Present* (Edinburgh: W. Green and Son, 1920).

[127] S. M. Molema, *Chief Moroka: His Life, His Times, His Country and His People* (Cape Town: Methodist Publishing House, 1951).

In the latter text he also articulated a view of precolonial life as an "abject condition of existence."[128] The historiographical projects of both Plaatje and Molema were driven by their perceptions of the need for cultural recuperation and the desire to contest the then-dominant representation of the Tswana past.[129]

Whereas black intellectual engagement with history was often framed in terms of a new nationalism opposing white domination, "tradition" was also supported by significant elements within African society as a means of fending off a capitalist economy.[130] The vision of the past underpinning the segregationist policies of the 1920s was not uniformly resisted. African leaders like J. T. Jabavu who sought to hold on to the limited franchise argued forcefully that black voters had "abandoned the position of barbarism and renounced tribal life."[131] Indeed, many African leaders traded their claims to political citizenship in return for the added lands promised. The package of traditionalism, communalism, and reserved lands proved attractive to some.[132]

Although considerable work has been done on the way in which black intellectuals of the late nineteenth and early twentieth centuries produced histories in a variety of written genres, we have, as yet, only tantalizing glimpses of the ways in which history was produced in more performative genres, including sermons, hymns, music, and praises, as well as topographically in the maintenance of grave sites and other ritual venues. These modes and sites of the production of history, manifestations of historical sensibilities, of popular historical consciousness, and even a historical unconscious, and their significance for our understanding of historiography invite sustained attention.

ETHNIC HISTORIES AND THE RATIONALE FOR APARTHEID

In the 1940s, a new basis for understanding population categorization was developed that underpinned apartheid. The African population, previously regarded as a relatively homogenous historical and social grouping, was

---

[128] *Montshiwa, Barolong Chief and Patriot* (Cape Town: Struik, 1966), pp. 191–2. This was published in the year following Molema's death. All three books deal with the history of the Barolong and their dealings with whites. Our thanks to Jane Starfield for access to elements of her unpublished work on Molema and for assistance in dealing with Molema's historiographical enterprise.

[129] The "New Africans" were in contact with, and influenced by scholars and intellectuals outside South Africa, and the effects of those influences on their historical writings awaits systematic investigation.

[130] Dubow, *Segregation*, p. 114.   [131] Cited in Dubow, *Segregation*, p. 151.

[132] Dubow, *Segregation*, Chapters 6 and 7.

broken into a heterogeneous assemblage of plural Bantu cultures, each understood to be historically based in territories encapsulated within existing reserves.

The political proposal was for each of these historical cultures to develop into a separate nation. Ethnic difference was mobilized to control the urbanization of Africans and to facilitate the division of African labor between urban industry and capitalist agriculture while suppressing claims for a common citizenship. As ethnic divisions began to be accorded centrality in official understanding of the "native question," and as policies for the development of the reserves as national homelands crystallized, a massive effort of research into those distinct identities was launched. The political project further required justification for European occupation of the interstitial spaces, a position no longer arguable in terms of the need for civilization alone. The key concept of self-determination for groups then began to draw on ideas of all the inhabitants of South Africa as immigrants. Bantu migrations and the devastations of the *mfecane* all attracted research interest. The departments of *Volkekunde* (ethnology) and archaeology in the Afrikaans universities and the ethnology section of the government's Native Affairs Department were especially productive in all of these endeavors.

Paul-Lenert Breutz was employed as a government ethnologist in Pretoria from 1948 until his retirement in 1977. During that period he carried out extensive oral research into the histories of all Tswana societies. He traveled to every identifiable Tswana grouping and personally conducted interviews in which he traced the origins, genealogy, settlement, and migrations of the group. The ethnology section then published his work in a book on each group.[133] At the same time other government ethnologists were working on various other African groups. W. D. Hammond-Tooke, for example, undertook the same exercise among the Xhosa-speaking peoples of the Mount Frere and Umtata districts.[134] Similarly, N. J. van Warmelo worked on the northern Transvaal and A. C. Myburgh on the northeastern Transvaal.[135] These studies generated a wealth of historical detail that added another distinctive and rich layer to the archive of material pertaining to the precolonial and colonial past, this time cast within an explicitly ethnic framework. The key theoretical concepts of culture and ethnos and an implied primordial link between them that underpinned this framework

---

[133] There are volumes on the "Tribes" of Marico, Mafeking, Ventersdorp, Lichtenburg, Rustenburg, Pilanesberg, Kuruman, Postmasburg, Taung, Herbert, and Vryburg districts, all published in Pretoria by the Government Printer between 1954 and 1963.

[134] See W. D. Hammond-Tooke, *The Tribes of the Mount Frere District* (Pretoria, 1955) and *The Tribes of the Umtata District* (Pretoria, 1956).

[135] N. J. van Warmelo, *Die Tlokwa en Birwa van Noord Transvaal* (Pretoria, 1953); A. C. Myburgh, *The Tribes of Barberton District* (Pretoria, 1949).

were largely developed within the discipline of *Volkekunde* in the Afrikaans universities. Theoretically aligned with evolutionism, *Volkekunde* was closely linked with physical anthropology, psychology, and what was termed prehistory. Many of this generation of ethnologists were the children of missionaries, and they brought to this strand of ethnology elements of the missionary tradition of historical work. Like many of the early administrators involved in the collection of African history and some of their own missionary parents, the ethnologists were typically fluent in the languages of the people they studied.

PROFESSIONAL HISTORY, ARCHAEOLOGY, AND THE EMERGENCE OF A GUILD

Like war, academic history in South Africa has often been the continuation of politics by other means. Thus the first chairs of history in the country, founded at the University of Cape Town in 1903 and Stellenbosch University in 1904 and funded by mining magnates and Western Cape Afrikaner farmers, respectively, began a tradition of institutionalized opposition between the Afrikaans- (at that stage, of course, still Dutch) and English-medium universities that continued throughout most of the twentieth century.[136] Anglophone history in the classrooms was initially imperialist, at least in the sense of concentrating on the constitutional history of the British Empire, but it was, in general, more concerned to discuss European topics than South African ones.[137] In contrast, in Stellenbosch a local and Afrikaner nationalist historiography was developed, initially heavily concerned with the economic and agricultural history of the Cape during the eighteenth century, as befitted the background of the university and its supporters.

Eventually, under the leadership of H. B. Thom, institutionally if not intellectually the most influential historian in South Africa in the first two-thirds of the century, the emphasis shifted in particular to more nationalist topics, notably the Great Trek. Where there was a concern with any precolonial history, scholars maintained the old myth, which lay deep in the justification of apartheid, that, as F. A. van Jaarsveld wrote, "White and Bantu met one another along the east coast as a result of independent movements in opposite directions . . . "[138] Within this tradition, the

---

[136] H. Philips, "100 Years Old and Still Making History: The Centenary of the Department of Historical Studies at the University of Cape Town," *South African Historical Journal*, 50 (2004), pp. 199–210.

[137] This trend was even stronger in Australia where there were hardly any courses in Australian, let along Asian, history until well after World War II.

[138] Quoted in Saunders, *The Making of the South African Past*, p. 43.

Stellenbosch History Department came to spread its ex-students throughout the country and, where necessary, notably at the University of Pretoria,
those who did not accede to the nationalist vision of history were driven
out. The result was the entrenchment in the heart of the historical establishment of a vision of history, which was at once heavily committed to a
specific Afrikanercentric and nationalist view of the past and determined to
maintain an "objective–scientific" view of that past. Not for nothing was
the most prestigious outlet for the works of this school considered to be the
Archives Year Book. Clearly, it was believed that such research would justify
the truth of Afrikaner nationalism, and works in which this view was not
evident were generally dismissed as poor scholarship. There was obviously a
potential contradiction between these aims, as historical research could, at
least in theory, have undermined a nationalist agenda, but until the 1970s
the consequences of this paradox were evaded.[139]

At the other end of the (white) political scale, at least before World
War II, were those whose historical drive came from a recognition of the
deep-rooted interconnectedness of all South Africans and their consequent
opposition to segregationist politics. The most notable of these were W. M.
Macmillan, C. W. de Kiewiet and, to a lesser degree, J. S. Marais. The intellectual influence of their work was considerable, but as both Macmillan and
de Kiewiet left South Africa, they were unable to found a "school" to rival
that emanating from Stellenbosch. Nevertheless, what came to be known
as the liberal version of South African history, with its stress on the interaction between races, was maintained, at least to some extent, in the Anglophone universities, where, indeed, some of the most prominent of its practitioners were members of the Liberal Party in the 1950s.

It was also a school that placed considerable emphasis on the importance
of the missionaries. Macmillan famously worked with the papers of John
Philip and, to a considerable degree, identified with the positions Philip
had taken, whereas Monica Wilson, who had been brought up in a mission
family, maintained the tradition when, in the 1960s, together with Leonard
Thompson, she planned (and wrote a good deal of) the *Oxford History of
South Africa*.[140] In Natal, in the absence of a local liberalism, settler history

---

[139] On this, see A. Grundlingh, "Politics, Principles and Problems of a Profession: Afrikaner
Historians and their Discipline, c.1920–c.1965," *Perspectives in Education, 12* (1990), pp.
1–19; N. Southey & F. A. Mouton, "'A *Volksvreemde* historian': J. A. I. Agar-Hamilton
and the Production of History in an Alien Environment," *South African Historical Journal,
44* (2001), pp. 72–98; F. A. Mouton, "Professor Leo Fouché, the History Department
and the Afrikanerisation of the University of Pretoria," *Historia, 38* (1993), pp. 51–63.
[140] See on this, H. Macmillan and S. Marks (Eds.), *Africa and Empire: W.M. Macmillan
Historian and Social Critic* (London: Temple Smith for the Institute of Commonwealth
Studies, 1989); C. Saunders, *C. W. de Kiewiet: Historian of South Africa* (Cape Town: Centre

continued as an unchallenged investigation into the European colonial experience in the province. After the Englishman A. F. Hattersley arrived in Natal as the founder and only member of the University of Natal's Pietermaritzburg History Department, he developed a historiography of nostalgia for "old Natal" that was something of a reaction to and an escape from Afrikaner nationalism on the one hand and the searching post-settler historiography that Macmillan and de Kiewiet were developing on the other.[141]

The positive evaluation of the missionaries by the liberal historians and, indeed, by certain African writers like Plaatje provoked vehement attacks from the first Marxist analysts of South African history, namely, the Cape Town Trotskyists associated with the Unity Movement of the early 1950s. The pamphlets *The Role of the Missionaries in Conflict*, written by Dora Taylor (under the pseudonym Nosipho Majeke), and *Three Hundred Years*, by Hosea Jaffe as "Mnguni," emerged from a Capetonian intellectual circle whose center lay in the colored schools and their staffs. It was, however, a critique originally advanced by black, mission-trained nationalists at the end of the nineteenth century, and one that resurfaced again in the more Africanist works of the 1960s and 1970s.[142]

On the other hand, it is perhaps ironic that an anthropologist like Monica Wilson was among the most distinguished of the liberal adherents. For Macmillan, the vision of cultures as bounded wholes that react against each other was anathema. This was something he saw in the practice of anthropologists in the 1920s, and it was in many ways theorized in the work of the leaders of British social anthropology, Bronislaw Malinowski and A. R. Radcliffe-Brown, both of whom had South African experience. Certainly there was a tendency to see cultures as timeless entities and to attempt to reconstruct their true essence as at the "zero-point" before contact. Although this was rejected by a younger generation of primarily South African anthropologists, of whom Monica Wilson was one, this tended to mean that their own practice attempts at historical reconstruction,

of African Studies Communications no. 10, 1986); M. Wilson and L. Thompson (Eds.), *Oxford History of South Africa*, 2 vols. (Oxford, Oxford University Press, 1968–1971).

[141] Our thanks to John Wright for this point.

[142] Mnguni' [Hosea Jaffe], *Three Hundred Years* (Cape Town: New Era Fellowship, 1952); Nosipho Majeke [Dora Taylor], *The Role of the Missionaries in Conquest* (Johannesburg: Society of Young Africa, 1953); G. Cuthbertson, "Christianity, Imperialism and Colonial Warfare," in J. Hofmeyr and G. J. Pillay (Eds.), *A History of Christianity in South Africa* (Pretoria: HAUM, 1994), p. 167; E. Mphahlele, *The African Image* (London: Faber and Faber, 1962); L. Zulu, "Nineteenth-century Missionaries: Their Significance for Black South Africa," in M. Motlhabi (Ed.), *Essays on Black Theology* (Johannesburg: University Christian Movement, 1972).

as in some of Wilson's chapters in the *Oxford History*, reverted to fairly static models of distinct societies and long-term cultures.[143]

Archaeological exploration of the country was, until then, virtually exclusively concerned with what was known as the stone age, that is to say, with the history of the country before the introduction of iron, agriculture, and pastoralism. Although collections of stone artifacts had been made as early as the 1850s, the professional study of South African archaeology did not begin until the 1920s and even then was the work of a couple of men, notably A. J. H. Goodwin, professor at the University of Cape Town, where he was the only teacher of the subject in the country from the 1920s to the 1950s, and Clarence van Riet Lowe, a civil engineer who became director of the Archaeological Survey in the 1930s. They were concerned to sort out, on the basis of lithic typology, the sequence of the various stone cultures in South Africa, initially on the basis of European analogues. Although they eventually came to appreciate that the earliest South African history had to be reconstructed on its own terms, it was the very long-term evolution that was central to their approach.[144]

In their concerns, and in their lack of interest in the African population, the early archaeologists were close to Jan Smuts, who himself had written an archaeological paper for the *South African Journal of Science* in 1932.[145] Smuts saw South Africa as the "cradle of mankind" and believed that archaeology was one way in which South African influence could be expanded throughout the continent. At the same time, he had a totally Eurocentric view of the South African past, seeing the San as living fossils whose relatives had died out in Europe. Indeed, South African paleoanthropological discoveries and contemporary Khoesan anatomical specimens and items of material culture were internationally prized sources of evidence in the discussion of human

---

[143] H. Macmillan, "'Paralyzed Conservatives': W. M. Macmillan, the Social Scientists and 'the Common Society,' 1923–48," in Macmillan and Marks (Eds.), *Africa and Empire, W.M. Macmillan, historian and social critic* (Aldershot: Temple Smith for the Institute of Commonwealth Studies, 1989), pp. 72–90. The strictures on Wilson's work for the *Oxford History* refer to her chapters entitled "The Hunters and Herders" pp. 40–74, "The Nguni People" pp. 75–130, and "The Sotho, Venda and Tsonga," pp. 131–86 rather than that on "Co-operation and conflict: the Eastern Cape Frontier," pp. 133–271.

[144] N. Shepherd, "State of the discipline: Science, Culture and Identity in South African archaeology, 1870–2003," *Journal of Southern African Studies*, 29 (2003), pp. 823–44; N. Shepherd, "Disciplining Archaeology: The Invention of South African Prehistory, 1923–1953," *Kronos*, 28 (2002), pp. 127–45; J. Deacon, "Weaving the Fabric of Stone Age Research in Southern Africa," in P. Robertshaw (Ed.), *A History of African Archaeology* (London: James Currey, 1990), pp. 39–58.

[145] J. C. Smuts, "Climate and Man in Africa," *South African Journal of Science*, 29 (1932), pp. 98–131; in general, see also N. Schlanger, "Making the Past for South Africa's Future; The Prehistory of Field-Marshal Smuts," *Antiquity*, 76 (2002), pp. 200–9.

development.[146] Smuts acted as patron for van Riet Lowe in particular, and in government circles archaeology came to be seen as Smuts's hobby. So plans for a second Pan-African archaeological congress, to be held in Johannesburg, had to be aborted after the National Party came to power in 1948. Nevertheless, it was under National Party rule that the number of archaeologists in South Africa increased dramatically.[147]

This expansion made possible, for the first time, the construction of a broad survey of what was tellingly referred to as the prehistory of the farming communities of South Africa. The term Iron Age was coined in 1952 by archaeologist Revil Mason, and archaeologists began to explore seriously the proposition that the Iron Age people were somehow ancestral to the modern African population. In the 1970s the basic chronology of the history of KwaZulu-Natal and the Highveld was worked out, aided, of course, by the technological advances that made possible relatively accurate dating.[148]

There are several paradoxes in this. First, it occurred despite, and in opposition to, the vision that white society in general and the National Party in particular had of the history of sub-Saharan Africa. It quickly became clear that the ancestors of most black South Africans had been in the region for at least a millennium before the arrival of the Europeans. As Martin Hall put it, "the liberal germ, from which the florescence of Iron Age research has stemmed, had been outrage at the conscious distortion of history to form part of apartheid ideology."[149] Secondly, however, the results of this work did not reach far beyond the charmed circle of the archaeologists themselves, both because the understanding of excavation data requires considerable skill and because those who could understand did not translate the information into forms that were widely comprehensible. As Mamphela Ramphele remarked at the opening of the 1999 World Archaeological Congress in Cape Town, the potential symbiosis between the Iron Age archaeologists and black consciousness, for instance, simply did not happen.[150]

By the late 1970s ideas drawn from structuralist anthropology were introduced into Southern African studies, above all by Adam Kuper.[151] Kuper began with the hypothesis that the social and spatial principles of

---

[146] Dubow, *Scientific Racism*, pp. 20–66.

[147] From a single professionally trained archaeologist working in South Africa in 1930, there were six in 1960, seventeen in 1970, and fifty-eight in 1987. See Deacon, "Weaving the Fabric," p. 51.

[148] See the Chapters II and III by Parkington and Hall and Hall in this volume.

[149] In Deacon, "Weaving the Fabric," p. 72.

[150] Shepherd, "State of the Discipline," p. 837.

[151] Notably in "Symbolic Dimensions of the Southern Bantu Homestead" *Africa*, 50 (1980), pp. 8–23; Kuper would always admit his debt to the early articles by Hans Holleman, "Die Zulu isigodi" *Bantu Studies*, 15 (1941), pp. 91–118 and 245–76, which were totally

those people who spoke one of the Bantu languages were fairly uniform, at least to the south of the Limpopo (plus Botswana). What was reported by observers and ethnographers between about 1850 and 1950 represented variations of a basic underlying pattern. His task, as he saw it, was to explain how what was seen could be derived, logically, from that pattern; there was another task, that of the historian, to explain how and why what was seen at a given time and place had come into existence, which he would expect to be the result of the specificities of political development and, perhaps, ecology. The danger of this approach is that it was very easy to slip from statements about, say, what anthropologist Isaac Schapera saw in Mochudi in the 1930s into statements about the customs of the Bakgatla, or the Batswana, and even easier for people to read such comments into the work. Nevertheless, the spatial elements of Kuper's model in particular have been widely used by archaeologists, as they provide a nontrivial way of linking the material remains of past societies to their political and social ideologies. A structurally informed history of the politics or economics of precolonial societies, let alone of their kinship structures, has, however, been singularly absent.

The 1970s also saw the development of cognitive archaeology in South Africa in the form of rock art studies. The work of the pioneering scholar in this field, David Lewis-Williams, also used ethnographic material (notably the Bleek/Lloyd archive and contemporary San ethnographies) to interpret, in this case, images. The primary theoretical approach was derived from symbolic anthropology, notably the work of Victor Turner, to interpret symbolism and ritual within San society and within the rock art, which could then be approached as a complex system of metaphors and symbols.[152] It was an approach that was to have an enormous international impact on the interpretation of rock art and early domestic art.

Despite its strong structuralist orientation, the establishment of a South African archaeology between about 1960 and 1980 was part of a general expansion of African history throughout the continent. This had to do with the establishment of universities throughout the continent, and with the necessity, at least as it was felt, to create a history for the new nations. The time depth of African history was steadily increased by the use of archaeology, historical linguistics, and the analysis of oral traditions as well as through the reinvestigation of such written sources as exist for the deeper African past. In South Africa, historical linguistics played a very minor role,

---

ignored, both having been written in Afrikaans and inspired by the theoretical ideas of Dutch Indonesian anthropology.

[152] D. Lewis-Williams, *Believing and Seeing: Symbolic Meanings in Southern San Rock Paintings* (London: Academic Press, 1981).

primarily because the linguistic situation was much less complicated than it was further north. The investigation of oral tradition was largely limited to the reanalysis of that which had been collected by people like Bryant, Stuart, and the ethnographers of the Native Affairs department, employing Vansina's oral tradition methodology. Nevertheless, there was a major push to write, effectively for the first time, the late precolonial history of African societies and their subjugation as part of the concerted revision of South African history from the late 1960s onward.

The centers of this work were initially outside South Africa, to some extent in the United States but above all at the seminar run by Shula Marks at the Institute of Commonwealth Studies in London. A large number of the participants in the seminar had grown up in South Africa, generally as Anglophone whites, had maintained their links with it, and, when not prevented from doing so by their political actions, did their research in the country of their birth. Many would eventually return to teach at South African universities. The slew of monographs produced by these scholars typically provided in their early chapters the first detailed accounts of regional political developments in the late precolonial era, giving close attention to the reasons for the rise and fall of local polities. They further provided elaborated accounts of colonial conquest and the resistance it encountered.[153]

To make sense of the precolonial history of African societies a number of theories from anthropology were employed by these scholars. By far the most influential were various forms of Marxist materialism. These had the advantage, greatly appreciated, of focusing attention on matters of production, on the penetration of capitalism, on exploitation, and eventually on gender relations, which in Southern African contexts have always been intertwined with production and exploitation. They also allowed an easy progression from precolonial to colonial and industrial periods – in fact, the reverse direction was more generally taken – and thus the link with leftist politics was evident. At a time when detailed empirical research into the current political, economic, and social situation of the mass of South Africans was exceedingly difficult, history that offered explanations of the present situation informed political analysis.

The new historiographies that followed the achievement of independence from colonial rule of much of the rest of sub-Saharan Africa by the mid-1960s were not without their effect on South Africa, despite the persistence of white rule south of the Limpopo. The Black Consciousness Movement, which emerged in the early 1970s, was critical of the kind of history that had been written about Africans by white writers. Steve Biko, the

---

[153] These works form much of the backbone of Chapter 7 in this volume.

movement's leading thinker, described such history as "distorted, disfigured and destroyed" and clearly in need of correction. "The history of African society was reduced to tribal battles and internecine wars. There was no conscious migration by the people from one place of abode to another. No, it was always flight from one tyrant who wanted to defeat the tribe not for any positive reason but merely to wipe them out of the face of the earth."[154] It is because of this negative image of African history that, according to Biko, "the African child learns to hate his heritage in his days at school." Biko saw black consciousness as a means of reexamining and rewriting the history of South Africa.

The alternative history that Black Consciousness called for may have had a different intellectual and political impulse from that which motivated the challenges expressed by more explicit African nationalists, but the nature of the two was similar. Writing in 1982, Bernard Magubane criticized official South African history for its settlerist orientation and its manipulation in its effort to justify land seizures and racial domination. He identified the key myths sustaining apartheid: the idea that segregation was the expression of primordial allegiances, that the so-called Bantu arrived in South Africa at the same time as the first whites, that the conflicts between the colonial powers and the independent African chiefdoms were wars between rival conquerors for possession of empty territory, and that the reserves were the original homelands of indigenous African societies, divided into Xhosa, Sotho, Zulu, Tswana, and so on. For Magubane, it was equally important that these ideas denied the historical evolution of concepts of African nationalism and the role of the African elite. He suggested that the key question to be asked of South African history was what had brought about the domination of blacks by whites and the subsequent abolition of this relationship. In a further twenty-five pages or so, Magubane offered some examples of areas that need further study to begin to answer the question he posed. Although the proponents of Black Consciousness and of African nationalism articulated the need for an alternative historiography, prior to 1994 relatively few historical works by black scholars flowed directly from those impulses. Expressly antisettler histories like Jay Naidoo's *Tracking Down Historical Myths*, which tackled key settler myths such as van Riebeek's relationship with the Cape Khoekoen, the death of Hintsa, the death of Retief, the Makapan Siege, and other examples, are relatively rare.[155]

[154] S. Biko, *I Write What I Like*, A. Stubbs Ed., (London: Bowerdean, 1978), p. 29.
[155] J. Naidoo, *Tracking Down Historical Myths: Eight South African Cases* (Johannesburg: AD Donker, 1989).

HOMELAND HISTORIES

Black historians based in the homelands, producing narrow nationalist accounts in the service of homeland identities, were only marginally more prolific. The ethnic identities that underpinned the apartheid system of so-called independent homelands depended on historical justification. The bulk of the research base for these identities was provided by the Ethnology Department. Nonetheless, homeland authorities were active in fostering history that promoted various ethnic identities. Their tactics ranged from aggressive assertions of the right to censor and control history production through strategic tweaking of historical details to outright invention.

Nowhere was the process of control more dramatic than in KwaZulu, where the chief minister, Mangosuthu Buthelezi, promoted a particular interpretation of the making of a unified Zulu nation focused on the figure and activities of the 1820s Zulu king, Shaka. Presented primarily in public speeches but also articulated in a host of commemorative sites and activities, this version of Zulu history placed a premium on a warrior ethos, discipline, male-dominated gender relations, Zulu achievements, the accommodation of whites, and traditionalism. Historical research conducted in support of this agenda by academics based in the homeland university struggled to gain professional recognition. Buthelezi was, in turn, assiduous in monitoring the academic research of historians of the Zulu kingdom based outside of KwaZulu and, on more than one occasion, succeeded in pressuring reputable historians into changing their texts to fit narrow Zulu nationalist interests.[156]

The then president of the former homeland of Bophuthatswana, Lucas Mangope, also appealed to and used history to legitimate his government and "state," characteristically manipulating specific historical details to advance his agenda rather than fostering new history production in the interest of the homeland. For example, Mangope authenticated the Bophuthatswana government's claim to the areas that officially constituted the apartheid Tswana homeland by referring to the settlement as early as AD 450 in areas of contemporary occupation and in areas from which they were subsequently displaced. He also cited archaeological findings on which the claim was based.[157]

---

[156] See G. Maré, *Brothers Born of Warrior Blood: Politics and Ethnicity in South Africa* (Johannesburg: Ravan Press, 1992), section 2; P. Forsyth, "The Past as the Present: Chief ANMG Buthelezi's use of history as a source of political legitimation," unpublished M.A. thesis, University of Natal, Pietermaritzburg (1989), especially pp. 200–5.

[157] L. M. Mangope, *Mandatory Sanctions: Bophuthatswana and Frontline OAU Nations* (Lagos: Emmcon, 1988), p. 23.

As with the Inkatha histories of KwaZulu, much is made in his single major published text of Tswana support for white activities. The text claims, rather disingenuously, that a military expedition sent on January 16, 1837, by the Voortrekker leader, Hendrik Potgieter, to punish Mzilikazi "was accompanied by an army of Tswanas."[158] The fact is that from October 1836 every Boer commando comprised considerable numbers not only of Batswana but also of Griqua and Korana groups, each of which had its own grievances against the amaNdebele.[159] Mangope's account was not simply one of white accommodation, however, as it focused in detail on how the lands of the Batswana were expropriated by whites despite a number of treaties entered into by both parties to curb the practice. In particular, Mangope indicted the British for splitting the Batswana by declaring Tswana country north of the Molopo River a "Bechuanaland Protectorate" and the south the "Crown Colony of British Bechuanaland," later incorporated into the Cape Colony.[160] In the case of the Ciskei homeland, which had absolutely no basis in ethnic, cultural, historical, or linguistic terms, pure invention, rather than manipulation, was the key strategy.[161] Nonetheless, control over archives remained significant: The establishment of the homelands required the transfer of archival holdings from South African state repositories into the homeland archives, constituting thus the historical foundations of their "independence."

By the mid-1980s black homeland ideologues and historians were locked in fierce debates with Marxist historians. Although the extent of the debate in academic fora was limited (the two parties seldom attended the same conferences or published in the same journals), it proliferated in the media, most actively in the KwaZulu and Natal press.[162]

This was in part a result of the escalating violence by supporters of the modern-day Zulu nationalist movement, Inkatha, and partly a consequence of the commitment of many of the Marxist historians to ensuring that their research was popularly accessible.[163]

---

[158] Mangope, *Mandatory Sanctions*, p. 24.

[159] See R. K. Rasmussen, *Migrant Kingdom: Mzilikazi's Ndebele in South Africa* (London: Rex Collings, 1978), pp. 123–5; see also B. Mbenga, "Forced Labour in the Pilanesberg: The Flogging of Chief Kgamanyane by Commandant Paul Kruger, Saulspoort, April 1870," *Journal of Southern African Studies*, 23(1) (March 1997), p. 130.

[160] Mangope, *Mandatory Sanctions*, pp. 30–1.

[161] Anonymous (J. Peires), "Ethnicity and Pseudo-Ethnicity in the Ciskei," in Leroy Vail (Ed.), *The Creation of Tribalism in Southern Africa* (London: James Currey, 1987) pp. 396–413.

[162] See Hamilton, *Terrific Majesty*, pp. 12–15.

[163] See, for example, their contributions to publications like *New Nation, New History*, and the "Learn and Teach" series.

However, the debates were not simply between the Marxist historians on the one hand and apartheid apologists on the other.

HISTORY PRODUCTION AND THE END OF APARTHEID

In 1988, Julian Cobbing published a provocative essay attacking the idea of the *mfecane* – by which is generally meant the period of upheaval across sub-Saharan Africa in the early nineteenth century caused by the expansion of Zulu power under Shaka. Cobbing argued that the idea of the *mfecane* proceeding as something separate from the colonial history of the time, as being driven by the Zulu king, and as disrupting much of the interior of Southern Africa, depopulating vast swaths of the country, was yet another settler myth. He suggested that the disruption of the time was rather the consequence of the labor demands of colonialism and concomitant growth in slaving activities and that settler demonization of Shaka was an attempt to shift the onus to the Zulu king. His thesis was challenged not by apartheid historians but by a range of scholars working within the revisionist paradigm. Their challenges came from a variety of perspectives: Some interrogated the evidence for slave trade in Southern Africa and found it unable to sustain the weight placed on it in Cobbing's argument; others queried whether his representation of the rise of settler views on Shaka was correctly periodized, suggesting that he missed key differences between early trader, settler, and colonial authorities' interpretations of the precolonial past.

The publication in 1989 of Edwin Wilmsen's *Land Filled with Flies: A Political Economy of the Kalahari* was a powerful salvo in a similar revisionist challenge that argued that prevailing discourse on the San, which presented them as isolated, pristine, egalitarian, and unchanging hunter–gatherer communities, ignored centuries of interaction between them and neighboring communities.[164] The revisionists' work offered accounts of the past that integrated the San into regional, even global, economies. Wilmsen, for example, argued that the San of the Kalahari were never a distinct cultural entity but an underclass in a patron–client relationship with the local Sotho–Tswana-speakers. This work was, in turn, criticized for having a weak evidentiary basis and for generalizing across too wide a grouping without taking account of spatio-temporal variation.

The lines in the two debates were not drawn on strictly ideological grounds. Rather, as the debates evolved they began to raise questions

---

[164] Earlier indications of this line of argument had arisen in the 1970s, notably in S. Marks, "Khoisan resistance to the Dutch in the Seventeenth and Eighteenth Centuries," *Journal of African History*, *13* (1972), pp. 55–80.

that moved beyond the political economy focus that marked much of the revisionist historiography of the late 1970s and early 1980s. Primarily, the perspective looked less at one-sided domination and more at processes of articulation, of the creolization of identity, and at the mix of newer and older ideas in culture, ritual, and religion.

The 1980s also witnessed the rise of historical archaeology, which consciously subverted the division of disciplines in terms of which history serviced the white past and archaeology and anthropology the black past. It did this by applying archaeological methods and material culture analyses to colonial topics, primarily to provide a new perspective on the experiences of slaves in colonial society.[165]

Whereas much history production in the 1980s focused with energy on the rise and development of the apartheid state in an effort to analyze it and to contribute to its demise, the first democratic elections, held in 1994, permitted a refocusing of attention on other historical questions. In this period questions of identity and subjectivity loomed large in public discourse as South Africans grappled with the challenges of reimagining themselves and breaking free of the institutions and inherited structures that had defined apartheid identities.

Khoesan identity, for example, was extensively explored in public discourse. In general, since the end of the Kat River rebellion in the 1850s, those of Khoesan descent had been careful to avoid emphasizing this affiliation. The old appellations "Hottentot" and "Bushman" had become insults (the latter particularly in its Afrikaans version as "boesman"). They were not used self-referentially and, under the post-1994 dispensation, the description of an individual as "Hottentot" became illegal. With the transition in the 1990s a number of those who had previously been described as "coloreds" claimed a Khoesan identity, and certain individuals put forward claims to being Khoesan chiefs. For some so-called colored supporters of the old apartheid regime, this movement offered a strategy for regaining political respectability. In this, much was made of the worldwide promotion of the rights of indigenous peoples and thus of the claim by the Khoesan to represent the earliest inhabitants of the region. The lead was taken by the Griqua, who had never hidden their Khoesan descent but who had tended to emphasize the white side of their ancestry.[166]

Although the South African state did not in any way respond to the political demands of the Khoesan – which related largely to the recognition

[165] M. Hall, *Archaeology and the modern world: colonial transcripts in South Africa and the Chesapeake* (London and New York: Routledge, 2000).

[166] Michael Besten, "Transformation and Reconstitution of Khoe-San Identities: AAS Le Fleur I, Griqua Identities and Post-apartheid Khoe-San Revivalism," unpublished Ph.D. thesis, Leiden University (2006).

of Khoesan chiefs as "traditional authorities" with salaries equivalent to those of other "traditional authorities" – it did take on board the symbolic reappraisal of the role of the Khoesan in the country's history. South Africa's new coat of arms has two Khoesan figures, copied from rock art, as its central symbols, and the motto, *!ke e:/xarra //ke*, is in /Xam. In his speech in 2000 inaugurating these symbols, South African President Thabo Mbeki stressed that the Khoesan were the first inhabitants of South Africa and stated that the choice of the extinct /Xam language to convey the sentiment "diverse people unite" was a protest against the genocide of the /Xam and others.[167] The same impulses led to government support for Khoesan claims for the return of the bodily remains of Sara Baartman, the woman shamefully exhibited in England and France in the early nineteenth century as "the Hottentot Venus." Various portions of her anatomy, which had been held in the *Musée de l'Homme* in Paris, were reburied with great ceremony and in the presence of Thabo Mbeki at Hankey, in the Eastern Cape, on August 9, 2002 (Women's Day). Again, the government recognized neo-Khoesan claims and aspirations in a manner that was essentially symbolic and relatively cheap.[168] The active engagement in the public arena with the ideas of Khoesan and colored identities was mirrored by similar sustained attention, though often with different inflections, in the arena of the production of professional history.[169]

Where the 1980s had seen the emergence of a new kind of historicized and radicalized anthropology influenced by historical materialism, it was in the 1990s that a ful-fledged historical anthropology emerged, offering a historical perspective not on "the natives," the historical preserve of the discipline, but on the colonial encounter itself. This work is perhaps most substantially represented in the work of the historical anthropologists John and Jean Comaroff.[170] Indeed, this period saw intensive investigation of

---

[167] See address by President Thabo Mbeki at the unveiling of the coat of arms, Kwaggafontein, April 27, 2000, to be found on http://www.sahistory.org.za/pages/mainframe.htm (accessed April 2005); see also Alan Barnard, *Diverse People Unite: Two Lectures on Khoisan Imagery and the State* (Edinburgh: Centre of African Studies, 2003).

[168] Besten, Transformation and Reconstitution, Chapter 13.

[169] C. Hendricks, "'Ominous' Liaisons: Tracing the Interface between 'Race' and sex at the Cap," in Z. Erasmus (Ed.), *Coloured by History, Shaped by Place: New Perspectives on Coloured Identities in Cape Town* (Cape Town: Kwela Books and SA History Online, 2001), Chapter 1. The literature on slavery feeds into this historiographical project, just as the public engagement about the representation of slavery links into the discussion of Khoesan identity. See further A. Bank (Ed.), *The proceedings of the Khoisan Identities and Cultural Heritage Conference, held at the South African Museum, Cape Town, 12–16 July 1997, organised by the Institute for Historical Research, University of the Western Cape* (Cape Town: Institute for Historical Research, University of the Western Cape, 1998).

[170] Comaroff and Comaroff, *Of Revelation and Revolution*; Hamilton, *Terrific Majesty*.

the workings of colonialism and the constitution of colonial subjectivity. Highlighting questions of race and gender identity and, most recently, sexuality, this work was, and is, highly varied in its inflections.[171] An important characteristic is the way in which it augmented the predominantly political economy approach of the 1970s and 1980s with sustained attention to issues of culture (now fully historicized and understood as a cultural field marked by change), symbolism, the production of meaning, and consciousness. Not surprisingly, the perspective led to a renewed engagement with the impact of the missionaries and Christianity on African societies and to attention to the significance and workings of faith as well as a new interest in ancestor and witch beliefs.[172] In the later 1990s, historical anthropologists and intellectual historians began critically to investigate colonial knowledge practices and to question the evidentiary paradigms that they put in place.[173]

The epistemological critique emerging from this work intersected with a clutch of allied concerns with different points of genesis. Notable among these has been the energetic thrust from within literary studies demanding that greater attention be given to the textual forms of the archive and of historical accounts, to their generic characteristics and key tropes, and to the implications of translation. The literary history contribution has been substantial in examining colonial impositions of subjectivity and the positioning of writing by Africans – often emerging from missionary training – seeking to establish identities for themselves. It further focused attention on the development of print culture, the politics of literacy, and the constitution of reading communities.[174] Another significant point of intersection has been with the increasingly vocal epistemological critique mounted by a new generation of black intellectuals alert to the exclusion of black intellectual history from formal historiography. An important angle

---

[171] A. McClintock, *Imperial Leather: race, gender, and sexuality in the colonial conquest* (New York, Routledge, 1994); Z. Magubane, *Bringing the Empire Home: Race, Class and Gender in Britain and Colonial South Africa* (Chicago: University of Chicago Press, 2004).

[172] P. Delius, "Witches and Missionaries in Nineteenth-century Transvaal," *Journal of Southern African Studies,* 27(3) (2001), pp. 429–43.

[173] See for example, Ashforth, *Politics of Official Discourse*; Dubow, *Scientific Racism*, pp. 246–83; Hamilton, *Terrific Majesty*, esp. Chapters 3 & 4.

[174] See, for example, De Kock, *Civilising Barabarians*; Attwell, *Rewriting Modernity*; Hofmeyr, *We Spend our Years*; I. Hofmeyr, *The Portable Bunyan* (Johannesburg: Wits University Press, 2004); also see the take up by historians, e.g., J. Guy, "'Making Words Visible': Aspects of Orality, Literacy, Illiteracy and History in Southern Africa," *South African Historical Journal, 31* (1994), pp. 3–27; P. Harries, "Missionaries, Marxists and Magic: Power and Politics of Literacy in South-East Africa," *Journal of Southern African Studies,* 27(3), 2001, pp. 405–27; H. Mokoena, "The Making of a Kholwa Intellectual: A discursive biography of Magema Magwaza Fuze," Ph.D. thesis, University of Cape Town, 2006.

in this work, and a point of direct overlap with historical anthropology, is the way in which it begins to confront and foreground the problem of ethnocentrism in the production of knowledge itself.[175]

At much the same time historians began actively to track the role of public presentations of history in the making of subjectivity and identity, and, more specifically, the role of history in creating nationalisms. Elements of this work focused on the public presentation of the preindustrial past in museums and theme parks and in acts of memorialization, notably celebrations of moments from the history of colonial expansion within South Africa, looking at the role of public history both in the past and in the post-1994 era.[176] Since 1994, not surprisingly, the emphasis in public history and the allocation of linked public monies has been on African nationalist projects. In respect of the preindustrial past, however, the developments have been slow, with the notable exception of the erection and celebration of a new monument at Ncome River, dedicated to attesting to the Zulu side of the battle and, more generally, reassessing the battle as a moment of violent settler conquest. Acknowledgment of "living heritage" and of the importance of oral histories in government policy documents and in a variety of heritage fora provides the basis for further endeavors.

The evidentiary status of oral histories, especially those that refer to the distant past, nonetheless remains ambiguous in post-apartheid South Africa. Accounts of the preindustrial past surfaced publicly in the oral testimonies of land claimants and in commissioned research presented to the Commission for the Restitution of Land Rights, set up by the new ANC-led government in 1994 to address the history of land alienation. A total of 67,314 claims were lodged with the commission by the deadline of December 31, 1998.[177] The claims were investigated (mainly by professional historians in tertiary institutions) using title deed records and other archival material. As many of the claimants were in illiterate rural communities, the submission of oral historical accounts was allowed and considered by the commission to be an important and legitimate form of

[175] See, for example, Mokoena, "Magema Magwaza Fuze."

[176] T. Dunbar Moodie, *The Rise of Afrikanerdom: Power, Apartheid and the Afrikaner Civil Religion* (Berkeley, Los Angeles, and London: University of California Press, 1975), pp. 180–1. On the *braaivleis*, and the Afrikaner context, see also Giliomee, *The Afrikaners*, p. 432; E. Delmont, "The Voortrekker Monument: Monolith to Myth," *South African Historical Journal*, 29 (1993), pp. 76–101; A. Grundlingh, "A Cultural Conundrum? Old monuments and New Regimes: the Voortrekker Monument as Symbol of Afrikaner Power in a Postapartheid South Africa," *Radical History Review*, 81 (2001), pp. 95–112; L. Witz, *Apartheid's Festival: Contesting South Africa's national pasts* (Bloomington & Cape Town: Indiana University Press and David Philip, 2003).

[177] *LANDinfo*, a journal of the Department of Land Affairs, Pretoria, 9(1) (2002), p. 4.

evidence, and many claimants relied entirely on oral evidence. Although only claims for land taken after 1913 were eligible, the oral testimonies supporting the claims were typically replete with details about circumstances of land holding until 1913 or a subsequent date of dispossession. The claimants, who were often third-generation descendants of the original owners, would relate to the researchers how their ancestors had originally come into the area, how they had gained access to the land, the physical structures they had erected, where they were buried, and how they were dispossessed. Many of these claims still await finalization, and it remains to be seen how the oral testimony will finally be evaluated. It is, of course, striking that colonial dispossessions of previous centuries are excluded from this process of redress.

The records of the commission, along with those of the Commission on Traditional Leadership Disputes and Claims, will constitute one of the new archives of the post-1994 period that refer to the preindustrial past, along with new archives envisioned for Freedom Park, the national historical theme park outside Pretoria, which deals with precolonial wars, genocide, slavery, and wars of resistance,[178] the huge Southern African Rock Art Digital Archive currently being developed at the University of the Witwatersrand,[179] and the New African Movement virtual archive currently under construction by the literary scholar Ntongela Masilela, which draws together into an archive of black intellectual history scattered newspaper articles written, often in vernacular languages, by the emerging black intellectuals dubbed the "New Africans."[180]

CONCLUSION

This chapter lays out some of the processes that underlie the transportation of elements of, or ideas about, the preindustrial past into modern South Africa, whether as historical reconstructions, archival residues, practices designated traditional, components of identities, in political arrangements, or as formally recognized historical knowledge. It illuminates a range of historical and historiographical developments and interventions designed to inhibit both processes of cultural articulation and the emergence of histories of such processes. The chapter also shows how, in spite of this, the various histories produced by the varied parties making up the two categories of "colonizer" and "colonized" were nonetheless complex acts of articulation. There was no sense in which the productions of either of

[178] See www.freedompark.org.   [179] See www.SARADA.co.za
[180] See www.pitzer.edu/academics/faculty/masilela/index/asp

these categories were homogenous or conceptually exclusive, even when the authors represented themselves as in opposition to, for instance, "white settler historiography."

History production and effacement were typically driven by agendas of domination and contestation but were seldom tightly sealed off from each other or neatly confined to those concerns. The historical accounts that resulted were not simply expressions of contested ideologies: The chapter reveals processes of hegemony at work where certain accounts changed shape, sometimes by appropriating the arguments of the opposition, at other times by seeking to neutralize them, expanding or contracting the available archive on which they drew, often undertaking complex work in engaging the key ontological and epistemological questions of the time.

In some instances the agenda of identity formation called forth rigid and simplified historical accounts, in other instances the accounts avoided direct engagement with the prevailing power relations. The chapter points to the role played by the discipline of history, and by its precursors, in the making of colonial, apartheid, and modern subjects.

The chapter draws attention to the very different ways in which the history of South African communities was produced in precolonial times, under early colonial conditions, in the heyday of imperialism, in subsequent national contexts, and in the immediate postapartheid era. Conceptualization of this historiography in terms of simple binaries of a version of history promoted by the colonizers and an alternative history advance by the colonized, or of domination and resistance histories, does not do justice to the changing forms of those histories over time. It also does not take account of the extent of their reciprocal determinations and mutual imbrication, their involvement in multiple processes and dialogue (what David Attwell has termed, in relation to black South African literature, "transculturation"),[181] and the elaborate devices and tactics, sources and sites, of history production at work in each period. In this, the production of South African history has been a metonym for that history itself.

The chapter has traced the processes of information gathering, archival creation, and the construction of historical narratives about preindustrial South Africa, examining how those processes came to be concentrated in the hands of a small band of white, mostly male, experts, whether colonial officials, anthropologists, or apartheid, liberal or radical historians. "Those who have not domesticated the information gathering process at the institutional level are doomed to receive information, even about themselves,

---

[181] Attwell, *Rewriting modernity.*

second-hand," commented Njabulo Ndebele, literary Critic and University vice-chancellor.[182]

Traditions of intellectual rigor founded on historical research by black South Africans concerned with the preindustrial past have yet to become firmly established in such institutions. The reasons for this are complex, many of them typical of the character of research more generally in the institutions, and occupy the minds of concerned academics like Ndebele. In addition to the institutional difficulties, historical research into the precolonial past presents particular challenges for reasons inherent to the practice of all historical inquiry. In particular, it requires a major intellectual effort to find and represent the voices of women and the colonized and, more generally, to supersede the demands of those who controlled knowledge production when the available archive, relatively slim as it is, was laid down.

---

[182] N. Ndebele, *Rediscovery of the Ordinary: Essays on South African Literature and Culture* (Johannesburg: COSAW, 1991), pp. 25–6.

2

THE APPEARANCE OF FOOD PRODUCTION IN SOUTHERN AFRICA 1,000 TO 2,000 YEARS AGO

JOHN PARKINGTON AND SIMON HALL

About 2,000 years ago domestic animals, first sheep and later cattle, and domestic plants, principally sorghum and millet, spread to Southern Africa from areas to the north where they were originally domesticated some thousands of years earlier. The retrieval of the remains of these domesticates has allowed archaeologists to develop narratives that describe the social events responsible for the material traces excavated. For historical reasons these events are referred to as "stone age" in the West or "iron age" in the East, depending on the absence or presence of traces of iron use and smelting as associated practices. There is a broad correspondence between this distinction and between the winter (and year-round) and summer rainfall zones of Southern Africa. Here we address the geographic and historical contexts under which people adopted some or other mix of domestic plants and animals, transforming hunter–gatherers into either farmers or herders. We follow Mitchell[1] and others in using the term herder for the (economic) practice of keeping domestic stock and pastoralist and farmer for the (cognitive) practice of developing a world view around mobile stock ownership and sedentary mixed agriculture, respectively.

THE NATURE OF ARCHAEOLOGY AS HISTORY

To explain the appearance of food production in Southern Africa, to document the arrival of domestic plants and animals, and to understand the addition of food production alongside hunting and gathering in certain areas and the replacement of hunting and gathering in others, it is necessary to establish in broad outline the nature of archaeology as history and the comparative relationship between the two.

[1] P. Mitchell, *The archaeology of southern Africa* (Cambridge: Cambridge University Press, 2002).

If conventionally history is the construction of a past or pasts from written documents, an archaeological history is constructed from material traces that have survived into the present. A number of implications of this distinction are relevant to the subject of this chapter. History, *sensu stricto*, is able to resolve the moment, the event, the place, and the person, albeit with the recognition that the information is manufactured from some specific perspective. Identities in documents are often, but not always, self-referential, names to which people would have responded positively, words people would have used for themselves. Issues raised are those appropriate to this resolution of time, place, and person. Though this process may be comparable to anthropological or ethnographic accounts, there are substantial differences when material traces, not documents or eyewitness accounts, form the record.

Archaeological histories are written from material remains such as artifacts, hearths, rock paintings, or engravings and the remains of settlements. The order of these residues in time and their distributions and associations across the contemporary landscape provide the structure for an archaeological narrative. Conventionally, archaeological constructs are site-based, meaning that narratives are developed from the understanding of material remains from particular places on the landscape and the linking of these "sites" into local, regional, or continental distributions. The result of these frameworks (material, site) is that the resolution of space is usually as good as, if not better than, that of an eyewitness account or an observation committed to writing, but that of time and person is almost always much poorer. Contemporaneity is assumed only by a similarity of radiocarbon dates, which may have error margins of some tens or a few hundred years. Although it is assumed that individuals lit fires and made stone artifacts, the narratives are usually written in terms of groups whose exact composition is uncertain. Names are imposed after the fact, and specific historical anonymity means that identities may only be inferred at a general level.

These differences in the focus and scale of written and material evidence are critical in time periods when both kinds of evidence are at hand, as occurs from the fifteenth century along the Atlantic Seaboard and in the Western and Southern Cape. Integrating the written accounts of early European travel writers encountering nonliterate communities with the approximately contemporary material traces of these same communities is fraught with problems, though obviously also steeped in narrative potential. Written sources may seem to speak with an authority that belies their geographically and temporally fragmented nature and upon which interpretive generalization may be dangerously built. More realistically, early written sources at the frontier of first encounters provide snapshots or events that are highly variable in their analogical power to infer a norm or pervasive cultural patterns. At best, such discontinuous observation provides suggestive scenarios about what indigenous people were doing at the point of those first encounters, and one role of material evidence is to critically test those scenarios rather than play handmaiden to them.

This critical relationship must also apply to the deeper past. Although the interpretation of material evidence is unavoidably always undertaken comparatively using historical and ethnographic frameworks, there is always the problem that we will never know the past other than in those terms. We can, however, exercise some control over contemporary observation by manipulating informing source and archaeological subject in a more recursive way. Indeed, writing archaeological narratives respects a continuous resonance between source and subject rather than imposing a contemporary framework on archaeological subject in a unidirectional way. Additionally, from our point of view the perspective provided by archaeological narratives contextualizes the indigenous viewpoint at the time of first colonial encounters, whether that is in the Western Cape during the fifteenth and sixteenth centuries or in the Kalahari in the second half of the nineteenth century. In so doing, archaeological sequences have the capacity to point out that there are also alternative ways of reading the written records of those encounters. In our view the inconclusive nature of debates about Kalahari identities and the transitions to herding in the Cape are the result of the uneven relationships that result when material- and text-based narratives are uncritically juxtaposed. This chapter consequently reviews two different transitions to food production that in our attempts at understanding, continually combine and involve different scales of evidence.

Despite the methodological caution posted previously, the history of various understandings of the appearance of food production in South Africa have tried to link archaeological sequences to the trajectory of identities that emerge historically. The concern with linking archaeological sequences to historic identities, albeit on a very broad scale, has required a continuous appeal to migration as the causal mechanism through which food production found its way into South Africa. Such an appeal is logically obvious from Later Stone Age (LSA) sequences that chronologically straddle the pre- and post-food production period. The pool of wild progenitors from which plant and animals domesticates were drawn does not occur locally and equally, the knowledge of iron and pottery production and lifeways based on sedentary homesteads are also not local innovations. In the eastern savannah summer rainfall regions of South Africa, therefore, archaeologists link a package of material residues that appear suddenly in the archaeological record between about AD 250 and 500, with Bantu-speaking farmers.

In the West there are the residues for sheep and a stylistically heteroge-
nous range of thin-walled ceramics. A continuous theme in the research of
anthropologists, linguists, historians, and archaeologists is that they represent the movement of Khoekhoe pastoralists into the western and southern
reaches of South Africa 2,000 years ago.

THE CULTURAL AND ENVIRONMENTAL SETTING
FOR FOOD PRODUCTION

The introduction of food production about 2,000 years ago marks a major
change in the South African sequence and had varying impacts on the
historical trajectories of hunter–gatherers. Prior to this event, and back to
about 10,000 years ago, when there is broad cultural continuity within
hunter–gatherers, the archaeological record is clear in generating no evidence of the presence of domestic plants or animals in Southern Africa. We
can conclude that wherever people lived they subsisted off wild, not domesticated or cultivated resources. The archaeological record for the millennia
before this time is geographically patchy in certain areas, but less so in others, and through time there are also dips and peaks in population densities.
This is a pattern most archaeologists take to mean that people distributed
themselves across the landscape broadly in proportion to their perception
of resource distributions. The rules of residence were presumably flexible
enough for people to redistribute themselves easily in both the long and
the short term in response to changes in rainfall and resource productivity.

The fact that there has been more research in certain areas than in others
(a relatively intense focus on the Western, Eastern, and Southern Cape,
for instance) is, in part, a function of preservation. Much of this work
prior to the mid-1980s emphasized adaptive relationships to environmental structure.[2] In many respects this work mirrored the ecological concerns of ethnographers working on the Dobe !Kung in the Kalahari,[3] and
archaeologists successfully outlined patterns of seasonal mobility, the com-
plementarity of plant and animal foods, and the technological package
through which resources were secured. In line with theoretical trends
elsewhere, however, some archaeologists were encouraged from the mid-
1980s to intensify their focus on the social structures within which environmental relationships were organized. Rock art studies, for example,
which underwent a significant reorientation guided by Lewis-Williams

---

[2] H. J. Deacon, *Where hunters gathered; a study of Holocene stone age people in the Eastern Cape*
(Claremont: South African Archeological Society, 1976).

[3] R. Lee, *The !Kung San: men, women and work in a foraging society* (Cambridge: Cambridge
University Press, 1979).

and Wadley,[4] explains the different subsistence and tool signatures between sites within the social framework of seasonally aggregating and dispersing bands. Another approach sought to shift the analytical scale away from principles of ecological adaptation to the details of how the tool, plant, and animal mix changed through time.[5] Terms such as intensification and extensification were used to suggest that hunter–gatherer subsistence was by no means static but apparently did not shift in the direction of the dramatic modification of person–plant and person–animal relations we would call domestication. Interpretation has focused on vital and complex links between resources, population densities and degrees of mobility,[6] and the social basis of managing these relationships.

However we wish to interpret the pre-2000 BP (before present) hunter–gatherer sequence, few would imagine the hunter–gatherers as socially passive and guileless. This is despite the apparent contrast between the relatively muted change through the pre-2000 sequence and the pace and scale of change that occurred when and after food production appeared. If the fundamental condition of hunting and gathering may be described as strategic flexibility, as evident from the varied and diverse ecologies that were exploited (Fig. 2.1), we would also expect the hunter–gatherers to have been flexibly strategic in their response to the elements of food production and food producers themselves.[7] Much of what follows poses a number of questions about this interface. Different archaeologists, however, using various comparative aids and theoretical positions, provide different answers to these questions, and there is by no means consensus.

---

[4] J. D. Lewis-Williams, "The economic and social context of southern African rock art," *Current Anthropology*, 23 (1982), pp. 429–49. T. A. Dowson and J. D. Lewis-Williams (Eds.), *Contested images: diversity in southern African rock art research* (Johannesburg: Witwatersrand University Press, 1994). L. Wadley, *Later Stone Age hunters and gatherers of the southern Transvaal: social and ecological interpretations* (Oxford: BAR, 1987).

[5] J. Parkington, "Time and place: some observations on spatial and temporal patterning in the the Later Stone Age sequence in southern Africa," *South African Archaeological Bulletin*, 35 (1980), pp. 75–83.

[6] A. D. Mazel, "People making history: the last ten thousand years of hunter-gatherer communities in the Thukela Basin," *Natal Museum Journal of Humanities*, 1 (1989), pp. 1–168. S. Hall, "Burial and sequence in the Later Stone of the Eastern Cape Province, South Africa," *South African Archaeological Bulletin*, 55 (2000), pp. 137–46. A. Jerardino, "Changing social landscapes of the western Cape coast of southern Africa over the last 4500 years," Ph.D. thesis, University of Cape Town (1996).

[7] For relatively early statements on hunter-gatherer flexibility, see M. G. Guenther, "The trance dancer as an agent of social change among the farm Bushmen of the Ghanzi District," *Botswana Notes and Records*, 7 (1975), pp. 161–6, and J. E. Yellen, "The integration of herding into prehistoric hunting and gathering economies," in M. Hall, G. Avery, D. M. Avery, M. L. Wilson, & A. J. B. Humphreys (Eds.), *Frontiers: Southern African Archaeology Today*, pp. 53–64 (Oxford: BAR International Series, p. 207, 1984).

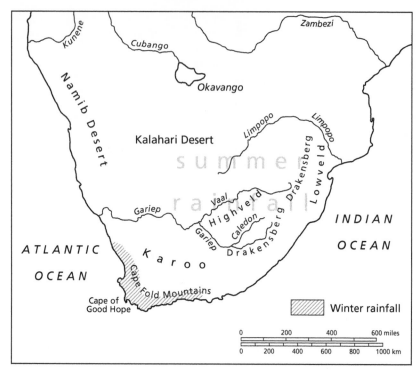

FIGURE 2.1. The physical and environmental setting for food production in South Africa. (Base map adapted from P. Mitchell, *The archaeology of southern Africa* [Cambridge, 2002], 2.2.)

How important were resident hunter–gatherers to the success of pioneer food production? In the western areas were hunter–gatherers marginal to the advent of ideologically committed pastoralists or did they flexibly attach diffused sheep and pottery to the basic condition of hunting and gathering? In the east, to what extent did hunter–gatherers attract pioneer farmers and facilitate their ecological passage or did migrating farmers have the power to pick and choose their habitats at will?

Although the establishment of mixed farming in the east is a slightly later event than the herder/pastoralist archaeology of the west, we deal with it first because on empirical grounds the archaeological visibility, coherence, and apparent cultural homogeneity of pioneer farming in the east is strong. This has led to an interpretive emphasis on the appearance of these residues early in the first millennium A.D. as a broad package introduced through migration, providing a comparative baseline for the patchy remains of food production in the west where there is ongoing debate about economic and cultural identities and the variable role of migration and diffusion. It is to these debates about the advent of food production that we now turn.

THE APPEARANCE OF FARMING IN THE EAST: MIGRATION AND PACKAGE?

Tending crops and managing animals is obviously constrained by climatic and ecological conditions, and the distribution and location of farmer[8] settlements, at several different geographical scales, reflects the tolerances of these resources (Fig. 2.1). The movement of farmers into the eastern summer rainfall areas of South Africa in the first millennium A.D. is an example of this phenomenon. Despite the evidence of the ideological importance of cattle and small stock, the eastern distribution of farmer settlements underpins the importance of day-to-day food security based upon the successful production of sorghum and millet. This distribution also reflects the primary rainfall and temperature conditions under which sorghum and millet were first domesticated in the Sahelian belt far to the north. Equally, sheep and goats were domesticated in the near east and cattle may have been domesticated in North Africa,[9] whereas pottery has a long history in North Africa and metal technologies were relatively recent introductions.[10] Consequently, whereas these basic elements have complex histories in Africa, their appearance in early first millennium seems to be as a preassembled package.

Migration of Bantu-speaking people is seen as the mechanism but does tend to reify a packaged genetic, economic, and cultural identity that seems to repeat the ahistoric and immutable identities of apartheid ideology. The idea of "Bantu migration" has been current ever since Wilhelm Bleek recognized in the mid-nineteenth century that over the vast expanses of Central, Eastern, and Southern Africa Bantu languages were closely related, and in the South African context, quite separate from "Bushmen" and "Hottentot." The classificatory homogeneity of Bantu languages was accounted for by rapid and recent migration, and in the colonial imagination, this could be

---

[8] The "Early Iron Age" is used as a shorthand label for mixed farmers in the first millennium. Some feel that the term is misleading for its emphasis on a technological attribute of a much more complex system and others deem it Eurocentric because its referents are outside of Africa. In this chapter we use early agriculturists or early farmers. See T. Maggs, "Name calling in the Iron Age," *South African Archaeological Bulletin,* 47 (992), p. 131.

[9] D. Gifford-Gonzalez, "Animal disease challenges to the emergence of pastoralism in sub-Saharan Africa," *African Archaeological Review, 17* (2000), pp. 95–139.

[10] For a review of metal in Africa see S. T. Childs and E. W. Herbert, "Metallurgy and its consequences," in A. Brower Stahl (Ed.), *African Archaeology*, pp. 276–300 (Oxford: Blackwell, 2005).

no less than the mindless southward movement of barbaric hordes. Under the apartheid government, recent meant contemporary with European settlers, and a history defined by writing removed the primacy of tenure. Conveniently, the apartheid view of history was difficult to undermine because the historical process evident in the Bantu linguistic classification could not easily be chronologically anchored. Archaeological research from the 1960s, coupled with the availability of radiocarbon dating, changed this dramatically. The distinctive archaeological residues long known from the summer rainfall Bushveld areas comprising the remains of wattle and daub huts in sedentary homesteads, cereal and animal domesticates, pottery and iron artifacts, and metal working debris, were seen to represent the materialization of the first South African Bantu-speaking farmers, with a time depth of almost 2,000 years.[11] The archaeological and linguistic data appear to correlate well in the South African context. Early farming residues have a general cultural and economic homogeneity that parallels an equal homogeneity in Bantu languages, and both indicate relatively recent and rapid movement. The earliest radiocarbon dates for farming place the process between about AD 250 and 450.

The appearance of farming and Bantu-speakers in South Africa appears to be two expressions of the same "event" and marks a substantial new lifestyle compared with that in the eastern summer rainfall areas. Whether this also tallies with new gene pools in South Africa, and whether the same compatibility between sources is evident to the north, are topics we return to briefly after discussing the archaeology of this "event."

With respect to archaeologically defined identity, South African mixed farmers can be traced northward to East Africa and northwestward into the archaeologically poorly known areas of Angola. These geographic links are drawn from stylistic continuities in pottery between these areas and South Africa. Early farmer pottery and directionality is indicated by a chronological trend from older to younger the further south one comes. The stylistic homogeneity of this pottery has long been recognized, and the term "Chifumbaze Complex" has been coined for it (Fig. 2.2).[12] Although there is general consensus about the stylistic homogeneity of the Chifumbaze Complex, there has been no agreement about stylistic variability within it. This variability is modeled in terms of streams of movement that represent cultural traditions and have been drawn as broad arrows across

---

[11] For a discussion of the political context of "Iron Age" archaeology see Martin Hall, "Hidden History: Iron Age archaeology in southern Africa," in P. T. Robertshaw (Ed.), *A history of African archaeology*, pp. 59–77 (London: James Currey, 1990), and T. Maggs, "Three decades of Iron Age research in South Africa: some personal reflections," *South African Archaeological Bulletin*, 48 (1993) pp. 70–6.

[12] D. Phillipson, *African Archaeology* (Cambridge: Cambridge University Press, 1993).

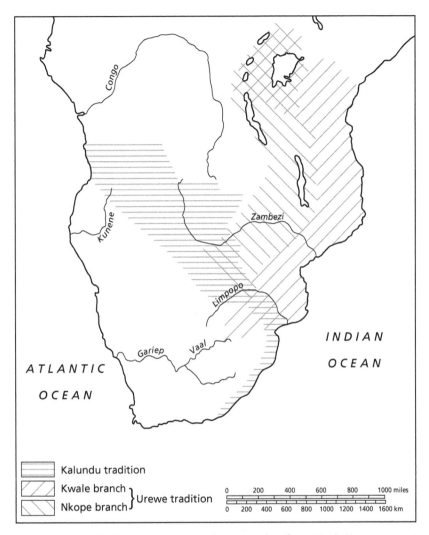

Kalundu tradition

Kwale branch ⎫
                ⎬ Urewe tradition
Nkope branch ⎭

FIGURE 2.2. The Chifumbaze Complex. (Base map taken from Mitchell, 2002, 10.3.)

the landscape of Southern and Central Africa. Disagreement stems from the way stylistic difference and similarity is measured on pottery,[13] and

---

[13] See D. Phillipson, *The later prehistory of eastern and southern Africa* (London: Heinemann, 1976) for an early synthesis of linguistic and archaeological data and a model of "Iron Age" movement into Central and Southern Africa. This is methodologically and theoretically critiqued by T. Huffman, "African origins," *South African Journal of Science,* 75 (1979), pp. 233–37. Huffman's alternative model is the one given here. For the details of ceramic analysis, see T. Huffman, "Ceramics, classification and Iron Age entities," *African Studies,* 39 (1980), pp. 123–74.

furthermore, it has been suggested that there has been too great an emphasis on classification (on pots rather than people) and that this has tended
to marginalize other aspects of agriculturist archaeology such as ecological
relationships, economic structure, and the symbolic meaning of material
culture. It is also suggested that a concern with ceramic classification simply extends apartheid thinking into the past.[14] Ceramic analysis, however,
provides one of the basic frameworks within which all "Iron Age" archaeologists orient themselves in time and space, some more explicitly than
others, before moving on to develop their narratives. The ability to distinguish different ceramic styles is also important because such distinctions
relate to historical processes. When placed in a broader archaeological and
ethnographic framework, continuity and change in ceramic style can be
linked to the construction of identities that relate to the regional politics of
precedence.[15] Ceramic sequences provide a basic but important spatial and
chronological structure, and consequently, it is worth making a few brief
statements about ceramic analysis.

Ceramic classification assumes that different ceramic styles represent
some form of cultural identity. Within a cultural milieu, decoration is not
random but is repeatedly applied in a structured and limited number of
ways. Although theoretically there is an infinite number of ways in which
decoration can be applied to a pot, analysis of pottery shows that this is
not the case. Style is discontinuous between groups, and this has been
tested on ethnographic pottery assemblages where potters with the same
cultural identity produce pots with the same style structure to a shared
cultural world.[16] The emphasis on ceramic style in archaeological analysis

---

[14] Martin Hall has questioned the assumptions that underpin ceramic classification and the
value of the culture history sequences that result. They still, however, structure his own
work. See M. Hall, "Tribes and traditions and numbers: the American model in southern
African Iron Age studies," *South African Archaeological Bulletin, 38* (1983), pp. 51–61,
and "Pots and politics: ceramic interpretations in southern Africa," *World Archaeology,
15* (1984), pp. 262–73.

[15] See Chapter 3 for a full discussion of this and I. Kopytoff, "The internal African
frontier: the making of African political culture," in I. Kopytoff (Ed.), *The African
frontier: the reproduction of traditional African societies*, pp. 3–84. (Bloomington: Indiana
University Press, 1987). J. H. N. Loubser, "Archaeology and early Venda history," *The
South African Archaeological Society Goodwin Series, 6* (1989), 54–61. J. H. N. Loubser,
"The ethnoarchaeology of Venda-speakers in southern Africa," *Navorsinge van die Nasionale
Museum Bloemfontein, 7* (1991), pp. 146–464. J. A. Calabrese, "Ethnicity, class and polity:
the emergence of social and political complexity in the Shashi-Limpopo Valley of southern
Africa, AD 900 to 1300," Ph.D. thesis, University of the Witwatersrand (Johannesburg,
2005).

[16] See Huffman, "Ceramics," and T. N. Huffman, "Ceramics, settlements and Late Iron
Age migrations," *African Archaeological Review, 7* (1989), pp. 155–82.

of culture–history sequences may be questioned because pottery is only one expressive medium through which style is made explicit. But Evers[17] has shown, again by analyzing ethnographic material, that much of the style structure on pots occurs on a wide array of other decorated items, such as wall and mural art, beadwork, and wood carving. Ceramic style, therefore, is not culturally trivial but part of a wider design field even though much of this is not preserved for archaeological recovery.

If style is not arbitrary and is deeply embedded, shared, expressed, and communicated within cultural systems, the difficulty for archaeologists is to establish what scale of identity is expressed through ceramic style and what social dynamics maintain or change it. Huffman argues that ceramic styles represent a form of macroethnicity that is produced by people who speak the same language because language is the medium through which cognitive codes, symbols, and behavioral values are communicated. Furthermore, although there is some consensus that ceramic style clusters have empirical integrity, the question remains how these clusters and the boundaries between them are theoretically conceived to operate "in the real world." Archaeological definitions of identity have been criticized for being vague, static, and perhaps interchangeably standing for culture because of a lack of rigor in demonstrating the social basis of these identities. Recognizing "groupishness," in whatever form or scale, should encourage archaeologists to think about what the sociology of a group might be and also about the historical context that requires its construction in relation to a boundary and to some other group.[18]

Historical analogues do provide some cautionary tales in this regard. In Zambia, for example, pottery from Kololo sites (originally Sotho groups who migrated during the *difaqane*, and referred to as the Linyati Tradition) is stylistically similar to Sotho pottery, and this continuity demonstrates their historical and cultural links. For the Ngoni, however (migrants from Nguni-speaking South Africa also during the *mfecane* early in the nineteenth century), this stylistic relationship is not straightforward. In Eastern Zambia, Ngoni pottery falls within what is called the Luangwa Tradition that was well established before the Ngoni arrived in the region. Although

---

[17] M. Evers, "The recognition of groups in the Iron Age of southern Africa," Ph.D. thesis, University of the Witwatersrand (1988).

[18] David Hammond-Tooke captures and distills this issue but prefers to label stylistic clusters "material culture units." This acknowledges their discontinuous nature but neutralizes any inference about identity that needs to be rigorously theorized. D. Hammond-Tooke, "'Ethnicity' and 'ethnic group' in Iron Age southern Africa," *South African Journal of Science*, 96 (2000), pp. 421–2.

this migration is not reflected in ceramic style, there is continuity in settlement style and organization.[19] This example needs to be contextualized within Nguni attitudes to cattle, agriculture, and women and the capacity of gendered material culture to maintain identity in the face of change. These examples highlight the fact that ceramic sequences must be read in conjunction with the wider array of archaeological data.

The distribution of stylistically homogenous Chifumbaze Complex pottery has been explicitly linked to the distribution of eastern Bantu languages, and by association, the archaeology dates this spread (Fig. 2.2). The associations, however, are unquestionably complex. Terms for iron-working, cereal production, and the tools of production and domestic animals in eastern Bantu are linguistic borrowings from central Sudanic or eastern Sahelian languages, and it is in this complex cultural milieu that the loan of these words may have taken place. For plant and animal domesticates this is not surprising because the archaeology shows that these Neolithic communities were well established before the appearance of "Iron Age" Chifumbaze pottery north of Southern Africa, and in East Africa in particular. Christopher Ehret, a linguist, has suggested that the conduit for livestock terms in eastern Bantu was through Khoe, who in turn acquired them from central Sudanic-speakers who had moved as far south as Southern Africa. Ehret has subsequently placed the emphasis on eastern Sahelian languages as the donor, but his linguistic reconstructions have been questioned.[20] The evidence does show that livestock predates the Chifumbaze Complex in Southern Africa, but it does not support that the livestock component of early agriculturists was locally grafted onto Iron Age society. The movement of livestock into Southern Africa may have been a continuous process, and this does not obviate a Chifumbaze "package" in which livestock were already embedded in a culturally specific and distinctive way.

What specifically encouraged the expansion of mixed farmers southward remains under debate. The addition of iron to this mix certainly correlates with the expansion of mixed farming south of Lake Victoria and an apparent rapid emplacement of mixed farming to the southern

---

[19] D. Collett, "A contribution to the study of migrations in the archaeological record: the Ngoni and Kololo migrations as a case study," in I. Hodder (Ed.), *Archaeology as long term history*, pp. 105–16 (Cambridge, UK: Cambridge University Press, 1987).

[20] C. Ehret, "Patterns of Bantu and Central Sudanic settlement in central and southern Africa (ca. 1000 BC–AD 500)," *Transafrican Journal of History* (1973), pp. 1–71. C. Ehret, *An African classical age: eastern and southern Africa in world history, BC 1000 to AD 400* (Oxford: James Currey, 1998). C. H. Borland, "The linguistic reconstruction of prehistoric pastoralist vocabluary," *South African Archaeological Society Goodwin Series,* 5 (1986), pp. 31–5.

limits of agricultural viability.[21] Iron would certainly have facilitated the domestication of landscape, and the prior Neolithic experience of managing domesticates and genetically modifying them to different conditions may also have helped.[22] To this mix of archaeological and linguistic reconstruction we can add genetic evidence. Although preliminary in nature, most mitochondrial DNA lineages in southern Bantu-speakers are derived from either West or East Africa with variable but low assimilation of indigenous populations.[23] We are mindful of the complexity and independence of language, population, and cultural/economic variables in discussions of migration that tend to reify the idea of "package." In our opinion, however, and focusing on archaeological evidence, there seems to be little that undermines a relatively direct association between the sudden appearance of Chifumbaze ceramics as part of an eastern Bantu-speaking farming complex in South Africa. We return to the eastern Bantu association in the following when we consider the worldview of early mixed farmers.

SEQUENCE AND STREAMS

On the basis of ceramic style three separate streams of movement into South Africa have been identified (Fig. 2.2). Together they make up Phillipson's Chifumbaze Complex, and it is clear that they represent migrations and the movement of people.[24] Two of these streams have a common origin in the interlacustrine region of East Africa and can be traced through their ceramic style back to pottery referred to as Urewe, and hence both these branches fall within the Urewe Tradition. From a stylistic point of view, the least controversial stream is referred to as the Kwale Branch. Ceramic analysis clearly distinguishes two phases in South Africa. An earlier phase (archaeologically known as Silverleaves) dates between AD 250 and 430 and marks the earliest mixed farmers in South Africa. The second phase is known as Mzonjani with dates between AD 420 and 580.

[21] For the historical analysis of Bantu languages, see C. Ehret and M. Posnansky (Eds.), *The Archaeological and Linguistic Reconstruction of African History* (Berkeley & Los Angeles: University of California Press, 1982), and for a recent review see M. K. H. Eggert, "The Bantu problem and African archaeology," in A. Brower Stahl (Ed.), *African Archaeology*, pp. 301–26 (Oxford: Blackwell, 2005).

[22] Gifford-Gonzalez, "Animal disease challenges."

[23] M. Richards, V. Macaulay, C. Hill, A. Carracedo, and A. Salas, "The archaeogenetics of the dispersals of the Bantu-speaking peoples," in M. Jones (Ed.), *Traces of ancestry: studies in honour of Colin Renfrew* (Oxford: Oxbow Books, 2004), pp. 75–87. Although these studies suffer from circularity by sampling DNA by language, the weight of evidence does indicate the East African origins of "Bantu" mtDNA.

[24] See Huffman, "African origins," p. 237; T. N. Huffman and R. K. Herbert, "New perspectives on Eastern Bantu," *Azania, 29/30* (1994/95), p. 32.

Initially this pioneer phase of agriculturist occupation was seen as specifically coastal in distribution. In KwaZulu-Natal, Mzonjani sites are distributed linearly along the coast and mostly within 6 km of it. This very specific locational preference has been interpreted in several ways. One is that it correlates with ancient Pleistocene dune systems that, once cleared of their low forest cover, expose sandy soils that supported brief bursts of agriculture before the soils wore out.[25] In addition, a coastal orientation was geared to the exploitation of rocky points and rich shellfish fields, particularly of the brown mussel (*Perna perna*), which provided an important supplement to the protein diet. These factors may have encouraged rapid relocation through a continuous cycle of slash and burn agriculture. Mzonjani sites are small, and limited material evidence implies that villages were moved frequently.[26] More recently, however, it has been suggested that the coastal orientation optimized the available coastal rainfall and that Mzonjani site location inland was also geared toward sources of iron ore.[27] The location of Silverleaves sites in the Mpumalanga escarpment[28] and in the Swaziland highlands also indicates a specific selection of high rainfall areas and ore. A recent reanalysis of ceramics from Broederstroom, west of Pretoria in the Magaliesberg Valley, clearly shows that Mzonjani communities had spread over the escarpment and well inland by the sixth century,[29] but they did not push further south than the position of present-day Durban (Fig. 2.2).

The second branch of the Urewe Tradition is referred to as Nkope. These ceramics follow a more inland distribution from southern Tanzania, through Malawi, the eastern areas of Zambia, and into Zimbabwe in the fifth century. Of relevance to Southern Africa is the Zhizo phase, which enters the Shashe/Limpopo Valley in the ninth century in pursuit of ivory for the growing east coast trade and the closely related Toutswe phase in eastern Botswana.[30]

There is less consensus concerning the origins and development of the second tradition, known in the archaeological literature as Kalundu. In Huffman's scheme, distinctive Kalundu ceramics were made by Bantu-speaking agriculturists who found their way into South Africa from the northwest. Ceramics from the site of Benfica, on the Angolan coast, provide

---

[25] M. Hall, *Settlement patterns in the Iron Age of Zululand* (Oxford: BAR, 1981).

[26] G. Whitelaw and M. Moon, "The distribution and ceramics of pioneer agriculturists in KwaZulu-Natal," *Natal Museum Journal of Humanities, 8* (1996), pp. 53–79.

[27] *Ibid.*, p. 70.

[28] M. Klapwijk, "A preliminary report on pottery from the north-eastern Transvaal, South Africa," *South African Archaeological Bulletin, 29* (1974), pp. 19–23.

[29] T. Huffman, "The antiquity of *lobola*," *South African Archaeological Bulletin, 53* (1998), pp. 57–62.

[30] Huffman, "African origins." pp. 57–62.

a link, but more observations are required.[31] In South Africa itself Kalundu ceramics were present in Limpopo Province by the fifth century, at the well-known Lydenburg site in Mpumalanga and in KwaZulu-Natal in the best-documented sequence from the seventh century through to the tenth century. In contrast to Mzonjani communities, Kalundu sites are found further to the south as far as the region of present-day East London (Fig. 2.2).[32] Various Kalundu phases occur in the Transvaal and in eastern Botswana, and the terminal phases range in date between the tenth century in KwaZulu-Natal and into the fourteenth century in Eastern Botswana. In some areas the terminal phases of the Early Iron Age are contemporary with the first phase of proto "Tswana"-speakers (see Chapter 3 on second-millennium archaeology).

The chronology of the Kalundu Tradition into South Africa means that it overlies stratigraphically the earlier Urewe Tradition sites where the two overlap. This is most clear in KwaZulu-Natal, where there is a significant break in the sequence between the two.[33] Some suggest, however, that the break is not clear cut, and many of the motifs present in Mzonjani ceramics continue in the Kalundu phases, thereby obviating the need to postulate a second significant inflow of new Early Iron Age communities.[34] This difference of opinion perhaps relates to the alternative classifications employed by different researchers. Huffman's methodology seeks to capture a style structure that combines profile, decorative layout, and position in a complex multivariate analysis. The scale and complexity of this analysis allocates pottery to one tradition or phase and seeks to optimize the assumption that ceramic style is discontinuous. The analysis is meant, at this scale, to isolate difference. In contrast, Maggs compares pottery assemblages through a matrix of attributes. Although this method still distills the fundamental stylistic differences between Mzonjani and early Kalundu ceramics, it highlights smaller-scale stylistic continuities. These continuities do hint at social, economic, and political interactions "on the ground" between Mzonjani residents and Kalundu newcomers that would otherwise be obscured when the scale of analysis is meant to emphasize

[31] J. Denbow, "Congo to Kalahari: data and hypotheses about the political economy of the western stream of the Early Iron Age," *African Archaeological Review*, 8 (1990), pp. 139–75.

[32] T. Nogwaza, "Early Iron Age pottery from Canasta Place, East London district," *Southern African Field Archaeology*, 3 (1994), pp. 103–6. J. Binneman, "Preliminary results from investigations at Kulubele, an Early Iron Age farming settlement in the Great Kei River valley, Eastern Cape," *Southern African Field Archaeology*, 5 (1996), pp. 28–35.

[33] Whitelaw and Moon "The distribution and ceramics."

[34] T. Maggs, "The Iron Age south of the Zambezi," in R. G. Klein (Ed.), *Southern African prehistory and palaeoenvironments*, pp. 329–60 (Rotterdam: Balkema, 1984).

discontinuity. Already established farmers did not simply disappear and, as suggested previously, archaeology must start questioning these stylistic boundaries.[35] What contextual conditions allowed "Kalundu" newcomers to impose their "stylistic" will and culturally absorb Mzonjani communities already resident? One suggestion simply emphasizes weight of numbers. When Mzonjani and Silverleaves communities entered South Africa it appears that there was relatively less rainfall. Settlement choices along the coastal belt and in the escarpment areas reflect the most optimal rainfall areas where crop agriculture could be practiced. Furthermore, Mzonjani site numbers are low compared to the dramatic increase recorded for first-phase Kalundu sites (Msuluzi). It is suggested that ameliorating climatic conditions were optimal for agriculturist expansion and success up to the eighth century, but that in the succeeding phases (Ndondondwane and Ntshekane), site numbers drop sharply, a downturn that may be equivalent to a similar paucity of later phase Early Iron Age sites in the Magaliesberg.[36]

By the sixth century, Early Iron Age farmers were well established south of the Limpopo. The general distribution of Early Iron Age sites clearly shows that they were constrained within the summer rainfall regions (Fig. 2.3). More specifically, they are generally in riverside locations and were placed on deep colluvial and alluvial soils within mixed bush and grass habitats (Bushveld/savanna) (Fig. 2.1). It is clear that the Highveld grassland habitats south of the Magaliesberg, for example, and the higher grassy interfluves above the Bushveld valleys of KwaZulu-Natal were avoided by Early Iron Age people.[37] The southernmost limits of the Early Iron Age range were reached along the coast near East London at Canasta Place, where summer rainfall conditions shift toward year-round patterns. This distribution must partly be tied to the climatic tolerances of staple carbohydrate crops that require $\pm$ 500 mm annual rainfall, with a minimum of 350 mm during the growing season, and a nighttime temperature average of $15°$ C. We can, however, speculate that as pioneers, the farmers were under no demographic or spatial pressure to innovate agricultural strategies outside

---

[35] See Hammond-Tooke, "Identity."

[36] R. Mason, *Origins of the Black people of Johannesburg and the southern, western and central Transvaal* AD *350–1880.* (Johannesburg: Occasional paper of the Department of Archeology, University of the Witwatersrand, 1986). F. E. Prins, "Climate, vegetation and early agriculturist communities in Transkei and KwaZulu-Natal,' *Azania,* 29/30 (1994/1995), pp. 179–86.

[37] Maggs, "The Iron Age." L van Schalkwyk, "Settlement shifts and socio-economic transformations in early agriculturist communities in the lower Thukela Basin," *Azania,* 29/30 (1994/1995), pp. 187–98. R. Mason, "Early Iron Age settlement at Broederstroom 24/73, Transvaal, South Africa," *South African Journal of Science,* 77 (1981), pp. 401–16.

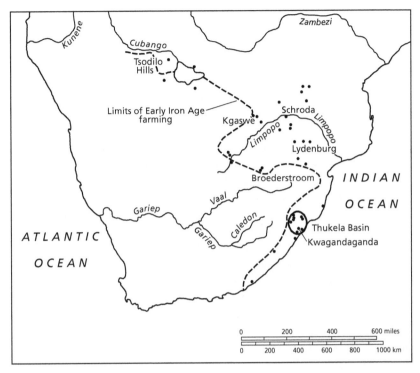

FIGURE 2.3. The geographic limits of Early Iron Age settlement in South Africa showing the location of some of the sites mentioned in the text. (Base map adapted from Mitchell, 2002, 10.1.)

these boundaries, even though crop tolerances allow this (see chapter on second-millennium A.D. farmers). Although the direct evidence for crop cultivation on Early Iron Age sites is limited, the identification of pearl millet (*Pennisetum americanum*) at Silverleaves indicates a wider presence in the pioneer phase. Within Kalundu phase sites, cow peas (*Vigna ungiculata*), ground beans (*Voandzeia subterranea*), sorghums (*Sorghum bicolor*), pearl millet, and finger millet (*Eleusine coracana*) have also been recognized, and the presence of characteristic Early Iron Age grindstones provides abundant indirect evidence of cereal processing. There is also good evidence of metalworking at the Silverleaves and Mzonjani sites and of the fact that the location of these sites was also tied to the proximity of iron ore.[38] The remains of cattle, however, appear to be more variable, and this variability is at the core of debates over the worldview of these first-millennium farmers.

[38] Whitelaw and Moon, "The distribution and ceramics."

SETTLEMENT ORGANIZATION AND THE NATURE OF EARLY FARMER SOCIETY

This brief empirical summary of the appearance of pioneer farmers suggests that a package comprising sedentary village life supported by domesticated cereal agriculture, livestock, and the whole supported by iron technology arrived intact. The evidence for South Africa does not indicate that the elements that make up early farming accreted serially. Although the bits and pieces of material evidence outline broad patterns of settlement choice, ecology, and subsistence, what they signify in terms of social structure has been the subject of some debate.

At the center is the question of the social and ideological role of cattle in Early Iron Age society. Martin Hall argues that Mzonjani farmers had few cattle and that cattle herds only increased significantly in size toward the end of the first millennium A.D. as Early Iron Age farmers created the necessary ecological conditions for successful cattle keeping. In contrast, Huffman argues that cattle were present in sufficiently high numbers from the inception of the Early Iron Age, and this underpinned a cattle ideology that was a central attribute of the package.[39] These interpretations draw attention to important methodological and theoretical differences. On the one hand, Martin Hall constructs a predominantly theoretical argument based on Giddens's structuration theory, which is developmental in nature. On the other hand, Huffman and others have tested ethnographic models of spatial organization against archaeological settlement plans within a structuralist framework. They argue that the ethnographic analogies are relevant because of a broad historical continuity between past and present and that a cattle ideology was an indivisible part of the package that more specifically included the institution of bridewealth exchanges through cattle (*lobola*).

The spatial organization of Early Iron Age settlements, omitted from this review so far, now becomes central to the way past social structure is read and worldview inferred. One spatial model, known in the literature as the Central Cattle Pattern, has been built around the synthesis of Southern

---

[39] M. Hall, "The role of cattle in southern African agropastoral societies: more than bones alone can tell," *South African Archaeological Society, Goodwin Series,* 5 (1986), pp. 83–7, and "Archaeology and modes of production in pre-colonial Southern Africa," *Journal of Southern African Studies, 14* (1987), pp. 1–17. T. N. Huffman, "Broederstroom and the origins of cattle-keeping in southern Africa," *African Studies,* 49 (1990), pp. 1–12. "Broederstroom and the Central Cattle Pattern," *South African Journal of Science,* 89 (1993), pp. 220–26. "The antiquity of lobola," *South African Archaeological Bulletin, 53* (1998), pp. 57–62. "The Central Cattle Pattern and interpreting the past," *Southern African Humanities, 13* (2001), pp. 19–35.

African but predominantly Nguni-speaking ethnographies.[40] This distillation demonstrated how core cultural principles were indissolubly expressed, enacted, controlled, and determined by the spatial form of settlements. For the archaeologist, the ethnographically observed relationship between social form and meaning and its spatial materialization offers a method whereby the ethnographic model can be used comparatively and tested against archaeological settlement plans and thereby explore, and "illuminate the values, ideals and beliefs of the past."[41] Space has structure, and that structure is another expression of social form and provides a map of worldview.

Briefly, the Central Cattle Pattern (CCP) model is an ideal representation of a settlement in terms of core social values such as status, life forces, and kinship (Fig. 2.4).[42] Cattle, which validate these principles, are symbolically central, and this is physically expressed by locating the byre centrally in the settlement. In the division of labor, cattle are the preserve of men, and consequently the byre is male space and is linked to a male court or assembly area that provides the forum to discuss and resolve community issues. Male craft production is also linked to this central zone and important people are buried there. The byre may also be associated with subterranean cereal granaries under the control of the head man. Cattle were always at the core and "were the pliable symbolic vehicles through which men formed and reformed their world of social and spiritual relations."[43] In contrast to the settlement center is the outer domestic ring, comprising productively independent households controlled by wives who in the spatial domain of huts, courtyards, kitchens, and private granaries processed the products of their agricultural labor. The domestic ring was also both spatially and economically marginal to the political center of men. Women through their labor managed the mundane day-to-day routines upon which homestead life was based, but it was men who controlled political life because all transactions were mediated and signified through cattle.

The relevance of the CCP model for animating the settlement layouts of second-millennium settlements that can, in broadest terms, be linked to ancestral Nguni and Tswana/Sotho-speaking communities is beyond doubt (see Chapter 3 on the archaeology of the second millennium). The ethnographic analogies and archaeological subject are historically, culturally, and geographically close. There has, however, been criticism of the

[40] A. Kuper, *Wives for cattle: Bridewealth and Marriage in Southern Africa* (London: Routledge, 1982).

[41] Huffman, "The Central Cattle Pattern," p. 19.

[42] *Ibid.*, p. 20.

[43] Jean Comaroff and John Comaroff, *Of Revelation and Revolution: Christianity, colonialism and consciousness in South Africa*, vol. 1 (Chicago: Chicago University Press, 1991), p. 145.

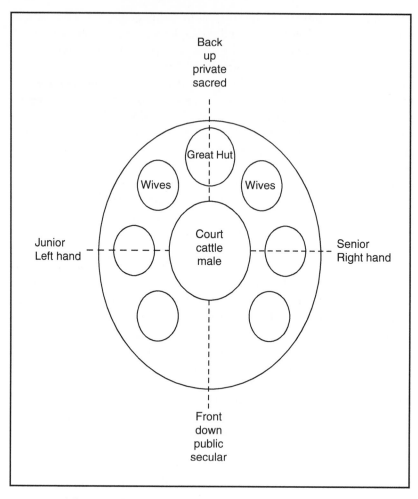

FIGURE 2.4. The Central Cattle Pattern model. (Adapted from T. N. Huffman, "The Central Cattle Pattern and interpreting the past," *Southern African Humanities, 13* (2001), pp. 19–35.

use of the model outside the bounds of its immediate cultural context and its relevance for the elucidation of early farmer settlement space.[44] Of greatest concern are assumptions about structuralism and the normative scale it employs. More specifically, its structuralist nature addresses ideal

[44] Hall, "Archaeology and modes of production". P. Lane, "The use and abuse of ethnography in Iron Age studies of southern Africa," *Azania, 29/30* (1994/1995), pp. 51–64, and "Engendered spaces, bodily practices in the Iron Age of southern Africa," in S. Kent (Ed.), *Gender in African prehistory* (London: Sage, 1998).

cognitive templates at the level of cultural principles that are believed to have endured timelessly and without modification. Furthermore, even if early farmer settlement structure conformed to the basic layout in the model, does this necessarily mean that the same social and ideological principles informed it? Can one assume that the basic amplifying function of the model in terms of the invisible social and ideological correlates is correct? Of concern is that extrapolating the CCP back into the first millennium paints the African past as a timeless place occupied by people with an invariant culture and with no history. Those who critique the CCP appeal to the theoretical notion that cultural and social form is constantly under negotiation in historically contingent ways.

In a response to these points, Huffman counters that the CCP is meant to be ahistorical and that discerning smaller-scale historical change requires models that are more culturally specific.[45] As a step toward arguing for the relevance of the CCP for first-millennium spatial interpretation he demonstrates an extremely close correspondence between the model and the spatial organization of Kgaswe, an eleventh-century Toutswe settlement in eastern Botswana (Fig. 2.5). The capacity of the CCP to explicate Kgaswe is highly relevant to Huffman's case, because on the basis of ceramic style the site falls within the Nkope Branch of the Urewe Tradition. This is significant because it falls outside the predominantly Nguni, Tswana, and Sotho-speaking cultural context that generated the CCP model. In terms of its normative scale, it culturally crosscuts these distinctions.[46]

The CCP model, in Huffman's opinion, successfully accounts for an early farmer social structure and worldview underpinned by a cattle complex and in which cattle as bridewealth was a central element of the package. If we were to consider only cattle bones recovered from these sites, the claim for the importance of cattle in this period would flounder on a lack of evidence. This point is a central thread in the argument developed by Hall, who points out that pioneer Mzonjani settlements have produced few cattle bones and that the livestock emphasis at Broederstroom is on sheep/goat rather than cattle.[47] The absence of cattle bone on Early Iron Age sites seems to undermine the central role posited by the package interpretation, and "cattle keeping of a scale and persistence sufficient for cattle to be employed in the signification of central power relations may not have been possible."[48] This occurred only toward the end of the first millennium A.D.

---

[45] Huffman, "The Central Cattle Pattern."

[46] It is worth noting that this underlines the importance of developing a sound ceramic sequence and having consensus about it.

[47] Mason, "Early Iron Age settlement."

[48] Hall, "Archaeology and modes of production," p. 84.

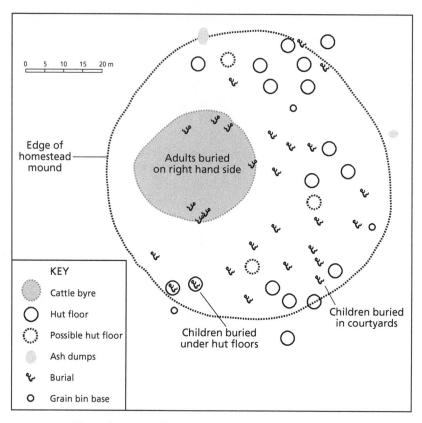

FIGURE 2.5. Plan of the twelfth-century Central Cattle Pattern settlement of Kgaswe, a commoner Toutswe site in eastern Botswana.

when a gradual rise in cattle numbers is attributed to bush and forest clearance through slash and burn agriculture that opened up the land and created a more favorable grazing habitat.[49] In Hall's view, cattle displaced agriculture as the medium that signified relationships between households and regionally between homesteads because cattle are more stable and storable.

[49] It would appear that pioneer farmers did change the environment if one compares the presence of forest-loving Nyala bones (*Tragelaphus angasi*) from a number of Thukela Basin Early Iron Age sites, with the more restricted range of this animal today. This is limited to the northern areas of KwaZulu-Natal, where it is "protected" by tsetse fly and which makes it out of bounds for cattle keeping, see T. Maggs, "The Early Iron Age in the extreme south: some patterns and problems," *Azania*, 29/30 (1994/1995), pp. 171–8. See also L. O. van Schalkwyk, "Settlement shifts and socio-economic transformations in early agriculturist communities in the lower Thukela Basin," *Azania*, 29/30 (1994/1995), pp. 187–98.

He also suggests that the stylistic homogeneity of Early Iron Age pottery, with its widespread and shared symbol sets, encouraged agricultural exchange.

Hall's argument is theoretically appealing in its emphasis on power and a people-centered framework rather than on abstract notions of enduring and timeless cognitive structures. On the basis of historical evidence, however, one might well ask why cattle constitute a more stable and secure medium. More fundamental is that the absence of cattle bone on early farmer sites cannot be taken at face value, and other pieces of empirical evidence must be given consideration. One aspect of the recent research at Broederstroom has been a reevaluation of Revil Mason's earlier work using the CCP (Fig. 2.3).[50] A result outcome of this reevaluation has been the separation of features into a series of individual homesteads, which is in sharp contrast to Mason's confusing palimpsest of features. At the center of homesteads, cattle dung deposits are associated with dung-lined storage pits and prestige burials.[51] Daga features encircling these centers comprise hut floors and collapsed granaries, which were incorrectly identified by Mason as raised hut platforms. The key issue is that the absence of cattle bones can be linked to preservation and cultural practices in the disposal of cattle remains. On the basis of the dung deposits it appears that cattle were a prominent and central component at Broederstroom. Compared to Broederstroom, coastal Mzonjani sites in KwaZulu-Natal are not well preserved, and this has an impact upon both the survival of bone and the settlement structure. The presence of some cattle bone indicates that larger breeding herds must have been present, and the identification of wild animals in the faunal mix that prefer open or mixed habitats suggests that the emphasis on closed habitats is overplayed.

Although the coastal sites are not clear-cut in terms of the CCP model, the fit at Broederstroom encourages Huffman to argue that there had not been a shift toward cattle keeping between the initial Mzonjani occupations and Broederstroom. Rather, cattle were an integral part of the Kwale Branch of the Urewe Tradition and ideologically deeply embedded. This is significant because as shown previously, the CCP applies to the Nkope Branch of the Urewe Tradition, and the evidence from Kalundu sites, particularly in

---

[50] Mason, "Early Iron Age settlement," *Origins of the Black people*. Huffman, "Broederstroom and the Central Cattle Pattern," "The antiquity of lobola." At a general level, this exercise provides a good example of the need to use ethnographic models to generate more rigorous hypotheses about spatial organization because Mason's original map of the distribution of features at Broederstroom has little explanatory power.

[51] Mason identified these deposits as ash dumps at face value, but chemical and phytolith analysis indicates that they were functional cattle byres. See Huffman, "Broederstroom and the Central Cattle Pattern."

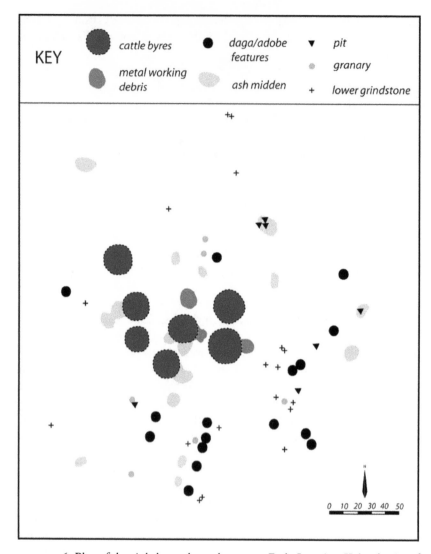

KEY

cattle byres   daga/adobe features   ▼ pit

metal working debris   ash midden   granary   + lower grindstone

0 10 20 30 40 50

FIGURE 2.6. Plan of the eighth- to eleventh-century Early Iron Age Kalundu site of KwaGandaganda near Durban. (Adapted from G. Whitelaw, "KwaGandaganda: settlement patterns in the Natal Early Iron Age," *Natal Museum Journal of Humanities,* 6 (1994), pp. 1–64.)

KwaZulu-Natal, indicate large central cattle byres surrounded by domestic debris (Fig. 2.6).[52] This implies that the relative stylistic homogeneity

[52] See G. Whitelaw, "KwaGandaganda: settlement patterns in the Natal Early Iron Age," *Natal Museum Journal of Humanities,* 6 (1994), pp. 1–64, and "Towards an Early Iron Age worldview: some ideas from KwaZulu-Natal," *Azania, 29/30* (1994/1995), pp. 37–50.

that is so obviously characteristic of early farmer pottery also underpins a broader cultural homogeneity, and consequently the CCP is part of the whole Chifumbaze Complex.[53] Furthermore, the archaeologically recognized expansion of the Chifumbaze complex represents the expansion of eastern Bantu-speakers.[54] One final implication of this association in South Africa is that a proto-Shona language (the majority language in Zimbabwe today) was a significant part of the Kalundu Tradition. This inference is based on ceramic continuity from early farmer Kalundu sites and the start of the K2 and Mapungubwe period in the Shashe/Limpopo region, which on additional archaeological grounds marks the start of the Zimbabwe Culture sequence.[55]

The general settlement structure of early farmer settlements seems to mesh with the CCP, but some of the more detailed predictions made by the model are not as clear-cut in the archaeology. The model, for example, expects that iron smelting took place in seclusion outside of the settlement because the transformation of ore into iron was understood and richly symbolic within the structural parallel of procreation and birth. Heat mediation is central to actual smelting and biological reproduction, and birth, the final process in this transformation, is spatially secluded because of the danger to community. The model successfully accounts for the spatial isolation of iron smelting in second-millennium sites, but the evidence for the Early Iron Age is equivocal. It depends on successfully differentiating smelting slag from forging slag, although the presence of both within early settlements does not necessarily refute the external origins of smelting slag. Smelting furnaces, however, may be present on some early farmer sites in KwaZulu-Natal, and the socially negative essence of smelting within settlements was possibly controlled in a different way. Such distinctions, however, underpin problems with normative models. Does one accept this spatial intimacy at face value as evidence that undermines the value of the model, or are the principles of seclusion and isolation still being applied, but on scales that cannot be archaeologically resolved?[56]

---

[53] This obviously includes the ethnographic Nguni and Tswana-speakers from whom the model is derived. See Chapter 3 in this volume.

[54] T. Huffman, *Iron Age migrations: The ceramic sequence in southern Zambia: Excavations at Gundu and Ndonde.* (Johannesburg: Witwatersrand University Press, 1989). T. Huffman and R. K. Herbert, "New perspectives on Eastern Bantu," *Azania, 29/30* (1994/1995), pp. 27–36.

[55] See Chapter 3 in this volume.

[56] T. Maggs, "The Early Iron Age in the extreme south." D. E. Miller and G. Whitelaw, "Early Iron Age metal working from the site of KwaGandaganda, Natal, South Africa," *South African Archaeological Bulletin, 49* (1994), pp. 79–89. H. Greenfield and D. Miller, "Spatial patterning of Early Iron Age metal working at Ndondondwane, South Africa: the question of cultural continuity between the Early and Late Iron Ages," *Journal of Archaeological Science, 31* (2004), pp. 1511–33.

Although the CCP has received valid criticism, much of it has focused on theoretical issues with little attempt made to reevaluate the data with alternative models that would have to be ethnographically grounded and, by the nature of hypothesis testing, provide a better explanation of the data. The CCP is a test of hypotheses about the past and not simply a device that affirms that the past was the same as the present. Debates about ideology, furthermore, and specifically about whether cattle and bridewealth were integral to early farmer society, have ranged around only a handful of sites. It may still be difficult to assess whether variability in the details between those sites marks significant departures from the CCP at the level of principle or whether that detail is a variation on a theme. The intensity of the debate about whether the structuralist model is relevant for an understanding of settlement organization, however, may dissipate as more data are accumulated and research focuses on contextually engaging with and accounting for variability rather than subduing it.

Such contextual considerations focus on the organization of early farming communities within regional relationships and, in particular, the identification of regional political hierarchy and longer distance contacts between regions. Again, ethnographic analogies are important in helping to identify which material provides evidence of political hierarchy and power. First is settlement size, which is a measure of status based on the relative power of authority to attract people and wealth (in cattle) that legitimates marriage and alliance. Some early farmer sites are bigger than others, suggesting ranking within a regional hierarchy. More specifically, this ranking is corroborated by large kraal complexes and associated middens.[57] The recovery of ritual prestige items at some of these larger sites elaborates on this theme and provides further strands of evidence that "speak" of their regional status. The presence of ceramic masks and figurines, for example, suggests that certain settlements were important ritual centers and had the power to conduct and control adolescent initiation rituals. The Lydenburg heads from Mpumalanga are the most dramatic examples of such ritual objects (Figs. 2.3 and 2.7). Specialization in crafting prestige material such as ivory, and the production of beads and cosmetic powder (most notably constrained to the formal "male" centers of early farmer sites), may also reflect differences in status between sites.[58] The conclusion is that although hierarchy is

---

[57] See Whitelaw, "Towards an Early Iron Age worldview" for how this is recognized at Kwagandaganda in KwaZulu-Natal.

[58] See R. Inskeep and T. Maggs, "Unique art objects in the Iron Age of the Transvaal, South Africa," *South African Archaeological Bulletin,* 30 (1975), pp. 114–38. T. Maggs, "Ndon-dondwane: a preliminary report on an Early Iron Age site on the lower Tugela River," *Annals of the Natal Museum,* 26 (1984), pp. 71–94. J. N. H. Loubser, "Ndondondwane: the significance of features and finds from a ninth-century site on the lower Thukela

FIGURE 2.7. One of the large Lydenburg "Heads" from the Lydenburg Heads Site, Mpumalanga.

relatively shallow it is nevertheless possible to identify differences in political power from early farmer settlements.

River, Natal," *Natal Museum Journal of Humanities*, 5 (1993), pp. 109–51. G. Whitelaw, "Customs and settlement patterns in the first millennium AD: evidence from Nanda, an Early Iron Age site in the Mngeni Valley, Natal," *Natal Museum Journal of Humanities*, 5 (1993), pp. 47–81. L. O. van Schalkwyk, "Wosi: an Early Iron Age village in the lower Thukela Basin, Natal," *Natal Museum Journal of Humanities*, 6 (1994), pp. 65–117.

There is good evidence to show that the status distinctions between settlements do not simply relate to local politics, but that certain sites grew in stature because of specific relationships to long-distance trade, particularly toward the end of the first millennium.[59] Seashells (both Atlantic and Indian Ocean in origin) occur in several early farmer settlements across the interior of Southern Africa and attest to far-reaching trade contacts, albeit probably of a simple "down the line" type. Certain areas, however, such as the Shashe/Limpopo, start to specialize in specific commodities. Here Schroda stands out as the capital of a ninth- to tenth-century polity that intensifies ivory acquisition for an increasingly acquisitive set of entrepôets on the East African coast, which were in turn networked into the wider Indian Ocean arena from at least AD 500, if not earlier.[60] The intensifying and reciprocal nature of this relationship is evident in the growing number of exotic glass trade beads found at interior sites in the Zimbabwe and Limpopo areas.

There was not the same scale of emerging political and economic change south of the Shashe/Limpopo, although the presence of a glass trade bead and a piece of ninth-century Islamic pottery from KwaGandaganda attest to marginal connections, perhaps at the southern limits of the east coast trade range. Further to the northwest in the Tsodilo Hills in Botswana, the early farmer sites of Divuyu and Nqoma dating between the sixth and twelfth centuries, respectively, preserve a variety of evidence of trade and exchange that is both local and regional in scale. Iron and copper jewelry, particularly at Nqoma, is evidence of exchange of either ore or metal from at least 200 km away.[61] The large amount of exotic material at Nqoma indicates that it came to be a dominant node in the structure of regional exchanges. Furthermore, sharp ecological gradients between Tsodilo, the deeper Kalahari hinterland, and the Okavango Delta also contributed to the structure of regional exchange networks between areas with

---

[59] See L. van Schalkwyk, "Settlement shift," p. 196, concerning the increase of social networks toward the end of the first millennium in KwaZulu-Natal when communities were "drawn into wider social networks."

[60] See P. J. J. Sinclair, J. M. F. Morais, L. Adamowics, and R. T. Duarte, "A perspective on archaeological research in Mozambique," in T. Shaw, P. J. J. Sinclair, B. Andah, and A. Okpoko (Eds.), *The archaeology of Africa: food, metals and towns*, pp. 409–31 (London: Routledge, 1993). This part of the sequence is covered in more detail in Chapter 3 of this volume because it is integral to the development of K2 and the Zimbabwe Culture System.

[61] See J. Denbow, "The dialectics of culture and identity in the Kalahari: AD 700–1700," in S. K. McIntosh (Ed.), *Beyond Chiefdoms: Pathways to complexity in Africa* (Cambridge, UK: Cambridge University Press, 1999).

different potentials in cattle, wild animal hides, ivory, fish, and freshwater shell.

INTERACTIONS BETWEEN AGRICULTURISTS AND FORAGERS

The Nqoma evidence shows that exchanges were not simply between farmers but that hunter–gatherers were deeply involved as well. The presence of stone tools of microlithic Later Stone Age type at Nqoma implicates hunter–gatherers, both in the acquisition of wild animals and the working of wild hides. Different positions concerning the nature of these interactions, however, have hardened into "the Kalahari revisionist debate" about what the same historic, ethnographic, and archaeological evidence means for the status of hunter–gatherers in these interactions with farmers. Some, although acknowledging that hunter–gatherers, even in the deepest reaches of the Kalahari, interacted with farmers, deny that this made hunter–gatherers their dependents. According to Wilmsen and Denbow, however, the anthropological work of Richard Lee and others among !Kung-speaking Ju/'hoansi of Dobe and Nyae-Nyae created an image of hunter–gatherers in the deepest reaches of the Kalahari as isolated exemplars of the Stone Age. Furthermore, this image is a function of a selective research framework couched in ecology and blinkered to the wider social and economic context of which hunter–gatherers were a part. Researchers simply found the ethnography that they wanted to find. Wilmsen and Denbow's alternative image is one of hunter–gatherers locked into relationships of subordination in which they form a lower tier within a predominantly domesticated landscape.[62]

The revisionist debate has created awareness that there are several different historic images of what ethnographic hunter–gatherers represent and what those images mean in relation to a prior history of shared landscapes. Whatever position is taken, though, the archaeology shows that few hunter–gatherers were not involved with the advent of food production, in whatever form. The key question, however, is not whether they interacted with food producers or took on some of the attributes of food production, either agriculturist or herder/farming, but whether this

[62] R. Lee, The !Kung San. E. N. Wilmsen, Land filled with flies: a political economy of the Kalahari (Chicago, 1989). E. N. Wilmsen and J. R. Denbow, "Paradigmatic history of San-speaking peoples and current attempts at revision," Current Anthropology, 31 (1990), pp. 489–524. R. Lee and M. Guenther, "Oxen or onions? The search for trade (and truth) in the Kalahari," Current Anthropology, 32 (1991), pp. 592–601. S. Kent, "The current forager controversy: real versus ideal views of hunter-gatherers," Man, 27 (1992), pp. 45–70.

fundamentally changed the basic political, economic, and social tenets of being a hunter–gatherer. In this regard revisionists are accused of generalizing the Kalahari context, and the !Kung in particular.[63] Similarly, there may also be a tendency to homogenize farmers into a generic category.[64] The danger for archaeology is the uncritical use of the !Kung, who come to stand as analogical surety for all southern African hunter–gatherer societies. The ethnography may reify the !Kung as typical, when on basic environmental grounds much of the region presented different challenges that must have encouraged different emphases in the way hunter-gatherers organised themselves. As suggested in the introduction to this chapter, the archaeology has a controlling role in relation to the nature of ethnographically and historically generated images, and each interaction context should be assessed individually and contextually. We outline briefly some of the archaeology of interaction and then return to the ethnography to suggest that interactions were forged and made predictable by the construction of mutually contrasting identities.[65]

As noted previously, first-millennium farmers were pioneers in a landscape that they were domesticating for the first time. This was not, however, simply a question of subduing nature and simplifying it to the needs of cattle and cereal, but of creating an ideological imprint, a landscape in the cultural sense of the term that could not ignore the presence of hunter–gatherers as "first peoples." Farmers were pioneers in their own idiom but newcomers to a landscape that had already been richly imprinted. It is probable that altering the landscape to their ecological and ideological will took some time and varied considerably over the areas settled by farmers. To what extent did they have to "learn" the landscape, and were

[63] See, for example, J. E. Parkington, "Soaqua and Bushmen: hunters and robbers," in C. Schrire (Ed.), *Past and present in hunter-gatherer studies*, pp. 151–74 (Orlando: Academic Press, 1984); S. Kent, *Ethnicity, hunter-gatherers, and the "Other": association or assimilation in Africa*, S. Kent (Ed.) (Washington, D.C: Smithsonian Institution Press, 2002).

[64] See W. D. Hammond-Tooke, "Selective borrowing? The possibility of San shamanistic influence on Southern Bantu divination and healing practices," *South African Archaeological Bulletin*, 53 (1998), pp. 9–15, and "Divinatory animals: further evidence of San/Nguni borrowing," *South African Archaeological Bulletin*, 54 (1999), pp. 128–32. F. E. Prins, "Living in two worlds: the manipulation of power relations, identity and ideology by the last San rock artist in Tsolo, Transkei, South Africa," *Natal Museum Journal of Humanities*, 6 (1994), pp. 179–93. P. Jolly, "Symbiotic interaction between black farmers and south-eastern San: implications for southern African rock art studies, ethnographic analogy, and hunter-gatherer cultural identity," *Current Anthropology*, 37 (1996), pp. 277–88. See Chapter 3 this volume for an elaboration of this point.

[65] The discussion of the interface between hunter–gatherers and food production that follows is limited to the first millennium and specifically focuses on "Iron Age" agriculturists. The nature of hunter–gatherer and herder/pastoralist relationships is a major issue in the archaeology of the western areas.

hunter–gatherers willing tutors? A consideration of site distributions coupled to change in hunter–gatherer sequences provides some insight into the way hunter–gatherers responded geographically to farmers. On a finer scale, the occurrence of farmer material culture in hunter–gatherer sites and vice versa suggests some of the different logic behind settlement distributions and the specific kinds of interactions, work, and exchanges that took place.

Also, as noted previously, several ecological factors influenced the distribution of early farmer settlements (Fig. 2.3). Although this specificity in part reflects the tolerances of basic farming needs we must not lose sight of the fact that, as pioneer farmers, the new settlers may have been in a position to pick and choose their locations at will. Rather than seeing early farmers as restricted by ecology, specific settlement distribution may reflect low population densities with little competition over first-choice locations. Whatever the case, early farmers did not saturate the summer rainfall area and Bushveld habitats with their settlements and did not "drift" over it like an all-embracing blanket. Hunter–gatherer settlement choices or mobility patterns consequently may not have been substantially disrupted by early farmers, and they may well have had room to move within and between agriculturist settlements and certainly had the option of retreating from the areas that farmers settled.

These choices are hinted at in several areas. Hunter–gatherers in the Thukela Basin, for example, may have actually intensified their use of rock shelters within the Valley Bushveld in order, perhaps, to better coordinate mutually beneficial exchange.[66] The key to this kind of interaction is possibly premised on the fact that hunter–gatherers were not necessarily spatially encapsulated or hemmed in.[67] The willingness to intensify occupation close to farmers may have related to the security of retreat to areas and habitats beyond the farmer frontier. The recovery of ostrich eggshell beads from early farmer settlements potentially elaborates this scenario, because ostrich shell was available only from the more open habitats away from these valleys. Furthermore, these beads were acquired through an exchange network because there is little debris in farmer sites associated with their manufacture. Hunter–gatherers may have supplied beads, perhaps on a seasonal basis, when they "retreated" from the immediate geographic distribution of the Thukela Basin, although this assumes that they, and not farmers, had a monopoly on this technology (Fig. 2.3). Kalundu-type early farmer pottery at an LSA context at Likoaeng, in Lesotho, and well beyond

---

[66] Mazel, "People making history."

[67] See J. E. Parkington and M. Hall, "Patterning in recent radiocarbon dates from southern Africa as a reflection of prehistoric settlement and interaction," *Journal of African History*, 28 (1987), pp. 1–25.

the range of Early Iron Age settlement attests to the widespread movement of material.[68]

An intensification of post-2,000-year-old Later Stone Age occupation in the Lowveld areas of Zimbabwe and the northern Limpopo Province in South Africa may partially be comparable but also suggests that hunter–gatherers may have retreated more permanently.[69] Along the Limpopo River there are only a few large caves and rock shelters that preserve longer pre-2,000-year-old Later Stone Age sequences. It is notable, however, that the many available small rock shelters and overhangs appear only to be first used in a flurry of occupation starting in the first millennium A.D. This intensification of LSA settlement along the Limpopo River correlates with the regional appearance of early farmers, but despite intensive surveys it appears that farming only took hold along the Limpopo River about AD 900, with the appearance of Zhizo settlements.[70] Early farmer ceramics from pre-AD 900 phases have been found along the Limpopo but in most cases come from Later Stone Age contexts. The actual settlements are more easily found around the better-watered fringes of the Soutpansberg, some 90 km to the south. It is also notable that the rich Later Stone Age sequences found in the large caves of the Matobo Hills in southwest Zimbabwe stop early on in the first millennium A.D. It appears that pioneer farmers settled more intensively in optimal higher rainfall areas and could afford to avoid the agriculturally marginal mopane and Lowveld habitats. This regional consideration of site distributions and sequences appears to parallel those of the Thukela Valley in that the Limpopo provided a spatial retreat outside the areas settled by pioneer farmers. On the basis of the Matobo evidence, however, it may be that in certain areas hunter–gatherers chose to retreat completely.

These settlement data indicate that the establishment of agriculturists on specific parts of the South African terrain reconfigured the hunter–gatherer approach to it. In certain areas hunter–gatherers withdrew more; in others they were drawn in. If hunter–gatherers were drawn into exchange

---

[68] P. J. Mitchell and R. L. C. Charles, "Later Stone Age hunter-gatherer adaptations in Lesotho," in G. N. Bailey, R. L. C. Charles, and N. Winder (Eds.), *Human ecodynamics* (Oxford: Oxbow, 2000), pp. 90–9.

[69] N. J. Walker, *Late Pleistocene and Holocene hunter-gatherers of the Matopos* (Societas Archaeologica Upsaliensis, 1995). S. Hall and B. Smith, "Empowering places: rock shelters and ritual control in farmer–forager interactions in the Northern Province, South Africa," *South African Archaeological Society Goodwin Series, 8* (2001), pp. 30–46. B. van Doornum, "Spaces and places: investigating proximity between forager and farmer sites," MSc thesis, University of the Witwatersrand, Johannesburg (1998).

[70] T. N. Huffman, "Mapungubwe and the origins of the Zimbabwe culture," *South African Archaeological Society Goodwin Series, 8* (2000), pp. 14–29.

relationships, as the Thukela and Tsodilo data suggest, what conditions, apart from the possible safety valve of free and agriculturally untrammeled space into which hunter–gatherers could "retreat" structured the face-to-face interactions between the two? We can start by listing briefly the kinds of material exchanges that took place, considering them in a common sense way and then briefly exploring some ethnographic frameworks that may amplify these data.

The recovery of early farmer pottery, iron, and other agriculturist artifacts in hunter–gatherer rock shelter deposits clearly underpin interaction.[71] But does this indicate a straightforward continuity and transfer of the original value and function? Can we assume, for example, that complete pots were transferred and not scavenged from abandoned farmer settlements?[72] What happened to function and meaning as pottery crossed through a cultural membrane into hunter–gatherer society? Furthermore, the presence of iron in hunter–gatherer contexts makes sense given that hunter–gatherers would have been quick to understand the value of iron artifacts over those made from stone. But how was iron wrested from farmers, given that farmers may have intensively curated it because of its pivotal role in agriculture and its complex range of symbolic meanings? Equally important is the return direction of hunter–gatherer material into farmer homesteads. A common observation in this regard is that stone tools occur on early farmer sites, and frequently the typological emphasis is on scrapers, which are functionally associated with working and preparing hides.[73] There is also evidence that these tools were made by contemporary hunter–gatherers because the absence of knapping debris on farmer sites indicates that the stone tools were made offsite and transported as finished tools. Furthermore, this typological emphasis is not limited to farmer contexts, and in contemporary hunter–gatherer sites the variety of types in precontact tool kits narrows

---

[71] See, for example, A. D. Mazel, "Mbabane Shelter and eSinhlonhlweni Shelter: the last two thousand years of hunter-gatherer settlement in the central Thukela Basin, Natal, South Africa," *Annals of the Natal Museum,* 27 (1986), pp. 389–453. L. Wadley, "Changes in the social relations of precolonial hunter-gatherers after agropastoral contact: an example from the Magaliesberg, South Africa," *Journal of Anthropological Archaeology,* 15 (1996), pp. 205–17. M. van der Ryst, *The Waterberg Plateau in the Northern Province, Republic of South Africa, in the Later Stone Age* (Oxford: BAR, 1998); Hall and Smith, "Empowering places." K. Sadr, "Encapsulated Bushmen in the archaeology of Thamaga," in Kent (Ed.), *Ethnicity, hunter-gatherers and the "Other."*

[72] K. Sadr, "Kalahari archaeology and the Bushmen debate," *Current Anthropology,* 38 (1998), pp. 104–12.

[73] Mason, "Origins of the Black People." F. E. Prins and J. E. Grainger, "Early farming communities in northern Transkei: the evidence from Ntsitsana and adjacent area *Natal Museum Journal of Humanities,* 5, 153–74 (1993). Whitelaw, "Customs and settlement patterns." Binneman, "Preliminary results."

significantly, and emphasis was also frequently placed on scraper manufacture. The presence of these tools in farmer sites may indicate that farmers supplemented some of their own needs with hunter–gatherer technology or had hunter–gatherers do the working for them.

This brief review highlights that hunter–gatherer practice was deflected more in certain areas than in others. The juxtaposition of hunter–gatherer material culture with the products from farmer settlements was relatively abrupt, but a spatial perspective offers a glimpse of the slight difference in approach of hunter–gatherers to landscape. This deflection may be a further comment on pioneer farmers as "package." We suggest, however, that simply sharing a landscape does not necessarily lead to intensive interaction, and there is a danger of overreading the first-millennium record through the synchronic instance of ethnographic observation. This may be more applicable as analogue for the archaeological evidence of interaction during the second millennium A.D.[74] Whatever the case, it is difficult to read the record in terms of any hard and fast dependencies. As far as archaeology can resolve, early farmers made choices driven by their own imperatives. Farmer populations in the first-millennium A.D. were probably initially low, and we know that their distribution was patchy. If hunter–gatherers had sufficient space for retreat, there may not necessarily have been any cauldron within which they were forced to become subordinate. We might speculate that interaction was for the most part conducted from a point of cultural independence in mutually beneficial ways. The exchange of commodities may have evened out resource gradients in which hunter–gatherers applied their expertise to the exploitation of the interstices between farmer settlements and the habitats beyond the limits of farmer settlement, and cooperation in certain areas may have raised the productivity of the landscape for the benefit of all. In such cases we may ask what common understanding existed between farmers and hunter–gatherers that placed value on the services and material culture that was exchanged? A brief excursion into the ethnography suggests that material exchanges are frequently forged within the realm of spiritual knowledge held by hunter–gatherers as "first people."

Generally, Bantu-speakers were ambivalent about the San. On the one hand they describe them as animals and "buffoonish, profligate, amoral

---

[74] The archaeological evidence suggests that interaction shifted significantly in the second millennium, and taking into account the warning about homogenizing farmers, we can conclude that it took very different directions depending on whether the farmers were of Sotho-Tswana or Nguni-speaking background. The interactions with Nguni-speakers, for example, based on the evidence of intermarriage (genetics) and linguistic and religious exchanges, seem to differ markedly in their intensity compared to interactions with Sotho/Tswana-speakers. See Hammond-Tooke, "Selective borrowing?" and Chapter 3 in this volume.

fools" who are like children when compared to farmers, whose stable values are underpinned by homestead and cattle. Hunter–gatherers are seen as the antithesis of all it means to be moral and human. As such, they are not bound by social rules and conventions and live freely in the bush and forest in the potentially polluting world of rank nature. On the other hand, the conditions of their existence are held in awe because they "live in the realm of witches and wild spirits, but also live in the presence of God."[75] Hunter–gatherers frequently appear in Bantu-speaking creation myths as implicated in fertility and reproduction. They are recognized for their power over nature, and most classically, among Nguni-speakers for their power over rain. In short, the ambivalence of hunter–gatherers in farmer eyes has great efficacy for the former and can occupy, and work within, the dangerous interstitial area of transformation. This characterization of hunter–gatherers by Bantu-speakers provides a means of defining identity and of structuring interactions between them. Thus, contact with farmers may have intensified hunter–gatherer identities.[76]

We have withheld one last piece of evidence that may have implications for the way hunter–gatherers in the Thukela region responded to pioneer farmers. This evidence comprises several pottery collections from Thukela Basin rock shelter sites that appear in the sequence a little over 2,000 years ago,[77] significantly before the first Mzonjani farmers arrived. At this stage, there is no evidence that this pottery is associated with domestic stock. The pottery is fragmented, but it is clear that it has no clearly defined stylistic features and is very different from the richly decorated Early Iron Age pottery. It forces us to confront the fact that some hunter–gatherers were already familiar with a central artifact of food production before Bantu-speaking farmers arrived and that its identification and dating blurs the neat chronological and economic sequence, showing that the interface with mixed Bantu-speaking farmers may not have been very pronounced. Whatever the case, the appearance of the pottery raises questions about its appearance, not least of which is that it falls outside the cultural and stylistic attributes of the mixed farming package.

What is distinctive about this pottery is that it is thin walled, an attribute that places it together with a number of other small and fragmentary pottery collections from rock shelter sites elsewhere in the summer rainfall Bushveld regions of South Africa and eastern Botswana (Jubilee Shelter,

[75] M. G. Kenny, "A mirror in the forest: the Dorobo hunter-gatherers as an image of the other," *Africa*, 51 (1981), pp. 477–95.

[76] *Ibid.*

[77] A. D. Mazel, "Early pottery from the eastern part of southern Africa," *South African Archaeological Bulletin*, 47 (1992), pp. 3–7.

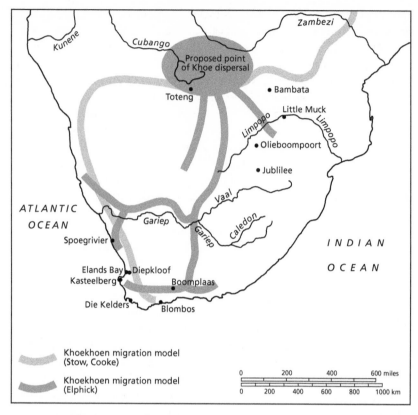

FIGURE 2.8. The location of pastoralist sites mentioned in the text. (Base maps adapted from Mitchell, 2002, 9.1 and 9.2.)

Olieboompoort, Little Muck; Fig. 2.8), and northern and southern Namibia and the Western Cape.[78] This pottery is also dated between about 2,100 and 1,700 years ago, and the early Thukela Basin pottery, therefore, seems to be a part of a horizon of thin-walled pottery that significantly pre-dates unequivocal mixed farmers. Compared to the stylistic homogeneity of first-millennium mixed farmer ceramics, most of this thin-walled pottery is stylistically heterogeneous. It occurs in distinctive stylistic patches

[78] See L. Webley, "The history and ethnoarchaeology of pastoralist and hunter-gatherer settlement in the north-western Cape, South Africa," Ph.D. thesis, University of Cape Town (1992); A. B. Smith, *Pastoralism in Africa: origins and developmental ecology* (London: Hurst, 1992); J. C. Sealy and R. Yates, "The chronology of the introduction of pastoralism to the Cape, South Africa," *Antiquity,* 68 (1994), pp. 58–67. C. Henshilwood, "A revised chronology for pastoralism in southernmost Africa: new evidence of sheep at c. 2000 b.p. from Blombos Cave, South Africa," *Antiquity,* 70 (1996), pp. 945–9.

that cannot be linked in a stylistic migrationary chain.[79] Furthermore, although early farmer pottery is securely attributable to Bantu-speaking mixed farmers in the east, there is much uncertainty over the cultural and economic identity of the makers of this thin-walled pottery.

The interpretation of one form of this pottery, known as Bambata after its first discovery in Bambata Cave in the Matobo Hills in southwestern Zimbabwe (Fig. 2.8), captures this ambiguity. Bambata fits stylistically within the Kalundu style structure, but the thin walls also place it within the character of early thin-walled ceramics in the west. The contexts of its discovery add to this economic and cultural uncertainty. Originally, most Bambata pottery was recovered from rock shelter sites, but because of its Iron Age style it was interpreted as farmer pottery that had been used by hunter–gatherers. More recently, however, early dates from the type site and a few other localities place the appearance of Bambata well before the Iron Age arrival, and its association with sheep and cattle and Later Stone Age lithic tools has encouraged the view that the makers were semisedentary stone tool-using hunter–gatherers who had some domestic stock.[80] The occurrence of Bambata pottery at sites along pan and river margins in Botswana suggests that the watering needs of livestock were an important factor in settlement choice. The expectation that a Bambata site at Toteng near Lake Ngami would present evidence of a sedentary village structure has not been entirely met (Fig. 2.8). The stylistic congruence with Kalundu pottery clearly links it to early farmers, but the earlier dates and thin walls place it outside this context. Clearly, the cultural and economic identity of the makers of Bambata pottery are ambiguous. The pottery is in part wrapped up in debates about the identity of its makers and in particular the origins of Khoe pastoralism in the west, which is the subject of the following section.

HUNTING, GATHERING, HERDING, AND PASTORALISM

The distinction between an eastern, well-watered summer rainfall zone with good soils in Southern Africa and a western, arid, largely winter rainfall zone with thin, poorly developed soils is critical to an understanding of the

---

[79] K. Sadr, "Kalahari archaeology."

[80] See the following for a range of views over the status of Bambata pottery. N. Walker, "The significance of an early date for pottery and sheep in Zimbabwe," *South African Archaeological Bulletin, 38* (1983), pp. 88–92. J. R. Denbow, "Congo to Kalahari." T. N. Huffman, "Toteng pottery and the origins of Bambata," *Southern African Field Archaeology, 3* (1994), pp. 3–9. A. Reid, K. Sadr, and N. Hansom-James, "Herding Traditions," in P. Lane, A. Reid and A. K. Segobye (Eds.), *Ditswa Mmung: the archaeology of Botswana* (Gaborone: Botswana Society, 1998).

spread of domesticates (Fig. 2.1). Agro-pastoralists farming both crops and domestic animals obviously preferred the former, whereas sheep-herding, and later cattle-herding pastoralists were able to manage and occasionally thrive in the latter. In this section we focus on the western zone, where both hunter–gatherer groups and those with domestic animals were using stone for their tools and did not develop metalworking as a practice.

From as early as the 1920s archaeologists have known that pottery, usually small fragments but occasionally whole pots, can be found in the later stages of the Stone Age sequence in the Cape.[81] By the early 1970s[82] they also knew that the bones of domestic animals, especially sheep, formed part of the final Stone Age faunal assemblages. Soon after this, radiocarbon dates began to accumulate showing that the earliest traces of both pottery and sheep appear not long. Sheep bones later dated directly by radiocarbon dating at Spoegrivier on the Namaqualand coast to 2105 and at Blombos on the southern Cape coast to 1960 years before the present (BP), overlap at two standard deviations, suggesting that the diffusion of sheep as a resource was rapid and extended through some 1,000 km of near coastal landscape.[83] Sheep bones appear rather later, probably not until 1,400 years ago, in the Karoo interior.[84] By 1,500 years ago sheep bones are also found at many other sites such as Diepkloof, Tortoise Cave, Elands Bay Cave, and Kasteelberg along the Atlantic coast, at Die Kelders in the Southwestern Cape, and at Boomplaas in the interior mountains of the Southern Cape (Fig. 2.8).[85] In most cases the bones of wild animal forms and shellfish

---

[81] H. J. Deacon, J. Deacon, M. Brooker, and M. L. Wilson, "The evidence for herding at Boomplaas Cave in the Southern Cape, South Africa," *South African Archaeological Bulletin, 33* (1978), pp. 39–65. J. Rudner, "Strandloper pottery from South and South West Africa," *Annals of the South African Museum, 49* (1968), pp. 441–663.

[82] F. R. Schweitzer and K. J. Scott, "Early occurrence of domestic sheep in sub-Saharan Africa," *Nature, 241* (1973), p. 547.

[83] L. Webley, "The re-excavation of Spoegrivier Cave on the west coast of South Africa," *Annals of the Eastern Cape Museums,* II (2001), pp. 19–49. C. Henshilwood, "A revised chronology for pastoralism in southernmost Africa: new evidence for sheep at *c.* 2000 b.p. from Blombos Cave, South Africa," *Antiquity, LXX* (1996), pp. 945–9.

[84] C. G. Sampson and J. C. Vogel, "Radiocarbon chronology of Later Stone Age pottery decorations in the upper Seacow valley," *Southern African Field Archaeology, 4* (1995), pp. 84–94.

[85] J. C. Sealy and R. Yates, "The chronology of the introduction of pastoralism to the Cape, South Africa," *Antiquity, LXVIII* (1994), pp. 58–67. R. G. Klein and K. Cruz-Uribe, "Faunal evidence for prehistoric herder-forager activities at Kasteelberg, Western Cape Province, South Africa," *South African Archaeological Bulletin, 44* (1989), pp. 82–97. M. L. Wilson, "The late Holocene occupants of Die Kelders: hunter-gatherer or herders?" *Southern African Field Archaeology,* V (1996), pp. 79–83. K. Sadr, A. B. Smith, I. Plug, J. Orton, and B. Mutti, "Herders and foragers on Kasteelberg: interim report of excavations 1999–2002," *South African Archaeological Bulletin, LVIII* (2003), pp. 27–32.

massively outnumber sheep, although larger concentrations of sheep are found at Boomplaas, Diepkloof, and Die Kelders. At Boomplaas the evidence of dung floors in the cave strongly supports the notion that sheep were kraaled inside the overhang. Wild plant food residues are very common at all sites. However these occupants of the Western and Southern Cape may have conceived of themselves, they were subsisting largely by hunting and gathering. With the exception of Kasteelberg, all of these sites are the kinds of rock shelters and caves occupied for millennia earlier by people without domestic stock. No cattle bones dating between 2,000 and 1,500 years ago have been found at these sites, and very few from later millennia.

From the beginning, ceramics have been integrated into the debate. First appearing at about 2,000 years ago, by 1,500 years ago ceramics, dated by association with hearths from archaeological contexts, have been found throughout the region from which the early sheep dates have come. Strongly influenced by the views of linguists,[86] who noted greater similarities between the traces of languages spoken by Khoekhoe people at the seventeenth-century Cape and between those from parts of northern Botswana than between those of the Khoekhoe and nearby Cape hunter-gatherers, referred to as Soaqua (Fig. 2.8), archaeologists began to think of a spread of pottery-using, sheep-owning Khoekhoe from north to south about 2,000 years ago. Pottery and sheep were viewed as a package, and both were identified with the appearance and spread of historically known and labeled pastoralists, the Khoekhoe.

For the next thirty years observations increased in number and quality, but differences of opinion emerged among archaeologists, anthropologists, and historians. One school of thought, let's call them lumpers, believed that once domestic stock appeared in the Cape region, everyone should be considered a herder and that it would not be sensible to distinguish between hunters and herders. Initiated by Marks, guided by Elphick, and promoted by Schrire,[87] these researchers, mostly those depending primarily on written documents, believed that Cape communities hunted and herded

H. J. Deacon, J. Deacon, M. Brooker, and M. L. Wilson, "The evidence for herding." J. E. Parkington and C. Poggenpoel, "Diepkloof Rock Shelter," in J. Parkington and M. Hall (Eds.), *Papers in the Prehistory of the Western Cape, South Africa.* Oxford BAR International Series 332(ii) (1987), pp. 269–93.

[86] E. O. J. Westphal, "The linguistic prehistory of southern Africa: Bush, Kwadi, Hottentot and Bantu linguistic relationships," *Africa, 33* (1963), pp. 237–65.

[87] S. Marks, "Khoisan resistance to the Dutch in the seventeenth and eighteenth centuries," *Journal of African History, 13* (1972), pp. 55–80. R. Elphick, *Khoikhoi and the Founding of White South Africa* (Johannesburg: Ravan, 1985). C. Schrire, "An inquiry into the evolutionary status and apparent identity of San hunter-gatherers," *Human Ecology, 8* (1980), pp. 9–29.

in cycles as a result of the loss and repossession of stock, thus appearing in the documents as hunters or herders depending on the timing of the colonial observation. Elphick referred to this as an "ecological cycle" and implied that all Cape inhabitants might have been herders at some point in their lives. Early accounts of people herding stock but bearing names that apparently labeled them hunters seemed to support this theory of behavior.

Splitters, however, often archaeologists basing their views on material excavated evidence, believed they could distinguish residual hunter–gatherers from those who had become herders. Small numbers of sheep could easily have been stolen or received in payment for services rendered as owned and herded. These researchers argued that the sharing ethic widely described by ethnographers from among Southern African San communities would impede the cycles of hunting and herding. Both ethnographic and historic accounts of hunters acquiring sheep illustrated the pressure on them to kill and share rather than keep and breed them.[88] Khoekhoe, the splitters pointed out, were marked by enthusiastic and socially sanctioned accumulative behavior. Herders who lost sheep were likely simply to borrow some stock from relatives and start accumulating again rather than become hunters. This argument reflected a belief that hunting is a cognitive rather than an economic label. Sites with few domestic animal bones, especially caves and rock shelters, could thus be seen as the camps of hunter–gatherers.

Clearly, the detail of the eyewitness accounts recorded in historic documents and ethnographic studies has played a major role in the attempt to discern precolonial identities. Historic accounts of Cape populations from the very late fifteenth century are notoriously complex but eventually hint at distinctions between those with and those without domestic stock. Seventeenth-century expeditions into the interior record encounters with Soaqua or Sonqua who arguably spoke a language different from that of the Khoekhoe at the Cape.[89] Splitters point to the extreme disdain with which the Khoekhoe interpreters spoke of the Soaqua, calling them robbers rather than relatives. The phrase "these small people" could imply some visible physical differences between the stature of herding Khoekhoe and the stockless Soaqua, especially as Khoekhoe near the fort were never referred to as small. Such stature differences are documented between people later referred to as "Hottentots" and "Bushmen," though we need to be mindful of the effects of changes in diet on growth. The Soaqua descriptions refer to bow-and-arrow-using people of small size, living off a range of wild game

[88] J. Marshall and C. Ritchie, *Where are the Ju/wasi of Nyae Nyae?* (Cape Town: Centre for African Studies [UCT] Communications, 1984).

[89] J. E. Parkington, "Soaqua and Bushmen: hunters and robbers."

and plant foods in the mountainous regions of the Cape. Archaeologists have excavated numerous small shelters with a pattern of bedding and ash deposits and artifactual and food debris that corresponds uncannily with these descriptions.[90] But even a site with almost no domestic stock bones could be viewed by lumpers as one occupied by herders out hunting.

There has been some debate about the extent to which sheep bones and pottery form a package of linked traits emerging as a result of the same dispersal event. Which appears first varies among individual sites and direct radiocarbon dating of sheep bones has shown on several occasions that the bones were more recent, often much more so, than the level in which they were apparently found.[91] Pottery cannot, of course, easily be dated in this way. Nevertheless, the earliest sheep and potsherds are contemporary at the regional scale, and it still seems reasonable to assume some association between the dispersal of the two. Cattle bones, however, are not found until about 600 years later, and even then in very small numbers, implying that cattle must be presumed to have entered Southern Africa some considerable time after sheep. It must be admitted, though, that there is more difficulty in distinguishing cattle bones from like-sized wild forms such as buffalo and eland than there is in distinguishing sheep from similar-sized wild bovids such as springbok or reebok. Given this minimal archaeological record of cattle bones, it is entirely possible that large numbers of herded cattle at the Cape barely predated their observation by Portuguese sailors at the end of the fifteenth century A.D.

This debate between splitters and lumpers simmered for a good while without really changing many minds. The evidence was simply too malleable to successfully debunk either of the hypotheses. By the 1990s archaeologists had begun to count numbers and densities of potsherds and sheep bones to distinguish the signatures of the supposed residual hunter–gatherers from those of the herders.[92] To the extent that assemblages were dominated by the bones of small wild bovids rather than sheep, or by formally retouched stone tools rather than potsherds, those responsible for the record were hunters. The reverse pattern characterized the herding signature. Almost all archaeological sites appeared on this scale to be the places occupied by hunter–gatherers.

Another material trace was introduced into the debate in the 1980s. Ostrich eggshell beads are almost ubiquitous in Later Stone Age sites, but the sizes of beads had been seen to vary somewhat systematically from site

[90] *Ibid.*   [91] Sealy and Yates, "The chronology."

[92] A. B. Smith, K. Sadr, J. Gribble, and R. Yates, "Excavations in the south-western Cape, South Africa, and the archaeological identity of prehistoric hunter-gatherer within the last 2000 years," *South African Archaeological Bulletin*, XLVI (1991), pp. 71–90.

to site and from level to level.[93] Before the appearance of sheep bones or pottery, beads are uniformly small and do not change in size for many millennia. Later beads were often, though not always, larger. After the appearance of sheep and pottery, sites vary dramatically in mean bead size. Careful study by various scholars of bead sizes and bead aperture sizes led to the suggestion that herders made larger beads than hunters. Bead size had become a material, metaphorical reflection of the splitter position. The assertion was based on the association of larger mean bead sizes with sites from which other evidence, according to splitters, pointed to herding as the preferred economic behavior. Interestingly, the persistence of both formal stone tool manufacture and the making of small beads is taken as evidence of the persistence of hunting and gathering practices and perhaps the mindset that underpinned them among supposed residual hunter–gatherers.[94]

Study of the faunal remains allowed some archaeologists to develop another argument about dog ownership in relation to the hunting–herding divide.[95] Noting that heavily gnawed bones from hunted animals, especially the fatty, spongy bones of seals, only occurs in assemblages that postdate 2,000 years ago, it is possible to argue for some domestic dog access to discarded bones. Not all late bone assemblages are gnawed, however, leading to the possibility in some researchers' minds of distinguishing herders with dogs from hunters without. The evidential support for such a difference is not persuasive in the historical records, although no canid bone is described as dog rather than jackal before the first appearance of sheep. It may be significant that no cave or rock shelter faunal assemblage has a high level of gnawed bone.

Underlying and paralleling this debate about the nature of late precolonial community distinctions has been another, separate but not unrelated, about the mechanisms of dispersal. After the early enthusiasm for identifying the emergence of Khoekhoe with the first sheep bones, some archaeologists began to flirt with the idea that stock and pottery might have dispersed without much population movement.[96] Distinguishing migration

[93] L. Jacobson, "The size variability of ostrich eggshell beads from central Namibia and its relevance as a stylistic and temporal marker," *South African Archaeological Bulletin*, 42 (1985), pp. 55–8. R. Yates and A. B. Smith, "Ideology and hunter/herder archaeology in the south-western Cape," *Southern African Field Archaeology*, 2 (1993), pp. 96–104. R. J. Yates in prep. "Ostrich eggshell bead sizes and the recent prehistory of the Cape Province."

[94] R. J. Yates, A. H. Manhire, and J. Parkington, "Rock Painting and History in the southwestern Cape," in T. Dowson and J. D. Lewis-Williams (Eds.), *Contested Images: diversity in Southern African rock art research*. (Johannesburg: Witwatersrand University Press, 1994), pp. 29–60.

[95] Klein and Cruz-Uribe, "Faunal evidence."

[96] K. Sadr, "The first herders at the Cape of Good Hope," *African Archaeological Review*, XV (1998), pp. 101–32.

from diffusion is a long-standing archaeological enterprise but not always a successful one. In this case, those in favor of a migration of people ask how successive groups of hunters with no previous experience of sheep could generate spare stock capacity to pass them on repeatedly over 1,500 km in a radiocarbon instant?[97] Similarly, they point out that the ceramics from sites with early sheep bones are well made, professionally fired, and hardly the products of learners. Surely, the rapid spread of sheep management and pyrotechnology imply that the minds that housed these skills moved, too.

Those in favor of diffusion expect that any migration should be accompanied by artifactual evidence for stylistically coherent elements such as requiring the movements of human carriers. Detailed analysis of the decorative motifs and motif placements on the pottery vessels from a series of first millennium A.D. sites from the Kalahari to the Cape shows greater variability than might have been expected from the movement of a group of stock-owning, pottery-using people.[98] Pottery from these sites is always thin walled and, thus, easily distinguishable from that of farmers, but the decorative details vary from region to region in a way regarded as inconsistent with a single movement of pottery makers. Thin walls, spouts, and lugs are functional elements that might be independent of a stylistic mindset. When seen alongside the very small numbers of sheep bones compared with those of wild forms, this evidence surely points to the dissemination of stock through a population of hunters who then became hunters-with-sheep, part-time herders but not yet pastoralists?

Diffusionists argue that a coherent stylistic pattern does appear from the Kalahari to the Cape somewhat later, perhaps as early as AD 1000, marked by the spread of thin-walled, lugged, conical-based pottery forms that may have been needed to store and carry milk (Fig. 2.9). Previous thin-walled forms had spouts but lacked lugs. These lugged forms resemble the pots observed among the historic Khoekhoe by colonial residents and travelers.[99] This later migration is likely to have originated north of the Orange River, perhaps in northwestern Botswana.

Rock paintings, a pervasive component of the later part of the Cape archaeological record, became incorporated in the arguments between lumpers and splitters by the mid-1980s.[100] A particularly significant observation was that handprints are distributed unevenly across the landscape and, whenever involved in superpositioning, are clearly late in the sequence

[97] Smith, pers. comm.   [98] Sadr, "The first herders."

[99] P. Kolb, *Caput bonae spei hodiernum, das ist Vollständige Beschreibung des Africanischen Vorgebürges der Guten Hoffnung,* 2 vols. (Nürnberg, Peter Conrad Monrath, 1719).

[100] J. E. Parkington, R. Yates, A. H. Manhire, and D. Halkett, "The social impact of pastoralism in the south-western Cape," *Journal of Anthropological Archaeological,* 5 (1986), pp. 313–29.

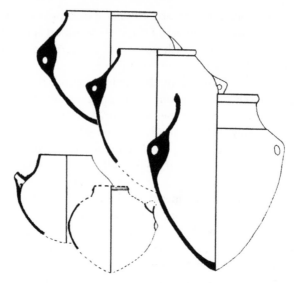

FIGURE 2.9. Examples of Khoe pottery. (Taken from E. Boonzaier, C. Malherbe, P. Berens, and A. Smith, *The Cape Herders: A History of the Khoikhoi of southern Africa,* 46 [Cape Town, 2000].)

of painting.[101] Handprints are particularly common, though not restricted to, the coastal plains along the Atlantic shore on which colonial observers had seen large flocks of sheep and some cattle. Additionally, paintings of sheep in the fine line tradition that evidently characterized predomestic stock paintings were more or less restricted to the mountainous regions east of these plains in a landscape patently not ideal for herding stock. Further, no known paintings of cattle, whether fine line or finger painted, are to be found in these Cape regions.[102] Could the sheep paintings be a response by supposed residual hunters to the appearance of competitive herding communities who confined them to the periphery? Could the handprints be the work of herders? Do they add the loss of figurative painting to the proposed demise of traditional skills implied by the increase in bead size and the disappearance of formally retouched stone tools from late, supposed herding, assemblages? No better integration of material and historically recorded identities could be wished for.

[101] A. H. Manhire, "The role of handprints in the rock art of the south-western Cape," *South African Archaeological Bulletin,* 53 (1998), pp. 98–108.

[102] A. H. Manhire, J. E. Parkington, A. D. Mazel, and T. M. O'C Maggs, "Cattle, sheep and horses: a review of domestic animals in rock art of southern Africa," *Southern African Archaeological Bulletin,* 5 (1986), pp. 22–30.

Interestingly, the debate seems to have been moved into a new dimension by the analyses of excavated and surveyed material from the important sites at Kasteelberg in the granite region of Saldanha Bay.[103] When initially excavated, the sites of Kasteelberg A and B on this hill appeared to have produced the evidence many felt should exist for the precolonial antiquity of the Cape Khoekhoe. Groups known to the early Dutch commanders at the Cape as "Saldanhamen" were thought to have ranged from the Cape Flats to the shores of St. Helena Bay. Kasteelberg, with very large numbers of sheep bones and lots of potsherds in some localities, seemed to fit the material signature of such historically known people. The sites, however, are characterized more by vast numbers of seal bones than by superabundant sheep or cattle bones. Cattle bones are almost completely absent. More problematically, all occupation of this area seems to have ended several hundred years before the colonial observations of the seventeenth century. Moreover, despite some assiduous searching, no other comparable sites have been found on other granite outcrops. The pastoralists so prominent in historic records are as invisible as ever!

The question remains how did, or perhaps did, some of these herders become fully fledged pastoralists as seen and described by fifteenth-century colonists? The variable pasturage potential of the Cape landscape surely played an important role in encouraging, promoting, or disadvantaging any attempts to develop larger flocks and herds. In Namaqualand and in the Swartland plains south of the Saldanha peninsula the shale bedrock is rich in nutrients and extremely valuable grazing land. Between these parts, approximately between the mouths of the Olifants and Berg rivers, loose sands blanket a landscape underlain by acid sandstone and quartzite bedrock, with little grazing potential. East of this lies the Cape Fold Belt mountains, parallel ranges of mostly nutrient-poor shallow soils in very rugged terrain. An exception, probably an important route, is the shale outcropping along the Olifants River valley that effectively links the attractive grazing areas of Namaqualand and the Swartland. Further east is the western karoo, extremely dry, remote from the coastal plains but nutrient rich, especially attractive in the winter. This combination of carrying capacity, accessibility, and connectedness produces a patchwork of landscape blocks that surely influenced the growth and development of herding in the Cape. In many areas it would not have made sense to try to develop advanced stock-rearing economies.

Even if small numbers of sheep spread through hunter–gatherer groups all more or less equally open to becoming small-scale herders, some groups

---

[103] Sadr et al., "Herders and foragers on Kasteelberg." Sadr, "The first herders at the Cape of Good Hope."

must by reason of access to highly nutritious vegetation have been able to increase herd sizes and contemplate life as full-time herders. Presumably, also as some groups became more fully committed to herding, perhaps even crossing the boundary to pastoralism, they began to see themselves as different from those who had remained hunters with sheep or, in some areas, hunters without sheep.

Currently, narrative reconstructions of the transition from hunting and gathering to some form of herding or pastoralism in the Cape vary from the purely diffusionist to the simply migrationist. At the latter end, there are few archaeologists prepared to argue that Khoekhoe as observed by seventeenth-century colonists arrived in the Cape 2,000 years ago, although some believe the Khoekhoe language may have appeared then. The material record shows that the kind of trace predicted from the colonial accounts is virtually absent from the excavated archive. Nor does it seem likely that archaeologists could sustain a version that viewed all developments as diffusion and subsequent *in situ* evolution of economies and cognitive mindsets. The most difficult observations for this kind of narrative are the suggestions in historical documents that there were significant differences between the languages spoken and in the stature of people thought to be hunters and herders. These differences are unlikely to have developed in a mere 1,500 years.

The most parsimonious explanation of these archaeological, historical, and ethnographic observations from Southern Africa is that an initial dispersal of sheep and ceramics, with a small but significant immigrant population, transformed some hunters, especially along the Western and Southwestern Cape coastal plains, into hunters with sheep. Hunter–gatherers further inland probably acquired very few sheep, and all, including those with a few sheep, may have retained an essentially hunter–gatherer view of the world, emphasizing sharing rather than accumulation. Notwithstanding some differentiation among these Cape people, brought about by variations in rainfall and pasture quality, the focus of these herding or pastoralist economies remained the management of small stock. Later, and how much later we cannot tell, an important influx of cattle, perhaps from the east rather than from the north, occurred some time before the first European eyewitness accounts of communities later termed "Hottentots," "Khoikhoi," "Quena," or "Khoekhoe."

CONCLUSION

The ability to outline the advent of food production in the first millennium A.D. in the eastern, summer rainfall areas of South Africa is in sharp contrast to the possibility of doing so in the western areas. In the latter, fragmentary remains of sheep and pottery are found in settlements that conform in most characteristics to hunter–gatherer occupations. There is little in the spatial organization of these sites that would encourage the view that sheep were formally managed in large numbers. Furthermore, the manner in which pottery and sheep were introduced remains obscure, and this ambiguity directly influences views on the identity of hunters and herders, their interactions, the way hunting and herding unfolds through the first millennium, into the second, and what continuities are represented by the early observations of European voyagers and colonists. In the east, the weight of evidence indicates the unequivocal appearance of crop and live-stock farmers. Despite some less clear economic variability on the margins of the summer rainfall areas, these residues constitute a relatively homoge-nous package that indicates the movement of a culturally cohesive breeding population that asserted, maintained, and perhaps intensified identities in relation to hunters as a basis for sharing the landscape.

This contrast in degrees of interpretive clarity can be attributed to a number of factors. Obviously, the nature of the empirical record plays a part. Farmers are sedentary and litter the landscape with cultural marks and stylistic signposts that are relatively easy to find and encourage both the construction of detailed sequences and an appreciation of spatiality at several different scales. Occupation of a single point on the landscape over an extended period offers the potential to capture residues that are more representative of cultural practice. From this stems a greater interpretive security. In the west there is less certainty about what rock shelter horizons and open camps represent in terms of time and behavioral scale, and conse-quently in terms of economic and social identity. The predominant picture is based on residues that fit more comfortably within a hunter–gatherer pattern. Do these, however, represent only one half of the first-millennium picture and suggest that the more elusive open settlements of transhumant herders or pastoralists will eventually be found? Or must we confront the evidence as it stands, with the view that it does provide evidence of absence of a committed pastoralism in the first millennium and that holding out for such settlements is illusory and will only continue to frustrate.

This last point is critical because it raises the influential, dominating, but unavoidable chain of relationships between present contexts and the interpretation of the past. We look for the remains of pastoralists camps in the first millennium because we are drawn to the historical images of thriving herds managed by committed pastoralists. We find it difficult for hunter–gatherers to shift ideological positions because the ethnography emphasizes the leveling power of sharing. Some emphasize migration and package in the west to account for the historic pattern. In the east, the scale of uncertainty is different. We can broadly marry present with past and assert some essential and fundamental continuities in the linguistic and social identities of the farmers. As we seek to refine our ideas about the detail of farming in the east, however, and test hypotheses about social structure, ideology, and the details of day-to-day life, we are still captive, as some maintain, to a problematic ethnographic present that continues to overpower the past in its own image. The question we continually confront is whether there is room to construct interpretations outside of historic images and the ethnographic present. Or do these realistically provide a broad range of interpretive possibility into which the meaning of material remains must fit?

As outlined in the introduction to this chapter, although no interpretation of an archaeological past is ever free from the straitjacket of present perspectives, interpretation of archaeological evidence has been made with specific historical identities in mind. Implicit in this is perhaps the desire to make archaeology relevant to the image of the historic period, and to history in general, by seeking to confirm it. The ambiguity about the meaning of first-millennium residues in the west, however, suggests that not all these residues fit comfortably within the images provided by the historic framework and must be approached with other options in mind. The current state of play shows that there is no direct and easy historical line between the past and present and that poor convergence is complicated by the different historical scales to which documentary and archaeological evidence appeal. It is obvious on the one hand that the synchronic observations made by seventeenth- to eighteenth-century Portuguese and the Dutch were snapshots in a much longer sequence. Although archaeology, on the other hand, stands further back in its historical scale, we suggest that it offers the opportunity to contextualize the meaning and value of these colonial snapshots rather than merely to be a "handmaiden" to them. Furthermore, the material remains provide more control over place and space than the patchy historical records. The apparent authority of a written document is undermined when one considers the complex anthropological realities. Hunters and herders move in response to seasonal rhythms and less predictable windfalls; they coalesce and fragment in response to those rhythms as well as to the political possibilities and pressures presented by living in relatively close proximity to one another. Cultural prejudices aside, early colonial observers glimpsed fleeting spatial and temporal nodes in complex regional networks, and their own presence rapidly presented a range of new tensions to which indigenous people were already responding flexibly. It seems dangerous to distill such a record into one of timeless and fixed identities and seemingly predictable generalities. The material record offers the opportunity to flesh out patchy historical records temporally and spatially and to contextualize them in terms of a longer record.

Ideally, however, the interpretive relationship between present and past must be one of continuous and critical comparison. The ability to discern the trajectory of hunter–gatherers and their historical emergence as the Sonqua/Soaqua is a case in point. In this instance a plausible bridge can be built between historical records and material residues because the scale of identity evident in the two sources resonates compatibly. For much of the first-millennium residues in the west, however, the transferral of historic, ethnographic, or even economic identities is not so straightforward, and consequently the assignation of identity remains weak. In contrast, the relative homogeneity of the farmer record in the east gives more security about these basic identities.

Finally, it must be remembered that the narrative presented here is based only on a handful of detailed observations, both in the east and in the west, although whereas large areas in the east are poorly served by detailed excavation, the identifiable cultural homogeneity in the material lends itself to greater extrapolation, and the ecological tolerances are also predictable. In the west, hunting and herding straddled different ecologies that must have encouraged people to be flexibly strategic in terms of where they placed their economic emphasis, and the expectation should be that first-millennium residues will not be easy to pigeonhole. But whereas at a certain scale each observation is unique, different ecological potentials offer a natural structure within which to make more observations and thereby build up more directed comparisons. It may be that, in contrast to farming in the east, where the menu appears to be fixed, the advent of food production in the west will continue to be a variable feast.

3

FARMING COMMUNITIES OF THE SECOND
MILLENNIUM: INTERNAL FRONTIERS, IDENTITY,
CONTINUITY AND CHANGE

SIMON HALL

This chapter outlines a narrative for precolonial farming societies of the second millennium A.D. in South Africa and highlights several themes. The first is that this is a period when trade relations with the wider world intensified, first with Swahili based in their East African coastal entrepôts and later with the Portuguese, Dutch, and English. The outcomes of these contacts vary, but a second theme draws attention to trade as an important factor in the growth of political complexity and the rise of social hierarchies. Some of these are referred to as state level in their complexity. In reviewing this complexity, however, the essay resists an inclination to reify steeply hierarchical systems over those that contextually combined factors of trade, wealth, and contact in different ways, that, although not monumental in scale, are no less important.

Third, the second millennium is a period when the identities that emerged historically can be identified, traced, and tracked fairly securely by a combination of archaeological, oral, and written sources. It is not a period of historical anonymity. This overlaps with the last theme, which relates to method, emphasizing in particular issues relating to analogy and the unavoidable and complex relationship between ethnographic models and their ampliative role. Ethnographic models extol cultural structure and capture historical context only in the broadest of ways. This characteristic is exacerbated when used in conjunction with structuralist assumptions. This chapter suggests there are good grounds for the extensive use of ethnography for analogical purposes but, as some work has already shown, the second millennium offers more scope for writing history. Throughout there is a concern to understand how cultural principles in South African societies were articulated with specific historical contexts.

INTRODUCTION

During the second millennium AD Southern African agropastoralist societies continued to farm using the basic elements introduced in the first millennium. Sorghum and millet agriculture provided for the essential day-to-day subsistence needs and cattle, in varying degrees, provided meat, milk, and ideological sustenance.[1] In contrast, however, to early and mid–first-millennium farming in which homesteads were predominantly self-sufficient and where political gradients between homesteads were relatively shallow, the second millennium saw significant political, social, and economic changes. At the junction of the Shashe and Limpopo rivers, for example, ancestral Shona-speakers molded into the Mapungubwe state the opportunities provided by the deepening trade relationships between the Southern African interior and the southeast African coast. This nascent political complexity set the tone for much of the second-millennium history of farmers in the northern areas of South Africa and in neighboring Zimbabwe and Botswana. To the south, Nguni- and Sotho/Tswana-speakers expanded their summer rainfall range beyond the Bushveld habitats favoured by first-millennium farmers into the predominantly grassland habitats of the Highveld. An increasing turbulence in farmer politics is indicated in eighteenth-century oral records and changes in settlements underpin processes of political centralization.

Although still general in outline, the interpretation of second-millennium archaeology has advanced toward a more fine-grained historical understanding. This contrasts with the review of food production for the first millennium, which identifies broad processes and debates about the nature of society and cultural form that are less rooted in explicit historical context.

Two interrelated factors contribute to this ability to shift the historical scale and these are thematic threads that run throughout this chapter. First is the increasing clarity with which we can discern the emerging historical identities of communities that snap into full view in the early nineteenth century. This is allowed by our ability to trace post-1800 A.D. material

---

[1] Much of the second millennium A.D. is generally referred to as the "Late Iron Age" as opposed to the "Early Iron Age" of the first millennium. The particular developments in the Shashe/Limpopo area have been given the label "Middle Iron Age." Among archaeologists it is acknowledged that the terms are European imports. Although the term does privilege iron and technology, it is a convenient shorthand label for a complete social system. More recently, other terms such as "Early Farming Communities" and "Later Farming Communities" have been used that emphasize economy and people as agriculturists. See, for example, G. Pwiti, "Continuity and Change: An Archaeological Study of Farming Communities in Northern Zimbabwe, AD 500–1700," *Studies in African Archaeology, 13* (Uppsala: Acta Arkeolgica Upsaliensis, 1996).

culture styles back through time and link these, by means of oral and some historical sources, to pre-1800 A.D. identities. Second is the growth of international trade links between interior African societies, the East African coast, and the many polities and states that border the wider shores of the Indian Ocean. It is against this backdrop that the places where, and the way in which, African polities developed can be understood in terms of more subtle political and economic choices. In addition, European expansion and intensified interactions with coastal and interior Southern African societies from the sixteenth century created new entanglements that drew Africans increasingly into the "modern" world.

Whereas the visibility in the archaeological record of political action, competition, and economic choice increased as the second millennium proceeded, it is obvious that the action of individuals, communities, and states was indivisibly embedded within cultural structures. Consequently, the use of ethnographic models and historical analogues remain critical to understanding these choices, despite the criticism that, in using them, the past is overpowered and simply painted in the image of the analogical present and that this encourages images of timelessness and cultural inertia.[2] But these models are comparative tools that not only identify critical continuities between past and present but also have the capacity to highlight what has changed. They help us recognize identities not as sealed cultural packages and archaeological abstractions, but, when framed within identifiable economic and political motive, as historically situated developments strategically linked to the rise and fall of political hierarchies and power over people and resources. The way in which historical circumstance contributes to an understanding of cultural structure is a central theme throughout this chapter.

The chapter is not universal in its coverage and, of necessity, places a selective emphasis upon periods and areas that have been reasonably well researched and that provide opportunities to discuss the themes mentioned previously. Consequently, the chapter is divided into two broad sections. The first begins in the early tenth century A.D. in the Limpopo Valley, with the growing engagement of subsistence scale farming societies with the wider world of Indian Ocean trade that contributed to a significant shift toward more complex state-level organization. In this region, and on the Zimbabwe plateau to the north, the scale of social, political, and economic organization that developed was significantly different from the Early Iron Age farming societies of the first millennium.

---

[2] It should be noted that a detailed understanding of archaeological sequences can equally inform on the degree of change from the early nineteenth century, the period of the ethnographic "present."

The second section traces the history of Venda-, Sotho/Tswana-, and Nguni-speakers, starting with their ancestral origins, followed by shifts within these societies, beginning in the seventeenth century, resulting from the growing influence of European mercantile interests. The end date of this review is the period of intense political reorganization of the early nineteenth century, referred to in much of the literature as the *difaqane*. It is at this time that most African societies became indissolubly enmeshed within European interests. Moreover, the *difaqane* is particularly appropriate as an end point because, although the scale of the event was unique, it is suggested that the nature of the response was not and that the archaeology indicates that there is continuity with the past in the structure and processes of political and cultural reformulation. The fragments of archaeological evidence outlined in the following sections can begin to identify these general processes and, in certain contexts, identify the specific political and economic imperatives that drove them.

THE ARCHAEOLOGY OF CLASS AND COMPLEXITY

Between AD 900 and 1290, farming communities near the junction of the Limpopo and Shashe rivers underwent changes that gave rise to a significantly greater scale of political, social, and economic organization than that seen in earlier first-millennium farming communities. Later Stone Age hunter–gatherers continued to share this landscape with farmers and although the evidence indicates that their basic social structure fragmented, it is likely that in their capacity as the ultimate "first people" they continued to play a ritual role in the critical relationship between farmers and landscape.

Between AD 1220 and 1290, political and ritual power was centralized in the hands of a ruling elite at Mapungubwe. The Mapungubwe state had influence and control over a large area of present-day northern South Africa, southern Zimbabwe, and eastern Botswana (Fig. 3.1). The rise of Mapungubwe was the first example in Southern Africa of a class-based social system sanctioned by sacred leadership and that contrasted with the ranked political systems that organized earlier farming polities. That this complexity was built upon the intensifying trade links with the East African coast is well attested to and its citizens can be identified as ancestral Shona-speakers. The Mapungubwe occupation was the first of three periods that together make up what Tom Huffman describes as the Zimbabwe Culture.[3] The distinctive settlement organization first established at Mapungubwe was

---

[3] T. N. Huffman, "Mapungubwe and the origins of the Zimbabwe culture," *South African Archaeological Society Goodwin Series*, 8 (2000), pp. 14–29.

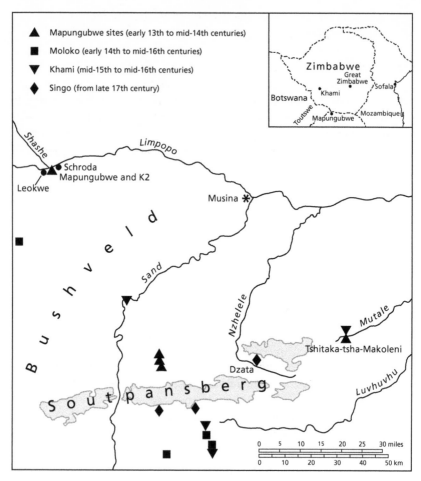

FIGURE 3.1. Map of northern South Africa and southern Zimbabwe showing the location of sites and places associated with the Mapungubwe, Venda, and ancestral Sotho/Tswana sequence.

a spatial expression of class and sacred leadership and was the formative model upon which the following two Zimbabwe Culture periods were based. These were Great Zimbabwe, dating between AD 1290 and 1450, and Khami, dating from AD 1450 until the early part of the nineteenth century (Fig. 3.1).[4]

---

[4] Space allows only for a brief treatment of the Zimbabwe periods north of the Limpopo. For a review, see T. N. Huffman, *Snakes and Crocodiles: Power and Symbolism in Ancient Zimbabwe* (Johannesburg: Witwatersrand University Press, 1996). For critical comment on this volume, see Review Feature of "Snakes and Crocodiles," *The South African Archaeological Bulletin*, 52 (1997), pp. 125–43.

The events that led to the prominence of Mapungubwe in the thirteenth century started in the tenth century when farmers referred to as Zhizo by archaeologists first settled the valley in significant numbers. This is recognized from many settlements that can be dated to this period and that preserve evidence of cattle dung deposits, domestic ash dumps, and the burnt remains of collapsed huts. Zhizo is an archaeological label, shorthand for a distinctive ceramic style that distinguishes it from other styles, such as K2 and Mapungubwe. That the appearance of Zhizo farmers in the valley was a new movement is clear because there is no evidence of farmers there between about AD 700 and 900. In addition, the first pioneer farmers who moved into northern South Africa between AD 400 and 500 left only a faint imprint in the Limpopo Valley. The key question, therefore, is what made the Limpopo Valley an attractive option for Zhizo farmers in the early tenth century?

One possibility is changes in climate and rainfall, obviously essential ingredients for farming. Today, the Shashe/Limpopo Valley is considered to be marginal for crop farming, but this has not always been the case because rainfall and temperature have varied in the past 2,000 years.[5] Consequently, it is reasonable to suggest that the geographic and temporal ebb and flow of farmers in the area varies in tandem with climatic change so it is possible that the colonization of the Shashe/Limpopo area by Zhizo farmers was encouraged by warmer and wetter conditions that started in 900 A.D.[6] Furthermore, the growth of political complexity and the parallel population increase seem to be based upon successful agricultural production allowed by favorable conditions until AD 1300. As one might expect, the collapse of the Mapungubwe state at this time seems to coincide with drier and colder conditions.

Additional evidence, however, suggests that these climate/cultural correlations were not so straightforward.[7] Rainfall in AD 900 was similar to the current marginal levels and this prompts us to think about reasons for the arrival of Zhizo farmers other than to take advantage of better farming conditions. The motivation for occupying the valley at this time may be sought rather in the growing importance of trade with the Swahili on the southeast African coast. The evidence for this trade comes from numerous

---

[5] P. D. Tyson and J. A. Lindesay, "The Climate of the Last 2000 Years in Southern Africa," *The Holocene*, 2(3) (1992), pp. 271–8.

[6] T. N. Huffman, "Archaeological Evidence for Climatic Change During the Last 2000 years in Southern Africa," *Quaternary International*, 33 (1996), pp. 55–60; Huffman, "Mapungubwe."

[7] J. M. Smith, "Climatic Change and Agropastoral Sustainability in the Shashe/Limpopo River Basin From AD 900," unpublished Ph.D. thesis, University of the Witwatersrand, Johannesburg (2005).

glass trade beads found in Zhizo settlements in the valley and in earlier
Zhizo settlements to the north and east in present-day Zimbabwe. The
relatively empty valley offered political independence for a community and
the opportunity to assert control over the exploitation of elephant ivory and
its export to the southeast African coast.[8] One Zhizo settlement, named
Schroda by archaeologists, was the largest in the valley and its size indicates
that it was the capital and exercised political control over other settlements
in the immediate region between AD 900 and AD 1000 (Fig. 3.1).

The ethnography makes the connection between settlement size and
political power explicit. Ethnographic studies of Southern African political
culture identified as traditional suggest a model of precolonial political
culture dominated by hierarchy in which, for example, no two people can
occupy the same status or rank. A chief is singular in his (very occasionally
her) position as the wealthiest man, his wealth expressed primarily through
the control of cattle which gives him access to and control over people from
whom he exacts tribute and labor. Political power is centered on the civil
functions of the most senior court in the settlement and in which power
is formalized through court fines and ritual duty.[9] Quite simply, chiefly
power meant wealth in people, and this translates physically into larger
settlements. Schroda, consequently, probably had this status.

Further evidence of Schroda's status comes from a remarkable collection
of broken clay figurines of animals, humans, and fantastical creatures that
was found in the central area of the town.[10] Their significance is again made
explicit by the ethnography. They were probably used as an instruction aid
at initiation rituals for boys and girls. Current knowledge indicates that
there are no equivalent collections at other Zhizo sites in the area, indi-
cating that initiation was centralized at the capital and under the control
of a chief. In addition, the same area at Schroda produced a concentration of metal working debris in the form of slag, furnace pieces, and clay
blowpipes that may represent actual smelting, or were used as additional
props during initiation.[11] Whatever the case, as with the figurines, the

---

[8] Huffman, "Mapungubwe."

[9] T. N. Huffman, "Archaeological Evidence and Conventional Explanations of Southern
Bantu Settlement Patterns," *Africa,* 56(3) (1986), pp. 280–98; T. N. Huffman, "Iron Age
Settlement Patterns and the Origins of Class Distinction in Southern Africa," *Advances
in World Archaeology,* 5 (1986), pp. 291–338; Huffman, "Mapungubwe."

[10] E. O. M. Hanisch, "An Archaeological Interpretation of Certain Iron Age sites in the
Limpopo/Shashi Valley," unpublished M.A. dissertation, University of Pretoria (1980);
E. O. M. Hanisch, "Schroda: The Archaeological Evidence," in J. A. van Schalkwyk and
E.O.M. Hanisch (Eds.), *Sculpted in Clay: Iron Age Figurines From Schroda, Limpopo Province,
South Africa* (Pretoria: National Culture History Museum, 2002).

[11] J. A. Calabrese, "Metals, Ideology and Power: The Manufacture and Control of Materialized Ideology in the Area of the Limpopo-Shashe Confluence, c. AD 900 to 1300,"

presence of metallurgical debris potentially underpins the centralization and control of initiation and fertility by the political leadership at Schroda. In Bantu-speaking Africa, smelting ore to produce a metal bloom is often a metaphor for procreation and, because fertility is granted through the ancestors of senior men, or, at a national level, through the ancestors of a king, the centralized remains of smelting debris may further represent political authority.

There is also abundant evidence of ivory-working at Schroda and this, too, probably underpinned authority because historically the possession and use of ivory was reserved for people of high status.[12] Some control over ivory production is indicated and this is obviously significant given that elephant ivory was a key trade commodity. Ninth-century documentary evidence indicates that Swahili found new ivory markets near Sofala and, both locally and internationally, ivory was a prestige material and much sought after.[13] Documentary evidence indicates that gold was also exported from the interior at this time, but there is no direct archaeological evidence for this from the Limpopo Basin until the thirteenth century.

If gold was exported during the tenth century it appears that this was done without it being symbolically representative within a local value system. The evidence unequivocally shows that glass trade beads were the common reciprocal trade items coming in from the southeast African coast. Similar beads to those at Schroda have been recovered from Chibuene (Fig. 3.1) and some ceramics have their origins in Persia, but the precise origin of these items is uncertain.[14] More recently, some of the Limpopo Valley glass trade beads have been chemically sourced to Indonesia and this indicates considerably more complexity in the trade route and perhaps, one destination of the ivory.[15] Very little is known about the structure of trade and the passage of goods between the Shashe/Limpopo region and the southeast African coast but it is probable that it took the form of down-the-line trade between independent polities. Although Schroda was the political center in the tenth century, important evidence from the wider

---

South African Archaeological Society Goodwin Series, 8 (2000), pp. 100–11. J. A. Calabrese, "Ethnicity, Class and Polity: The Emergence of Social and Political Complexity in the Shashi-Limpopo Valley of Southern Africa, AD 900 to 1300," unpublished Ph.D. thesis, University of the Witwatersrand, Johannesburg (2005).

[12] Hanisch, "An Archaeological Interpretation."

[13] Huffman, "Mapungubwe."

[14] M. Wood, "Making Connections: Relationships Between International Trade and Glass Beads From the Shashe-Limpopo Area," *The South African Archaeological Society Goodwin Series*, 8 (2000), pp. 78–90.

[15] M. Wood, "Glass Beads and Pre-European trade in the Shashe-Limpopo Region," unpublished M.A. dissertation, University of the Witwatersrand, Johannesburg (2005).

region suggests that participation in this trade was not limited to the elites at the capital.

Whatever the case, the key factor is that the tenth-century farming communities in the Limpopo Basin and on the Zimbabwe plateau became increasingly embroiled within the Indian Ocean trade nexus that was coordinated, in part, by Swahili traders on the coast. There is nothing comparable in the farmer record to the south of the Limpopo. Despite the recovery of one Islamic shard dating to the ninth century, and a glass trade bead from Kwagandaganda, an Early Iron Age settlement near present-day Pietermaritzburg, no contemporary early farmer settlements elsewhere participated in international trade with the intensity evident at Schroda and other Zhizo settlements at the time.[16]

At the start of the eleventh century A.D., the intensity of trade links with the East African coast increased and the evidence indicates that elites consolidated and exercised more control over it. The identity of those elites, however, changed, because new communities moved into the valley and imposed themselves on the Schroda polity. This event is recognized through the rapid appearance of a new ceramic style, referred to as Leopards Kopje, in the Shashe/Limpopo Valley. As Schroda's local power waned, a new capital (K2) was established nearby (Fig. 3.1).[17] This change marked the development of an altogether different scale of hierarchy, and social and political power was premised increasingly upon the control of exotic trade goods.[18] Continuities in Leopards Kopje ceramic style and settlement organization through to Mapungubwe in the thirteenth century and Great Zimbabwe, established early in the fourteenth century, show that K2 people were ancestral Shona-speakers.

On stylistic grounds few query the sharp disjunction between Zhizo and Leopards Kopje pottery or the fact that the rapid appearance of the latter in the Shashe/Limpopo region represents the arrival of new people, or at least the core of a new lineage.[19] Furthermore, it appears that many of the Zhizo settlements in the Limpopo Basin ended early in the eleventh

---

[16] G. Whitelaw, "Kwagandaganda: Settlement Patterns in the Natal Early Iron Age," *Natal Museum Journal of Humanities*, 6 (1994), pp. 1–64.

[17] K2 was the name given to this site by early excavators because the massive central midden reminded them of North African tells called *Kom*. The 2 indicates that it is the second settlement in the immediate vicinity.

[18] Huffman, "Mapungubwe."

[19] T. N. Huffman, "The Origins of Leopard's Kopje: An 11th Century Difaqane," *Arnoldia* (Rhodesia) 8(23) (1978), pp. 1–23; T. N. Huffman, "Archaeology and Ethnohistory of the African Iron Age," *Annual Review of Anthropology*, 11 (1982), pp. 133–50; T. N. Huffman, *Iron Age Migrations: The Ceramic Sequence in Southern Zambia: Excavations at Gundu and Ndonde* (Johannesburg: Witwatersrand University Press, 1989).

century, and it is inferred that these new arrivals undermined the Schroda chiefdom and displaced Zhizo communities from the area.[20] The wider regional settlement evidence, for example, suggests that there was a contemporary increase in settlement density and population growth in eastern Botswana.[21] This sequence of events has been interpreted as a sharp cultural disjunction that resulted in little constructive economic or social exchange between the newly established K2 polity in the Shashe/Limpopo region and chiefdoms in eastern Botswana.[22] More recent work, however, has begun to complicate this interpretation. Some Zhizo communities (known as Leokwe), persisted in the Shashe/Limpopo area until the early thirteenth century and continued to express a distinctive ceramic identity throughout the K2 period, even though they were living immediately adjacent to K2 communities.[23] Furthermore, at Leokwe, a large settlement some 12 km west of the K2 capital (Fig. 3.1), K2 and Zhizo people lived close to each other but not together. This ethnic co-occurrence directs attention to the nature of the relationship between them and the nature of roles and interactions that encouraged both stylistic continuity and active differentiation between the two.

An informing framework for the evidence of this conjunction is provided by a historical model of African ethnic interaction and political reformulation generated by Kopytoff.[24] He provides numerous historical examples in which the growth, collapse, and reformulation of African polities has played out in generally similar ways. This is because within the internal African frontier an almost continuous process of segmentation, fission,

---

[20] Huffman, "Mapungubwe."

[21] J. Denbow, "The Toutswe Tradition: A Study in Socio-economic Change," in R. R. Hitchcock and M. R. Smith (Eds.), *Settlement in Botswana* (Gaborone: Heinemann, 1982), pp. 73–86; J. Denbow, "Congo to Kalahari: Data and Hypotheses About the Political Economy of the Western Stream of the Early Iron Age," *African Archaeological Review*, 8 (1990), pp. 139–76; J. Denbow, "The Dialectics of Culture and Identity in the Kalahari: AD 700–1700," in S. K. McIntosh (Ed.), *Beyond Chiefdoms: Pathways to Complexity in Africa* (Cambridge: Cambridge University Press, 1999).

[22] Huffman, "Origins."

[23] J. A. Calabrese, "Interregional Interaction in Southern Africa: Zhizo and Leopard's Kopje Relations in Northern South Africa, Southwestern Zimbabwe and Eastern Botswana, AD 1000 to 1200," *African Archaeological Review*, 17(4) (2000), pp. 183–210; Calabrese "Ethnicity, Class and Polity"; J. C. Vogel "Radiocarbon Dating of the Iron Age Sequence in the Limpopo Valley," *South African Archaeological Society Goodwin Series*, 8 (2000), pp. 51–7; J. C. Vogel and J. A. Calabrese, "Dating of the Leokwe Hill Site and Implications for the Regional Chronology," *South African Archaeological Society Goodwin Series*, 8 (2000), pp. 47–50.

[24] I. Kopytoff, "The Internal African Frontier: The Making of African Political Culture," in I. Kopytoff (Ed.), *The African Frontier: The Reproduction of Traditional African Societies* (Bloomington: Indiana University Press, 1987), pp. 3–84.

movement, and the creation of new encounters between groups is premised upon a broadly shared set of cultural principles. These principles give some predictability to how those encounters are managed and the processes by which new identities and polities emerge.

A central theme in the political development and ambitions of immigrant communities (newcomers) is the way they acquire power over farmers who are already resident in the region into which they move (firstcomers). Military force and the accumulation of people through intermarriage, who then become classificatory kin rather than competitors, are two strategies. There is, however, a potentially delicate period to negotiate before newcomers can exercise a more confident political primacy. Consequently, a dual system can develop in which the residential primacy of firstcomers and their historical intimacy with the land is acknowledged by according them ritual ownership of that land and the political ambitions of newcomers, as "owners of people," depends upon this recognition.[25] In this regard the firstcomers par excellence are hunter–gatherers and their ritual interventions in the affairs of Bantu-speaking farmers are well documented. With increasing political confidence, however, newcomers may manipulate genealogical history and cast aspersions on the cultural status of firstcomers by aggrandizing their civilizing role, for example, in the provision of iron, pottery, or stable political systems, and ultimately invert their historical position.

There is much more complexity in Kopytoff's discussion of the political and cultural dynamics of the internal African frontier, but this brief outline of one of its characteristics provides a framework within which to develop the significance of the archaeological evidence for ethnic co-occurrence in the Shashe/Limpopo region between AD 1000 and 1200. Furthermore, the development of sharper social distinctions and steeper political hierarchies over this period may be situated within the dynamics of dual ethnicities and driven by political ambition and the advantages of controlling international trade.[26] There is, consequently, an obvious congruence between this aspect of the model and the archaeological identification of K2 people as newcomers and Zhizo people as firstcomers. Additionally, the continuity of a Zhizo ethnicity in these circumstances may be strategically related to their ritual power over landscape and the dependency of K2 people upon it, but also a relationship increasingly differentiated by status, as expressed at Leokwe. These relationships not only played out between farmers but also between farmers and hunter–gatherers. In this regard it is possible that, within the same framework, there were relatively intense interactions between hunter–gatherers

[25] *Ibid.*, p. 55.
[26] Calabrese, "Interregional interactions"; "Ethnicity, class and polity."

and early Zhizo farmers.[27] However, as first Zhizo, and then K2 farmers imposed their political and cultural will upon the Shashe/Limpopo region, the ideological role played by hunter–gatherers may have slipped off the base of an ever-steeper social and economic pyramid.

It is within this duality that the seeds of social distinctions may have taken root. The archaeology of the capital at K2 certainly attests to its growing status. Between the establishment of K2 early in the eleventh century A.D. and its abandonment 200 years later, the capital grew in size and spatial changes took place that actively accommodated the rapid growth of an economic, social, and political hierarchy. At its inception, K2 was organized according to the principles of the Central Cattle Pattern.[28] Although it is difficult to extrapolate complete settlement organization from small excavations, it is clear that when the capital was established there was a central cattle byre surrounded by domestic areas. Toward the end of the eleventh century, however, cattle dung stopped accumulating in the central byre and it became partially smothered by a large ash midden. This space became the central focus of the capital; the cattle were moved elsewhere. This midden would have been associated with the court and male activity, including craft production, which continued centrally despite the fact that the sanctioning presence of cattle was no longer there. Its considerable size, seemingly impractical, became a symbol of status and political power at K2.[29]

The social and political logic of the spatial shift at K2 becomes apparent with the abandonment of the town early in the thirteenth century when the community moved only 1 km away to Mapungubwe (Fig. 3.1), which provided the physical conditions to express the social distinctions that had developed during the K2 period. At Mapungubwe, elite rulers expressed their status spatially by isolating themselves on top of the hill. Commoners lived in the town at the base of the hill to the south and north. The rapidity of the move from K2 to Mapungubwe suggests that the social and structural move toward a burgeoning class-based system had already been completed

---

[27] S. Hall and B. Smith, "Empowering Places: Rock Shelters and Ritual Control in Farmer-forager interactions in the Northern Province, South Africa," *South African Archaeological Society Goodwin Series*, 8 (2001), pp. 30–46; B. van Doornum, "Spaces and Places: Investigating Proximity Between Forager and Farmer Sites," unpublished M.A. dissertation, University of the Witwatersrand, Johannesburg (2000).

[28] The Central Cattle Pattern, a normative ethnographic model of spatial organization, is used as a comparison with the archaeology of Southern African farmer spatial organization. It is divided into the central area of cattle and the court and is conceptually linked to the activities of men and the surrounding domestic ring which is the conceptual domain of women and children. This organization is associated with patrilineal Eastern Bantu-speakers who practice bridewealth in cattle. See Chapter 2 for a fuller description of it and a discussion of its analogical use.

[29] Huffman, "Mapungubwe."

at K2 and eventually the location and settlement plan became inadequate to express that system.

Several other linked changes encourage a more detailed interpretation of this shift. The first is that the 200-year juxtaposition of Zhizo and K2 communities ended when Mapungubwe was occupied, and secondly, there was an isolated period of lower rainfall.[30] Very broadly this suggests a cusp in the political assertiveness of K2 newcomers whereby the need to accommodate the services of Zhizo ritual specialists lapsed. It was no longer necessary to configure identity in relation to a dual system because the ritual of rainmaking and the fertility of the land were taken over by K2 elites. Indeed, Huffman suggests that elite occupation on top of Mapungubwe actually appropriated rainmaking sites and that the responsibility for national fertility and rain became vested in sacred leaders through the parallel rise in power of their own ancestors.[31] The timing of the climatic "wobble" may have been critical in that it encouraged an ideological shift toward centralization and hierarchy through the perceived need for greater power in ritual intercessions for rain.[32] In summary, sacred leadership and the development of a class-based system at Mapungubwe had its roots "in the far more modest embryonic polity shaped by the frontier," of which the interplay between K2 newcomers and Zhizo firstcomers was one important ingredient.[33]

The growing asymmetry between K2 elites and Zhizo commoners through the eleventh and twelfth centuries must have been played out with one eye on the competitive advantages of controlling trade. The removal of cattle from K2, for example, suggests that trade beads, cloth, ivory, and later, gold, were woven into the fabric of exchange values and became additional instruments of exchange for wives. The differentials in wealth visible in the archaeology of settlements away from the capital encourages the view that control of their circulation became centralized and exclusive to an alliance of the upper class.[34] Furthermore, glass beads were recycled during the K2 period to manufacture large and exclusive "garden roller" beads. This innovation created another signifier of status. Clearly, trade goods expanded prestige and status well beyond the signifying power of cattle.[35]

At the Mapungubwe site the material expression of class and status is clear. The new settlement structure there, known as the Zimbabwe Culture Pattern, attests to a rearrangement of some of the cultural principles that

---

[30] Calabrese, "Ethnicity, Class and Polity"; Smith, "Climatic change."

[31] Huffman, "Mapungubwe."   [32] Smith, "Climatic Change."

[33] Kopytoff, "The Internal African Frontier," p. 62.

[34] M. Hall, *The Changing Past: Farmers, Kings and Traders in Southern Africa, 200–1860* (Cape Town: David Philip, 1987); Calabrese, "Ethnicity, Class and Polity."

[35] Hall, "The Changing Past."

underpinned the Central Cattle Pattern, most notably the link between height and status, and the formalization of an east/west axis that associates private ritual activity with the eastern end of the hill.[36] The spatial expression of status and the greater social distance between elite and commoner also was expressed in the differential access to and manipulation of gold. The iconic gold-plated rhino, bowl, and "sceptre," for example, were found in the graves of the "royal" cemetery on the hilltop. The status of this location can be further embellished because, in Shona ethnography, the black rhino is a symbol of political leadership, and the other prestige grave goods must have carried similar meaning.

The fact that some of these royal burials were smothered with thousands of gold and glass trade beads completes the picture. In sharp contrast, gold is absent from commoner areas. Furthermore, there is evidence that exotic trade goods and other craft activities, such as metallurgy, were also centralized and controlled by elites.[37] As indicated previously, ideology and religion underwrote transformation toward social complexity that was inseparably linked to the sacred leadership role of the head of the ruling family. This parallels the political status of leadership, and elite ancestors were elevated to a national role.[38]

The spatial pattern at Mapungubwe expressed the social distance between elites and commoners, and smaller elite political centers within the Mapungubwe state used the same spatial code. Commoner homesteads at the base of the hierarchy were, however, organized according to the Central Cattle Pattern, a sharp reminder of the social distance between classes. The geographic extent of the Mapungubwe state and its influence is indicated by the presence of Mapungubwe ceramics in eastern Botswana, south toward the Soutpansberg and well into Zimbabwe to the northwest.

We have already identified the fact that Zhizo communities regrouped in eastern Botswana in the eleventh century and melded into what is archaeologically called the Toutswe Tradition. In their new home, farmers developed shallower political hierarchies, which were contemporary with K2 and Mapungubwe. These were based on smaller polities that developed political economies predominantly around livestock production and extensive local trade with the Kalahari hinterland and the Okavango area in northwest Botswana and involved many pastoralist and hunter–gatherer communities.[39] The presence of freshwater resources at Toutswe sites that

---

[36] See Huffman, "Mapungubwe" for the details of spatial organisation at Mapungubwe.

[37] Calabrese, "Ethnicity, Class and Polity."   [38] Huffman, "Mapungubwe."

[39] Denbow, "Dialectics"; A. Reid and A. Segobye, "Politics, Society and Trade on the Eastern Margins of the Kalahari," *South African Archaeological Society Goodwin Series, 8* (2000), pp. 58–68.

could only have come from the west and distinctive pottery indicates contacts as far afield as Tsodilo in northwest Botswana. The wealth and political status of capitals such as Toutswe and Bosutswe contrast sharply with those of the Shashe/Limpopo capitals. Toutswe homesteads continued to be organized according to the principles of the Central Cattle Pattern, so there was no sharp separation between rulers and commoners.[40] Although there are indications that there were regional links between eastern Botswana and the Shashe/Limpopo region at this time it is possible that the control held by K2 and Mapungubwe elites over trade goods coming from the east meant that little of this trade continued further to the west.

As with any complex system, the Mapungubwe state required a scale of agricultural production sufficient to support the day-to-day subsistence needs of its people. In an area identified today as marginal for crop production, food security and predictability must have been an issue. The location of elite and commoner settlements throughout the tenth- to thirteenth-century occupation of the region sheds some light on how the necessary scale of agricultural production was achieved. Apart from access to alluvial gold washing down the rivers, which drained the gold rich geology of the Zimbabwe Plateau to the north, Schroda, K2, and Mapungubwe also commanded access to extensive flood plains adjacent to the Limpopo River and, in particular, just upstream of its junction with the Shashe River.

The evidence of the importance of flood plain agriculture comes in part from the distribution and density of commoner homesteads within and immediately adjacent to these flood plains, where both the needs of the commoners and their agricultural tribute responsibilities to elites must have been met.[41] Predictability of production was based upon annual flood and recession cycles and the nutritional rejuvenation of flood plain soils, and this balance must have been delicate, particularly during the Mapungubwe period. Indeed, it has been suggested that the collapse of the Mapungubwe state resulted from a downturn in rainfall toward the end of the thirteenth century and this destabilized the pivotal relationship between flooding and predictable agricultural production. Newer climatic data, however, indicate that the end of Mapungubwe occurred at a time when there was an upturn in rainfall levels.[42] Even so, it is possible that even slight perturbations in climatic conditions had significant repercussions for food security. Whatever the case, this signals that relationships between climatic and agricultural systems are complex and, although not minimizing the

[40] J. Denbow, "Cows and Kings: A Spatial and Economic Analysis of a Hierarchical Early Iron Age Settlement System in Eastern Botswana," in M. Hall, G. Avery, D. M. Avery, M. L. Wilson, and A. J. B. Humphreys (Eds.), *Frontiers: Southern African Archaeology Today* (Oxford: BAR. International Series 207, 1984), pp. 24–39; Denbow "Dialectics."
[41] Huffman, "Mapungubwe."   [42] Smith, "Climatic Change."

obvious importance of suitable conditions for farmers, this fact alerts us to consider in more detail the political and social ramifications of those conditions.

With the collapse of Mapungubwe, Great Zimbabwe to the northeast (Fig. 3.1) rose to immediate prominence from the early fourteenth century as the capital of a new Shona-speaking state that started the second phase of the Zimbabwe Tradition. The location of Great Zimbabwe, and other Zimbabwe period sites, on the southern slopes of the Zimbabwe Plateau makes good sense if rainfall was a factor because these areas would have received what rain there was. Equally, however, the shift in political power to the northeast may also relate to the strategic advantage of competitors who were closer to the east coast trade. In this position, a new polity could have strangled the flow of trade goods to the west, and would also have been well placed to exploit the gold fields of the Zimbabwe Plateau.

Whatever caused the demise of the Mapungubwe state, there is cultural continuity between Mapungubwe and Great Zimbabwe. The basic social, political, and economic structures established at K2 and Mapungubwe at the start of the Zimbabwe Tradition were repeated at Great Zimbabwe but were elaborated on a monumental scale. The continuities evident between Mapungubwe and Great Zimbabwe do not mean that there was large-scale population movement to that area. In fact, the evidence shows that although the Shashe/Limpopo area experienced a significant downturn in farmer numbers, Mapungubwe settlements continue, for example, in eastern Botswana in the fourteenth century when Mapungubwe ceramics and identities came to dominate. More importantly for this chapter, Mapungubwe settlements continued on the northeastern side of the Soutpansberg and this is significant for the next stage of this narrative.

Before turning to this next stage, however, it is worth noting that in the past decade the eleventh- to thirteenth-century archaeological sequence described previously has been increasingly exposed to the South African public, particularly through reformed school history curricula, the press, documentary productions, and, most recently, the repatriation of burials. The award of World Heritage status to the Mapungubwe complex has intensified this positive exposure and the freedom to explore African achievement. The golden rhino recovered from the royal cemetery at Mapungubwe, for example, is a central icon of this achievement, and it is frequently extolled in public as a model for current economic and social aspirations; a model that has also been encouraged by archaeologists.[43] The Mapungubwe state unquestionably represents significant African achievement. It does not, however, represent a yardstick against which other Southern

[43] See T. Maggs, "African Naissance: An Introduction," *The South African Archaeological Society Goodwin Series,* 8 (2000), pp. 1–3.

African farming societies are measured. Although they were not organized
in an equivalently complex way, other farming societies to which we now
turn were different in the way they were contextually structured to confront, accommodate, and solve particular issues within specific historical
contexts.[44]

CONTINUITY AND CHANGE FROM THE
FOURTEENTH CENTURY

A central theme throughout this section is that of the increasing ability
of archaeologists to link sites, their occupants, and material culture to
historical identities. This is a potential noted relatively early in the history of systematic agropastoralist studies.[45] The archaeology contributes to
tracking these identities through to the nineteenth century and contrasts
with the more opaque historical identities of farmers in the first millennium A.D.[46] Regional chronologies, stylistic ceramic sequences, variability
in lifeways, and economic emphases and cultural form can be matched,
linked, and correlated with identities documented in the eighteenth and
nineteenth centuries. Oral records make a critical contribution to this.
Furthermore, the continuing trade links with the southeast African coast,
particularly with Europeans from the sixteenth century, brought literate
observers to the region. Their documents refer to the identities of coastal
and interior communities. The historical anonymity that veils much of the
first millennium begins to slip. Consequently, the main focus in this section
is to discuss very broadly the genesis and development of Sotho/Tswana-,
Venda-, and Nguni-speakers.

Ancestral Sotho/Tswana- and Nguni-speakers

Tracing the origins of Sotho/Tswana- and Nguni-speakers in Southern
Africa appeals, once more, to migration, because there are major ceramic dis-
continuities between the styles of terminal Early Iron Age farmers ("Eiland"
in the Soutpansberg area, for example, and "Ntshekane" in KwaZulu-Natal)
and those of ancestral Sotho/Tswana- and Nguni-speakers. Cultural remains
of people likely to be ancestral Nguni-speakers, first appear about AD 1100
in the coastal regions of KwaZulu-Natal, and Sotho/Tswana-speakers in

---

[44] See S. McIntosh (Ed.), *Beyond Chiefdoms: Pathways to Complexity in Africa* (Cambridge,
New York: Cambridge University Press, 1999).
[45] T. Maggs, *Iron Age Communities of the Southern Highveld* (Pietermaritzburg: Natal Museum,
1976), p. 186.
[46] See Chapter 2 in this volume.

the Bushveld habitats north and south of the Soutpansberg, from about AD 1300.[47] The evidence gleaned from ceramic and settlement style indicates continuity into historically documented societies. As the second millennium progressed, these identities became even more recognizable when the archaeology chronologically overlaps with the oral records and written sources.[48]

The earliest sites linked to ancestral Sotho/Tswana-speakers, dating to the early fourteenth century, are found in Limpopo Province (Fig. 3.2). From the mid-fifteenth century, there was expansion of these settlements southward into the North-West province and eastern and southeastern Botswana. From the early seventeenth century, a further phase of expansion pushes beyond the mixed Bushveld habitats onto the predominantly High-veld grasslands of KwaZulu-Natal and the eastern Free State. Within South Africa and Botswana, therefore, the chronological trend of Sotho/Tswana settlement is from north to south. There is less clarity about Nguni settlement history than about the Sotho/Tswana past. Enough is known to show that there is no continuity between the early farmer phase (Ntshekane) in KwaZulu-Natal and pioneer Nguni settlements.[49] Consequently, the origins of Sotho/Tswana- and Nguni-speakers appear to be broadly related phenomena.

The impetus for these origins must have come from further north of the Limpopo. Some archaeological evidence, for example, links early Nguni pottery and thirteenth-century pottery from Ivuna in Tanzania.[50] Furthermore, on linguistic grounds, both Nguni and Sotho/Tswana languages have features that could only have developed in East Africa.[51] On anthropological grounds, kinship terminology, the practice of *hlonipha* (the respect shown

---

[47] The ancestral Sotho/Tswana sequence is archaeologically referred to as Moloko ("to shift one's village"), and is subdivided into several phases (see Huffman, "Regionality"). Other archaeological labels describe the Nguni sequence (see Huffman, "Archaeology of the Nguni Past"). These labels may be used where necessary but, for the sake of clarity, the linguistic terms Sotho/Tswana and Nguni are used more often.

[48] See, for example, Maggs, "Iron Age Communities," N. Parsons, "Prelude to the Difaqane in the Interior of Southern Africa c. 1600–c. 1822," in C. Hamilton (Ed.), *The Mfecane Aftermath: Reconstructive Debates in Southern African History* (Johannesburg and Pietermaritzburg: Witwatersrand University Press and University of Natal Press, 1995), pp. 322–49.

[49] T. N. Huffman, "The Archaeology of the Nguni Past," *Southern African Humanities, 16* (2004), pp. 79–111.

[50] Huffman, "Iron Age Migrations," p. 176.

[51] J. A. Louw and R. Finlayson, "Southern Bantu Origins as Represented by Xhosa and Tswana," *South African Journal of Languages, 10*(4) (1990), 401–10; R. K. Herbert and T. N. Huffman, "A New Perspective on Bantu Expansion and Classification: Linguistic and Archaeological Evidence Fifty Years After Doke," *African Studies, 39* (1993), 123–74; Huffman, "Archaeology of the Nguni Past."

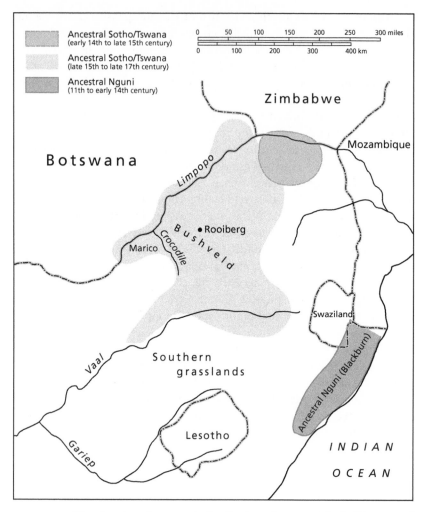

FIGURE 3.2. Map showing the general distribution of ancestral Sotho/Tswana and Nguni-speakers up to the mid-sixteenth century.

by married women for her husband's patrilineal family and expressed in the avoidance of words associated with their names), and specific pollution concepts are also linked to historic cultural practices in East Africa. The importance attached to cattle over agriculture and a material culture that follows East African patterns (notably beehive houses) suggests that although they were mixed farmers, they lived in an area surrounded by ideologically committed pastoralists.[52] Identification of these links is hampered by the fact that there is little known evidence of movement.

---

[52] Huffman, "Archaeology of the Nguni Past."

The relatively rapid early nineteenth-century movement of Ngoni from northern KwaZulu-Natal to northern Malawi and southern Tanzania is not an appropriate analogue for the north to south appearance of Sotho/Tswana- and Nguni-speakers. It does remind us, however, that people on the move may not leave much evidence of their passage.

The East African origin of Sotho/Tswana- and Nguni-speakers supports, in Tom Huffman's view, the Central Cattle Pattern model as an appropriate ethnographic model from which to infer the worldview of first-millennium farmers.[53] It will be remembered that this model is based on a synthesis of Nguni and Tswana ethnography and that African linguists place these languages within the larger group of patrilineal Eastern Bantu-speakers who share specific beliefs about cattle, ancestors, and bridewealth.[54] It must also be remembered that the only recognized linguistic continuity in South Africa between first- and second-millennium farmers is derived from the stylistic chain between early ninth-century farmers (Klingbeil), K2/Mapungubwe, and the later Zimbabwe Culture sequence. Consequently, it is accepted that first-millennium farmers spoke an early form of Shona. If Nguni and Sotho/Tswana derive from earlier Eastern Bantu-speakers (Chifumbaze) in East Africa there is, in Huffman's view, a general continuity in worldview and belief systems and the first Nguni and Sotho/Tswana settlements do conform to the organizational principles of the Central Cattle Pattern.[55]

The current evidence indicates that the origins of Nguni- and Sotho/Tswana-speakers are to be sought in East rather than Southern Africa. What motivated and sustained this movement over such a distance is uncertain. Climatic downturn in East Africa may have been a factor. Whatever the initial motive, the rapid appearance of Sotho/Tswana in northern South Africa in the fourteenth century appears to have been during a slightly wetter phase.[56] Once established in South Africa, distinctive Sotho/Tswana settlements are relatively easy to find and dating them shows that there was a steady expansion southward through the fourteenth and fifteenth centuries.

There is nothing in the archaeology to suggest that this was driven by events other than the normal process of fission within kin groups.[57] This was

---

[53] See Chapter 2 in this volume.

[54] A. Kuper, *Wives for Cattle: Bridewealth and Marriage in Southern Africa* (London: Routledge, 1982).

[55] See Chapter 2 for a discussion of the Chifumbaze Complex and the implications for settlement organization in the first millennium A.D.

[56] Smith, "Climatic Change."

[57] T. M. Evers, "The Iron Age in Eastern Transvaal, South Africa," in E. A. Voigt (Ed.), *Guide to Archaeological Sites in the Northern and Eastern Transvaal* (Pretoria: Transvaal Museum, 1981).

again an internal frontier. Because Sotho/Tswana communities south of the Soutpansberg obviously did not expand onto an empty landscape, internal frontier dynamics must have been in operation. The interface between these traditions, however, has received little attention. The scale of ceramic analysis isolates major identities but offers little comment on the nature of the boundaries between those identities. Interaction is hinted at in some areas through the subtle incorporation of some Early Iron Age decorative motifs into the style structure of Sotho/Tswana pottery.[58] Furthermore, in southeastern Botswana there is good evidence for distinct chronological overlap between the terminal phase of early farmer settlements and pioneer Sotho/Tswana-speakers, and it is clear that both traditions briefly shared the landscape.[59]

The nature of interactions with these newcomers is unknown, but it is legitimate to ask why early farmer identities, as represented by ceramic style, offered little resistance to newcomers and under what conditions existing farming communities lost their identity to them? This clearly resonates with the Zhizo/K2 interface discussed previously. In KwaZulu-Natal, the evidence indicates that eleventh-century early farmer settlement density dipped markedly in response to deteriorating climatic conditions, and early Nguni-speakers may, therefore, have met very little cultural or demographic "resistance."[60]

THE ORIGINS OF VENDA IDENTITY

At this point we halt the discussion of early Sotho/Tswana- and Nguni-speakers and stay in Limpopo province in order to outline the origins of a Venda identity in the sixteenth and seventeenth centuries. Venda origins provide a reasonably well-resolved example of the dynamics of the internal African frontier and the politics of newcomer and firstcomer interaction.[61] The ability to recognize this process resides, in part, in precise ceramic classification and the capacity to recognize contemporary

---

[58] J. C. A. Boeyens, "The Late Iron Age sequence in the Marico and early Tswana history," *South African Archaeological Bulletin, 58* (2003), pp. 63–78.

[59] J. Denbow, "Broadhurst: A 14th Century AD Expression of the Early Iron Age in South Eastern Botswana," *South African Archaeological Bulletin, 36* (1981), pp. 66–74; C. van Waarden, "The Late Iron Age," in P. Lane, A. Reid, and A. Segobye (Eds.), *Ditswa Mung: The Archaeology of Botswana* (Gaborone: Botswana Society, 1998).

[60] F. E. Prins, "Climate, Vegetation and Early Agriculturist Communities in Transkei and KwaZulu-Natal," *Azania, 29/30* (1994/95), pp. 179–86; J. C. Vogel and A. Fuls, "The Spatial Distribution of Radiocarbon Dates for the Iron Age in Southern Africa," *South African Archaeological Bulletin, 54*(170) (1997), pp. 97–101.

[61] Kopytoff, "The Internal African Frontier."

but distinct identities in the past. Furthermore, the archaeology contributes to debates about the origins of Venda identity and how the claims made in the oral record can be assessed. Oral, archaeological, and some written evidence combine to paint a broader historical landscape in which the logic of identity formation and collapse can be understood. Venda is a combination of a predominantly western Shona (Kalanga) grammar and a dominant Sotho vocabulary. This indicates that the origins of Venda identity are to be found in this cultural amalgam and the archaeology contributes significantly to this search.

It is necessary first to return to the Zimbabwe Tradition sequence because it was from that context that several identifiable contributions by Shona-speakers to the origins of Venda can be traced. The first can be linked to the collapse of the Mapungubwe state. As noted previously, the fallout from Mapungubwe was not restricted to cultural continuity at Great Zimbabwe. Mapungubwe pottery and sites also occur on the northern aspects of the eastern Soutpansberg (Fig. 3.1) until about AD 1450.[62] Settlement structure indicates that some of these Mapungubwe sites were occupied by elites and walling signals the residences of rulers. These elites followed the precedents set at K2 and Mapungubwe and cattle were kept elsewhere. Significantly, the continuity of Mapungubwe sites into the fifteenth century means that these communities were contemporary with pioneer Sotho/Tswana communities, who were well established by the fourteenth century. From about AD 1450, there was a second injection of Shona-speakers southward. Judged on the basis of a distinctive settlement and ceramic style this had its origins within the domain of the trading state centered on the capital at Khami, near present-day Bulawayo in southwestern Zimbabwe. These Khami-style settlements expanded south of the Limpopo and lapped up against the north-facing slopes of the Soutpansberg.[63]

From the fourteenth century, Shona- and Sotho-speakers were in close proximity in the Soutpansberg. Other evidential strands for this relationship are drawn from the ethnographic record and oral records. The latter, however, account for Venda origins through the politically dominant traditions of the Singo.[64] The Singo traditions outline a dispute with Shona Rozvi rulers as the motivation for their departure from southwestern Zimbabwe, but the Singo claims are at odds with the archaeological

[62] J. H. N. Loubser, "Archaeology and Early Venda History," *The South African Archaeological Society Goodwin Series*, 6 (1989), pp. 54–61; J. H. N. Loubser, "The Ethnoarchaeology of Venda-speakers in Southern Africa," *Navorsinge van die Nasionale Museum Bloemfontein*, 7(8) (1991), pp. 146–464.

[63] See T. N. Huffman and E. O. M. Hanisch, "Settlement Hierarchies in the Northern Transvaal: Zimbabwe Ruins and Venda History," *African Studies*, 46 (1987), pp. 79–116.

[64] Loubser, "The Ethnoarchaeology of Venda-speakers," p. 151.

evidence because the first Singo capital, Dzata near the Nzhelele River in the eastern Soutpansberg, was only occupied between AD 1680 and AD 1700 (Fig. 3.1).[65] It seems that Singo traditions overpowered fainter pre-Singo "voices," and remodeled events into a firstcomer charter that legitimates their political authority in the region by claiming to be the first Venda. These traditions imply that the Venda language and civilized cultural practice were introduced by the Singo in the seventeenth century. This would mean that class distinction and the distinctive settlement pattern that evokes it was also brought to the region by the Singo.

The archaeological evidence from the ceramic and settlement sequence outlined by Loubser provides a critical foil to the claims of Singo primacy. This evidence recognizes that a pre-Dzata Venda identity had already developed from intense interaction between Shona- and Sotho-speakers. The mid-fifteenth century A.D. spread of Khami communities south of the Limpopo is supported by oral traditions that suggest that this expansion took place when southwestern Zimbabwe was under the authority of the Torwa dynasty centered at Khami. The oral records are clearly those of chief lineages linked to sites such as Tshaluvhimbi and Tshitaka-tsha-Makonei (Fig. 3.1), which have prestige walling marking the "palace" (known in the Venda language as *musanda*), with extensive areas outside these walls where commoners lived. An even earlier layer of oral tradition suggests that this Khami incursion subdued local Ngona and other communities, perhaps linked to the earlier Mapungubwe settlements. Indeed, the stratigraphic evidence indicates that these Mapungubwe settlements were still occupied at the time of the Khami incursion. The combination of oral and archaeological evidence therefore indicates that, from the thirteenth century A.D. the Shona cultural substrate upon which Venda identity developed was well in place.

Although these Shona incursions brought Zimbabwe Culture Pattern settlements to the north of the Soutpansberg, on the southern side of this range contemporary Sotho/Tswana settlements were organized according to the center/surround principles of the Central Cattle Pattern. The mountains were not a barrier and interaction is evident through the exchange of ceramics. These exchanges take on more complex social meaning when stylistic attributes of Khami and Sotho/Tswana pottery were merged on the same vessels. Because women were the potters, this must indicate that social exchanges included intermarriage. The stylistic fusion of Khami and Sotho/Tswana pottery (called Tavhatshena by Loubser) is relatively short lived and it was replaced by a new ceramic style (called Letaba) that developed from Tavhatshena by AD 1550, and potters stopped making

[65] Loubser, "Archaeology and early Venda history," p. 58.

Sotho/Tswana and Khami styles. Letaba ceramics are stylistically stable up to the historic and the present time, and Venda potters still make them today. The conclusion is that Tavhatshena represents an early stage of ethnogenesis resulting from intermarriage between Shona- and Sotho-speakers, whereas the widespread replacement of all styles in the region with Letaba ceramics marked the rapid development of a full-blown Venda language and cultural identity.[66]

The later but dominating Singo traditions attempt to mask the earlier development of a Venda identity that the Singo lay claim to. Close scrutiny of Singo oral records and comparison with the traditions of marginalized groups highlight the deculturizing strategy the Singo employed.[67] The Singo depict the pre-Singo Mapungubwe period Ngona communities as having been chiefless (i.e., without civilized leadership) and without fire, pottery, metal, or agriculture.[68] The Singo attained firstcomer status because they brought these practices with them. The pre-Singo archaeological evidence obviously shows that these claims are not literally true. This strategy inverts chronology by asserting firstcomer status based on the claims of political and cultural enlightenment, a process that resonates with the co-occurrence of Zhizo and K2 communities in the Shashe/Limpopo region, but with the benefit of extant oral evidence.

Venda totemic names (*mitupo*), furthermore, have a distinct hierarchy that relates to the political fortunes of chiefs who were subdued by the Singo, and consequently, they preserve historical sequences and a relative chronology. The Singo *mitupo*, for example, underpins political power expressed through mountain imagery and Singo chiefs are also buried on mountains. Those stripped of political power have lost these references but retain *mitupo* with pool imagery, which relates to procreation and fertility. As a result of the Singo incursion, the Khami period Mbedzi palace, for example, changed into a pool and alludes to the loss of political independence but the retention of procreative power. This pecking order plays out in ritual function whereby the Mbedzi chiefs in their capacity as original occupants of the land were allocated specialist niches such as the securing of fertility. As first people their status is implicitly secured as "owners of the land," as opposed to the Singo, who were "owners of people."[69] At the social base are people such as the Dzivhani Ngona, who occupy the outer margins of Venda society and are reviled through their *mitupo* as "dry ones." Their

---

[66] *Ibid.*, 58.
[67] Kopytoff, "The Internal African Frontier."
[68] Loubser, "The ethnoarchaeology of Venda-speakers," p. 405.
[69] See C. S. Lancaster, "The Frontier as Regional System: Political Structure and Ethnicity in an Immigrant Society: The Goba of Zambia," in Kopytoff, *Internal African Frontier*, pp. 101–20.

ancestors were the early Shona-speakers (Mapungubwe period), who were progressively submerged, first by pre-Singo (Khami period) and secondly by Singo newcomers. The *mitupo*, therefore, signals their regressive status, brought about by a sequence of political change and ethnogenesis.[70]

With the comparative aid of historical analogues, the cultural rationale of Venda origins can be outlined, but what specific material conditions drove this process? At Mapungubwe and Great Zimbabwe, prestige trade goods were centralized in the elite areas, and the same applied at the fifteenth- and sixteenth-century Khami settlements in the Soutpansberg. Trade, therefore, was controlled by elites. In contrast, the evidence from the fourteenth-century Mapungubwe sites indicates that they were relatively poor in prestige goods. This is not surprising, given that Great Zimbabwe must have dominated trade relations with the southeast African coast at this time. With the fifteenth-century expansion of Torwa period chiefs southeastward across the Limpopo and the collapse of Great Zimbabwe, the intensity of trade contacts with the East African coast picked up. In addition, the Portuguese wrested control of the coastal trading entrepôts early in the sixteenth century and changed the dynamics of trade with the Zimbabwe interior by trying to establish a more direct approach.[71]

Ambitious Khami polities in the eastern Soutpansberg were consequently well placed to initiate new trading links, whereas the Portuguese pursued the mythical Ophir further to the north. The initial motivation behind the fifteenth-century Khami expansion south across the Limpopo may have been to locate and acquire new gold, copper, and ivory sources for trade. The end result was their independence, which, as the archaeology shows, was modeled on the political and cultural forms to the northwest of the Limpopo. Increasing dislocation of this internal frontier from the Khami "metropole" may have driven interaction, intermarriage, and ethnogenesis between Shona- and Sotho-speaking communities. The appearance of a consolidated Venda identity in the sixteenth century may have been a full expression of economic and political independence that facilitated control of regional resources and coordinated production. Whatever the case, this period was one of intense trade in which copper, gold, ivory, and less tangible commodities such as salt were traded out.[72] Copper mining and export

---

[70] *Ibid.*

[71] I. Pikirayi, *The Archaeological Identity of the Mutapa State: Towards an Historical Archaeology of Northern Zimbabwe* (Uppsala: Societas Archaeologica Upsaliensis, 1993).

[72] M. Kusel, "A Preliminary Report on Settlement Layout and Gold Mining at Thula Mela, a Late Iron Age Site in the Kruger National Park," *Koedoe, 35*(1) (1992), pp. 55–64; M. Steyn, S. Miller, W. C. Neinaber, and M. Loots, "Late Iron Age Gold Burials From Thulamela (Pafuri region, Kruger National Park)," *South African Archaeological Bulletin, 53* (1998), pp. 102–6.

were centered on the rich but localized ore deposits at Musina, Phalaborwa, Gravelotte, and Leydsdorp.[73] At the interstices of Venda identity, specialist providers, such as the Lemba, were closely linked to the Venda through copper production at the Musina mines (Fig. 3.1).[74]

The Singo State, established late in the seventeenth century, continued the external trade along much the same lines, with the help of co-opted pre-Singo traders. Metal production was still a major focus and the capital at Dzata was a point of central control. The benefits from trade still accrued to elites, as indicated by the presence of prestige goods at royal settlements. Those who adopted the Singo *mitupo* and shifted their ethnic allegiance gained an economic advantage.[75] Mahumane directly observed the Singo trading state in 1728 and 1729, a time when the Singo must have been near the height of their power, and a reference to "Palaote" (the Phalaborwa area) in the eastern Lowveld indicates the relatively large area under the control of the Singo at this time.[76] It is significant, however, that in the early eighteenth century, the Singo state traded more intensively through the Dutch and some English at Delagoa Bay, whereas the outlet for earlier Venda trade was through Sofala and Inhambane. Dutch records show that a fluctuating, but at times significant, amount of copper and tin arrived at Delagoa Bay from the interior.[77] The copper came from the Phalaborwa mines in the eastern Lowveld and the Musina mines on the Limpopo in the far north, and the tin probably came from Rooiberg to the southwest (Fig. 3.2).

The shift in trade outlets southward along the coast to Delagoa Bay and the competition between Dutch and British traders for goods from the interior stretched trade routes from the Singo state to this outlet. The balance of trading power tilted increasingly toward the interior Sotho/Tswana-speaking communities of the Lowveld and escarpment areas to the south, who were closer to the outlet. With diminishing authority over the east coast trade, Singo power declined and, in the second half of the eighteenth

[73] T. M. Evers, "Iron Age Trade in the Eastern Transvaal," *South African Archaeological Bulletin, 29* (1974), pp. 33–7; Loubser, "The ethnoarchaeology of Venda-speakers," p. 413.

[74] The Lemba identity may also have been premised on "first people" status and their ritual relationship with the land. In order to consolidate their occupation of a specialized productive niche, and move freely and unencumbered by ethnic affiliation, they constructed an independent identity bolstered by endogamy.

[75] Loubser, "The ethnoarchaeology of Venda-speakers," p. 415.

[76] G. Liesegang, "New Light on Venda Traditions: Mahumane's Account of 1730," *History in Africa* IV (1977), pp. 172–3.

[77] H. M. Friede and R. H. Steel, "Tin mining and smelting in the Transvaal during the Iron Age," *Journal of Southern African Institute for Mining and Metallurgy,* 74 (1976), pp. 461–70.

century, there were succession disputes, political fragmentation, and settlement relocations to defensive hilltop settlements that continued into
the nineteenth century.[78] With this shift of trading power further to the
south during the eighteenth century, we now turn our attention back to
the interior Sotho/Tswana- and coastal Nguni-speaking communities of
KwaZulu-Natal, the escarpment areas, the far western interior, and the
predominantly grassland habitats south of the Vaal River.

SOTHO/TSWANA- AND NGUNI-SPEAKERS FROM THE SEVENTEENTH CENTURY

From the early sixteenth century, the identities represented by the archaeology of these later farming communities can be increasingly resolved through
the oral records, and detailed ethnographic comparisons can be made
with some confidence because of the close historical proximity between
ethnographic source and subject. However, the first fourteenth-century
Sotho/Tswana settlements identified in the northern areas south of the
Limpopo lie beyond the recall of oral records.[79] By the mid-fifteenth and
early sixteenth centuries, Sotho/Tswana-speakers had pushed southward
and settled as far as the southern edge of the mixed Bushveld habitats that
lie against the grasslands of the Highveld immediately to the south. At
this time, dry stone walling starts to be used to mark essential settlement
boundaries and by the early seventeenth century Sotho/Tswana people had
extended their range even further and settled south of the Vaal River in the
northern and eastern grasslands of the Free State.[80] This was the first time
mixed farmers had breached the Bushveld boundary (Fig. 3.2).

Early Sotho/Tswana Settlement of the Bushveld

The oral records describe a migration from the north, perhaps from
Botswana, and the emplacement of a founding Tswana identity in the core
Tswana areas of present-day Rustenburg and Marico by the late fifteenth

---

[78] Loubser, "Archaeology and early Venda history," p. 58.

[79] See E. O. M. Hanisch, "Excavations at Icon, Northern Transvaal," *South African Archaeological Society Goodwin Series, 3* (1979), pp. 72–9; T. N. Huffman, "Regionality in the
Iron Age: The Case of the Sotho-Tswana," *Southern African Humanities, 14* (2002), pp.
1–22; Vogel and Fuls, "The Spatial Distribution of Radiocarbon Dates."

[80] Maggs, "Iron Age Communities"; R. Mason, *Origins of Black People of Johannesburg
and the Southern Western Central Transvaal* AD *350–1880*, Occasional Paper No. 16
(Johannesburg: University of Witwatersrand Press, 1986); J. J. B. Dreyer, "The Iron Age
Archaeology of Doornpoort, Winburg, Orange Free State," *Navorsinge van die Nasion-
ale Museum, Bloemfontein, 8*(7) (1992), pp. 261–390; J. C. A. Boeyens, "In Search of
Kaditshwene," *South African Archaeological Bulletin, 55* (2000), pp. 3–17.

century. The emphasis on the western areas of the trans-Vaal and adjacent eastern Botswana as the growth point of a core Tswana identity is elaborated in the creation myth of Matsieng, an apical Tswana ancestor who is described as emerging from a hole in the earth. Rock cavities and sumps in riverbeds immediately to the northeast of present-day Gaborone are commonly linked to the myth.[81] Associated with these holes are petroglyphs of human and feline footprints that have a hunter–gatherer (Later Stone Age) authorship and may exemplify Tswana appropriation of signs of the quintessential "first peoples."[82] The myth has several variants, one of which describes how animals, followed by the San and lastly by Matsieng, emerged serially to populate the earth. Although this myth is widespread within the western Tswana world and was recorded by early European travelers north of the Gariep River, there is a hint that the possession of the myth originally lay primarily within the Hurutshe and Kwena lineages and, consequently, is a historical resource that establishes their political precedence.[83] Archaeologically derived dates rein in oral claims of the presence of specific Tswana identities, such as the Barolong, in the thirteenth and fourteenth centuries, and discourage the view that chiefdoms entered this area with their historically defined identities intact.[84] The oral records begin to contribute specific detail for the mid-second millennium onward, from which point more detailed correlations can be made with the archaeology.[85]

By the late fifteenth and sixteenth centuries ancestral Tswana settlements were well established in the Bushveld habitats below the 1,500 m contour line and to the north of the southern grasslands. The preference was for building homesteads along the basal contours of low hills and, in contrast to Early Iron Age settlement location, riversides were avoided.[86] Homesteads

[81] N. Walker, "In the Footsteps of the Ancestors: The Matsieng Creation Site in Botswana," *South African Archaeological Bulletin*, 52 (1997), pp. 95–104.

[82] S. Ouzman, "Spiritual and Political Uses of a Rock Engraving Site and its Imagery by San and Tswana-speakers," *South African Archaeological Bulletin*, 50 (1995), pp. 55–67.

[83] J. Campbell, *Travels in South Africa, 1813*, 3rd ed. (London: Black and Perry, 1815); J. C. A. Boeyens, "The Late Iron Age Sequence in the Marico and early Tswana history," *South African Archaeological Bulletin*, 58 (2003), pp. 63–78; I. Schapera, *The Tswana* (London: International African Institute, 1943).

[84] P. L. Breutz, *The Tribes of the Rustenburg and Pilanesberg Districts*, Department of Native Affairs, Ethnological Publication No. 28 (1953).

[85] See, for example, T. N. Huffman, "Regionality in the Iron Age: The Case of the Sotho-Tswana," *Southern African Humanities*, 14 (2002), pp. 1–22; A. Manson, "Conflict in the Western Highveld/Southern Kalahari, c. 1750–1820," in Hamilton (Ed.), *The Mfecane Aftermath*, pp. 351–61; N. Parsons, "Prelude to the Difaqane in the Interior of Southern Africa c. 1600-c. 1822," in Hamilton (Ed.), *The Mfecane Aftermath*.

[86] See Chapter 2 in this volume; T. Maggs, "The Iron Age South of the Zambezi," in R. Klein (Ed.), *Southern African Prehistory and Palaeoenvironments* (Rotterdam: A. A. Balkema, 1984), pp. 329–60.

conform to the Central Cattle Pattern layout, with central cattle byres and a surrounding domestic circle of households. Although preservation at early Sotho/Tswana sites is frequently poor, direct evidence for sorghum and millet agriculture has been recovered by Mason at Olifantspoort and further to the west at Magozastad.[87] The relatively high visibility of early ancestral Tswana homesteads in this area reflects the success of a mixed agricultural economy in a well-resourced habitat.

It is possible that in the Marico area these early Sotho/Tswana sites are associated with early Hurutshe oral records.[88] Barolong are also associated with this region and would, therefore, possibly predate fission and the later independent establishment of these identities, particularly of the BaRolong, to the south. The archaeology, however, does not encourage the view that the core Hurutshe and Kwena lineages in the west were a united confederacy, or that the expansion of Tswana lineages in the seventeenth century can be viewed as state growth, because settlements are small and relatively dispersed.[89] There is no evidence on the basis of settlement size, cattle enclosure size, or the presence of extravagant midden deposits associated with central courts, to indicate marked wealth, status differences, or political hierarchy. Most early Sotho/Tswana homesteads appear to be self-sufficient and no glass trade beads have been reported for this region.[90] There are, however, clear cultural continuities between the organization of early Tswana settlements and the ethnographic present, most notably in the organization of space and architectural detail.[91]

Developments in the Seventeenth Century

Between AD 1550 and 1650 there were further developments in the Sotho/Tswana world. One was their expansion southward across the Vaal River and onto the southern grasslands of the eastern Free State. By the end of

[87] Mason, "Origins"; Boeyens, "The Late Iron Age Sequence in the Marico."

[88] Boeyens, "The Late Iron Age Sequence in the Marico."

[89] See A. Manson, "Conflict in the Western Highveld/Southern Kalahari, c. 1750–1820," in C. Hamilton (Ed.), *The Mfecane Aftermath*, pp. 351–61; Parsons, "Prelude," p. 331.

[90] Mason, "Origins"; Boeyens, "The Late Iron Age Sequence in the Marico."

[91] For detailed discussion and debate about the use of ethnographic models to identify settlement organization and architectural features and to infer the associated social structure and worldview they represent, see, for example, T. N. Huffman, "The Central Cattle Pattern and Interpreting the Past," *Southern African Humanities, 13* (2001), pp. 19–35; S. Hall, "A Consideration of Gender Relations in the Late Iron Age 'Sotho' Sequence of the Western Highveld, South Africa," in S. Kent (Ed.), *Gender in African Prehistory* (Walnut Creek, London, New Delhi: Altamira Press, 1998) pp. 235–58; P. Lane, 1998, "Engendered Spaces and Bodily Practices in the Iron Age of Southern Africa," in Kent (Ed.), *Gender in African Prehistory*, pp. 179–203.

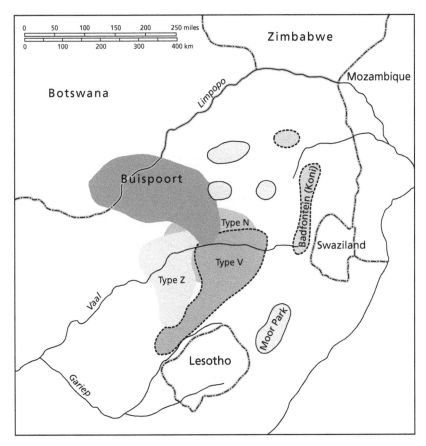

FIGURE 3.3. Map showing the distribution of Sotho/Tswana and Nguni stone-wall settlements after the mid-fifteenth century.

the seventeenth century, Sotho/Tswana-speakers had pushed against the southern climatic limits of viable sorghum and millet agriculture, marked by the 500 mm edge of the summer rainfall region (Figs. 3.3 & 3.4). This was the first systematic exploitation of these southern grasslands by farmers, and therefore the question of timing and motivation is of interest. One possibility is that movement was encouraged by a period of warmer and wetter climatic conditions during the Little Ice Age.[92] It must be remembered that African farming systems are resilient and adaptable and many varieties of sorghum and millet have been developed to

[92] Vogel and Fuls, "The Spatial Distribution of Radiocarbon Dates"; Huffman, "Archaeological Evidence for Climatic Change"; see also Huffman, "Archaeology of the Nguni past," for correlations between second-millennium climatic changes and Nguni-speaking diasporas from present-day KwaZulu-Natal.

FIGURE 3.4. Map showing the location of some late eighteenth and early nineteenth century western and southern Tswana towns.

reduce risk in conditions of low predictability and uncertainty. Further-more, a return to drier conditions after AD 1675 did not seriously hamper settlement.[93]

A second trend was the increasing use of drystone walling as a replace-ment for pole and thatch boundaries to enclose cattle enclosures, homestead edges, and other activity areas within homesteads. Walling shows up clearly on aerial photographs, particularly in the open grassland environments onto which farmers moved. In the context of the relatively wood-poor habitats of the Highveld, this innovation makes good sense, particularly if climatic conditions restrained tree growth and the availability of wood. Walling, however, is also a parallel innovation in Bushveld regions where wood must have been readily available. In such cases, the move toward stone bound-aries may be an index that farmers were perceptibly placing pressure on

[93] Breutz, *Tribes of the Rustenburg and Pilanesberg Districts*; P. J. Quinn, *Food and Feeding Habits of the Pedi* (Johannesburg: Witwatersrand University Press, 1959); H. O. Monning, *The Pedi* (Pretoria: Van Schaik, 1967); Boeyens, "The Late Iron Age Sequence in the Marico."

key resources and the use of walling provides an obvious way of creating sustainability in wood. In addition, the high visibility of stone-wall settlements may give a false impression of increasing settlement density because they were obviously not all occupied at the same time. It is nevertheless reasonable to infer that the population was increasing at this time and, consequently, the relationship between space, resources, and sustainability had to be managed. Within this relationship, it may have become more important to mark homesteads more firmly.[94]

The high visibility of these settlements on aerial photographs was first systematically exploited by archaeologists in the late 1960s. Large numbers of settlements were identified, distributions mapped, and variability in settlement densities noted.[95] The visibility also encouraged the identification of different settlement types or styles which, like pottery, was expressive of identity. The distribution of settlement types was linked to smaller-scale Sotho/Tswana identities through the oral records. Consequently, the earliest distinctive settlements (known as Type N; Fig. 3.3) in the northeastern Free State date to the sixteenth century, and the "type-site," Ntsuanatsatsi, can be linked through oral records to the Bafokeng, who were later joined by Kgatla and Kwena lineages. Origin myths recall that people first emerged from a marsh at Ntsuanatsatsi and this is conceptually similar to the creation myths of Matsieng. The construction of beehive-shaped huts at Type N settlements and ceramic features that recall Nguni style suggest, however, considerable Nguni influence in the cultural complexion of Type N settlements.[96] Obviously, there were considerable interethnic exchanges between Nguni-speakers east of the escarpment and Sotho/Tswana-speakers to the west. A "Makgwareng" settlement type (Maggss Type V; Fig. 3.3), dating between the seventeenth and early nineteenth centuries overlay Type N settlements but also expanded beyond the southern distribution of Type N settlements. These settlements can be linked to southern Sotho lineages (Taung). In the southwest a "Thabeng" type (Maggs Type Z) is associated with seventeenth- and eighteenth-century Tlhaping and Rolong lineages that had their origins in the Tswana core area in the region of present-day

[94] See Hall, "Gender Relationships."

[95] Maggs, "Iron Age Communities"; T. Maggs, "Iron Age Patterns and Sotho History on the Southern Highveld," *World Archaeology*, 7(3) (1976), pp. 318–32; for the early use of aerial photography to identify the distribution of Sotho/Tswana settlements, see R. Mason, "Iron Age Settlement in the Transvaal and Natal Revealed by Aerial Photography and Excavation," *African Studies*, 27 (1968), pp. 181–8.

[96] M. Legassick, "The Sotho-Tswana Peoples Before 1800," in L. Thompson (Ed.), *African Societies in Southern Africa* (London: Heinemann, 1969), pp. 6–125; Dreyer, "The Archaeology of Doornpoort"; see also Huffman, "Regionality."

Zeerust. In the Marico and Rustenburg areas, distinctive stonewall settlements with scalloped boundaries and "Buispoort" pottery is associated with western Tswana Hurutshe and Kwena lineages (Figs. 3.3 & 3.4).[97] Overall, there is a general concordance between historically recorded identities and the distribution of distinctive settlement types.

Nguni-speaking Diasporas

It has already been noted that the expansion of farmers south of the Vaal River in the sixteenth and seventeenth centuries was not linked solely to Sotho/Tswana identities. The derivation of Type N settlements and the Fokeng occupants also points to Nguni origins and is one example of movements of Nguni-speakers from east to west over the escarpment, and described as "The Trans-Vaal Ndebele (Tebele) Diaspora."[98] These movements to the west break down the escarpment as an axiomatic boundary between the two major linguistic identities. Nguni-speakers, labeled with the Sotho/Tswana term "Matebele," are negatively cast in the mold of mercenaries and brigands, despite the fact that most were assimilated by the dominant Sotho/Tswana matrix into which they moved. The term has some time depth and is not reserved only for the early nineteenth-century incursions of Mzilikazi's amaNdebele west of the escarpment. In order to discuss the history of Nguni-speakers west of the escarpment it is necessary to outline briefly the Nguni archaeology of KwaZulu-Natal, which is contemporary with the archaeology west of the escarpment that has been reviewed so far.

Compared to the relatively detailed picture we currently have of the early history of Sotho/Tswana-speakers, Nguni archaeology in KwaZulu-Natal is less well known. This is the result, in part, of the difficulty of locating earlier Nguni settlements and to variable preservation. Furthermore, the establishment of the Zulu state early in the nineteenth century erased much of the earlier oral record. In contrast, our knowledge of Nguni-speakers in the context of Sotho/Tswana-speakers west of the escarpment prior to the nineteenth century is clearer.

The first Nguni settlements in KwaZulu-Natal are dated to the eleventh and twelfth centuries. There is a complete break from the terminal phase of the Early Iron Age in terms of ceramic and settlement style and settlement location, and there is no cultural continuity between the two. The first phase of Nguni settlement (Blackburn) lasts until about AD 1300. The

---

[97] Maggs, "Iron Age Communities"; Mason, "Origins"; Huffman, "Regionality."

[98] Parsons, "Prelude," p. 331; Huffman, "Archaeology of the Nguni Past."

coastal settlement of Mpambanyoni also indicates that gathered marine resources were relatively important when settled in coastal locations.[99]

A second phase, referred to as Moor Park, is longer-lived and dates between the fourteenth and eighteenth centuries. During this phase farmers expanded into the KwaZulu-Natal midlands and occupied higher grassland spurs and were the first to use stone to construct settlement boundaries. Although the evidence at Moor Park sites is limited, full mixed farming was practiced despite the settlement locations on steep slopes at some distance from water and arable land. These locations suggest a concern with defense that may have prompted competition in the less favorable cooler and drier conditions at the start of the Little Ice Age.[100] Moor Park ceramics are also found to the south on the Pondoland coast and in the Eastern Cape borderlands near Grahamstown by the fifteenth century, if not earlier.[101] Contrary to the colonial version that saw the southern Nguni arrival as contemporary with their own, the ancestors of the amaXhosa had long settled these areas at the southern limits of mixed cattle and crop farming.

Early Moor Park sites fall outside the range of oral records, but the archaeological evidence identifies an early sixteenth-century movement of Moor Park Nguni-speakers out of KwaZulu-Natal. Some of these farmers moved into the Waterberg of Limpopo province and, once again, selected defensive locations on the tops of steep-sided hills. Their arrival clearly created competition with the established Sotho/Tswana matrix into which they had moved because some contemporary Sotho/Tswana settlements were also perched on top of defensive hilltop aeries.[102] This stand-off probably persisted only for a short time before these Nguni immigrants were integrated into Sotho/Tswana society, presumably through intermarriage, and their distinctive settlement style fades from the record. Although we have no details about this process, the familiar conditions of the internal frontier were once again created by the juxtaposition of newcomers with firstcomers. Interestingly, in this case, the newcomers acceded to the cultural structures of those already in residence.

---

[99] R. T. Mpambanyoni, "A Late Iron Age Site on the Natal South Coast," *Annals of the Natal Museum*, 24(1) (1980), pp. 147–64.

[100] Huffman, "Archaeology of the Nguni Past."

[101] R. M. Derricourt, *Prehistoric man in the Ciskei and Transkei* (Cape Town: Struik, 1977). S. Hall, "Pastoral adaptions and forager reactions in the eastern Cape," *South African Archaeological Society Goodwin Series*, 5 (1986), pp. 42–9.

[102] S. Hall, "Archaeological Indicators for Stress in the Western Transvaal Region Between the Seventeenth and Nineteenth Centuries," in C. Hamilton (Ed.), *The Mfecane Aftermath*, pp. 307–21.

It was also during the later Moor Park phase that the most significant movement of Nguni-speakers from KwaZulu-Natal occurred. This gave rise to the so-called Northern and Southern Ndebele, based around present-day Mokopane and Pretoria (Tshwane), respectively. Seemingly two separate movements occurred.[103] The Southern amaNdebele trace their descent to a mythical ancestor called Musi, whereas the Northern amaNdebele are linked to the Langa who left from an area in northern KwaZulu-Natal. A combination of archaeological and oral evidence dates these parallel movements to between 1630 and 1670 A.D.[104] The motivation for these movements of Nguni-speakers westward over the escarpment has again been attributed to one of the worst climatic periods of the Little Ice Age.

Manala and Ndzundza Southern Ndebele settlements are well known in the Pretoria area and in Mpumalanga, near Steelpoort. Descendants are also known for their characteristic dress, adornment, and mural art. Although this distinctive expression of identity has its roots in the colonial politics of the nineteenth century, it does have greater time depth. Settlement organization emphasizes certain Moor Park principles that contrast with Sotho/Tswana settlements. In contrast, Ndzundza amaNdebele in the Steelpoort area made ceramics that are stylistically the same as eastern Sotho Pedi pottery.[105] The archaeology confirms a certain degree of insularity among amaNdzundza in relation to eastern Basotho. Settlements expressed the continuity of external origins, whereas the similarities of pottery style show that women could be assimilated through intermarriage, particularly if the principles of exogamy were stringently applied.[106] The contextual subtlety and complexity of interethnic relationships along the borderlands between Nguni- and Sotho/Tswana-speakers is underlined by variable responses of immigrant Nguni communities elsewhere. Other Southern Ndebele lineages and their settlements to the west of Tshwane, for example, such as the Batlokwa, Bapo, and Bamalete can

---

[103] See J. H. N. Loubser, "Ndebele Archaeology of the Pietersburg Area," *Navorsinge van die Nasionale Museum (Bloemfontein), 10* (1994), pp. 61–147, for a summary of the oral evidence for these movements.

[104] Huffman, "Archaeology of the Nguni Past."

[105] M. Schoeman, "Excavating Ndzundza Ndebele identity at KwaMaza," *Southern African Field Archaeology, 7* (1998), pp. 42–52; M. Schoeman, "Material Culture 'under the animal skin': Excavations at Esikhujuni, a Mfecane Period Ndundza Ndebele Site," *Southern African Field Archaeology, 7* (1998), pp. 72–81; Huffman, "Archaeology of the Nguni Past."

[106] Huffman, *Ibid.* For a discussion of relationships between gender dynamics and settlement and ceramic style among Nguni chiefdoms in KwaZulu-Natal, see also M. Hall and K. Mack, "The Outline of an Eighteenth Century Economic System in South-east Africa," *Annals of the South African Museum, 91* (1983), pp. 163–94.

be identified through oral records but are distinctively western Tswana in organization. In these areas, a certain degree of cultural expediency is evident and cultural assimilation must have facilitated the growth of their own economies as independent Tswana chiefdoms in the eighteenth century in a context where resident Kwena lineages were dominant.[107]

Northern Ndebele groups (Langa) such as the Ledwaba settled in the Pholokwane and Mokopane areas, as did the Bamphahlele and Bakgaga, who were all assimilated by various Sotho groups. Pottery, for example, was made in the style of either Sotho/Tswana (North Sotho) or Letaba (Venda) and this again must have downplayed previous connections and aided social and political integration in the wider region. In the Badfontein area of Mpumalanga, there are extensive stone-wall complexes comprising homesteads, long cattle tracks, and large areas of hill-slope agricultural terracing.[108] These complexes are also linked to "Sothoized" Nguni (Koni in Sotho) who were settled in the region before the Pedi, or at least before the development of a historically recognized Pedi identity. The extensive terrace agricultural system on the slopes of the escarpment may indicate a strategy to optimize runoff during dry periods.

This brief survey indicates that the conventional historical divide between Nguni-speakers in KwaZulu-Natal and Sotho/Tswana-speakers to the area west of the escarpment was not fixed. It does seem, however, that exchange between Nguni and Sotho/Tswana was always unidirectional – that is, from east over the escarpment to the west and not the other way round. The seventeenth and eighteenth centuries were a period of significant movement from KwaZulu-Natal and this also may correlate with expansion and developments in the Sotho/Tswana world. Oral records for later periods describe, for example, Nguni movement over the escarpment and into the Caledon Valley, which provided a "bolt-hole" that alleviated ecological and climatic pressures experienced east of the escarpment.[109] Although the gross underlying causality in these exchanges may well be situated in the fluctuating climatic conditions through the Little Ice Age, it nevertheless continually recreated conditions for the physical juxtaposition of different identities, and their coincidence had to be socially and politically negotiated. The details of negotiation within these internal frontiers are, however, still only dimly perceived.

---

[107] Parsons, "Prelude," p. 334.

[108] D. Collett, "Ruin Distributions in the Stone-Walled Settlements of Eastern Transvaal," *South African Journal of Science*, 78 (1982), pp. 39–40; T. Maggs, "Neglected Rock Art: The Rock Engravings of Agriculturist Communities in South Africa," *South African Archaeological Bulletin*, 50(162) (1995), pp. 132–42.

[109] N. Etherington, *The Great Treks: The Transformation of Southern Africa, 1815–1854* (Edinburgh: Pearson Education Limited, 2001).

We also must speculate that demographic dynamics below the escarpment to the east may also have been further complicated by the Portuguese on the southeast African coast from the early part of the sixteenth century. If, for example, the introduction of maize was rapidly integrated into the agricultural mix of coastal Tsonga and Nguni polities and bolstered food production that encouraged population growth, this would have to have been politically managed. Given that the climate in the eighteenth century was better, maize agriculture is likely to have had a significant impact in this period. Maize is a sensitive plant compared to the more robust sorghums and millets, but with the right rainfall conditions the plant can produce significantly more cereal per area cultivated, and because the cob is sheathed, it does not require the intensive labor of crop-watching to keep birds at bay. In the southern Mozambique and KwaZulu-Natal coastal regions, however, the early history of maize is poorly known, and the impact of its presence has not yet been determined.[110] On the basis of distinctive lower grindstones found on sites well to the west of the escarpment, however, and which are interpreted as maize grindstones, maize could have been in use by the seventeenth century.[111]

POLITICAL CENTRALIZATION DURING THE EIGHTEENTH CENTURY

West of the escarpment there was a process of settlement growth during the eighteenth century. This trend climaxed at the end of the eighteenth and early in the nineteenth centuries with the emergence of the large, aggregated towns around which Tswana chiefdoms had developed a more centralized political system. This process of aggregation is most evident in the grassland areas of the Witwatersrand, south into the grasslands across the Vaal River, and along the escarpment areas to the east.[112] The most distinctive aggregations occurred in the southern Bushveld areas of the Magaliesberg, Rustenburg, and Marico areas west of Pretoria (Fig. 3.4). This process of aggregation and town formation was well developed by the early nineteenth century when early European travelers such as William Burchell visited the Tlhaping capital of Dithakong near Kuruman in 1812 (Fig. 3.4).

[110] See, for example, I. Pikirayi, *The Archaeological Identity of the Mutapa State: Towards an Historical Archaeology of Northern Zimbabwe* (Uppsala: Societas Archaeologica Upsaliensis, 1993).

[111] T. N. Huffman "Maize grindstones, Madikwe pottery and ochre mining in precolonial South Africa," *Southern African Humanities*, 18 (2006), pp. 51–70.

[112] M. O. V. Taylor, "Late Iron Age Settlements on the Northern Edge of the Vredefort Dome," unpublished M.A. dissertation, University of the Witwatersrand (1979); Huffman, "Archaeological evidence"; Maggs, "Iron Age Communities."

John Campbell spent a week at the Hurutshe capital of Kaditshwene in 1820 and both provided important eyewitness accounts. The organization of these Tswana towns was very different from that of the capitals in the Shashe/Limpopo area and, whereas the homesteads of chiefs within the towns were characteristically large, they still lived within the body of commoner homesteads with no sharp separation between them.[113]

A central element of the growth of these towns is that they were a defensive response to the *difaqane* (time of troubles), which, in a more expansive definition, started to develop in the mid-eighteenth century and became particularly acute in the early nineteenth century.[114] The archaeological evidence certainly indicates that the classic western Tswana preference for large-town living was not an inherent cultural adaptation to the more arid climates to the west but developed in response to these specific historical conditions.[115] It has also been argued that the construction of large towns emphasized hilltop locations and this also underpinned defense. This cannot be generalized, however, because the open location of several large early nineteenth-century towns in the Rustenburg area suggests less concern with defense (Figs. 3.4 & 3.5). The specific circumstances of each town require individual consideration. Although the contrast with the Sotho/Tswana settlement patterns of the earlier eighteenth and seventeenth century is certainly marked, and the scale of early nineteenth-century western Tswana towns in particular is unique, it is possible that the principle they elaborate is not. There is some evidence that the principle of aggregation was part of Sotho/Tswana organization from a relatively early period.[116] Events in the second half of the eighteenth century may simply have elaborated on this principle.

The historical character of the eighteenth century is captured by Tswana oral histories, which describe the period as one of war and violence.[117] The reality was probably somewhat less stark but there was a growing competitive aggression in which chiefdoms were constantly jostling for ascendancy. The power of senior Tswana chiefdoms such as that of the Bahurutshe in the Marico area was eroded toward the end of the nineteenth century in the face of increasingly assertive chiefdoms immediately to the east. Still

---

[113] For a detailed description of a Tswana town, see J. C. C. Pistorius, *Molokwane, an Iron Age Bakwena Village: Early Tswana Settlement in the Western Transvaal* (Johannesburg: Perskor Printers, 1992).

[114] See Huffman, "Archaeological Evidence"; Manson, "Conflict."

[115] See B. Sansom, "Traditional Economic Systems," in W. D. Hammond-Tooke (Ed.), *The Bantu-speaking Peoples of Southern Africa* (London: Routledge and Kegan Paul, 1974), pp. 135–76; Huffman, "Archaeological Evidence."

[116] See, for example, Maggs, "Iron Age Communities."

[117] Breutz, *Tribes of the Rustenburg and Pilanesberg Districts*.

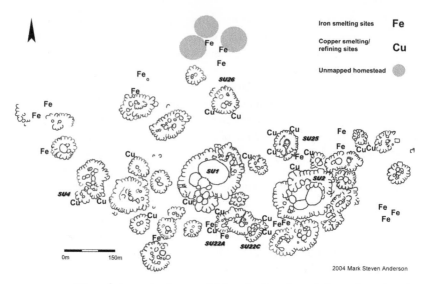

FIGURE 3.5. Map of the central area of Marothodi, a late eighteenth and early nineteenth century Tlokwa town near the Pilanesberg.

further to the east, the Pedi state had considerable regional influence, which was felt as far west as present-day Rustenburg.[118] The Ngwaketse chiefdom grew in power to the northwest and Tlhaping power grew in the south (Fig. 3.4).

Two main reasons have been suggested for these tensions. One focuses on relationships between population, climate, and agricultural production. As indicated previously, there are large numbers of Sotho/Tswana stonewall settlements in the grassland areas south of the Vaal River and in the Bushveld and mixed habitats to the north. Many of these date to the eighteenth century and probably reflect absolute population growth. It is not clear, however, if this was a specific population spurt or whether growth was continuous from the seventeenth century. This is possible because the southward expansion of Sotho/Tswana-speakers in the seventeenth century described previously may reflect natural processes of homestead fission as populations grew in the agriculturally core areas of the southern Bushveld.

In a sense, expansion to the south was into an open frontier, which closed when the southern ecological limits of viable agriculture were reached (Fig. 3.4). Similarly, the agricultural frontier was closed to the southwest, where the Kalahari fringes became marginal for agriculture, as well as to the north, where vectors such as tsetse fly set limits on production.

[118] P. Delius, *The Land Belongs To Us: The Pedi Polity, the Boers and the British in the nineteenth-century Transvaal* (Johannesburg: Ravan Press, 1984).

To the east, Bapedi and Bakgatla were undergoing similar adjustments to some of the same boundary conditions. Once the limits of geographic expansion had been reached, the political and social strategies associated with accommodation within internal frontiers must increasingly have come into play.

The growing tensions through the eighteenth century may reflect continuing but more intense structural adjustments to diminishing land and space and the formulation of political and social strategies that adjusted the limits of production and the way that production was organized. Specific factors hurried these changes along. By the end of the eighteenth century, when some of these Tswana towns had populations of more than 10,000 people, the scale of agricultural production and resource exploitation and its management from single points on the landscape must have required very different strategies from those employed in earlier periods when populations were lower and less densely clustered.

It is clear that for the western Batswana this process was inextricably linked to the centralization of political power. The usual equation applied – wealth in cattle for exchange meant more wives, more children, and more labor. Political security through marriage alliance among elites, however, created longer-term problems because, as elite polygyny increased, so too did conflict over succession, and conflict was further exacerbated by limited space for agnatic fission.[119] Everything about western Batswana developments at this time concerned centralized organization of people, labor, and resources and their control and management.

This process, however, must have been encouraged and complicated by climatic change and agricultural potential. Throughout the eighteenth century, for example, conditions for agriculture appear to have been good and this, in turn, may have encouraged the uptake or intensification of maize agriculture. By the early nineteenth century, maize agriculture may have significantly contributed to and sustained western Tswana political growth.[120] This issue is not satisfactorily resolved. On climatic grounds, these western areas may have been marginal for maize, although the higher than average rainfall conditions through the eighteenth century could have encouraged greater all-around cereal production. Furthermore, although lower grindstones found in late eighteenth-century Tswana towns have the typical "bird-bath" morphology for grinding maize, there is no direct evidence for maize from these settlements. Also, the writings of early nineteenth-century European travelers to the western Tswana areas reveal

[119] Manson, "Conflict," p. 357.
[120] Huffman, "Archaeological Evidence for Climatic Change"; "Archaeology of the Nguni Past."

few references to maize, and it is possible that maize agriculture only intensified after 1826, with the arrival of Mzilikazi from the KwaZulu-Natal area.[121] Whatever the case, a climatic downturn in the early years of the nineteenth century must have exacerbated the competitive violence between chiefdoms caused by dwindling food security. In 1821, for example, Stephen Kay described a general "spiritlessness" at Kaditshwene, induced by food shortage and war.[122] By this time some Tswana towns had grown to a considerable size. Campbell estimated a population of about 20,000 people at Kaditshwene. Estimates for Molokwane (Bakwena) and Marothodi (Batlokwa; Fig. 3.5) near Rustenburg are 12,000 and 7,000 people, respectively, and there were many more contemporary large settlements.[123]

The oral records also frequently refer to cattle raiding and the settlement plans of towns such as Molokwane, Marothodi, and Kaditshwene vividly indicate that powerful chiefs successfully amassed considerable cattle holdings.[124] Raiding, furthermore, was not only about cattle, but also aimed at capturing women. This is not surprising given the competitive advantage that large cattle holdings, as the currency of political power, and women as instruments of labor and fertility, would confer on chiefs. Another aspect to this jostling for power was the increasing strategic and political advantage of location in relation to the control of resources, both for internal and external trade. It seems that an interest in acquiring and controlling ivory, fur, hides, wood, and metal increased and networks deep into the Kalahari and north into the resource rich, but agriculturally less desirable, Limpopo area intensified.[125]

A second factor in political centralization was the encroaching demands and desires of Europeans as they bartered and raided their way north from the Cape Colony in the south and from the coast to the east. Central here was the international demand for elephant ivory – summary statistics show that the quantity of ivory exported from Sofala peaked in 1762, but demand continued into the nineteenth century.[126] The Bangwato were well positioned to expand their influence over key elephant habitats in the Limpopo and across the Kalahari to the northwest and to control production, not only of ivory, but also of prestige fur and feathers (Fig. 3.4). There was also competition over critical copper sources in the Dwarsberg, for example,

---

[121] Boeyens, "The Late Iron Age sequence in the Marico."

[122] S. Kay, *Travel and researches in Caffraria* (London, Mason, 1833), p. 198.

[123] See Mason, "Origins."

[124] Parsons, "Prelude"; Manson, "Conflict"; Pistorius, *Molokwane*; S. Hall, D. Miller, M. Anderson, and J. A. C. Boeyens, "An Exploratory Study of Copper and Iron Production at Marothodi, an Early 19th Century Tswana Town, Rustenburg District, South Africa" (n.d.); Boeyens, "In search of Kaditshwene."

[125] Parsons, "Prelude," pp. 335, 338.   [126] *Ibid.*, p. 341.

and the scale of mining and the archaeological evidence of smelting indicates that much of this production exceeded local needs. Another center of intensive and, possibly, specialized copper and iron production has been identified at Marothodi, an early nineteenth-century Tlokwa town near the Pilanesberg (Fig. 3.5).

In contrast, at Molokwane, a contemporary Kwena town near Rustenburg with a population in excess of 12,000 people, there is no evidence of either copper or iron production.[127] The scale of consumption at towns such as Molokwane must have been immense and underpinned regional resource gradients and complementary production skills. Copper was also a specialist product of the Bahurutshe and the Bangwaketse. They supplied it, along with iron, to the Batlhaping to the south and even further afield, into the Eastern Cape. Tin bronze jewelry found at Marothodi suggests that the Rooiberg tin fields, which were first exploited in the sixteenth century, continued to be an important resource in the eighteenth and early nineteenth centuries. Despite the aggression evident in the oral records, within the western Tswana world of the late-eighteenth and early nineteenth century it appears that the rhythm of day-to-day agricultural and commodity production continued.

Mercantile demands were also intensifying from the Cape Colony (Fig. 3.4). The development of frontier identities in the form of the Griqua and Kora vanguard of the colonial frontier made life along the southern margins of the Sotho/Tswana world increasingly difficult. Their desires focused both on trading and raiding for cattle and people. Ivory, hides, iron, copper, and ochre were all traded south and, in return, the Sotho/Tswana received pack oxen and any goods they could convert into cattle, which were still the premier currency in all aspects of political and social life. The Griqua and the Kora also had a particular advantage over the Sotho/Tswana because, as an extension of the Cape world, they possessed both guns and horses, which southern Tswana were desperate to acquire. Their possession, however, had the effect of fragmenting Tswana communities rather than uniting them because those who acquired guns and horses used them against Tswana rivals. The raiding exploits of people like Jan Bloem from the early 1790s are well known.

Early travelers such as John Campbell noted the immense appetite among the western Tswana for glass trade beads and that, at Kaditshwene, people were somewhat dismissive of his other trinkets. Beads were clearly a currency of trade but this documented profile has not yet been matched archaeologically and most regional trade must have been transacted with cattle, hides, and copper.

---

[127] Hall *et al.*, "An Exploratory Study of Copper"; Boeyens, "The Late Iron Age Sequence of the Marico."

To the east of the western Tswana region, parallel processes of change and centralization were under way among the Bapedi.[128] This is attributed to a similar mix of causal factors that included population pressure, changed relationships between agricultural production, and the weather and competition over trade resources. The latter is particularly important for it highlights the growing influence on interior resources of European mercantile demands from the east coast and the strategic importance of location in relation to the Delagoa Bay outlet in the east and the areas from which those resources were obtained to the west. The Bapedi were clearly at an advantage in terms of controlling the flow of trade goods and the routes that passed through their domain from east to west.

When the vanguard of Mzilikazi's amaNdebele started raiding in the Rustenburg area between 1826 and 1827, strife-weary and fragmented western Tswana chiefdoms offered little resistance and Mzilikazi rapidly imposed himself and a new political order on the region. Some Tswana chiefdoms had already succumbed to inter-Tswana rivalry before his arrival. As suggested by Etherington, Mzilikazi and the amaNdebele eventually brought a certain degree of stability to the western Tswana world because they provided the military structure to repel Griqua and Kora raiders.[129] Many Batswana entered the structures of Mzilikazi's state but others retained some independence within tributary relations to Mzilikazi and still others fled to eke out a precarious living in extreme circumstances.[130] The period from the early 1820s among the western Tswana is considered to be the start of what has been termed the *difaqane*, and Mzilikazi, as both destroyer and nation builder, represents an important part of the *difaqane* in this region. This essay suggests rather that within this region, the time of troubles conventionally identified as the *difaqane* ended a longer period of Tswana political centralization across the eighteenth century. This process was a local response to colonial expansion, intensified trade, and climatic shifts that presented a wider set of opportunities that were challenges most other farmers also had to meet.

Eighteenth-Century Nguni

The mention of Mzilikazi turns attention back to KwaZulu-Natal in the east and the archaeology of the eighteenth century and the leadup to the

---

[128] Delius, "The Land Belongs to Us."

[129] Etherington, "The Great Treks."

[130] Hall, "Archaeological Indicators for Stress"; for preliminary work on the archaeology of Ndebele sites in the Rustenburg area, see J. C. C. Pistorius, "The Matabele Village Which Eluded History (Part 1)," *South African Journal of Ethnology*, 20(1) (1997), 26–38; J. C. C. Pistorius, "The Matabele Village Which Eluded History (Part 2)," *South African Journal of Ethnology*, 20(2) (1997), pp. 43–55.

formation of the Zulu state in the early nineteenth century. This event occurred at the interface with an ever-increasing colonial presence and the colonial imagination highlighted the ruthless and predatory nature of the Zulu state. In part, because of this colonial gaze, the widespread political and social upheavals of the early nineteenth century, described by the term *mfecane* (*difaqane* in Sotho), was singularly centered on the Zulu state and events elsewhere in the interior of South Africa were naturally seen as driven by it. As outlined previously for the western Tswana, this view cannot be sustained because this was a parallel and earlier response to some of the same factors. These comparative perspectives decenter the rise of the Zulu state as prime *mfecane* motor.[131] The origins and establishment of the Zulu state, therefore, were also a response and not the cause of the *mfecane*.[132] Events that preceded the Zulu state in the later eighteenth century are, therefore, important. They focus on the increasing intensity of ivory trade (noted previously) with the Dutch and British through the outlet at Delagoa Bay. Cattle trade also intensified and there was heightened raiding in an effort to meet demands.[133] Mention has been made previously of the potential demographic impact of maize agriculture and it is probable that maize was well integrated into Nguni-farming systems at this time.[134] It was within this context that Zwide's forceful political ambitions in northern KwaZulu-Natal were among the factors that precipitated the events that led to the Zulu response.

What can the archaeology contribute to an understanding of these events? Given that trade, population expansion, intensive cattle production for trade, and ecological imbalance all have material correlates the potential exists for archaeology to explore these attributes of rising tension in the pre-Zulu period.[135] The archaeological phase within which the events unfolded has been labeled the Nqabeni phase, after a type site of that name.[136] Within this phase several settlement types have been identified

---

[131] Hamilton (Ed.), *The Mfecane Aftermath*.

[132] See Chapter 5 by John Wright for details of the late eighteenth- and nineteenth-century history of KwaZulu-Natal.

[133] J. Wright and C. Hamilton, "Traditions and Transformations: The Phongolo-Mzimkhulu Region in the Late Eighteenth and Early Nineteenth Centuries," in A. H. Duminy and B. Guest (Eds.), *Natal and Zululand From the Earliest Times to 1910: A New History* (Pietermaritzburg: University of Natal Press and Shuter & Shooter, 1989), pp. 48–82.

[134] See T. Maggs, "The Iron Age Farming Communities," in A. H. Duminy and B. Guest (Eds.), *Natal and Zululand From The Earliest Times To 1910: A New History* (Pietermaritzburg: University of Natal Press and Shuter & Shooter, 1989), pp. 28–48.

[135] Hall and Mack, "Outline," pp. 163–94.

[136] See M. Hall and T. Maggs, "Nqabeni: A Late Iron Age site in Zululand," *South African Archaeological Society Goodwin Series, 3* (1979), pp. 159–76; Huffman, "The Archaeology of the Nguni Past."

by means of the visibility of stone-walling to make boundaries. These types differ in spatial arrangement from Zulu homesteads. Stone is used only to construct the central cattle byres and associated enclosures and not to define the domestic ring. Settlement style, therefore, was explicitly expressed in the arrangement of male areas. Furthermore, the distribution of these settlement styles occurs in relatively small areas and can be correlated with individual chiefdoms, the boundaries of which have been reconstructed with the help of oral records.

Type B (after Babanango) sites, for example, mostly fall within the reconstructed boundaries of the Khumalo chiefdom as it was toward the end of the eighteenth century.[137] In contrast to the relatively small-scale male expressions of political identity, ceramic style crosscuts these boundaries, and this must relate to the practice of exogamous marriage practices and the wider geographic exchange of wives. The boundaries of these chiefdoms also have been analyzed in relation to carrying capacity, and the conclusion is that most enclose a complementary mix of seasonal grazing types, and consequently most chiefdoms were configured to optimize cattle production. Analysis of cattle bone and the age at which the cattle were slaughtered backs this up. It is difficult, however, without a longer chronological sequence with which to compare it, to be categorical about whether the optimal production identified was specific to the period, and consequently ask whether it was rising or declining, or was normal Nguni practice, irrespective of time. The reconstructed chiefdoms, however, and the density of settlements within them suggest that conventional models of dispersed settlement patterns have been overemphasized to the detriment of recognizing a more aggregated scale of political organization "beyond the lineage segment."[138] On most counts, therefore, the archaeology successfully contributes to outlining the structure of pre-Zulu state economic and political systems, but without a comparative perspective it is difficult to say whether this structure was part of a trend.[139]

One point emphasized in this work is that the distinctions between Nguni settlement organization in the eighteenth century are at odds with the patterns that would be predicted from the ethnographic present, and this has implications for interpretation because the ampliative role of analogy for inferring the form of features that are beyond archaeological recovery is potentially false. The assumption that Type B huts, which were archaeologically invisible, were beehive in form, for example, is questioned because

[137] Hall and Mack, "Outline"; Hall and Maggs, "Nqabeni."

[138] M. Hall, "The Myth of the Zulu Homestead: Archaeology and Ethnography," *Africa, 54* (1984), pp. 65–76.

[139] Hall and Mack, "Outline," pp. 163–94.

the visible analogical relationship at the scale of homestead organization breaks down.[140] The analogical method is problematic because it imposes a static "presentism" upon the past. However, in this case, and in line with the comparative rather than imposing role of analogy suggested in the introduction to this chapter, change and difference have been identified. It remains for the historian to ask why this is so. The issue of congruence between historic and archaeological observation forms part of the approach used by archaeologists working in the context of the Zulu state. Excavations at Mgungundlovu, occupied by Dingane between 1829 and 1838, verify the structure and organization of this military town and add detail to eyewitness accounts and sketch maps of the settlement.[141] At this shallow time depth and specific context, the congruence between historical records and archaeology is high.

THE SAN AS HISTORICAL PLAYERS

Up to this point San hunter–gatherer interactions with farmers have been mentioned only in passing. To omit them would seriously misrepresent their presence and role in the context of second-millennium farmers and perpetuate images of the San as marginal to the mainstream histories of agropastoralists. This is clearly not the case. Excavated evidence and rock art provide a more complex insight into the way the San reworked the relevance of their world for themselves and for farmers. The rock art in particular provides insight into San relationships from their own point of view.[142]

As discussed in Chapter 2, any understanding of the roles, rivalries, and exchanges farmers and the San entered into need specific contextual understanding. There are some areas where the evidence allows this and specific historical interactions with farmers can be outlined in more detail. Furthermore, we cannot assume that second-millennium interactions continue the patterns broadly outlined for the first millennium.[143] Does, for example,

[140] Hall, "Myth of the Zulu Homestead," p. 78.

[141] J. E. Parkington and M. Cronin, "The Size and Layout of Mgungundlovu 1829–1838," *South African Archaeological Society Goodwin Series, 4* (1979), pp. 133–48.

[142] C. Campbell, "Images of War: A Problem in San Rock Art Research," *World Archaeology, 18* (1986), pp. 255–68; T. A. Dowson, "Reading Art, Writing History: Rock Art and Social Change in Southern Africa," *World Archaeology, 25* (1994), pp. 332–44; T. A. Dowson, "Hunter–gatherers, Traders and Slaves: The 'Mfecane' Impact on Bushmen, Their Ritual and Their Art," in C. Hamilton (Ed.), *The Mfecane Aftermath*; see also J. Kinahan, *Pastoral Nomads of the Central Namib Desert: The People History Forgot* (Windhoek: New Namibia Books, 1991).

[143] See Chapter 2 in this volume.

the general model of hunter–gatherers as the ultimate "first people" and the ritual role this status confers on them and their relations with farmers hold in the second millennium? Indeed, it may be that the model intensifies as farmers increasingly domesticated the landscape, and this placed more constraint on the economic independence of huntergatherers. As described previously, new areas were settled by Tswana-, Sotho- and Nguni-speaking farmers, and previously farmed areas were exploited more intensively, thereby continually redefining and constraining frontiers and the interactive setting. In addition, the details of Nguni and Sotho/Tswana and San social structure must have differed from those of the first millennium and this must also have created new possibilities and conditions for interaction. What follows is a brief summary of two general areas. The first is the areas north of the Vaal River, and the second concentrates on the areas to the south of the Vaal, in particular the foothills and higher ground of the Drakensberg escarpment in the east and the Caledon River Valley to the west of Lesotho.

North of the Vaal River, rock shelter sequences provide some comparisons between the hunter–gatherer occupations of the first and second millennium. In general, although first-millennium deposits contain obvious indices of interaction with farmers, such as pottery, there is much continuity in hunter–gatherer material culture in the form of microlithic stone tools, bone work, and ostrich eggshell beads. If this continuity in the norms of tool manufacture represents cohesive hunter–gatherer systems, the breakdown of these artifactual norms, which is widespread in the second millennium A.D., indicates considerable change in hunter–gatherer society. In southeastern Botswana, for example, the second millennium is referred to as the Late Contact period in which "degraded," "ex-Late Stone Age" hunter–gatherers lived in varying degrees of dependency upon neighboring Tswana farmers, a pattern that seems to be described by European observers in the nineteenth century.[144] It may be, however, that these records, although emphasizing the marginal and degraded status of the San in the context of Tswana farmers, pay less attention to the continuing ambiguity of the San as "first people" and the reciprocal advantages this status may have conferred on both.[145]

Although a focus on rock shelters gives a powerful impression of hunter–gatherer change through time and some idea of what kinds of interactions

---

[144] K. Sadr, "Encapsulated Bushmen in the Archaeology of Thamaga," in S. Kent (Ed.), *Ethnicity, Hunter–gatherers and the 'Other': Association or Assimilation in Africa* (Washington, D.C.: Smithsonian Institution Press, 2002), pp. 28–47.

[145] See, for example, E. Cashdan, "Coping With Risk: Reciprocity Among the Basarwa of Northern Botswana," *Man*, 20 (1985), pp. 454–74.

took place, it is difficult to construct the specific nature of these. Clearly, a focus only on the hunter–gatherer rock shelter side of the frontier provides only one-half of the picture, whereas the identification of San residues in farmer settlements provides an opportunity to examine interaction that is unequivocally face-to-face.

In early Tswana settlements dating to the sixteenth century A.D. in the Madikwe area, for example, San tool residues have been found in the back courtyards of individual households. This provides a method of assessing how Tswana farmers socially constructed hunter–gatherers by identifying the kinds of spaces hunter–gatherers were allowed to enter when inside a Tswana homestead. On ethnographic grounds, for example, the back court-yard position for the San is entirely appropriate because it is, essentially, a female space. This is where women store and can grind cereal, prepare food, and store kitchen utensils. The close proximity between the back courtyard, agricultural transformation, and the "wild" domain outside the homestead where women work is also appropriate for hunter–gatherers, because they live within that wild domain. Like women, they are not "complete" people. Neither women nor the San were ever fully socialized and therefore could not formally possess or control cattle, and the residues of San presence in back courtyards cast them in this less than social guise. The proximity to the bush, however, fundamentally underpinned the power of the San to live in that world and also potentially to influence its transformation in favor of farmers. These residues may, in fact, represent ritual, rather than practical work.[146]

The decay evident in second-millennium San material culture suggests that farmers increasingly complicated the landscape for them. Reductions in space and resource shortfalls were more intensively transferred to their rela-tionships with farmers. Further to the east, in the Magaliesberg, this trend is visible in hunter–gatherer sequences that also capture the disintegra-tion of traditional hunter–gatherer mobility patterns. Again, identifying this disintegration depends upon comparison with the first-millennium sequence. This indicates that an annual cycle of formal band aggregation and less formal dispersal phases was progressively fractured and ultimately broke down.[147] In this context, and probably many others, the organic residues upon which a seasonal round is evident and upon which the social imperatives of aggregation and dispersal were indivisibly linked indicate

---

[146] S. Hall, "Forager Lithics and Early Moloko Homesteads at Madikwe," *Natal Museum Journal of Humanities, 12* (2000), pp. 33–50.

[147] L. Wadley, "Changes in the Social Relations of Precolonial Hunter–gatherers after Agropastoralist Contact: An Example from the Magaliesberg, South Africa," *Journal of Anthropological Archaeology, 15* (1996), pp. 205–17.

progressive resource and spatial disruption and, by the fourteenth century, the formal material signatures of San aggregation dissipate.[148]

Similar sequences of decay and fragmentation are discernable in the context of the increasingly complex farming systems of the Shashe/Limpopo. Here hunter–gatherers appear to become only seriously disrupted at the start of the second millennium. Until about AD 1000, hunter–gatherers in close proximity to Zhizo homesteads possessed toolkits that suggest intense hide-working, possibly in client relations with their farmer neighbors. It would seem, however, that as the agriculturist hierarchy in the Shashe/Limpopo area grew, the client niches San conventionally exploited were taken over by commoner farmers at the base of this pyramid.[149]

As discussed previously, the status of firstcomers potentially passed to Zhizo communities in the complex interethnic juxtaposition between the eleventh and thirteenth centuries. In the core areas of K2 and Mapungubwe, power conventional hunter–gatherer material culture disappears rapidly. At face value this would suggest that hunter–gatherers were progressively marginalized as farmer communities attained greater levels of social, economic, and political complexity. As indicated previously, ivory was a key trade resource in this period, and if hunter–gatherers participated in its acquisition they may have moved to regions outside the core areas, which were less heavily exploited. There is, however, also the obvious possibility that hunter–gatherers were still present but had completely shed their conventional material identity and taken on the material persona of farmers. If so, the archaeological recognition of assimilated identities poses an interesting challenge. It is apparent that in areas further to the west in the context of Toutswe settlements, and further west still into the Kalahari, hunter–gatherers were part of regional economies.[150] Their deeper desert hunting abilities must have been welcomed by farmers in terms of acquiring prestige fur and hides, and was a pattern that continued into the nineteenth century when new Tswana polities, such as the Bangwato and Batawana, were also in part supplied by hunter–gatherers. Although the archaeological evidence shows that most key areas of the Kalahari during the second millennium did not fall outside the influence of farmers and their trade networks, revisionists still debate whether hunter–gatherers served these regional systems as a dependent underclass or as agents who interacted and exchanged but retained their ideological independence.[151]

---

[148] See van Doornum, "Spaces and Places."   [149] Hall and Smith, "Empowering Places."
[150] Denbow, "Congo to Kalahari"; "Dialectics."
[151] E. N. Wilmsen, *Land Filled With Flies* (Chicago: Chicago University Press, 1989); Sadr, "Kalahari Archaeology and the Bushmen Debate."

Although hunter–gatherer occupation of Shashe/Limpopo rock shelters ceased, shelters within relatively close proximity to major K2 and Mapungubwe period towns continued to be used, but by farmers. The evidence suggests that this use was not casual or expedient but that shelters were also important places in farmer cosmology. It is possible that there was a deliberate appropriation of hunter–gatherer places because, again, the ambiguity "first people" possessed in relation to living in and, therefore, commanding power over nature, made hunter–gatherer places efficacious in terms of the farmers' own ritual needs. This also may have been a consideration in the choice of rainmaking hills by K2 farmers.[152] The well-documented use by Southern Sotho farmers of paint pigment from eastern Free State rock art sites is a further example of the power the essence of San spirituality had for farmers.

In all these contexts the increasing grip of farmers on the land through the second millennium must have had a serious demographic impact on the viability of San communities. Intermarriage, perhaps dominated by San women marrying into farmer society, must also have contributed to the fragmentation of hunter–gatherers' social structure. Historical records indicate some of the outcomes of intermarriage. In the mountains of the Waterberg to the south of the Shashe/Limpopo, there was a complex sequence of change in a shared landscape that started in the eleventh and twelfth centuries, when both farmers and hunter–gatherers moved in tandem into the Waterberg uplands in response to a decrease in rainfall.

The correlation between a synchronous increase in both farmers and hunter–gatherers in the Waterberg points to mutual dependencies. The historical records for this area and the Soutpansberg, however, suggest that relationships were varied but sequentially shifted toward conflict and subjugation. One outcome that emerges historically is a hybrid category of people referred to as "Vaalpense," a derided mixture of San and farmers who lived and served at the social base of Tswana and Ndebele communities.[153] Their marginal identity was compounded in the nineteenth century by being traded and bartered into Boer society.[154] The development of these new identities is potentially well documented in rock art sequences of the area, where the decay and change documented in

---

[152] M. H. Schoeman, "Imagining rain-places: rain-control and changing ritual landscapes in the Shashe-Limpopo confluence area, South Africa," *The South African Archaeological Bulletin*, 61 (2006), pp. 152–65.

[153] "Vaalpense" – literally "grey stomachs" – describes the menial status of people who are so low they cannot help but be smothered by ash.

[154] M. M. van der Ryst, *The Waterberg Plateau in the Northern Province, Republic of South Africa, in the Later Stone Age*, BAR International Series, 71 (1998).

everyday artifacts also are reflected in what has been referred to as "Art of the Apocalypse."[155]

In the Tswana world on the fringes of the Kalahari to the west and southwest, the San also historically emerge as a menial and exploited category ("Balala"). It remains to be seen whether western Tswana centralization in the second half of the eighteenth century exacerbated this process or whether this status was long lived. In the rock shelters of the Waterberg, Blaauberg, Magabeng, and Soutpansberg, a relatively recent "Late White" rock art tradition emerges that, in its images and cruder finger-painted style, falls completely outside the conventions broadly identifiable as Khoisan art. These images are the work of Sotho/Tswana-speakers and underpin initiation and issues of fertility.[156]

To the south of the Vaal River, a set of new frontier conditions developed through the second millennium A.D. with the arrival of Nguni-speakers, whose cultural approach and attitude to the landscape differed markedly from those of first-millennium farmers. As outlined previously, their settlement ranges expanded onto the higher lying grasslands and, by the sixteenth century, they had pushed the range of farming well outside the Bushveld habitats favored by first-millennium farmers. Furthermore, the parallel expansion of Sotho/Tswana-speakers south of the Vaal River and up to the southern environmental limits of sorghum and millet agriculture further complicated these areas, where the San, up to this point, had not been directly confronted. Prior to this southward expansion these areas potentially provided a physical retreat for the San although there is evidence for the existence of networks with the San well beyond the Bushveld boundaries of fourteenth- and fifteenth-century farmers.[157] By the seventeenth century, farming expansion lapped up against the mountains of Lesotho and increasingly a series of well-resolved frontiers developed on the western, northern, and eastern edges of this high ground.

Rock art imagery that explicitly depicts cattle, Sotho shields, horses, riders, Europeans, and guns tells of a complex creole in which Nguni, Sotho, and a growing colonial presence, including Kora and Griqua raider/herders/traders, increasingly pressed upon the independence of the San.[158] An important theme in much interpretation of the San during this period is that

[155] S. Ouzman and J. H. N. Loubser, "Art of the Apocalypse," *Discovering Archaeology, 2* (2000), pp. 38–44.

[156] See Hall and Smith, "Empowering Places."

[157] C. Thorp, *Hunter–gatherers and Farmers: An Enduring Frontier in the Caledon Valley, South Africa* (Oxford: British Archaeological Reports, 2000).

[158] T. A. Dowson, G. Blundell, and S. Hall, "Finger Paintings in the Harts River Valley, Northern Cape Province, South Africa," *Southern African Field Archaeology, 1* (1992), pp. 27–32; L. Wadley, "Who Lived at Mauermanshoek Shelter, Korannaberg, South Africa," *African Archaeological Review, 18* (2001), pp. 153–79.

rock art provides a window into their own action in this world as historically relevant and socially dynamic in their accommodation to change. This approach vigorously seeks to dismantle enduring colonial stereotypes of the San as passive, irrelevant, and marginal players who occupied the nooks and crannies of the farmer and colonial worlds as isolated relics. A more serious interpretive challenge is aimed at the image portrayed by ardent revisionists of the San as a dependent lower class within farmer society.[159] The rock art imagery provides a subtle but increasingly penetrating commentary on the active strategies employed by San communities to accommodate their condition and mold new opportunities through their own cultural filters and action. The rock art, and the specifically exotic nature of the images, also provides some chronological anchors and much of this "contact" art may be relatively recent. Indeed, it is within the context of the increasingly turbulent colonial politics of the late eighteenth century, and continuing through the nineteenth, that much of this contact art finds its meaning.

Clearly, a key question is what motivated the San to include animal domesticates in their art and what were the social and historical implications of these inclusions? First, however, it seems probable that depictions of sheep are chronologically earlier than those of cattle. The distribution of sheep images on the northern edge of the Drakensberg borders in the areas occupied by first-millennium farmers suggests that the two are chronologically equivalent and so documents a frontier between the two. The meaning of sheep paintings, therefore, needs to be found in that context. Equally, it seems that in the Western Cape and in the Shashe/Limpopo area, sheep images may also date to the first millennium A.D.[160] Cattle images, however, are common in shelters in the Drakensberg foothills and have a second-millennium date.[161] Various interpretations of these animals and the associated imagery have been suggested. Negative constructions of the San underpin ideas that they were not actually the authors of domestic ungulate paintings, or that the paintings were simply depictions of what the San saw or literal recollections of cattle raids. More recently, however, interpretation has sought to understand and explain exotic images from the perspectives offered by the ethnography of Bushman cosmology. It was San values and beliefs that made exotic elements relevant within a corpus of imagery that constructed syncretic meaning which rationalized new

---

[159] Dowson, "Reading Art, Writing History."

[160] R. Yates, A. H. Manhire, and J. E. Parkington, "Rock Painting and History in the South-Western Cape," in T. A Dowson and J. D. Lewis-Williams (Eds.), *Contested Images: Diversity in Southern African Rock Art Research* (Johannesburg: Witwatersrand University Press, 1994), pp. 29–60.

[161] A. D. Mazel, "People Making History: The Last Ten Thousand Years of Hunter–gatherer Communities in the Thukela Basin," *Natal Museum Journal of Humanities*, 1 (1989), pp. 1–168.

relationships with farmers and the additional pressures of the encroaching colonial world.

In the eastern Free State, for example, particular attention has been given to the distribution of paintings of domestic ungulates, Sotho shields, and horses found in rock shelters that fall outside the distribution of seventeenth- and eighteenth-century Sotho stone-wall settlements. It has been suggested that this imagery was incorporated as new sources of potency with which medicine men made rain and healed within their own communities.[162] It would seem that in this context the San participated flexibly with agropastoralism and could retreat seasonally into the higher mountains across the Caledon River to the east. Beyond the frontier of southern Sotho farmers to the southwest, different stone-wall settlements along the Riet River mark an altogether more committed shift to livestock keeping by the San.[163]

By contrast, interaction with the Nguni-speakers on the eastern side of the Drakensberg took on a somewhat different form. The absence of San clicks in Sesotho but their strong presence in Nguni languages emphasizes an altogether different form of interaction between the two, and one that must have been continuous and intense because Nguni-speakers have only been on this landscape since about the twelfth and thirteenth centuries. Furthermore, the nature of interaction between southern Nguni- and Khoisan-speakers on the southern margins of viable mixed farming was different compared to more northern Nguni-speakers. On linguistic and genetic grounds and in issues of divination, southern Nguni and Khoisan interaction was more intense.[164] Very broadly, this intensity may have been driven by the increased unpredictability of farming in these southern areas. A key to understanding the structure of relationships between Nguni-speakers on the one hand, and Sotho/Tswana on the other, is to be found in the different emphasis they placed on certain social institutions. As mentioned previously, understanding variability in the structure of shared landscapes requires that farmers are differentiated and not homogenized as a generic category. It has been suggested, for example, that the institutionalized marginality of Nguni wives, and more specifically of women as diviners, placed them at the interface with the less than human world of

---

[162] J. H. N. Loubser and G. Laurens, "Depictions of Domestic Ungulates and Shields: Hunter/Gatherers and Agro-pastoralists in the Caledon River Valley Area," In Dowson and Lewis-Williams (Eds.), *Contested images*, pp. 83–118.

[163] T.M. O'C. Maggs, "Pastoral Settlements Along the Riet River," *South African Archaeological Bulletin*, 26 (1971), pp. 37–63.

[164] W. D. Hammond-Tooke, "Selective Borrowing? The Possibility of San Shamanistic Influence on Southern Bantu Divination and Healing Practices," *South African Archaeological Bulletin*, 53 (1998), pp. 9–15

San hunter–gatherers. Nguni women, therefore, became a conduit through which linguistic and certain spiritual exchanges took place, with influence running from San into Nguni society.[165] This is the same relationship suggested previously on the evidence from the early Tswana homesteads at Madikwe. Another domain of interaction between San and Nguni farmers was in rainmaking and historical records accord some status and importance to San rainmakers, although their power and ideological hold over farmers has possibly been overemphasized.[166]

Such contracts were paid for with livestock and this is potentially documented in the rock art of the southeastern Drakensberg, where cattle and horses appear in proprietary relationships to San, in contrast to the situation among Sotho-speakers. Individuals in San society became more important because of their skill and this became a pivot around which increasing differentiation within San society developed through their central role in economic exchanges. The rock art sequence of the southeastern Drakensberg makes a powerful and penetrating statement about the historical development of these relationships and the significance of painting and the images in redefining roles and status. It has been recognized, for example, that in earlier phases of the rock art sequence human figures are undifferentiated. By contrast, in later phases certain figures began to be fantastically individualized and, in the context of farmer interactions, the head is enlarged in complete disproportion to a diminutive body, and eventually only heads are emphasized. Such a sequence, it is suggested, is deeply embedded in the changing role of San diviners away from conventional healing, where the healer worked upon the community through the body, to emphasising individual potency owners who worked as paid rainmakers.[167] In this changing world, wrought, in particular, by the pressure exerted by the colonial world upon indigenous society, images underwrote changing historical relationships that elevated the importance of diviners, both as individuals within their own communities and within southern Nguni society. Much

---

[165] W. D. Hammond-Tooke, "Divinatory Animals: Further Evidence of San/Nguni Borrowing," *South African Archaeological Bulletin*, 54(170) (1991), pp. 8–132; F. E. Prins, "Living in Two Worlds: The Manipulation of Power Relations, Identity and Ideology by the last San Rock Artist in Tsolo, Transkei, South Africa," *Natal Museum Journal of Humanities*, 6 (1994), pp. 179–93; P. Jolly, "Symbiotic Interaction Between Black Farmers and Southeastern San: Implications for Southern African Rock Art Studies, Ethnographic Analogy, and Hunter-gatherer Cultural Identity," *Current Anthropology*, 37 (1996), pp. 277–88.

[166] G. Whitelaw, "Their village is where they kill game": Nguni interactions with the San. In: P. Mitchell and B. Smith (Eds.), *The eland's people: new perspectives on the rock art of the Maloti/Drakensberg Bushmen. Essays in memory of Pat Vinnicombe* (in press).

[167] G. Blundell, *Nqabayo's Nomansland: San rock art and the somatic past* (Studies in Global Archaeology, 2. Uppsala, 2004). For earlier developments of this theme, see Dowson "Reading art, writing history" and "Hunter–gatherers, traders and slaves."

of the second-millennium farmer sequence rightly emphasizes that local economies are structured in part around global forces. It is apposite that hunter–gatherers' local responses are also seen as integral to this wider world.

CONCLUSION

The material reviewed in this chapter highlights the second millennium as a period during which farmers of the eastern areas of South Africa constructed opportunities that increasingly connected them to a wider world. From AD 1000, the more complex polities of the Shashe/Limpopo region were based upon intensified trade relationships with the East African coast and the Indian Ocean trade routes. From the sixteenth century, European colonialism progressively changed the character of these earlier trade structures and coastal and interior farmers responded accordingly, until the nineteenth century, when African political and social structures could no longer absorb and adapt to the intense demands of an encroaching colonialism. There are a few further points to be made about the writing of precolonial history with archaeological material as the evidential base.

The chapter has attempted to foreground the contribution of archaeological material to the writing of a larger-scale historical narrative that emphasizes the strategic abilities of precolonial Africans. In doing so, there is perhaps a danger of drawing too sharp a distinction between the historical nature of the second millennium, on the one hand, and the more anonymous nature of the first millennium, on the other. As this chapter indicates, there is more resolution for the second millennium in terms of discerning real historical identities, their trajectories through time, and their emergence in the nineteenth century. An equivalent resolution for the first millennium is beyond the grasp of material evidence alone and this is perhaps why intense debates about this period have emphasized theory and methods and the interpretation of cultural structures as a dominant theme. As a matter of principle, the first millennium is obviously no less historical and the division in this volume between the advent of food production and the second millennium should not obscure the clear continuities across this divide.

The ability of the second-millennium evidence to support a more historical narrative should also not obscure the fact that economies, production, strategic settlement moves, the rise of political power, and so on are all anchored within cultural systems. There is possibly a danger of losing sight of this by overresponding to allegations that agriculturist archaeologists have written the past only in terms of static cultural models and systems. One of the threads this chapter has tried to articulate is that there seem to be considerable continuities in African cultural principles and these are contextually used again and again in redefining identities and creating new political structures. The manipulation of firstcomer and newcomer status resonates throughout the second millennium (and is a principle that may become increasingly relevant to thinking about the first millennium) and provides a cultural trope that clearly does not exclude hunter–gatherers. The challenge for archaeology is not simply to recognize and identify cultural principles but to show how they are contextually employed to suit the needs of specific historical circumstance. Both farmers and hunter–gatherers often redefined their position in the wider world through these principles. The contextually specific turmoil of the early part of the nineteenth century, for example, during which political power ebbed and flowed and people changed their affiliations and recast their identities, is an extreme example of what precolonial farmers did over and over again and it is these dynamics that the archaeology of the second millennium is beginning to outline.

The ability to move, resettle, shift allegiance, and create new identities in the pursuit of political and economic advantage is an enduring theme within African political culture. Although we would not wish to draw too great a distinction between the first millennium and the second, so too must we be wary of isolating the early nineteenth century as something that was totally new in the experience of South African farmers. The scale of these events was certainly unprecedented, but the responses to them perpetuated deeper time cultural strategies. In this regard, as the archaeology increasingly looks forward into the ethnographic present, we may find that it will highlight cultural continuities into this period, rather than assuming that, from the perspective of a colonially ravaged population, the past was a significantly different place.

4

KHOESAN AND IMMIGRANTS: THE EMERGENCE OF COLONIAL SOCIETY IN THE CAPE, 1500–1800

ROBERT ROSS

In the last years of the fifteenth century, Southern Africa's contacts with the world outside the South African subcontinent took on new forms. No longer was maritime trade maintained only on the shores of the Indian Ocean. In this chapter the first results of that change are discussed, primarily with regard to the period after the establishment of a Dutch colony at the Cape of Good Hope. This was a period that saw the destruction of Khoesan independence through most of the region to the south of the Gariep River and simultaneously, in close relation to this, the establishment of colonial society within the same space. That system was a relatively minor part of the empire of the Vereenigde Oost-indische Compagnie, the Dutch East India Company, or VOC, but it increasingly developed its own dynamics based on the land of the dispossessed Khoesan, and on the labor in part of the Khoesan but primarily of imported slaves and employees of the company.

Initially, the historiography of this period celebrated European colonization and was concerned with the details of colonial rule and settlement.[1] As might be expected, the revitalization of the historiography came in the first instance through discussions of the Khoesan,[2] of slave society,[3] and of the

---

[1] This did, however, produce a number of important works on the Cape economy and also notable forerunners of South Africa's modern environmental history, particularly P. J. van der Merwe's three major works, *Die Noordwaartse Beweging van die Boere voor die Groot Trek (1770–1842)* (The Hague: Van Stockum, 1937); *Die Trekboer in die Geskiedenis van die Kaapkolonie, 1657–1842* (Cape Town: Nasionale Pers, 1938); *Trek: Studies Oor die Mobiliteit van die Pioniersbevolking aan die Kaap* (Cape Town: Nasionale Pers, 1945).

[2] R. Elphick, *Kraal and Castle: Khoikhoi and the Founding of White South Africa* (New Haven and London: Yale University Press, 1977); N. Penn, *"The Forgotten Frontier: Colonist and Khoisan on the Cape's Northern Frontier in the 18th Century* (Athens and Cape Town: Ohio University Press and Double Storey, 2005); S. Newton-King, *Masters and Servants on the Cape Eastern Frontier, 1760–1803* (Cambridge: Cambridge University Press, 1999).

[3] R. Ross, *Cape of Torments: Slavery and Resistance in South Africa* (London: Routledge, 1982); N. Worden, *Slavery in Dutch South Africa* (Cambridge: Cambridge University Press, 1985); R. C.-H. Shell, *Children of Bondage: A Social History of the Slave Society at the*

historical geography of colonial farming and pastoralism.[4] Much of this work came together in the two editions of *The Shaping of South African Society*.[5] Nevertheless, neither these works nor the subjects with which they deal can be considered distinct from each other.

The sharpest debates have been over the extent to which a slave community evolved distinct from, or incorporated with, the masters; the degree to which Khoesan resistance to the Dutch was driven by the experience of the Khoesan as farm laborers and was thus a form of class struggle; and, more generally, the degree to which the forms of stratification to be found in the Cape were essentially racial, and thus the origin of later South African patterns. Increasingly, therefore, it has become necessary to view the history of the Cape Colony as an integrated, if conflictual, whole. However, the strength of such work has been in reconstructing microhistories, which as yet await full incorporation into a wider understanding of Cape society.[6]

EARLY CONTACTS

In 1488, a Portuguese ship under the command of Bartholomew Dias rounded the Cape of Good Hope and put into Mossel Bay. As the Portuguese were loading drinking water, there was a short confrontation with the Khoekhoen who had gathered there. In the course of the struggle one of the Khoekhoen was killed. The Portuguese had interpreted the Khoekhoen's actions as hostile – whether correctly or otherwise is hard to say.

Cape of Good Hope, 1652–1838 (Hanover and London: Wesleyan University Press for the University Press of New England, 1994).

[4] L. Guelke, "The Early European Settlement of South Africa," unpublished Ph.D. thesis, University of Toronto (1974); P. van Duin and R. Ross, *The Economy of the Cape Colony in the Eighteenth Century* (Intercontinenta, Leiden: Centre for the History of European Expansion, 1987).

[5] R. Elphick and H. Giliomee (Eds.), *The Shaping of South African Society, 1652–1820* (London: Longmans, 1979), republished as *The Shaping of South African Society, 1652–1840*, 2nd ed. (Cape Town: Maskew Miller Longman, 1989).

[6] N. Penn, *Rogues, Rebels and Runaways: Eighteenth-Century Cape Characters* (Cape Town: David Philip, 1999), particularly "The Fatal Passion of Brewer Menssink: Sex, Beer and Politics in a Cape Family, 1694–1722," pp. 9–72; N. Penn, "The Wife, the Farmer and the Farmer's Slaves: Adultery and Murder on a Frontier Farm in the Early Eighteenth Century," *Kronos, 28* (2002); S. Newton-King, "For the Love of Adam: Two Sodomy Trials at the Cape of Good Hope," *Kronos, 28* (2002), pp. 21–42; N. Worden, "Forging a Reputation: Artisan Honour and the Cape Town Blacksmith Strike of 1752," *Kronos, 28* (2002), pp. 43–65; exceptions to the general rule can be seen in W. Dooling, *Law and Community in a Slave Society: Stellenbosch District, c. 1760–1820* (Cape Town: Centre of African Studies University of Cape Town, 1992) and *idem, Slavery, Emancipation and Colonial Rule in South Africa* (Scottsville, University of KwaZulu-Natal Press, 2007, Chapter 1).

The Portuguese had come to South Africa in the hope of discovering a sea route from Europe to the southern coast of Asia and its associated islands. A few years later, on a subsequent expedition under Vasco da Gama, they succeeded in this aim. For the next century and a half, European ships regularly put into the bays along the southern and southwestern coasts of Africa to take on water and to trade with the Khoekhoen for cattle and sheep. From about 1590, the Portuguese were joined by northern Europeans, particularly English and Dutch. From the early seventeenth century, the latter would become by far the more frequent visitors.

The early contacts were sporadic and often hostile. The defeat of a Portuguese force on the shores of Table Bay in 1510, which resulted in the death of the admiral, Francesco d'Almeida, and fifty of his men, confirmed for the Portuguese their distrust of the Khoekhoen. Moreover, as the center of their Asian enterprise was in Goa on the west coast of India, and their sailing route ran through the Mozambique channel, harbors further north in Africa suited their purpose better. Only after about 1610 did the Dutch discover the advantages of sailing due east from the Cape before swinging north to reach what had become the hub of their trading network, namely, Java. As a result, contacts between the Khoekhoen and the Europeans steadily increased, particularly around Table Bay.

In the first half of the seventeenth century, a regular system of trade developed between the Khoekhoen of the Southwestern Cape and the visiting sailors. In essence, sheep and cattle were exchanged for metals – initially iron, but later more brass and copper. The former was used primarily for the manufacture of assegais and thus had a relatively restricted market, as the Khoekhoen of the Southwest Cape would not have wanted to pass their weapons of war on to their potential rivals further upcountry. The latter, used above all for personal adornment, had a much wider distribution.

It might be surmised that this trade would have led to some degree of political concentration among Cape Khoekhoen.[7] Political power in Khoekhoe society is generally recognized to have been dependent on wealth and only contingently on such ascriptive matters as descent. A man might have inherited wealth in stock, and thus influence, from his father, but it does not appear that this process was institutionalized into hereditary chiefly lineages. Once the material basis of power disappeared, that power itself evaporated.

In these circumstances efficient use of the resources made available by the trade with Europeans could have resulted in a considerable increase in political scale. This does not seem to have happened. The Khoekhoe groups

---

[7] This is a suggestion put forward by K. Sadr, "The First Herders at the Cape of Good Hope," *African Archaeological Review, 15* (1998), p. 124.

who were in the best position to profit from European presence were, of course, those living in the neighborhood of Table Bay itself. These were known as the Goringhaicona, the Goringhaiqua, and the Gorachouqua. However, despite the advantages they possessed in relation to the external sources of wealth, they remained poor. The Goringhaicona, indeed, had no cattle at all, and the other groups had relatively few. Presumably the territory through which they moved – effectively, in modern terms, the Cape peninsula, the Durbanville hills, and the winelands – was too poor to allow a massive buildup of stock, and their neighbors, the Cochoqua to the north in the Swartland and the Chainouqua across the mountains to the east, were powerful enough to contain them.

In the mid-seventeenth century the two largest and most powerful Khoekhoe groupings were the Hessequa, who controlled the rich pastorage east of the Chainouqua from about modern Swellendam to Mossel Bay, and the Inqua, otherwise known as the Hamcunqua, whose base seems to have been in the southern kloofs of the Great Escarpment, and from there they ranged over the plains of the Camdeboo, which were probably greener and better watered than they are now. The Inqua were the richest of the Khoekhoen, both because of their extensive pastures and because they controlled the trading networks of the interior, bringing copper from the Orange River, and ultimately Namaqualand, and exchanging it for dagga (and no doubt stock and agricultural goods) produced by amaXhosa and others, which, in turn, was passed on as far as the Western Cape.[8] They were also accorded political and ritual preeminence by their fellows, although in reality this recognition of superiority had no further consequences.

Still further east, in the ecological shadow zone between the Khoekhoen and the agriculturalists, which runs from the Eastern Cape in a wide curve to the Namibian highlands, lived groups known as the Gonaqua, the Damaqua (the "black people," who are described as living in clay houses),[9] and the Damasonqua ("Black San"). These people were generally bilingual in isiXhosa and Khoekhoe and were able, if circumstances allowed and made it advantageous, to switch from one side of the cultural and economic divide to the other.

Surrounding these Khoekhoe groups were those known as San, or Soaqua. Essentially they lived as hunter–gatherers, frequently in the mountains, and often as bandits. It has been a matter of some debate as to whether

[8] G. Harinck, "Interaction between Xhosa and Khoi: Emphasis on the Period 1620–1750," in L. Thompson (Ed.), *African Societies in Southern Africa* (London, Ibadan, and Nairobi: Heinemann, 1969).

[9] E. E. Mossop (Ed.), *Journals of the Expeditions of the Honourable Ensign Olof Bergh (1682 and 1683) and the Ensign Isaq Schrijver (1689)* (Cape Town: Van Riebeeck Society, 1931), p. 111.

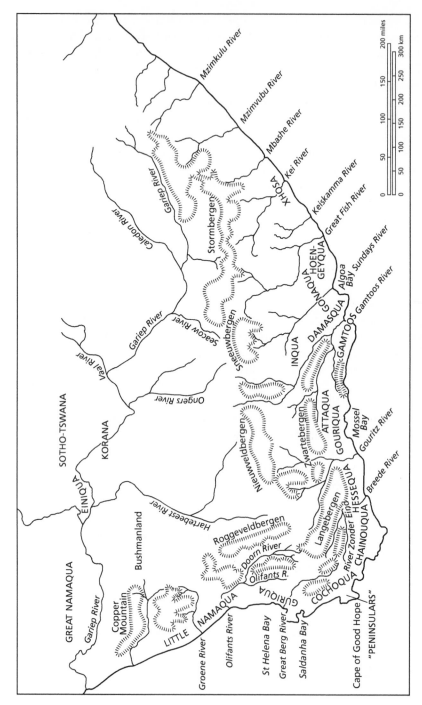

FIGURE 4.1. Approximate locations of Khoikhoi before contact with whites.

they were descendants of the aboriginal, pre-Khoekhoe populations of the Cape or whether they were Khoekhoen who had lost their stock and had, perhaps only temporarily, taken on a hunter–gatherer lifestyle to recoup their position.[10] As is often the case with such debates, examples can be found to support both propositions. Certainly, in the semideserts to the north of the Great Escarpment, for instance in the Zak and the Seekoe river valleys, and in the mountains of the Eastern Cape and Lesotho, the /Xam and the N//ŋ still spoke non-Khoekhoe languages, and, in the latter case, the tradition of rock art lasted into the nineteenth century. Equally, even in the Western Cape, where there is no evidence of a separate aboriginal language surviving into the seventeenth century and where the "Soaqua" spoke Khoekhoe, the material culture of the mountain-dwelling hunter–gatherers would seem to have been distinct from that of the Khoekhoe pastoralists of the plains. On the other hand, the boundary between the two groups was almost certainly permeable, and many of the hunters acted from time to time as clients of the Khoekhoen, although what the stockholders saw as gifts to clients may, as ever, have been interpreted by the recipients as proceeds of a protection racket.

The problem in resolving this argument lies in the nature of the evidence. Those who would claim that the Khoekhoen and the San acted according to different logics and that a hunter–gatherer would have great difficulty in acquiring the mindset of a pastoralist, with its emphasis on the maintenance of the herd, have had to rely on ethnographic analogies to modern groups, often well outside South Africa.[11] However, such analogies show that it has been usual in historic times for hunter–gatherers to live in some sort of symbiotic relationship with food producers of various types. On the other hand, those who have argued that individuals and families could move between the two modes of life have almost invariably had to present examples from the early decades of Dutch rule, and even then can only provide cases of stock loss, not of recovery or of acquisition of a herd or a flock on the part of those who had been without them. The problem is that relationships between hunter–gatherers and pastoralists were heavily affected by the advent of colonialism at the Cape. As a result, it is virtually impossible to read back from after the arrival of the Portuguese, let alone the Dutch, to fully precolonial times.

THE FOUNDATION OF THE COLONY

In 1651, the Heren XVII, the board of the VOC, decided to establish a permanent base in Table Bay "in order to provide that the passing and

---

[10] On this debate see *ibid.*, Chapter 2.

[11] A. Smith, *Pastoralism in Africa* (Johannesburg: Witwatersrand University Press, 1992).

re-passing East India ships, to and from Batavia, respectively, may, without accident, touch at the said Cape or Bay, and also upon arriving there, may find the means of procuring herbs, flesh, water, and other needful refreshments, and by this means restore the health of their sick."[12] They therefore dispatched three ships to set up the station. They were under the command of Jan van Riebeeck, who had previously been employed as a merchant in Vietnam but had fallen temporarily into disgrace for engaging in forbidden private trade. They arrived in April 1652 and began to build a fortified stockade.

In the mid-seventeenth century, the VOC was the most important trading company in the world. Founded in 1602, it had been granted monopoly rights by the Dutch States-General over all trade between the Netherlands and places to the east of the Cape of Good Hope. By the time van Riebeeck set off for the Cape, the VOC had developed an intricate system of commercial relations, so organized that the trade within Asian waters largely financed the purchase of the goods that were to be sent to the Netherlands. The VOC profited from the monopolies it was able to acquire by territorial conquest, or at least by the use of force. This was particularly the case for the production of spices, notably nutmeg and mace in the Banda archipelago, cloves in the Moluccas, and cinnamon in Sri Lanka. It was also the only foreign company allowed by the Shogun to trade in Japan, but only under very restrictive conditions. Elsewhere, particularly on the Asian mainland, it was merely one of many competitors, although it was generally in a strong position because of its economies of scale and ability to dominate a given market.

At the center of this web of trading relations was the city of Batavia (Jakarta). This was the seat of the governor-general and council, the ruling body of the VOC in Asia, and it increasingly became a city with a distinct colonial culture, which was later to have its effect on the Cape. Batavia was also the point of arrival and departure for most of the Dutch ships to Asia, as the goods that were eventually to be sent to Europe were collected there for shipment. After 1670, a fair number of ships sailed directly from Sri Lanka to the Netherlands and, from the 1730s, also from India and China. In total, over the nearly two centuries of its existence, the VOC dispatched 4,721 ships from Europe and 3,354 from Asia. This obviously required vast personnel. In total nearly a million men (and a handful of women) sailed east. They came primarily from the Netherlands and from

---

[12] D. Moodie, *The Record; or a Series of Official Papers Relative to the Condition and Treatment of the Native Tribes of South Africa* (Cape Town: A. S. Robertson, 1838–1845; reprinted Amsterdam and Cape Town: Balkema), part I, p. 7.

what is now Germany. Approximately a third returned.[13] From the middle of the eighteenth century they were supplemented by sailors of Asian background: "Moorish" (largely from the Indian east coast), Javanese, and Chinese.[14] After 1652, almost all of these would put into Table Bay and visit Cape Town for a few days or weeks. Cape Town was thus a cosmopolitan town and the colony as a whole an important, if minor, part of the Dutch imperial and commercial system.

Table Bay was chosen as the base of the VOC in South Africa because it was the safest anchorage in the region (at least in the late southern summer, when VOC ships would be passing in both directions), with a sufficient supply of water. Firewood, too, could be obtained in sufficient quantities from the slopes of Table Mountain.[15] The other requirements of the fleets, essentially meat, bread (or rice), and vegetables and wine as antiscorbutics, had to be produced or traded locally if they were not to be imported.

In the first instance, meat was obtained through trade with the Khoekhoen. Between 1652 and 1699, the VOC obtained a total of around 20,000 cattle and 40,000 sheep from the Khoekhoen by means of trade. Given the extended period over which the purchases were made, these are not totals beyond the amounts that could have been sustained by the natural increase of the Khoekhoe flocks and herds.[16] If the VOC at the Cape had been content to remain a small establishment engaged in acquiring stock for its fleet, this pattern of potentially mutually beneficial exchange could have lasted for a long time. That this did not happen was, in essence, the consequence of the unconscious decision on the part of the VOC to transform the post at the Cape of Good Hope from a small trading factory to what was, in embryo, a colony.

There were two complexes of reasons for this. First, the VOC was inherently an expansionist organization. At least since the days of Jan Pieterszoon Coen, its employees believed that territorial sovereignty gave it the best chance to achieve the monopolistic super-profits it desired. Especially in the Moluccas and Banda, but also, to some extent, in Java and Sri Lanka, this was the policy it pursued. Elsewhere it was constrained by the presence of powerful monarchies, which it was forced to consider as its equals or its local superiors. At the Cape, such monarchies did not exist. Moreover, in common with other visitors to the Cape, the Dutch had come to have a low

---

[13] J. R. Bruijn, F. S. Gaastra, and I. Schöffer, *Dutch-Asiatic Shipping in the 17th and 18th Centuries*, 3 vols. (The Hague: Martinus Nijhoff, 1987), vol. I, p. 144.

[14] *Ibid.*, p. 153.

[15] A. Appel, "Die Ontginning van die Inheemse Houtbosse op die Kaapse Skiereiland 1652–1795," *Historia*, 22 (1977).

[16] Elphick, *Kraal and Castle*, pp. 169–70.

opinion of the Khoekhoen. Although their ideas were in part constrained by their day-to-day interactions, the Dutch saw the Khoekhoen as savages, and generally as ignoble savages at that.[17] They were not going to be limited by the Khoekhoen to the role forced upon them by, for instance, the Moghul emperor or the shogun of Japan.

Second, trade in livestock was not the only, perhaps not even the major, preoccupation of the Dutch at the Cape. They also needed cereals, vegetables, and fruit, perhaps conserved by alcohol as wine. The move to creating an agricultural colony to ensure the production of these products was easily made. Within five years after van Riebeeck's arrival, a group of nine men were discharged from the service of the VOC and granted land along the Liesbeeck River, near what is now Rondebosch, in order that they might begin farming. Shortly afterward a number of other men were also granted their release in order to work independently as artisans or retailers of drink in Cape Town. So the Cape began to shift from being a simple fort to being a colony.[18]

THE EARLY COLONY

The new colony remained very much under the control of the Dutch East India Company. Its successive governors were relatively low-level officials within the VOC hierarchy, although as the Cape grew in importance and size, their status improved. In 1690, Simon van der Stel was promoted from commander, the rank all his predecessors had enjoyed, to governor, and a year later appointed "Raad Extra-Ordinaris van Indië,"[19] a symbolic honor but nevertheless one of considerable importance within the status-driven world of the company. However, certainly in the early years of the colony, the commanders of the VOC's fleets on their return from Asia to the Netherlands were regularly commissioned to inspect the new colony. These men, who had achieved high office within the VOC, ensured that the Cape was governed in accordance with the principles employed throughout its empire and for the benefit of the company.

---

[17] M. van Wyk Smith, "'The Most Wretched of the Human Race': The Iconography of the Khoikhoin (Hottentots) 1500–1800," *History and Anthropology*, 5 (1992), pp. 285–330; E. Bassani and L. Tedeschi, "The Image of the Hottentot in the Seventeenth and Eighteenth Centuries: An Iconographic Investigation," *Journal of the History of Collections*, 2 (1990), pp. 157–86; E. de Groot, "The Earliest Eyewitness Depictions of Khoikhoi: Andries Beeckman in Africa," *Itinerario*, 29(1) (2005), pp. 17–50.

[18] G. C. de Wet, *Die Vryliede en Vryswartes in die Kaapse Nedersetting, 1657–1707* (Cape Town: Historiese Publikasie-Vereniging, 1981).

[19] "Councillor-Extraordinary of India." See Gerrit Schutte, "Company and Colonists at the Cape, 1652–1795," in Elphick and Giliomee (Eds.), *Shaping*, p. 295.

In the first instance they were, of course, interested in the defense of new possessions and had the castle built following the best model of the time – although, in the event, the Cape did not suffer a foreign attack until the 1780s. They were further concerned to ensure that the fleets of the VOC in Cape Town, which reached an average of forty-five vessels a year in the first decade of the eighteenth century,[20] were sufficiently provisioned. As a result, culverts were built to bring the water to the quay, and regulations were made to protect Cape Town's wood supply.[21] Providing sufficient food for the fleets was, however, a longer-term problem.

The population of the small settlement grew slowly. The company's establishment increased steadily, from just more than 100 in 1657 to more than 700 by 1695. The number of so-called free burghers who had been granted release from company service also increased. In 1672 half the free burghers were called back to help in the defense of the colony against the possibility of a French attack. By this stage, their numbers were increasing sharply, aided by the immigration of about 150 Huguenots, a miniscule part of the 400,000 who left France subsequent to the revocation of the Edict of Nantes in 1685. Cape Town was, by now, beginning to develop into a town with a variety of urban occupations, notably innkeepers and drink salesman, but also masons, carpenters, smiths, wagonmakers, potters, shoemakers, and tailors. The richest were those who were able to get company contracts as butchers and brewers.[22]

Alongside the company officials and free burghers was an increasing population of slaves. The few early slaves had been in the households of the first Dutch settlers, including van Riebeeck, but the first large contingents only arrived in 1658 – one group on a vessel that had been sent on a clandestine expedition to Dahomey, the others a cargo of Angolan slaves captured from the Portuguese off Brazil. These were the last slaves imported into the Cape from further north on the western coast of South Africa. From then on slaves were regularly imported from the various shores of the Indian Ocean. The company sent twelve expeditions to Madagascar before 1700 to acquire, in total, 1,069 slaves for its own use. The free burghers also began to purchase slaves, quite legally, but not through company channels. Indeed, the *fiscaal*, the company law officer, took a personal fee for the importation of private slaves. By the beginning of the eighteenth century private slaves numbered about 891, excluding those who were in the private

---

[20] C. Beyers, *Die Kaapse Patriotte gedurende die Laatste Kwaart van die Agtiende Eeu en die Voortleving van hul Denkbeelde*, 2nd ed. (Pretoria: J. L. van Schaik, 1967), p. 333.

[21] A. Böeseken, *Nederlandsche Commissarissen aan die Kaap, 1657–1700* (The Hague: Martinus Nijhoff, 1938).

[22] De Wet, *Vryliede en Vryswartes*.

possession of company officials, a group that was virtually never counted and who thus escape the vision of historians. About 80 percent of these slaves were men.

The extension of the colony outside the confines of Table Valley, where Cape Town was founded, depended on the progress of the Dutch relationship with the Khoekhoen. The initial settlement in the Liesbeeck River Valley precipitated a Khoekhoe attack on the colony and a war that lasted for about a year. The Peninsula Khoekhoen, led by a man called Doman who had been an interpreter and had even traveled to Batavia, were attempting to drive the colonists away by stealing stock and destroying the nascent crops. However, the loose coalition he had been able to assemble against Dutch settlement was not strong enough to absorb the relatively mild defeats the Dutch were able to inflict upon them. Doman himself was wounded and the various peninsula groups sued for a peace, which left the Dutch in clear control of the immediate surroundings of Cape Town.[23]

This proved to be the pattern of Khoekhoe–Dutch relations in the subsequent half-century. In some ways the level of stock owned by the Khoekhoen, and their consequent power in what was always a plutocracy, was finite and thus slowly diminished as the trade with the insatiable Dutch fleets continued. There is no indication of a concerted Dutch plan to excise Khoekhoe leadership and political authority from the Southwestern Cape. Had there been, the Dutch would have been much more brutal, at least on the evidence of their actions in various parts of the Indonesian archipelago, notably the Banda islands. The point, of course, is that there was no need for them to behave in such a way. The slow Dutch pressure on Khoekhoe polities led to the latter's collapse without the necessity for drastic action on the part of the Netherlanders. By the end of the century, the Dutch had gained control of the whole area to the west of the first main range of mountains, north at least to the Piquetberg, at the cost of one further military campaign.

The campaign, which has become known in the historiography as the Second Khoekhoe–Dutch war, was fought by the Cochoqua of the northern borderlands during the 1670s. It was brought on by a series of incidents between Khoekhoen and colonists, in which the major problems were the decision of the company to punish Khoekhoe malefactors itself (instead of returning them to their chiefs) and a number of raids on the colonists by San, who may or may not have been under the control of the Cochoqua chief, Gonnema. Even this period of hostilities, which lasted for some four years, was rather desultory, though it did lead to the capture of nearly 1,800 cattle and 5,000 sheep by joint expeditions of the Dutch and the Cochoqua's

---

[23] Elphick, *Kraal and Castle*, pp. 110–16.

Khoekhoe enemies, primarily Chainouqua. This was a severe blow to the power of what had been one of the most powerful of the Khoekhoe polities in the Southwest Cape. It was, however, not sufficient to account for the total collapse that followed, after the death of Gonnema, let alone explain how it came about that those Khoekhoe groups against whom the Dutch did not make war also disintegrated, particularly as a proportion of the stock captured from the Cochoqua were dispersed to other Khoekhoe groups. In response to these questions, other arguments are needed.

At the base of such arguments must always be questions of stock. Khoekhoe society was only held together by the ties of patronage provided by the leaders being able to dispense cattle and sheep and by the prestige that substantial flocks and herds conferred on these men. As the Khoekhoen lost their stock, so they lost the ability to maintain social cohesion and, eventually, to resist further impositions on the part of the colonists. To some extent the losses were the result of the trade the Khoekhoen carried on with the company. In total, between 1662 and 1713, the company purchased 14,363 head of cattle and 32,808 sheep from the Khoekhoen. Increasingly these purchases came from the peoples of the southern plains, the Chainouqua and the Hessequa. Of those cattle whose origins could be determined, 69 percent came from the eastern Khoekhoen and, of the sheep, 47 percent.[24] Initially at least, this trade was on a willing-seller basis, although eventually it degenerated into something approaching remunerated tribute. The problem was that the goods the Khoekhoen acquired in exchange, primarily copper beads, tobacco, and alcohol, were not such as to allow for a replenishment of the herds, and thus for the power, of the Khoekhoe leader, presumably on the basis of an organized system of trade with groups further to the east. However, it is at least debatable whether Dutch trade greatly exceeded the natural reproduction of the Khoekhoe herds and flocks, and thus whether on its own it had a substantial lasting effect on their size. What is clear, though, is that the combination of the trade with a degree of illegal, and violent, seizure of stock from the Khoekhoen by colonists, or by cattleless Khoesan, and the necessity of slaughtering stock to maintain prestige and thus power, drove the herds into a downward spiral from which there was no recovery.

This process was best illustrated by the fate of the Chainouqua.[25] In the early years of Dutch settlement, these people, who lived mainly in the region between the Hottentots Holland Mountains and modern Swellendam, were led by a man named Soeswa. He ruled over some sixteen settlements – it is impossible to say how large each of these settlements would have

---

[24] *Ibid.*

[25] In this analysis I am following Elphick, *Kraal and Castle*, Chapter 7.

been – in close alliance with the rulers of the Hessequa, a rather larger group somewhat further to the east. Soeswa was said to be the second-most senior chief in the region, after the ruler of the Inqua. Certainly, with their control of the rich pastures of the Southern Cape forelands, the Chainouqua and Hessequa were the richest Khoekhoen, probably anywhere on the subcontinent. They were also involved in a continual feud with the Cochoqua, of the type known as "traditional" – which only means that no one now knows what its origins were – and were thus in no way averse to aiding the Dutch during the Second Khoekhoe–Dutch war.

Chainouqua power succumbed, before about 1700, to the divisive consequences of the relation with the Netherlanders. One of the settlement heads, Dorha,[26] became the main agent for the Dutch in their cattle trade to the interior. The conditions involved were immensely advantageous for the VOC but also allowed Dorha to climb from the position of settlement head to one where he was married to a daughter of the Hessequa chief, Gaukou, and was clearly the leader of the Chainouqua. It is at least probable, though, that the conditions of trade had led to a steady deterioration in the overall prosperity of the Southern Cape Khoekhoen while allowing a single individual to accumulate much wealth. In any event, Dorha was not able to convert his wealth into lasting power or to eliminate his enemies. He was thus particularly vulnerable to the capriciousness of Dutch policy. In 1693, then, the governor of the Cape, Simon van der Stel, abandoned a twenty-year friendship with Dorha, listened to the complaints of his Khoekhoe enemies, and sent an expedition against him. Cattle and sheep were seized, Dorha was arrested and put on Robben Island, and his followers were ordered to become the followers of his competitor, known only by his Dutch name, Koopman. The evidence, meager though it is, suggests that van der Stel took this measure to ensure the continuance of official dominance in the cattle trade.[27] At any event, even though Dorha was shortly released on the orders of the Heren XVII, he was unable to regain his former position – or even his wife, who absconded to Koopman – and shortly afterwards he was assassinated on a visit to his enemy.

This was the last time the Dutch had to take account of individual Khoekhoe leaders in the Southwestern Cape. Henceforth they are not even named in the sources, and clearly no longer had any significant power. But at the same time it was significant that Dorha's demise was seen as the result of the attempt on the part of van der Stel to dominate the cattle trade. This was, in its way, symptomatic of the ways in which colonial political and economic relations developed at the turn of the seventeenth

---

[26] Always known to the Dutch as Klaas.   [27] Elphick, *Kraal and Castle*, p. 146.

century. These relations derived from a paradox that could only be resolved through political struggle. This was that the colony was becoming richer, so the rewards of official domination were becoming greater, but only on the basis of the expansion of the settlement and economic interests of the burghers, which provided the latter with both the need and the means to combat that very domination.

This expansion was the consequence of a shift in the VOC's policy toward land grants and, as a consequence, of the form of agriculture that was to be pursued. Until 1679, the assumption was that the company's needs would be best served by the burghers' cultivation of relatively small plots in the immediate neighborhood of Cape Town. The elimination of any threat from the Peninsula Khoekhoen and, indeed, the Cochoqua, made possible the settlement of free burghers across the Cape flats, on the shale hills of the Tijgerberg and the southern Zwartland and in the valleys surrounding the new town, which was named Stellenbosch after the governor. Here they would develop an agricultural system whose prime products were wheat and wine, the classic crops of the Mediterranean complex, but which had not previously been grown in Southern Africa. Surprisingly, the third main component of the Mediterranean complex, the olive, was not introduced into South Africa to any degree until late in the twentieth century. Presumably the availability of animal fats – sheep tallow and butter above all – precluded the necessity for developing the production of vegetable oils.

In 1679 Simon van der Stel opened the region that was to become Stellenbosch for the staking of farms, initially on full freehold tenure. The first farmers of the region naturally took the prime sites, largely along the river frontages. Within a decade, about sixty grants had been made in the Stellenbosch area. As they averaged only about fifty hectares each, these made up no more than a fifteenth of the land area in question but, by controlling the waterfronts, these farmers effectively controlled the whole district, including the theoretically unclaimed grazing land surrounding the farms. A visiting VOC official attempted to systematize the settlement pattern in the subsequent areas to be distributed, laying out adjoining rectangular pieces of ground in the Paarl Valley, but this had little long-term effect. The Southwest Cape, between the Cape flats and the mountain chain, was being claimed by a nascent gentry.[28]

[28] L. Guelke, "Freehold Farmers and Frontier Settlers, 1657–1780," in R. Elphick and H. Giliomee (Eds.), *The Shaping of South African Society, 1652–1840*, 2nd ed. (Cape Town: Maskew Miller Longman, 1989), pp. 73–83; see also L. Guelke, *The South Western Cape Colony 1657–1750: Freehold Land Grants*, Occasional Paper No. 5, Geography Publication Series (Waterloo: Geography Department, University of Waterloo, Ontario, 1987).

Those who received land in this fashion came from a variety of origins. Many of the Huguenot immigrants settled in certain of the Stellenbosch district valleys, notably Franschhoek, and around what was later to be known as Wellington, then the Wagenmakers Vallei. But there were also men who had come to the Cape from Germany and the Netherlands, and a sprinkling of men of Asian descent. In general, relations between the various groups were not antagonistic, in part because the VOC engaged in a conscious policy of assimilation and soon arranged for the dismissal of the French-speaking clergyman who had accompanied the Huguenots. Church services in French continued for another generation, until the 1730s, and even a century later the descendants were aware of their Huguenot heritage,[29] but well before then the VOC's policy had borne fruit, and any ethnic antagonism there might have been given way to accommodation and the creation of a singular colonial community.

This solidarity was forged, or at least strengthened, in the struggle between the burghers and company officials, which came to a head in 1705. In essence, this was a struggle for control of the colony's economy. On the one hand, the governor, Willem Adriaan van der Stel, attempted to dominate the supply of meat and other products to the VOC. He did this together with a group of his associates, most of whom were either still or had recently been company officials, for instance the governor's father, Simon, from whom Willem Adriaan had taken over the office.

Many of them had acquired land and were developing their farms, notably Constantia on the eastern slopes of the Cape Peninsula and Vergelegen in the Hottentots Holland Valley, into substantial estates able to monopolize the sale of wine. The fact that these men could ensure that their goods were bought by the company and that they could make private use of company employees and even slaves obviously gave them enormous advantages. On the other hand, there were a number of burghers, now excluded from such riches, who objected to van der Stel's actions. They were led by Henning Husing, who had himself grown rich on contracts to supply the company. Around him were a number of men who farmed in the Stellenbosch area or who had become substantial butchers, in part because they had organized and profited from raids on the Khoekhoen. Van der Stel was to describe his opponents as anarchic, almost democratic, while they complained about his dictatorial tendencies. At least the latter may have been true, but neither was particularly relevant to the outcome of the contest. This was decided by the Heren XVII in the Netherlands on the basis of their need to maintain some control over their servants, even those who had risen to be governors. Enrichment was tolerated, but not such enrichment that the

---

[29] See the journal of Prosper Lemue, December 7, 1829, in *Journal des missions évangeliques*, 5 (1830), p. 109.

company might be faced by a monopoly from which it was forced to buy at inflated prices. When these factors were combined with a shift in the factional composition of the Amsterdam directors of the VOC, with the consequent removal of those who had got van der Stel his job, the victory of the burghers was assured – a relative victory, as the governor was merely dismissed and in no way either disgraced or ruined, though most of his associates remained in office at the Cape.[30]

The defeat of van der Stel meant that the last opportunity to contain the colony had disappeared. It is difficult to say whether this had ever been a genuine possibility, but hereafter there was no longer any chance that the VOC would exercise its powers to restrict either the number of those who took the opportunity to set up as free burghers or how far from the Cape they settled. The victory of the established gentry of the Stellenbosch area also did not mean that either they or the company had any reason or opportunity to control the movement of stock farmers across the mountains into the interior of the Cape. On the contrary, both had every reason to profit from it, as the interior farmers became suppliers of meat and draught oxen to those of the southwest and to Cape Town. The losers, of course, were the Khoekhoen.

It is conventional to ascribe the final collapse of the Western Cape Khoekhoen to the smallpox epidemic that struck the colony in 1713. Certainly the loss of life was considerable, although the contention of Khoekhoen arriving in Cape Town from the Piketberg in February 1714 that scarcely one member in ten of their society had survived needs to be treated with considerable statistical skepticism. The population decrease of the non-Khoesan population of the Cape was, in general, in the order of 20 percent in the year of the epidemic, and that of the Khoekhoen may well have been significantly higher because few, if any, would have acquired immunity to the disease from a former infection. Against this it is not by any means certain that every Khoekhoe community would have been touched by the infection. Perhaps in total a third of those in the neighborhood of Cape Town and in the Southern Cape died. However, it is also very clear that the ravages of the smallpox epidemic were merely the last in a series of disasters to hit the Khoekhoen and that the European incursions onto Khoekhoe grazing land and Khoekhoe-held water sources, which were at least as disastrous for a pastoral society, were beginning to speed up before the epidemic struck.[31] Khoesan were henceforth on occasion a threat to

---

[30] Schutte, "Company and Colonists," pp. 303–07.

[31] For the debate on the effects of the smallpox epidemic, see R. Ross, "Smallpox at the Cape of Good Hope in the Eighteenth Century," in *African Historical Demography* (Edinburgh: Centre of African Studies, 1977), pp. 416–28; R. Viljoen, "Disease and Society: VOC Cape Town, Its People and the Smallpox Epidemics of 1713, 1755 and 1767," *Kleio, 27* (1995), pp. 22–45; R. Viljoen, "Medicine, Health and Medical Practice in Pre-Colonial

individual farmers, but at least in the southwest their collective political might had largely been destroyed.

THE STRUCTURE OF COLONIAL RULE

Following the recall of Willem Adriaan van der Stel and the emasculation of the Southwestern Cape Khoekhoen, the colony developed a dynamic pattern that was to last for most of the rest of the eighteenth century.

In the first place, the Cape Colony was clearly a part of the empire established by the Dutch East India Company, albeit for a variety of reasons an anomalous part. In particular there were no other areas (except the Banda archipelago) in which large numbers of Europeans organized the agricultural production, nor any (except to some extent Batavia itself) whose function within the VOC was not, in the first instance, the procurement of products for export, either to Europe or within Asia. From the point of view of the VOC, the Cape had to fulfill its original function, namely, the provisioning of the fleets that swung every year between Europe and Asia, the number of which fluctuated between around forty-five and sixty. The company, of course, had no objection to the Cape being used by the ships of other nations. Indeed, the VOC cut its expenses at the Cape by requiring foreign ships to buy meat from the butchers who had tendered to supply the company. These butchers could thus charge the former monopoly prices to recoup the subeconomic rates for which they contracted to sell to the VOC. Also, the presence of foreign ships in Cape Town made the concessions to sell wine extra attractive and thus lucrative for the VOC. The number of foreign ships increased slowly as the century wore on until, in 1772, for the first time, it exceeded that of the VOC ships.[32] Further, the Cape could be used to refurbish ships as a hospital for sailors who had fallen sick on the journey to Cape Town. Also, by no means unimportantly, the Cape could be used as a place to which those who had fallen foul of the company in the Indonesian archipelago could be banished.[33]

The colony as a whole was ruled by a governor and council according to the laws promulgated in the company's headquarters in Batavia and further within the Netherlands. The governor and council could also issue

Khoikhoi Society: An Anthropological Perspective," *History and Anthropology*, 11 (1999), pp. 515–36; L. Guelke and R. Shell, "Landscape of Conquest: Frontier Water Alienation and Khoikhoi Strategies of Survival, 1652–1780," *Journal of Southern African Studies, 18* (1992), pp. 803–24; A. B. Smith, "Khoikhoi Susceptibility to Virgin Soil Epidemics in the 18th Century," *South African Medical Journal,* 75 (1989), pp. 25–6.

[32] Beyers, *Kaapse Patriotte*, pp. 333–5.

[33] K. R. Ward, *Networks of Empire: Forced Migration in the Dutch East India Company* (Cambridge, Cambridge University Press, 2008).

such proclamations for local use as they saw fit. In large measure, the high officials filled the seats of the law court, although from 1685 two burghers also held seats in the court, at least when cases concerning a burgher were being heard. The governor, who could grant mercy as the representative of the Heren XVII, did not himself sit in judgment. Certainly, the punishments imposed and the use of torture to extract confessions seem barbaric by today's standards, but they were nevertheless in line with those employed in the Dutch Republic, although exacerbated by the presence of a large slave population, whose offenses were dealt with harshly to preserve order.[34]

The Cape was never seen as a prize posting within the system of the VOC. The opportunities for self-enrichment on the part of the governor and his subordinates were too limited, certainly by the avaricious standards of company officials in Bengal or Batavia. The various governors, notably Hendrik Swellengrebel and Rijk Tulbagh, were able to accumulate considerable sums,[35] but the lesser officials were unable to do so. The consequence was that they remained at their posts in the colony throughout their lives and, more importantly, ensured that their sons followed them into VOC service. By 1779, more than half of those employed by the central administration in Cape Town had been born in the Cape, all of them as the children of VOC officials.[36] A specific social category was developing.

Those who held higher positions within the company hierarchy looked with disdain on those below them. In 1717 they were confronted with the question of whether the company should attempt to run its affairs as far as possible on the basis of slave labor or whether efforts should be made to introduce a European work force in sufficient numbers to cover its needs. Almost unanimously the members of the Council of Policy chose the former option.[37] In general, they felt the slaves could be controlled, whereas European laborers were likely to be nothing more than drunken and rebellious louts. As is always the case with such attitudes among members of a ruling group, the view from below was substantially different. Cape Town in particular came to see the growth of an artisanal culture among the lower- and middle-level employees of the VOC, many of whom were of German origin, and whose ideas of honor and respect were brought

---

[34] R. Ross, "The Rule of Law at the Cape of Good Hope in the Eighteenth Century," *Journal of Imperial and Commonwealth History, IX* (1980), pp. 5–16; P. Spierenburg, *The Spectacle of Suffering: Executions and the Evolution of Repression: From a Pre-Industrial Metropolis to the European Experience* (Cambridge: Cambridge University Press, 1984).

[35] Van Duin and Ross, *The Economy of the Cape Colony*, p. 81.

[36] Schutte, "Company and Colonists," p. 297.

[37] *Reports of De Chavonnes and His Council, and of Van Imhoff, on the Cape*, Cape Town (Van Riebeeck Society, 1918).

with them from Europe.[38] A few members of this group moved out of company service to become part of the burgher population of the growing town, just as a number of those who had been hired out by the company as farm servants (*knechts*) also remained permanently in the Cape outside VOC employ.

Certainly, the harshness of the discipline the VOC imposed through the legal system weighed as heavily on the European soldiers and sailors as on the slaves, at least in the early years of the colony. Later, though, those of European descent were spared the more extreme forms of capital punishment – in which the death process was extended over hours or days – which was thought necessary to keep the slaves in check.

The population of the Cape Colony grew steadily throughout the eighteenth century, although it is not possible to provide exact figures of the rates of growth for the totality. In particular, it is unclear how many Khoesan were under colonial rule and thus should be counted in the totals. Probably the number was increasing, not for reasons of natural growth but rather because more were being forced by the loss of their grazing lands to live on the farms and under the control of the invading settlers. In addition, the company employees never had to register the number of members of their families or other dependents, nor of their slaves. An attempt has been made to estimate the number of the latter, on the basis of slave transfer figures, or rather to provide total numbers for the slave population of the colony.[39] These have to be combined, together with the fairly certain numbers for the free non-Khoesan population, both in company service and among the burghers. This shows that the total population rose steadily from about 3,700 at the beginning of the century to about 22,500 in 1775, a rate of just under 2.5 percent per year. In general, slaves made up around half of that population, though a somewhat higher proportion in the middle of the first half of the century than either before or subsequently.

These raw figures hide within them very substantial differences, particularly with regard to the sex ratio of the various groups. Company servants were, by definition, all male, and the absence of their womenfolk from the figures somewhat distorts information on the colonywide ratio. For the rest, the proportion of men among adult slaves was always higher than 75 percent, whereas among the children there was also a light predominance of males. In relation to the free population, in contrast, the proportion of adult males declined steadily from about 67 percent of the adult population at the beginning of the century to about 60 percent by 1775.[40]

---

[38] Worden, "Forging a Reputation."   [39] Shell, *Children of Bondage*, pp. 149–51.

[40] These figures are based on calculations that include the number of *knechten* among the adult male population, thus skewing the numbers toward a higher sex ratio.

In other words, although the proportion of slaves in the colony remained relatively constant, and thus the growth rate of both slave and free populations remained more or less equal, the causes of that growth rate differed sharply. The slave population grew entirely as a result of the slave trade and would have declined but for that forced immigration. Only from the second half of the eighteenth century was half the slave population, including the children, Cape born. The free population did have a substantial component of immigrants, both men from Europe who had left the service of the VOC and those ex-slaves, predominantly women, who entered the free population on the basis of their manumission,[41] but in general the sharpness of colonial expansion derived from natural population growth as a result of high levels of fertility and relatively low mortality rates.[42]

The slave trade to the Cape Colony remained split into two segments. On the one hand was the trade of the VOC itself, for its own use. In total, during the eighteenth century the company sent out twenty-one expeditions, primarily to Madagascar, and five to the east coast of Africa.[43] Between them they brought about 3,000 slaves back to the Cape and, in addition, nearly 300 from the short-lived post the VOC had established in Delagoa Bay (Maputo) in the 1720s.[44] On the other, there was the trade for the company officials and the burghers. Very occasionally the VOC sold slaves it had purchased on the local market, but the great mass came through the private trade. The best estimate we have is that during the whole period of Cape slavery, from 1652 to abolition in 1808, a total of about 58,500 slaves were imported for the private sector.[45] Until the last quarter of the eighteenth century they came in approximately equal proportions from Madagascar, India, and the Indonesian archipelago, with a smattering from the East

---

[41] See R. Elphick and R. Shell, "Intergroup Relations: Khoikhoi, Settlers, Slaves and Free Blacks, 1652–1795," in Elphick and Giliomee (Eds.), *Shaping*, pp. 204–13.

[42] R. Ross, "The 'White' Population of South Africa in the Eighteenth Century," *Population Studies, 19* (1975), pp. 210–22; L. Guelke, "The Anatomy of a Colonial Settler Population," *International Journal of African Historical Studies, 21* (1988), pp. 453–73. That mortality rates were low has had to be inferred, as deaths, unlike baptisms and marriages, were not registered.

[43] The distinction was not absolute. For instance, the expedition of 1776 in the *De Zon* traveled to Zanzibar and indeed to what is now southern Somalia but nevertheless acquired most of its sixty-eight slaves on the coast of Madagascar. R. Ross, "The Dutch on the Swahili Coast, 1776–1778: Two Slaving Journals," *International Journal of African Historical Studies, 19* (1987), pp. 305–60, 479–506.

[44] J. C. Armstrong and N. A. Worden, "The Slaves, 1652–1834," in Elphick and Giliomee (Eds.), *Shaping*, p. 112; C. G. Coetsee, "Die Kompanjie se Besetting van Delagoabaai," *Archives Year Book for South African History* II (1948).

[45] Shell, *Children of Bondage*, p. 40. I have subtracted the 4,300 slaves imported for the company from his figure.

African coast, mainly Mozambique.[46] Some of the Malagasies and Mozambicans were offloaded from slaving vessels on their way to the Americas,
and from the 1770s onward there seems to have been a dedicated trade in
African slaves conducted from Mauritius in exchange for foodstuff.[47] The
Indians and Indonesians, by contrast, came on the ships of the Dutch East
India Company and, to some extent, of the French, on their way from Asia
to Europe. On average a VOC ship might carry some twenty slaves for
private sale in Cape Town, and this was, in general, an accepted perquisite
for skippers and repatriating officials. Only in 1767 was an attempt made
to prohibit the importation of Indonesian, particularly Bugis, slaves as a
result of a number of violent crimes committed by the Bugis in Cape Town,
but these repeated ordinances do not seem to have had much effect.[48]

The slaves who were imported into the Cape were put to work, in very
large measure either within the economy of Cape Town or in that of the
wine and wheat farms of the Southwestern Cape. Both of these sectors of the
Cape economy grew steadily through the eighteenth century. The number
of burgher-owned slaves in Cape Town can, to some extent, be used as an
indicator of its prosperity because, presumably, the continual investment
required to maintain a given level of slave holdings, let alone to increase it,
would have been impossible without the steady growth of colonial wealth.
At a rough estimate, the number of slaves owned by burghers who did not
have any agricultural holdings rose from 468 in 1723 to 2,123 in 1773, a
rate of 3.1 percent a year. They formed an increasingly large proportion of
the total population of the town, which can be estimated at about 2,000 in
1720. But it had risen to 7,400 by the 1770s.

The occupations of Cape Town's inhabitants were much the same as
those of any port city. A census taken of the free burghers in 1731 shows
a variety of craftsmen, including plumbers, wagonmakers, shoemakers,
tailors, blacksmiths, saddlemakers, coopers, and thatchers, plus some more
skilled artisans, including a coppersmith and a silversmith. The largest
single category, though, were lodging-house keepers, and there were also
a number of shopkeepers, innkeepers, and wine sellers.[49] As the century
wore on, at least some of the more specialized crafts began to increase in

---

[46] After about 1775 the number from the East African coast increased sharply. See Shell,
Children of Bondage, p. 41; Ross, "The Last Years of the Slave Trade to South Africa,"
Slavery and Abolition, 9 (1988), pp. 209–20.

[47] Ross, "Last Years."

[48] Armstrong and Worden, "Slaves," p. 117; S. Koolhof and R. Ross, "Upas, September and
the Bugis at the Cape of Good Hope: The Context of a Slave's Letter," *Archipel*, 70 (2005),
pp. 281–308; the Bugis are one of the largest ethnic groups in Southern Sulawesi.

[49] N. Worden, E. van Heyningen, and V. Bickford-Smith, *Cape Town: The Making of a City*
(Cape Town: David Philip, 1998), p. 57.

number, as Cape society was able to sustain more skilled craftsmen.[50] Some of the slaves labored in the workshops of these men, others dominated the retail trade in foodstuff and in vegetables, working as independent entrepreneurs but required to provide for their owners a weekly sum of money, known as *koeligeld*. There were other ways in which *koeligeld* could be acquired, including prostitution and the trade in stolen goods.[51] Slaves also functioned as the main domestic servants and, indeed, as the cooks of the town, something that still can be appreciated in the eastern basis of traditional Cape cuisine. The majority, however, had more menial tasks: cutting wood on Table Mountain, fetching water, and so forth. In particular, the slaves owned by the company had heavy tasks, many of them working in the harbor, in forests above Cape Town, maintaining the fortifications, or clearing Cape Town of its rubbish.[52]

The majority of the slaves, on average about two-thirds of those owned by the burghers, worked in the wheat and wine farms of the Boland and Swartland. Here, too, there was a steady growth in the levels of production and in the wealth of the farmers. From the early eighteenth century, but for a few exceptional years when bad weather struck, the Cape was able to produce all the wheat it needed for its own consumption and for the needs of the ships putting into Table Bay harbor. There was also, at least from the 1740s on, a regular export of wheat, largely to Batavia and to the other Dutch factories in the East. Clearly, the Mediterranean climate of the Cape, which precluded agricultural exports to Europe on any large scale, was advantageous in supplying populations of European origin in those parts of Asia that did not, for instance, produce bread grains, primarily wheat, which exceeded barley and rye by a ratio of about five to one.[53]

The production methods employed at the Cape did not need to be sophisticated. To some extent beans and peas were planted in rotation with the wheat and other grains. Ploughs were heavy, drawn by as many as twelve oxen, and cut a deep furrow. Weeds were therefore ploughed in and formed a green manure on lands that were left fallow at least every other year. By this means some considerable proportion of the virgin fertility the Cape had possessed before the arrival of the Dutch was preserved. Yields

---

[50] D. Viljoen and P. Rabe, *Cape Furniture and Metalware* (Cape Town: privately published, 2001). It is by no means certain how many of the furniture makers were resident in Cape Town as, by the later eighteenth century, and certainly in the early nineteenth, regional styles began to be evident, showing that the producers were living in the countryside.

[51] In an attempt to curb the latter, an ordinance was issued in 1754 prohibiting slaves from selling any goods aside from eatables, but this remained a dead letter.

[52] R. Ross, "The Occupations of Slaves in Eighteenth Century Cape Town," *Studies in the History of Cape Town*, 2 (1980), pp. 1–14.

[53] Van Duin and Ross, *Economy*, pp. 17, 129.

were low when measured against the acreage of land under cultivation, but were nevertheless relatively high in comparison to those in Europe when measured against the amount of seed sown. Harvesting was primarily by means of a sickle. The shale lands of the region to the north of Cape Town, long cleared of their Cochoqua inhabitants, were being brought into another sector of the world economy.

The same could be said of the hill slopes on the eastern side of the Cape Peninsula and around Stellenbosch, which provided the locus for the wine industry. Again, there was a steady increase in the level of production, from around two million vines in about 1720 to four million in about 1750 and close to seven million by the 1770s. Again, the steady increase, and therefore the continual investment, makes it clear that there was a sufficient market for the wine produced on the basis of these vines. This market was primarily in Cape Town, where the licence to sell wine by the glass was heavily contested, but where nevertheless sales by the barrel were common. In addition, from the midcentury wines were exported from the colony, again largely to the east, with the exception of those from the Constantia estates on the peninsula, which, by a remarkable feat of marketing, became the first estate wines to gain prominence in Europe and were widely desired in royal courts and elsewhere.[54]

Slave holdings were, in general, not large. In 1753, for instance, 74 percent of those burghers who owned any slaves owned fewer than ten, and twenty years later this proportion had risen slightly, to 76 percent. Only 3.6 percent of owners (27 of 748) owned thirty or more slaves in 1753, and only 3 percent (34 of 1,138) in 1773. Obviously, when looked at from the point of view of the slaves, matters are somewhat different. In 1753, 34.9 percent of slaves lived in holdings of fewer than ten, and 19.6 percent in holdings of thirty or more; in 1773, the equivalent percentages were 44.0 and 17.6.[55] It appears that only one man, Maarten Melck, ever owned more than 100 slaves, although Willem Adriaan van der Stel may also have done so before his dismissal.[56] The Cape was never a country of large plantations; farms were always substantial but not very large. In terms of slaveholdings, at least, the largest were in the Cape district and the wine-farming parts of Stellenbosch district, and those farmers who lived

[54] J. J. Steur, *Herstel of Ondergang: De Voorstellen tot Redres van de VOC, 1740–1795* (Utrecht: Hes, 1984); G. J. Schutte (Ed.), *Hendrik Cloete, Groot Constantia and the VOC, 1778–1799* (Cape Town: Van Riebeeck Society, 2003).

[55] These figures were constructed from the so-called *opgaafrollen* in the National Archives in The Hague, in VOC 4193 and 4276.

[56] Between 1699 and 1707 he bought at least 121 slaves. J. L. Hattingh, "Die Klagte oor Goewerneur W. A. van der Stel se Slawebesit – 'n Beoordeling met Behulp van Kwantitatiewe Data," *Kronos, VII* (1983), pp. 40–1.

across the mountains in Swellendam or in the further parts of Stellenbosch and Drakenstein were likely to own the fewest slaves. There were also a few very large slave owners in Cape Town itself (who may, in fact, have been primarily market gardeners on the slopes of Table Mountain), but in general urban slaveholdings were low, averaging scarcely more than those in Swellendam. On the other hand, the proportion of farming households with at least one slave was always very high, over 95 percent in the Cape District and over 50 percent even in pastoral Swellendam.[57]

These figures give a somewhat distorted view of the labor available to the Cape farmers. In the first place they do not include the Khoesan, who worked in increasing numbers on the farms. The stock farmers of the interior, although they may have had a few slaves, had to rely primarily on Khoesan. The investment in slaves was higher than most of them could permit, and the danger that slaves would escape to the independent African polities grew as the colonial farmers came to live further to the east. In addition, Khoesan worked on the wheat and wine farms, though primarily as additional labor in harvest time.[58] Here they joined slaves who were sent from one type of farm to another, with somewhat different seasonal labor requirements, as the wheat was harvested between December and February and the grapes largely in March. These slaves might have moved between the various farms of a single very rich owner, but more generally on an arrangement, either in terms of reciprocity or of hire, between two farmers. The result was that even those slaves who seem to have lived on isolated farms had more contact outside their immediate living space than might at first sight appear.

THE STRUCTURE OF COLONIAL SOCIETY

As the colony expanded it became necessary to develop some level of administration below that of the Council of Policy. In Cape Town, the independent *fiscaal* doubled as chief prosecutor of the colony, responsible to the Heren XVII and theoretically able to keep a check on all the officials as well as the burghers, and as magistrate of Cape Town. He had under his control a contingent of so-called *kaffirs*, who were men exiled to the Cape from Indonesia for some crime. They patrolled the town at night and arrested those whom the *fiscaal* ordered to be detained. In this they were aided by the *burgherwagt*, a civilian force under the control of the Burgher

---

[57] Armstrong and Worden, "Slaves," p. 135.
[58] A. Biewenga, *De Kaap de Goede Hoop, Een Nederlandse Vestigingskolonie, 1680–1730* (Amsterdam: Prometheus/Bert Bakker, 1999), pp. 105–08; R. Elphick and V. C. Malherbe, "The Khoisan to 1828," in Elphick and Giliomee (Eds.), *Shaping*, pp. 28–35.

Council, a body nominated by the governor but was nevertheless supposed to represent the opinions of the free burghers in the government of the city, which was also required to inspect the water channels through the town. Burgher counselors also served on the Court of Justice and on the body that gave men and women permission to marry. From 1722, on the other hand, fires were to be fought primarily by the freed slaves, who, in one of those symbolic inversions beloved of *ancien-regime* societies, were to combat the arson that was one of the major weapons of resistance of their erstwhile fellows in bondage.

Outside of Cape Town, magistracies were set up in Stellenbosch in 1682 and in Swellendam in 1743. Here the *landdrost*, as the magistrate was known, was assisted by leading figures among the locally resident farmers, who acted as the board of *heemraden*. These individuals had, in general, a much greater influence over the working of the district than the Burgher Council in Cape Town had over the administration of the town. Obviously the pressure they could bring to bear on the single figure of the local magistrate could be considerable, and they were involved in matters of law enforcement and land granting. Although *heemraden* only served for a single year, they could be reappointed with some regularity. The *heemraden* were thus the temporary representatives of a much wider class, namely, the Cape gentry, which established itself in the Southwest Cape countryside during the first half of the eighteenth century.[59] They had first come to prominence as the adversaries of Willem Adriaan van der Stel, but thereafter, quietly, their relations with the officials of VOC improved very considerably as the two groups came to realize that neither could succeed without the other.

The same group of men came to dominate the church as deacons and elders. The Dutch Reformed Church was the public church of the colony. The company paid for its buildings and its clergymen were on the company's payroll. A similar situation existed in the Netherlands and throughout the VOC empire, but, in contrast to both these regions, the Reformed Church held a monopoly over formal religious observance in the colony at least until the 1780s. This did not mean, however, that all the Europeans within the colony were fervent Calvinists. In 1700 about 8 percent of the European population of Cape Town, and a slightly higher proportion of that of Stellenbosch, were full members of the Dutch Reformed church. Probably because it had seen the influx of the Huguenots, who were after all religious refugees, the proportion in Drakenstein was substantially higher. During the course of the century the numbers of church members would increase,

---

[59] R. Ross, "The Rise of the Cape Gentry," *Journal of Southern African Studies*, 9 (1983), pp. 191–217; L. Guelke and Robert Shell, "An Early Colonial Landed Gentry: Land and Wealth in the Cape Colony 1682–1731," *Journal of Historical Geography*, 9 (1983), pp. 265–86.

both absolutely and relative to the growing population of European descent, at least in the countryside, but even by the end of the century the proportion remained below 50 percent.[60]

Baptism was a different matter. Christian baptism was seen as a necessary, though not sufficient, condition for acceptance into the higher levels of free society. Men and women from Europe baptized their children if they accepted them as their offspring, legitimate or otherwise. The tenets of the Calvinist theology of baptism required that a master bring up all those born in his (or her) household as Christians, which would have required the infant baptism of all slave children. Nevertheless, relatively few of the slaves belonging to other owners were baptized at birth. The belief that the baptism of a slave precluded his or her sale, whether strictly imposable by law – there is no known case of a slave contesting his or her sale on these grounds – made such a procedure unacceptable to most slaveowners. In the event, the only major slaveowner to baptize slaves on a systematic basis was the Dutch East India Company itself, whose officials ensured that all those born in the lodge were baptized and, in theory, received some instruction in the Christian religion. Because the company never sold its slaves, certainly not those who were born in the Cape, problems relating to possible sales did not affect it. However, those who came into the lodge as a result of the slave trade, no matter what their age, were not baptized.

Attempts at mission work at the Cape failed. The fairly half-hearted start made in the early eighteenth century by the Rev. Petrus Kalden came to nothing and probably would have been done even if he had not been recalled to Europe as one of those too closely associated with the regime of Willem Adriaan van der Stel. In 1736 Georg Schmidt, a member of the Moravian Brotherhood, arrived at the Cape to work among the Khoekhoen. He had a degree of support from Amsterdam, so he could not, in the first instance, be refused, and the Cape government allowed him to begin preaching in Baviaans Kloof, near Swellendam. A small congregation developed around him, which, half a century later was to form the kernel of the Mission community, which was established in the same place, later renamed Genadendal ("the valley of grace"). The Khoekhoen who had come into contact with Schmidt were able to maintain their Christianity even after Schmidt was expelled from the colony as a result of the complaints of the Dutch Reformed Ministers. However, those Khoekhoen did not, themselves, continue to proselytize, nor would they have been able to.[61]

---

[60] G. Schutte, "Between Amsterdam and Batavia: Cape Society and the Calvinist Church under the Dutch East India Company," *Kronos: Journal of Cape History*, 25 (1998–1999), pp. 17–45.

[61] H. C. J. Bredekamp, "Construction and Collapse of a Herrnhut Mission Community at the Cape, 1737–1743," *Kronos: Journal of Cape History*, 24 (1997).

The ministers of the Dutch Reformed Church were thus able to maintain their monopoly over the organized religion of the colony. This included preventing the establishment of a Lutheran church until 1780, despite the fact that a high proportion of company employees had been brought up in the Lutheran areas of Germany. It also meant that the slaves, and most of the Khoekhoen, were cut off from organized Christianity, and there is no sign that they compensated for this by developing any independent Christian congregations.

There are indications, though, that in the course of the eighteenth century Islam was taking root among the Cape Town underclasses. This came about in two ways. First, some of the newly imported slaves may have been Muslim before their enslavement or may have converted in the course of their slavery before arriving in South Africa. Probably there were rather fewer of these than would be apparent from the toponyms of Cape slaves, as even those described as "van Bugis" or "van Java" may have come from the non-Muslim populations of Indonesia and have acquired their designations as they passed through Bugis and Java. Nevertheless, there was certainly a Bugis community at the Cape in which respected elderly slaves functioned as doctors and in which the country of origin could help in the development of that trust necessary for slave resistance. All the same, this trust is nowhere stated to have been based on the shared belief in, and practices of, Islam.[62]

Secondly, Islam came to the Cape through a number of members of the Indonesian elite exiled there by the Dutch, primarily for leading various movements of resistance against VOC overlordship. The Cape functioned as a most convenient penal colony, both because transport was easily arranged and because the chances of escape back to the east were small. In the century and a half of company rule, over a thousand men and women were so exiled. Many of those sent west were incarcerated on Robben Island, further limiting their ability to escape, but there were also those who were settled on the mainland. As early as 1667 two sufi shaykhs were placed in the forests of Constantia, and, most famously, in 1694 Shaykh Yusuf al-Taj al-Khalwati al-Maqasari, with a party of fifty followers, was settled at Zandvliet on the False Bay coast. Attempts were made to isolate these men from the mass of the Cape population, but these would seem to have failed. It may be that their very isolation allowed them to maintain contact with the Cape Town slaves, particularly woodcutters, which the authorities were unable to control or even to know about.

The indications are that during the eighteenth century there developed a small but growing Islamic community, based primarily on Sufi brotherhoods, and probably a wider circle of sympathizers. There are even

---

[62] Koolhof and Ross, "Upas, September and the Bugis," pp. 287–9.

indications that returning exiles brought to the Javanese courts elements of the religious ideas and organizations they had developed in South Africa. Be that as it may, the activities of one Shaykh Nuruman in providing written charms to facilitate slave escapes illustrates both the use made of Islamic learning and the breadth of the shaykhs' influence in and around Cape Town. Only right at the end of the period of VOC rule would it prove possible for Islamic leaders to found Cape Town's first mosques and initiate the institutionalization of the faith. The Cape was being linked to Asian as well as European intellectual and political networks.[63]

Aside from its intrinsic importance in providing the inhabitants of the Cape Colony with the means to make sense of their world and with the strength to endure it, religion, both Islam and, in particular, Christianity, mattered because of the role it played in the definitions of status, and thus in effectively determining the social stratification of the colony. Again, this has been a matter of some contention in the historical writing about early colonial South Africa. The arguments were driven by the question of to what extent the roots of later forms of racial oppression are to be found in the Dutch-ruled Cape. The answer to such a question, naturally, lies as much in the period after Dutch rule ended as during that period and is primarily determined by the particular interpretation chosen of the most salient features of later South African society. Nevertheless, historians who work on the Dutch period have been heavily concerned with questions of how far the European domination of the colony, which no one can deny, involved racial stratification. The essential problem is whether the rulers of the colony saw themselves as Europeans, or, even more narrowly, as whites, and whether that fact, if it was a fact, in any way influenced their actions. Conversely, of course, the question is whether those whom later generations would consider to be "colored" or "nonwhite" were seen at the time as such, or, in other words, whether such a categorization had any social meaning during the eighteenth century. In other words, the problem

[63] J. E. Mason, "'A Faith for Ourselves': Slavery, Sufism and Conversion to Islam at the Cape," *South African Historical Journal*, 46 (2002), pp. 3–24; M. A. Bradlow, "Imperialism, State Formation and Establishment of a Muslim Community at the Cape of Good Hope, 1770–1840: A Study in Urban Resistance," unpublished M.A. dissertation, University of Cape Town, 1988; F. Bradlow and M. Cairns, *The Early Cape Muslims: A Study of Their Mosques, Genealogy and Origins* (Cape Town: Balkema, 1978); R. Shell, "The Establishment and Spread of Islam at the Cape from the Beginning of Company Rule to 1838," unpublished B.A. Hons dissertation, University of Cape Town, 1974; A. Davids, "The 'Coloured' Image of Afrikaans in Nineteenth Century Cape Town," *Kronos: Journal of Cape History*, 17 (1990), pp. 42–5; Ward, "The Bounds of Bondage." On Nuruman van Marantu, see Nigel Worden and Gerald Groenewald, *Trials of Slavery, Selected Documents Concerning Slaves from the Criminal Records of the Council of Justice at the Cape of Good Hope, 1705–1794* (Cape Town: Van Riebeeck Society, 2005), 537 ff.

is whether the ways of thought and the mainsprings for action, which have been all too common in the South Africa of the twentieth century, can be found two centuries earlier, or whether historians erroneously read back such categorizations into the earlier period.

With this in mind, it is striking that the main distinctions were not between "white" and "black" but rather between "Christian" and "heathen," between "slave" and "free," between "burgher" and "company official," or between "burgher" and "Khoesan" – at least to give modern translations of the original Dutch, and to ignore those between "adult" and "child" and between "man" and "woman," which are close to universal, in application if not in content.[64] Evidently these were sufficient to organize the social world. But then the question arises: How far were such appellations in some way surrogates for unconsciously adopted and rigid ideas of race, or an analysis of early colonial South Africa in terms of race merely an anachronism?

In attempting to solve such questions, historians have looked in particular at the two groups known as "free blacks" (*vrije swarten*) and as "baptized Bastards." The former were primarily to be found in and around Cape Town. It would seem they were all freed slaves or time-expired convicts, or at least the descendants of such people. This does, to some extent, explain why they constituted only a small proportion of the population of Cape Town.[65] In comparison with at least the South American port cities, levels of manumission at the Cape were always low. Fewer than 2 Cape slaves per 1,000 could expect to be freed every year, by the decision of their owners or by the provisions of a will. This was a sixth of the rate that obtained, for example, in Brazil or much of Spanish America. Rural slaves were virtually never freed, except by running away, and even urban slaves could generally not expect to receive their legal freedom. Those who were freed were disproportionately likely to be young, to have been born at the Cape (or if not to have been of Asian origin) and to be female (particularly if the manumitter was himself male). They were also disproportionately likely to have been owned, at least at the end of their slavery, by a free black and quite likely to have been his or her relative.[66]

What all this means is that it was probable that a slave on his or, more likely, her, manumission would be absorbed into some kinship network

---

[64] Biewenga, *De Kaap de Goede Hoop*, 28–9; R. Ross, *Status and Respectability in the Cape Colony, 1750–1870: A Tragedy of Manners* (Cambridge: Cambridge University Press, 1999), Chapter 2.

[65] In 1770 free blacks and their dependent children made up 11 percent of the free, noncompany population of the Cape District. Calculated from van Duin and Ross, *Economy*, Appendix 2.

[66] Elphick and Shell, "Intergroup Relations," pp. 208–10.

among the free, either because he or she already belonged to such a network on the basis of birth or because the freed slave would marry into such a network. The exceptions were those who were able to purchase their own freedom on the basis of the profits from the commercial or artisanal activities in which they were engaged in Cape Town, a process that would eventually lead to something approaching the disintegration of slavery within the city.[67] In any event, the manumitted were not cast loose on society, largely because a substantial sum had to be paid to the deaconry of the Dutch Reformed Church as a guarantee against the freed slave becoming a charge on Cape Town's poor funds, with the result that those slaves who could no longer work were not thrown out onto the streets; they might of course be sold upcountry if there was a market for them.

Thus the manumitted became part of Cape Town's wider society, although the stigma of their having been slaves remained. It is at least arguable that "free black" was not a heritable status and that the children of free blacks were no longer seen as "black," which referred to the infamy of slavery or of criminal conviction, rather than to somatic type.[68] This was more particularly the case when the union in question was that of an ex-slave woman married to a burgher man, at any rate when the children were born after their mother's manumission and their parents' marriage.

Similarly, the category of "baptized Bastards" (*gedoopte bastarden*), which came into existence in the east of the colony in the later eighteenth century, found its prime justification in the nonmarriage of the parents as well as in the mixture of the various stocks inherent in the term. "Bastard" in Dutch means "mongrel" rather than "illegitimate." It was an extension of the term "Bastard," which referred to those with a white father and a Khoekhoe mother, in contrast to those known as "*Bastard Hottentotten*," whose fathers were slaves and mothers Khoekhoe and on whom farm owners could make claims to labor until the age of twenty-five, in theory as compensation for the cost of raising them.[69] By the end of the century there were about forty such families in Graaff-Reinet district, taxonomically anomalous because they should have been accepted into full burgher status and society according to one criterion, that of their Christianity, but not by others – their illegitimacy and, by this stage, perhaps their Khoesan origin. It was a group that was to survive into the nineteenth century, with the women probably mainly being accepted through marriage into what was

[67] A. Bank, *The Decline of Urban Slavery at the Cape, 1806 to 1843* (Cape Town: Communications 21, Centre for African Studies, University of Cape Town, 1991).

[68] Ross, *Status and Respectability*, pp. 30–5.

[69] V. C. Malherbe, "Indentured and Unfree Labour in South Africa: Towards an Understanding," *South African Historical Journal*, 24 (1991), pp. 3–32.

coming to be seen as white society, whereas the men remained outside that select group.

THE EXPANSION OF THE COLONY

As the colonists began to move away from the Southwest Cape, they could no longer rely on the forces of the Cape government for their protection. The natural result was the development of citizen militia, which were extensions of the practice of including civilians in the armed patrols of the Cape's military. These militias, largely horse-borne and well armed, came to be known as commandos. They were commanded by senior and respected local figures who held the office of *veld-kornet* and whose area of authority, the *veldcornetcy*, became the lowest level of administrative division within the colony. Above them, in major commandos, was the *veld-commandant*, who commanded the militias of a complete district when such was necessary.

The first really substantial employment of the commando system occurred in the late 1730s, in the northwest of the colony. Colonial intrusion into the Oliphants River valley, which had been continuing since the mid-1720s,[70] created a zone of conflict, in part because the originally relatively open and egalitarian relations between farmers and Khoesan became increasingly hierarchical and exploitative as settlement became more intense. Attempts by the Cape authorities to dampen down the conflict only led to unrest among the frontiersmen, who temporarily took arms against the Cape Town government under the leadership of a disaffected French soldier named Etienne Barbier. Barbier himself was eventually captured and put to death for treason. However, in their attempts to regain the allegiance of the frontiersmen, the Cape authorities reneged on an agreement with a number of Khoesan leaders. Cattle that had previously been confiscated and then returned to the Khoekhoen were reappropriated by the Dutch.

In consequence, the Khoesan launched attacks on a number of the most isolated of the northwest farms. At least ten were attacked and a further forty-eight abandoned. A commando was sent out, led by Johannes Cruywagen, a man with large-scale meat interests in the northwest – he was one of the contractors who supplied meat to the company and had ranches of about 40,000 hectares near St. Helena Bay. This and subsequent commandos included both Europeans and Khoesan among their number. Many of the former were attracted by the promise of amnesty for their part in

[70] L. J. Mitchell, "Contested Terrains: Property and Labor on the Cedarberg Frontier, South Africa 1725– c. 1830," unpublished Ph.D. thesis, University of California Los Angeles (2001).

the Barbier unrest and were thus able to realize at least some of the aims of Barbier's followers. The commandos swept through the Sandveld and the mountains around the Oliphants River and on to the Bokkevelden. They destroyed many settlements, captured cattle and sheep, and effectively forced the Khoesan still living there either to move to the north or to take service on the European-owned and run farms.[71]

The latter was indeed, often, whence they came. The events of 1739 are designated the "Bushman war" by historians,[72] but this is the consequence of assuming that all Khoesan who fought guerrilla wars against the colonists were in some way "Bushmen." Clearly, this was not the case. In the first place, many of the leaders of the resistance were themselves stockholders, though, in this arid region, both they and their predecessors were considerably poorer than, for instance, the Hessequa of the southern coastal forelands. Secondly, many of the others had worked for a time as farm servants. Indeed, what seems at first sight to be the primary resistance of autochthonous hunter–gatherers turns out to have been in part a conflict between Trekboers attempting to assert their control over the landscape and over its inhabitants, on the one hand, and the Khoesan who had worked for them, had often been maltreated, and who had revolted in an attempt to retain some independence, on the other. In so doing, the latter behaved as "Bushmen," but the Bushmen wars were as much class struggle as anything else.[73]

This is clear in the major struggle for the conquest of the Cape, which took place along the mountain ranges of the Cape Fold Belt, from the region of the Bokkeveld in the west to the Sneeuberg to the north of Graaff-Reinet in the east. Perhaps it is not the whole story. There are indications that the various San groups of the Escarpment and the plains between it and the Gariep River, which included the /Xam of the Zak River valley and the "Houswana" of the Seekoe River, had a deep history as substantive entities. Certainly they had maintained a non-Khoekhoe language and, together with the "Mountain Bushmen" of the Drakensberg, were also still painting on the rocks when the Europeans encountered them. Against this,

---

[71] N. Penn, "Land, Labour and Livestock in the Western Cape During the Eighteenth Century," in W. James and M. Simons (Eds.), *The Angry Divide: Social and Economic History of the Western Cape* (Cape Town: David Philip, 1989), pp. 2–19; Penn, *Forgotten Frontier*; Newton-King, *Masters and Servants*, pp. 68–9.

[72] P. L. Scholtz, "Die Historiese Ontwikkkeling van die Onder-Olifantsrivier (1660–1902); 'n Geskiedenis van die Distrik Vanrhynsdorp," *Archives Year Book for South African History* (1966).

[73] J. Wright, "San History and non-San Historians," *Collected Seminar Papers of the Institute of Commonwealth Studies, London: The Societies of Southern Africa in the 19th and 20th Centuries*, 8 (1977), pp. 1–10.

they were certainly not isolated from the rest of the Khoesan population of the Cape, or, indeed, by the mid-eighteenth century, from the invaders. Thus, a series of concerted attacks, by groups of several hundred fighters, drove the Europeans from a wide swath of land to the south of the escarpment and elicited the launch of the largest and most savage commandos the colony had ever seen.

In 1774, 250 men – 150 of whom were themselves Khoekhoen or Bastards – divided into three groups, swept through the country from the Ceres Karoo to the Sneeuberg, killing, according to their own figures, 499 San men, women, and children and capturing another 231, who were distributed among the farmers in a status equivalent to slavery. However, even this bloodletting, inflicted by commandos, who apparently only lost a single man, did not end the war. Attacks on isolated farms continued. The frontier farmers even believed that they had labored with too many restrictions, so that a subsequent commando, in 1777, demanded and received permission from the Council of Policy in Cape Town to "extirpate" their enemies.[74] It was, in its way, an invitation to genocide, and the opportunity was taken up with great energy by the colonists. The war continued until at least 1791, and at times the colonists were driven out of large areas of the escarpment and the Sneeuberge. In the end, though, the wars did not end in the physical elimination of the San but rather in the incorporation into colonial society at the lowest possible level, that of distrusted and exploited servant, of those who did not succeed in fleeing beyond colonial control.

There is little mystery about why the Khoesan resisted European intrusion as vigorously as they did. Those who remained more or less as independent hunter–gatherers saw their hunting grounds alienated and what was once one of world's largest concentrations of mammalian fauna steadily reduced to a tiny fraction of what it had been.[75] Guns and horses made the colonists much more efficient slaughterers than the Khoesan had ever been, nor did the colonists have any idea that they should preserve game stocks for following generations – it is doubtful whether the Khoesan did either, but their capacity for mass destruction was much more limited. The game was replaced by the colonists' cattle, sheep, and horses, with a much lower total biomass and, in theory, protected from Khoesan predation. Those who had spent time as laborers on colonists' farms and had experienced the

---

[74] Newton-King, *Masters and Servants*, pp. 74 ff; van der Merwe, *Noordwaartse Beweging*; on extirpation, Robert Ross "Donald Moodie and the Origins of South African Historiography" in *Beyond the Pale: Essays on the History of Colonial South Africa* (Hanover and London: Wesleyan University Press, 1993).

[75] See, for example, van der Merwe, *Trek*, pp. 27–42.

near-slavery and regular physical punishment this often entailed, had every reason to turn against their erstwhile masters, especially as many of them had been captured by previous commandos and put to work in the most unstable of servile relations.

There is a larger question with regard to the motivation for colonial invasion, that is to say both the reasons for colonial settlement so far from Cape Town and for the great brutality with which it was accomplished. The answer to the second part of the question is only partially dependent on that of the first, as the very processes of colonial conquest, undertaken for whatever reason, were likely to produce the sort of mindset that could justify genocide. On the other hand, there are good reasons to argue that both the continual expansion of the Trekboers toward the northeast and the brutality this entailed related to the microeconomics of the farming households.

Microeconomics cannot entirely be separated from macroeconomics. The Trekboers have been described as relatively self-sufficient and isolated from the market, or alternatively as driven by a close dependency on market forces.[76] Two matters stand out in this regard. First, there was clearly a steady expansion of the pastoral sector of the Cape economy. The sheep holdings of the colony more than tripled between 1730 and 1780, and cattle holdings grew by at least 287 percent between the same dates.[77] The growth in sheep holdings occurred primarily in the east of the colony, so that by the last decade of the eighteenth century well over half the colony's sheep were held in the Graaff-Reinet district. While the flocks and herds were used in part for household consumption, there was also a very considerable market throughout the century for butcher's meat, draught oxen, and so forth, and this probably grew to a sufficient extent to absorb the steadily increasing potential production of mutton and beef, and of the by-products of pastoralism: hides, tallow, and butter.[78]

Nevertheless, the development of the pastoral economy in the interior was far from simple or certain. Whereas there were those whose initial capital, luck, and skill ensured that they were able to build up a reasonable fortune, by Cape standards, there were also those for whom the

---

[76] S. D. Neumark, *Economic Influences on the South African Frontier, 1652–1836* (Stanford: Stanford University Press, 1957); L. Guelke, "Frontier Settlement in Early South Africa," *Annals of the American Association of Geographers* 66 (1976), pp. 25–41; van der Merwe, *Trekboer*.

[77] Van Duin and Ross, *Economy*, pp. 58–81. These figures derive from tax assessments, so that the absolute figures are untrustworthy. However, underreporting is likely to have increased with the greater distance from Cape Town. If this is so, the proportional growth could only have been higher.

[78] *Ibid.*, pp. 58–80.

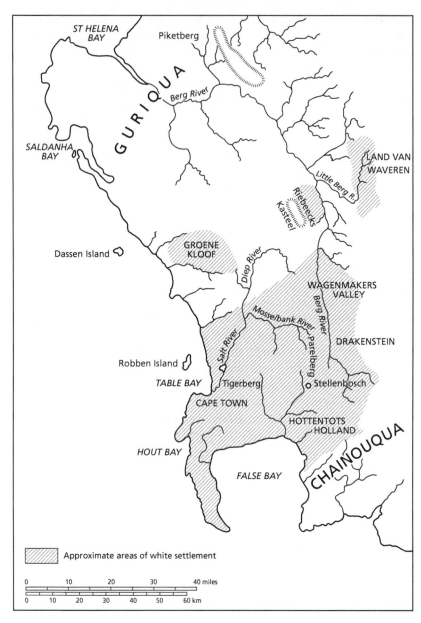

FIGURE 4.2. Approximate area of white settlement c. 1710.

establishment of a business of significant size was a problem. Drought, disease, and the attacks of San were always potentially ruinous. The major butchers of Cape Town were, in effect, both monopolists and monopsonists, selling the consumer needs of the frontier farmers while acquiring their sheep and, moreover, their promissory notes circulated as currency. A butcher's bankruptcy in Cape Town could bring down several Graaff-Reinet farmers. In circumstances of such vulnerability it is perhaps not surprising that what was in effect a counterproductive level of violence was employed, in the vain hope of maintaining order and, with it, the chance of economic growth. The consequence, however, was that farm laborers regularly took up arms against their masters, both in the incessant Bushman wars and, at the end of the century, in the so-called Servants' Revolt in the Eastern Cape.[79]

By the last quarter of the eighteenth century the potential conflict between the Trekboers, ever in search of more land to the east, and the amaXhosa became a reality. It was first fought in the summer grazing lands of the Zuurveld, around what was later to become Grahamstown, after the effective elimination of the Khoekhoe chieftaincy of the Hoengeiqua, founded some short time previously by Ruyter, a man who had moved from the mountains of the Roggeveld to avoid charges of murder. It was also fought in the lands around the headwaters of the Fish River, near modern Cradock. In neither area did the established Xhosa chiefdoms, subject to members of the royal house, hold sway. In particular, the amaGqunukwebe, who were of at least partial Khoekhoe descent and were led by men who were not of the Xhosa royal lineage, felt threatened by both the Trekboers, who were moving into their grazing lands, and by the Rharhabe amaXhosa, who were trying to subject them to the rule of the Xhosa royal house.

Thus, one of the earliest conflicts took place between the amaGqunukwebe, on the one hand, and the amaRharhabe, in alliance with Trekboers, on the other. More generally, the barter system, which had been grown, illegally, between the easternmost Trekboers and the amaXhosa, encouraged, ultimately, by the links of the farmers to the Cape Town market, could deteriorate into mutual raiding. Whereas the first of the frontier wars is conventionally dated to 1779–1781, it was only in 1793 that the conflict between the colony and major sections of the amaXhosa, under the control of the royal house, broke out, as part of the massive breakdown of order along the frontier that occurred in the last decade of the century.[80]

Given the aridity of the Cape interior, certainly to the north of the great escarpment, it is not in the least surprising that colonial expansion along

[79] See Chapter 6 in this volume.   [80] See Chapter 6 in this volume.

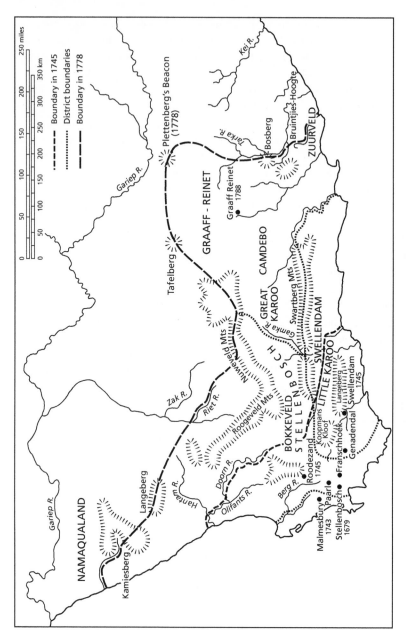

FIGURE 4.3. The shifting Cape frontier in the eighteenth century.

the western coast took on very different characteristics from that in the east, in at least two main ways. First, it was much less commercial. The regular visits of butchers' *knechts* and the droving of cattle and sheep, which were so common in Graaff-Reinet district, did not occur in the mountains of Little Namaqualand. Secondly, and not unconnected, a far larger proportion of the settlers through the western hills and in the valley of the Gariep were recognized as being of partial, or indeed total, Khoesan descent. This was not the case in the early years, as Legassick has pointed out,[81] but became so increasingly after the 1730s, because many of the original male settlers of European descent in this area formed long-term relations with Khoesan women, and the children of such unions became the dominant figures in the region.[82]

This stream of colonial expansion was no less violent than that to the east and northeast. It was initiated in the aftermath of the Bushman war of 1739, whereupon European settlers began moving into the Oliphants River valley and further into the Bokkevelde, the Roggeveld, and the Nieuwveld mountains.[83] There was a period of relative peace, largely because those Khoesan who could have formed the core of resistance to settler advance had either been killed or had retreated to the north. The lull, though, was temporary. By perhaps 1765, and certainly by the 1770s, war had broken out again, beginning with an uprising of farm servants in the Roggeveld and continuing as a drawn out and murderous war in the mountains and the plains of what is today the Northern Cape province. The General Commando of 1774, described previously, was in many ways the most concentrated colonial action in this war, but in the two decades that followed it spread from the Nieuwveld north to the Gariep. In the beginning the war was more or less under the control of the Cape authorities, at least as delegated to the various *veldkornets* and *veldcommandants*. In the ensuing few years, as the site of struggle moved north, it moved outside the law and became the province of individual colonial ruffians.

This was most evident with regard to the Einiqua, or River People, the Khoekhoen who lived along the Gariep River itself. In the region above the Augrabies Falls, the Gariep spreads out to create a tangle of islands covered with thick bush. It forms a long oasis in what is otherwise a region of semidesert. It had therefore become the center for groups of Khoekhoen who ran their cattle and sheep over a wider area of Bushmanland and the southern Kalahari, but who could retreat to the islands during the

[81] M. Legassick, "The Northern Frontier to c. 1840: The Rise and Decline of the Griqua People," in Elphick and Giliomee (Eds.), *Shaping*, p. 363.

[82] Penn, *Forgotten Frontier*, 164f.

[83] Mitchell, "Contested Terrains," esp. Chapter 3; Penn, *Forgotten Frontier*, Chapter 5.

regularly recurring periods of drought and grazing shortage. They could also act as intermediaries in the trade between the Southern Tswana and the Khoekhoen of the Karoo and the southern plains. In the 1770s, when Hendrik Wikar, a Swedish deserter from the service of the company service, lived among them, they were still flourishing. In subsequent years, however, they were the victims of a series of raids from the colony, led by a number of frontier farmers who had become most separated from the colonial order, notably Adriaan van Zyl and Pieter Pienaar.

The actions of a few colonial ruffians had a disastrous effect on the Einiqua but did not lead to the establishment of colonial control along the Gariep. Rather, whereas van Zyl was tried in absentia for his part in the raids, Pienaar was eliminated by Jonker Afrikaner, leader of the Khoekhoen, with whom the raiders had been associated. Nevertheless, even so far to the north, a degree of collaboration with the colony was essential for political survival. The result was that Afrikaner and his immediate associates eventually left the Gariep valley to establish themselves as warlords in what was to become Central Namibia. The valley and the springs in the slightly better-watered area to the north of it became the bases for the other large clans of so-called Bastards, who had emerged in Namaqualand in the last half of the eighteenth century, centred on the extended Kok and Barends families. They were tainted neither by the raids on the Einiqua nor by the subsequent murder of Peter Pienaar. Employing both the colonial and the Khoekhoe sides of their ancestry as political resources, which gave them legitimacy both through their wealth and their trading connections, they were able to establish hegemony in the region and form the nuclei of what were to become the Griqua captaincies.[84]

POLITICS AND THE COLONIAL COMMUNITY

In the historiography of the Cape Colony in the eighteenth century there has always been a tension between the center and the frontier; between Cape Town and the Southwest Cape, with the government and the colony's connections to the world of the Dutch commercial empire, on the one hand, and the valleys of the Gariep and the Fish, with the colony's connections to the rest of Africa, on the other. The former was the world of trade and farming, of slavery, of government, of administration, and of control; the

---

[84] Legassick, "Northern Frontier"; Legassick, "The Griqua, the Sotho-Tswana and the Missionaries, 1780–1840: The Politics of a Frontier Zone," unpublished Ph.D. thesis, UCLA, 1969; Penn, *Forgotten Frontier*, 157ff.; Penn, "The Orange River Frontier Zone, c. 1700–1805," in A. Smith (Ed.), *Einiqualand: Studies of the Orange River Frontier* (Rondebosch: University of Cape Town Press, 1995), pp. 21–100.

latter of pastoralism, of exploited Khoekhoen, of minimal government and, if not of anarchy, at least of the right of the strongest. Eventually, from the beginning of the nineteenth century, the center would reincorporate the periphery and impose its version of order on it. But before it could do so, the relations between the rulers and their subjects had to change profoundly. Colonial South Africa had to shift from a country dominated formally almost exclusively by its foreign rulers to one in which the established settlers had a significant say in the running of affairs. This process could be described as the empowerment of a ruling class, by now native to the colony if of settler descent.

The political making of a colonial ruling class was a threefold process. In the first place, there was a profoundly ambivalent relationship between the burgher elites, whether in Cape Town or in the Western Cape countryside, and the officials of the VOC. In the late 1770s the Cape Patriot movement developed within the colony. It took its name, and to some extent its inspiration, from the Patriot movement in the Netherlands, but its goals were strictly local. The initial trigger was the arrest and banishment of Carel Hendrik Buitendag. Buitendag was an unsavory character, whose earlier career, mainly in the Bokkevelde, had been marked both by great violence toward his Khoekhoe servants and by his alienation of various members of the extended van der Merwe family, which, at that point, dominated the area. He had been convicted of the unlawful killing of one of his servants and sentenced to be banned from the colony. The governor had remitted part of the sentence and allowed him to remain in Cape Town, on condition of his good behavior.[85] However, when his wife came to complain of her husband's actions, the fiscal, W. C. Boers, had him arrested and summarily shipped off to Batavia.

This was the pretext on which a major agitation was hung. A petition was drawn up and sent to the Heren XVII. It was signed by 400 burghers, led by both the private merchants of Cape Town and the richer farmers of the Western Cape. It stressed not so much the high-handedness and dubious legality of the fiscal's actions but, more importantly, the stranglehold the officials were said to have over the Cape's economy. Essentially, their role as managers of by far the largest enterprise in the colony, which doubled as the government, allowed a number of officials, as partners in private firms, to dominate the trade in wheat and wine, particularly that destined for

---

[85] N. Penn, "The Beast of the Bokkeveld: The Banishing of Carel Buitendag, 1770–1780," in N. Penn, *Rogues, Rebels and Runaways*, pp. 131–147; S. Newton-King. "In Search of Notability: The Antecedents of Dawid van der Merwe of the Koue Bokkeveld," *Collected Seminar Papers of the Institute of Commonwealth Studies, London: The Societies of Southern Africa in the 19th and 20th Centuries*, 20 (1994).

export, not as farmers – the gentry of the Southwestern Cape had become far too efficient for this to be possible – but by inserting themselves into the chain of purchase and resale. At the same time, the burghers demanded that they be granted the right to run their own shipping, which would primarily have exported agricultural produce and imported slaves, and that Chinese and free black stallholders on the shores of Table Bay be restricted in their activities.[86]

The sharpness of the conflict between the burghers and the company officials was tempered by the fact that the years after the presentation of the petition were ones of great prosperity for the colony, as the War of American Independence[87] brought many extra ships, mainly French, into Cape Town harbor, thus causing the market for Cape products to boom. Nevertheless, it dragged on throughout the remaining years of VOC rule of the Cape. Petitions and counterarguments were regularly sent from the Cape to the Netherlands, in the hope of bringing about, or indeed preventing, an overhaul of the colonial structure. In the 1790s, a series of commissions were sent out from Amsterdam to attempt to restore the profitability of the company, which had been severely hit by the war from which the Cape burghers had profited. They were unsuccessful. Thus the VOC government in Cape Town could no longer count on acquiescence from the colonial elite, nor did it have the strength to impose its unconditional will.

As against this, there was a steady rapprochement between the local elites and the district magistrates, particularly in the Stellenbosch district, but also around Swellendam. This was manifested in the full cooperation of the officials in the maintenance of the control of the master class over the slaves and Khoekhoe laborers, at times even in opposition to the specific wishes of the central government in Cape Town. Thus, in 1788, a movement among the Khoekhoen of Swellendam to regain the lands they had lost, which included considerable millenarian features, including the slaughtering of cattle, was triggered by the failure of the local magistrate to execute the orders of the governor in a conflict between a group of Khoekhoen and a farmer over land ownership and use. Further, the dangers of a Khoekhoe uprising were stressed by the local magistrate, with good reason, whereas in Cape Town it was generally assumed that the warnings were wildly exaggerated. At the same time, those farmers from among whom the board of *heemraden* – and the deacons and elders of the churches – were chosen

---

[86] R. Ross, "The Cape Economy and the Cape Gentry," in Ross, *Beyond the Pale*, pp. 28–32; G. J. Schutte, *De Nederlandse Patriotten en de Koloniën: Een Onderzoek Naar hun Denkbeelden en Optreden, 1770–1800* (Groningen: H. D. Tjeenk Willink, 1974), pp. 60–88; Schutte, "Company and Colonists," pp. 309–315.

[87] The Fourth Anglo-Dutch War in South African (and Dutch) historiography.

were able to establish their hegemony over the less fortunate of those of settler descent much as they did over the slaves and Khoekhoen.[88]

Although the relationship between the local elites and the local representatives of government was fairly secure in the settled districts of the colony, this was not the case on the frontier. Thus the attempts of the Cape Town government in the mid-1790s to impose order over Graaff-Reinet, primarily as a way of regulating relations with the amaXhosa, led to a revolt by specific groups of frontier farmers who considered that their needs had been insufficiently addressed. The magistrate, H. C. D. Maynier, was expelled from the district and central government control was only restored after the British conquest of the Cape in September 1795. Something similar occurred in Swellendam, where a short-lived republic was proclaimed in the final days of VOC rule, influenced both by the example of Graaff-Reinet and by the economic difficulties in which the farmers found themselves. These difficulties were themselves primarily the consequence of the company closing a depot at Mossel Bay for the purchase of grain grown on the southern plains, thus greatly increasing the costs of bringing the corn to market. The revolt was thus not a consequence of Swellendam's distance from the colonial system but rather a symptom of its intense involvement with the colonial economy.

By the last years of the eighteenth century, then, a colonial economy had been definitively established in the Cape Colony. The relationship between the creole elite and the colonial masters was strained, but their interdependence was unquestioned by either side. Together they had built the foundations of a commercial colonial economy and thereby established class rule over the slaves and laborers of the Western Cape, which was steadily being extended into the interior, away from Cape Town. This rule was in fact very largely that of those of European descent over Africans and (the descendants of) men and women imported from Asia, but this was not as yet justified by a racist ideology.

Independent Khoesan communities interspersed among the farmers were few and impoverished, although in Namaqualand and north of the Gariep new communities were developing and a few /Xam maintained a hunter–gatherer existence in the dry plains of Bushmanland. Elsewhere, they had largely been reduced to the status of farm laborers or were living as bandits in the hills. The establishment of the first permanent mission at Baviaans Kloof in 1792 provided the kernel of the means of escape, at least for some fortunate Khoekhoen. In the east of the colony the first clashes in the long battle between colonists and amaXhosa for the land between the Fish and

---

[88] Dooling, *Law and Community*; R. Viljoen, *Jan Paerl, a Khoikhoi in Cape Colonial Society, 1761–1851* (Leiden and Boston: Brill, 2006).

the Kei rivers had begun, but without the use of European regular troops the contest was still even, in fact probably more in favor of the Xhosa than of the colonists. In part, though not totally, then, the foundations of at least the colonial portions of South African history as they would develop over the next three-quarters of a century had been laid when, in 1795, the British navy brought an expeditionary force to False Bay and, after a short battle at Muizenberg, conquered Cape Town and forced the capitulation of the colony. The period of company rule was over, and, with a short intermezzo, the Cape, at least, would henceforth constitute part of the British Empire.

5

TURBULENT TIMES: POLITICAL TRANSFORMATIONS IN THE NORTH AND EAST, 1760s–1830s

JOHN WRIGHT

"THE WARS OF SHAKA," THE *MFECANE*, AND BEYOND

This chapter focuses on the nature and causes of the major political transformations that took place in the later eighteenth and early nineteenth centuries in the region bounded roughly by the Orange River, the Kalahari Desert, and the Indian Ocean. The notion that the years from the 1760s to the 1830s constitute a discrete period in this region's history, a period defined by the working-out of an identifiable set of transformations, is of very recent origin. Before the 1970s, historians had long been treating the three decades after about 1810 as a period on its own, one defined primarily by the rise and supposedly explosive expansion of the Zulu kingdom under Shaka, the supposedly consequent destabilizing of much of the eastern half of Southern Africa, and the emergence of a number of new kingdoms in this area. With few exceptions, historians paid very little attention to the decades before 1810 except to describe briefly the emergence of Shaka's supposed precursor, Dingiswayo of the abakwaMthethwa. In the 1970s and 1980s, as historians began to develop new approaches to the study of African pasts, and to tap more widely into the available source material on precolonial Southern Africa, they began to investigate the political and social history of specific African societies of the later eighteenth century in more detail and over a wider area. However, they still tended to see these years as forming a kind of preface to the Zulu expansion and the "wars of Shaka," or *mfecane*, as they came to be called from the late 1960s onward. It was not until the late 1980s, when this Zulu-centric historiography first began to come under fire,[1] that historians generally were

---

[1] The prime galvanizing text was by Julian Cobbing, "The mfecane as alibi: thoughts on Dithakong and Mbolompo," *Journal of African History*, 29 (1988), pp. 487–519.

My thanks go to Johannes du Bruyn for discussion of a preliminary plan of this chapter, and to Julian Cobbing and Dan Wylie for their comments on a draft of the chapter.

galvanized into starting to think about more broadly based explanations of change, and, in the process, to push the beginnings of the processes that led to state formation further and further back into the eighteenth century.

The often fierce *mfecane* debates, which took place among academic historians in the first half of the 1990s served, if not finally to demolish, at least seriously to weaken the long-established Zulu-focused line of explanation.[2] It was further undermined by the development in the same period of radically revisionist analyses of the historical process in which images of Shaka had been produced.[3] At the same time, senior academic historians began publishing studies that implicitly or explicitly abandoned Zulu-centrism altogether.[4] By the early 2000s, the controversies over the *mfecane* were dying down and something of a new consensus on approaches to the history of the late eighteenth and early nineteenth centuries had begun to emerge. Its most important feature was agreement that the upheavals of the 1820s and 1830s could no longer be adequately explained in terms of "the wars of Shaka," and that they needed to be set in the much wider context of increasing interaction since at least the mid-eighteenth century between indigenous communities and settlers and traders on the frontiers of European colonial and commercial expansion. This does not mean that historians were necessarily all in agreement about the nature of the roles that should be attributed to Shaka and the Zulu kingdom. Some now saw the emergence of the kingdom as a product of the conflicts of the times; others wanted to hold on to the older idea that the amaZulu were at least partly responsible for the conflicts. Some wanted to abandon the term *mfecane* altogether as being inextricably linked to an outdated Zulu-centric line of argument; others wanted to retain it while seeking to give it new meanings. But overall there was a growing acceptance that a thorough rethinking was needed of received, colonial-era notions about the history of Southern Africa in the late eighteenth and early nineteenth centuries.

---

[2] Carolyn Hamilton, (Ed.), *The Mfecane Aftermath: Reconstructive Debates in Southern African History*, (Johannesburg: Witwatersrand University Press and Pietermaritzburg: University of Natal Press, 1995); John Wright, "Mfecane debates," *Southern African Review of Books*, September/October and November/December (1995), pp. 18–9.

[3] Carolyn Hamilton, *Terrific Majesty: The Powers of Shaka Zulu and the Limits of Historical Invention* (Cape Town: David Philip, 1998); Dan Wylie, *Savage Delight: White Myths of Shaka* (Pietermaritzburg: University of Natal Press, 2000).

[4] Robert Ross, *A Concise History of South Africa* (Cambridge: Cambridge University Press, 1999); Norman Etherington, *The Great Treks: The Transformation of Southern Africa, 1815–1854* (Harlow: Longman, 2001).

TRADING, RAIDING, AND POLITICAL EXPANSION, 1760S TO 1810S

The Interior

Historians have long recognized that the later eighteenth century saw the emergence and expansion of a number of increasingly centralized chiefdoms in the region between the northern and central Drakensberg and the Indian Ocean. It is only recently that they have begun to recognize that similar – if less pronounced – processes were taking place at much the same time among the Tswana-speaking societies on the southeastern fringes of the Kalahari Desert.[5] To a large extent this lag has been a product of the relative paucity of documented evidence on the history of the interior regions before 1800, and of the difficulties of interpreting what evidence there is. The consensus among modern-day students of Tswana history is that the final decades of the eighteenth century were a period of growing conflict among the chiefdoms of the region between the middle reaches of the Vaal River and the Kalahari. The most important of these polities appear to have been those of the Bafokeng, Bahurutshe, Bakgatla, Bakwena, Bangwaketse, Barolong, and Batlhaping. Conflicts between these and other chiefdoms had no doubt been a pronounced feature of political life in the region before this, but in the later eighteenth century they seem to have acquired a new dynamic. Archaeological evidence indicates that this was a period of generally higher rainfall across much of Central and Eastern Southern Africa, which has led some scholars to speculate that there was a consequent increase in agricultural output and in livestock numbers and, hence, in the size of the human population. The introduction of maize at this time may also have been a factor in population growth. The result, particularly in years of below average rainfall, would have been an increase in competition for resources of land and livestock.[6]

At the same time, the politics of the southern Tswana chiefdoms were more and more being shaped by the expansion of trade with the European colonial world and by the northward advance of the frontier of colonial

---

[5] Neil Parsons, *A New History of South Africa*, 2nd ed. (London: Macmillan, 1993), Chapter 3; Neil Parsons, "Prelude to *difaqane* in the interior of southern Africa c.1600–c.1822," in Hamilton, (Ed.), *Mfecane Aftermath*, pp. 323–49; Andrew Manson, "Conflict in the western highveld/southern Kalahari," in Hamilton, (Ed.), *Mfecane Aftermath*, pp. 350–61.

[6] Simon Hall, "A consideration of gender relations in the Late Iron Age 'Sotho' sequence of the western highveld, South Africa," in Susan Kent, (Ed.), *Gender in African Prehistory* (Walnut Creek: AltaMira Press, 1998), p. 247.

settlement in the Cape. Evidence from colonial documentary records, travelers' accounts, and recent archaeological research indicates that the southern Tswana region lay at the convergence of several long-distance trade routes. Cowrie shells and beads from Muslim and, later, Portuguese traders on the Indian Ocean coast had been reaching the interior, if in small quantities, for many centuries before the period under discussion. From the south, Khoekhoe intermediaries had been bringing beads and iron goods obtained from European callers and settlers at the Cape since the early 1500s. Along a third route came beads from the Portuguese sphere of influence in Angola. In exchange, traders on the coast sought ivory, copper, skins, and pelts. Goods passed back and forth between numerous local trading networks dominated by political leaders who sought to use the new forms of wealth brought by trade with the outside world to increase their status and power. Attempts to control trade routes and the disposal of trade goods were probably a frequent cause of conflict among chiefs and between chiefs and local community leaders.

In the later eighteenth century, volumes of trade were increasing on the routes that led into the interior both from the Cape and from Delagoa Bay. By the 1760s, the frontier of colonial settlement in the south had reached the Nuweveld and Sneeuberg mountains, and Dutch stock farmers were seasonally grazing their livestock further north toward the Orange River. More and more frequently they came into contact with the groups of Khoekhoe pastoralists who lived along the river. Though it was illegal for the colonists to trade across the colonial boundary, frontier farmers bartered beads, firearms, and horses to the Khoekhoen in exchange for cattle. In turn, the Khoekhoen traded beads and other manufactures for cattle with the Batlhaping to the north of the Orange.

To the east a marked expansion of trade through Delagoa Bay was taking place. From the 1760s onward, English, Indian, and other merchants were coming in growing numbers to buy ivory from the chiefs round the bay in exchange for cloth, beads, and metal. Though it was the chiefdoms in the vicinity of the bay who were most directly affected by this trade, some historians have suggested that its impact reached as far inland as the southern Tswana region. In the same period, trade between the southern Batswana and chiefdoms to the north also may have been expanding, stimulated by an increase in Portuguese trading activities in southern Angola.

It was not only through the expansion of trade that influences from the outside world were felt among the southern Batswana in the later eighteenth century. The advance of the Cape frontier of settlement brought closer the frontier of raiding. Official and unofficial commandos marauded northward for livestock and for San women and children whom Dutch colonists wanted as domestic workers and shepherds on their stock farms.

As the area dominated by the Dutch expanded, groups of Khoekhoen and San were pushed toward the arid regions along the middle and lower Orange River, where they came into competition and conflict with groups already living there. The result was the breakdown of established pastoralist and hunting and gathering communities, and the emergence of fluid, unstable groupings of Khoekhoen, San, and Batswana who lived by combinations of hunting, gathering, herding, trading, and raiding. Some of these groups were joined by runaway slaves and by bandits and deserters of various shades of color from the Cape Colony. Some acquired guns and horses from the colonial farmers by trade and theft and raided livestock from one another and from the farmers and for women and children from surviving San communities. By the 1780s, at least, they were making depredations on Tswana communities to the north. By the early years of the nineteenth century, these groups, which have become known as Kora or Korana in the literature, were a major destabilizing force in the interior north of the middle and lower Orange.[7]

Toward the end of the 1790s, a new element was added to the politics of the middle Orange region with the arrival of several of groups of pastoralists of mixed descent from lower down the river. These people, who came to be known to themselves and others as Griqua from the early years of the nineteenth century, were seeking to escape from the disturbances that were being caused along the lower Orange by the expansion of Dutch stock farmers into the region. They settled along a line of springs near the confluence of the Orange and Vaal rivers in territories occupied by groups of Kora and San, numbers of whom had little option but to join them as clients. Like some of the Kora, the Griqua were equipped with guns and horses, and some parties soon took to raiding neighboring communities. The more important Griqua leaders, however, were interested less in raiding than in livestock-keeping, in hunting, and in trying to break into the well-established trade between the Batswana and the Cape Colony. Some groups even tried to cultivate crops. In 1801, one leader, Berend Berends, seeking protection from rival groups, and also wanting to establish closer trading links with the Cape, arranged for missionaries to begin work among his followers.

In this same period, small groups of amaXhosa were quitting the increasingly unstable regions on the frontier of the eastern Cape and were establishing themselves in the already volatile regions along the middle Orange.

[7] Martin Legassick, "The northern frontier to c. 1840: the rise and decline of the Griqua people," in Richard Elphick and Hermann Giliomee., (Eds.), *The Shaping of South African Society, 1652–1840* (Cape Town: Maskew Miller Longman, 1989), pp. 364–76; Nigel Penn, "The Orange River frontier zone, c.1700–1805," in Andrew Smith, (Ed.), *Einiqualand: Studies of the Orange River Frontier* (Cape Town: University of Cape Town Press, 1995), pp. 38–89.

They were joined by numbers of Kora, San, and refugees from the Cape, and, with the firearms which they had acquired, raided widely in the region round the Orange and lower Vaal. Though they mostly avoided attacking the stronger Griqua groups, the raids which they made against the Batlhaping threatened to disrupt the trade that these groups were trying to establish to the northward.[8]

It is against this background of expanding trade to the south, east, and north, and of increasing political instability along the Orange River to the south, that we need to place the history of the southern Tswana chiefdoms in the last two decades of the eighteenth century and the first two of the nineteenth. Recorded histories indicate that in these years nearly all these chiefdoms became caught up in a series of raids and counterraids, which left some of them stronger than before, whereas others fragmented into different sections. In the mid-eighteenth century, the dominant chiefdom had been that of the Bahurutshe, prior to its breakup into subgroupings later. Its center of gravity lay in the upper Marico region, which was good cattle country and which also lay at the intersection of important trade routes to the east and south. Toward the end of the century, Hurutshe power was increasingly challenged by the Bangwaketse, who lived to the northwest on the fringes of the desert and seem to have been seeking to gain a greater share of long-distance trade. To the southwest, the Batlhaping were establishing control of the trade route to the Cape. To the east, in the region of what is now Pretoria, the Bahurutshe were facing competition from the expanding Maroteng or Pedi chiefdom, whose heartland lay south of the Olifants River, well outside the southern Tswana territories.

It was probably during these years of growing political instability that there began the concentration of settlements that produced the large southern Tswana towns remarked on by European visitors in the early decades of the nineteenth century. There has been a good deal of debate in the literature about their origins, but archaeologists and historians now seem broadly agreed that the growth of these towns most probably began in the mid-eighteenth century and was due primarily to defensive needs in a time of increasing insecurity.[9] By the early nineteenth century, when the first European travelers visited them, some of these towns had populations estimated at 10,000 or 15,000. The biggest of them seems to have been

---

[8] Peter Kallaway, "Danster and the Xhosa of the Gariep: towards a political economy of the Cape frontier 1790–1820," *African Studies*, 41 (1982), pp. 143–60; Elizabeth Anderson, *A History of the Xhosa of the Northern Cape 1795–1879* (Cape Town: Center for African Studies, University of Cape Town, 1987), Chapter 2.

[9] Tom Huffman, "Archaeological evidence and conventional explanations of Southern Bantu settlement patterns," *Africa*, 56 (1986), pp. 280–98; Hall, "Gender relations in the Late Iron Age," pp. 238–48.

Kaditshwene, the capital of a major section of the Bahurutshe, situated 25 km northeast of what is now Zeerust. In 1820–21 its population was estimated by two visiting missionaries as numbering between 13,000 and 20,000, which would have made it much the same size as Cape Town.[10]

How such concentrations of population affected the structure of homesteads and the functioning of the economy is a topic that needs detailed research. It is likely that this factor intensified conflicts over grazing and agricultural land and contributed to the social and political tensions of the time. So too, very probably, did the depredations of white freebooters like the well-known Coenraad de Buys and the political interventions of the missionaries who were beginning to operate in the region. In the early nineteenth century, fighting between chiefdoms was becoming fiercer as chiefs sought not only to seize cattle from rival polities but also to subjugate them and to eliminate their leaders. "By 1820," one historian writes, "warfare was so widespread among the western Tswana that hardly a chiefdom had not seen its chief killed in battle."[11]

Though the evidence is very thin, it is likely that chiefdoms in the territories to the south and east across the Vaal River were also caught up in the intensified conflicts among the southern Batswana. In the late eighteenth century, the Bataung were beginning to attack and subjugate their neighbors in what is now the northern and central Free State. Further to the east, one of the Tlokwa chiefdoms also seem to have been growing in power at this time, possibly because it was situated in a locality from which its leaders could control an east–west trade over the Drakensberg escarpment. By the late 1810s, the leaders of this chiefdom felt confident enough of their strength to raid a section of amaHlubi living to the east of the Drakensberg. Pressures on the Sotho-speaking chiefdoms of the Southern Highveld came not only from the zone of conflict among the Batswana to northwest but also from what has been called the "firearm frontier" along the middle Orange to the southwest.[12] By the 1810s, Boer farmers were expanding toward the river in what is now the Colesberg area, and raiding by parties of Boers, Kora, and Griqua for cattle and slaves may by this time have been reaching as far as the Caledon Valley.[13]

---

[10] Jan Boeyens, "In search of Kaditshwene," *South African Archaeological Bulletin*, 55 (2000), pp. 3–17.

[11] Parsons, *A New History of South Africa*, p. 52.

[12] Legassick, "The northern frontier to c. 1840," in Elphick and Giliomee, (eds.), *The Shaping of South African Society*, Chapter 8.

[13] Elizabeth Eldredge, "Slave raiding across the Cape frontier," in Elizabeth Eldredge and Fred Morton (eds.), *Slavery in South Africa: Captive Labor on the Dutch Frontier* (Boulder, CO: Westview Press, and Pietermaritzburg: University of Natal Press, 1994), pp. 93–114.

A clear outcome of the intensified conflicts of the late eighteenth and early nineteenth centuries was the expansion and political centralization of certain chiefdoms to a much greater degree than before. A successful ruler like Makaba (c. 1790–1824) of the Bangwaketse seems to have wielded considerably more power than his predecessors. At the same time, weakened chiefdoms often split up into rival segments, as did the Bahurutshe, the Barolong, and several of the Kwena, Kgatla, and Fokeng chiefdoms. Another outcome was the development in many chiefdoms, particularly the more centralized ones, of marked social and political differentiation between the various groups that had been brought together under the rule of the chief. Broadly speaking, the populations of these polities were divided into three tiers. At the top was the ruling family, together with the families that had come to be closely associated with it. In the middle tier were the various subordinate groups that recognized the authority of the chief and that looked to him for rights in land, for protection of themselves and their livestock, for adjudication of major disputes, and for providing leadership in the sphere of ritual. At the bottom were low status groups of clients, dependents, and menials, usually without livestock of their own and often in positions of servitude that were close to slavery. Membership of the chiefdom was relatively fluid, with groups not infrequently hiving off to establish their political independence or to go and give their allegiance to another chief, and with other groups arriving to give their allegiance and seek incorporation into the body of the chief's adherents. Even the most markedly centralized chiefdoms, then, were far from being tightly bounded and monolithic entities; rather, they were composite polities in which different groups identified themselves and were identified by others, primarily in terms of genealogical descent.

Ruling houses sought to establish different generic identities for the different tiers of society. Use of convenient generic labels for particular chiefdoms in the historical literature should not be allowed to obscure the fact that many of the people who gave allegiance to a chief would not necessarily have claimed, or have been allowed to claim, the same identity as he did. For example, numbers of people who gave allegiance to the Hurutshe chief would not have been called Bahurutshe. By the same token, some people might have called themselves Bahurutshe in certain circumstances but not in others. The formation of identities in the pre-colonial societies of Southern Africa is a topic that needs to be much more widely researched, but case studies from the region east of the Drakensberg indicate that ruling families in centralizing chiefdoms reserved particular generic names exclusively for themselves and closely associated groups and sought to confer other names on the various categories of people subject to their rule in order to mark them off clearly from the ruling group.[14] It is more than likely that the same kind of practices were obtained among the chiefdoms, which were jostling for domination among the southern Tswana in the late eighteenth and early nineteenth centuries. Identities in all these societies were not fixed features with a timeless history; they cohered under particular circumstances and then might be remade under different circumstances.

The East

In the territories east of the Drakensberg, patterns of political and social change cannot be firmly traced before the mid-eighteenth century. Some historians have speculated that, as was the case in what is now the Zimbabwe-central Mozambique region, relatively large and centralized states had existed round Delagoa Bay for several centuries before this,[15] but there is little evidence to support this notion. Recorded oral histories suggest that in the second half of the century, as was happening in the interior, ruling groups in chiefdoms over a wide region were beginning to acquire relatively more power over their adherents and to enlarge the territories under their authority. Clashes between chiefdoms seem to have become more serious matters than before.[16]

Since the 1940s, a number of different hypotheses, some based more on speculation than on firm evidence, have been put forward by researchers to explain these developments in terms that move beyond the simplistic Great Man theories of the nineteenth century. Some scholars attribute them to growing pressure on resources caused by growth in human population, or else by the cumulative effects of unsuitable agricultural and livestock-keeping practices. Others, as in the case of the southern Tswana in the interior, invoke the impact of climatic changes, whether of drought or increased rainfall, or both, though too often the impact of these factors is described in very generalized terms without sufficient account of its variation from one society to another. The introduction of maize cultivation, with a consequent increase in population, is sometimes also seen as having been significant.

[14] See pp. 223, 229–30 following.

[15] Norman Etherington, "Were there large states in the coastal regions of southeast Africa before the rise of the Zulu kingdom?" *History in Africa*, 31 (2004), pp. 157–83.

[16] John Wright and Carolyn Hamilton, "Traditions and transformations: the Phongolo-Mzimkhulu region in the late-eighteenth and early nineteenth centuries," in Andrew Duminy and Bill Guest (Eds.), *Natal and Zululand from Earliest Times to 1910: A New History* (Pietermaritzburg: University of Natal Press and Shuter & Shooter, 1989), pp. 57–66.

More recently, some historians have sought to ascribe the political changes of the times primarily to the impact of external trade, whether in ivory, cattle, slaves, or a combination of these commodities. As already indicated, the growth of trade at Delagoa Bay from the 1760s onward is well attested in the literature. Portuguese from Mozambique had operated a spasmodic trade at the bay from the mid-sixteenth to the early eighteenth century, but it had been on too small a scale to have had any significant and lasting effect on local politics. By contrast, the trade that opened up in the 1760s and 1770s was on a much larger scale and seems to have kept growing through the 1780s. The export of ivory seems to have dropped off in the 1790s, but some historians argue that it was compensated for by an increase in the sale of cattle to American whaling ships, which by then were using Delagoa Bay as a base of operations in growing numbers.

The evidence leaves little doubt that the Tembe and Mabhudu chiefdoms were drawn into increasing competition at Delagoa Bay and conflict with each other, and with other chiefdoms in the region, as a result of their attempts to establish control over routes to the ivory- and cattle-producing regions to the west and south. Both chiefdoms grew larger and stronger; they extended their domination over some of the neighboring chiefdoms and pushed out others, like that of the abakwaDlamini.[17] In the same period, 300 km to the northwest of the bay, the Maroteng chiefdom seems to have been raiding more widely and establishing control over trade routes to the interior and laying the foundations of what came to be the Pedi kingdom. In the process, the Maroteng came up against chiefdoms such as those of the amaNdzundza Ndebele, Masemola, Magakala, Bamphahlele, and Balobedu.[18] Further north, round the Soutpansberg, lay the expanding sphere of influence of the Venda kingdom, which was the product of a quite separate set of political dynamics centered in the territories north of the Limpopo in what is now Zimbabwe.[19]

To the south of Delagoa Bay, in the territories between the Phongolo and Thukela rivers, the rulers of the Nxumalo and Nyambose chiefdoms were enlarging the territories under their authority and forming what came to be, respectively, the Ndwandwe and Mthethwa kingdoms. Attempts to

[17] Philip Bonner, *Kings, Commoners and Concessionaires: The Evolution and Dissolution of the Nineteenth-Century Swazi State* (Cambridge: Cambridge University Press, 1983), pp. 9–12.

[18] Peter Delius, *The Land Belongs to Us: The Pedi Polity, the Boers and the British in the Nineteenth-Century Transvaal* (Johannesburg: Ravan Press, 1983), pp. 11–19.

[19] D. N. Beach, *The Shona and Zimbabwe 900–1850,* (London: Heinemann, 1980), pp. 209–18, 260–3; Thomas Huffman, *Snakes and Crocodiles: Power and Symbolism in Ancient Zimbabwe* (Johannesburg: Witwatersrand University Press, 1996), pp. 12–13, 195–7.

control the trade in ivory and cattle to the bay from the south may have been a factor in their expansion. On the margins of these territories, other chiefdoms began expanding, possibly as a defensive response; among the more important were those of the abakwaDlamini north of the Phongolo, the amaHlubi on the upper Mzinyathi, and the abakwaQwabe near the lower Thukela. The expansion of the abakwaQwabe in turn pushed sections of the abakwaCele and amaThuli chiefdoms southward along the coast. The establishment of an enlarged chiefdom by the amaThuli in the area between the lower Mngeni and the lower Mkhomazi rivers pressured other groups into moving further south across the Mzimkhulu. Their movements may have been a factor in stimulating the defensive amalgamation of a number of local chiefdoms into a loosely structured kingdom dominated by the amaMpondo.

In the more centralized of these polities, such as those of the abakwa-Ndwandwe and the abakwaMthethwa, the expanded powers of the chiefly house to a greater or lesser extent were based on the control that it had been able to establish over age sets of young men known (in what later came to be called the Zulu language) as *amabutho*.[20] This term has frequently been translated as "regiments," but this military inflection gives a misleading idea of the composition and social functions of these age sets. They seem originally to have been groups brought together by chiefs for short periods to be taken through the rites of circumcision, and perhaps to engage in certain services, such as hunting. It is likely that chiefs used *amabutho* to obtain the ivory that they traded to Delagoa Bay in the later eighteenth century, and, by extension, to pursue their conflicts with rival chiefs. From there it was a short step for chiefs to use *amabutho* to bring their own adherents more firmly under control and to extract from them increased amounts of tribute. This took the form not only of cattle but also of the labor power of more cohorts of young men, who were used to expand the *amabutho* system still further. In the process of transforming the system, chiefs were able to do away with circumcision rites. Previously these rites had served to mark an important step in the transition from boyhood to autonomous manhood. By doing away with them, chiefs were able to prolong the period for which they could keep young men under their direct authority. In some of the bigger chiefdoms, tribute also took the form of young women. These latter were maintained in sections of chiefs' homesteads known (in Zulu) as *izigodlo* (sing.: *isigodlo*) until they were married off to wealthy or politically important adherents of the chief in return for large payments of bridewealth to the chief.

[20] John Wright, "Pre-Shakan age-group formation among the northern Nguni," *Natalia*, 8 (1979), pp. 22–30.

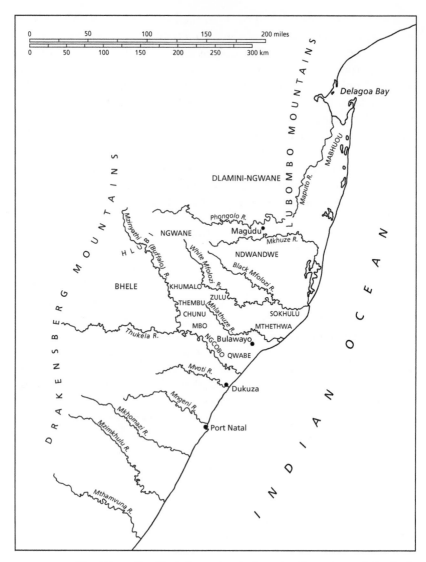

FIGURE 5.1. The Phongolo–Thukela region before the formation of the Zulu kingdom.

In the more centralized chiefdoms, the *amabutho* increasingly served as fighting and policing units under the control of the paramount. They also were used to build homesteads for the chief, to cultivate his fields, and – most importantly – to guard his cattle. In effect, they constituted a new kind of production unit that enabled the chief to take direct control of the labor power of the chiefdom's young men and to use it to the benefit of the ruling family and the aristocracy of associated families that was forming round it. Most day-to-day production remained in the hands of the chiefdom's numerous commoner households, but the efforts of the chief to extract from them a growing tribute in cattle and in the labor power of young men was a source of increasing tensions inside the chiefdom. In less politically centralized chiefdoms – probably the great majority – fighting forces continued to be composed, as it seems they had long been, of *amabandla*, that is, groups of men of all ages drawn from the same local community and under their own local leaders. Generally speaking, in the business of raiding and fighting, those chiefs who had *amabutho* at their disposal had a major advantage over chiefs who did not.

Political centralization also entailed new ways of structuring identities within chiefdoms. Research into the documented sources on the history of the Mthethwa chiefdom indicates that in the earliest stages of the chiefdom's expansion, in about the third quarter of the eighteenth century, groups subordinated to the abakwaMthethwa were incorporated into the chiefdom as putative kinsfolk of the ruling house. They were encouraged to recast their traditions of origin along lines that enabled them to claim to be genealogically related to their new rulers. By the end of the century, however, newly subjected groups were being prevented from making such claims and were coming to form a distinct and subordinate stratum within the chiefdom.[21] What generic names were used to identify rulers and ruled from this time on is not on record, but it is likely that a similar pattern of discrimination was becoming established in all the chiefdoms that were developing more centralized institutions of government in this period, not only east of the Drakensberg but in Southern Africa more generally. Everywhere, identities were subject to being made and remade according to circumstance.

An important factor in the politics of the Delagoa Bay hinterland would fairly certainly have been the activities of the Portuguese. They had established a small force, mainly of black soldiers, at the bay in 1782 to try to prevent trading by foreign ships in what the Portuguese regarded as their own sphere of influence. The garrison had been expelled by a French expedition from Mauritius in 1796, but had been reestablished in 1799, even though, owing to disruptions of international commerce by the European wars of the period, the export trade at the bay had fallen off. Though the

---

[21] Wright and Hamilton, "Traditions and transformations," in Duminy and Guest (Eds.), *Natal and Zululand from Earliest Times*, pp. 63–4; John Wright and Carolyn Hamilton, "Ethnicity and political change before 1840," in Robert Morrell (Ed.), *Political Economy and Identities in KwaZulu-Natal: Historical and Social Perspectives* (Durban: Indicator Press, 1996), pp. 22–3.

Portuguese did not have the power to intervene decisively in the politics of the region, they constantly sought to play off the chiefdoms near the bay against one another to try to maintain control over the trade in ivory and, later, in slaves.

The development of a trade in slaves from the northern parts of the Portuguese sphere of influence in Mozambique to sugar plantations on the French-controlled islands of Mauritius and Reunion in the later eighteenth century is well attested, but there seems little to show that slaves were traded in any significant numbers at Delagoa Bay at this time.[22] After 1810, however, increasing numbers of traders from Brazil were turning to Southeast Africa as a source of slaves to compensate for the closing off of sources in West Africa that followed Britain's abolition of the slave trade in 1807 and the signing in 1810 of an Anglo–Portuguese treaty that confined the buying of slaves by Portuguese citizens to Portugal's own colonies in Africa. Brazilian slavers concentrated their activities mainly in the established slaving zones in central and northern Mozambique, but by at least the later 1810s some may have been trading at Delagoa Bay, as may smugglers from Reunion and Mauritius, which had recently been annexed as a British colony. The number of slaves traded at this stage is a matter for debate, but is likely to have been low until 1823–24, when the trade expanded markedly, reaching a minimum of 1,000 to 2,000 slaves a year in the later 1820s.[23] Most of the slaves exported by the Portuguese from Delagoa Bay were probably obtained by purchase from African slavers in neighboring chiefdoms rather than through raiding by the Portuguese themselves. The small, badly equipped, fever-ridden garrison at the bay was hardly able to defend itself against hostile forces, let alone engage actively in slaving expeditions. Its function was less to seize captives than to hold those purchased from African merchants until the arrival of slave ships.

Debating the dating and size of the slave trade at Delagoa Bay has tended to divert the attention of historians away from what is perhaps a more important topic: the nature of relations between the Portuguese and their neighbors, such as the Tembe and Mabhudu chiefdoms and the impact of periodic attempts made by the Portuguese to enlarge the sphere in which they exercised political influence. It seems more than likely that Ndwandwe leaders would have kept a close watch on the politics of the area round the bay, about 200 km away, and the expansion of the Ndwandwe kingdom

---

[22] For sharply contrasting views see Cobbing, "The mfecane as alibi," pp. 503–07; Elizabeth Eldredge, "Delagoa Bay and the hinterland in the early nineteenth century: politics, trade, slaves, and slave raiding," in Eldredge and Morton (Eds.), *Slavery in South Africa*, pp. 127–65.

[23] Patrick Harries, "Slavery, social incorporation and surplus extraction: the nature of free and unfree labor in southeast Africa," *Journal of African History*, 22 (1981), p. 316.

may have been in some measure a defensive reaction to the activities of the Portuguese. A comprehensive integration of the "Portuguese factor" into the history of the eastern half of Southern Africa in the period under discussion is long overdue.

By the 1810s, the most actively expanding polities in the Delagoa Bay hinterland were those of the abakwaNdwandwe under Zwide kaLanga and the abakwaMthethwa under Dingiswayo kaJobe. A little before 1820, the rivalry between them for domination of the Phongolo–Mfolozi region came to a head. A series of raids and counterraids ended with the defeat of the abakwaMthethwa and the killing of Dingiswayo. These events effectively opened the way for the emergence of a new political force in the regions south of the White Mfolozi. This was the rising Zulu chiefdom under the leadership of Shaka kaSenzangakhona.[24] In Senzangakhona's reign, the small Zulu chiefdom had been brought under the domination of Dingiswayo and on the former's death Dingiswayo had installed Shaka as chief of the amaZulu in opposition to a number of rival candidates. The Mthethwa chief had encouraged Shaka to restructure and expand the *amabutho* at his disposal, and to establish himself as the dominant power in the western marches of the Mthethwa sphere of influence in order to set up a bulwark against the expansion of the abakwaNdwandwe. Some traditions state that when summoned by Dingiswayo to assist the Mthethwa forces against Zwide's attack, Shaka had deliberately held back from doing so. If this was a ploy to shake off Mthethwa domination, it proved successful, for after the death of Dingiswayo the Mthethwa paramountcy rapidly broke up into its constituent parts, enabling Shaka to establish himself as the strongest leader south of the White Mfolozi.

The expanding Zulu chiefdom was clearly the remaining obstacle to the consolidation of Ndwandwe domination over the former Mthethwa territories. Soon after the defeat of the abakwaMthethwa, Zwide launched a major raid against the amaZulu, who managed to survive it only with heavy losses of cattle. The common view in the literature is that a further Ndwandwe attack was beaten off by the amaZulu, who then proceeded to advance into Ndwandwe territory, destroy Zwide's capital, and break up his kingdom. This view is based very much on the traditions of the amaZulu rather than those of the abakwaNdwandwe; recent research into the surviving traditions of the latter suggest that Zwide's polity broke up primarily as a result

---

[24] On Shaka and the early Zulu kingdom see Carolyn Hamilton, "Ideology, oral traditions and the struggle for power in the early Zulu kingdom," M.A. dissertation, University of the Witwatersrand, (1985); John Wright, "The dynamics of power and conflict in the Thukela-Mzimkhulu region in the late-eighteenth and early nineteenth centuries: a critical reconstruction," Ph.D. dissertation, University of the Witwatersrand, (1989); Chapters 4–6.

of internal political tensions rather than of conquest by the amaZulu. The evidence indicates that Shaka's forces were able to hold off those of Zwide and to make a successful counterraid into Ndwandwe territory, but it seems unlikely that at this stage the Zulu leader had anything like the means to overcome Zwide's much larger and longer-established kingdom. A more credible scenario is that the failure of Ndwandwe attacks on the amaZulu brought tensions in Zwide's ruling house to the point where sections of it broke away to establish their independence from the senior section. Two breakaway groups under Soshangane and Zwangendaba moved into the Delagoa Bay region, whereas another under Msane moved to eastern Swaziland. In all but the most recent literature, these groups have invariably been seen as refugees from Shaka; they are more likely to have been seeking to escape from what had for some years been a zone of intensifying conflicts, first between the abakwaMthethwa and the abakawaNdwandwe and then between the latter and the amaZulu.

After the failure of his attacks on the amaZulu, Zwide moved away from the Mkhuze region northward across the Phongolo, apparently into what is now southern Swaziland. He had already brought this area under his domination by driving out the abakwaDlamini, and here he sought to reconsolidate his kingdom. The shift of the Ndwandwe ruling house opened the way for the amaZulu under Shaka to extend their domination north across the White Mfolozi. The conventional view is that he was soon able to bring the whole region as far as Delagoa Bay and even beyond under his sway. There is no evidence to support this notion, and it is likely that for some years effective Zulu rule did not extend much beyond the Mkhuze River. Whereas Shaka later sought to extend his sphere of influence further northward into the region dominated by the abakwaMabhudu, at no stage of his reign did he have the military or political capacity to rule it directly. Contrary to the common view, the emergent Zulu polity did not have the capacity to pursue a policy of active expansion to the southward either. In this direction, Shaka's main aim was to establish a stable and secure border roughly along the line of the lower Mzinyathi and Thukela rivers. To this end he sought to break up or drive away chiefdoms which he regarded as posing a threat while allowing several client chiefs to rule with a degree of autonomy in return for recognizing his overlordship.

CONQUESTS AND UPHEAVALS IN THE 1820S

The Northeast

In the early 1820s, three kingdoms were emerging as the dominant powers in the region between the Drakensberg and the Indian Ocean. These were the kingdoms of the abakwaNdwandwe under Zwide, the abakwaGaza under Soshangane, and the amaZulu under Shaka. Alongside them, the Portuguese at Delagoa Bay also played an increasingly important role in the politics of the region.

The sources on the history of Zwide's kingdom in these years are very thin. As will be discussed in the following, the abakwaNdwandwe were defeated and broken up by the Zulu in 1826, and very little information about their history has come down in the oral and written record. Snippets of evidence suggest that Zwide did not remain for long in the southern Swaziland region. Situated as he was between the Portuguese and the breakaway sections of the abakwaNdwandwe to the northeast, the defeated but not destroyed abakwaDlamini to the north, and the expanding Zulu power to the south, Zwide seems soon to have decided to move to a more secure region. This time the migration of the abakwaNdwandwe main house took it and its adherents northwest to the vicinity of the Nkomati River on the borders of present-day Swaziland and South Africa.[25] Here, it seems, Zwide was rapidly able to reestablish a large following by successfully raiding surrounding chiefdoms for cattle and attracting adherents from weaker and poorer polities. Some sources suggest that his forces were able to defeat and break up the long-established Maroteng or Bapedi kingdom, and that for a brief period the abakwaNdwandwe settled in the former Pedi heartland south of the Olifants River.[26] At all events it is likely that by the time of Zwide's death in about 1825 the revived Ndwandwe polity dominated much of the interior between the Olifants in the north and the Phongolo River in the south.

To the east, much of what is now southern Mozambique was at this time coming under the sway of the section of abakwaNdwandwe that had broken away from Zwide under his kinsman Soshangane.[27] Again, there is very little evidence to go on, but it seems that in the early 1820s his adherents, together with those of other groups that had split off from Zwide, were raiding for food, cattle, and slaves in the region round Delagoa Bay and were fighting one another as well as the chiefdoms near the bay. They also came into conflict with the Portuguese and, in 1822, with elements of a British naval expedition that had been sent out supposedly to survey the coast of Southeast Africa. By the mid-1820s, Soshangane had established himself on the lower Nkomati River, where his Ndwandwe

[25] Bonner, *Kings, Commoners and Concessionaires*, p. 29.

[26] Delius, *The Land Belongs to Us*, pp. 20–6.

[27] On the history of the Gaza kingdom, see Gerhard Liesegang, "Nguni migrations between Delagoa Bay and the Zambezi, 1821–1839," *African Historical Studies*, 3 (1970), pp. 317–37; G. J. Liesegang, "Aspects of Gaza Nguni history 1821–1897," *Rhodesian History*, 6 (1975), pp. 1–14.

followers formed the nucleus of an expanding polity that became known as that of the abakwaGaza, after one of Soshangane's ancestors. Rival groups under Zwangendaba, Nxaba, and Msane had by this time moved or been pushed further north into what are now central Mozambique and eastern Zimbabwe. With the abakwaNdwandwe and the amaZulu extending their spheres of influence to the west and south, respectively, the main line of expansion for Soshangane's growing kingdom was to the north and east. His *amabutho* raided widely among the small Tsonga-speaking chiefdoms north of Delagoa Bay for such cattle as they could find in what was largely a tsetse-infested area and for ivory and slaves. By this time the trade in slaves at the bay, though now illicit, was growing rapidly, with Portuguese officials deeply involved in promoting it. Continued attempts by the Portuguese to assert control of the chiefdoms round the bay added to the instability of the region.

Much more is known about the history of the amaZulu than of the abakwaNdwandwe or abakwaGaza at this time. Recent academic research has begun to give us a picture of the history of Shaka's kingdom that is in many respects very different from the stereotyped versions – settlerist, Zuluist, African nationalist – that have come down from the colonial era and have long predominated in the literature. Shaka had been able to establish the domination of the Zulu chiefly house over the territories between the Thukela and Mkhuze rivers not only through the use of force but also through his skills in diplomacy and his ability to seize political opportunities which came his way. The scale of his conquests has been greatly exaggerated. In his recorded praises, most of the celebrated battles and victories refer to the subjugation not of great potentates but of local petty chiefs. On occasion his forces were able to raid long distances beyond the confines of his kingdom, but not always successfully. In the literature he is often said to have had up to 50,000 armed men at his command; in reality, his forces are unlikely to have numbered more than 10,000 or 15,000, which in those times would have been a formidable complement. The notion, which is still cited from time to time in the popular literature, that he was responsible for the deaths of up to a million people, is a pure fabrication. Unlike the Ndwandwe, Gaza, and Ndebele kingdoms, the Zulu polity did not take shape in the course of a series of highly disruptive migrations; it expanded outward from a secure territorial core and, once its brief formative period was over, constituted a zone of relative stability in a region of widespread upheaval.

Shaka did not rule, as is often supposed, over a politically united nation. Like other African states, the kingdom that emerged under his rule was an amalgamation of discrete chiefdoms, each with its own hereditary chiefs, its own customs, often its own dialect, and its own memories of the times before the establishment of domination by outsiders. The idea is deeply entrenched in the literature that power in the Zulu kingdom flowed outward and downward from the center, with the monarch ruling the chiefdoms under his authority through a hierarchy of *izinduna* and headmen appointed by himself. This notion in fact reflects the structure of bureaucratic administration that was established in Zululand under colonial rule from the late nineteenth century onward: It does not reflect the system of rule that existed in the independent Zulu kingdom. Under the Zulu kings, the *izinduna* were primarily officials who controlled the king's *amabutho*; they did not function as administrators of subordinate chiefdoms. The latter remained under the immediate rule of their own chiefs, who, even in Shaka's time, might seek to resist aspects of Zulu rule where they felt they could get away with doing so. Shaka was certainly a despotic ruler, and in many cases was able to promote to chiefships his own candidates from within local ruling houses, but even he did not act unchecked, at least by the mightier of his subjects. The apparently arbitrary violence that he often employed against his adherents was as much a sign of the insecure bases of his rule as of the power that he wielded.

The dominance that the Zulu ruling house was able to establish in the 1820s over the chiefdoms subordinate to it was based largely on its ability to maintain direct control over the kingdom's armed men through the *amabutho* system. The increasing militarization of this system under Shaka's rule still needs detailed research, but it is clear that Shaka was able to tighten it significantly during his reign.[28] At the same time he extended it to include the formation of *amabutho* of young women, and made marriages across the kingdom contingent on his giving permission to specific men's *amabutho* to choose wives from designated women's *amabutho*. He also greatly increased the number of marriageable young women who were kept in the royal *izigodlo*. How he was able to establish this dispensation in the face of what must have been considerable popular opposition is a subject that still needs to be investigated.

The society that emerged under Zulu domination consisted of three broad tiers. At the top were the king and the cluster of related families that had dominated the former Zulu chiefdom, together with the closely associated groups that had been incorporated into the kingdom in the early stages of its expansion. Also forming part of this aristocracy were the *izikhulu*, the chiefs and notables of the more powerful subordinate chiefdoms. The second tier of society consisted of the rest of the population of the chiefdoms that formed the core of the kingdom; from these chiefdoms were drawn the

---

[28] Hamilton, "Ideology, oral traditions and the struggle for power in the early Zulu kingdom," Chapter 6.

young men who filled the ranks of the *amabutho*. The lowest tier consisted of members of low-status groups on the geographical margins of the kingdom. They were despised as outsiders and inferiors by members of the other two tiers, their leaders were excluded from the councils of the *izikhulu*, and their young men were put to menial tasks like herding cattle at outlying royal cattle posts.

Contrary to widespread belief, the people of Shaka's kingdom did not call themselves after the ruling house, the abakwaZulu, or "people of the place of Zulu." This name was reserved strictly to members of the ruling Zulu descent group; for them to have extended it to their subjects would have entitled the latter to claim the same status as their rulers. As had long been the practice, people referred to themselves, and were referred to by others, primarily by the name of their own descent groups. To promote the political integration of the kingdom, however, Zulu leaders were concerned to promote the idea that the peoples of the top two tiers belonged together by virtue of a common descent and a common culture in a vaguely defined ethnic category of amaNtungwa people. This was seen as being of different – and superior – descent and culture from the despised peoples of the kingdom's third tier, who were given contemptuous designations like *amalala* (menials), *amathonga* (subservients), *amanhlwenga* (beggars), and others.[29] It is not clear when or how the generic designation amaZulu for the inhabitants of the kingdom came into existence. It may first have been used in this sense by outsiders, including Europeans, and only later have come to be used by the people of the kingdom and their descendants. Later still it came to be used to refer to speakers of the Zulu language more generally.

The territories ruled by Shaka had long formed part of the trading hinterland of Delagoa Bay, though at the time of his access to power in the late 1810s the trade in ivory and cattle seems to have been at much lower levels than it had been in the later eighteenth century. Whether or not a trade in slaves ever penetrated to his domains is not clear. For his part, the Zulu king seems to have encouraged the continuation of the trade in ivory and cattle to the Portuguese at Delagoa Bay as a means of obtaining manufactured goods, but there is very little evidence as to the scale of this commerce. From 1824, the kingdom's trading links with the

---

[29] Wright and Hamilton, "Traditions and transformations," in Duminy and Guest (Eds.), *Natal and Zululand from Earliest Times*, pp. 72–3; Carolyn Hamilton and John Wright, "The making of the *amalala*: ethnicity, ideology and relations of subordination in a precolonial context," *South African Historical Journal*, 22 (1990), pp. 3–23; John Wright and Carolyn Hamilton, "Ethnicity and political change before 1840," in Robert Morrell (Ed.), *Political Economy and Identities in KwaZulu-Natal: Historical and Social Perspectives* (Durban: Indicator Press, 1996), pp. 24–9.

outside world were expanded with the advent at Port Natal of small parties of British trader–adventurers from the Cape. These men were seeking to tap into the existing trade in ivory and possibly to smuggle out slaves as well. Their bases at Port Natal lay to the south of the territories ruled directly by Shaka but well within his sphere of influence, and from the start he sought to maintain a firm control over their trading activities. He valued the traders' presence not only for the manufactured goods that they brought – he was particularly interested in obtaining firearms – but also for the access that they seemed to offer to the British colonial government in the Cape and for their potential usefulness as political allies.

From about 1826, the traders began to play a more and more important role in the king's political calculations. By this time internal resistance and external threats were beginning to combine to make his hold on power more uncertain. A key factor in this development seems to have been the expansion of the Ndwandwe kingdom, now ruled by Zwide's son Sikhunyana, toward the northwestern borderlands of the territories dominated by the Zulu. The new Ndwandwe chief, who was described by the trader Henry Fynn as "equal in power to Chacka,"[30] was probably seeking to challenge Shaka's control of the former Ndwandwe homeland, where numbers of Zwide's former adherents still lived. By the middle of 1826, Shaka seems to have made up his mind to mount a major offensive against the abakwaNdwandwe and summoned the traders to provide assistance. The latter were no doubt happy enough to have the chance to win the favor of the king and to gain booty in the form of cattle and captives. Several of the traders, together with a number of their African retainers who had been trained in the use of muskets, joined Shaka's forces in their advance into Ndwandwe-dominated territory. The Zulu army came up with the abakwaNdwandwe north of the upper Phongolo at the Izindololwane hills, and, in a fierce fight in which the gunmen from Port Natal were involved, routed Sikhunyana's forces, killed numbers of women and children, and seized large herds of cattle.

After this defeat the Ndwandwe kingdom fell to pieces. Sikhunyana, with numbers of his adherents, is said to have made off toward the country of the abakwaGaza, ruled by his kinsman Soshangane, in southern Mozambique, but thereafter he is lost to view. Numbers of former Ndwandwe subjects went to give their allegiance to Shaka while others took refuge with Mzilikazi, ruler of the rising Ndebele polity to the west. From this time, Zulu domination of the region from the Phongolo southward toward

---

[30] Percival Kirby (Ed.), *Andrew Smith and Natal: Documents Relating to the Early History of That Province* (Cape Town: Van Riebeeck Society, 1955), p. 68.

the Mzimkhulu was unchallenged until the advent of new groups of British traders from the Cape in the mid-1830s.

The Southeast

Since it was first articulated in print by British settlers in Natal and the eastern Cape in the late 1820s and the 1830s, the idea that in the late 1810s and early 1820s the region south of the Thukela River was devastated and depopulated in a series of bloody attacks by Shaka's armies, and by refugees from Shaka's armies, has gained virtually universal acceptance in the literature. A critical reexamination of the evidence points to very different conclusions.[31] The amaZulu were only one of the agents of the upheavals that took place in this region. The others – mainly the Ngwane,[32] Thembu, Chunu, Memela, and Nhlangwini chiefdoms – were moving out of a zone of instability and conflict in which not only the amaZulu but the abakwaNdwandwe and the abakwaMthethwa before them were major actors. The stereotyped view that the Zulu had the power to intervene more or less at will in the region's affairs is not supported by the evidence.

The history of the period was characterized not so much by the destruction of populations as by the displacement and breakup of communities and the fragmentation of political units. The territories dominated by chiefdoms that could provide security became relatively more populated whereas other areas became relatively denuded of inhabitants. In these latter regions numbers of small groups clung on in the more broken or forested parts. They lived largely by hunting and gathering, and kept cultivation and the keeping of livestock to a minimum to avoid attracting the attention of larger and stronger groups. Others took advantage of the breakdown of previously established authority structures to turn to banditry. Groups of this kind, which lived mainly by raiding, were often described by more settled communities as *amazimu*, or people outside the law. Later the word was translated into settler literature as "cannibals" and fed into stereotyped stories about the widespread existence of cannibalism south of the Thukela in Shaka's time.

The conventional literature on the devastation of Natal sees a large number of refugees from the region as having fled from roving Zulu armies

---

[31] John Wright, "Political transformations in the Thukela-Mzimkhulu region in the late eighteenth and early nineteenth centuries," in Hamilton (Ed.), *Mfecane Aftermath*, pp. 163–81.

[32] These were the *amaNgwane*, i.e., "the Ngwane people," who lived in the northwest of what is now the KwaZulu-Natal province of South Africa. Some historians confuse them with the entirely unrelated *abakwaNgwane*, "the people of the place of Ngwane," who formed the nucleus of what became the Swazi kingdom.

southward across the Mzimkhulu River toward the Cape frontier. According to this view, most of these groups ended up as clients of the abaThembu and of the amaGcaleka Xhosa, or as so-called Fingoes, or amaMfengu, in the eastern regions of the Cape Colony. Recent research suggests that although some elements of these Fingoes were migrants from Natal, many were socially marginalized amaXhosa who had been dispossessed by British cattle raids and land seizures on the eastern frontier of the Cape Colony.[33] During the frontier war of 1834–35, numbers of Fingoes took the opportunity of breaking away from the amaGcaleka and abaThembu and establishing themselves as autonomous communities in the eastern border regions of the Cape Colony. Subsequently, to provide themselves with distinct identities, their leaders, together with the missionaries who had settled among them, evolved collective histories of having been pushed out of Natal by Shaka and having fled southward. These histories fed easily into a settler historiography that was seeking to cover up settler aggressions against the amaXhosa.

Most of the groups that migrated southward out of Natal in the late 1810s and early 1820s seem to have established themselves between the Mzimkhulu and Mzimvubu rivers rather than moving on further south. Here they found themselves within the sphere of influence of the relatively large Mpondo kingdom under Faku kaNgqungqushe. Their choices were to give their allegiance to Faku, to fight the amaMpondo for dominance, or to attempt to reestablish themselves on the margins of the Mpondo sphere of influence. Most of the larger migrant groups seem to have chosen the third course, thus inaugurating a long period of violence and instability in the region south of the Mzimkhulu. By the end of the 1820s, the two dominant powers in the region were the Mpondo and Bhaca chiefdoms. Numbers of smaller groups had moved out of the zone of conflict to settle north of the Mzimkhulu or across the Thukela in the Zulu kingdom. Others had moved away southward to Thembu and Xhosa country.

By this stage, the territories south of the Mzimkhulu were more and more experiencing the impact of British expansionism from the Cape frontier regions. British forces had fought destructive wars against the southwesternmost Xhosa chiefdoms in 1811–12 and again in 1819, and on both occasions pushed these chiefdoms back into territories occupied by others. The 1820s had seen rising tensions between Xhosa communities and the newly established British settler communities of the Suurveld region round Grahamstown. In 1828, a force of British regulars and Boer frontiersmen had marched 300 km beyond the frontier in a major show of strength in Xhosa

[33] Alan Webster, "Unmasking the Fingo: the war of 1835 revisited," in Hamilton (Ed.), *Mfecane Aftermath*, pp. 241–76.

and Thembu territories. At Mbholompo, west of present-day Umtata, it attacked and broke up a large group under Matiwane of the amaNgwane, which had moved in from the Caledon Valley to the northwest (see pp. 243–5 following). This event sent shock waves through African communities across a wide region and signaled that British power was becoming a major factor in the politics of the regions beyond the borders of the Cape Colony.

The Interior

By the late 1810s, the chiefdoms of the Caledon Valley and the open plains north of the Orange River were being squeezed between three expanding zones of instability and conflict. From the south and southwest, parties of Griqua, Kora, and Boers were periodically raiding for cattle and slaves. To the northwest, the rivalries of Batswana chiefdoms were spilling across the Vaal River. To the east, the conflicts of the abakwaNdwandwe and abakwaMthethwa, and then of the abakwaNdwandwe and amaZulu, were beginning to push displaced groups across the Drakensberg. Evidence on these events is thin and contradictory and has been subject to varying interpretations. But it is clear that in the early 1820s a disruptive series of raids and population migrations spread over the interior north of the Orange. Numerous communities broke up while others became successful predators. A few, after a period of warfare, were able to establish themselves as focal points of stability. As in the regions south of the Thukela River, groups attacked one another not so much to destroy populations as to expel them from their territories and seize the grain and cattle needed for survival and for maintaining social cohesion. In the hilly country of the Caledon Valley, groups also fought one another for control of defensive strongholds. Numbers of people scattered over the landscape and found refuge, temporary or permanent, in communities far from their original homes. Many migrated as far as the Cape Colony, where they ended up as laborers on the farms of white settlers.

The conventional view is that these upheavals were set in motion by the irruption into the Highveld south of the Vaal River of two groups from east of the Drakensberg, the amaHlubi of Mpangazitha and the amaNgwane of Matiwane. But, as indicated previously, it is clear that the chiefdoms of the southern Highveld had for years been coming under increasing pressure from the raids of Kora and other bandits from the southwest, and from the conflicts of the Tswana chiefdoms to the northwest. The amaHlubi themselves had previously been raided by Batlokwa from the Highveld. The advent of Mpangazitha's and Matiwane's followings may well have served to further destabilize an already unstable situation; it did not inaugurate fighting and migrations in the region.

In the east the main rival groups were those under Mpangazitha, Matiwane, and MaNthatisi of the Batlokwa. All three moved southward into the Caledon Valley, where they could raid among the small local chiefdoms and, crucially, establish themselves on defensible hilltops. By the mid-1820s, Matiwane had defeated and broken up Mpangazitha's people and was emerging as the dominant leader on the middle Caledon. MaNthatisi's people were ensconced on the upper Caledon. Clinging on in nooks and crannies round about were a number of smaller groups, such as the Bamokotedi, that maintained a precarious autonomy by paying allegiance to one or both of their two bigger neighbors.

To the west, the zone of raiding, fighting, and population displacement extended across the Vaal River to the Kuruman area and the southeastern reaches of present-day Botswana.[34] Particularly disruptive raids were carried out by groups of Maphuthing, Bafokeng, and Bataung who had originally lived south of the Vaal. Some of the Kora on the lower Vaal and the Griqua further to the west also became caught up in the upheavals, as were a number of missionaries and traders from the Cape. The best-known instance of missionary involvement occurred in mid-1823, when Robert Moffat persuaded a party of Griqua to help beat off an impending raid by a group of Maphuthing and Bahlakwana on the Batlhaping. The Griqua were lured by the prospect of booty in cattle and captives, both of which they obtained in some numbers. On other occasions, communities of southern Batswana sought the assistance of Griqua and Kora against raiding groups, and it is likely that parties of both became involved in unrecorded raids on communities made vulnerable by the upheavals of the time.

By the mid-1820s, the adherents of Sebetwane of the Bafokeng and Moletsane of the Bataung had emerged as the main raiders in the southern Tswana territories. The former were active mainly in the upper Molopo region and the latter mainly on the Vaal. Both groups had in effect taken to a life of brigandage. From the east, the abakwaKhumalo of Mzilikazi were also raiding more frequently.[35] Most of the chiefdoms – Bahurutshe, Bakgatla, Bakwena, Barolong, Bangwaketse, and others – which suffered from the depredations committed by Sebetwane, Moletsane, and Mzilikazi were able to hold on to their territories in the face of repeated attacks, even if they lost large numbers of cattle. An exception was the group under Sefunela of the Barolong, which was driven backward and forward between the Vaal and upper Molopo, until eventually, in 1833, with the assistance

---

[34] Margaret Kinsman, "Hungry wolves: the impact of violence on Rolong life, 1823–1836," in Hamilton (Ed.), *Mfecane Aftermath*, pp. 363–80.

[35] Ibid., pp. 380–7; R. Kent Rasmussen, *Migrant Kingdom: Mzilikazi's Ndebele in South Africa* (London: Rex Collings and Cape Town: David Philip, 1978), pp. 49–52.

of Wesleyan missionaries, it moved across the Vaal to settle at Thaba Nchu in the comparatively quiet zone of the present-day central Free State.

THE NDWANDWE AFTERMATH, 1826–36

The defeat of the abakwaNdwandwe by the amaZulu at the Izindololwane in 1826 marked a major turning point in the history of the territories on both sides of the Drakensberg. It removed a long-established power from the scene and left the amaZulu and abakwaGaza kingdoms as the dominant polities in the east. It opened the way for the emergence of a major new political force in the interior in the form of the amaNdebele kingdom, and for the reemergence, in a precarious position between the amaZulu, abakwaGaza, and amaNdebele, of the Swazi and Pedi kingdoms.

The East

Shaka's defeat of the abakwaNdwandwe removed from the circle of his opponents what the trader Nathaniel Isaacs described as "the most powerful tribe with which he had ever contended."[36] Paradoxically it also opened the way for the spread of internal opposition to the king's rule, particularly within the Zulu royal house itself. So long as there were threats from outside the kingdom to the domination exercised by the royal house, resistance to Shaka's rule from hostile internal factions remained largely muted, but once the main external enemy had been disposed of, opposition in these quarters seems to have begun growing, if largely in secret.

That there was a high degree of political tension in the Zulu kingdom at this time is indicated by the killings that apparently followed the death of the king's mother Nandi in August 1827. The eyewitness account of this episode written by Henry Fynn, a Port Natal trader, is well known; exaggerated though it undoubtedly is, it suggests that these events had important political dimensions. They may well have been a consequence of deliberate attempts on the part of Shaka to rouse popular feeling against his enemies so that he could rid himself of opposition elements. More and more by this time he seems to have been turning to the traders for support. He allowed them to take in refugees from the Zulu kingdom and to establish themselves as heads of growing followings. In April 1828, the Zulu king despatched two envoys to the Cape on a boat built by the traders, and the following month himself set off with a number of his *amabutho*, together

---

[36] Nathaniel Isaacs, *Travels and Adventures in Eastern Africa* (Cape Town: Struik, 1970, first published London, 1836), p. 71.

with strong contingents from the traders' settlements, on a major raid into the Mpondo country.

Why Shaka should have launched this raid just when he was in the process of trying to establish diplomatic contacts with the Cape is not clear,[37] but in the event his forces, actively assisted by some of the traders, penetrated beyond the lower Mthatha River and seized large numbers of cattle from the Bomvana and Mpondo chiefdoms. But the expedition's successful outcome did nothing to head off a conspiracy that was developing among several of Shaka's brothers, possibly with the knowledge of some of the Port Natal traders, to kill him. It seems likely that Shaka had wind of the plot, for even before his *amabutho* had returned from the expedition against the amaMpondo he issued orders for his forces, including his brothers, to proceed at once to raid the chiefdoms far to the north in the region beyond Delagoa Bay. The launching of a new expedition so soon after the conclusion of a previous one was unprecedented and caused much dissension in the kingdom. It may have constituted an attempt by Shaka to put the conspirators at a distance pending the return of his embassy to the Cape with a hoped-for agreement of friendship with the British. But his envoys were unable to establish satisfactory relations with the British, largely because of the interference on their own account of the traders who had accompanied them. The return of the ambassadors with news of their failure probably played a key role in the conspirators' decision to make their move. The absence of most of Shaka's forces may have been another important factor. In late September, he was stabbed to death at kwaDukuza, 70 km north of Port Natal, by a party led by his brothers Dingane and Mhlangana.

The assassination of Shaka is an event that has been heavily dramatized in the literature; seen from a contemporary perspective, it marked little more than the success of a palace coup organized by an opposing faction of the Zulu royal house. After seeing to the murder of Mhlangana and other possible rivals for the succession, Dingane was able to win the support of most of the kingdom's *izikhulu* and become king in Shaka's place.[38] The only overt act of opposition that he faced took place at the beginning of his reign when a large group of abakwaQwabe broke away and made off with numbers of cattle into the region south of the Mzimkhulu. Here, at the end of 1829, they were attacked and broken up by the amaMpondo. The relative smoothness of the transition to Dingane's reign was an indication

[37] Wright, "Dynamics of power and conflict," pp. 353–71; Carolyn Hamilton, "The character and objects of Chaka: a reconsideration of the making of Shaka as mfecane motor," in Hamilton (Ed.), *Mfecane Aftermath*, pp. 189–203.

[38] Wright, "Dynamics of power and conflict," pp. 371–80; Peter Colenbrander, "The Zulu kingdom, 1828–79," in Duminy and Guest (Eds.), *Natal and Zululand from Earliest Times*, pp. 83–9.

of the degree to which the Zulu ruling house had by this stage achieved legitimacy in the eyes of its subjects, and perhaps also of the degree to which growing outside pressures were serving to hold the kingdom together. To the south, the British had recently broken up the Ngwane chiefdom at Mbholompo; on the southern Highveld, Griqua and Kora were raiding widely; to the northwest Mzilikazi's Ndebele polity was starting to fill the vacuum of power left by the breakup of the abakwaNdwandwe in 1826; to the north were the Portuguese at Delagoa Bay and the growing Swazi and Gaza kingdoms.

The most immediate problem Dingane faced at the start of his reign was to ensure the continued loyalty of the *amabutho* and their leaders. He proceeded to remove some of the major grievances that had been building up under Shaka by relaxing the marriage laws far enough to enable men of the senior *amabutho* to marry and set up their own homesteads. He also made them generous presentations of cattle. At the same time he was turning to the business of getting rid of Shaka's favorites. He found excuses for putting to death several chiefs who owed their positions to Shaka and replaced them with his own supporters. To remove potential rivals for the kingship, he also killed off all but two of his surviving brothers.

Although this combination of policies enabled Dingane to establish his authority over the kingdom in the short term, in the long term he faced the same problem that the rulers of all the emerging polities of southern Africa had to cope with: how to acquire large enough resources of cattle to retain the loyalty of their fighting men and of politically important subordinate chiefs. Few, if any, rulers had enough cattle of their own or were able to squeeze enough cattle from their subjects to be able to do this; sooner or later most had to turn to raiding cattle from other chiefs. In the Zulu kingdom this problem seems to have become acute by the end of Shaka's reign, and his successor was constrained to send out regular raiding expeditions. Dingane is known to have attacked the amaBhaca to the south in 1830, the amaNdebele in the Magaliesberg in 1832, the amaBhaca again in 1833, the amaSwazi in 1836, and the amaNdebele again, this time 500 or 600 km away on the Marico, in 1837. Not all these forays were successful, which may account in part for what seems to have been an increase in the authoritarian nature of Dingane's rule as time went by.

On his advent to power, Dingane's first impulse seems to have been to try to reduce contact with the Port Natal traders. He abandoned the cattle posts that Shaka had recently established south of the port and established his main residence at Mgungundlovu near the White Mfolozi River about 200 km away. But, like Shaka, he needed the traders as sources of manufactured goods and as intermediaries with the Cape, and by 1830 he was actively courting them again. At the same time, he also sought to expand trade with the Portuguese at Delagoa Bay and to play them off against the British at Port Natal. His relations with both entrepôts remained tense: Zulu forces clashed briefly with the Port Natal traders on two occasions in the early 1830s, and in 1833 Dingane went as far as sending an expedition to attack the fort at Delagoa Bay and put to death the Portuguese governor in order to keep open the trade route to the bay.[39] His dealings with the Port Natal traders were complicated by the advent of British and American missionaries in his kingdom in the later 1830s.

The Northern Interior

The history of the Ndebele kingdom begins with the emergence in the late eighteenth and nineteenth centuries of several distinct Khumalo chiefdoms in the region about the sources of the Black Mfolozi. By the 1810s, these chiefdoms were being brought under the domination of the abakwaNd-wandwe immediately to the east. Upon the breakup of the first Ndwandwe kingdom in about 1820, a group of abakwaKhumalo under their young chief Mzilikazi moved away from the zone of conflict between the abak-waNdwandwe and the amaZulu and migrated toward the upper reaches of the Vaal River. There is very little evidence on their history over the next half-dozen years or so, and historians have come up with a number of dif-ferent stories about their movements and raiding activities in this period. None of these versions takes much account of the increasingly powerful presence of the reconsolidating Ndwandwe kingdom to the east, but it is likely that for some years the Khumalo leaders would have kept a wary eye on their much stronger neighbor. Meanwhile, they were gradually build-ing up their own chiefdom by seizing grain and cattle and incorporating refugees from Tswana and Sotho chiefdoms in the increasingly unstable zone of conflict to the west and south. Here the erosion of the power of the Bahurutshe, together with the ending of Pedi influence after their defeat by the abakwaNdwandwe, enabled Mzilikazi to raid with relative ease.

By 1823, Mzilikazi's adherents were becoming known among Sotho-speaking people as "Matebele" (amaNdebele, in the Nguni languages), that is, marauders. In the colonial literature of the time they were frequently and confusingly referred to as "Zulus." Mzilikazi's power was consider-ably augmented when numbers of abakwaNdwandwe came to give him their allegiance after their defeat at the hands of the Zulu in 1826. As the Ndebele kingdom expanded, it developed into the major predator polity

---

[39] Gerhard Liesegang, "Dingane's attack on Lourenco Marques in 1833," *Journal of African History*, 10 (1969), pp. 565–79.

in the interior.[40] To the north, Mzilikazi's forces raided as far as the Venda kingdom in the Soutpansberg. In the northeast, groups like the Maroteng, the amaNdzundza, and the Balobedu were able to cling on mainly because they were able to find places of refuge in the broken country of the Drakensberg escarpment. In the west, the amaNdebele drove out Sebetlwane and his people and raided as far as the territories of the Bangwaketse beyond the Marico River. On the southern Highveld, they attacked Moletsane and drove him and his followers toward the Orange River; they raided Matiwane and his people in the Caledon Valley.

In 1827 or 1828, Mzilikazi led his adherents in another move, from the upper Vaal region to the good cattle country on the northern slopes of the Magaliesberg near present-day Pretoria. From this area, his forces continued to raid long distances for cattle, particularly into the territories of the southern Batswana, who had already suffered severely from the depredations of Sebetlwane and Moletsane. Nearby chiefdoms, such as that of the Bahurutshe, were forced to become tributary to Mzilikazi; more distant ones, like the Bangwaketse, suffered repeated raids. By about 1830, the Ndebele zone of influence had expanded to the point where Mzilikazi could forbid the Tswana chiefdoms to the west to trade with Europeans and Griqua without his permission.

Such were the Ndebele successes in raiding cattle that their herds began attracting the attention of other predators. In mid-1828, a party of Kora, Griqua, Bataung, and other Sotho and Tswana groups under Kora leader Jan Bloem raided from the southwest into the Ndebele heartland and made off with large numbers of cattle. On its way back, the Kora and Griqua contingent was overtaken and scattered by a force of amaNdebele, and its share of the booty recovered. Three years later, Griqua *kaptyn* Berend Berends organized a similar raid. A formidable force of perhaps 300 Griqua and Kora horsemen, supported by several hundred Batswana on foot, penetrated deep into Ndebele territory, seized large herds of cattle, and took a number of women as captives. Soon after setting out on its return trip the commando was surprised by the pursuing amaNdebele and many of its members killed. The captured cattle were recovered. Then in 1832, Dingane sent a strong force of amaZulu to raid Mzilikazi's territories. After some fierce fighting, the amaZulu withdrew, having captured relatively few cattle.

Soon after this attack the Ndebele polity moved once again, this time to the upper Marico River, roughly 200 km to the west. It is unlikely that they made the move to try to escape Griqua and Kora attacks from the lower Vaal region, as some writers have suggested, for in the Marico region

[40] Rasmussen, *Migrant Kingdom*, pp. 59–109 passim.

the amaNdebele were, if anything, closer to Griqua and Kora country than they had been before. The main reason for the move was probably to make it easier for the amaNdebele to raid cattle from Batswana communities. Fear of more attacks by the amaZulu may have been another motivating factor. In the event, the amaNdebele pushed into what had up till then been Bahurutshe territory and proceeded to settle in it. Mzilikazi established his headquarters at eGabeni, not far from the ruins of Kaditshwene, which had been abandoned by the Bahurutshe in the face of Ndebele raids a few years before. Many Bahurutshe remained to give their allegiance to Mzilikazi; others scattered southward into the territories of the Batlhaping and Griqua, once again destabilizing wide areas about the lower Vaal. Soon afterward, Mzilikazi launched raids southward against the Barolong and northward against the Bakwena and Bangwaketse.

In moving to the Marico region, Mzilikazi and his adherents were obtruding into territories that some Griqua and Kora leaders saw as lying within their own spheres of influence. By 1834, Kora leader Jan Bloem was once again organizing a major expedition of Kora, Griqua, and Batswana against them. The attack followed much the same pattern as the two previous ones: the advance of the raiders, seizure of cattle, retreat, surprise counterattack by Ndebele, defeat of raiders, recovery of cattle. Mzilikazi did not follow up, as he could easily have done, with attacks aimed at eliminating the menace of Kora and Griqua raids, probably because he wanted to avoid pressing too close to the Cape Colony's sphere of influence. Instead he seems to have adopted the policy of maintaining an empty buffer zone beyond the southern marches of his kingdom and chasing out hunting and trading parties that ventured into it without his permission.

Mzilikazi's first encounter with Europeans had taken place in his territories north of the Magaliesberg in 1829, when he was visited by two traders. Later that year, he sent emissaries to the London Missionary Society's station among the Batlhaping at Kuruman to make contact with its head, Robert Moffat. Moffat duly paid a visit to the Ndebele king, no doubt with an eye to the prospect of extending mission activities further into the interior, and established a relationship with him that survived until Mzilikazi's death in what is now Zimbabwe in 1868. But Mzilikazi's concerns in initially inviting Moffat to visit him were less to encourage missionaries to work in his country than to set them up as intermediaries between himself and the colonial authorities in the Cape. Like Dingane, he remained largely aloof from the handful of missionaries whom he eventually allowed to work in his territories.

In 1835, Mzilikazi was visited by Andrew Smith, leader of a government-supported exploring expedition from the Cape, who left the first detailed written description of the Ndebele kingdom. He estimated the number of armed men in the kingdom to be 4,000. From this figure one historian has deduced that the total Ndebele population at this time would have been on the order of 20,000.[41] From Smith's and other contemporary accounts, we get a broad idea of the political and social structures of Ndebele kingdom in the mid-1830s. The ruling group consisted of the abakwaKhumalo and other families that had accompanied Mzilikazi during his flight from the Ndwandwe sphere of influence in the late-1810s. It is likely that they were already beginning to refer to themselves as *abasenzansi*, "those from down below," meaning the lower-lying country east of the Drakensberg, from which they originated. The language of the king's court was what would now be called isiZulu or isiNdebele. Under the domination of the abakwaKhumalo were the various groups, mostly of Sotho/Tswana-speakers, which had given their allegiance to Mzilikazi during the early stage of his migrations. They were collectively referred to as *abasenhla*, those from the higher country. From these groups were drawn the men of the *amabutho* who raided for cattle and had the responsibility of looking after them. The quarters of the *amabutho* were mostly concentrated in a relatively small territory round the king's own residences. In the outlying districts of the kingdom were the low-status tributary groups, or *amahole*, which had been subjugated in the later phases of Ndebele migration and expansion; as in the Zulu kingdom, their function was to guard the marches of the kingdom and to man outlying royal cattle posts. Territorial chiefs seem to have had much less political influence than in the Zulu kingdom, whereas commanders of *amabutho* seem to have had considerably more. This was a function mainly of the kingdom's origins as a migrant, predatory polity rather than as a partly defensive, sedentary one. Overall, it was probably responsible for more violence and disruptions than any of the other states that emerged in the period from the 1810s to the 1830s.

Particularly hard hit by the expansion of Mzilikazi's kingdom were the Tswana chiefdoms of the territory between the Vaal River and the Kalahari Desert, a region that had already been devastated by the depredations of Sebetwane and Moletsane. In this mostly flat terrain there were no defensible mountain strongholds: The only way to escape Mzilikazi's raiders was to move away altogether, as Sebetwane and his people did after their defeat at the hands of the Ndebele, or to retreat into the deserts to the west where Ndebele forces found it difficult to pursue. This tactic was successfully used on several occasions by the Bangwato of the Shoshong area and by the Bangwaketse of the upper Molopo. Though both chiefdoms lost many cattle to Ndebele raiders, and both at times paid nominal tribute to Mzilikazi, they were able to preserve their political autonomy.

---

[41] Rasmussen, *Migrant Kingdom*, p. 92.

Not so fortunate were the peoples of the regions that were directly occupied by the Ndebele. The Bakwena and Bakgatla chiefdoms of the Magaliesberg area, together with the once-powerful Bahurutshe of the Marico, were thoroughly subjugated and forced to become tributary to Mzilikazi. Groups within raiding distance, like the Barolong chiefdoms of the Vaal–Molopo area and the Bakwena of the Madikwe, were broken up and scattered. Some fragments gave their allegiance to Mzilikazi; others moved away to the south to seek refuge with the Batlhaping or with the Griqua of Griquatown and Philippolis. Of all the major Tswana groups, only the Batlhaping escaped Ndebele raids, almost certainly because of the presence among them of the well-established LMS mission under Robert Moffat.

The Southern Highveld

As we have seen, by the mid-1820s displaced communities of the Caledon Valley were beginning to cohere round a number of leaders who were able to offer some measure of protection against raiding groups. Dominant among them was Matiwane of the amaNgwane.[42] By this time the main zone of conflict in the interior had shifted to the region round the middle Vaal, but the communities along the Caledon were still far from secure. Griqua, Kora, and Boer freebooters from the middle Orange and lower Vaal were raiding more frequently, and in about 1827 Matiwane's people lost numbers of cattle in a raid probably made by a force of Mzilikazi's amaNdebele. (Some historians have mistakenly blamed this raid on the amaZulu, who were often confused with the amaNdebele by colonial writers at this time: see earlier.) Matiwane proceeded to try to make up his losses by raiding the abaThembu over the Drakensberg escarpment to the southeast, but chiefdoms in the Caledon Valley were clearly still vulnerable to predatory groups from the west and north, and in 1828 the amaNgwane chief decided to move away with his adherents and resettle in Thembu territory.

The ensuing migration brought Matiwane and his people into a region that colonial officials in the Cape were more and more coming to see as lying within the British sphere of influence. In the middle of the year, alarmed by reports of increasing conflict in the northeastern border zone, the colonial authorities sent out a strong contingent of troops to reestablish stability and make a show of force in the region. The troops were accompanied by

[42] For contrasting accounts of the history of Matiwane and his following at this time, see Jeff Peires, "Matiwane's road to Mbholompo: a reprieve for the mfecane?" in Hamilton (Ed.), *Mfecane Aftermath*, pp. 213–39; and Elizabeth Eldredge, "Migration, conflict and leadership in early nineteenth-century South Africa: the case of Matiwane," in Robert Harms et al. (Eds.), *Paths Towards the Past: African Historical Essays in Honor of Jan Vansina* (Atlanta: African Studies Association, 1994), pp. 39–75.

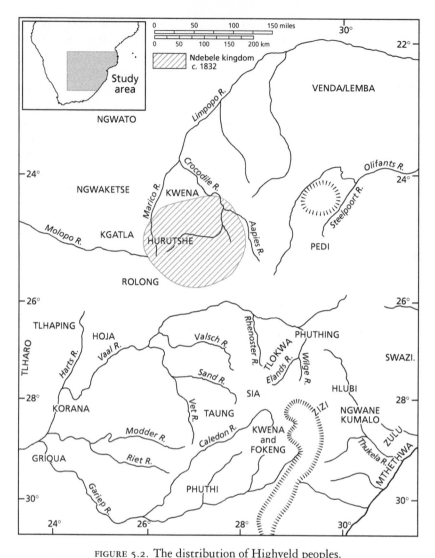

FIGURE 5.2. The distribution of Highveld peoples.

a commando of frontier farmers eager for the chance to seize cattle and captives and were joined by large parties of amaGcaleka, amaMpondo, and abaThembu with the same objective. In August 1828, the combined forces fell upon Matiwane's people at Mbholompo to the west of present-day Umtata, routed them, captured large herds of cattle, and took numbers of men, women, and children captive.

This attack completely broke Matiwane's chiefdom and ended its existence as a significant political force. The way was now open for new groups to fill the power vacuum that Matiwane's departure had left in the Caledon Valley. Sekonyela of the Batlokwa had the largest following in the region, but he faced increasing competition for domination from Moshoeshoe of the Bamokotedi, whose adherents occupied the region round the mountain stronghold of Thaba Bosiu on the middle Caledon. Under his leadership, the Mokotedi polity had been able to establish itself as a focal point of stability for displaced communities in the Caledon Valley, and Moshoeshoe's following had grown rapidly. By 1827–28, it seems, his chiefdom was strong enough to beat off an attack by that of Matiwane, and after the breakup of the latter in 1828, Moshoeshoe was quick to seize the opportunity of further expanding his power. In 1829, he successfully raided the relatively untouched reservoir of cattle in the Thembu country across the Drakensberg, so providing himself with resources for attracting the allegiance of numbers of the refugees who by this time were beginning to return to the Caledon Valley from the Cape border regions to the south. The Tlokwa chiefdom, for its part, was less favorably located for benefiting from the return of these refugees and for raiding into cattle-rich areas. In addition, Sekonyela seems to have been a less-capable diplomat and tactician than Moshoeshoe. By the early 1830s, the Mokotedi chiefdom was rivaling that of the Batlokwa for dominance in the Caledon Valley.[43]

From 1833, missionaries of the Paris Evangelical Missionary Society (PEMS) were active in Moshoeshoe's chiefdom, and the following year a Wesleyan mission was established among Sekonyela's people. In sharp contrast to rulers like Dingane and Mzilikazi, Moshoeshoe welcomed the arrival of missionaries and encouraged the PEMS to expand its activities among his people. In more centralized polities like those of the amaZulu and the amaNdebele, whose rulers were highly sensitive to perceived threats to the powers accumulated by the monarchy and maintained largely by force, missionaries tended to be regarded by rulers with deep suspicion. In the much less centralized polity of Moshoeshoe, the presence of missionaries constituted not so much a threat to the chief's powers as a source of support. Apart from anything else, the Sotho king's willingness to accept them was a major factor in earning him a generally good press, then and later, in the world of European colonialism and imperialism. By contrast, historians have generally treated his rival, Sekonyela, with little sympathy or insight.

---

[43] Peter Sanders, *Moshoeshoe: Chief of the Sotho* (London: Heinemann, and Cape Town: David Philip, 1975), Chapters 4–6; Leonard Thompson, *Survival in Two Worlds: Moshoeshoe of Lesotho 1786–1870* (Oxford: Oxford University Press, 1975), Chapters 2, 3; Elizabeth Eldredge, *A South African Kingdom: The Pursuit of Security in Nineteenth-Century Lesotho* (Cambridge: Cambridge University Press, 1993), Chapters 3, 4.

From records left by missionaries we can get some idea of the nature of the polity ruled by Moshoeshoe in the later 1830s. His adherents, who by now were becoming known as Basotho, numbered about 25,000, as against the 14,000 or so of Sekonyela. Most of the communities that had given Moshoeshoe their allegiance had done so to obtain protection in a time of great instability and to acquire cattle to rebuild lost herds. At the heart of the political and social system in his kingdom was the *mafisa* system, through which the king and other great cattle-owners – mostly his senior kinsmen – entrusted cattle to adherents. The latter had the use of them in return for giving political loyalty and, when called on to do so, military service. Men fought under their local leaders; unlike Shaka and Mzilikazi, Moshoeshoe had not inherited a centrally controlled and partially militarized *amabutho* system, and the ad hoc manner in which he had gained adherents from numerous fragmented refugee communities had not provided him with the opportunity to establish such a system himself. His kingdom was a relatively loose confederation in which the monarch had a relatively limited authority over his more powerful subordinates. It did not constitute a nation, as some historians have described it.

Most of the more important subordinate chiefs in Moshoeshoe's kingdom were close kinsmen – brothers and sons – of the king whom he had located at strategic points and under whose rule he placed many of the communities that came to give him allegiance. These kinsmen were at one and the same time the major recipients of cattle distributed by the king under the *mafisa* system and the main leaders of opposition to him. The tendency among them – especially among the politically more ambitious – was always to seek more autonomy for themselves, but in the unstable times of the 1820s and early 1830s, when the polity faced serious threats from outside to its very existence, they retained their allegiance to the king in the face of common enemies. Of the chiefs outside the Mokotedi royal house who were tributary to Moshoeshoe, probably the most important was the Baphuthi leader Moorosi, who ruled with a high degree of autonomy over a following of Baphuthi, Basotho, abaThembu, San, and others in the far south in the Orange River–Kraai River region.

In the semiarid territories on the southern peripheries of Moshoeshoe's kingdom and in the mountainous regions that extended east of it to the Drakensberg range and its foothills, where few if any farming communities had settled, groups of San sought through a variety of strategies to retain what autonomy they could.[44] In the remoter highlands, some were able

---

[44] John Wright, *Bushman Raiders of the Drakensberg 1840–1870* (Pietermaritzburg: University of Natal Press, 1971); John Wright, "*Bushman Raiders* revisited," in Pippa Skotnes (Ed.), *Claim to the Country: The Archive of Lucy Lloyd and Wilhelm Bleek* (Johannesburg:

to pursue a way of life based primarily on hunting and gathering. Others, particularly in the valley of the upper Orange and on the adjoining plateau of what was later called East Griqualand, became involved in networks of hunting and trading that extended to the Cape Colony in one direction and Port Natal in another. They exchanged ivory for items such as cattle, horses, firearms, and tobacco. Further south, numbers of San in Moorosi's country joined others of his adherents in raiding livestock from abaThembu and other communities across the Drakensberg and from white graziers on the northeastern borders of the Cape Colony. Throughout these regions, San notables continued to acquire livestock and earn prestige through providing services as rainmakers and healers to neighboring groups – Basotho, Baphuthi, abaThembu, amaMpondomise, and amaBhaca. Changes in political and social relations among the San were reflected in the development of new styles and new motifs in the rock paintings that their shaman artists continued to make.[45]

The Northeast

Another effect of the collapse of the Ndwandwe kingdom in 1826 was to leave the way open for the consolidation of the Dlamini or Swazi kingdom under Sobhuza and the reemergence of the Pedi kingdom under Sekwati. Since the early 1820s, the abakwaDlamini had gradually been expanding their domination over the small chiefdoms of the southern and central regions of present-day Swaziland. A number of fortified caves in the Mdimba Mountains near the modern capital of Mbabane provided them with a degree of security against attack from stronger powers like the amaZulu. The overthrow of Shaka in 1828, together with the shift of the Gaza kingdom's center of gravity from the Nkomati to the lower Limpopo, encouraged Sobhuza to expand his rule more aggressively, and in the early

Jacana; and Athens, Ohio: Ohio University Press, 2007), pp. 118–29; Jannie Loubser and Gordon Lourens, "Depictions of domestic ungulates and shields: hunter/gatherers and agro-pastoralists in the Caledon River valley area," in Thomas Dowson and David Lewis-Williams (Eds.), *Contested Images: Diversity in Southern African Rock Art Research* (Johannesburg: Witwatersrand University Press, 1994), pp. 83–118; Pieter Jolly, "Interaction between south-eastern San and southern Nguni and Sotho communities c.1400-c.1880," *South African Historical Journal*, 35 (1996), pp. 30–61.

[45] Loubser and Lourens, "Depictions of domestic ungulates and shields," in Dowson and Lewis-Williams (Eds.), *Contested Images*, pp. 83–118; Thomas Dowson, "Hunter–gatherers, traders and slaves: the mfecane impact on Bushmen, their ritual and their art," in Hamilton (Ed.), *The Mfecane Aftermath*, pp. 51–70; Geoffrey Blundell, *Nqabayo's Nomansland: San Rock Art and the Somatic Past* (Uppsala: Department of Archaeology and Ancient History, Uppsala University; and Johannesburg: Rock Art Research Institute, University of the Witwatersrand, 2004.)

1830s he extended his sphere of influence as far north as the Sabi River. His power was based largely on the authority that he exercised over his polity's *amabutho* or *emabutfo*, and as in other similar kingdoms, a clear political and social distinction came to be established between conquerors and conquered. The abakwaDlamini and the groups closely associated with them became known as *bemdzabuko*, or "first people," whereas the subordinated groups were known as *emakhandzambili*, which is often glossed as "those found ahead" (a literal translation is "those with two heads"). Preferred marriage with kin kept wealth in cattle largely in the hands of the Dlamini aristocracy, which led to growing political tensions within the kingdom. But the combination of firm rule from the center and the existence of outside threats from the amaZulu to the south, the amaNdebele to the west, and Gaza and Portuguese slavers and their allies to the east gave the emerging Swazi state a relatively high degree of cohesion. By 1836, Sobhuza's kingdom was strong enough to survive a raid made by a large force of amaZulu, assisted by a party of gunmen from the British trading settlement at Port Natal.[46]

The Pedi polity that was reestablishing itself in the same period was structured on very different lines. The breakup of the kingdom after its defeat at the hands of Zwide's abakwaNdwandwe in the early 1820s had taken place in a period when the Maroteng ruling house was deeply divided in a succession dispute that followed the death of the king, Thulare. After the Ndwandwe conquest of the Pedi heartland, the Maroteng split into a number of fragments under Thulare's sons. Several of these migrated northward into the region across the Olifants River, where they tried to reconsolidate. The most successful group was led by Sekwati, one of Thulare's junior sons. Some time after the defeat of the abakwaNdwandwe by the amaZulu in 1826, Sekwati was able to return to the vicinity of the Steelpoort River and begin trying to rebuild a following. He did so in much the same way as Moshoeshoe was doing in the Caledon Valley: by establishing a reasonably secure base on a fortified hilltop and offering protection to the large number of communities in the region that had been displaced by the ravages of stronger powers like the amaZulu, abakwaNdwandwe, amaNdebele, and amaSwazi, and by Gaza and Portuguese slave raids in the region to the north of Delagoa Bay. He was not able to establish the centralized institutions of power, which the ruling houses of these other kingdoms had been able to do, and expanded his authority largely through diplomatic means. The following that cohered round him was nevertheless strong enough to ward off a major Swazi raid in the late 1830s.[47]

---

[46] Bonner, *Kings, Commoners and Concessionaires*, pp. 30–41.
[47] Delius, *The Land Belongs to Us*, pp. 26–30.

The late 1820s and 1830s were also a time of expansion for the Gaza kingdom. In about 1827, Soshangane moved his headquarters from the lower Nkomati to the lower Limpopo. From here, he continued to trade ivory and slaves to Delagoa Bay to the south and opened up contact with the Portuguese at Inhambane to the northeast. In the latter part of 1828, he defeated the large Zulu force that Shaka had sent to raid north of Delagoa Bay and had become enfeebled by malaria and dysentery. Soshangane seems to have courted the Portuguese at Delagoa Bay as allies against the rival Zulu power, which, under the rule of Dingane, was actively seeking from about 1830 onward to bring the territories round the bay under its domination. Both Dingane and Soshangane regarded trade with the Portuguese as important enough to take forcible measures when necessary to retain control over it; in 1833, as mentioned above, Dingane sent an expedition to execute the governor of Delagoa Bay for refusing to comply with his demands and in 1834 Soshangane destroyed a force of Portuguese from Inhambane seeking to contest his control of trade in the hinterland of that port. After this, Soshangane's domination of the territories from Delagoa Bay far to the northward was largely unchallenged. The area over which his *amabutho* raided and extracted tribute ultimately reached to the Zambezi, making Soshangane's sphere of influence much the largest of any of those dominated by the kings who held power in southern Africa in the turbulent years of the 1820s and 1830s.[48]

THE POLITICAL SCENE IN THE MID-1830S

In the seventy years or so after 1760, the political face of the region north of the Orange and east of the Kalahari was profoundly transformed. At the beginning of the period, the farming communities of the region were organized into possibly several hundred chiefdoms, the great majority of them small, fluid, and politically decentralized. By the 1830s, the area had come to be dominated by three large and centralized kingdoms, those of the amaZulu in the east, the abakwaGaza in the northeast, and the amaNdebele in the west. The first of these had more or less stabilized their borders; the other two, notably that of the abakwaGaza, were still expanding. Lodged uncomfortably between them or on their borders were several smaller and less centralized kingdoms – those of the Bapedi, amaSwazi, Batlokwa, Basotho, and amaMpondo. Of the previously existing chiefdoms, most had either been incorporated into, or become dominated by, one or other of

---

[48] Liesegang, "Aspects of Gaza Nguni history 1821–1897," pp. 1–14; Gerhard Liesegang, "Notes on the internal structure of the Gaza kingdom of southern Mozambique 1840–1895," in Peires (Ed.), *Before and after Shaka*, pp. 178–209.

these larger polities. Others had fragmented and disappeared altogether as discrete entities. A small number – on the edges of the Kalahari Desert; in the malaria- and tsetse-ridden eastern Lowveld; on the plains of the southern Highveld; in the broken country south of the Thukela – managed to cling to an uncertain autonomy on the margins of their bigger neighbors. A number of chiefdoms or offshoot elements had migrated out of the region altogether.

In all the new kingdoms, the authority of rulers, even the most autocratic of them, continued to depend ultimately on their ability to provide their subjects with protection, adequate agricultural and grazing land, and the opportunities for building up the holdings of cattle crucial for the establishment and reproduction of autonomous homesteads. Powers exercised by individual kings varied widely. The strongest of them – Shaka, Soshangane, Mzilikazi – ruled societies in which the monarchy had been able to establish centralized control over male age grades (*amabutho*) and, to a high degree, to militarize them. These rulers thus disposed of forces that enabled them to establish domination over relatively large territories and to use pronounced degrees of violence, or threats of violence, to overcome opposition and extract tribute from subjected peoples. By contrast, the kingdoms of the Bapedi, Basotho, Batlokwa, and amaMpondo were essentially defensive polities that had formed, and continued to hold together, in the face of outside threats. Their rulers maintained their authority over subordinate chiefs less by force than through diplomatic maneuverings and the manipulation of access to resources of land and cattle. The Swazi polity occupied a position somewhere in between: It had begun life in the later eighteenth century as an expansionist migrant chiefdom, had then been forced onto the defensive by its bigger Ndwandwe, Zulu, and Gaza neighbors, and was able to turn its *emabutfo* toward effective expansion again only in the 1830s.

Centralized and less-centralized kingdoms alike were characterized by more or less clear divisions between three social tiers. At the top was an aristocracy consisting of the ruling family and a number of other families closely bound to it by ties of descent, or of political loyalty, or both. Beneath it was a stratum consisting of the commoner families of the kingdom's heartland: These formed the main part of the kingdom's body politic. At the bottom was a category of despised and generally poorer families of clients and dependants who recognized the king as their overlord but were usually excluded from participation in the kingdom's political affairs.

Throughout the homestead remained the basic unit of social and economic organization, though differences of wealth between aristocratic and commoner homesteads were now much more marked than had been the case half a century before. Heads of homesteads were subjected by their political rulers to heavier demands for tribute in the form of cattle, grain, marriageable young women, and the labor power of young men. But even the most authoritarian rulers held back from exploiting subject homesteads beyond a certain point, for otherwise the economy that sustained the whole society would have been endangered. The ability of homesteads to function effectively on a day-to-day basis and to produce the surplus of cattle and labor power that underpinned the existence of the aristocracies lay at the very heart of the social and economic order.[49] Kings and subordinate chiefs were expected to render assistance to poorer homesteads in bad times, and young men might be released from service in the king's *amabutho* in cases where their own homesteads had especially urgent need of their labor.

Gender identities and relations were transformed in important ways with the emergence of more centralized – and in some cases, militarized – systems of government. Though there is little historical evidence for the existence of figures such as that of the "noble Zulu warrior" beloved of modern authors and filmmakers, the rise of militarized conquest states would have provided a ripe setting for the emergence of male warrior cults. For their part, wives and daughters were probably brought more firmly under the domination of male homestead heads as systems of authority in general became tighter. In the Zulu kingdom, as previously indicated, the choosing of marriage partners and the timing of marriages became subject to direction by the state. At the same time, in some kingdoms, individual women could and did become powerful political figures in their own right. Usually they were senior members of the ruling house or senior wives in the ruling house, who had first become influential in its internal – and invariably highly factional – politics, and subsequently in state affairs. For their part, kings who were concerned to prevent male relatives from establishing themselves as rivals, and subordinate chiefs from becoming overmighty, often sought to establish senior women relatives in positions where they could act as political counterweights. Well-known examples of politically powerful women in the early nineteenth century are Ntombazi, variously given as the mother or sister of Zwide of the abakwaNdwandwe; MaNthatisi, mother of Sekonyela of the Batlokwa; and Mnkabayi, sister of Shaka's father Senzangakhona.

Rulers of the new kingdoms had to find new ways of integrating into the body politic the various groups that came under their domination, or, to put it another way, of turning potentially resistant subjects into more or less willing adherents. Importantly, this meant the development or elaboration of state rituals and ideologies, such as those associated with "first fruits"

---

[49] Jeff Guy, "Analyzing pre-capitalist societies in southern Africa," *Journal of Southern African Studies*, 14(1), pp. 18–37.

ceremonies and with preparing fighting men for war, which were designed to win general acceptance of the notion that the ancestors of the ruling house were ultimately the sources of the welfare of the whole society. At the same time, rulers were concerned to preserve, and even accentuate, the social and political distinctions between ruling houses and the peoples over which they ruled. These contradictory aims entailed complex and ongoing manipulations, by both rulers and ruled, of genealogical memories and of group identities.

If these emerging states were held together in part by new institutions of government and by new ideologies, to a large degree they were also propped up by outside pressures. On the one hand, they faced the threat of raids from rival states. On the other, they faced the expansion, real or potential, of European colonial domination from the Cape in the south and, to a much weaker extent, from the Portuguese sphere of influence in the northeast. In the far southwest, on the Orange and Vaal rivers, three unstable herding, hunting, trading, and raiding polities under the leadership of Griqua "captains" had developed as outliers of Cape frontier society. Further to the east, graziers from the Cape were beginning to push across the Orange River into the southern Highveld, and to the north hunters and traders from the colony were penetrating well beyond the Vaal. At Delagoa Bay, a small and ramshackle but politically important outpost of Portuguese colonial rule sought to control a long-established trade in ivory and a rapidly expanding trade in slaves. At Port Natal, a growing group of British traders was nominally subject to Dingane, but in effect was acting with more and more autonomy. Groups of missionaries had been working among the southern Batswana since early in the century, and in the 1830s others were establishing themselves in the Caledon Valley, in the territories between the Fish and Mzimkhulu rivers, and in the Zulu kingdom. In Cape Town and Grahamstown, British colonial officials sought to gather information about the powerful new states that had emerged to the north and wondered how best to deal with them. Most of these polities were still in the process of consolidating themselves when, in the later 1830s, the migration of parties of Boers and their retainers from the Cape into the territories across the Orange and Vaal inaugurated a new era of violence and instability across much of the subcontinent.

6

FROM SLAVE ECONOMY TO SETTLER CAPITALISM: THE CAPE COLONY AND ITS EXTENSIONS, 1800–1854

MARTIN LEGASSICK AND ROBERT ROSS

In the first half of the nineteenth century the Cape Colony became not merely a colony of European settlement based on coerced black labor but one capable of expelling the agricultural amaXhosa from their land, annexing it, and driving them into the colony for work. In 1795 the colony, characterized by slavery and near slavery (of the indigenous pastoral Khoekhoen), as well as racial hierarchy, was ruled by the senescent mercantilist VOC, its furthest frontier of cattle, and sheep farmers recently having encountered resistance from San and amaXhosa in the East. VOC rule was replaced by the rising industrial power of Britain. Britain initially occupied the Cape in 1795 as a strategic wartime naval base in the Napoleonic wars. In 1803 the Cape reverted temporarily to the Batavian Republic but was retaken by the British in 1806 and permanently ceded in 1814.

In global terms, these shifts in the position of the Cape derived from the Napoleonic wars, themselves the consequence of political revolutions in France and America – which also triggered off a successful slave revolt in Haiti. This "age of democratic revolution" gave rise to new universalist ideas about freedom. The same era saw industrial capitalism emerge from a new factory system, chiefly in Britain. The new, "autocratically ruled yet uncentralised"[1] British Empire had as its premise the central role of overseas markets in sustaining industrial development. India was the central market, and China the huge, untapped market to be aspired to. "Free trade" was projected as the way for the British to dominate the world. Within this, the Cape was taken over above all as a way station on the route to the east.

What were the effects of this new world situation on the peoples who were already in, or became embraced within, the colony? This is the main question this chapter tries to address. In so doing, it attempts to reconcile

---

[1] T. Keegan, *Colonial South Africa and the Origins of the Racial Order* (Cape Town: David Philip, 1996), p. 45; C. A. Bayly, *Imperial Meridian: The British Empire and the World* (Harlow: Longmans, 1989).

three distinct narratives of the Cape's history, which frequently seem to be in conflict with each other and which certainly are rarely integrated in the historiography: the liberal line of progress through the emancipations of slaves and Khoekhoen to the establishment of constitutional rule in the early 1850s, a line linked to the expansion of the economy and the transition from a governmental system based on patronage and corruption to one where the rules of bourgeois respectability held sway, and also to the development of a new colored identity; the systemic violence of the conflicts between the colony and the amaXhosa, linked to the increased racism of colonial society; and the expansion of colonial settlement into Transorangia, into what was to become the Transvaal and into Natal.[2] The dynamic of South African colonial history before 1850 derives from the interaction of these lines of development.

HISTORIOGRAPHY

During the early nineteenth century, the intellectual life of the Cape Colony began to take on recognizably "modern" forms. The first printing press was introduced into the country in 1800. In 1820 the first newspapers were founded and also the first monthly journals. The South African Library and the South African Museum were established in Cape Town in 1818 and 1825, respectively. Within this intellectual milieu, which was both Dutch and English, the two main concerns were, on the one hand, the biology of South Africa, which led to a number of major expeditions and to the increasing colonial knowledge of the interior, and, on the other, the recent history of the colony. This was, of course, in essence a scarcely transformed political argument. As argued in Chapter 1, it was this historical writing, set in train by the Rev. John Philip, that set the parameters for the historical debate that has continued more or less ever since.[3] For a long time the dominant discourse justified colonial expansion, which could form the basis both for an English South African nationalism, as with George McCall Theal or Sir George Cory, or an Afrikaner one. Such interpretations never went unchallenged. Xhosa ideas about their past, and their confrontation with colonialism, have remained a powerful voice, though only intermittently on the same stage as that of the whites.[4] Missionary liberalism, Janus-faced

---

[2] It is notable that the *Oxford History* covers the material for this chapter in four separate sections, entitled "Co-operation and Conflict: The Eastern Cape Frontier," "The Consolidation of a new society: the Cape Colony," "Cooperation and Conflict: the Zulu Kingdom and Natal," and "Co-operation and Conflict: The High Veld."

[3] See Chapter 1 in this volume.

[4] J. Peires, *House of Phalo* (Johannesburg: Ravan Press, 1981), pp. 170–80; N. Mandela, *Long Walk to Freedom: The Autobiography of Nelson Mandela* (London: Little, Brown, 1994), pp. 21–2. On Xhosa oral tradition, see also J. Opland, *Xhosa Poets and Poetry* (Cape Town:

as ever, has had its descendants in the academic world and has perhaps even become dominant, if in a transmuted and secularized version. Marxism, specifically Trotskyism, in the radical circles of twentieth-century Cape Town, produced a couple of important, if underused, accounts of this period.[5]

In the 1980s and early 1990s an emphasis on social history resulted in a series of more specialized studies of slavery and its abolition, of the Khoekhoen, and of farm workers.[6] Matters of respectability and of gender have come to the fore here, as have attempts to understand the religious experience of converts.[7] The 1990s also saw a series of important syntheses, by Clifford Crais and Tim Keegan, as well as the mammoth work of more than 1,300 pages by nonacademic historian Noel Mostert. They were building on the first sympathetic academic account of Xhosa history, that was published in 1981 by Jeff Peires.[8]

The main significance of this work has been their attempt to integrate the story of the (partial and ambivalent) liberation of the slaves and Khoekhoen with that of the conquest of the amaXhosa.[9] Crais and Keegan in particular have insisted that the racism of the nineteenth century highlighted the role of British settler leaders in the Eastern Cape in promoting a new discourse of racism, different from that of the eighteenth century. They have exposed the paradox of Cape liberalism – that from the late eighteenth century, conquest, exploitation, and subjugation by European powers coexisted and coincided with increasingly powerful claims in political discourse to universal principles as the basis for organizing a polity.[10] Together with this,

---

David Philip, 1998), and on the interpenetration of written and oral versions of history, see Chapter 1 in this volume.

[5] See particularly N. Majeke [Dora Taylor], *The Role of the Missionaries in Conquest* (Johannesburg: Society of Young Africa, 1953).

[6] Particularly N. Worden and C. Crais (Eds.), *Breaking the Chains: Slavery and Its Legacy in the Nineteenth-Century Cape Colony* (Johannesburg: Witwatersrand University Press, 1994).

[7] Of particular importance were the works of P. Scully, *Liberating the Family? Gender and British Slave Emancipation in the Rural Western Cape, South Africa, 1823–1853* (Oxford, Hanover and Cape Town: Heinemann, James Currey, and David Philip, 1997); E. Elbourne, *Blood Ground: Colonialism, Missions, and the Contest for Christianity in the Cape Colony and Britain, 1799–1853* (Montreal and Kingston: McGill-Queens University Press, 2002); see also R. Ross, *Status and Respectability at the Cape of Good Hope, 1750–1870: A Tragedy of Manners* (Cambridge: Cambridge University Press, 1999).

[8] Peires, *House of Phalo.*

[9] C. Crais, *The Making of the Colonial Order: White Supremacy and Black Resistance in the Eastern Cape, 1770–1865* (Johannesburg: Witwatersrand University Press, 1992); N. Mostert, *Frontiers: The Epic of South Africa's Creation and the Tragedy of the Xhosa People* (London: Cape, 1992); T. Keegan, *Colonial South Africa.*

[10] C. Crais, "Race, the State and the Silence of History in the Making of Modern South Africa: Preliminary Departures," (Africa Seminar, Centre for African Studies, University

Crais and Keegan have emphasized the incipiently capitalist land-grabbing activities of the British settlers and pointed to the model provided by the early nineteenth-century Cape for other colonial societies in Africa, from the Rhodesias to Kenya.[11] In addition, Crais charts the early phases in the formation of a rural working class molded from former slaves, Khoesan, and the unfree within the colony and those becoming unfree outside of it, even while they were being pulled "within."[12] This chapter is indebted to the narrative strength of Mostert's account, the theoretical insights of Keegan, and the more pointillist approach of Crais. Keegan and Crais's concern is with the impact of the Cape Colony on the wider formation of South Africa. This chapter, although not oblivious to this, tries to take further the integration of Xhosa history into that of the rest of the colony, and the country, by focusing on the factors that determined Khoekhoe (and slave and "Baster," as the half-castes were often known) consciousness and that of the amaXhosa and the relations between them (or, as they became, colored–black relations.)

THE 1799–1803 XHOSA-KHOEKHOE REVOLT AND BETHELSDORP

The period with which this chapter is concerned began and ended, significantly, with revolts by amaXhosa and Khoesan together against the colonial order (1799–1803 and 1851–53) and was punctuated by four further wars between the amaXhosa and the colony (1812, 1819, 1834–5, 1846–7).

The state established initially by the British as a state of occupation therefore remained essentially military, ruled until midcentury by

---

of Cape Town, July 1992); see also W. Dooling, "'The Good Opinion of Others': Law, Slavery and Community in the Cape Colony, c. 1760–1830," in Worden and Crais (Eds.), *Breaking the Chains*, pp. 25–45, esp. p. 28; M. Legassick, "The State, Racism and the Rise of Capitalism in the Nineteenth Century Cape Colony," *South African Historical Journal*, 28 (May 1993), pp. 329–68; F. Cooper and A. L. Stoler, *Tensions of Empire: Colonial Cultures in A Bourgeois World* (Berkeley: University of California Press, 1997). See also the essay on "The Janus Face of Merchant Capital," in E. Fox-Genovese and E. D. Genovese, *Fruits of Merchant Capital: Slavery and Bourgeois Property in the Rise and Expansion of Capitalism* (New York: Oxford University Press, 1983), pp. 3–25.

[11] Noel Mostert's military history of the colonial wars against the Xhosa is masterly in its description and analysis. Keegan was the first to integrate Legassick's evaluation of the state-building aspects of the program of John Philip into the history of the Cape, and he also has a particularly innovative interpretation of the role of the British settlers in distorting the grievances of Afrikaners of the Great Trek so as to incorporate their own complaints at the retrocession by Colonial Secretary Lord Glenelg of Queen Adelaide Province, annexed by Governor D'Urban in May 1835.

[12] See Legassick, "The State, Racism and the Rise of Capitalism," p. 349.

masculinist white governors with military backgrounds.[13] Marx, in *Capital*, wrote of the role of the colonial state as "to hasten, hothouse fashion" the transformation of social relations to those of capitalism.[14] To facilitate primitive accumulation, and to generate markets, however, it had also to function as an instrument of conquest and the crushing of resistance. Until after the Napoleonic wars this was the main function of British rule. At the core of the state were British troops, some 4,000–5,000 until the end of the Napoleonic wars, declining thereafter to 1,500 in 1834, but increasing again to some 6,200 after the 1846–7 war. In 1850, after Smith had reduced the garrison, there were 4,068, but this number had doubled to 8,660 by the end of 1851.[15] (They were supplemented by Boer and Khoesan levies and, later, British settlers.) Rather than transforming the social order, British rule based itself politically on the old Dutch order, with local government by notables rooted in the Dutch landed slave-owning class.[16] Masculine militarism at the top consolidated and reinforced the tendencies to patriarchy among Boer settlers, coloreds and amaXhosa. At the same time the British sought to consolidate the rule of law around a rhetoric of equality before the law.[17]

The colony's population in 1806 was estimated at 26,768 white "free burghers" (14,074 men to 12,694 women), some 1,200 free blacks, 29,861 slaves (with 19,346 men against 10,313 women), and 20,426 Khoekhoen (9,781 men and 10,642 women).[18] Wine was by far the most important export commodity – produced by slaves (80 percent of them living in

---

[13] Keegan, *Colonial South Africa*, p. 43; S. Dubow, "An Empire of Reason: Anglophone Literary and Scientific Institutions in the Nineteenth Century Cape Province," (UWC Dept of History and IHR seminar, 4/5/1999), p. 3. Until Grey in the 1850s, only Caledon (1807–11) was not a military man, although Pottinger (1847) was only a colonel in the army of the East India Company, and thus could not exercise military rank at the Cape. See H. Bradford, "Through Gendered Eyes: Nongqawuse and the Great Xhosa cattle-killing," (IHR, UWC, SA, and contemporary history seminar, cohosted with AGI, UCT, 9/10/2001), p. 3 and passim; Peires on Grey, *The Dead will Arise: Nongqawuse and the Great Xhosa Cattle-Killing Movement of 1856–7* (Bloomington: Indiana University Press, pp. 45–53).

[14] K. Marx, *Capital*, vol. I (London: Lawrence and Wishart, 1970), p. 751.

[15] E. Walker, *History of South Africa* (London: Longmans Green, 1928), p. 148.

[16] Keegan, *Colonial South Africa*, esp. pp. 42–3, 47, 53, provide the best treatment. See also, more generally, J. Lonsdale and B. Berman, "Coping with the Contradictions: The Development of the Colonial State in Kenya," *Journal of African History*, 20 (1979), pp. 487–506.

[17] See Crais, *Colonial Order*, pp. 58–9.

[18] S. Patterson, "Some Speculations on the Status and Role of the Free People of Colour in the Western Cape," in M. Fortes and S. Patterson (Eds.), *Studies in African Social Anthropology* (London: Academic Press, 1975), pp. 159–207, table on pp. 172–3.

Cape Town and the arable southwest), who constituted a big capital investment. In 1808 and 1825 there were abortive and localized slave revolts.

The revolt by the amaXhosa and Khoekhoen in 1799 was precipitated
by the arrest by British troops of the leaders of a renewed Boer frontier
rebellion in Graaff-Reinet. The divisions were thought of as a sign of
colonial weakness.[19] Frontier Khoekhoen, facing a hardening of labor relations with their landowning Boer masters and the growth of violence in
those relations, seized the opportunity to break from them.[20] Equally, the
amaGqunukhwebe under Chunga were resisting attempts by the British to
push them out of the Zuurveld across the Fish River. San hunting bands in
the mountains were also struggling to maintain independence. The resulting combined revolt forced the colonists to evacuate much of the eastern
frontier and even led to a British defeat in one battle.[21] A temporary peace
concluded at the end of the year broke down and the revolt continued until
the takeover of the Cape by the Batavian regime in 1803.[22] Colonial order
was seriously threatened.

The Batavian regime made peace by leaving the amaXhosa in occupation of the Zuurveld. It also established a new magistracy at Uitenhage,
to the south and east of Graaff-Reinet and closer to the Zuurveld.[23] And
it confirmed the allocation of land by the British to the Khoekhoen at
Bethelsdorp, under the supervision of missionaries of the London Missionary Society (LMS), Dr. J. T. van der Kemp and James Read.[24] Van der Kemp,

---

[19] See Chapter 4 in this volume. On negative appraisals of Boers at this time, see Crais,
Colonial Order, pp. 56–7.

[20] S. Newton-King, *Masters and Servants on the Cape Eastern Frontier, 1760–1803* (Cambridge: Cambridge University Press, 1999). On forms of Khoekhoen resistance in the
late eighteenth century, see Crais, *Colonial Order*, p. 64.

[21] Peires, *House of Phalo*, p. 58; L. Switzer, *Power and Resistance in an African Society: The
Ciskei Xhosa and the Making of South Africa* (Madison: University of Wisconsin Press,
1993), p. 49.

[22] For interpretations of the revolt, see S. Newton-King and V. C. Malherbe, *The Khoikhoi
Rebellion in the Eastern Cape (1799–1803)* (Cape Town: Centre of African Studies, 1981);
H. Giliomee, "The Eastern Frontier, 1770–1812," in R. Elphick and H. Giliomee (Eds.),
The Shaping of South African Society, 1652–1840, 2nd ed. (Cape Town: Maskew Miller
Longman, 1989); Newton-King, *Masters and Servants*, pp. 210–31; Elbourne, *Blood
Ground*, Chapter 2.

[23] See Newton-King, *Masters and Servants*, pp. 49–52, 63, for the reasons why the initial
thrust of colonial settlement had moved inland, via Graaff-Reinet, and then turned south
rather than moving along the coast. Also, Mostert, *Frontiers*, p. 334.

[24] Rebel Klaas Stuurman also received a small grant of land, though after his death, his
brother was dispossessed of it by the British in 1808 and sent to Robben Island; David
Stuurman was also dispossessed and exiled to Botany Bay, and the land was divided
among white farmers: see B. Maclennan, *A Proper Degree of Terror: John Graham and
the Cape Eastern Frontier* (Johannesburg: Ravan Press, 1986), pp. 92–3; J. Sales, *Mission*

who arrived in 1799, had initially established a mission with the Rharabe chief Ngqika but retired from it at the end of 1800. Having taken up the cause of the Khoekhoe rebels, he persuaded the British to establish Bethelsdorp, which they agreed to do in an attempt to reconcile the rebellious Khoekhoen and divide them from the amaXhosa. The struggle between the Bethelsdorp missionaries and the government was the most significant development in shaping social relations in the colony in the first decade of British rule, and resonated thereafter.

The missionary societies in Europe grew out of a renewed proselytizing Protestant movement, reacting against secularization of Christian beliefs and the relaxation of moral norms, which has been linked by some to the insecurities associated with industrial transformation and by others to the results of political and religious conflict. From reviving religion among the domestic working class grew the idea of converting the "heathen" around the world. The London Missionary Society, founded in 1795, was part of this reinvigoration of dissenting denominations in Britain with roots in seventeenth-century Puritanism. Many missionaries added the concerns of the Enlightenment to these roots, and the evangelical movement came to take the form of humanitarianism and, particularly in the late eighteenth century, of antislavery. By 1783 the Quakers had established a committee to work for abolition, and others followed. However, the dissenting societies were viewed with extreme suspicion in Britain by the Anglican establishment prior at least to 1810, suspected of being in league with French revolutionaries.

If this chapter dwells on the various forms of mission activities and ideas it is because missionaries were the main mediators of colonial politics and culture among the Khoisan and amaXhosa. Correspondingly, most voices of the Khoesan and the amaXhosa are heard through their mediation. There has been considerable debate about whether and in what sense missionaries were agents of colonial conquest. Undoubtedly, as we shall see, many were. As Xhosa oral tradition has it to this day, "when the missionaries came, they carried a Bible in front, but behind their backs a musket."[25] At the same time the important point made by Elbourne should not be ignored: Religious ideas – like all ideas – were plastic and could be used by the oppressed as well as the oppressor.[26]

Stations and the Coloured Communities of the Eastern Cape, 1800–1852 (Cape Town: Balkema, 1975), pp. 37–8.

[25] Opland, *Xhosa Poets and Poetry*, p. 29.

[26] The quotation is from Elizabeth Elbourne, "A Question of Identity: Evangelical Culture and Khoisan Politics in the Early Nineteenth Century Eastern Cape," *Collected Seminar Papers of the Institute of Commonwealth Studies, London: The Societies of Southern Africa in the Nineteenth and Twentieth Centuries, 18* (1992), pp. 14–30; Elbourne, *Blood Ground;*

Van der Kemp laid down an exceptional tradition, especially when it is viewed against the other main missionary society then present in the Cape Colony – from 1737 to 1743 and again after 1792 – the conservative, quasi-Anglican, and obeisant Moravians.[27] He was Dutch, from a well-off family, and well educated. Profligate as a young man, he turned to missionary life perhaps to expiate a sense of guilt. His religiosity was strongly millenarian: His belief in the imminent intervention of God on the side of the oppressed resonated closely with rebelliousness among the indigenous people. This millenarianism echoed that of the dissenters of the seventeenth-century English revolution, and even that of peasants in medieval Europe – and it would be passed down to the Khoekhoen as well as the amaXhosa.[28] He was both nonracial and an abolitionist. He purchased the freedom of and then married a 14-year-old slave girl from Madagascar. He stressed the inwardness of conversion rather than (as did later missionaries) the outward signs of civilization. Faith rather than good works. In 1814, it was even alleged by another LMS missionary that van der Kemp had said "all civilization is from the Divil [Devil]."[29]

Van der Kemp's ideas first became rooted in Bethelsdorp. The mission started as a refugee camp for Khoekhoen displaced during the revolt or fleeing brutal masters. At a minimum, Bethelsdorp provided shelter for women, children, and the old while Khoekhoen (mainly) men sought work with farmers. It came to reflect the thirst for Christianity among many Khoesan, whose indigenous institutions had largely been destroyed and who were now brutally oppressed by the Boers. Of perhaps 12,000 Khoesan in the Eastern Cape at this time, some 450 came to live at Bethelsdorp by 1812. The mission was, by its very existence, subversive to the Boer master–servant order. It stood for an egalitarian, nonracial Christianity as opposed

E. Elbourne and R. Ross, "Combatting Spiritual and Social Bondage: Early Missions in the Cape Colony," in R. Elphick and R. Davenport (Eds.), *Christianity in South Africa: A Political, Social and Cultural History* (Cape Town: David Philip, 1997), pp. 31–50; D. Stuart, "'Of Savages and Heroes': Discourses of Race, Nation and Gender in the Evangelical Missions to Southern Africa in the Early Nineteenth Century," unpublished Ph.D. thesis, University of London (1994), cf. below, Chapter 8.

[27] R. Ross, "The Social and Political Theology of Western Cape Missions," in H. Bredekamp and R. Ross (Eds.), *Missions and Christianity in South African History* (Johannesburg: Witwatersrand University Press, 1995), pp. 97–112.

[28] C. Hill, *The World Turned Upside Down: Radical Ideas During the English Revolution* (London: Temple Smith, 1972); Elbourne, *Blood Ground*, pp. 197–232; Crais, *Colonial Order*, p. 83. At the same time, of course, there were indigenous intellectual contributions to subsequent Khoekhoe and Xhosa millenarianism.

[29] See F. A. Steytler (Ed.), "Minutes of the First Conference Held by African Missionaries at Graaff-Reinet, 1814," *Hertzog-Annale van die Suid-Afrikaanse Akademie vir Wetenskap en Kuns*, 3 (1956), p. 111.

to the exclusivist version of the Boers, demarcating membership in the moral community and access to the law. Boers tried to prevent Khoekhoen from going to Bethelsdorp. They also tried to break up the institution and to kill van der Kemp and his close colleague, Read. The mission also served as a place where remnants of traditional lifestyle, even if not the whole of a herding transhumant economy, could be sustained.

From the start, van der Kemp and Read constituted the Bethelsdorp as an *imperium in imperio* – a place with its own moral code. As early as April 1804 van der Kemp refused to cooperate with government in dispatching labor to farmers or compelling inhabitants to join the military. The Batavian government accused them of fomenting dissension and revolt, recalled them to the Western Cape, and refused to allow the teaching of literacy at the mission. With the second British takeover, in January 1806, however, they were allowed to return.[30] From this time Bethelsdorp was to become a center of equality and literacy. Khoekhoe native agents spread religion far and wide among the Khoekhoen. Van der Kemp and Read believed in making the greatest possible use of indigenous people in spreading the gospel.[31] Moreover, Bethelsdorp was closely linked from the start to the amaXhosa. Not only was the son of the chief of the amaNtinde, Jan Tshatshu, an early resident and convert, the village's Gona (part-Khoe) residents provided a link to the Gqunukhwebe amaXhosa.[32]

The LMS had sent van der Kemp to South Africa to, in LMS terms, deliver the heathen from idolatry and barbarism. As Elbourne has remarked, however, van der Kemp found Satan not among the "wild savages" but among the Boers! As early as 1801 he warned the British authorities that "there is no way of saving this country, other than by the government doing justice to the natives" – which would also allow the Boers to save their own souls.[33] From at least the second British occupation, both van der Kemp and Read bombarded government officials with complaints about the treatment of Khoekhoen by the Boers. They clashed repeatedly with the newly appointed landdrost of Uitenhage, the American, Colonel Cuyler, so that relations degenerated totally.

---

[30] According to Elbourne, *Blood Ground*, p. 154, van der Kemp regarded the British reoccupation as brought about by the providence of God, and immediately offered advice to the authorities on the treatment of the Khoekhoen.

[31] See, e.g., Keegan, *Colonial South Africa*, pp. 84–5; V. C. Malherbe, "The Life and Times of Cupido Kakkerlak," *Journal of African History,* 20(3) (1979), pp. 365–78.

[32] R. S. Levine, "Sable Son of Africa: The Many Worlds of an African Cultural Intermediary on the Eastern Cape Frontier of South Africa, 1800–1848," unpublished Ph.D. thesis, Yale (2004); also Elbourne, "Question of Identity," p. 16.

[33] Elbourne, "Question of Identity," p. 15, citing S. Bannister, *Humane Policy: Or Justice to the Aborigines of New Settlements* (London: T. & G. Underwood, 1830), p. cxxxi.

In March 1807, the British government withdrew the country from its major share of the slave trade. Eventually, the metropolitan impulses that had led to this move would also temper Cape slavery by the legal paternalism of "amelioration," particularly as slaves attempted to make use of the law.[34] In the short term, though, for most rural slaves and the Khoekhoen, the abolition of the slave trade may well have worsened their situation because it reduced the inflow of labor.[35] Khoekhoen did not wish to live on the colonial farms and wanted to be hired. But farmers were extremely reluctant to pay them cash wages and tried by every means to tie them to their farms for a lifetime of service. The abolition of the slave trade also stimulated transfrontier raiding by colonists for slave substitutes, mainly across the northern border.[36]

In 1809, in an attempt to bring Boer–Khoekhoen relations under regulation, Governor Caledon issued a code hailed at the time as the "Magna Carta of the Hottentots," but which in fact entrenched coercive labor practices. It demanded that each Khoesan should have a "fixed place of abode," whose alteration must be approved by a local official. It provided for mandatory contracts of service and in fact entrenched the oppressive controls of the Boer farmers. It lacked explicit recognition of Khoesan rights to land. Attempting to suppress the violent private oppression of the Boers, it instead submitted Khoesan to the more systematic oppression of the colonial order through the state and the law as a means of social control – and locally it was Boer notables who were the "state." Soon the missionaries objected to the code as such as well to the fact that little attention was paid to verifying contracts, and that the pass laws formalized in the code were abused to keep the Khoesan in service.[37]

---

[34] J. E. Mason, *Social Death and Resurrection: Slavery and Emancipation in South Africa* (Charlottesville: University of Virginia Press, 2003); M. I. Rayner, "Wine and Slaves: The Failure of an Export Economy and the Ending of Slavery in the Cape Colony, 1806–1834," unpublished Ph.D. thesis, Duke University (1986).

[35] S. Newton-King, "The Labour Market of the Cape Colony, 1807–1828," in S. Marks and A. Atmore (Eds.), *Economy and Society in Pre-industrial South Africa* (London: Longman, 1980); cf. Keegan, *Colonial South Africa*, pp. 52–3; see Crais, *Colonial Order*, pp. 65–70, for a description of the situation of the "unfree" (slave, peon, etc.) in the Eastern Cape at this time.

[36] Crais, *Colonial Order*, p. 96; M. Legassick, "The Griqua, the Sotho-Tswana and the Missionaries, 1780–1840: The Politics of a Frontier Zone," unpublished Ph.D. thesis, UCLA (1969); E. A. Eldredge, "Slave Raiding Across the Cape Frontier," in E. A. Eldredge and F. Morton (Eds.), *Slavery in South Africa: Captive Labor on the Dutch Frontier* (Boulder, CO, San Francisco, Oxford, and Pietermaritzburg: Westview Press and University of Natal Press, 1994).

[37] John Philip, *Researches in South Africa: Illustrating the Civil, Moral, and Religious Condition of the Native Tribes: Including Journals of the Author's Travels in The Interior, Together with*

These complaints were first investigated by Cuyler at Caledon's request. He found little basis for further inquiry, but van der Kemp and Read continued with their accusations, finally presenting 113 cases of injustice to a commission under the fiscal, John Truter.[38] At this point, but perhaps not as a direct consequence of the missionaries' complaints, Caledon instituted a circuit court to travel annually around the districts of the Cape to judge crimes – a first attempt to override local abuse of the law and the first step toward wide-ranging legal reform.[39] The second such commission, which became known as the "Black Circuit," did not find that the Khoekhoen accusations had been proved, hardly surprising as Khoekhoen testimony under oath was not allowed. Moreover, the report of the court went out of its way to make a scathing condemnation of Bethelsdorp for encouraging laziness, idleness, and filth, in contrast with the praiseworthy Moravian stations.

While adopting the rhetoric of the "rule of law," it projected the Khoekhoen as an inferior order of beings enjoying inferior natural rights, with an obligation to serve the colonists.[40] Bethelsdorp, it stated, had "established such an overstrained principle of liberty as the ground work, that the natural state of barbarism appears there to supersede civilization and social order."[41] At about the same time, the new governor, Sir John Cradock, issued supplementary regulations to the Caledon Code, compelling Khoekhoe children to be apprenticed to farmers until the age of 18.[42] This demonstrated how little the government was really concerned with the abuse of the Khoekhoen. Nevertheless, the institution of the

Detailed Accounts of the Progress of the Christian Missions, Exhibiting the Influence of Christianity in Promoting Civilization, 2 vols. (London: J. Duncan, 1828), vol. I, pp. 147–8; W. W. Bird, *The State of the Cape of Good Hope in 1822*, p. 6, cited in H. Giliomee, "Die Administrasietydperk van Lord Caledon, 1807–1811," *Archives Year Book for South African History* II (1966), p. 277; R. Ross, *Beyond the Pale: Essays on the History of Colonial South Africa* (Hanover and London: Wesleyan University Press, 1993), pp. 94–102; Crais, *Colonial Order*, p. 60.

[38] Giliomee, "Caledon," p. 304; van der Kemp warned Caledon that if justice was not obtained he would publicize the cases or communicate them to the Colonial Office.

[39] Proclamation of May 16, 1811. Such a circuit court had already been recommended by W. S. van Ryneveld during the first British occupation. H. Giliomee, *Die Kaap Tydens die Eerste Britse Bewind, 1795–1803* (Cape Town: H.A.U.M., 1975), p. 98; Giliomee, "Caledon," 310.

[40] Elbourne, *Blood Ground*, pp. 207–11; Keegan, *Colonial South Africa*, pp. 55–6; cf., e.g., Giliomee, "Caledon," 312–3. The first circuit court had also praised Genadendal and criticized Bethelsdorp, though not so strongly: see G. McC. Theal (Ed.), *Records of the Cape Colony*, 36 vols. (London: Clowes for the Government of the Cape Colony, 1897–1905) (hereafter *RCC*), vol. VIII, pp. 303–4.

[41] Theal, *RCC*, vol. IX, pp. 74–5.

[42] Proclamation of April 23, 1812, in Theal, *RCC*, vol. VIII, p. 385.

circuit court, which was largely the consequence of this struggle, was of major importance for the establishment of central authority throughout the colony.

Van der Kemp had died on December 19, 1811, without seeing the results of the "Black Circuit." But his influence persisted – on his colleague James Read and, in a certain way, on John Philip.[43] His memory continued to be treasured among the Khoekhoen, and for a long time he remained respected among the amaXhosa.

THE NORTHERN FRONTIER AND TRANSORANGIA

The conflict on the eastern frontier of the colony derived in essence from the expansion of colonial society across the ecological boundary, which marked the western limit of summer rain-fed agriculture, and thus of Xhosa and Thembu settlement. At the same time, there was a steady colonial advance northward, through the dryer stretches of the South African interior. The defeat of the San by the end of the eighteenth century had opened up wide areas north of the escarpment, in particular in the Sneeuberge and Zeekoe River valley, to settlement by Afrikaner farmers.[44] However, the main thrust of the colonial advance came from the Griqua, of at least partial Khoesan descent, several of whose major families had settled around a number of springs to the north of the Gariep, where they also collected a large number of Korana Khoekhoen (and no doubt the descendants of the Einiqua of the Gariep River bush) around them. Here, from 1800, they were in contact with missionaries of the LMS who attempted to convert them not merely to Christianity but also to adherence to the colonial order and to what was held to be civilized behavior. The group, previously known as Bastards, were renamed Griqua under missionary pressure. Coinage, with the dove insignia of the LMS, was issued. An attempt was made to settle the population close to the church in what was now renamed Griquatown. A constitution for the new statelet was adopted in 1813, with the leaders of the most important families, Adam Kok II and Barend Barends, as controlling captains.[45]

---

[43] W. M. Freund, "The Career of J. T. van der Kemp and his Role in the History of South Africa," *Tijdschrift voor Geschiedenis, 86* (1973); see also Elbourne, *Blood Ground*, p. 199, quoting LMS 5/3/C Thom to Burder CT, 16/2/1814: Thom was jealous of the way van der Kemp was presented. Philip had, in fact, a condescending attitude to van der Kemp. See, for example, *RCC* vol. I, pp. 133–41, where he praises van der Kemp but regrets his too easy intimacy with his charges and his marriage to a slave woman.

[44] P. J. van der Merwe, *Die Noordwaartse Beweging van die Boere Voor die Groot Trek (1770–1842)* (The Hague: Van Stockum, 1937).

[45] Legassick, "The Griqua, the Sotho-Tswana and the Missionaries."

The formation of political units did not proceed easily. Within a few years both Kok and Barends had abandoned Griquatown, and control of the settlement devolved on Andries Waterboer, a man of San descent whose rule was not uncontested. Waterboer's attempts, in conjunction with the mission, to impose a sedentary agricultural lifestyle on the Griqua led to a series of revolts, known as the Hartenaar and Bergenaar uprisings, against his rule. The participants in these revolts were trying to maintain their raiding way of life, directed primarily against Tswana groups to the north of Griqualand, and were also engaged in a surreptitious slave trade of, mainly, San children into the colony.[46] The exploitation of their northern frontier was a serious option for the Griqua during the 1830s, as indeed it had been ever since they aided the Batlhaping at the battle of Dithakong in 1823.[47] Later, Barend Barends led a number of large-scale cattle raids on Mzilikazi's amaNdebele, and even the Griquatown polity attempted to establish its hegemony over the Kuruman Valley in particular and the Sotho-Tswana in general.[48] Both these attempts failed, and the Griqua were to become increasingly settled, particularly in the region around Philippolis in the southern Free State, where Adam Kok II came to settle in 1826 and where it later became possible to breed merino sheep in some quantities.[49] The raiding life was primarily maintained by a number of Korana groups further to the north, but even they were increasingly forced to become more sedentary under mission influence and as the land became more peaceable.

The Expulsion of the amaXhosa from the Zuurveld, 1812, and the "Agreement" with Ngqika, 1819

The dynamics of Xhosa society militated in favor of constant expansion into new territory. By the late seventeenth century they had penetrated much of the area between the Kei and Fish rivers, where they had absorbed many Khoekhoe pastoralists. Until the mid-eighteenth century, the inhabitants of the Zuurveld had been the Khoesan Gona, but they were then joined by the amaGqunukhwebe, the amaNtinde, the amaGwali, the imiDange, and the amaMbala. In the 1770s the chief, Rharabe, crossed the Kei to settle between it and the Keiskamma River, absorbed Khoesan, and tried to assert his dominance over the area. However, it was his son, Ndlambe, as regent for Ngqika from about 1782, who established the power in the area

[46] Eldredge, "Slave Raiding Across the Cape Frontier," pp. 93–126.

[47] See also Chapter 5 in this volume, p. 235.

[48] Legassick, *The Griqua, the Sotho-Tswana and the Politics of a Frontier Zone*, esp. Chapters VII and VIII.

[49] R. Ross, *Adam Kok's Griquas: A Study in the Development of Stratification in South Africa* (Cambridge: Cambridge University Press, 1976).

of the political entity still named after his father, driving other amaXhosa westward. In 1795, Ngqika rebelled against Ndlambe and attempted to construct a centralized Xhosa state against centrifugal pressures that were eventually too great. By 1800, Ngqika was at the height of his power.[50]

When the amaXhosa encountered the Boers they assumed they would come to absorb them as they had the San, Khoekhoen, and abaThembu. Between the 1770s and the 1790s there was mutual skirmishing and cattle raiding, including two "frontier" wars that were minor affrays, at least in comparison to what was to follow. In 1800 Ndlambe escaped from virtual captivity under Ngqika across the Fish River to the Zuurveld, where he came to dominate along with Chungwa of the Gqunukhwebe – who, by September 1807, was settled near the Gamtoos River west of Algoa Bay. In the same year, Ngqika, having failed to lure the colony into an alliance to crush Ndlambe, abducted one of his wives, provoking a revenge attack. Though peace between Ngqika and Ndlambe was concluded, this was the start of the decline of Ngqika's power.[51] At this time there were some 38,000–40,000 amaXhosa west of the Kei River, and there may have been similar numbers to the east of it, as well as abaThembu, amaMpondo, etc. – as against only some 1,500 Boers dispersed across the Cape.[52]

The British attack was fought with small forces, at most 2,000 men, of whom more than a third were Khoesan. Many of these men were fighting old acquaintances, and indeed relatives, among the amaXhosa. Many of the Khoesan recruited into the newly formed Cape regiment had lived on the mission stations, and James Read and the other missionaries had not opposed war.[53] The British success derived from their concentrated brutality and totally alien viciousness.[54] More amaXhosa were killed than wounded – among them many women and children. Up to 20,000 amaXhosa were driven out of an area of 4,000 square miles. Ndlambe's people were pushed back onto Ngqika's, eventually intensifying the conflict between them. To assuage a reluctant Colonial Office in London, Cradock, however, wrote that "there has not been shed more Kaffir blood than would

[50] Peires, *House of Phalo*, pp. 50–61; Stapleton, *Maqoma*, p. 21.

[51] Peires, *House of Phalo*, pp. 57–60; Maclennan, *Proper Degree of Terror*, p. 95. For Ngqika, see Peires, "Ngqika, c. 1779–1829," in C. Saunders (Ed.), *Black Leaders in Southern African History* (London: Heinemann, 1979), pp. 15–30.

[52] See *Oxford History*, I, pp. 254–6; Maclennan, *Proper Degree of Terror*, p. 228; Switzer, *Power and Resistance*, p. 41. In 1800 van der Kemp estimated 38,400 Xhosa west of the Kei; in 1809 Colonel Collins estimated 40,000 west and 10,000 (an underestimate?) east of the Kei. In 1826 Thompson estimated the total Xhosa population at 100,000.

[53] Different figures are given by Giliomee in Elphick and Giliomee (Eds)., *Shaping*, p. 448; Elbourne, "To Colonise the Mind," p. 182; Maclennan, *Proper Degree of Terror*, p. 89.

[54] Maclennan, *Proper Degree of Terror*, p. 111.

seem to be necessary to impress on the minds of these savages a proper degree of terror and respect."[55] For the first time, the arable – and thus female – base of Xhosa society was attacked. The persistent cattle raiding between colonists and amaXhosa involved solely the men, but in the real wars of the nineteenth century the whole of society was attacked. Grahamstown was then founded as the headquarters of the military operations in the Eastern Cape, and of the Cape Regiment.

In the aftermath of the 1812 war there was a change in British colonial policy toward the amaXhosa. The amaXhosa were to be culturally assimilated, not merely excluded militarily, and the missionaries were to be among the agents of this assimilation. Thus, instead of being viewed as potential rivals to government's authority, the missionaries became seen as potential allies and even agents. The rapprochement between government and missionaries took place in the context of a concentrated reconceptualization of the meaning of the civilization imparted by the missionaries. Over time, the meaning of this word was worked out, not in armchairs in Britain, but in practice, through contestations that included both debate and rebellion. The main aim of the state was to turn from the millenarianism of van der Kemp to a more respectable Christianity. New missionaries who had arrived from Britain, notably George Thom, could be enlisted for this project and the (temporary) sidelining of James Read following a sexual scandal made it easier. Thus, Joseph Williams was allowed to settle near Ngqika as a missionary to aid in this.[56]

This was a longer-term plan. In the shorter term the British were firmly committed to Ngqika as the senior chief west of the Kei. In April 1817, the governor, Lord Charles Somerset, met Ngqika – together with Williams – at the Kat River and offered him sole rights to permit Xhosa access to the colony to trade and active military assistance against his supposed subordinate chiefs – provided that he consent to allow colonists to track stolen cattle to kraals and seize suspect animals. Ndlambe tried but failed to make a separate agreement with the colony.[57] The result was an attack on Ndlambe, led by the young Maqoma, on behalf of his father, Ngqika. But Ndlambe was reinforced by the amaGcaleka of Hintsa, and the colony refused Ngqika's request for assistance. At the battle of Amalinde, Ndlambe's and Hintsa's forces were led by the millenarian war prophet Nxele (Makana), with syncretic Christian and Xhosa beliefs – the first to prophesy the rising of the

---

[55] Maclennan, p. 128, from Theal, *RCC*, VIII, p. 160.

[56] D. Stuart, "The 'Wicked Christians' and the 'Children of the Mist': Missionary and Khoi Interactions at the Cape in the Early 19th Century," *CSPSSA*, vol. 18 (University of London, ICS), pp. 1–13; Elbourne, *Blood Ground*, pp. 227–32.

[57] For the conference, see Theal, *RCC*, XI, pp. 295–321; Stapleton, *Maqoma*, pp. 25–6.

dead and their cattle. A severe defeat was inflicted on Ngqika, killing many of his men and wounding Maqoma near-fatally. In retaliation, in December 1818 colonial forces responded to Ngqika's pleas and joined him in a counterattack on Ndlambe, seizing 23,000 cattle of which 11,000 were given to Ngqika. This triggered a new frontier war, with the amaXhosa invading the colony and besieging Grahamstown during the early months of 1819. On April 22, Nxele led 6,000 of Ndlambe's forces in a daylight attack on Grahamstown itself. They were repulsed and severely defeated. In late July colonial forces counterattacked and, in August, Nxele surrendered and was exiled to Robben Island, where he drowned while trying to escape.[58] Virtually all amaXhosa were driven across the Keiskamma. The amaXhosa learned from the experience the dangers of mass frontal attack against the colony and, in the future, resorted to guerrilla methods of fighting, using the dense bush (where British guns and horses were less effective) and the mountains.

In October, Governor Lord Charles Somerset and Andries Stockenström, now landdrost of Graaff-Reinet in place of his father, met again with Ngqika and declared that the colony's boundary would be moved east to the Keiskamma River, and all amaXhosa within the colony must move with it. This meant, *inter alia*, abandoning the fertile Kat River valley, where Maqoma was situated. Though the rhetoric was that the territory was to be held neutral, from the beginning it was seen as an area for systematic colonization.[59]

The combined effects of the war and this agreement were a blow to the amaXhosa and particularly to Ngqika. With colonial support, he had asserted his supremacy over Ndlambe – and in some measure over Hintsa – only to be forced from his land by the British. The agreement with the colony was never set down and signed but remained verbal. Essentially it was rejected by the amaXhosa as invalid and unfair.[60] As Read wrote in 1833, "All the chiefs knew of the transaction was that Gaika [Ngqika] proposed to them that part of the country should be neutral and that soldiers should be stationed in the neighbourhood till Slambie [Ndlambe] was reconciled and Peace restored – but by no means finally to lose their country."[61] For Maqoma, as Stapleton relates, "the disaster at Amalinde, the collaboration of his father, and the treachery of the whites became

---

[58] Stapleton, *Maqoma*, pp. 31–2; Switzer, *Power and Resistance*, p. 53; Peires, *House of Phalo*, pp. 62–3, 143–5; Crais, *Colonial Order*, p. 104; Bradford, Through Gendered Eyes," p. 6.

[59] J. B. Peires, "The British and the Cape, 1814–1834," in Elphick and Giliomee (Eds.), *Shaping*, p. 483.

[60] Peires, "The British and the Cape," p. 483.

[61] Elbourne, *Blood Ground*, p. 429, citing CA A50 Read to Philip, Kat River, 1/4/1833.

the formative experiences of [his] early adult life" – and by 1821 he had defiantly returned to his home in the ceded territory.[62]

British Settlers and the 1820s Revolution in Government

The 1819 agreement with Ngqika ushered in fifteen years of uncertainty in colony–Xhosa power relations, altered only by the 1834–5 war and its aftermath, though the shift began with Maqoma's expulsion from the Kat River area in 1829. In the meantime a revolution took place in the Cape Colony – economically, in the character of government, and in the legal position of the Khoekhoen and the slaves.

The revolution represented the working out in the colony of the changes flowing from the industrial revolution in Britain. These involved the ideas of free trade and of civilization. A new sense of British imperial mission, developed in the first half of the nineteenth century and significantly fostered by missionaries, promoted the ideas of "Christianity, commerce, and civilisation." These acted as a justification for the evangelicals of colonial conquest. At the Cape in the 1820s missionary propagation of these ideas was spurred and materially underpinned by the interests of a local merchant class that had grown up under British rule and was oriented to trade with Britain. They were ideas above all associated with Dr. John Philip, superintendent of the LMS from 1819, and with John Fairbairn, who arrived in 1823 and, after a struggle with the government to establish a free press, became editor of the humanitarian *South African Commercial Advertiser*. An arch-champion of free trade, Fairbairn became a leading spokesman for the (changing) interests of the Cape merchant class in commercial expansion. He also became Philip's son-in-law. Both had polemical skills and were enthusiastic in promoting their views.[63]

At the same time some 5,000 other British settlers were aided by the government to establish themselves in the Zuurveld. From the point of view of the colony, this furthered Somerset's plans to establish a rural buffer against the amaXhosa – though most moved to the towns within two years. In the early 1820s it was even argued by colonial officials that British settlement on the frontier would stop the spread of slavery. However, the government in Britain was prepared to spend the money not primarily to defend the Cape but rather to generate expanding demand for British

---

[62] Stapleton, *Maqoma*, pp. 33–4, 38.

[63] For Fairbairn, see H. C. Botha, *John Fairbairn in South Africa* (Cape Town: Historical Publication Society, 1984); L. Meltzer, "Emancipation, Commerce and the Role of John Fairbairn's *Advertiser*," in Worden & Crais, *Breaking the Chains*, pp. 169–200.

products and to drain Britain of "redundant" population, in part in reaction to post-Waterloo domestic unrest. The 1820 settlers, as they became known, came to develop in South Africa "an ideology of accumulation and dispossession that was a new force in colonial society."[64]

In the 1820s missionary and merchant interests – and even, at first, British settler interests – became closely fused in campaigning for colonial reform. The movement gained sustenance from the appointment by the British government in 1822 of a commission of inquiry into the affairs of the colony, with the aim of liberalizing and Anglicizing social relations. Lord Charles Somerset, friend of horse racing and jackal hunting, was then governor of the colony. He had arrived in 1814 and was to serve longer than any other British governor. His rule was effete and corrupt, riddled with monopoly and patronage. At the start settlers, missionaries, and merchants together challenged Somerset's autocratic government with demands for freedom of speech and of the press. As time passed, however, the interests of the "humanitarian alliance" diverged from that of the settlers. Although all wanted the removal of obstacles to free enterprise and trade, missionaries (and merchants, too, at this time) wanted the Khoekhoen and the slaves freed and to try to create peasant consumers with new "wants." As Fairbairn put it: "To stimulate Industry, to encourage Civilisation, and convert the hostile Natives into friendly Customers is . . . a more profitable speculation than to exterminate or reduce them to Slavery."[65]

A material basis for the revolution that transpired consisted in the removal, after 1825, of preferential tariffs in Europe that destroyed the main export of wine, produced by Dutch notables in the Western Cape who were Somerset's strongest supporters. The economy of slavery was thereby undermined.[66] Meanwhile, the British settlers pioneered the opening up of trade both in Xhosaland and in the hinterland of Port Natal. They broke down the state-regulated "trade fair" system by penetrating deeper into Xhosa territory, knocking out Xhosa middlemen. (In parallel, Griqua and Boers traded northward.) Ivory and arms and ammunition (illegally) were central items.

Central to the humanitarian standpoint was Philip. When he arrived in the Cape he tended to support the views of Thom and to disparage Read. But on a trip to Bethelsdorp in 1821 he discovered documents that vindicated Read and began a crusade against the entire labor system and its underpinnings in government. "The Hottentots are acknowledged to be a free people," he wrote in October 1822, "but labour is every day becoming

---

[64] Keegan, *Colonial South Africa*, p. 62; Crais, *Colonial Order*, pp. 88–90.

[65] Cited in Keegan, *Colonial South Africa*, p. 98

[66] Rayner, "Wine and Slaves," 190 ff.

scarcer and the colonists are resolved to indemnify themselves for the loss of the slave trade by reducing the Hottentots to a condition of slavery the most shocking and oppressive."[67] The philosophy that underpinned his crusade, however, differed from van der Kemp's. Its full statement is in his *Researches*, written in Britain and published in April 1828, mentioned previously as a founding history of the colony. The philosophy was important not only in reshaping the concept of civilization to suit the combined purposes of merchants, missionaries, and government, it was also to have lasting effects on the consciousness of the evolving colored community.

Its strong side was its universalist concept of human nature; of the capacity of each individual, given freedom from confining regulations, to progress spiritually and materially, thus contributing to the greater good of society. But the prescriptions were spelled out in a particular way. Philip never had any qualms about the expansion of colonial rule, even as personified by the British military. Economic progress was no longer seen merely as a pragmatic means to minimize poverty and hunger. Rather colonial interest, the idea that British rule was beneficent, and the civilization of the Khoesan were interwoven.[68]

Settler stereotypes of indigenous peoples were condemned, but the latter still had to be saved from the inferiority and barbarity of their own culture. Missionaries controlled to save. This was reflected in the rectangular, clean houses of the mission stations. The missions stressed that it was the women's task to maintain these, to sew and clean clothes, and to raise the children. The male inhabitants of the stations were encouraged to serve the British state. In sum, Philip aimed for the missionaries "to raise uncivilized and wandering hordes, which formerly subsisted by the chase or by plunder, to the condition of settled labourers and cultivators of the soil, to lead them to increase the sum of productive labour and to become consumers of the commodities of other countries, to convert such as were a terror to the inhabitants of an extended frontier into defenders of that frontier against the inroads of remoter barbarians."[69] Read endorsed these ideas.

The philosophy as a whole created an ideology of respectability for colored artisanal and peasant classes and formed a basis on which there emerged a self-consciously Khoekhoe elite. The ideas were spread between Bethelsdorp and Griquatown and far wider by native agents and others.

---

[67] Cited in Keegan, *Colonial South Africa*, p. 93.

[68] Keegan, *Colonial South Africa*, pp. 102–3; Elbourne, *Blood Ground*, pp. 238–41, argues that Philip's coupling of missions to empire was a defensive reaction against the previous idea that they were a threat to empire, which only "later, in different hands," changed to an aggressive pro-empire stance. But Philip, too, came to take that stance.

[69] Memorial of LMS January 22, 1827, Theal, *RCC*, 30, p. 121; Keegan, *Colonial South Africa*, pp. 102–3; Elbourne, *Blood Ground*, pp. 238 ff.

For the Khoekhoen, the reformation of manners, in housing, clothing, sexual mores, and schooling, allied to the realignment of belief, provided a new order of society when the old was crumbling[70] – whereas for the still unconquered amaXhosa they would appear as an assault on their core social institutions.

Meanwhile, the tide of reform had forced Somerset out of the governorship by 1826. His successor, Acting Governor Richard Bourke, following the recommendations of the commission of inquiry, carried out a virtual political revolution in the colony. Bourke did away with remaining monopolies and all restrictions on free economic activity. He established new taxes and devalued the rixdollar. He remodeled the civil and judicial establishments, creating a new system of administration, an independent judicial system, and a Legislative Council with changed composition, displacing the Dutch notables from government. The legal system was not only reworked but partly Anglicized. By 1829, freedom of the press was also firmly established, creating an important new arena of public discourse. From January 1827, moreover, to encourage British immigration, English became the colony's only official language.

Moreover, Bourke secured the passage of the famous Ordinance 50 of 1828, which removed from the Khoekhoen all pass laws, compulsory service, and summary punishment without trial. At the same time, as Crais emphasizes, it reaffirmed "the virtues of private property and wage labour."[71] Bourke had just promulgated Ordinance 49, which encouraged Xhosa migrant labor into the colony. Though abolition of passes for the Khoekhoen had been floated from early 1826, according to his biographer, Bourke felt it particularly unjust to favor extracolonials when indigenous people within the colony were oppressed.[72] Hence, Ordinance 50. The actual measure was prompted by a memorandum by Andries Stockenström, now commissioner-general on the eastern frontier, whose ideas had come to agree with those of the missionaries and who was to be an influential actor in the colony for the next ten years and again in the late 1840s and early 1850s.

---

[70] Ross, *Status*, p. 124; Elbourne, *Blood Ground, passim*; Keegan, *Colonial South Africa*, p. 85; Sales, *Mission Stations*.

[71] Crais, *Colonial Order*, p. 61.

[72] H. King, *Richard Bourke* (Melbourne: Oxford University Press, 1971), pp. 118–21; Newton-King, "Labour Market," pp. 171–207; B. le Cordeur and C. Saunders, *The Kitchingman Papers: Missionary Letters and Journals, 1817 to 1848* (Johannesburg: The Brenthurst Press), p. 135. Andries Stockenström, *Light and Shade as Shown in the Character of the Hottentots of the Kat River Settlement, and in the Conduct of the Colonial Government Towards Them* (Cape Town: Saul Solomon, 1854); LMS 10/1/C Foster to Burder, Bethelsdorp, 17/6/1826; LMS 10/3/C C. van der Kemp to Hankey, Bethelsdorp, 28/12/1827; Elbourne, p. 27.

Philip's achievement, in London, was its constitutional entrenchment. The victory, however, such as it was, belonged to Philip and the humanitarians who had created the climate for it.[73] The Khoesan welcomed it, and it precipitated "a flight from the estates" to the towns and the missions (whose populations rocketed): It provided, as Andries Stoffels was to say, "a taste of freedom."[74] The settlers, both Boer and British, were enraged. Even those who might have profited from the freeing up of labor were "most reluctant for the Hottentots to enjoy their liberty," as James Read wrote.[75] This part of the government revolution, in fact, created a backlash, preparing the way among other things for the Trek of 1834–7.

The Colonial Office in London had confirmed Ordinance 50 in part because it could be extended throughout the empire. Thus, color, as opposed to slave status, could no longer be used as legal grounds for discrimination. The measure formed part of a concerted attempt to reform the structure of slave societies, in particular by limiting the power of slaveowners to punish their slaves and by providing, in the Protectors of Slaves, someone to whom the slaves could complain of maltreatment. In the event, the Cape Protectors of Slaves proved more willing to defend the interests of the masters than those of the slaves. Certainly they were not encouraged to be liberal by the minor but violent slave revolt led by Galant, in the Cold Bokkeveld to the north of Cape Town in 1825.[76] Nevertheless, the increased opportunities for complaint forced farmers to treat their slaves in ways determined by the law and not merely in such a fashion as to prevent their deserting or murdering their masters.[77]

The bifurcation of the slave population between those who lived in the countryside and were generally harshly treated[78] and those in Cape Town was maintained. In the city, slavery was slowly disappearing, both because of developments internal to the city and because, before 1825, slaves were sold in some numbers from the city to the booming wine farms.[79] Manumission

---

[73] For an assessment of the discussion, see Elbourne, "To Colonise the Mind," pp. 292–6; also King, *Bourke*, pp. 122, 274; Keegan, *Colonial South Africa*, pp. 103–4; Ross, *Status*, p. 117.

[74] *South African Commercial Advertiser*, September 3, 1834.

[75] King, *Bourke*, pp. 118–21; LMS 11/2/A James Read, Bethelsdorp, 28/8/1828.

[76] R. Ross, *Cape of Torments: Slavery and Resistance in South Africa* (London: Routledge, 1982); N. Worden, *Slavery in Dutch South Africa* (Cambridge: Cambridge University Press, 1985), pp. 105–16; P. van der Spuy, "'Making himself Master': Galant's rebellion revisited," *South African Historical Journal*, 34 (1996).

[77] Mason, *Social Death and Resurrection*, Chapter 3.

[78] But cf. J. E. Mason, "Fortunate Slaves and Artful Masters: Labor Relations in the Rural Cape Colony during the Era of Emancipation, ca. 1825–1838," in Eldredge and Morton (Eds.), *Slavery in South Africa*.

[79] Dooling, "'The Good Opinion of Others,'" pp. 25–44.

rates had always been higher in the city than in the countryside. Many slaves worked independently, both as craftsmen and as retailers, paying their owners a fixed rent for their own time, as it were. In the process they were able to accumulate the funds necessary to buy themselves free.[80] Between 1806 and the late 1820s, the free black population of Cape Town quadrupled. Some of these free blacks were "liberated Africans" who had been taken off slave ships the British had captured en route from Mozambique to the Americas. Some 2,000 ex-slaves were introduced into the colony in this way between 1807 and 1816. Thereafter they were indentured for fourteen years and may thus have performed the manual labor from which, slowly, the Cape-born slaves in the city were beginning to escape.[81]

The erosion of urban slavery led to the establishment of a slave and ex-slave community in the city. Before emancipation, the central institutions of this community were the mosques. Although there may have been a Muslim, primarily Sufi, presence in Cape Town and its surroundings dating to the late seventeenth century, and there were certainly Islamic gatherings in the town in the 1770s, the great expansion of Islam only began with the establishment of the first madrasah (Islamic school) in 1793 and the first mosque in 1804. By 1839, immediately after the end of slavery, there were said to have been nearly 6,500 Muslims, above all in Cape Town, under the tutelage of nine imams. The mosques, and presumably their adherents, were concentrated to the west of Cape Town's city center in what was to become known as the Bo-Kaap. Here and elsewhere converts heard the word expounded and performed the Sufi rituals of the *ratiep*, which entailed the piercing of the body with knives while in a state of trance, in itself a metaphor for rebirth out of slavery.[82]

---

[80] A. Bank, *The Decline of Urban Slavery at the Cape, 1806 to 1843* (Cape Town: Communications, 21, Centre for African Studies, University of Cape Town, 1991).

[81] C. Saunders, "Liberated Africans in Cape Colony in the First Half of the Nineteenth Century," *International Journal of African Historical Studies, 18* (1985); C. Saunders "'Free, Yet Slaves': Prize Negroes at the Cape Revisited," in Worden and Crais (Eds.), *Breaking the Chains*; P. Harries, "Cultural Diasporas and Colonial Classification: A History of the Mozbieker Community at the Cape," *Social Dynamics, 26* (2000) (Eds.).

[82] See R. C.-H. Shell, "From Rites to Rebellion: Islamic Conversion, Urbanization, and Ethnic Identities at the Cape of Good Hope, 1797 to 1904," *Canadian Journal of History, 28*(3)(1993), pp. 410–57; A. Davids, "'My Religion is Superior to the Law': The Survival of Islam at the Cape of Good Hope," in Y. da Costa and A. Davids (Eds.), *Pages from Cape Muslim History* (Pietermaritzburg: Shuter and Shooter, 1994); Y. da Costa and A. Davids, *The Mosques of Bo-Kaap* (Athlone: The South African Institute of Arabic and Islamic Research, 1980); S. Jeppie, "Leadership and Loyalties: The Imams of Nineteenth Century Colonial Cape Town," *Journal of Religion in Africa, 26* (1996), pp. 139–62; J. E. Mason, "'A Faith for Ourselves': Slavery, Sufism and Conversion to Islam at the Cape," *South African Historical Journal, 46* (2002), pp. 3–24.

The Expulsion of Maqoma and the Kat River Settlement, 1829

Save for the continued patrol system and the opening up of trade, the revolution within the colony distracted attention from relations with the amaXhosa. During the 1820s Maqoma, having returned to the Kat River area, became the most important chief west of the Kei. His father Ngqika's power was eroding. In 1825 Ngqika even lost the sole recognition he had enjoyed from the colony in favor of a policy of recognizing different chiefs. He died – as did Ndlambe – in 1828. The tragedy for Maqoma was that, though he was Ngqika's first son he was not his first son by the Great Wife, whom Ngqika had married later for diplomatic reasons. He could not succeed Ngqika but would have to leave the succession to the club-footed and frail Sandile.[83]

Maqoma was a selective modernizer and requested a missionary from the LMS, which did not oblige. Rather, agents of the Glasgow (Presbyterian) and Wesleyan societies established a chain of stations through Xhosaland and on across the Kei. The Wesleyans arrived along with the 1820 settlers, had congregations among them, and drew financial support from them and, over time, were to play a crucial role in shaping their identity. They were both prosettler and highly conservative, quite different from the LMS.[84] The Glasgow missionaries were less politically constrained and would, in time, found Lovedale, an important educational center. In general, though they might like Xhosa people individually, they had nothing but contempt for Xhosa society and saw no value in the religious innovations of the millenarian prophet Nxele, or even van der Kemp. Their conversions would be few until much later and were limited mainly to outcasts from Xhosa society.[85]

By the later 1820s, the colonial government was again attempting to impose the order it desired across the frontier. The first salient example of this was the expulsion of Matiwane and the amaNgwane from the Transkeian highlands in 1828. Matiwane, who originally came from the Mfolozi Valley in what is now KwaZulu-Natal, had moved into the Transkei

---

[83] CO 165 Thomson to Scott 10/6/1822, quoted in Stapleton, *Maqoma*, p. 41.

[84] See the characterization in Keegan, *Colonial South Africa*, pp. 65–7. For a view that regards William Shaw, at least, as more complex in his racial views, see B. E. Seton, "Wesleyan Missions and the Sixth Frontier War, 1834 to 1835," unpublished Ph.D. thesis, University of Cape Town, 1935.

[85] Donovan Williams, *When Races Meet: The Life and Tiems of William Ritchie Thomson, Glasgow Society Missionary, Government Agent and Dutch Reformed Church Minister, 1794–1891* (Johannesburg: A.P.B. Publishers, 1967), Chapter 7; N. Erlank, "Re-examining Initial Encounters Between Christian Missionaries and the Xhosa, 1820–1850; the Scottish Case," *Kleio, 31* (1999), pp. 6–32.

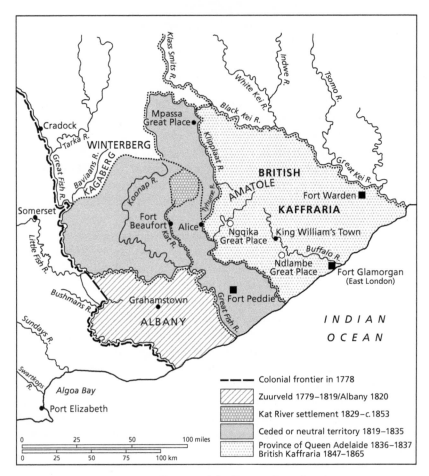

FIGURE 6.1. Albany and the Eastern Cape frontier.

from the Highveld in the wake of a failed attack on Moshoeshoe at Thaba
Bosiu. There he was attacked at Mbholompo by a coalition orchestrated
by Ngubencuka, the Thembu king, who had the most to lose, and including amaGcaleka, amaMpondo, and the British. There were, of course, by-
products of such an attack in the form of cattle and a number of semislave
laborers, but the main impulse, at least for British participation, was the
desire to maintain their grip on political relations across the border.[86]

[86] J. Peires, "Matiwane's Road to Mbholompo: A Reprieve for the Mfecane?" in C.
Hamilton (Ed.), *The Mfecane Aftermath: Reconstructive Debates in Southern African History*
(Johannesburg and Pietermaritzburg: Witwatersrand University Press and University
of Natal Press, 1995); J. Cobbing, "The Mfecane as Alibi: Thoughts on Dithakong and
Mbolompo," *Journal of African History*, 29 (1988), pp. 487–520. E. Eldredge, "Migration,

If this were the case, it was of a piece with the next major intervention by the British to the east, namely the expulsion of Maqoma, then probably with more than 16,000 subjects, from the Kat River area, ostensibly for raiding the abaThembu.

Maqoma's expulsion proved a turning point in Xhosa–colony relations, adding greatly to Xhosa mistrust. In Maqoma's place Stockenström established a settlement of coloreds: the Kat River settlement. His main aim was, as he put it, to turn "the better and more efficient part of the Hottentots into a breastwork against an exasperated, powerful enemy in the most vulnerable and dangerous part of our frontier."[87] At the same time, it was, paradoxically, the culmination of the dreams of the humanitarians for the Khoesan.

The LMS acquiesced in the expulsion of Maqoma, though they denied their complicity in the actions. The Rev. W. R. Thompson, an old Glasgow missionary who had had an unfortunate time as a government agent among the amaXhosa, was the only colonial to protest.[88] All the same, Thompson was appointed to the settlement as a government clergyman, but attempts to prevent Read from living there too failed, as the Khoekhoen who had come to the Kat River requested his presence. Read had incurred the hatred of the colonists both because of his opposition to oppression and because he did not maintain the racially desired social distance from his charges. Equally, many of his fellow missionaries, notably Robert Moffat, never forgave his earlier adultery.

The original settlers of the Kat River included, besides 144 families from Theopolis and Bethelsdorp (Khoekhoe), Gona who had been living in the area as clients of Maqoma's people, who were placed under the Gona leader Andries Botha, seventy to eighty families of Basters from the Somerset and Graaff-Reinet districts, placed under Christian Groepe; and others from

Conflict and Leadership in Early Nineteenth-century South Africa: The Case of Matiwane," in R. W. Harms et al. (Eds.), *Paths toward the Past: African Historical Essays in Honor of Jan Vansina* (Atlanta, GA: African Studies Association Press, 1994), pp. 66–7, accepts Thembu initiative in the construction of the coalition against Matiwane. As yet the affair has not been investigated from the perspective of the abaThembu or other Transkeians.

[87] Stockenström, *Light and Shade*, p. 5; *Autobiography*, II, p. 358. His memorandum of 17/4/1829 on the subject is reprinted in *Light and Shade*, pp. 3–5. His "desire for a dense buffer settlement in the Ceded Territory preceded his concern for the Khoikhoi," according to Peires, p. 484. See also Crais, *Colonial Order*, p. 79; B. A. Le Cordeur, *The Politics of Eastern Cape Separatism, 1820–1854*, (Cape Town, Oxford University Press, 1981), p. 47; J. D. Pitman, "The Commissioner Generalship of Andries Stockenström," unpublished M.A. dissertation, University of Cape Town (1939), p. 35.

[88] James Read to Directors, Philipton, 19.11.1839, LMS 16/4/B; Thomson to Cole, 1/7/1829, Cape Archives Depot, CO 362/36.

Enon and elsewhere. Some were converts, from the LMS, WMS, and GMS. In 1853 some inhabitants were still using a Khoekhoe language. In about 1831 Read mentioned thirty-three locations – some named after abolitionists such as Wilberforce, Lushington, Buxton, and van der Kemp – with on average 100 persons in each, 21 of them occupied by LMS people. By 1834 there appear to have been 5,000 inhabitants. By then the LMS dominated the settlement, with Thompson's congregation confined largely to Basters. Within the settlement, there was considerable differentiation of wealth and property, and many of the wealthy maintained Khoekhoe or Xhosa clients. The aim was to turn it into a prosperous cash crop community. As among the amaXhosa, the agriculture was carried out by women.[89] In 1831 Read wrote, "I expect our improvements will be rapid, as we have from our stations all kinds of mechanics: masons, smiths, carpenters, sawyers, wheelwrights, shoemakers, etc. We have excellent forests of timber, extensive markets in the Colony, and easy of access." As at Bethelsdorp earlier, the settlement served as the center of a "coloured diaspora" of traders, transport riders, artisans, and teachers. And until the 1834–5 war at least it prospered.[90]

The rest of the ceded territory was distributed by Stockenström to Boers and British settlers "at least, three or four times as much as was allotted to the Hottentots." When land near the Kat River, the area which was to become the prosperous wool-producing district of Fort Beaufort, was sold by government the coloreds were prohibited from buying it.[91]

Philip soon extended the frontier defense concept of the Kat River settlement into concrete proposals for the statelet at Griquatown, which had been nurtured by the LMS since early in the century and to which his protégé, Peter Wright, had been transferred as missionary in 1825. In 1830 he recommended to government the appointment of a magistrate to the Griqua who would form "a kind of frontier militia" to prevent aggressions by the Boer farmers who were moving into Transorangia. He was, in other words, for their incorporation in the colony.[92] In the ensuing decade he would promote Griqua expansionism from Griquatown and Phillipolis in

---

[89] Stockenström, *Light and Shade*, p. 15.

[90] Kirk, "Progress and Decline in the Kat River Settlement, 1829–1854," *Journal of African History,* XIV (3) (1973), pp. 411–6; Elbourne, *Blood Ground,* pp. 262–71; James Read Sr. to J. Campbell, LMS 12/4/C Philipton, "No date but probably August 1831"; Stockenström, *Light and Shade,* pp. 44–54; Crais, *Colonial Order,* pp. 69–70. For the consciousness of the peasant inhabitants, see, e.g., Crais, *Colonial Order,* pp. 83–4; Keegan, *Colonial South Africa,* p. 118.

[91] Crais, *Colonial Order,* pp. 85, 115.

[92] Legassick, "The Griqua, the Sotho-Tswana and the Missionaries," p. 459 and generally; Keegan, *Colonial Order,* pp. 180–2.

Transorangia, exerting hegemony over Sotho-Tswana peoples. At the same time Philip supported in the area the state of increasing size and wealth built by Moshoeshoe through the *mafisa* system since the 1820s around the Caledon River Valley. In 1833 he sponsored the French Protestant missionaries who would establish themselves with Moshoeshoe. In the same year, because government did not support annexation, he and Wright worked out a proposal for a treaty arrangement between the colony and the Griqua chief, Andries Waterboer.[93]

Thus, the realization of Philip's vision in the Kat River settlement was used to promote the interests of coloreds on the northern frontier as well. All this had been at the expense of the amaXhosa (and would be, for a period, of Sotho-Tswana groups). The contradiction this entailed, between forcible civilization and individual upliftment was inherent within philanthropic thought. The more civilized were set against the less civilized, and the LMS missionaries at this stage favored the emerging coloreds at the expense of Bantu-speaking peoples.

Meanwhile, settler reaction to the liberation of the Khoesan was growing apace. In fact the ideas of freedom became a two-edged sword. As taken up by Dutch farmers and British settlers in contrast to the humanitarians, they concerned principally more settler self-government, based on a system of labor coercion. In the Dutch case at least freedom included a defense of the property rights of slaveholders. Agitation for representative government began in the 1820s but received a setback when, after Boer farmers met and passed proslavery resolutions, Fairbairn withdrew his support for it in 1832 on the grounds that the settlers could not be entrusted with it. (There was also mistrust between British settlers and Afrikaners.)[94] Settlers found voices in the Dutch *De Zuid Afrikaan* (from 1830) and the British *Graham's Town Journal* (from 1831). Both newspapers denounced Ordinance 50, for which they held Philip and Fairbairn responsible. Afrikaners in particular resented the merchant–humanitarian alliance because of the removal of their role as agents of the Somerset autocracy. At the same time, members of the British settler elite were developing themselves as the rising agrarian capitalists of the Eastern Cape and, with Robert Godlonton as their leading spokesman, were demanding racial subjugation of labor and dispossession

---

[93] Legassick, "The Griqua, the Sotho-Tswana and the Missionaries," pp. 461–5, Chapters IX–XI; on the *mafisa* system and Moshoeshoe's rise to power, see previously pp. XXX (Wright chapter).

[94] Le Cordeur, *Eastern Cape Separatism*, pp. 51–4; Keegan, *Colonial South Africa*, p. 113; A. Ross, *John Philip (1775–18/51): Missions, Race and Politics in South Africa*, (Aberdeen, Aberdeen University Press, 1986), p. 210; A. Du Toit and H. B. Giliomee, *Afrikaner Political Thought: Analysis and Documents, Volume I: 1780–1850* (Cape Town and Johannesburg: David Philip, 1983), pp. 247–9, 275–82.

of the indigenous of their land. In this they were developing a discourse of an exclusive and racist English nationalism to underpin an emergent colonial identity.[95]

In 1833 the British government in London announced that slavery would be abolished throughout the empire the following year. To deal with the problems it foresaw as a consequence, the Cape Legislative Council passed an antivagrancy act only to have it vetoed by London as contrary to Ordinance 50. Significantly, the resolutions that accompanied this act were couched in the language of civilization appropriated from the humanitarians. The attempt to pass it, together with the failure to do so, provoked opposite reactions from Khoesan and settlers. On the one hand, the defeat intensified settler demands for self-government, on the other, the act's passage in the Cape served to sharpen the identity of the Khoekhoen, in what has been described as "Hottentot nationalism." At public meetings at the mission stations they recalled their harsh treatment by farmers and claimed the act would be a forced labor measure that would "seal the[ir] degradation" and "defeat the end of the labours of missionaries." The opposition of the British settlers to their rights changed the Khoekhoen's perceptions of them. However, the disallowance of the act by the British government reinforced Khoekhoen perceptions of British justice.[96]

In 1834, then, slavery was abolished as from December 1 – though with a four-year apprenticeship period so the full effects were not apparent until 1838. Some 3,000 Boer slaveowners had resisted many amelioration measures and wanted gradual abolition.[97] Abolition, like the failure to pass the vagrancy act, increased their discontent and sowed the seeds of the Trek, during which many left the colony. In their eyes the "proper relations between master and servant" were being disturbed.[98] However, for the colonial government, the goals of emancipation were the establishment of state regulation of labor in place of arbitrary slaveowner power. Thus could racial hierarchy be maintained.

[95] Keegan, *Colonial South Africa*, p. 119; Crais, *Colonial Order*, pp. 127–39; Ross, *Status*, pp. 43, 45–6.

[96] E. Elbourne, "Freedom at Issue: Vagrancy Legislation and the Meaning of Freedom in Britain and the Cape Colony, 1799 to 1842," *Slavery and Abolition,* 15 (1994); S. Trapido, "The Emergence of Liberalism and the Making of 'Hottentot Nationalism,' 1815–1834," *Collected Seminar Paper of the Institute of Commonwealth Studies, London: The Societies of Southern Africa in the Nineteenth and Twentieth Centuries,* 17 (1992), pp. 34–6; R. Ross, "The Kat River Rebellion and Khoikhoi Nationalism: The Fate of an Ethnic Identification," *Kronos: Journal of Cape History,* 24 (1997), pp. 91–105.

[97] Retief's manifesto, in the *Graham's Town Journal,* 2.2 (1837), is reprinted, for instance, in Du Toit and Giliomee, *Afrikaner Political Thought*, p. 213 and, in facsimile, in C. F. J. Muller, *Die Britse Owerheid en die Groot Trek* (Johannesburg: Simonium, 1963), p. 86.

[98] Crais, *Colonial Order*, pp. 62–3.

Humanitarians welcomed the idea of monetary compensation for slave-owners because of their defense of the rights of property and did not oppose the four-year apprenticeship period. Perhaps they did not need the opprobrium of fighting a battle already won. But Philip's main concerns were with the eastern frontier, where he and James Read slowly became aware of the devastation of western Xhosaland, and also the northern frontier, whence Andries Waterboer from Griquatown came to Cape Town to sign a treaty with the governor, Sir Benjamin D'Urban, by which, in return for a salary, arms, and ammunition, he would defend the colony and return fugitives.[99] D'Urban at this stage seemed to be in accord with the LMS, as indeed did Maqoma, whose rapprochement with James Read in the course of 1833 and 1834 only increased settler hatred of him. But whatever his real opinions, D'Urban, dallying at the Cape to settle matters following emancipation, was unable to implement a liberal policy on the frontier. He was preempted by the military and the settlers.

Maqoma's War, or the War of Hintsa, 1834–6

On December 21, 1834, three weeks after the abolition of slavery in the colony, 12,000–15,000 amaXhosa, divided into small guerrilla units, invaded the Cape Colony along a ninety-mile front from the Winterberg above the Kat River to the sea, starting a war that was to prove the most vicious to date. For the first time the amaXhosa used substantial numbers of firearms. The war was sparked by the wounding by British troops of Xhoxho, a full brother to Tyhali, who had assumed de facto leadership over the amaNqika. "I am a bushbuck," stated his half-brother Maqoma to the missionary Friedrich Kayser on December 22, "for we chiefs are shot like them, and are no more esteemed as chiefs."[100] Maqoma's tactics were governed by the failure of Ngqika's attempts to collaborate with the colony and, equally, the failure of the frontal assault of 1819.

Behind the war lay the Xhosa grievances about loss of land, expulsions from the ceded territory, the patrol and reprisal system, and all the other oppressions and indignities meted out to them. But behind this again lay settler bellicosity, in the expectation both of massive profiteering from the war and of eventual accumulation through the dispossession and subjugation of the Africans, and in the hope of alleviating labor shortages by using amaXhosa. Putting pressure after pressure on the amaXhosa until they

---

[99] Legassick, "The Griqua, the Sotho-Tswana and the Missionaries," pp. 480–532; John S. Galbraith, *Reluctant Empire: British Policy on the South African Frontier, 1834–1854* (Berkeley and Los Angeles: University of California Press, 1963), p. 107.

[100] Cited in Stapleton, *Maqoma*, pp. 86–7.

launched into war was one of the means employed, followed by putting pressure on the governor to undertake retribution.[101]

Hintsa had been consulted by the Ciskeian chiefs and, clandestinely at least, approved of the war. Of the principal Xhosa chiefs west of the Kei only Pato of the Gqunukhwebe, among whom the Wesleyans had a station, stood aside. He was later to send forces to join the colonial side – although many of his men fought on the Xhosa side.[102] The amaXhosa initially hoped that even the Khoekhoen in the colony would join them. In the event the coloreds marched off to war, from the Kat River settlement and elsewhere, with the encouragement of Philip. As Read said of those of the Kat River during the war: "As a political body they were moderate, and their *attachment to the British government* unquestionable" (though questioned). They fought hard, and were praised, in particular by Stockenström. The cost, though, was the devastation of the Kat River settlement.

The colony's defenses were at first in disarray, and settler paranoia exaggerated the extent of the Xhosa attacks. On January 1, Maqoma put out a peace feeler, but it was rejected by the brash Lieutenant Colonel Harry Smith, who, arriving on the frontier on January 6, drafted all available Boers and British settlers and the Cape Mounted Rifles (as the Cape Corps, the British army regiment recruited from among the Khoekhoe, had been renamed in 1827) to join the 1,500 or so British soldiers then in the colony. The amaXhosa aimed at a limited war to force a negotiated settlement of their grievances. As Xhosa detachments retired with captured cattle across the Kei, they established their main positions in the Amatole Mountains and the Fish River bush, whence they pursued harassing guerrilla tactics. Colonial forces made an initial unsuccessful attempt to clear the Fish River bush and then undertook an unsuccessful invasion of the Amatoles.[103] Thereafter (in April) Smith and D'Urban led a British army for the first time against the amaXhosa across the Kei, thereby declaring war on Hintsa, and seized many cattle. Eventually, after coming voluntarily to the British, Hintsa was taken prisoner and, on May 11, murdered while trying to escape and his body mutilated – an act that the amaXhosa have never forgotten.[104]

D'Urban arrived in Grahamstown on January 20. His views had been strongly modified there by the British settler lobby led by Robert Godlonton of the *Grahamstown Journal* and their allies in the military. Godlonton had attacked the LMS for its supposed fomenting of the war and, in general,

[101] Keegan, *Colonial South Africa*, pp. 74, 101.

[102] Stapleton, *Maqoma*, p. 92; Peires, *House of Phalo*, pp. 94, 109, 160.

[103] Peires, *House of Phalo*, pp. 146–8; Mostert, *Frontiers*, pp. 684–5, 688, 690–4, 702–9; Maclennan, *Proper Degree of Terror*, p. 224.

[104] Peires, *House of Phalo*, pp. 146–8; Stapleton, *Maqoma*, pp. 90–1; Mostert, *Frontiers*, pp. 658–64, 684–728; Macmillan, *Bantu, Boer and Briton*, pp. 131–2; Crais, *Colonial Order*, p. 116; Keegan, *Colonial South Africa*, p. 143.

supported the Wesleyans. Thus, in May, publicly blaming the amaXhosa for the war, D' Urban declared the ceded territory the district of Victoria, annexed amaXhosa territory between the Fish and the Kei as Queen Adelaide Province, and simultaneously described the amaXhosa as "treacherous and irreclaimable savages."

He demanded the expulsion of all Ciskeian amaXhosa across the Kei, out of the new province. But Maqoma and the other chiefs immediately rejected this, and British forces could not achieve it against Xhosa resistance. They continued their scorched earth tactics, destroying homes, grain stocks, crops, and stock, ensuring that the amaXhosa were unable to plant new crops and beginning to face starvation. By September, though, Xhosa military action had forced D'Urban to abandon his May policy. A peace agreement signed by D'Urban and the chiefs on September 17 left the amaXhosa within Queen Adelaide Province as subjects of the crown, with resident agents.[105] The Wesleyan missionaries had played a part in brokering the peace. Maqoma had shown himself to be a skilled tactician. Although against British power, the amaNgqika had been driven back once again, they retained land in the Ciskei, including their defenses in the Amatolas. The aristocrats remained in control. However, there was an increasing drain of Xhosa commoners to labor in the colony.[106] Among these were some 16,000 to 17,000 "Mfengu" resettled from Hintsa's territory to the Fort Peddie area and made British subjects, to act as frontier buffers against the entry of the amaXhosa to the Fish River bush. Already they had been drafted into the colonial forces in the later stages of this war.[107] They were also intended to provide a labor supply for the colonists and, indeed, their introduction brought a downturn in wages.[108]

For the next forty years the amaMfengu performed these roles admirably – and a core of them became successful peasants and the vanguard of a new African elite.[109] Some of them were refugees from Natal, others may have been Xhosa commoners.[110] What is certain is that the amaMfengu, liberated from slavery among the amaXhosa and becoming civilized under

---

[105] Stapleton, *Maqoma*, pp. 92–7; Mostert, *Frontiers*, p. 749; Macmillan, *Bantu, Boer and Briton*, pp. 149–50; Le Cordeur, *Eastern Cape Separatism*, pp. 75–6.

[106] Stapleton, *Maqoma*, pp. 97–8.

[107] *Ibid.*, p. 93; see Chapter 5 in this volume.

[108] Crais, *Colonial Order*, p. 152.

[109] Peires, *House of Phalo*, pp. 110–1; Crais, *Colonial Order*, p. 117; Keegan, *Colonial South Africa*, pp. 145–7; Mostert, *Frontiers*, pp. 697–8, 714–5, 719–20, 722; Switzer, *Power and Resistance*, p. 60.

[110] Stapleton, *Maqoma*, pp. 90–3; A. Webster, "Unmasking the Fingo: The War of 1835 Revisited," in Hamilton (Ed.), *Mfecane Aftermath*, pp. 241–74; Crais, *Colonial Order*, pp. 99, 118 and, for critique, Keegan, *Colonial South Africa*, pp. 330–1; Switzer, *Power and Resistance*, pp. 58–60.

British rule, were set ideologically against the resistant and barbarous amaXhosa who had to be dominated to be reformed.

In Queen Adelaide Province, in addition to 18,500 amaMfengu there were 56,000 amaNgqika, 9,200 amaNdlambe, and 7,500 amaGqunukhwebe to be ruled as British subjects by Wesleyan and Glasgow Missionary society missionaries, as well as by secular officials appointed as commissioners to the tribes.[111] Colonel Harry Smith, named civil commissioner, placed the tribes in defined locations, gave the chiefs the title of magistrates – with Maqoma as "Chief Magistrate" – and intended to teach them to administer English law and live off salaries rather than fines. Witchcraft executions were banned. The territory was to be filled with schools, missionaries, and trade commodities to civilize the ama Xhos Xhos Xhos Xhosa. By June 1836, with characteristic self-glorification, Smith was writing: "Everyone kisses my hand and greets me, not by outward show but inwardly, with his heart and voice, as his *Inkosi Inkulu* . . . and never was the authority of the Normans more thoroughly established over the Saxons, than the British over this mass of human beings from the Keiskama to the Umzimvooboo; for it is not only on this side of the Kye but beyond it that I am looked up to as the Great Chief."[112] Nevertheless, these were pipe dreams. On the one hand, the chiefs had not yet been conquered, on the other, war had resulted in widespread dispossession and proletarianization.[113]

Settler identity had already crystallized into "othering" the amaXhosa, but during the war attitudes hardened. Settlers were reassured that even in Queen Adelaide Province there would be large tracts of land for "the occupation and speculation of Europeans."[114] In South Africa the settler agenda seemed to have triumphed. In London, by contrast, humanitarian pressure through the Select Committee on Aborigines and Lord Glenelg, the evangelical colonial secretary of Scots Jacobite descent (and thus conscious of the effects of colonial conquest), led to disavowal of this agenda.[115]

---

[111] From an 1835/6 census, cited by Seton, "Wesleyan Missions," 322.

[112] Smith, 4/6/1836 in Theal, *Records of the Province of Queen Adelaide*, II, p. 625 [Cory Library] quoted in Seton, "Wesleyan Missions," 324. See also Peires, *House of Phalo*, p. 114

[113] In general, see A. Lester, "Settlers, the State and Colonial Power: The Colonization of Queen Adelaide Province, 1834–37," *JAH*, 39 (1998).

[114] Quoted in Le Cordeur, *Eastern Cape Separatism*, pp. 75–6.

[115] E. Elbourne, "The Sin of the Settler: The 1835–36 Select Committee on Aborigines and Debates over Virtue and Conquest in the Early Nineteenth Century British White Settler Empire," *Journal of Colonialism and Colonial History*, 4 (2003); Zoë Laidlaw, "'Aunt Anna's Report': The Buxton Women and the Aborigines Select Committee, 1835–1837," *Journal of Imperial and Commonwealth History*, 32 (2004), pp. 1–28; R. Vigne, "'Die Man Wat die Groot Trek Veroorsaak Het': Glenelg's Personal Contribution to the Cancellation of D'Urban's Dispossession of the Rarabe in 1835," *Kleio, 30* (1998), pp. 28–45.

On December 26, 1835, Glenelg sent a dispatch ordering the retrocession to the amaXhosa of Queen Adelaide Province (unless D'Urban could justify his actions). This arrived at the Cape on March 21, 1836, though Glenelg had to send another dispatch in August to insist on it. In the end, Queen Adelaide Province formally deannexed on February 2, 1837. This event, perhaps more than any other, was at the root of the British settlers' evolving political consciousness, strengthening their opposition to the interference of (some) missionaries in politics.

The Aftermath of War – Emancipation and the Great Trek

The retrocession of Queen Adelaide Province occurred during the period between the formal abolition of slavery at the Cape and the ending of the period of apprenticeship, which would genuinely allow the slaves freedom, building on the abolition of all racial discrimination, which was the basis of Ordinance 50. Vagrancy measures had been defeated, and it seemed that the humanitarian, missionary-based campaign was succeeding. Indeed, several thousand Afrikaner farmers were leaving the colony to the north in what was, in part at least, a protest against these humanitarian measures. In the event, the humanitarian victories between 1828 and 1837 were not conclusive. In their various ways, they contributed to the entrenchment in power of the colony's capitalist class and, eventually, to its extension to the Limpopo.

Sir Andries Stockenström (then in Europe) was appointed lieutenant-governor of the Eastern Cape by Glenelg and returned to Cape Town on July 25, 1836, with a policy of signing treaties with the Xhosa chiefs as a substitute for the patrol and reprisal system. Treaties were signed in December. The whole of the ceded territory was restored to the amaXhosa, making the Fish and Kat rivers the boundary. AmaXhosa were permitted to return to the area between the Fish and the Keiskamma, though the British insisted that the Mfengu remain in their settlements in the ceded territory – where they would be challenged and partly ousted by the returning Maqoma as well as by Pato of the amaGqunukhwebe.[116] This system never had a chance – the amaXhosa were already too tightly bound to the colony by trade, missionary activity, and labor migration.[117] Equally, the land-hungry British settlers, their appetites whetted by D'Urban's annexation in May 1835 and extremely frustrated by the retrocession, were determined that the treaty system should not succeed.

[116] Peires, *House of Phalo*, pp. 131–2.   [117] Peires, "British and the Cape," 490.

The settlers gained strength from the fact that the humanitarian–merchant alliance that had characterized the 1820s had begun to break up – precisely on the issue of policy toward the amaXhosa. The Cape Town merchant elite and Afrikaner professional and business class (save, at first, for Fairbairn) were now beginning to see more opportunities in colonial capitalism built on racial exploitation than in an independent brown and black peasant–artisan economy. Cape Town capital was flowing eastward into the new wool-based economy. Slave abolition hastened this shift in the center of gravity to the Eastern Cape: Money paid as compensation to indebted slaveowners passed to merchants, who used it to promote the wool economy.[118] Significantly, the first private commercial bank was established in 1837.

The period after the war was one of prosperity as Cape wool production increased in response to the demand created by the expanding textile industry in Britain. Governor Napier wrote in 1841 that "no merchant of any importance in Grahamstown has not within the last few years invested considerable sums of money in the purchase of farms along the immediate border, and in stocking these farms with sheep."[119] Already nearly 1 million pounds at the end of the 1830s, wool production, dominated by a small number of wealthy farmers, grew to 5.5 million a decade later.[120] Wool production, moreover, was more labor intensive than earlier forms of agricultural production in the Eastern Cape and created a huge demand for labor. It was not a climate conducive to success for Stockenström and, in 1839, he was relieved of his post as lieutenant-governor after a vindictive, personalized, and slanderous campaign waged by the Eastern Cape British settlers. The treaty system remained, but its desultory administration by Colonel John Hare, Stockenström's successor, essentially defeated it.

At the other end of the colony, some of the Boers to the north of Graaff-Reinet had, for some years, been moving their flocks across the Gariep on a regular basis. This had resulted in clashes with the Philippolis Griqua, to whom the region nominally belonged. From about 1834 some of the Boers who opposed the reforms of the 1820s began to trek out of the colony to preserve their old practices and seek new opportunities beyond the colonial boundaries. This movement (the "Great Trek") reached its peak in 1836.

---

[118] It also found its way to other places, including the building of houses in Cape Town's Bo-Kaap, which were inhabited by those who had left their masters' houses.

[119] Le Cordeur, *Eastern Cape Separatism*, p. 89, citing Napier to Stanley 21/12/1841 CA GH 23/13.

[120] Keegan, *Colonial South Africa*, pp. 115–6, 151–2, 181–2; Crais, *Colonial Order*, pp. 134–6. See also Meltzer, "Emancipation, Commerce," pp. 169–200.

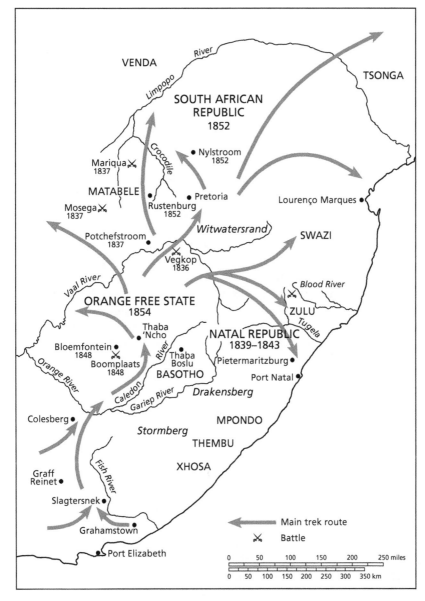

FIGURE 6.2. The Afrikaner Great Trek, 1836–54.

Settler propaganda at the time blamed the Trek on Glenelg's decision about retrocession of Queen Adelaide Province. However, recent historiography sees the cause of the Trek as lying in the political revolution of the 1820s – Ordinance 50, the abolition of slavery, Anglicization, and so on. Since their arrival and the crushing of the frontier rebellions the British had successively demolished most of the institutions of eighteenth-century Boer society. Many Boers felt a sense of resentment, powerlessness, bewilderment, and alienation because of the breakdown of their personal rule over their "servants," whereas the Trek leaders may have been frustrated as a leveled-down elite still anxious for accumulation and keen to explore the frontiers of trade and opportunity – though the Boers, unlike British settlers, were not generally agitating for military expansion against the amaXhosa. Although the early treks were inclined to break ties with Britain, those who left from 1836 continued to cling to colonial trade links: They were not fleeing but carrying the colonial nexus into the interior.

Later Afrikaner nationalist ideologists depicted the Trek – and the depiction is frozen in the friezes of the Voortrekker Monument near Pretoria – as a heroic flight from British oppression, taking the ideals of Christian civilization into a barbarous and unknown interior, and helping to forge the Afrikaner nation. At the same time, though, there was no evident sense of a national mission. Moreover, most of the territory into which the Trekkers moved – Transorangia and Natal – was already well known to white traders and missionaries. British merchants and settlers were already agitating for the settlement of Natal. At the time, Philip believed that the propaganda of *The Graham's Town Journal* contributed greatly to the Trek.[121]

The Trek nevertheless entailed a substantial movement of population. By 1840, about 10 percent of Cape whites had left the colony, and some Eastern Cape districts had lost a fifth of their white inhabitants. At this stage, most were living south of the Vaal and in Natal. This was made possible by the military successes of the early Trekker parties. The combination of the offensive power of mounted horsemen and the defensive strength of corraled wagon laagers was generally decisive against African kingdoms whose military successes had been on the basis of infantry assaults. Technology could trump numbers. Thus, in 1836, a small party of Trekkers under Andries Potgieter was able to beat off an attack by most of Mzilikazi's Ndebele army, though most of the Trekkers' cattle were captured. Potgieter and those under his leadership, together with the followers of Gert Maritz from Graaff-Reinet, responded by attacking the Ndebele capital at Mosega. A subsequent attack, led by Potgieter and Piet Uys, together with a raid by the amaZulu, was sufficient to convince Mzilikazi that his long-term

---

[121] Keegan, *Colonial South Africa*, pp. 186–97; Le Cordeur, *Eastern Cape Separatism*, p. 90; Muller, *Oorsprong, passim*; for a recent narrative, see Giliomee, *Afrikaners*, Chapter 6.

future lay further to the north, eventually in what was to become south-west Zimbabwe. The result was, at least potentially, white control over the grasslands on both sides of the Vaal River and over parts of the southern Bushveld.[122]

Initially, though, the Trekkers were more concerned to establish themselves in Natal. In the course of 1837, substantial parties crossed the Drakensberg, under Gert Maritz and Piet Retief, leaders elected by a *Burgerraad* (citizens' council), which had been unable to impose its authority on all the emigrants, notably on Potgieter who, with his family and immediate followers, moved into the highlands of what is now known as Mpumalanga. Until late 1838 the continued existence of Trekker society in Natal was in doubt after Dingane, the Zulu king, had ordered the killing of those, notably Retief, who had gone to negotiate with him. Isolated groups of Trekkers were then systematically mopped up by the amaZulu. However, the amaZulu failed in their attempt to crush the Trekkers, by now under Andries Pretorius, at the Ncome (Blood) River. The defensive strength of the laager proved decisive. As a result the Trekkers were able to establish their presence to the south of the Zulu kingdom, in the region centred on Pietermaritzburg and Port Natal, later renamed Durban.

Once the Trekkers had opened up Natal to European settlement, the British were quick to move in, both for the standard strategic reasons that impelled imperial policy throughout the nineteenth century and because of pressure from those who foresaw opportunities for land speculation. The independent *maatschappij* (society), which the Trekkers had organized, was annexed despite their protests. Eventually, this led to the return across the Drakensberg of many, but not all, of those who had gone to Natal. Andries Pretorius himself moved to the region of Rustenburg in 1847. There he would be at the head of slowly intensifying European control over what became the Transvaal, in a tense collaboration with the remnants of Potgieter's followers in the east, and based on cattle, the ivory trade to the far interior, and the extraction of rent from African societies. It was not necessarily a racial hegemony. Both Retief and Potgieter attempted to build alliances with the Griqua, the first against Mzilikazi and the second to stem further British involvement north of the Orange.[123] But the whole

---

[122] For details, see P. J. van der Merwe, "Die Matabeles en die Voortrekkers," *Archives Year Book,* 49(2) (1986).

[123] Letters in Du Toit and Giliomee, *Afrikaner Political Thought,* pp. 172–3. The Griqua, who were involved in a conflict with colonial emigrants who were threatening their lands, did not trust Potgieter enough to break their long alliance with the Cape colonial government.

process had produced a major geographical expansion of European control within the subcontinent.

Paradoxically, the real effects of emancipation came in 1838, when the Trek was already over. In that year 25,000 slaves were freed and fled from the farms – to vacant land, to missions, northward to the Griqua, and above all into town – joining the already emancipated Khoekhoen. Broken slave families were reconstructed, with men as head, and ex-slave women and children were largely withdrawn from the labor market. On farms during this period and after, a whole variety of social relations developed. Many people became labor–tenants. By the 1840s a bifurcated labor force had developed – on the one hand, permanent workers, and, on the other, seasonal workers with a resident base outside the farm, a division that has persisted to the present. It was a division of labor that allowed the landowners to maintain and even increase production levels of wine and wheat in the years after emancipation, at the cost to themselves of a continual struggle against bankruptcy.[124] By the early 1840s, the local state, under the control of settlers, was attempting to dispossess squatter and peasant communities. Rural resistance, particularly of squatters and peasants, increased from this time, according to Crais. Indeed, both squatting and theft, "the most primitive form of protest" as Engels put it, were a rejection of primitive accumulation and colonization.[125]

Emancipation and the move to the missions also provided the basis for the establishment of respectable communities of ex-slaves, following the model already developed for the Khoesan. These were highly gendered societies. Women and children acquired the opportunity to withdraw from the labor process on the farms, at least for most of the year, though at the cost of maintaining a lifestyle, both in terms of sexual morality and daily behavior, which was acceptable to the missionaries.[126] At the same time, the men might acquire a degree of status and prestige within church structures that they would not have had in the secular world. The struggle for political emancipation began within the mission churches. The opposition to it came, also, from certain missionaries, who saw their monopoly over the

---

[124] Worden and Crais (Eds.), *Breaking the Chains*, pp. 14–15; J. Marincowitz, "Rural Production and Labour in the Western Cape, 1838 to 1888, with Special Reference to the Wheat Growing Districts," Ph.D. thesis, University of London, 1985, p. 38; R. Ross, "'Rather Mental than Physical': Emancipations and the Economy of the Cape Colony," in N. Worden and C. C. Crais (Eds.), *Breaking the Chains: Slavery and its Legacy in the Nineteenth Century Cape Colony* (Johannesburg: Witwatersrand University Press, 1994), pp. 145–67; W. Dooling, "The Decline of the Cape Gentry, 1838–c.1900," *JAH*, 40 (1999).

[125] Crais, *Colonial Order*, pp. 148–9, 157, 163–4, 184.

[126] Scully, *Liberating the Family?*

Word of God challenged by recent converts.[127] The development not even of an African clergy but of African and ex-slave auxiliary missionaries was long drawn out and heavily contested.

In part these objections derived from the attempts of both Kat River Khoekhoen and Griqua to expand their field of influence over the Thembu and Tswana communities, respectively. In both cases this was justified by a nationalism not merely defensive but also expansionist. Griqua political expansion was predicated on expelling Robert Moffat, the long-established and authoritarian LMS missionary in Kuruman, from his post.[128] In the event this failed, as did attempts by John Philip in the early 1840s to solve the problems caused by the clash of Griqua and Batswana and the establishment of Trekboers north of the Gariep by arranging for the annexation to the colony of much of Transorangia. When the plans of the Trekboers to raise the flag of their Natal republic at Allemans Drift on the river reached the ears of Justice Menzies, by chance on circuit in Colesberg, he took it upon himself to annex a large area of Transorangia to the British crown. This did not accord with general British policy in the aftermath of the Glenelg dispatch, and the governor, Sir George Napier, disavowed his actions. Instead, treaties between the British and Adam Kok III in Philippolis, and with Moshoeshoe to complement that already signed with Waterboer, were supposed to guarantee the peace.[129]

In 1842 the British annexed the Republic of Natalia. The destabilizing effects of Boer rule was the excuse, but the pressure of local mercantile and land-speculative interests, publicized as usual by Godlonton, was strong and richly rewarded. Many Boers moved back to the Highveld during the 1840s. Meanwhile, the new colony strengthened its trade links with the Cape Colony along the land route through Xhosaland to Grahamstown. As in the Eastern Cape, settlers and Wesleyans established a special relationship, including in the promotion of immigration to the new colony. In 1846 Theophilus Shepstone, son of a Wesleyan missionary and 1820 settler, with experience as an interpreter and "paramount chief" of the amaMfengu, was appointed diplomatic agent to the native tribes in Natal. He was compelled to recognize existing settlement realities when he segregated the Africans in 1846–7.[130]

The retrocession of Queen Adelaide Province allowed Maqoma to reclaim his lands on the east bank of the lower Kat River, establishing his own

[127] Elbourne, *Blood Ground*, Chapter 9.
[128] Legassick, "The Griqua, the Sotho-Tswana and the Missionaries," Chapter 12.
[129] Ross, *Adam Kok's Griquas*, pp. 51–2.
[130] Keegan, *Colonial South Africa*, pp. 204 ff; T. McClendon, "The Man Who Would be *Inkosi*: Civilising Missions in Shepstone's Early Career," *JSAS*, 30 (2004), pp. 339–58.

residence near the colony at the junction of the Kat and Blinkwater rivers. Meeting Governor Napier in May 1838, however, Maqoma complained "with great force and pertinacity" that the lands around the upper Kat River (where coloreds were settled) had not been returned to him. Despite settler instigations against him, he also made serious attempts to cooperate with the colony, including strenuously implementing the terms of the treaties until 1844. In January 1839, he took a case of theft of his horse by a settler to the court in Grahamstown and was delighted to win. Whereas in general the amaXhosa turned away from the missions at this time, Maqoma preserved his relationship with the LMS, sending two of his young children to be cared for by the mission.[131] Subsequently, though, he fell out with Henry Calderwood, the LMS missionary assigned to his station. Maqoma also finally had to relinquish to Sandile his position as regent of the amaNgqika. He did instigate "smelling-out" intrigue in 1842 against Suthu, Sandile's mother, with the intention of discrediting Sandile, a plan that was foiled by colonial intervention.[132]

Particularly after the war, the situation of colored mission stations in the colony deteriorated, with entire families engaging as laborers for the surrounding farmers. In 1838, for the first time, Bethelsdorp inhabitants were unable to pay taxes. Hankey, in the Gamtoos Valley, was viewed in the 1840s as the model mission.[133] By the 1840s the fertile area of the Kat River settlement (very suitable for sheep) was surrounded by the farms of wealthy settlers, with whom there were occasional flare-ups. The fixed property of the settlement was valued at £36,000 to £40,000, despite the fact that Khoekhoen had little access to credit, and the settlers' movable wealth was also increasing.[134] In 1842 the valley had some 4,876 inhabitants and was quite diversified by wealth and descent, particularly reflected in the prevalence of clientship relations. Those dispossessed by conquest or the growth of capitalist agriculture from all over the Eastern Cape flocked to the area. After the 1834–5 war, D'Urban granted a part of the Blinkwater Valley to Hermanus Matroos, also known by the Xhosa name of Ngxukumeshe. He was the son of a slave who had fled across the border and a Xhosa woman, who now had a mixed ethnic following, largely

[131] Stapleton, *Maqoma*, pp. 106–16, 121; H. C. Hummel (Ed.), *F.G. Kayser, Journal and Letters* (Cape Town: Maskew Miller Longman, 1990), pp. 140–51; Le Cordeur and Saunders (Eds.), *Kitchingman Papers*, pp. 201–3.

[132] Peires, *House of Phalo*, p. 129; Stapleton, *Maqoma*, pp. 120–6; LMS 5/4/1842 Philipton, James Read Jr.

[133] Crais, *Colonial Order*, pp. 152–3; Sales, *Mission Stations*, pp. 121–34.

[134] Stockenström, *Light and Shade*, p. 72; Crais, *Colonial Order*, p. 159; Le Cordeur and Saunders, *Kitchingman Papers*, p. 191; CA LG 592, Borcherds report on KRS 10/2/1842; Kirk, "Progress and Decline," pp. 415–8.

amaGqunukhwebe. Over time, the Blinkwater became a halfway house between the Colony and Kaffirland – to which Xhosa women came to buy maize with which they returned to Xhosaland. Government officials began to try to enforce the signs of civilization: stone or brick houses, fencing, and the planting of trees. Aspirations to respectability among the residents coexisted with a certain simmering rebelliousness among the poor, who were growing increasingly destitute. The settlement was an area of intermingling of all the peoples of the Eastern Cape. As they strained to make a living from irrigated agriculture, stock keeping, and forestry, the settlement's inhabitants each individually made their personal accommodation between the competing demands of the Christian God and His preachers, of colonial officialdom, of the capitalist market, and of the social and cultural worlds inherent in Xhosa custom.[135]

The Road to War, 1844–6

The 1840s were a high point of British settler power in the Eastern Cape, as the state expanded, driven by the capitalization of wool production for export. By 1851 Fairbairn could report that "a large proportion of the money in Cape Town is derived from mortgages on frontier farms and frontier estates; a large proportion of the trade of Table Bay is connected with the frontier, and a great many people in Cape Town have an interest in estates in the eastern province."[136] The development of capitalism in South Africa, which this represented, took a predominantly landlord-dominated labor-repressive mode rather than a black peasant road. This entailed massive state coercion and the deracination of what was to become the black working class from what the whites increasingly saw as a culturally repugnant society. All this required that the amaXhosa come under direct imperial rule, along with the expansion of European settlement. Confident in the growing world ascendancy of Britain, settlers called vociferously for military action to acquire the resources of land and labor for accumulation and for the crushing of the amaXhosa, on the basis of a new racist ideology of dispossession.

Appropriating the language of civilization, the *Graham's Town Journal* declaimed that if Xhosaland was annexed, "Colonization would then be synonymous with Civilisation, and the natives instead of being depressed or destroyed, would be raised from their wretched grovelling condition, and participate in all the advantages which civilized government is calculated to

---

[135] Crais, *Colonial Order*, pp. 159–63, 166; Stapleton, *Maqoma*, p. 110; Peires, *House of Phalo*, pp. 129–30; R. Ross, "Hermanus Matroos, aka Ngxukumeshe: A Life on the Border," *Kronos,* 30 (2004), pp. 47–69.

[136] Cited in Le Cordeur, *Eastern Cape Separatism*, p. 129.

bestow."[137] British settlers, whose identity as such reached maturity with the twenty-fifth anniversary of their settlement, came close to viewing themselves as sent by God to civilize Africa, which, in effect, meant having Africans work for them. The combination of British power, settler drive, and the resilience of the colonial economy provided the force and the means in the decade after 1846 to conquer and subdue the Ciskeian amaXhosa and to destroy the Griqua states in Transorangia and consolidate new white states there and in Natal.

The contradiction between the free labor ideology promoted by Britain and the need of the Cape economy to subordinate and control workers was exposed by the passage in 1841 of a new stringent Masters and Servants Ordinance. Despite its theoretically nonracial character, it was directed at binding the new colored and Xhosa labor force to the farms. Workers were to receive contracts but in return were bound with severe criminal sanctions for breaches thereof; thus deference, corporal punishment for desertion or subordination, long working hours, poor living conditions, and low wages were promoted by criminal law. Women were subordinated to men as head of the family.[138] Increasing settler control of the local state only exacerbated the oppression. The establishment of the Fort Beaufort magistracy in 1844, for example, went along with the destruction of squatter communities, the extension of private property rights over African-held land, and the enforcement of requirements for building proper houses, fencing, and so forth.[139]

The passage of the 1841 Masters and Servants Ordinance, viewed by Fairbairn as removing the inferior status of coloreds, was the reason he gave for recommencing agitation for representative government. He had allied with the merchant interest in the expansion of a racial colonial capitalism – which wanted representative government because it believed that the fiscal conservatism of officialdom (and the lack of power of the legislative council on spending matters) was preventing the investment necessary for development. By the 1840s, too, the colony's Afrikaner elite had adopted the essentially bourgeois view of the colonial British and saw alliance with the more liberal English-speakers as the way to recover their preeminence. The humanitarianism of their potential allies (such as Fairbairn) had disappeared. By the time of the 1846–7 war with the amaXhosa, Fairbairn had

---

[137] Cited in Crais, *Colonial Order*, p. 141; Le Cordeur, *Eastern Cape Separatism*, pp. 128–9; Ross, *Status*, pp. 65–6.

[138] Keegan, *Colonial South Africa*, pp. 108, 126–7; Crais and Worden (Eds.), *Breaking the Chains*, p. 14; Scully, *Liberating the Family?*

[139] Crais, *Colonial Order*, p. 164; Peires, *House of Phalo*, p. 121 on the increase in Xhosa labor in the colony in this period.

become an ardent militarist. The British government had yet to be convinced about representative government. In 1842 Colonial Secretary Lord Stanley had replied to a petition from the Cape Town municipality, fearing that it could be "perverted into a means of gratifying the antipathies of a dominant caste, or of promoting their own interests or prejudices at the expense of those of other and less powerful classes." Six years were to pass before Governor Harry Smith effectively answered Stanley's reservations.[140]

In the meantime, the colony was reorganized administratively. It had built up a big debt as a result of the 1834–5 war, and the imperial government bore almost the whole cost of the military between 1836 and 1842, as well as a part of civil spending. The situation was turned round thereafter (as the result of wool), particularly under the administration of John Montagu, who became head of the Cape civil service[141] in 1843. Closely allied to the Eastern Cape settler elite, whose views on the amaXhosa he shared, Montagu paid off the colonial debt in two and a half years, professionalized and streamlined the civil service, and organized posts, harbors, and a program of road- and pass-building by means of convict labor, establishing lines of communication for the wool economy.[142]

In May 1843, Maqoma had told Capt. C. L. Stretch, diplomatic agent among the amaXhosa, "I will hold by Stockenström's word until I die and my people put me in the grave. If the treaties are forced from us, nothing can preserve us from war."[143] However, in September the following year, under settler pressure, the new governor, Maitland, abrogated the treaties unilaterally and imposed new agreements on the Xhosa chiefs. In particular, the hated patrol system was reintroduced. Also, amaXhosa living at mission stations were no longer to be subject to traditional law. At first, Maitland treated with the lesser chiefs, even refusing to see Maqoma and the other Ngqika chiefs, and then merely informed them of the abrogation.[144] The settlers rejoiced and burnt an effigy of Stockenström. The lieutenant-governor, Hare, offered his resignation in February 1845 because he said he was left with nothing to do: It was accepted in September 1846.

[140] Ross, *Status*, p. 167; Le Cordeur, *Eastern Cape Separatism*, pp. 136–7; Keegan, *Colonial South Africa*, pp. 108–09; for Afrikaner positions on representative government at this time see Du Toit and Giliomee (Eds.), *Afrikaner Political Thought*, pp. 249–50, 288–91.

[141] A position, confusingly also known as colonial secretary, but not to be confused with that of secretary of state for the colonies, a British minister.

[142] LMS 26/2/A, Glen Anan, 11/6/51, Stretch to Freeman; Keegan, *Colonial South Africa*, p. 211; Le Cordeur, *Eastern Cape Separatism*, pp. 130–2.

[143] Quoted in Stapleton, *Maqoma*, p. 126.

[144] Le Cordeur, *Eastern Cape Separatism*, p. 110; Peires, *House of Phalo*, p. 133; Stapleton, *Maqoma*, pp. 128–9; Mostert, *Frontiers*, pp. 842–4; Switzer, *Power and Resistance*, p. 61; Crais, *Colonial Order*, p. 143; A. Ross, *Philip*, pp. 196–7.

The Xhosa chiefs' alienation from the colonial powers was an inevitable result; equally, relations with the missionaries were seriously soured, not surprisingly because at this stage the missionary community in the Eastern Cape was in the grip of antihumanitarian sentiment.[145] Even Philip and James Read, both growing old, would offer no opposition to the war with the amaXhosa when it finally came. This derived from a combined post-emancipation backlash against the apparent failure of ex-slaves and Khoesan to become productive workers,[146] a settler land and labor hunger directed at the amaXhosa, and a burning missionary desire to civilize the amaXhosa under British rule – all against Xhosa resistance and recalcitrance.

The War of the Axe,[147] 1846–7

By the mid-1840s, there was virtually no productive farming land remaining to be granted in the colony, and the attention of the British settlers was more urgently directed to the lands of the amaXhosa. In late 1845 there arose what Le Cordeur calls the first political movement in the history of Eastern Cape separatism. Significantly, it was catalyzed around the issue of the "leniency of frontier policy," in other words, the settler desire for labor and land. What they wanted was more direct access to British military power, the means of subjugating the amaXhosa.[148]

In mid-January 1846 a party of military engineers provocatively crossed the Keiskamma to survey a site for a fort at Block Drift, a site that would later become Fort Hare. Sandile objected and a military confrontation threatened. The British withdrew, and Maqoma attempted to restrain Sandile. The pressures built up. In February, Governor Maitland contemplated a preemptive strike against the amaXhosa. On March 7 the *Grahamstown Journal* demanded annexation of the old ceded territory. On March 16 an iDange man was arrested for theft of an axe, but the party escorting him to Grahamstown for trial was ambushed by Xhosa warriors and the

---

[145] E. Elbourne, "Whose Gospel? Conflict in the LMS in the Early 1840s," in J. De Gruchy (Ed.), *The London Missionary Society in Southern Africa: Historical Essays in Celebration of the Bicentenary of the LMS in Southern Africa, 1799–1999* (Cape Town: David Philip, 1999), pp. 132–55.

[146] A. Bank, "Losing Faith in the Civilising Mission: The Premature Decline of Humanitarian Liberalism at the Cape, 1840–60," in M. J. Daunton and R. Halpern (Eds.), *Empire and Others: British Encounters with Indigenous Peoples, 1600–1850* (London: UCL Press, 1999), pp. 364–83.

[147] Called by Xhosa "the war of the whites" or "the war of the boundary."

[148] Le Cordeur, *Eastern Cape Separatism*, pp. 145, 216–7; Mostert, *Frontiers*, pp. 857–60; Keegan, *Colonial South Africa*, p. 215.

culprit released. The chiefs refused to deliver up the amaXhosa responsible. On March 21 Lieutenant-Governor Hare announced his intention to march into Xhosaland, and this was backed up by a declaration of war by Maitland on April 1. Maqoma asked Stretch for land for himself and his people further north in the colony, among the abaThembu, where they could sit the war out, but Stretch unwisely refused.[149]

The British ordered the missionaries out of Xhosa territory and three British columns invaded on April 11, aiming to camp at the foot of the Amatole. The amaXhosa, with firearms and horses in significant numbers for the first time, attacked the columns' baggage trains at Burnshill (an abandoned Glasgow Missionary Society station) and captured sixty-five wagons. Only the actions of the Kat River settlers, 250 men under the command of Andries Botha, prevented the amaXhosa from capturing the ammunition and completing their victory. As the British withdrew, the amaXhosa – appealing to the Boers to stand aside – swept into the colony, burning farms and missions, and besieged Fort Peddie. Every chiefdom in Ciskeian Xhosaland joined with Sandile's forces, including the amaGqunukhwebe of Pato, who attacked the amaMfengu settlement around Fort Peddie, which was on their former land. Jan Tshatshu, early chiefly convert and pride of the LMS, joined also, asserting that it was the British and not the amaXhosa who had broken the treaties. Sarhili of the Gcaleka was also supportive. The unity was a remarkable achievement, given the Xhosa history of separatism, of feuding chiefs, and of being driven back onto each other's land. Only the amaMfengu, shaped as collaborators, took the British side. They began the war fighting with assegais but ended it with guns. Also, some 1,100 of the Kat River people fought on the British side throughout the war.

The amaXhosa besieged Fort Peddie until May 28, when they launched an attack on it. The British deployed the amaMfengu outside the fort to repulse the assault, while all whites retreated inside. The amaXhosa seized many cattle. Some ten days later a cavalry force led by Somerset killed several hundred amaXhosa in an unusual open fight, known as the battle of the Gwangqa. Meanwhile, Maitland had taken command, declared martial law, and ordered burgher commandos to be called up from all over the colony. The Boers would have no one but Andries Stockenström to lead them – and even his British settler enemies such as Godlonton and J. M. Bowker supported him as more competent than the British military leadership.[150] The commandos took months to assemble, but by the end

---

[149] Except where otherwise indicated, this section is based on Mostert, *Frontiers*; Stapleton, *Maqoma*; Keegan, *Colonial South Africa*; Peires, *House of Phalo*.

[150] Mostert, *Frontiers*, pp. 887–8; Le Cordeur, *Eastern Cape Separatism*, p. 154. Stockenström's appointment was also supported by Calderwood and Read: LMS 22/1/D Fort Beaufort,

of June Maitland had at his disposal 14,000 men – 3,200 British regulars, 5,500 burghers, 800 Khoekhoe levies, and 4,000 Mfengu and Khoekhoen labourers, but they had few supplies and their leaders had no discernable strategy.

Much of the next phase of the war was a British attempt at an antiguerrilla campaign in the Amatole, attempting to starve the amaXhosa out. Learning from previous wars, however, the amaXhosa captured stock to ensure their food supply once the British had burned their crops and targeted British supplies.[151] For the first time in war the amaXhosa inflicted huge suffering on British wounded – Xhosa women, apparently, tortured them to death. Conflict was becoming sharper. Settlerdom saw the conflict in Manichaean terms, as a conflict of order and confusion that only British supremacy over Xhosaland and a strong state within the colony in the hands of the landed and wealthy could resolve.[152]

To avoid giving an impression of failure, Stockenström, in August, proposed an offensive across the Kei against Sarhili's amaGcaleka, and Maitland eventually agreed. He wanted Sarhili to acknowledge British conquest up to the Kei. Stockenström and his force met Sarhili at his Great Place, where they reached an agreement peacefully. However, when Maitland heard of the agreement he immediately repudiated it and demanded that Sarhili pay reparations for the damage his people had done to missions and trading stations. Stockenström, in frustration and anger, then decommissioned his burgher force and resigned from his post. The Boers were simply not interested in conquest of the amaXhosa or land expansion there.

Maqoma had been dragged reluctantly into the war, and indeed his biographer finds it hard to reconstruct whether he participated or not during the first five months. He wanted a brief war and by September was suing for peace – at a time when the colonial army was virtually unable to continue the war. The amaXhosa, meanwhile, were adopting, in the face of Maitland's threat of mass resettlement, a sit-down strike, which Mostert calls "passive resistance." Maitland had enlisted the aid of the Wesleyan, Shaw, and Calderwood of the LMS to advise him, and he now sent Calderwood to negotiate with Maqoma. Calderwood met Maqoma and the other Ngqika chiefs near Block Drift. He commented that Maqoma had much influence, but the chiefs refused to give up their firearms. The negotiations failed and the chiefs returned to their lands to plant crops.

5/5/46 Calderwood; LMS 22/1/A Eilands River post, Kat River, 31/8/46 Read. Keegan, *Colonial South Africa*, p. 216, is wrong to claim that the British settlers disliked the appointment of Stockenström.

[151] Stapleton, *Maqoma*, p. 135; Peires, *House of Phalo*, p. 153.

[152] Quoted in Crais, *Colonial Order*, p. 146.

A sort of stalemate set in, "both peace and war" (in Calderwood's terms), and in January, Maitland – on a renewed expedition against Sarhili – received a dispatch recalling him. He immediately revoked martial law.

In Britain, because of delayed communications, the war was essentially dealt with by Lord John Russell's Whig government, which replaced the conservatives under Peel in June 1846. The new government set about dismantling the final bulwarks of protectionism on the basis of the ideology of free trade. Russell and his colonial secretary, Earl Grey, were influenced by the ideas of Edward Wakefield on colonial affairs – responsible local government by free settler communities, with financial self-sufficiency as the goal. This left little room for humanitarianism, and the general attitude was that British settlers would not oppress the natives. "Civilization" was part of Earl Grey's vocabulary – because, for him, stabilizing the Xhosa frontier once and for all was the necessary condition for conceding representative government to the colony. And peace demanded British conquest. If peace could be maintained by a "strict and even severe system of government," religion, education, and commerce would gradually civilize the amaXhosa. With all the confidence of a mid–nineteenth-century British politician, he wrote: "The authority of the British Crown is at this moment the most powerful instrument, under Providence, of maintaining peace and order in many extensive regions of the earth, and thereby assists in diffusing amongst millions of the human race the blessings of Christianity and civilization." This was to be the justification for imperialism and British self-interest for the rest of the century.[153]

To stabilize the frontier, Grey replaced Maitland with Sir Henry Pottinger, whose colonial experience was mainly in India but who had lately obliged the Chinese to open up their ports to trade. Grey instructed Pottinger to pacify the frontier by proclaiming British sovereignty up to the Kei and subjugating the amaXhosa. His legal experts pondered over how to exercise British rule without giving the amaXhosa colonial citizenship rights and came up with the idea of a protectorate. Grey also called for a report on whether the colony was prepared for constitutional advance to representative government. Pottinger, who arrived on January 27, 1847, also became the first to hold the post of high commissioner, giving him powers to act across colonial boundaries. Sir Henry Edward Fox Young was appointed as the new lieutenant-governor. Pottinger had asked for a temporary appointment only, wishing to return to India. He was apparently a man of great intellect but also great rage and impatience.

---

[153] Quoted in Mostert, *Frontiers*, p. 909; see also T. E. Kirk, "Self-Government and Self-Defence in South Africa: The Inter-relations Between British and Cape Politics, 1846–1854," Ph.D. thesis, University of Oxford, 1972.

When Pottinger arrived, the war was in a state of stalemate, which frustrated the settlers. The amaXhosa were not fighting, and it was the British who took up the war again. Like his predecessors, Pottinger aimed to expel the amaXhosa across the Kei, although, unlike D'Urban and Maitland, he did not want to abolish the chiefs. His aim was to settle matters with Pato of the amaGqunukhwebe and Sarhili in order to put pressure on other chiefs, particularly Sandile – whom Calderwood was anxious to bring to heel. However, he was handicapped by the lack of interest of the Boers in pursuing the war, which made mass Xhosa expulsion impossible. The pretext for resumption of the war was the theft of fourteen goats by a follower of Sandile in June – which soon led to Sandile being declared a rebel. Pottinger was disgusted by war profiteering among the British settlers. But to raise the necessary forces, he proclaimed that amaMfengu, Boers, and coloreds could take whatever cattle or other booty they wanted. The aim was to clear the amaNgqika out of the Amatole Mountains. On September 29, the offensive began – in time to prevent the amaNgqika from sowing. The war ended in October when Sandile allowed himself to be taken into custody on the understanding that he would be treated as a negotiating equal but was instead made a prisoner. At the same time (September) Maqoma was deported by the government from Block Drift to Port Elizabeth. Pottinger wound up the war by attacks on Pato and by a further campaign across the Kei against Sarhili. However, by the end of September the governor knew that he was leaving for a coveted post in Madras.

Under Pottinger, the government also launched a serious assault on the Kat River settlement. Kat River residents had played a major role in the first part of the war – providing 90 percent of its males for service when every other area of the colony provided at most 3 percent, and their contribution was thought of as vital to British success.[154] Even at the end they played a major role in the clearing of amaXhosa from the Amatole. However, in the meantime, Pottinger had been angered by their reluctance to rejoin the military because they had been badly treated by Maitland. His attitude resonated with that of the settlers, who coveted the fertile Kat River pastures for their sheep – Godlonton and others had, for some time, criticized the settlement for locking up land and labor. Pottinger appointed T. J. Biddulph, a leading settler figure, as magistrate to the settlement, and Biddulph soon produced a scathing report that was eagerly publicized by the *Graham's Town Journal*. Pottinger endorsed the report in his correspondence with London, but in the colony itself it was criticized in at least three newspapers, including the *Eastern Province Herald*

---

[154] Mostert, *Frontiers*, p. 919.

(November 17, 1847),[155] where Stockenström, appalled because of the strategic importance of the Kat River settlement, attacked it.

Matters were not helped when, in another break from the humanitarian tradition, in late 1847 William Elliott of the LMS wrote a long letter to his directors in London arguing for breaking up the mission stations and converting their land to freely transferable individual ownership. The letter was then published in *Evangelical Christendom*. His rationale was the cost of the stations and the fact that the law now extended "protection to the black man as well as the white." Heavy use was made of his arguments in the settler press in their campaign against the Kat River settlement and the mission stations, as Elliott seemed to confirm that the stations locked up labor. Moreover, despite Philip's opposition to it, Elliott maintained his stance, even going to Britain in February 1849 to press his case.[156]

Smith's Governorship: The First Years, 1848–50

Sir Harry Smith arrived as governor on December 1, 1847. The arrogance he had demonstrated during his first tour of duty in South Africa had been further puffed up by his victory against the Sikhs in India. Within three weeks he had set out on a grand tour, first to the eastern frontier – where he was met with huge celebration by the settlers – and then north into Transorangia and to Natal. By February 1848 he had annexed the former ceded territory as the district of Victoria (East), established the new protectorate of British Kaffraria between the Keiskamma and the Kei, extended the colonial boundary in the northwest to the Orange River, and annexed Transorangia up to the Vaal River as the Orange River Sovereignty. He had also instructed William Porter, the attorney general, to draw up a memorandum on representative government for the colony.

Arriving in the Eastern Cape, Smith was committed to reinstating the D'Urban system, with which he had been associated and which Glenelg had rejected. To do this, he appointed members of the settler elite to official positions; Richard Southey, for example, a close colleague of Godlonton,

---

[155] Le Cordeur and Saunders (Eds.), *Kitchingman Papers*, p. 27: Biddulph's report appeared in the *Graham's Town Journal* on November 6, 1847; Kirk, "Progress and Decline," pp. 419–20; Mostert, *Frontiers*, p. 919. Also, Crais, *Colonial Order*, p. 164; Read Snr to Tidman, LMS 23/3/C Philipton 21/1/1848. See also Read to Directors, LMS 23/3/B, Philipton, 1/12/1847.

[156] A. Ross, *Philip*, pp. 203–5; Le Cordeur and Saunders (Eds.), *Kitchingman Papers*, pp. 244–5; Mostert, *Frontiers*, p. 987. However, as Le Cordeur and Saunders point out, Read had made the same proposal privately to his Bethelsdorp colleague and friend James Kitchingman in 1844: *Ibid.*, pp. 244–5: Philipton, 25/3/1844 Read sr to Kitchingman; Bank, "Losing Faith," p. 274.

became Smith's secretary. He then humiliated Maqoma, who was in Port Elizabeth, forcing him to the ground and putting his foot on Maqoma's neck.[157] He then dealt with other Xhosa chiefs in similarly theatrical fashion, tearing up the treaties in front of them, blowing up a wagon of gunpowder, and announcing a series of measures to revise all aspects of Xhosa lives and customs. In the new province of British Kaffraria everyone was to learn English, ploughing, and the "art of money." Cattle-keeping would be discouraged in favor of sheep. *Lobola* and witch-finding were banned. He, Harry Smith, and not Sarhili, was now the *Inkosi Inkhulu*, the Great Chief of the amaXhosa – though Sarhili retained independence in the Transkei. He did seem to favor the Khoekhoen side of the humanitarian program, making the Khoekhoen-descended Commandant Groepe of the Kat River a justice of the peace and praising the missionaries, but soon they would be disappointed in him.

The amaXhosa were finally expelled from the new Victoria East district, which was allocated mainly to settlers and to some amaMfengu (and aba-Thembu) locations. Land speculation and absentee ownership flourished, while some British settlers established wool farms in the northern areas of Victoria East where Maqoma and Sandile had once lived.[158] Maitland had not only promised the amaMfengu their lands in perpetuity but more land for fighting in the 1846–47 war, but this had been forgotten by the end of the war. Only late in 1848 did Smith make some additional provision for amaMfengu to settle on land taken from amaXhosa in the war.[159]

British Kaffraria was ruled as a military protectorate. The rebuilt town of King Williams Town, center of a grid of forts around the mountains, and the new port of East London were settler enclaves within the territory. In 1848 a census was taken of the protectorate's newly permanent British subjects. The amaNgqika – who still were in possession of the strategically significant Amatole Mountains – numbered 27,179 – in contrast to 56,000 in 1835. The rest were in the colony or in Gcalekaland. Of those in British Kaffraria Sandile had 14,915 followers and Maqoma 2,066. Maqoma had been allowed to return from Port Elizabeth to his people around Fort Hare, though his request for land at Blinkwater was denied. Most of the Ngqika

---

[157] Maqoma's comment (in Xhosa) was, "You are a dog and you behave like a dog. This thing was not sent by Victoria who knows that I am of royal blood like herself," cited in Stapleton, *Maqoma*, p. 145.

[158] Switzer, *Power and Resistance*, pp. 62–3; Crais, *Colonial Order*, pp. 144, 174; Keegan, *Colonial South Africa*, pp. 221–2.

[159] R. Moyer, "A History of the Mfengu of the Eastern Cape," unpublished Ph.D. thesis, London (1976), p. 217; R. Moyer, "The Mfengu, Self Defence and the Cape Frontier Wars," in C. Saunders and R. Derricourt (Eds.), *Beyond the Cape Frontier: Studies in the History of the Transkei and Ciskei* (London: Longman, 1974), p. 116.

cattle were concentrated in the top quartile of ownership; the bottom quartile owned only 5 percent.

There were 35,179 amaNdlambe. In addition, about 20,000 to 25,000 in total were thought to be absent. The amaGcaleka of the Transkei numbered 70,000. A tax of £1 was levied on African plot holders to try to induce labor, and a system of fines was established to suppress traditional customs, and a system of rewards for promoting "European attitudes."[160] Smith attempted to incorporate the missionaries into his plans, and they took the opportunity to wage an assault on polygamy and *lobola*, central structures of Xhosa patriarchy. However, Smith's plans for the transformation of agriculture were unrealistic and would have required big state inputs to succeed.

The war and the settlement drove large numbers of men to take up the "women's work" of agriculture. At the same time increasing numbers of amaXhosa – perhaps half the Ngqika population – sought work in the colony, some moving to the Mfengu locations on the way to "pass as Mfengu."[161] Calderwood, once an LMS missionary now the first magistrate of Victoria East and stationed at Alice, as well as being a zealous flogger of amaXhosa for minor offences, sent many, including women and children, to the colony to work.[162] There was a large demand in the Western Cape for the labor of children under ten. Terms of labor contracts were altered: Instead of entering the colony and seeking work on the free market, amaXhosa were now indentured to particular employers, at unspecified wages, even before they entered the colony.[163] Meanwhile, the fabric of peasant life, once based on marriage and female fertility, was unraveling; bridewealth for even one son was unattainable and abortion allegedly universal.

Smith also intervened in Transorangia, where tensions over land were building up between the Boers on the one hand and the Philippolis Griqua and Moshoeshoe on the other. Maitland had installed a British resident in

[160] J. Lewis, "Class and Gender in Pre-Capitalist Societies: A Consideration of the 1848 Census of the Xhosa," *Collected Seminar Papers of the Institute of Commonwealth Studies, London: The Societies of Southern Africa in the Nineteenth and Twentieth Centuries*, 17 (1990), p. 64; Stapleton, *Maqoma*, p. 148; Keegan, *Colonial South Africa*, p. 221; Mostert, *Frontiers*, pp. 939, 979–80.

[161] See Lewis, "Class and Gender," p. 64; Peires, *House of Phalo*, pp. 160, 167; Stapleton, *Maqoma*, p. 148.

[162] Peires, *House of Phalo*, p. 167; Mostert, *Frontiers*, pp. 948–9; Switzer, *Power and Resistance*, p. 63. In 1849 Calderwood instituted an agricultural system for the Xhosa, which was the prelude to the Glen Grey system of the 1890s: see Brownlee J. Ross, *Brownlee J. Ross: His Ancestry and Some Writings* (Lovedale: Lovedale Press, 1948), pp. 28–9. See also LMS 25/4/C Alice, 2/7/1850 H. Calderwood to Freeman, a self-righteous letter defending his conservative "native policy."

[163] Peires, *House of Phalo*, p. 168; Crais, *Colonial Order*, pp. 142, 174.

Bloemfontein, but the provisions of land division were becoming unwork-
able. Moreover, Eastern Cape British settlers desperately wanted the annexation of Transorangia to provide a legal basis for their land speculations.
Smith, under the impression that the Boers also wanted annexation, proclaimed the annexation of the Orange River Sovereignty, which entailed
the highhanded alteration of the treaty with Adam Kok III. Smith also
confirmed the Boers in possession of the land they had claimed from
Moshoeshoe. The hardliners of the Afrikaner *maatschappij*, particularly
those living around Potchefstroom, did rebel under Andries Pretorius as
soon as Smith had left the interior, but they were defeated in August
1848 at Boomplaats, though this required denuding the Xhosa frontier of
troops.

Land in the Orange River Sovereignty was gobbled up by the Eastern
Cape elite, including Godlonton, who bought five farms, and speculators from Natal. A total of 139 people, mainly from the Eastern Cape,
bought up over 2.5 million acres of land in the new colony. Absentee
ownership was rife. By September 1850, land prices had risen 400 percent
since the Pretorius rebellion. Godlonton established a new newspaper in
Bloemfontein, *The Friend of the Sovereignty*, to promote landed interests. The
economy became more closely tied to the larger colonial economy in the
Cape and Natal. Grain from Lesotho fed the town of Bloemfontein and
even rural areas. British settler strategy, pursued notably by the resident,
Major Warden, was designed to undermine Moshoeshoe's role as the pillar
of British hegemony, initially by supporting the weaker communities in
the eastern part of the colony against him. The ultimate goal, though, was
to break Sotho power and gain control over the fertile arable land of the
Caledon River Valley.[164]

Meanwhile, within the Cape Colony, pressures on the coloreds mounted,
particularly at the Kat River. In 1848 British settlerdom and Smith agi-
tated for a new vagrancy law, but it was disallowed by the imperial
government.[165] Smith wrote off the Kat River experiment as a failure.
Its inhabitants came under greater pressure from the settlers and their
representatives within the state. Successive magistrates raised the duties
on the cutting of wood, the main means by which the Kat River people,
their lands devastated by war, could acquire an income. They also burned
out the huts of the Xhosa clients of leading Kat River men while land in
and around the valley was allocated to whites, including Godlonton. All
this was done in the name of civilization, but by 1850 the coloreds were
experiencing the government as violently oppressive, not at all likely to

---

[164] Keegan, *Colonial South Africa*, pp. 259–271, 353; Crais, *Colonial Order*, pp. 143–4.
[165] Crais, *Colonial Order*, p. 142; Keegan, *Colonial South Africa*, pp. 221, 237–8.

redress their grievances.[166] The tinder was there for rebellion, and the spark was soon to come in the War of Mlanjeni.

The Struggle for Representative Government and the War and Rebellion of 1850–53

In the course of the 1840s, opposition to the autocratic forms of government orchestrated by John Montagu as head of the Cape administration was growing among those in the white settler elite, who should have been its main supporters. The system of patronage he exercised was too evidently designed to favor a small group of cronies and the aggressively English settlers of the Eastern Cape. In reaction, the old Dutch-speaking elite, particularly those centered in the Masonic Lodge, "De Goede Hoop," in Cape Town and including the editor of *De Zuid-Afrikaan*, had foresworn ethnic politics and were building an alliance with at least some of Cape Town's British merchants. Disputes between the municipality and the executive over road rates and market regulations, relatively trivial in themselves (although affecting merchants' balances), soon began to assume the character of a general challenge to the government, especially as the political after-effects of the abolition of slavery were waning.[167]

In 1848 Smith had sent to London a constitution drafted by the attorney general, William Porter. It was based on a nonracial qualified franchise: All adult males (inevitably) who had occupied property worth £25 for at least a year were eligible to vote. Porter was a (utilitarian) liberal, not a democrat. Two years later he denounced the option of universal manhood suffrage as threatening the colony with "communism, socialism and red republicanism which had caused so much mischief in France" in the 1848 revolution there. Smith's dispatch to London, however, crossed at sea with a dispatch from Grey that proposed sending Irish convicts to the Cape.[168]

This proposal, made public on November 8 by Smith, aroused a storm of agitation in the Cape Colony against the government, which intersected with and popularized the struggle for representative government. Almost all sections of society joined the agitation, as the impending arrival of the colonists was seen as a threat to the respectability of those who had

[166] A. Ross, *Philip*, p. 207.

[167] J. C. Visagie, "Willem Fredrik Hertzog, 1792–1847," *Archives Year Book for South African History* (1974); D. Warren, "Merchants, Commissioners and Wardmasters: Municipal and Colonial Politics in Cape Town, 1840–1854," *Archives Year Book for South African History* (1992); H. C. Botha, "Die Rol van Christoffel J. Brand in Suid-Africa, 1820–1854," *Archives Year Book for South African History* (1977); H. C. Botha, *John Fairbairn in South Africa* (Cape Town: Historical Publication Society, 1984).

[168] Keegan, *Colonial South Africa*, p. 244; Ross, *Status*, p. 167; Mostert, *Frontiers*, p. 973.

achieved it and to the livelihood of those who had not.[169] It was also a weapon with which to attack the oligarchy that ran the colony from the Legislative Council. The convict crisis itself simmered on until, in early 1850, the *Neptune*, carrying the convicts, was ordered to sail away after a five-month stay in Simon's Bay. The response from conservatives like Montagu, alarmed by the radicalism of the movement, demanded that Smith assert the government's authority. On the grounds that the movement was anti-English, Smith secured a delay for representative government.

Very soon, two tendencies had crystallized. On one side were the conservatives, represented by the governor and most of the Executive Council, led by Montagu; the big merchants of Cape Town and the Eastern Cape settlers led by Godlonton together with the newly arrived Anglican bishop, Robert Gray. They established a new conservative newspaper, the *Cape Monitor*, in October 1850. On the other side were the radicals, both British and Afrikaner, led by Fairbairn, Christoffel Brand, Reitz, and Andries Stockenström. They were united in their crusade against the corruption and nepotism of oligarchy but divided on frontier policy, at least until war broke out. Then Fairbairn joined Stockenström in criticizing Smith's policy as serving the interests of a war-profiteering elite of merchants and settlers.[170]

In the Eastern Cape the Godlontonians were not only disliked by the Boers but also by increasing numbers of British. Port Elizabeth, for example, was coming into its own as the main commercial rival of Grahamstown, and a "midlands axis" was arising, aligning Afrikaner Graaff-Reinet and English Port Elizabeth against the settler Albany district. Godlonton's diehard support for Smith further discredited him in the east.[171]

Early in 1850, Earl Grey submitted to Smith his constitutional proposals on behalf of the Colonial Office in London and instructed him to summon the Legislative Council to fill in its details. But even Smith could see that the existing Legislative Council was discredited and he turned to municipalities and district road boards (the only elected institutions in

---

[169] K. McKenzie, *Scandal in the Colonies: Sydney and Cape Town, 1820–1850* (Melbourne: Melbourne University Press, 2004), pp. 174–9.

[170] Le Cordeur, "Eastern Cape Separatism," p. 214; Keegan, *Colonial South Africa*, pp. 222–4, 235–6, 245, 282, 348, 350; Mostert, *Frontiers*, pp. 947, 975–6, 988–9; Legassick, "The State, Racism and the Rise of Capitalism," p. 357. On Stockenström's views at this time, see Du Toit and Giliomee, *Afrikaner Political Thought*, pp. 140, 180–181; on Afrikaner thinking on representative government see *ibid.*, pp. 250–1, 291–9, and on frontier policy, see *ibid.*, pp. 183–8; A. Du Toit, "The Cape Afrikaner's Failed Liberal Moment," in J. Butler, R. Elphick, and D. Welsh (Eds.), *Democratic Liberalism in South Africa* (Cape Town: David Philip, 1987), pp. 35–63.

[171] B. A. Le Cordeur, "Robert Godlonton as Architect of Frontier Opinion, 1850–57," *Archives Year Book for South African History*, I (1959), p. 2.

the colony) to nominate new candidates for it. Those thus unofficially elected overwhelmingly represented the popular party – Stockenström, in particular, enjoying overwhelming support in the east as well as some in the west. Smith, however, appointed Godlonton to the fifth seat on the council, though he had not received the fifth-largest number of votes. The four popular members soon resigned from the council. Smith promptly accused them of wanting to be without any government whatever." Together with the Cape Town municipality, they drew up and promoted a popular draft constitution, delegating Fairbairn and Stockenström to travel to London to lobby for it.[172] Those who backed the move fell into two camps: Some wanted to ensure that all the Dutch males had the vote, even at the expense of enfranchising a number of the coloreds; others saw the enfranchisement of the coloreds as a way of redressing Dutch numerical preeminence over the English.

There were two counterarguments. The first was the conservative fear that the low franchise would lead to the British being swamped at the polls by coloreds, under the influence of the despised missionaries, and, indeed, by the "uncivilized" Boers.[173] At the other end of the social spectrum, many coloreds feared that any form of representative government would entrench their oppressors in power and establish vagrancy laws and other coercive labor legislation. Similar viewpoints were expressed even at conservative missions like Genadendal and formed the main ideological basis of the Kat River Rebellion.[174]

Thus, the arguments over constitutional developments became entangled in the renewed war between the colony and the amaXhosa, in many ways the resumption of the War of the Axe, which was precipitated by Smith's decision to depose Sandile, part of a concerted campaign to emasculate Xhosa chiefs and household heads. In consequence, there was space for a war prophet. Mlanjeni, a teenager who found relief from his tuberculosis by spending most of his time in the river, proclaimed new ways to counteract witchcraft and gave hope to those who, having lost everything, had gone to work on the white farms. In large numbers they began to return to Xhosaland where they were incorporated into military plans of Maqoma, who became the real war leader. Mlanjeni's influence declined after the war began.

---

[172] Keegan, *Colonial South Africa*, pp. 230–1; Le Cordeur, "Eastern Cape Separatism," p. 225; A. Ross, *Philip*, pp. 211–2; Ross, *Status*, p. 170; A. H. Duminy, "The Role of Sir Andries Stockenström in Cape Politics," *Archives Year Book for South African History*, 22 (II) (1960).

[173] Le Cordeur, "Eastern Cape Separatism," pp. 268–9.

[174] Ross, *Status*, pp. 168, 170; Crais, *Colonial Order*, p. 185; Williams, *When Races Meet*, p. 132.

At its outset, the amaXhosa overran the frontier, destroying the new settler villages of Woburn, Auckland, and Juanasberg and bottling Sir Harry Smith up in Fort Cox. An attempt to relieve the siege was beaten off, but eventually Smith escaped, disguised as a private Khoekhoe soldier. The amaXhosa were particularly concerned to attack the English, whom they (rightly) considered responsible for their plight. They were joined, for the first time since 1799, by some of the Khoekhoen, in what was known, metonymically, as the Kat River Rebellion. It was led first by Hermanus Matroos, who had been humiliated by the British during the War of the Axe. As a result, he had made his peace with Maqoma and acted as a Xhosa chief in the Blinkwater Valley. He was able to build a following both from among some of those in the settlement who had been enraged by the treatment by successive magistrates and from among the Khoekhoe farm laborers. All in all, their rebellion was driven by the treatment of coloreds by British settlers; the devastation caused by the frontier wars (with no or belated compensation); the fierce desire not to return to a condition of slavery; the fear of representative government; and the fact that they had little to lose. As Elbourne intimates, whereas many rebels had lost faith in the government of Queen Victoria, others still looked to it as the fount of justice, their natural protector against the dangers of representative government. The revolt began to gather strength despite attempts by the missionaries to quell it. Between a third and half of the Kat River's inhabitants went into revolt. Residents of the Moravian missions at Enon and Shiloh joined, as did some from Bethelsdorp and all but two from Theopolis. Besides these, some Cape Mounted Riflemen deserted, or in some cases, mutinied to join. The paramilitary Xhosa police, who had been recruited after the War of the Axe to control the frontier and had been used, for instance, to burn huts in the Kat River in the winter of 1850, joined Maqoma with their weapons and ammunition in what was evidently a preplanned action. Mfengu at first refused to reenlist for military service.[175]

At this stage, the British were severely short of military manpower. The Boers, angry at British settler profiteering from war, refused to turn out.

---

[175] Ross, "Hermanus Matroos"; R. Ross, "Ambiguities of Resistance and Collaboration on the Eastern Cape Frontier: The Kat River Settlement, 1829–1856," in J. Abbink, M. de Bruijn, and K. van Walraven (Eds.), *Rethinking Resistance: Revolt and Violence in African History* (Leiden & Boston: Brill, 2003), pp. 117–41; E. Elbourne, "'Race,' Warfare and Religion in Mid-nineteenth Century Southern Africa: The Khoikhoi Rebellion Against the Cape Colony and its Uses, 1850–1858," *Journal of African Cultural Studies, 13* (2000), pp. 17–42; Stapleton, *Maqoma*, p. 153. Also, Crais, *Colonial Order*, pp. 177–180, 183–4; Sales, pp. 135–55; Williams, *When Races Meet*, pp. 154–95; Keegan, *Colonial South Africa*, pp. 238–9; K. I. Watson, "African Sepoys? The Black Police on the Eastern Cape Frontier: 1835–1850," *Kleio, 28* (1996), pp. 62–78.

The British were compelled to place a greater reliance on Mfengu troops, some 400 of whom participated. Hostility between amaMfengu and colored rebels was sharp, with coloreds acting out their resentment of Mfengu labor undercutting and pressure on land. In July, moreover, Read noted: "The Fingoes have done great service for Government, and the Colony in this war, but have made themselves odious to the Caffres, and should there be an opportunity the revenge will be fearful."[176] The British also had the support of the amaGqunukhwebe, which was fortunate for them because Gqunukhwebe territory lay across the crucial supply line from the port of East London to King Williams Town in the center of the war zone. Moreover, the amaNdlambe, save for one minor chief, remained neutral, and some chiefs joined the colonial side.[177]

The initial Ngqika-colored strategy, with the Kat River valley, and particularly the Waterkloof (Mtontsi),[178] as the center of its operations, was to besiege and try to capture the principal British forts – Fort Cox, Fort White, Fort Beaufort, Fort Hare, all of which were more camps than forts and were weakly fortified. It was essential for the British to hold these forts. If they lost them, it would probably swing the amaNdlambe, and even the amaGqunukhwebe, to enter the war against them as well as persuading wavering coloreds to join the rebellion. Attacks on Fort White, led by Sandile, and Fort Beaufort, led by Maqoma and Hermanus Matroos, failed, and Matroos was killed. A later attack on Fort Hare also failed, despite the presence of 5,000 to 6,000 amaXhosa. Only Fort Armstrong, in the Kat River valley and garrisoned by the Kat River militia, surrendered on January 22, 1851, to Willem Uithaalder, Matroos's successor, who had served in the Cape Mounted Rifles. Though it was strategically irrelevant, the British were determined to recapture the fort. On February 22, they launched an attack. Both the regular army and British settler levies marched through the valley, burning crops and houses, whether of rebels or loyalists, in an orgy of revenge. The settlers advocated "Extermination" on the flag they flew. As a result, a number of the Kat River people who had been wavering were driven into revolt and others, notably Andries Botha, who took to the bush to avoid the columns, were later unjustly accused of rebellion.

Thereafter, the main theater of the war centered on the Waterkloof, between the Kat and the Koenap valleys. This, with its thick jungle-like bush and steep ravines – brilliantly described by Mostert – was a far

---

[176] Read to Freeman, LMS 26/2/B Alice, 9/7/1851; Moyer, "The Mfengu, Self Defence and the Cape Frontier Wars," pp. 116–7; Mostert, *Frontiers*.

[177] Stapleton, *Maqoma*, pp. 151–2; Mostert, *Frontiers*, pp. 1071–2; Peires, *The Dead will Arise*, p. 16.

[178] This account follows Stapleton, *Maqoma*; Mostert, *Frontiers*; Peires, *The Dead will Arise*; Crais, *Colonial Order*.

more difficult terrain for the British to negotiate in their fight with the amaXhosa than even the Fish River bush or the Amatole. Thence, and from the other fastnesses, small bands of amaXhosa issued to attack white farms. The campaign to reduce the kloof began in September 1851 and lasted until March 1853. Maqoma was joined by Uithaalder and the other main Khoekhoe leader, Hans Brander, in a war within a war, in which the British troops experienced unrelieved hardship, which eventually led to serious disquiet. In this war 4,000 troops were tied down – against possibly few more than 200 poorly equipped men. Maqoma's successes in defeating crack British troops marked him as the greatest Xhosa soldier, and his feats are remembered in many oral traditions.[179]

With the amaXhosa still in occupation in the colony, and with the troops stymied against Maqoma, British forces were ordered in November across the Kei, as they had been in 1835 and 1847, to invade Gcaleka territory. One officer called it "the Great Cattle Patrol." Sarhili offered little resistance, and some 30,000 head of cattle were seized.

While the war was being fought out in the Eastern Cape, it reverberated in the west. Prisoners from the Kat River were being used to build the road over Bain's Kloof. At the same time, the government had introduced an ordinance to prevent the practice of squatting on government land, which was seen as a means of restricting the independence of colored laborers. The agricultural community of the Western Cape became convinced that a revolt of its laborers was brewing, and rumors to this effect spread through, in particular, the district of Malmesbury, to the north of Cape Town. Farmers even took their families into laager to defend themselves against the uprising, which was said to be planned for December 1, 1851, the anniversary of emancipation. In the event, although the panic proved baseless, the government did withdraw the planned squatters ordinance.[180]

At this stage, the various strands of policy and action became even more intertwined. The British government in London decided to retreat from Transorangia and sent out two commissioners to arrange the abandonment of the Orange River Sovereignty. The Boer elite of the southwest Transvaal was able to begin, as the "forward representatives of colonial capitalism,"[181] the negotiations that would lead to the Sand River Convention and the formal independence of what was to be the South African Republic, with

[179] Peires, *The Dead Will Arise*, p. 15; Stapleton, *Maqoma*, pp. 160, 166–7, 219–21; Mostert, *Frontiers*, p. 1127.

[180] E. Bradlow, "The 'Great Fear' at the Cape of Good Hope, 1851–2," *International Journal of African Historical Studies*, 22(3) (1989), pp. 401–52; J. Marincowitz, "From 'Colour Question' to 'Agrarian Problem' at the Cape: Reflections on the Interim," in H. Macmillan and S. Marks (Eds.), *Africa and Empire, W. M. Macmillan, Historian and Social Critic* (London: Temple Smith, 1989), pp. 153–67.

[181] Keegan, *Colonial South Africa*, pp. 271–5.

the British forewear all alliances with black rulers and giving the Transvalers a monopoly over colonial arms. Attempts to make peace with Moshoeshoe failed, and it was believed that the British "are beaten at all points, in the Fish River bush, in the Waterkloof, and across the Orange River."[182] Smith was recalled, and the costs of war brought down the British government. The amaXhosa, who had sued for peace, withdrew their offer, emboldened by the wreck of the *Birkenhead*, bringing new troops to the Cape in the hope of receiving better terms from the new governor.

The British army responded with a murderous campaign, executing all the amaXhosa they captured, irrespective of age or sex, scorching the earth – as had been their tactic as far back as 1812 – and launching a successful expedition up the Waterkloof under Lieutenant-Colonel Eyre, who had become a specialist in counteracting the jungle-war tactics of the amaXhosa. The settler elite made a last attempt to maintain its power with a propaganda campaign. The Stockenström–Fairbairn mission to Europe and the argument for a low franchise were attacked for their supposed and spurious connection with the Kat River Rebellion. Because Stockenström's farm near Bedford was the only one in the area not ransacked (Sandile had posted a guard on it), anonymous settlers burned the farmhouse to the ground while Stockenström was in London.[183] But the settler elite was fighting a rear-guard action on the constitution.

Settler imperialism, assisted by the "rogue governor" Smith, failed in its objectives of colonial expansion because it evoked massive resistance from both Boers and black people. Attempts to dispossess independent chiefdoms brought not support but intensified resistance from the Boers. British politicians in midcentury were not prepared to foot the bills for the wars that resulted and wanted to shift financial and military responsibilities to the colonists. The settlers' "ambitions for self-aggrandizement outstripped the economic potential that could be realized." Britain's interests should be secured through free trade and representative government to broaden the base of white rule rather than the 1840s and early 1850s militarization of colonial society. This was what the new Governor Cathcart, arriving at the Cape on March 30, 1852, was sent to bring about.[184]

The Establishment of Representative Government

As Cathcart arrived, Montagu, like Smith, departed from office, harassed by numerous petitions for his dismissal. Cathcart established himself on the frontier to end the war, with a lieutenant-governor, Charles Darling,

---

[182] Mostert, *Frontiers*, pp. 1132–3.

[183] Keegan, *Colonial South Africa*, p. 235; Le Cordeur, "Eastern Cape Separatism," p. 246; Mostert, *Frontiers*, pp. 1100–02, 1159.

[184] Keegan, *Colonial South Africa*, pp. 244, 278, 285–6.

in Cape Town. Together they initiated a political revolution comparable to that of Bourke in 1827–8. This entailed, first, the establishment of peace, or, in other words, the defeat of the amaXhosa and Khoekhoen. In the process, the Kat River Khoekhoen were further harried. Andries Botha, longtime pro-British military and, at most, a reluctant and short-term rebel, was convicted for high treason in South Africa's first political show trial and sentenced to death, though he was later reprieved. Then Cathcart and Eyre launched a particularly vicious campaign through the Waterkloof and into the Amatole Mountains, finally breaking Xhosa resistance. Sandile's deposition was rescinded and peace was concluded on March 2, 1853, after the second-longest war in South African history, which had left at least 16,000 amaXhosa and 1,400 on the British side dead. Before this, Cathcart had gone to revenge Moshoeshoe's victory at Viervoet but, in December 1852, Basotho cavalry had overwhelmed Cathcart's smaller force though Moshoeshoe tactfully allowed him to claim a victory and return to the colony. A couple of years later, the British would, by the Bloemfontein convention, allow the establishment of the Orange Free State to the fury of the Eastern Cape land speculators, but not to their long-term disadvantage.

The war had been brutal, with a "no prisoners policy" on the part of the British and gruesome torture practiced by the amaXhosa on prisoners.[185] It has been described as a war of race, but it was directed by the amaXhosa against the British and their black collaborators, not against the Boers.[186] In pitting the colonized proletariat against their colonial masters, it was also a war of class during which attempts were made to forge black nationalisms, transcending the distinctions of chief and commoner, landowner and landless; between amaXhosa and Khoekhoen; on the basis of the histories of oppression that they had all had experienced and discussed together.[187] However, the war was lost, and with it, for the amaNgqika, the Amatole. Maqoma's and Sandile's lands finally fell into the hands of the speculators, and border tracts were handed to the loyalist chiefs and their subjects, such as the amaGqunukhwebe, and to the amaMfengu. British Kaffraria remained a separate dependency, despite settler pressures for its incorporation into the colony. Colonel Maclean was appointed as its lieutenant-governor. In 1859, more than 6,000 Germans were settled along the supply line between East London and King Williams Town.

On April 21, 1853, little more than a month after the signing of peace with the amaXhosa, the new representative government constitution for the colony arrived in Cape Town. In Britain, a coalition of Whigs and Peelites

[185] Peires, *The Dead Will Arise*, pp. 23–5; Mostert, *Frontiers*, pp. 1096, 1117, 1142.
[186] Mostert, *Frontiers*, p. 1077.   [187] Crais, *Colonial Order*, pp. 174, 186–8.

had taken over government and broken the deadlock on the constitution that had prevailed throughout the war. The new colonial secretary, the Duke of Newcastle, advised Cathcart to stop all consideration of separatism or removal of the capital and to ratify the constitution immediately. He also restored the £25 property franchise (or a £50 salary a year) but agreed with the conservatives to double the financial qualification for membership of the Upper House. The Upper House, however, was to be elected, not nominated. The franchise in the Cape Colony was, in fact, lower, that is, more liberal, than that in Britain at the time. Conservative settlers were mortified. In a private letter Newcastle explained to Cathcart that the concessions were to prevent "the revival of political agitation at the close of the war," arguing the need to preserve the "rising commercial classes" at the Cape as allies. The aim, in other words, was the empowerment of the development-oriented classes that supported the popular party: They wanted stable conditions in which capital could be raised for infrastructure and company formation.[188]

The low franchise was based on a double calculation. On the one hand, it was intended to consolidate the stress of Afrikaners on their status as subjects of a British colony, rather than of Dutch descent. Thus, in 1850, Christoffel Brand complained that the attorney-general regarded the Eastern Cape British as "the only true British portion of the Colony," whereas he, too, was an adopted British subject. He was to become the first speaker of the House of Representatives. On the other, it was to recapture many of the small colored property owners who had rebelled and to break the colored–Xhosa alliance of unfree labor that had begun to develop in the uprising.

"I would rather meet the Hottentot at the hustings, voting for his representative," declared the attorney general, Porter, a defender of the low franchise, "than meet the Hottentot in the wolds with his gun on his shoulder."[189] It is at least arguable that the low franchise would not have been driven through had it not been for the Kat River Rebellion. Thus philanthropy and humanitarianism played little part in the passage of the low and nonracial franchise. Equally, no humanitarianism remained with regard to the fate of the people of the chiefdoms – "savages," as Fairbairn continued to call them. Only in 1865, when British Kaffraria was finally incorporated in the colony, could the black propertied become voters.[190]

---

[188] Le Cordeur, "Eastern Cape Separatism," pp. 265–7; Keegan, *Colonial South Africa*, pp. 245, 247.

[189] Quoted by Ross, *Status*, pp. 50–1, 171; on Brand, see also Du Toit and Giliomee, *Afrikaner Political Thought*, pp. 250–1.

[190] Keegan, *Colonial South Africa*, pp. 245, 289, 357; Legassick, "The State, Racism and the Rise Of Capitalism," p. 358.

CONCLUSION

Had it been left to the Boers and indigenous people to work things out for themselves, South Africa might have become a different place. Instead, it was the British, at the height of their world power, who were in command in the first half of the nineteenth century. The first effect was to inflict, from the time of the war of 1812, serious damage upon the balance of Xhosa society with nature – a far cry from the effects of the desultory skirmishes that had been the "first" and "second" frontier wars. By mid-century, at least the Ciskeian amaXhosa were under British rule, crowded onto insufficient land, and had become cheap labor for the colony.

Historians, writes Crais, have, in the past, "danced around the period, chanting praise for the enlightenment and exalting the arrival of liberalism, forgetting how the former was enormously paradoxical and the latter profoundly Janus-faced."[191] Together with the humanitarian anti–forced-labor side (itself riddled with contradictions), British rule and the increased integration of South Africa into the world economy of nineteenth-century capitalism brought the radically new idea that African societies should be subjugated and ruled in the interests of the colonial economy. Thus, British influence hardened the hierarchies of race and strengthened the hegemony of white colonists.[192]

Militarily, there was a progressive displacement of the Boer commando, the classic colonial fighting instrument of the eighteenth century, until, by the 1846–7 and 1850–53 wars against the amaXhosa, the Boers were uninterested in fighting, at least in the Eastern Cape – wars for the expansion of Afrikaner control north of the Gariep were normal enough. Correspondingly, the brunt of the front-line fighting came to be undertaken by Khoekhoen or colored and, later, Mfengu soldiers, strengthened by the core of the British regulars and, sometimes, by British settler levies.

After the government authorities' hostility to early Bethelsdorp they came to see Christianity and respectability, as preached by the missionaries, as necessary to secure the loyalty of the Khoekhoen/coloreds, and later the amaMfengu, to the colony in fights against the amaXhosa. Contrary, however, to the hopes of Philip that coloreds would act as intermediaries in the efforts to civilize the amaXhosa, their military force was used to clear land for white settlement, both on the eastern and (in a more complex way) northern borders of the colony. In 1870, no longer needed, the colored

---

[191] C. Crais, "Race, the State, and the Silence of History in the Making of Modern South Africa: Preliminary Departures," (Africa Seminar, Centre for African Studies, University of Cape Town, July 1992), pp. 3, 7–8.

[192] Keegan, *Colonial South Africa*, p. 292.

Cape Mounted Rifles was disbanded, replaced by the white Frontier Armed and Mounted Police.[193]

The idea of civilizing in fact served to create "the other," the barbarian. In this way Philip's adaptation of the early egalitarianism of van der Kemp – together with his support for British annexations – prepared the way for conquest. At the same time, many of the missionaries assisted in empowering the Khoesan, transforming them into coloreds and creating an independent elite. By midcentury a self-conscious Christianized colored community had emerged, formed from slaves and Khoesan, with a certain infusion of European descent as well as of amaXhosa. Their Christianity entailed civilization, according to the tenets of their white patrons, not merely in terms of values and ways of life but also totally abandoning independence and submitting to the paternalism of their white patrons. This submission began with the Wesleyans, pandering to their part-settler flock, and by the 1840s only the Reads actively resisted the missionaries' consensus. After the earlier hostility between state and missionaries there was now no longer simply cooperation but the interchange of personnel between mission and state, as in the case of Calderwood.

A similar process occurred with regard to the law. A new legal system took shape in the 1820s and 1830s, initially on the basis of formal equality. To the extent that the Great Trek was a rebellion, it was against this. However, as the British settlers came to be the motivating force of colonial society during the 1830s, the legal system was turned by white colonist pressure into an instrument of racial subjugation – directed also against the amaXhosa. This was a colonial postslavery society in which the key point of coercion lay in the law rather than in the personal authority of the master.

By midcentury a new concept had become popular – that of "extermination," which, as we have seen, appeared on a banner carried by British settler levies in the 1850–53 war, after Smith had called for the extermination of the amaXhosa. Smith did not mean in the polite way in which the term has often been interpreted by historians, merely displacing people geographically – driving the amaXhosa across the Kei. He meant killing people off. At the time Charles Stretch, former diplomatic agent to the amaXhosa, wrote of Smith's "extermination" policy that he "invited the colonists to come and shoot the Caffres without mercy."[194] The settlers, with J. M. Bowker as the main ideologue[195] and Smith following behind them, moved from humanitarian fear that European settlement would lead

---

[193] Maclennan, *Proper Degree of Terror*, p. 224.

[194] Mostert, *Frontiers*, p. 1096. See also Peires, *House of Phalo*, p. 113, for Smith's use of the term in August 1835.

[195] Ross, *John Philip*, pp. 189–91, remains the best description of this intellectual movement.

to the disappearance of the aboriginal inhabitants to the belief that it was a law of nature that indigenous peoples *would* disappear against the onward march of "European civilization" and then, as with the settlers, that they *should* disappear. The model for the expanding Cape Colony became, in other words, not India, but Australasia and North America. The only argument was whether the higher civilization of the British would reverse the process.

These ideas were to be belied by the continued resistance of the amaXhosa (despite the cattle-killing) and the failure, ultimately, to exterminate the blacks of South Africa (a prominent theme in the writings of de Kiewiet).[196] Maqoma set the precedent, his adaptation of new tactics for dealing with the British being compared by Stapleton with that of Samori Toure in West Africa later.[197] But in the nineteenth century, buttressed by British power, the ideas of extermination persisted among whites, no longer dressed up as history but eventually as evolutionary science, drawing on the ideas of Social Darwinism – of survival of the fittest, of British race pride, and of South Africa as a "white man's country."

From about 1844 a new era of imperial expansion began in Southern Africa. Its impetus was the rise of local rural capitalism with its needs for land and labor and with it the rise of a racist discourse. This grew into an expansionist drive, essentially of capital accumulation, in land, trade, wool, and finance, that was partially curtailed in the 1850s but in which the speculators would once again harness the imperial machine in the 1870s in Kimberley and later on the Witwatersrand. As a result of, and together with this, the colony entered between 1846 and 1853 a more severe crisis than that of 1799–1803, beset by divisions at the top, rebellion within and from the Boers outside, two bitterly fought wars against the amaXhosa both inside and outside, and the beginnings of military confrontation with Moshoeshoe. Indeed, far from stabilizing Southern Africa, Smith plunged it into its biggest conflicts to that time and put British rule at risk – while also militarizing the region.

The rescue for the British government was the institution of representative government – on a basis that involved the defeat of the Godlontonian elite by the "popular party." Nevertheless, the kind of government that emerged under representativity on the basis of the low nonracial franchise was certainly one in which the old power of settler capitalism and white

---

[196] C. W. de Kiewiet, *A History of South Africa, Social & Economic* (Oxford: Clarendon Press, 1941).

[197] Stapleton, *Maqoma*, p. 221; M. Legassick, "Firearms, Horses, and Samorian Army Organisation, 1870–1898," *Journal of African History*, VII (1) (1966), pp. 95–115; Peires, *House of Phalo*, p. 160.

supremacy was maintained. Throughout the period from 1800, in fact, "abstractions of freedom and equality existed in, served to reproduce, and were unable to explain, capitalist society as a class society."[198]

Conservatives defending white agrarian interests dominated representation in parliament and in the local state. Already in the first session of parliament there was discussion of vagrancy and other coercive legislation. The 1856 Masters and Servants Act was a notoriously severe measure that, through amendments to pass laws in 1857, brought blacks as well as browns under it.[199] Whereas coloreds at the Kat River voted overwhelmingly for Stockenström, in parliament he too was influenced by whites demanding repressive legislation. Coloreds, in fact, "were to be a marginal factor in the electoral politics of the Colony."[200] Some Africans, at first particularly amaMfengu, succeeded in becoming, for a period, acculturated and prosperous rich or middle peasants who, with the incorporation of British Kaffraria in 1865, allowed them to vote.[201] By the time in the 1880s that the Afrikaner Bond challenged British domination of the legislature, the Eastern Cape was able to defeat Afrikaners with the assistance of the black vote.[202]

Though both coloreds and Africans were marginal, the extension of the nonracial franchise at first differentially to colored and amaXhosa strengthened the differences between them, in particular between their elites. Crais, as we have seen, believes the elements of a cross-ethnic proletarian consciousness were coming into being during the 1850–53 revolt. However, these were a scattered rural proletariat, not yet a working class in factories producing collectively. The 1850–53 revolt had far more in common with the methods of "Captain Swing" – the rural revolt in Britain in 1830 – than with the German Social Democratic Party from the 1890s, for example, though it was far more organized and sharpened by the military experience of the Khoekhoen and the skillful military tactics of the amaXhosa.

If this is the case, then the events of the early 1850s, both the war and the new constitutional arrangements, sharpened the divisions within those

---

[198] Legassick, "The State, Racism and the Rise of Capitalism," p. 338; Ross, *Status*, p. 175.
[199] Crais, *Colonial Order*, pp. 193–4.   [200] Keegan, *Colonial South Africa*, p. 247.
[201] *Ibid.*, pp. 289–90; C. Bundy, *The Rise and Fall of the South African Peasantry* (London: Heinemann, 1979); H. Bradford, "Peasants, Historians and Gender: A South African Case Study Revisited, 1850–1886," *History and Theory, 39*(4) (2000), pp. 86–110; J. Lewis, "An Economic History of the Ciskei, c. 1848–1900," unpublished Ph.D. thesis, University of Cape Town (1984); Switzer, *Power and Resistance*, pp. 80–96.
[202] S. Trapido, "'The Friends of the Natives': Merchants, Peasants and the Political and Ideological Structure of Liberalism at the Cape, 1854–1910," in S. Marks and A. Atmore (Eds.), *Economy and Society in Pre-Industrial South Africa* (London: Longmans, 1980), pp. 247–74.

whom the colonial authorities and the white elite increasingly came to see as coloreds. On the one hand, there were the agricultural proletarians, whose limited capacity for collective resistance was finally crushed by the failure of the revolt. On the other, there were those who were claiming respectability and acceptance and whose political (though not social) aspirations within the new structures had not yet been disappointed. It was a bifurcation that went back to the aftermath of Ordinance 50 and emancipation, and which long survived the period discussed in this chapter. It was also a process that would be mirrored among the amaXhosa and other African groups. In both cases, the racial categorization of colonial society obscured the increasing social diversity of coloreds and Africans, but that very diversity long precluded the formation of a unified opposition to colonial hegemony.

James Read Jr., son of a Khoekhoe mother, forlornly watching smoke rising over Fort Hare on January 21, 1851, wrote "who that was acquainted with the facts of history, could for a moment think otherwise than that the Colony would at last conquer the Kaffirs? Though for a time the Kaffirs and Hottentots might triumph, that triumph would be ephemeral and short-lived, and soon would England reassert her supremacy as the mistress of Southern Africa . . . Insane must have been the man that could have thought otherwise."[203] Read's conclusion was correct. Incorporation for the indigenous was inevitable. The real question was the terms on which it would occur, with what history, and what consciousness of that history. The destruction of the Khoesan social fabric already by 1800 gave them a susceptibility to the Christian culture of the missionaries, and this, together with the role of the mission stations and the vote, gave them an advantage in the colony over the amaXhosa. Ironically, having been conquered, very many of the amaXhosa converted to Christianity – on their own terms, often syncretic, often semimillenarian "Zionist" terms, but also often in precisely the ways, no longer fashionable among missionaries, that van der Kemp and James Read Sr. had propagated.[204] Moreover, despite the mineral revolution and segregation, industrialization, apartheid, and Bantustanization, which undermined it economically and politically, the efforts of colonialism to destroy the cultural roots of Xhosa society have not succeeded to this day.

---

[203] Mostert, *Frontiers*, p. 1089.
[204] On this, see i.a. Chapter 8, in this volume.

7

FROM COLONIAL HEGEMONIES TO IMPERIAL
CONQUEST, 1840–1880

NORMAN ETHERINGTON, PATRICK HARRIES,
AND BERNARD K. MBENGA

The period covered by this chapter is marked by the expansion of power exercised by Europeans or their descendants in South Africa. In the Cape Colony, power shifted from a series of military governors to local officials elected under a nonracial, qualified franchise. A more original form of government emerged in Natal, where representatives of the metropolitan government ruled the African population while colonists of European descent exercised only limited political powers. In the interior, Boer settlers built two fragile republics on the basis of a racial franchise limited to white men. The growth and expansion of these very different settler states was conditional upon the conquest of the original inhabitants and the alienation of their land. Wool-farming and plantation agriculture, and later the mining of diamonds in the interior, brought a new urgency to the development of the British colonies and to demands for land and labor. The swell of change was carried far beyond the confines of British rule as people adopted new identities more suitable to their changed situation. Race grew into a primary factor of social classification, belonging, and exclusion and, over time, came to be regarded by many as a scientific means of explanation. The delineation and transcription of languages divided people into ethnic groups that rapidly developed their own values, practices, and histories. During this period, Christianity spread up the coast and into the interior. Many converts adopted the Christian beliefs and practices brought to Africa from Europe whereas others adapted them to local conditions. In some areas class-consciousness grew in importance whereas gender relations, based on the social practices associated with sexual difference, underwent extensive change. As the labor market expanded, many young African men returned home with wages and freedoms that challenged the gerontocratic structure of rural life.

For many, the forced march of progress quickened the rhythm of existence and undermined the stability of an older, more secure world. Original answers had to be found to new problems that affected the most isolated villages as much as they did the urban centers. Perhaps most notably, economic change and movement started to give a unity to the extended spaces that would one day find a political coherence as South Africa.

CONFLICT ON THE CAPE'S EASTERN FRONTIER

A brief period of peace came to the troubled area east of the Fish River during the late 1830s and early 1840s. The influence of humanitarians on the British government had caused the annexation of the area between the Fish and Kei rivers to be rescinded, after which direct rule was limited to amaMfengu immigrants settled by the British in the vicinity of Fort Peddie. Elsewhere, a series of treaties governed the relations between the British colonial government and the leaders of independent Xhosa and Griqua communities. These treaties deflected the Boers' drive for land away from the coastal plain to the dry interior, where they settled alongside immigrant Griqua communities and native Sotho-Tswana speakers. The treaties also placed the onus on the remaining white farmers to protect their herds and prohibited them from sending armed commandos to retrieve their stolen cattle or to extort compensation from frontier chiefs. The British further consolidated their recognition of Xhosa sovereignty by installing diplomatic agents, without the support of soldiers or police on the chiefs' lands, to oversee the application of the treaties.[1] This sudden reversal of policy underlined the tension between direct rule and assimilation, on the one hand, and various shades of indirect rule and territorial separation, on the other. It was to color life on this frontier over the next forty years by juxtaposing a policy of economic and cultural intercourse with that of intrusive military rule. The one was a cheap means of colonizing the consciousness of the amaXhosa; but its results were less immediately visible than those imposed by military conquest. The Cape's frontier politics would slew between these two poles throughout the period covered by this chapter.[2]

Powerful commercial interests wanted a stronger British presence on the frontier, as an army consumed local goods created a climate of confidence for investment and immigration and, in general, was expected to advance the interests of the settlers. Many farmers had benefited from slave compensation payments and the availability of cheap land vacated by Dutch-speaking emigrants in the mid-to-late 1830s. When the price of wool boomed in the

---

[1] J. B. Peires, *The House of Phalo* (Johannesburg: Ravan Press, 1981), pp. 119–21; John Frye (Ed.), *The War of the Axe and the Xhosa bible: The journal of the Rev. J. W. Applewood* (Cape Town: C. Struik, 1971).

[2] A point particularly made by T. Keegan, *Colonial South Africa and the origins of the Racial order* (Cape Town: David Philip, 1996).

early 1840s, and with it the cost of land, these farmers called on government to abandon the treaty system and annex unproductive African lands. They had strong ties to commercial interests in garrison towns along the frontier and, being mainly British settlers, had stronger links to government than the established Boer farmers. As their confidence grew with their wealth, these sheep farmers exercised an increasing influence on the administration.[3]

Metropolitan interests were also changing at this time. The humanitarian lobby declined in importance when slavery finally came to an end throughout the empire in 1838. The mighty experiment engendered by the costly liberation of slaves seemed to falter and fail as workers left the West Indian plantations and the price of sugar soared in Britain, and when free traders sought to open the British market to sugar produced by slaves in Cuba and Brazil, humanitarians found themselves politically marginalized. Intellectuals like Carlyle and Dickens would soon pour scorn on the hypocrisy of the "telescopic philanthropy" that favored inscrutable pagans in foreign lands rather than the poor at home. The humanitarians at the Cape had advocated the adoption of a package of freedoms by native peoples. These included freedom from slavery and servitude, free enterprise and free trade, freedom of religion and worship. But an integral part of this package was freedom from what was seen as the dark superstitions of tribal life, such as polygamy and bridewealth, and from dancing and the consumption of liquor. Most Africans found it difficult to abandon customs that, in the case of bridewealth, provided the payments needed for a son to marry and establish his own homestead. Through the consumption of liquor, and by participating in dancing, people constructed community ties that extended beyond those of kinship. For many, the power of ancestors or witches seemed more immediate than the interventions of a transcendent Supreme Being. However, the humanitarians saw these practices in starkly different ways. Bridewealth and polygamy enslaved African women, drinking and dancing were considered to be signs of ascendant savagery, and witchcraft and ancestor worship were products of diabolical agency. When Africans refused to abandon these practices and beliefs, or when Christian converts slid back into the dark maw of paganism, humanitarians experienced a sense of betrayal. The refusal of Africans to accept the leadership of the missionaries, or their cultural absolutism, would gradually undermine the strength of the humanitarian movement at the Cape.[4]

---

[3] B. le Cordeur, *The Politics of Eastern Cape Separatism, 1820–1854* (New York: Oxford Univeristy Press, 1981).

[4] L. Switzer, *Power and resistance in an African Society: the Ciskei Xhosa and the Making of South Africa* (Pietermaritzburg: University of Natal Press, 1993), pp. 115–35.

These changes reverberated on the eastern frontier as early as 1839 when an impetuous British colonel, John Hare, replaced Stockenstrom as lieutenant-governor. They grew in magnitude as the influence of James Read was all but effaced by a new generation of missionaries that, led by Henry Calderwood, threatened to impose Christianity on the amaXhosa by force. The decline of the humanitarian lobby also was felt at Cape Town where aging liberals like John Philip and his son-in-law, John Fairbairn, mounted little resistance when, in July 1844, Hare proposed a military reoccupation of the lands west of the Kei. Two months later a new governor, Lieutenant-General Sir Peregrine Maitland, finally annulled the treaty system and allowed farmers once again to follow their stolen cattle. At the same time, he prohibited independent Xhosa chiefs from applying tribal law and custom to Christians living in their areas.

By extending the thin wedge of colonial rule across the Fish River in this manner, Maitland effectively brought the dynamics of conflict back to the frontier. The vicious cycle of drought, cattle rustling, and armed reprisals grew during the summer of 1845–46 when the rains failed to fall. When a Xhosa rescue party freed a prisoner accused of stealing an axe, the British sent a force of regulars, Cape Mounted Rifles and colonial militia across the Fish River. The Seventh Frontier War marked a new level of viciousness on the frontier. The amaXhosa were far better armed, albeit with old flintlock guns, than a decade earlier. They fought out of desperation to prevent the British from expelling them from their lands and out of fear that they would be broken up, like the Khoekhoen, and scattered across the farms, like the amaMfengu. They tortured and killed prisoners, mutilated the corpses of their enemies and, when they crossed the frontier, burned settler homes. In their turn, the British mobilized the biggest army ever assembled in South Africa, about 14,000 men, of whom regulars made up less than one-third. Most of the fighting fell to amaMfengu and Khoekhoe auxiliaries, based on the Indian "Sepoy" model, or to colonists who despised inexperienced imperial troops. During the fighting, British commanders refused to extend the concept of chivalry to what they saw as a barbarous enemy and pursued an active strategy of burning Xhosa homes, seizing cattle, and destroying food stores.[5]

This scorched earth policy brought the amaXhosa to the edge of starvation and, without the logistics needed to pursue the war, immobilized their fighters. As the amaNgqika entered the hungry period before the rains, first Maqoma and then Sandile sued for peace. But without a clear military

---

[5] N. Mostert, *Frontiers: The Epic of South Africa's Creation and Tragedy of the Xhosa People* (London: Jonathan Cape, 1992), pp. 874, 878, 896, 899–90; Peires, *House of Phalo*, pp. 153–8.

victory, the British were unable to end the war. In the face of continuing Xhosa resistance, particularly from the amaNdlambe who crossed the Kei with impunity, the secretary of state for the colonies, Lord Grey, turned to a policy of military rule and cultural assimilation. When a new governor, Sir Henry Pottinger, arrived at the Cape to implement this policy, he was persuaded by the settler elite to force the amaXhosa across the Kei River. However, he had neither the means nor the ability to achieve this and was soon replaced by Sir Harry Smith, the veteran soldier who saw discipline, rather than diplomacy, as the solution to the frontier problem.[6]

Smith's objective was to pacify and subdue the amaXhosa in the shortest time possible. In December 1847, he threatened and humiliated a gathering of Xhosa chiefs, warning them of the consequences of taking up arms again. He then brought the territory between the Fish and Keiskamma rivers into the Cape Colony as the district of Victoria East. The amaXhosa were expelled from this area and their land was either settled by Mfengu or Khoekhoe immigrants or it was sold to sheep farmers, many of whom came from the Albany district. Africans who chose to reside on farms owned by settlers or missionaries were expected to conform to the values and practices of British civilization. Although cultural assimilation proved the rule in the Cape, Smith introduced a form of martial law, combined with indirect rule, in the territory between the Keiskamma and the Kei (the eastern section of D'Urban's old province of Queen Adelaide) that he named British Kaffraria. In this Crown Colony, the amaXhosa were squeezed into reserves, or rural locations, and subjected to a head tax. Humanitarians raised little objection to these policies, at least partly because they were coming to see the imposition of British civilization as the only means of assuring the freedoms associated with Christianity and commerce. Smith rewarded their inactivity by bullying the chiefs into prohibiting polygamy and witchcraft, and by placing the resolution of important contraventions of the law in the hands of military courts or magistrates who ruled alongside the chiefs.

The position of the Kat River settlement was soon threatened by the flagging energy of the humanitarian lobby and the turnaround in British opinion that allowed this expansion of the colony. During the Seventh Frontier War, the settlement's position as a buffer against Xhosa expansion had been underlined when large numbers of men were conscripted into the British army. But following the incorporation of Victoria East into the Cape Colony, the Kat River settlement lost much of this military function and the weapons of its occupants were called in. At the same time, amaMfengu

---

[6] A. Lester, *Imperial Networks: Creating Identities in Nineteenth-century South Africa and Britain* (London and New York: Routledge, 2001), Chapter 6.

displaced by white farmers in Victoria East, and amaXhosa looking for work, or pastures for their cattle, started to crowd into the area. Already a dumping ground for displaced peoples, the Kat River was unable to accommodate these new immigrants. Poverty in the area grew, particularly because the settlement's farmers were unable to sell their land on the open market or acquire the mortgages and capital needed to convert to sheep farming. White settlers traced the rise in cattle rustling to the anonymous newcomers and, ever critical of the endemic poverty in the area, called for the Kat River settlement to be disbanded as a distinct, self-governing territory under the tutelage of the LMS. The government responded to these requests when, during the harsh winter of 1850, police evicted what they regarded as illegal immigrants from the settlement. For the Kat River farmers, this seemed to presage their future if, through discussions entered into at the Cape, Britain agreed to hand the government of the colony to the settlers.[7]

Matters came to a head along the frontier when the amaXhosa, squeezed into locations and menaced by drought, began to respond to the messages of a prophet, Mlanjeni, who traced the ills of his people to witchcraft. If the amaXhosa sacrificed their dun-colored cattle, he promised, the English would disappear. Smith returned to the frontier to address the chiefs; but when Sandile failed to attend a meeting, he deposed the Ngqika chief in October 1850 and replaced him with a government magistrate, Charles Brownlee. This extension of direct rule brought the amaXhosa into open rebellion. Through their improved proficiency in the handling of firearms, they were able to inflict considerable casualties on British troops. The war spread as the amaXhosa mobilized the support of kinsmen living as tenants on farms in the frontier districts, as well as Thembu fighters living to the west of the Kei. It took a new and more serious direction when a large section of disaffected coloreds from the Kat River settlement, as well as deserters from the Cape Mounted Rifles, took up arms against their erstwhile British allies. The paternalism of their British officers and the racial abuse of a growing stratum of colonial society had caused these men of Khoekhoe and mixed race descent to defend their patriarchal honor and, at the same time, to fight for the preservation of the last vestiges of a Hottentot culture and identity.[8]

[7] T. Kirk, "The Cape economy and the expropriation of the Kat river Settlement, 1846–1853," in S. Marks and A. Atmore (Eds.), *Economy and Society in Pre-Industrial South Africa* (London: Longman, 1980), pp. 226–46.

[8] E. Elbourne, *Blood Ground. Colonialism, Missions, and the Contest for Christianity in the Cape Colony and Britain, 1799–1853* (Montreal: McGill-Queen's University Press, 2002), pp. 58–61; R. Ross, "The Kat river Rebellion and Khoikhoi nationalism: the fate of an ethnic identification," *Kronos*, 24, 1997.

The Eighth Frontier War was drawn out, marked by numerous frightful atrocities, a high loss of life, and a growing racial hatred. The British soldiers' grisly practice of taking trophy skulls from their enemies increased markedly at this time, at least partly because these objects had become items of phrenological study. This callousness was repaid in full by the Xhosa practice of torturing captured soldiers to death and dismembering their corpses.[9] The war lasted for twenty-seven months, required the presence of almost 9,000 British regulars, and cost the lives of some 16,000 amaXhosa. The Eighth Frontier War also led to the recall of Sir Harry Smith, the public execution of Kat River rebels, and the breakup of their settlement. It finally came to an end when, in February 1853, the British withdrew the order of deposition on Sandile. However, whereas the Ngqika chief was restored to his prewar position, his people were excluded from some of the most fertile land in British Kafraria. The fears of the Kat River rebels, that they would be disadvantaged by responsible government, materialized when the new representative government passed a Masters and Servants Law in 1856 that treated defaulting workers as criminals.[10]

The deprivation caused by the Eighth Cape Frontier (or Mlanjeni's) War grew more serious when an epidemic of lungsickness tore through the Xhosa herds in 1855 and the maize crop faltered due to excessive rain and insect infestation. These reverses undermined the structure of Xhosa society and left it open to extremist solutions. In April 1856, Nongqawuse, a young woman of about fifteen, had a dream in which a New People promised to come to the rescue of the amaXhosa but only if they destroyed their contaminated cattle and goods. Nongqawuse's vision combined traditional forms of divination and ways of purifying society through sacrifice with Christian ideas of resurrection and the battle between good and evil. When lungsickness ravaged the cattle herds to the east of the Kei, the prophecy took on a new urgency, and Sahili called on the chiefs of the Gcaleka amaXhosa to follow Nongqawuse's instructions. On the eastern side of the Kei, Sandile originally adopted the position of a passive unbeliever; but as the lungsickness destroyed his cattle he was driven to adopt the

[9] Mostert, *Frontiers*, pp. 1040, 1051–3, 1077, 1083, 1096–7, 1102, 1117, 1142, 1152–3; A. Bank, "Of 'Native Skulls' and 'Noble Caucasians': Phrenology in Colonial South Africa," *JSAS*, 22(3), (1996), p. 401. On warfare more generally, see C. Crais, *White Supremacy and Black Resistance in Pre-Industrial South Africa: The Making of the Colonial Order in the Eastern Cape, 1770–1865* (Cambridge: Cambridge University Press, 1992), pp. 173–88.

[10] The act would be amended in 1873, 1874, and 1875. This law replaced the Masters, Servants and Apprentices Ordinance of 1841; it would remain on the statute book until 1974. S. van der Horst, *Native Labour in South Africa* (London: Frank Cass, 1942), pp. 34–8.

position of an active believer. Xhosa society was divided between "soft" believers (*amathamba*) who awaited the coming millennium and "hard" unbelievers (*amagogotya*) whom they held responsible for its delayed arrival. Many people refused to sow crops in the spring of 1856 in anticipation of the Resurrection day due to arrive in the coming months. But by the following winter the New People had still not arrived, food stocks were depleted or destroyed, and soon people started to die. Hunger and exposure eventually killed between 35,000 and 50,000 amaXhosa in this "national suicide" and forced perhaps 150,000 to leave their land in search of food.

As many as 60,000 starving amaXhosa crossed into the Cape Colony in search of work. Sir George Grey's government attempted to control this immigration in 1857 through legislation requiring work-seekers to register at magistrate's offices where their contracts were attested. At the same time, it became a criminal offence for "Kafirs or other Native Foreigners" to enter the colony without a pass.[11] With their lands drained of population and their society shattered, the amaXhosa could only look on as the governor of the Cape, Sir George Grey, opened British Kaffraria to white settlement. German mercenaries, who had fought for the British during the Crimean War, and later German peasants were settled in the area where they established small towns with names like Stutterheim, Berlin, Braunschweig, and Hamburg. Although the Xhosa cattle killing should be viewed, as J. B. Peires suggests, as "a popular mass movement of a truly national character," it was an event that advanced the interests of the British far more than any military victory.[12]

Far from the violent upheavals on the eastern frontier, Cape Town's merchants drew some benefit from the supply to British armies of food and equipment. By the early 1840s, Cape Town was a recognizably British colonial town with a population of more than 30,000. In 1846, gas lighting was introduced and, two years later, the town welcomed its first Anglican bishop, Robert Gray, who encouraged the establishment of church schools based on the British model. The introduction of civil service exams encouraged the spread of formal schooling and caused several Dutch families to adopt the language and culture of the English. Local knowledge was reflected in newspapers and bookshops that tied Cape Town into an empire of learning dominated by Britain. The *Cape Monthly Magazine*, established

---

[11] J. Peires, *The Dead Will Arise* (Johannesburg: Ravan Press, 1989), pp. 249–50; van der Horst, *Native Labour*, pp. 29–34.

[12] J. Peires, *The Dead Will Arise*. In 1969, Monica Wilson judged the cattle killing a "pagan reaction," *Oxford History of South Africa* (Oxford: Oxford University Press, 1969), pp. 256–60, while, thirty years earlier, C. W. de Kiewiet declared it "an incredible madness," *Cambridge History of the British Empire*, 8, p. 403.

in 1859, mixed politics and history with investigations of climate, irrigation, and evolution. The town reflected a new self-confidence in its substantial buildings and original architecture. In 1859, a handsome edifice was erected, in the Greek-revival style, on the north side of old Company Gardens to house the South African Public Library and the museum. These institutions provided employment for well-connected intellectuals who brought the ideals of metropolitan scholarship to the Cape. Ernst Haekel's cousin, Wilhelm Bleek, initiated research into the languages and customs of the Bushmen. His collaborator and sister-in-law, Lucy Lloyd, would continue this work after his death in 1875 and, particularly through her *Folk-lore Journal*, provide inspiration for some of the first ethnographic essays to appear in South Africa.[13] Robert Owen supported the candidature of the ornithologist Edgar Layard for the post of museum curator, a position he occupied from 1855 to 1872, when the entomologist Roland Trimen replaced him. The South African College was established in 1841 on the grounds formerly occupied by the zoo at the southern end of Government Avenue. Housed in a single building, the institution was initially little more than a center for examinations and the conferring of degrees. But when the college became the University of the Cape of Good Hope in 1875, two new buildings were erected and, in 1881, a chemistry laboratory. The university complex at the one end of Government Avenue, and the museum–library at the other, formed the intellectual heart of the city. The establishment in 1877 of a South African Philosophical Society, with its own transactions, secured the link to metropolitan sites of knowledge. Grahamstown formed another core of settler intellectual activity with its own, Albany, museum (founded in 1855), public library, and short-lived *Eastern Province Monthly Magazine* (1856–58). Collections were built on the work of men in the field who, like the frontier entomologist and botanist Mary Barber, were sometimes women.[14] During the late 1830s, Andrew Geddes Bain, while building roads in the Fort Beaufort district for the Royal Engineers, discovered the fossilized bones of prehistoric (mammal-like) reptiles that Owen, in London, identified as dicynodants from the

[13] R. Thornton, "'This dying out Race': W. H. I. Bleek's "Approach to the languages of South Africa," *Social Dynamics*, 9, 1983; A. Bank "Evolution and racial theory: the hidden side of Wilhelm Bleek," *South African Historical Journal*, 43, 2000; Mario di Gregorio, "Reflections of a non-political naturalist: Ernst Haeckel, Wilhelm Bleek, Friedrich Müller and the meaning of language," *Journal of the History of Biology*, 35, 2002.

[14] W. Beinart, "Men, Science, Travel and Nature in the Eighteenth and Nineteenth Century Cape," *Journal of Southern African Studies*, 24, 1998; A. Cohen, "Mary Elizabeth Barber, the Bowkers, and South African Prehistory," *South African Archaeological Bulletin*, LIV, 170, 1999.

Permo-Triassic Age preceding that of the dinosaurs. The work of these collectors helped the metropolitan experts uncover and explain the vast diversity of species and gauge the enormous depth of time.[15] But these colonial footsoldiers of science were often experts themselves who, through their close contacts with the metropolitan world, brought to the Cape new ways of understanding the natural and human environment.

Much of this work had unexpected political consequences. First, European scientists saw their findings and explanations as universal and brushed aside those of the indigenous inhabitants. Second, the discoveries of geologists, palaeontologists, botanists, and zoologists showed Africa to be an ancient continent harboring primitive species made extinct in more advanced parts of the world. Third, these new ideas rapidly influenced the way scientists looked at the human population. Missionary linguists made tremendous advances in these years; the New Testament appeared in Setswana in 1840, isiXhosa in 1846, and South Sesotho in 1855. The following year, Bleek grouped these, and other, languages into a new classificatory category: the Bantu family of languages.[16] The missionaries' linguistic work was paralleled by their attempts to order and understand the indigenous peoples of South Africa. By midcentury, their monographs and essays had developed an ethnographic genre that divided the native population into a clear patchwork of tribes. These advances allowed Gustav Fritsch to produce, in 1872, the first ethnographic survey of the Bantu peoples of South Africa.[17] This reification of linguistic categories into tribes and then into an overarching social group, "the Bantu," provided science with categories that could be examined and analyzed in the manner

---

[15] The fossil collections sent to the British Museum by Bain are still being identified and have, only recently, helped scientists uncover the catastrophe that destroyed the trilobites and most other forms of life some 250 million years ago, M. Benton, *When Life Nearly Died: the greatest extinction of all time* (London: Thames and Hudson, 2003), pp. 206–8; S. Dubow, "Earth history, Natural history, and Prehistory at the Cape, 1860–1875," *Comparative Studies in Society and History*, 2004.

[16] W. Bleek, "South African languages and books," *Cape Monthly Magazine*, 3, (1858), p. 325. W. H. I. Bleek, *Comparative Grammar of South African Languages* (London: Trubner, and Cape Town: Juta), I (1862) and II (1869).

[17] Starting with works like J. Campbell's *Travels in South Africa: Being a Narrative of a Second Journey in the Interior of That Country* (London: Westley, 1822), pp. 193–222, J. Philip's *Researches in South Africa Illustrating the Civil, Moral, and Religious Condition of Native Tribes* (London: James Ducan, 1828), and R. Moffat's *Missionary Labours and Scenes in Southern Africa* (London: Snow, 1842), pp. 234–55. See especially E. Casalis, *The Basutos: or Twenty-three years in South Africa* (published in French, 1859, translated in London, 1861); W. Holden, *The Past and Future of the Kaffir Races* (reprinted Cape Town: C. Struik, 1963); H. Callaway, *The Religious System of the AmaZulu* (Springvale: Blair, 1868–70). G. Fritsch, *Die Eingeborenen Sud-afrika's* (Breslau: Hirt, 1872).

of plants and animals. Much of this work portrayed Khoesan and Bantu languages as little developed, weak, or feminine whereas the ethnographic work often sought to find the origins of language, religion, or the family in the primitive customs of African people living in a land that seemed to have undergone little change since the beginning of time. So, whereas this knowledge ordered and domesticated the human environment and gave government the intellectual resources needed to administer and control tribal peoples, it also extended the social distance between whites and Africans. It also portrayed colonized people as tribesmen living at an early stage of evolution or as dying out or inferior races in need of Christian care and colonial tuition. History as a discipline tended to confirm these ideas, particularly at the end of the 1870s and early 1880s, as the field moved in a professional direction following the appointment of the first state archivists.[18]

The intrusion of the state into the daily lives of individuals was particularly noticeable during the governorship of Sir George Grey, who replaced military rule with enlightened civil administration.[19] This was reflected in his labor legislation as much as in the construction of the Roeland Street jail in Cape Town and the impressive government hospitals erected in the capital and in King William's Town. It also was reflected in a campaign to build and extend schools, most notably Lovedale (established on the eastern frontier in 1841) and Zonnebloem (in Cape Town), and to provide an education for young women.[20]

When a hard road was built across the sandy Cape Flats in 1845, Cape Town's gaze turned hesitantly from its old, maritime hinterland and looked northward to the interior along new lines of contact, control, and commerce. New roads linked Cape Town to its hinterland, encouraged regular omnibus services with rural towns, and facilitated the movement of agricultural

---

[18] H. C. V. Leibbrant was appointed colonial archivist and parliamentary librarian in January 1881. G. M. Theal had started to work through, and order, state archives a few years earlier. C. C. Saunders, *The Making of the South African Past* (Cape Town: David Philip, 1988), pp. 12–14. On the earlier historiography, cf. Robert Ross, "Donald Moodie and the origins of South African historiography," in *Beyond the Pale: Essays on the History of Colonial South Africa* (Hanover and London: Wesleyan University Press and University Press of New England, 1993).

[19] The ambivalence of this term is reflected in historians' starkly divergent opinions of Grey. The role played by the institutions of the British colonial state in filtering power throughout civil society is stressed by C. Crais, *White Supremacy and Black Resistance.*

[20] D. Gaitskell, "At Home with hegemony: Coercion and consent in African girls' education for domesticity in South Africa before 1910," in D. Engels and S. Marks (Eds.), *Contesting Colonial Hegemony* (London: British Academic Press, 1994); N. Erlank "'Raising up the degraded daughters of Africa': the provision of education for Xhosa women in the mid-nineteenth century," *South African Historical Journal, 43,* (2000).

produce. Secure mountain passes soon allowed these lines of contact, control, and commerce to extend into the interior. The first railways were built in the early 1860s and, once diamonds were discovered, lines were extended to Beaufort West and Cradock in 1881. Kimberley would be reached four years later. By 1850, it took three days for troop reinforcements to travel from Cape Town to East London by coastal steamer; and a further day to reach King William's Town overland. Steamships reduced the length of the voyage from Britain to the Cape by a third and a telegraph linked the two countries for the first time in 1885. Much of Cape Town's energy grew out of a new political confidence. Colonists were able to exercise some political influence through road boards, school committees, and church synods. In 1846, they were able to enter into electoral politics for the first time with the establishment of a two-tiered form of municipal government dominated by wealthy town notables.[21] Three years later, the municipality brought together various groups calling for representative government when, in direct opposition to popular wishes, the metropolitan government attempted to bring convicts to the Cape to work on roads and other public works. The broad agitation provoked by this issue isolated the governor and his conservative allies, as well as political leaders, in the eastern district who feared the dominance of Cape Town and, in the wake of the Kat River rebellion, an unrestricted franchise. The constitution passed in 1853 was the product of notions of liberal democracy imported from Britain as well as economic interests that bound white merchants and black peasants into a single, prosperous class.[22] It introduced a color-blind franchise open to all males who earned £50 a year or owned property worth £25. They were not required to be literate. Men who met the low franchise qualification were eligible for election to the House of Assembly; but a relatively high property qualification (£2,000 fixed or £4,000 unfixed property) restricted entrance to the Upper House, or Legislative Council.

The first representative government was elected in 1854 but, for the next twenty years, failed to raise substantive new issues, beyond the competition between eastern and western districts or the shape of the budget, and succeed in mobilizing few voters, whether black or Dutch, in rural areas. For these reasons, responsible government came quietly to the Cape in 1872 when the colony was, for the first time, able to choose its own

---

[21] V. Bickford-Smith, *Ethnic Pride and Racial Prejudice in Victorian Cape Town* (Cambridge: Cambridge University Press, 1995).

[22] Historians remain divided on the benefits brought to the black population by the franchise. Compare Mostert, *Frontiers*, pp. 1160, 1273, 1275 with Trapido, "'The friends of the Natives': merchants, peasants and the political and ideological structure of liberalism in the Cape, 1854–1910," in Marks and Atmore (Eds.), *Economy and Society in Pre-Industrial South Africa*, pp. 267–8.

FIGURE 7.1A. The Eastern Cape frontier area 1858–66.

prime minister. A large and imposing building was constructed, between 1875–84, to house the new parliament. Situated at the head of Adderley Street, the main thoroughfare in Cape Town (named after a member of the British parliament opposed to the settlement of convicts at the Cape), this building, and the neighboring slave lodge turned supreme court, looked across government avenue to the library–museum, modeled on the Fitzwilliam Museum in Cambridge, and the Anglican cathedral, built in the early 1830s after the model of St. Pancras Church in London. The four institutions seemed to unite politics, law, knowledge, and religion in an apex of settler power.

FIGURE 7.1B. Eastern Cape and Transkei 1895.

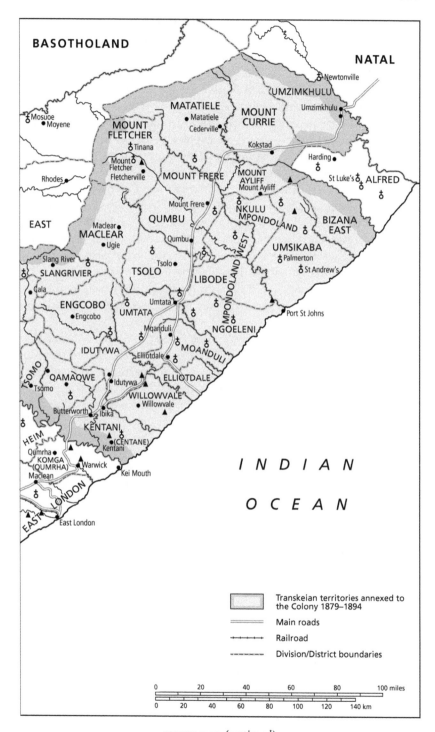

FIGURE 7.1B (*continued*)

The elected government was expected to contribute to the defense and expansion of the colony. Soon after the Xhosa cattle killing, Thembu and Mfengu emigrants crossed the Kei where they came into conflict with the local Gcaleka amaXhosa. As the fighting intensified, the British came to the aid of their allies and pushed Sahili and his followers further eastward. A decade later, in the mid-1860s, Thembu and Mfengu immigrants had, with the encouragement of their British allies, occupied the heart of the old Gcaleka territory. This movement of peoples created new frontier districts on the eastern side of the Kei: Emigrant Thembuland in the foothills of the Drakensberg, Fingoland, and, when Sahili returned to a severely reduced area on the coast, Gcalekaland. In 1866, the Cape Colony brought to an end its long annexation of the Ciskei when it took possession of British Kaffraria and divided the territory into two districts: East London and King William's Town. The Cape's annexation of this area swelled the numbers of isiXhosa-speakers in its population and, the following year, this change was reflected in a redrafted pass law. This no longer regarded "Kaffirs" as automatic foreigners and, as the need for land and labor changed after the discovery of diamonds, prepared the way for the piecemeal annexation of the Transkein territories.[23]

The last Cape Frontier war took place in 1877–78 as the amaXhosa mounted a final, futile struggle against British rule. The cost of this war, which resulted in the annexation of Fingoland, and particularly the disarming of the Basotho two years later, fell heavily on the Cape's taxpaying voters. This increased the disaffection of Dutch farmers who were suffering from free-trade policies and a growing dependence on imperial banks. In 1879, J.H. Hofmeyr started a political movement aimed at protecting the interests of largely Dutch farmers while S. J. du Toit established a political party, the Afrikaner Bond, and launched the first Afrikaans language movement. Although Cape Muslims had written some of the earliest Afrikaans texts in Arabic, they were not welcomed by du Toit's followers.[24] The more moderate Hofmeyr initially stressed the importance of Dutch and, when he took over the Bond a few years later, successfully established the right to use the language in Parliament, the civil service, and the higher courts. However, his mobilization of Dutch-speaking colonists did not seek to

---

[23] C. C. Saunders, "The Annexation of the Transkei," in C. C. Saunders and R. Derricourt (Eds.), *Beyond the Cape Frontier: Studies in the History of the Transkei and Ciskei* (London: Longman, 1974).

[24] A. Davids, "'My Religion is Superior to the Law': The Survival of Islam at the Cape of Good Hope," in Y. da Costa and A. Davids, (Eds.), *Pages from Cape Muslim History* (Pietermaritzburg: Shuter and Shooter, 1994) pp. 12, 68, 152; A. van Selms, "'n Arabiese Grammatika in Afrikaans," *Tydskrif vir Wetenskap en Kuns, 16*(1), (1956).

bring about confrontation with English-speakers, and Hofmeyr and his followers remained staunch members of the British Empire.[25]

Another consequence of the last frontier war was the transportation of prisoners to the Western Cape where they labored on farms and railways. Until this time, the descendants of slaves brought from Mozambique, Madagascar, and other areas of Africa constituted the major part of the black population in the Western Cape. The anti-slavery squadron established at Simonstown in 1808 liberated about 2,000 slaves in the first two decades of the nineteenth century and, between 1839–46, as the indentures of freed slaves expired, and the need for labor soared, brought another 4,000 of these "prize negroes" to Cape Town. The introduction of assisted immigration from Britain brought an end to this scheme; but the need for labor rose sharply after the discovery of diamonds and, between 1876 and 1883, another 3,200 contracted laborers were brought from southern Mozambique to the Cape. These men soon contributed to the ethnic mosaic clustered around churches like St. Paul's, constructed on the slopes of Signal Hill in 1880 and, later, St. Phillip's in Woodstock.[26] Islam flourished in the neighboring Bo-Kaap where a Turkish missionary of Kurdish origins, Abu Bakr Effendi, helped revitalize the religion after his arrival in Cape Town in 1862. The wealth and confidence of the Muslims grew, like that of most sectors of the population, with the growth of the economy occasioned by the diamond discoveries. In the 1884 House of Assembly elections, the Muslims indicated, for the first time, their ability to influence local politics.[27] Meanwhile, much further north in what was to become the Transvaal, another "ethnic mosaic" was taking place involving Boer and African communities.

THE SOUTH AFRICAN INTERIOR

From the mid-eighteenth century, the South African central and western Highveld was destabilized, both politically and economically, by general conflict among Tswana societies. This uncertainty reached a climax in the 1820s and 1830s with the invasion of the region by the Ndebele

[25] H. Giliomee, *The Afrikaners: Biography of a People* (Cape Town: Tafelberg, 2003), pp. 212–23.

[26] Saunders, "'Free, yet slaves': Prize Negroes at the Cape revisited," in N. Worden and C. Crais (Eds.), *Breaking the Chains: Slavery and its legacy in the nineteenth-century Cape Colony* (Johannesburg: Witswatersrand University Press, 1994); Harries, "Culture and Classification: a history of the Mozbieker community at the Cape," *Social Dynamics*, 26(2), (2000).

[27] N. Worden, E. van Heyningen, and V. Bickford-Smith, *Cape Town: the Making of a City* (Cape Town: David Philip, 1998), p. 221.

impis of Mzilikazi, resulting in the physical displacement of thousands of Sotho-Tswana speaking communities.[28] The Africans and the Boers were pastoral and agricultural societies. Both needed to recover after the equally disturbing periods of the Ndebele invasion and Great Trek, respectively. The frontier of Trekker expansion was a volatile region as both the Boers and the local African populace wanted to gain control over important resources, particularly land and workers. This situation made for a competitive and potentially hostile relationship between the Boers and the African groups. Yet, as will be shown in this chapter and as a number of other works on the history of the Transvaal have shown, there were also times when Boers and Africans cooperated and worked together.[29] From the late 1970s, historians have been especially concerned to shade in these specific nuances and differences, so that we now have a more detailed and complex picture of the Zuid Afrikaansche Republiek (ZAR) and how it functioned or failed to. What becomes manifestly apparent from these analyses is that the African population was able to dictate, to a significant degree, the nature of the ZAR.

Following the defeat and expulsion of Mzilikazi and the amaNdebele in 1837 from what was later to be called the Transvaal, the Voortrekkers under the leadership of Andries Potgieter proclaimed the area as Boer territory, by right of conquest. The creation of a new state on the South African Highveld was an arduous task for the Trekkers due to a number of problems. From the 1830s, the Voortrekkers on the Highveld lived in scattered communities in far-flung areas. The problem of such scattered Boer communities was worsened by disunity, manifested by internal splits. In April 1844, for example, Potgieter and his followers established a new Voortrekker "republic" with its own set of rules, the Thirty-Three Articles, as its basis of government. These articles were basically about issues of order and security in a fledgling society still grappling with the creation of a territorial government. As a pointer to the racial policy of the Voortrekkers to Africans, parts of these articles specifically excluded "half-castes, down to the tenth degree" while "natives" would "[not] be permitted to take

---

[28] This is more detailed in A. Manson, "Conflict in the western highveld/southern Kalahari," in C. Hamilton (Ed.), *The Mfecane Aftermath* (Johannesburg: Witswatersrand University Press, 1995), Chapter 13.

[29] See P. Bonner, *Kings, Commoners and Concessionaires* (Johannesburg: Ravan Press, 1982); P. Delius, *The Land Belongs to Us: The Pedi Polity, the Boers and the British in Nineteenth Century Transvaal* (Johannesburg: Ravan Press, 1982); R. Wagner, "Zoutpansberg: The Dynamics of a Hunting Frontier," in Marks and Atmore (Eds.), *Economy and Society in Pre-Industrial South Africa*; A. Manson, "The Hurutshe in the Marico District," Ph.D. thesis, University of Cape Town (1990).

up their residence near any townlands to the detriment of the [white] inhabitants of the town . . ."[30]

Potgieter stayed briefly at Potchefstroom and in August 1845, he and his followers left to establish the new settlement of Andries Ohrigstad. This was partly due to personal ambition, but also in order to establish a commercial outlet to the Mozambican coast, to ward off Portuguese territorial ambitions and move beyond the reach of British authority at the Cape. The Ohrigstad community, however, was faced with problems such as the tsetse fly, malaria, Portuguese and African opposition, as well as dissension within its leadership. Consequently, in 1848, Potgieter and a small following broke away and moved north to found another new settlement, Soutpansberg, leaving J. J. Burgers and others in charge of Ohrigstad. Some of the Ohrigstad community also moved out to found yet another new settlement about 10 km to the south, which they named the Republic of Lydenburg. Another group of Trekkers had struck out to the Madikwe region where they founded the settlement of Zeerust. Thus, by 1844, there were four distinct Voortrekker communities. Although all of them were motivated by the same social, political, and theological concerns, they were fundamentally disunited and split into factions based on loyalty toward certain leaders. Pretorius, for example, had his own following whereas many other Boers who were opposed to him refused to serve under him. He eventually settled at what later became Rustenburg. Those who were loyal to him gradually came to settle in the Magaliesberg, but the Boers of Ohrigstad, Olifants River, and Derdepoort insisted that they would never serve under him.

Following an earlier decision to unite, the Potchefstroom and Soutpansberg groups formed a united Volksraad at Hekpoort in the Magaliesberg in 1849. The Volksraad agreed to meet thrice a year. The four Boer communities of Mooi River and the Magaliesberg, Soutpansberg, Lydenburg, and Madikwe would each have its own commandant–general, but all of them under one united Volksraad. Whereas the envisaged Volksraad never met due to lack of a quorum, Pretorius, nevertheless, negotiated the Sand River Convention in 1852, explained in the following, on behalf of all the others.

As already indicated previously, initially the Trekkers were only a concentration of a few thousand inhabitants in centers far removed from each other, and it took nearly fifteen years to agree upon the need for, and basic characteristics of, the ZAR. The Sand River Convention of 1852 had done little to unite the three Boer communities in the area north of

[30] G. W. Eybers, *Select Constitutional Documents Illustrating South African History, 1795–1910* (London: Routledge, 1918), pp. 349–56.

the Vaal: at Potchefstroom, Lydenburg, and Schoemansdal. The Sand River Convention granted the Boers the right to govern themselves and buy arms and ammunition from the British colonies. It also undertook to repudiate all previous treaties with African communities north of the Vaal and not to sell arms or ammunition to them.[31]

Gathered around patriarchal leaders, Boers communities at times resorted to arms to settle their differences. It was only in 1860 that they were able to form a common government with its own constitution and infrastructure. Even after this, it took decades to unify and strengthen the new state and, despite its later resistance to British imperial advancement and attempts to dismantle it, the ZAR never stamped its authority firmly over the local black population.[32] The policies and laws of the ZAR were unevenly applied, varying from region to region according to a range of factors, among them the physical landscape, the nature of the local economy, the dispersion of disease-free areas, the density of black and white settlement, and the character of individual leaders, both Boer and African.

VOORTREKKER APPROPRIATION OF AFRICAN-OCCUPIED LAND

As the new authorities and "owners" of the land in the Transvaal, the Voortrekkers considered the Africans to be under their jurisdiction. If they found African-occupied land suitable for their occupation, "the natives were obliged to either regain possession by purchase or to become farm servitors."[33] Land in the Transvaal was given to the original Voortrekkers "on a very generous basis" and, up to 1870, two 6,000-acre farms were given to each one "as of right."[34] In about 1841, for example, when Paul Kruger, later president of the ZAR, was only sixteen years old, he was entitled to choose two farms for himself, one for grazing and another for growing crops.[35] From the 1850s, title-holders such as veldkornets

---

[31] Eybers, *Select Constitutional Documents*, p. 359.

[32] S. Trapido, "The South African Republic: Class Formation and the State, 1850–1900," *Collected Seminar Papers on Societies of Southern Africa in the 19th and 20th Centuries, 3* (hereafter *SSA*). (1971); S. Trapido, "Aspects in the Transition from Slavery to Serfdom: The South African Republic, 1842–1902," *SSA, 6* (1975); S. Trapido, "Reflections on Land, Office and Wealth in the South African Republic, 1850–1900," in Marks and Atmore (Eds.), *Economy and Society in Pre-Industrial South Africa*.

[33] L. V. Praagh, *The Transvaal and Its Mines: The Encyclopaedic History of the Transvaal* (Johannesburg: Praagh and Lloyd, 1906), p. 79.

[34] Trapido, "Aspects in the transition from slavery to serfdom," p. 27.

[35] S. J. P. Kruger, *The Memoirs of Paul Kruger*, vol. I (London: Unwin 1902), p. 13.

and commandants in particular, were able to acquire "substantial land holdings" easily. Such officials in positions of power had inside information about the workings of the land market and therefore could more easily ensure that their rights or titles were validated. In the 1850s and 1860s, white officials of the state were paid in land rather than in money because of the chronic shortage of cash in the ZAR government.[36] That is how in the Lydenburg district, for example, as Peter Delius records, H. Bührmann who was *landdrost* in the period 1849–51 and subsequently member of the Volksraad had acquired eighteen farms by 1869. But quite apart from state officials, there were other individuals who acquired incomes from hunting and trading and then invested them in land as a way of speculation. Thus, by 1877, one D. J. G. Coetzee, a prominent trader in the eastern ZAR, had bought and sold seven farms.[37]

In 1859, land appropriation by the Boers was facilitated further by a government decision which, in addition to a freehold farm which each burgher was entitled to, gave each one at least one more quitrent farm. This decision enabled those in positions of authority and influence to acquire, as Delius states, "truly massive landholdings." That is how, for example, by 1866, one Johannes Vos, then the landdrost clerk to Marthinus Wesselstroom in the Lydenburg district, had accumulated a staggering 120 farms.[38] Although such a large number of farms may have been an exception, it is nevertheless a pointer to the ease with which Boer individuals of influence could acquire a lot of farms.

A feature of Boer land acquisition in the Transvaal is that some of it was passed on to individuals and companies based outside the territory, notably the Cape and Natal. This incidence became so widespread, at least in the Lydenburg district, that in 1873 the residents there wrote a petition to the government complaining against this practice by "people residing in the neighboring colonies and in Europe who have no interest in the development of the country . . ."[39] The significance of the foregoing pattern and rate of Boer appropriation of African-occupied land in the northeastern Transvaal lies in the fact that:

It applied as markedly in areas of predominantly African settlement and within the domains of effectively independent African polities, and in contested areas, as it did in zones of white settlement and control . . . Even those societies sufficiently strong to resist Boer exactions were nonetheless unable to prevent the process whereby

---

[36] See Trapido, "Aspects," 27; Trapido "The South African Republic," p. 56.
[37] Delius, *The Land*, p. 128.   [38] Delius, *The Land*, pp. 128–9.
[39] Quoted in Delius, *The Land*, p. 129.

the land upon which they lived was transformed into [white-owned] freehold and quitrent farms.[40]

Appropriating land that had Africans already living on it had obvious and important advantages for the Boers. First, it was likely to be fertile and well watered. Second, the Africans on it had to pay rent in labor, kind, or cash as tenants. This general pattern, it should be noted, was very similar to land appropriation elsewhere in the ZAR, the difference being that in the western and southern parts, the process occurred earlier.

The missionaries were not to be left out of the ongoing land appropriation. Some began to acquire land from as early as the 1860s. The Rev. Henri Gonin of the Dutch Reformed Church, for example, bought four farms for himself in the Pilansberg during the 1860s.[41] It is unclear why, but it may have been "for better security in old age, or simply for sale at a profit in future." But, meanwhile, he settled the ex-slave Christian members (*Oorlams*) of his church on one of his four properties, Welgeval. Except for one other property, Schaapkraal, inherited by his children after his death in 1915, Gonin eventually sold all of his farms. Similarly, during the 1870s in the eastern Transvaal, the Berlin Mission Society (BMS) missionary, Alexander Merensky, personally owned many thousands of acres of land, whereas the Hermannsburg missionaries in the Rustenburg district also owned land and farmed, as did the BMS missionaries in nearby Kroondal. There were various reasons for missionaries owning land. Before the Second World War, the BMS missionaries, for example, were paid extremely small salaries which were, for example, "only a third of what Reformed and Methodist missionaries were paid" and, therefore, resorted to owning land, farming, and livestock production to survive as some of them "lived in great poverty."[42] Whereas missionaries in the Transvaal were involved in acquiring land for their future security, the fledgling Boer societies were engaged in processes of both conflict and accommodation with African societies.

BOER–AFRICAN RELATIONS

Up to the 1880s, incursions into, and settlement in, what later became the Transvaal resulted neither in an easy victory by, nor a complete dominance of the Boer colonists over African societies. There was, instead, a complex set of

---

[40] Delius, *The Land*, p. 130.

[41] B. Mbenga, "The Bakgatla-baga-Kgafela in the Pilanesberg District of the Western Transvaal, from 1899 to 1931," Ph.D. thesis, Unisa (1997), p. 213.

[42] F. Hasselhorn, *Mission, Land Ownership and Settlers' Ideology* (Johannesburg: South African Council of Churches, 1987), pp. 18–20.

relations between the two societies, ranging at various times between conflict and cooperation. In practice, the existence and continued livelihoods of the ZAR's inhabitants were as a result of agreements and compromises reached in the various districts of the Transvaal by local Boer officials and African leaders. This did not imply that there was an absence of violence but rather that such violence was a symptom of the Boers' inability to impose their dominance over the local population. Their initial attempts to subjugate African societies met with stiff resistance. In the northern Transvaal during the 1840s, as Delius has shown, the amaNdzundza Ndebele resisted Boer demands for their labor. With guns acquired through migrant labor, trade, and raiding, the amaNdzunza successfully beat off Boer attempts to subdue them. Delius further records that "by the late 1860s, many farmers [i.e., Boers] who had settled in the environs of the amaNdzundza trekked away in despair" while "those who remained recognized the authority of the Ndzundza rulers and paid tribute to them."[43] Following the annexation of the Transvaal in 1877 and defeat of the Pedi by the British in 1879, however, the balance of power swung greatly against African states in the region. Shortly afterward, the amaNdzundza came under the rule of the ZAR. Subsequently, a combined force of Boers and some African auxiliaries surrounded the amaNdzundza in a siege that lasted until July 1883, by which time they had been starved into submission and surrender. To press their victory home, the Boers torched the Ndzundza capital and imprisoned most of the ruling family, including Chief Nyabela, in Pretoria.[44]

Elsewhere in the Transvaal, Boer–African relations followed a similar pattern. In the Marico district in the early 1850s, as Andrew Manson has shown, following the continual raiding of cattle on Boer farms and the killing of three Boers by Bahurutshe, the Boers were forced to abandon their farms and go "into laager before finally leaving for Potchefstroom and Magaliesberg in January 1853."[45] Although the Boers returned to the Marico the following year, instability continued with the murder of several more of them over the next few years. The ZAR authorities were clearly unable to dictate terms to the Bahurutshe. In fact, they were too weak to exert hegemony over the Bahurutshe or any other Tswana community in the region. This factor and the importance of keeping open the crucial "Hunter's Road," which ran from the Marico north through Tswana territory into

[43] P. Delius, "The Ndzundza Ndebele: Indenture and the making of ethnic identity, 1883–1914," in P. Bonner et al. (Eds.), *Holding Their Ground: Class, Locality and Culture in 19th and 20th Century South Africa* (Johannesburg: Ravan Press and Witwatersrand University Press, 1989), p. 229.

[44] Delius, "The Ndzundza Ndebele," p. 231.

[45] A. Manson, "The Hurutshe and the Formation of the Transvaal State, 1835–1875," *The International Journal of African Historical Studies*, 25(1) (1992), p. 91.

Matabeleland, forced the Boers into a relationship of dependence upon African groups in the western Transvaal as allies.[46] This ambivalent Boer–African relationship of conflict and cooperation was commonplace in the rest of the Transvaal. In the northern Transvaal, for example, as in the Marico, African groups such as the Bakopa under Boleu, the amaNdzundza Ndebele under Mabhogo, and the Bapedi under Sekwati were also initially able to successfully resist Boer attempts to subjugate or extract forced labor from them at will.[47]

Boers and Tswana groups had been allies in a number of ways that were mutually beneficial. In this relationship, Tswana regiments were used by Boer commandos as auxiliaries in their many raids against other African groups in far-flung parts of the Transvaal.[48] At a time when the Sand River Convention of 1852 expressly prohibited Africans from possessing firearms, the Boer leader, Paul Kruger, allowed Tswana chiefs such as Kgamanyane of the Bakgatla and Mokgatle of the Bafokeng and their followers to own guns and participate in profitable ivory trading across the Limpopo River. Guns were given as a reward for participating in these raids and this enabled these groups to take part in the still lucrative ivory trade in the 1840s and 1850s. According to the historian Fred Morton, Mokgatle and Kgamanyane "acquired wealth in cattle, plantations, tools, buildings, and dependants."[49] In the northern Transvaal, Chief Sekwati had a similar relationship with the Trekker leaders, particularly Potgieter, "which was reflected in the mounting of joint hunts and raids."[50] As in the Eastern Cape during an earlier period, the leaders of immigrant and indigenous communities often exploited the open nature of the frontier to the benefit of their two communities. Another way to accumulate wealth was through trade, particularly in liquor and guns. Through this trade in guns, Africans were able to partake more fully in the slaughter of game that was threatening several species of animals with extinction. Independent chiefs also were able to arm their followers with these guns and either bought powder or acquired the skills needed to manufacture it. In the north, Boers gave guns to local hunters during the summer months when malaria increased the dangers of hunting, and tsetse fly prevented the use of horses and wagons. Black

---

[46] Manson, "The Hurutshe," p. 91.　　[47] Delius, *The Land*, pp. 36–7.

[48] About *Voortrekker* military expeditions using surrogate African groups against independent African polities in the Transvaal during the nineteenth century, see, for example, War Office General Staff, *The Native Tribes of the Transvaal* (London: War Office, 1905), pp. 100–6; J. Meintjes, *President Paul Kruger: A Biography* (London: Cassell, 1974), pp. 64–7; M. Juta, *Pace of the Ox: A Life of Paul Kruger* (Cape Town: Human and Rousseau, 1975), pp. 46–55.

[49] Morton, "Slave Raiding," p. 107.　　[50] Delius, *The Land*, p. 37.

hunters, known as *swart skuts*, acquired guns in this way and eventually grew strong enough to turn on their erstwhile employers and, in 1867, eject them from their northern capital of Schoemansdal. The northern frontier then retreated southward to leave the area immediately south of the Soutpansberg in the hands of Joao Albasini, a Portuguese trader by origin, and a disparate group of immigrants, many of them his followers. Pushed from the coast by famine, war, and disease, these immigrants were attracted to the transfrontiersman by his control of a profitable trade in slaves and ivory.[51]

On this frontier, isolated Boer communities seemed to experience a "reverse colonization" as they came to depend for their survival on African allies and assistants. With growing frequency, missionaries came across whites who, separated from their institutions and beliefs, employed slaves and traded in "black ivory."[52] European immigrants like Coenraad de Buys and Joao Albasini had married Africans, or taken local concubines, and they, together with other people of European descent, consulted rainmakers, diviners, and healers, or personally threw the bones.[53] The mode of production practised on this impoverished frontier seemed to have regressed after 1867 from a form of settled farming to a shiftless, itinerant hunting. Whites trekked after migrating game, lived from their rifles, and squatted in the same insalubrious conditions as the natives. The sight of a black servant teaching his master to read appalled one Swiss missionary, for whom this image encapsulated the astonishing ignorance to which the Boers had reverted in this northern wilderness.[54]

In areas where the Boers settled in greater numbers, they were likely to impose a more servile relationship on the local population. From the early years of their settlement in the Transvaal, the Voortrekkers were faced with what they perceived to be an acute shortage of labor. In the Cape where they earlier came from, they had built up a tradition of dependence upon slave labor. But such labor was not readily available in their new environment

---

[51] J. C. A. Boeyens, "'Black ivory': The Indenture System and Slavery in Zoutpansberg," in *Slavery in South Africa*, in E. Eldredge and F. Morton (Eds.), *Slavery in South Africa: Captive Labor on the Dutch Frontier* (Boulder, CO: Westview Press and Pietermaritzburg: University of Natal Press, 1994).

[52] Boeyens, "Black ivory," pp. 195–7.

[53] Swiss Mission Archives, Lausanne: 8.10.B Paul Berthoud to Mission Council, 28 December 1876 and 22 December 1877; *Bulletin de la Mission vaudoise,* 5 (1875), p. 73. *Nouvelles de nos missionaires* 10, 1, 1887, 8. Arthur Grandjean would refer to Albasini as an "Africanised Portuguese," "L'Invasion des Zoulous dans le Sud-Est Africain," *Le Globe, 36* (1897), p. 20.

[54] P. Berthoud, *Nègres Gouamba* (Lausanne, 1896), p. 20. On the Cape's eastern frontier the British prosecuted farmers who turned to African diviners for protection against witchcraft, cf. *South African Commercial Advertiser* 21 October 1843, pp. 163–4.

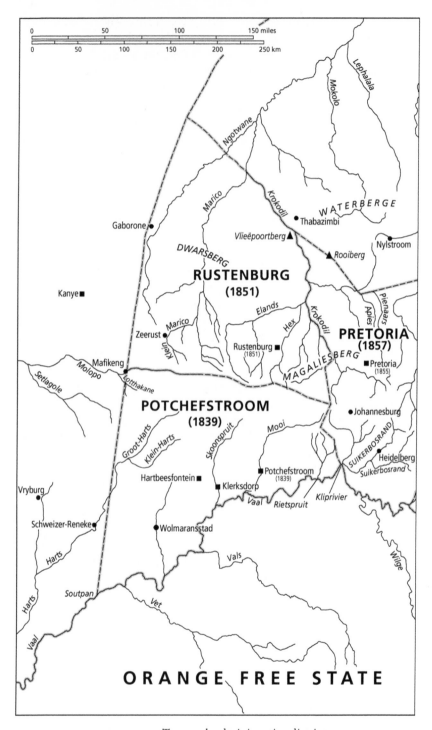

FIGURE 7.2A. Transvaal, administrative districts.

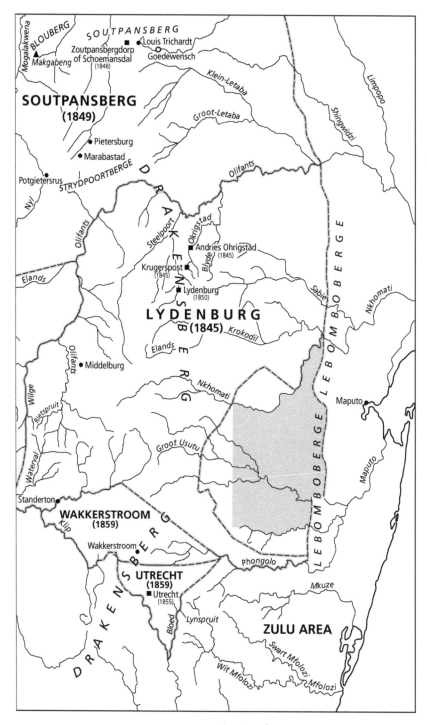

FIGURE 7.2A (*continued*)

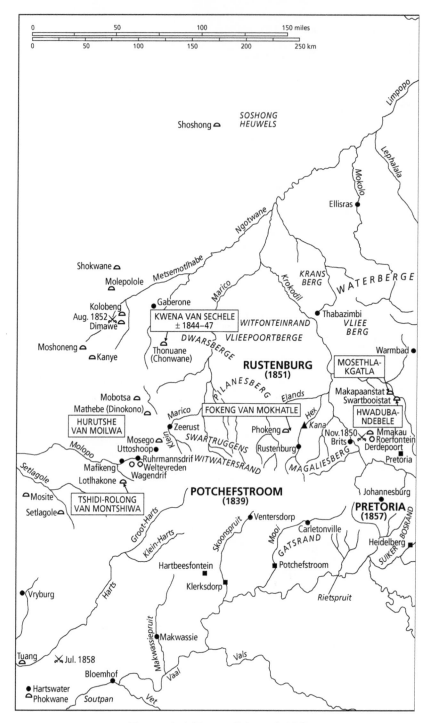

FIGURE 7.2B. Transvaal, African polities and Afrikaner towns.

FIGURE 7.2B (*continued*)

of the Transvaal and they resorted to coercing it from the surrounding African communities. This is one of the reasons that brought the Boers into conflict with their African neighbors. Some voluntary labor of three- or twelve-month contracts was available and paid for. However, the Boers considered labor obtained in this manner both insufficient and lacking in the requisite skills they needed.[55]

There was therefore another means by which the Boers obtained the sort of African labor that would be both skilled and permanent. As soon as they arrived in the Transvaal, Boer commandos periodically raided weaker and less organized African communities and captured their little children. In commando raids against communities such as the Bakgatla of Chief Mosielele, Bakwena of Sechele, the Bapedi of Sekwati, Bakgatla of Mankopane, Balaka of Mokopane, and the Balobedu of Modjadji, children were captured specifically in order to use them as "bonded laborers."[56] Sometimes they were demanded as tribute, traded or secured through exchange. Such captive children, referred to in the contemporary Dutch parlance as *inboekelinge* (registerees) who were "booked in" and notionally seen as "orphans," were indentured to their masters.[57] Rustenburg commandos, for example, raided African groups in the far northern Transvaal. Indeed, Rustenburg has been described as "a slave trading center with its own resident dealer."[58] Young captives were shared amongst the Boer commandos, who brought them up on their farms.

The practice was common at the time throughout what was to become the Transvaal. The cooperation of the Batswana who assisted in the commando raids was no different from that of the amaSwazi, Bapedi, and Vhavenda in this regard.[59] The amaSwazi themselves participated in slave raiding and traded in slaves. In the early stages of this practice, in the 1850s, Swazi regiments captured slaves during attacks on communities within the Swazi kingdom and on its outskirts. Later, Swazi raids were extended into the Lowveld and southern Mozambique. Bonner states, for example, that "several hundred children a year" were captured mostly

---

[55] Delius, *The Land*, pp. 34–5.

[56] Morton, "Slave Raiding and Slavery in the Western Transvaal after the Sand River Convention," *African Economic History*, 20 (1992), pp. 102–3.

[57] Delius, *The Land*, p. 35.

[58] Cited in Morton, "Slave Raiding and Slavery," p. 107; "Captive labor in the western Transvaal after the Sand River Convention," in Eldredge and Morton (Eds.), *Slavery in South Africa*, p. 175.

[59] See Morton, "Slave Raiding and Slavery," pp. 99–118; P. Delius and S. Trapido, "*Inboekselings* and *Oorlams*: The Creation and Transformation of a Servile Class," *Journal of Southern African Studies*, 8(2) (April 1982).

from the Lowveld communities and traded with the Boers of the eastern Transvaal.[60] In November 1869, a Swazi army incursion into the Soutpansberg, for example, netted, among a variety of other booty, about "400 women and children."[61] The child captives obtained from these raids were supplied to the eastern Transvaal Boers from whom, in return, "the Swazi rulers received hunting dogs, cattle, blankets, and to a lesser extent, at the beginning, guns and horses."[62] As servants on the Boer farms, they were trained in a variety of skills, such as, stonecutting and building, brickmaking, cookery, veterinary and folk medicine, literacy in Dutch, wagon repair, hunting, gun maintenance, making cheese, and plow farming. But perhaps the most important use of these servants is that, as Delius has said, "they could be trusted with firearms and placed in supervisory positions over herders and hunting and trading expeditions." It was in this status that these servants were known as *inboekelinge*. In using this kind of labor, the Boers were in fact continuing an old tradition they had brought with them from the Cape; there, indentured Khoekhoen and colored laborers were used as "cooks, herders, and laborers, wagon drivers, and interpreters," who were also "fine shots and horsemen . . ." in their auxiliary role "as soldiers on commando against the San and the amaXhosa."[63]

The male *inboekelinge* were manumitted at the age of 21 and the females at 25. But because of the lifelong separation from their geographical and family origins, they generally remained working on labor contracts on their ex-master's farms or, as in the Rustenburg and Pilansberg areas, settled as tenants on missionary-owned land or bought their own farms and settled as peasant producers. It was in this status that they were known as *Oorlams*.[64] The children of *inboekelinge* were treated in the same manner as their parents by their Boer masters. Where they settled and what happened to them after manumission, however, differed from one area to another. Delius has shown that in the northern Transvaal during the 1850s, for example, some would settle among the local African communities. Yet others were bonded once again on further contracts to their masters.[65]

---

[60] Bonner, *Kings, Commoners and Concessionaires*, p. 92.

[61] J. C. A. Boeyens, "'Black ivory': The Indenture System and Slavery in Zoutpansberg, 1848–1869," in Eldredge and Morton (Eds.), *Slavery in South Africa*, pp. 200–1. Quotation, p. 201.

[62] Cited in P. Delius and S. Trapido, "*Inboekselings* and *Oorlams*," pp. 228–9. Quotation, p. 229.

[63] Quoted in Delius, *The Land*, p. 36.

[64] Mbenga, "The Bakgatla-baga-Kgafela," pp. 56–8; Morton, *Slavery in South Africa*, pp. 167–214

[65] P. Delius and S. Trapido, "Inboekselings and Oorlams," pp. 235–6.

In the Rustenburg and Pilansberg areas, after manumission, the *Oorlams* tended to drift on to a farm called Welgeval, owned by the local Dutch Reformed Church missionary, Henri Gonin, which they eventually bought at the beginning of the twentieth century. Here, men like Cornelius Moloto, Cornelius Sefara, and many others prospered as peasant farmers, cultivating crops like wheat, rearing livestock, and making cheese for sale in the nearby Rustenburg market. Most of the missionary work of spreading the gospel and Western education was done by ex-*inboekelinge* teacher–evangelists. Whereas the central mission stations in the region were staffed by a few white missionaries, the African teacher–evangelists were entrusted with the running of the many "outer stations" dotted all over the region. By the end of the nineteenth century, for example, the DRC teacher–evangelist Stephanus Moloto was in charge of the school on the farm Welgeval, and Zacharia Tihira on Kruidfontein, Martha Moloto and Karl Thabole on Holfontein, while Leoke Mariri ran a school in the border village of Malolwane. All these were *Oorlams* upon whom Gonin heavily depended for his missionary work.[66] Among African communities in the western Transvaal, the *Oorlams* acted as interpreters, skilled artisans, and hunters. Socially, it was common practice for the *Oorlams* to marry within their own core community. This could be explained by their shared bonds of historical background, Dutch literacy, western education, and Christianity, factors which distinguished them from the rest of the Africans around them.[67] On the whole, by the end of the nineteenth century, they had integrated well into the African communities. However, the issues of Boer–African accommodation as well as the roles and socioeconomic status of the *Oorlams* might belie the more contentious question of land and land acquisition.

AFRICAN ACQUISITION OF LAND

On the premise that the Voortrekkers had defeated and expelled the Ndebele from the Transvaal, land in the western Transvaal was now the property of the ZAR government. Official policy therefore was that land could only be "given" to Africans as a "grant" for "services rendered" to them. In the western Transvaal, for example, the earliest known such cases date back to the beginning of 1837 when the Commandants Andries Potgieter, Gerrit Maritz, and Piet Uys gave land grants to some Tswana

---

[66] Mbenga, "The Bakgatla-baga-Kgafela," pp. 66–8.

[67] F. Morton, "Manumitted slaves and the Dutch Reformed Church Mission in the Western Transvaal and eastern Bechuanaland at the time of the colonization of southern Africa, 1864 to 1914," paper to symposium, "Manumission: the promise of freedom," Twelfth International Congress of Anthropological and Ethnological Sciences, Zagreb, Yugoslavia (July 28, 1988), pp. 10–18.

chiefs who had assisted the Boers in expelling Mzilikazi from the Transvaal. Thus, the Rolong chiefs Moroka, Montshiwa, and Gontse, and the Hurutshe chief, Moiloa, were "rewarded" with grants of land by Potgieter in the same localities they had occupied before the Ndebele invasion. Chief Mokgatle of the Bafokeng was similarly rewarded.[68] Indeed, after the expulsion of Mzilikazi, these groups were allowed back only with the permission of the Boers.[69] In fact, throughout the Transvaal, the Voortrekker commandants gave land grants to black groups "for services rendered" or loyalty.[70]

Africans therefore could not acquire land they could legally call their own as it was merely "loaned" to them. This was confirmed by Article 124 of a *Volksraad* Resolution 28 of November 1853, which stated that land was given to Africans "conditionally as long as they behave in accordance with the law and obediently."[71] According to another *Volksraad* Resolution 159 of June 18, 1855, Africans in the Transvaal were expressly forbidden to buy land.[72] Indeed, up to 1871, the issue of Africans buying land was never even considered by the ZAR government. This complete lack of security of tenure deeply concerned many Africans. In the western Transvaal, for example, the people of Rustenburg district were perhaps the first to persistently request the government for permission to buy land. In 1868, the Commandant of Rustenburg echoed this concern that "certain Natives in his district wished to purchase land from a burgher." At first the authorities agreed in principle to the idea of Africans buying land and suggested that its legal ownership be held in trust by the government on behalf of the African people concerned, "as long as they conducted themselves according to the law."[73] Due to repeated African requests to buy land, especially from the Rustenburg area, the government of President T. F. Burgers did consider the issue in 1874, but then after further debates in the Volksraad, rejected it because of Article 9 of the *Grondwet*, which stated that: "The [Boer] people will not permit any equalisation of colored persons with white inhabitants."[74]

Arising from this frustration therefore, Africans resorted to the practice of buying land through the white missionaries working among them.

---

[68] General Staff, War Office, *The Native Tribes of the Transvaal*, p. 20.

[69] For details, see the government *Report by the Commissioner for Native Affairs, relative to the Acquisition and Tenure of Land by Natives in the Transvaal* (Pretoria: Native Affairs Department, 1904), pp. 15–16.

[70] *Acquisition and Tenure*, pp. 18–20.

[71] *Acquisition and Tenure*, p. 20. The *Volksraad* was the parliament of the ZAR.

[72] T. R. H. Davenport and K. S. Hunt (Eds.), *The Right to the Land* (Cape Town: David Philip, 1974), p. 4.

[73] *Acquisition and Tenure*, p. 21.

[74] For details, see *Acquisition and Tenure*, pp. 21–2.

Each able-bodied adult male in a community contributed at least one cow toward the purchase of a farm. However, those who could not afford were not compelled to, nor were they denied a share of the land.[75] The Africans would give the purchase price through their chief to the missionary who would buy the land from a white owner but register it in his name on behalf of that community.[76] This practice seems to have started quietly from as early as the mid-1860s and lasted until the early 1880s. Since the practice lasted for about a decade, the Boer authorities must have been aware of it but perhaps turned a blind eye to it. But what seems clear is that the government neither checked nor stopped it. Eventually, however, as it became more and more prevalent, the government realized the need to regulate and standardise the practice. Following the Pretoria Convention of 1881, a Location Commission was formed in order to demarcate African locations, take transfer of, and hold in trust, land previously privately bought through missionaries by Africans. This responsibility was transferred to the secretary for native affairs in the early 1880s, to the superintendent of natives in 1886, the commissioner for native affairs (during the Crown colony government) and, in 1907, to the minister of native affairs.[77] Closely connected with the issue of land was that of forced labor.

FORCED LABOR

The issue of forced labor, however, took a more general and coercive form that in turn brought about widespread distress among the African communities. The Boers considered the labor they obtained voluntarily from Africans in the manner we have noted previously to be insufficient. Hence, the resort to forced labor. Boer requirements for African labor were procured through the local veldkornet, who has been described by Jeremy Krikler as a "sinister landowning representative of the [white] farmers in each district who hovered above the tenantry, *violently intervening* – when necessary – to ensure the rendering of labor service."[78]

The Boer practice of forced labor was pervasive throughout the Transvaal. Following the founding of the town of Andries Ohrigstad in the northeastern Transvaal in August 1845, for example, the Voortrekkers there came to depend upon black "apprentices" and a "labor tax" forcibly extracted

[75] S. D. Matshego and B. N. O. Pilane, joint interview by Bernard Mbenga, Koedoesfontein, the Pilanesberg, February 7, 1993.
[76] *Acquisition and Tenure*, p. 22.
[77] E. Brookes, *The History of Native Policy in South Africa* (Pretoria: J. L. van Schaik, 1927), pp. 126–7.
[78] J. Krikler, *Revolution from Above, Rebellion from Below: the Agrarian Transvaal at the Turn of the Century* (Oxford: Clarendon Press, 1993), pp. 135, 235–6. Our emphasis.

from the surrounding African communities for agricultural and domestic purposes.[79] A contemporary writer had the following to say about Africans in the Transvaal generally:

The Tribes . . . are forced to perform all the labour of the fields, such as manuring the land, weeding, reaping, building, making dams and canals, and at the same time to support themselves. I have myself been an eye-witness of Boers coming to a village, and, according to their usual custom, demanding twenty or thirty women to weed their gardens, and have seen the women proceed to the scene of unrequited toil.[80]

The economic malaise of the ZAR during the 1860s exacerbated tensions between the Boer authorities and the African communities.[81] In this period, as Roger Wagner has shown for the Soutpansberg area, previously profitable sources of income for the Boers (such as hunting) were declining.[82] With diminishing resources, ZAR officials, such as Paul Kruger and Andries Potgieter, resorted to ever harsher methods of extracting tax from the Africans. As Stanley Trapido has stated: "Between 1850 and 1868, various Volksraads attempted to raise taxes by exhortation, fines, proclamations, and hectoring instructions to landdrosts, with little or no effect."[83] According to Trapido, the Boer need for more African labor at this time led to territorial expansion through military expeditions westward, eastward, and northward. However, although these expeditions were in themselves disruptive,[84] they do not seem to have procured enough labor from the northern and eastern parts of the Transvaal where Africans had not yet come under white hegemony. Therefore, until the 1880s and 1890s when such expeditions yielded much larger numbers of captive Africans,[85] the Boer authorities got their labor requirements from conquered African groups that were already under their jurisdiction, such as the various Tswana groups in the western Transvaal.

Both Trapido and Delius have shown how holders of high office in the ZAR were well placed to take advantage of not only accumulating personal

---

[79] Cited in Mbenga, "Forced labour," p. 134.

[80] W. E. Garrett Fisher, *The Transvaal and the Boers, A Brief History* (reprinted: New York: Negro University Press, 1969), p. 275.

[81] S. Trapido, "Reflections on land, office and wealth in the South African Republic, 1850–1900," in Marks and Atmore (Eds.), *Economy and Society in Pre-Industrial South Africa*, p. 356.

[82] For details, see R. Wagner, "Zoutpansberg," pp. 323–37.

[83] Trapido, "Land, office and wealth," p. 356.

[84] Trapido, "Aspects in the transition from slavery to serfdom," p. 26.

[85] For details of these later Boer military campaigns, see especially T. J. Makhura, "The Bagananwa polity in the north-western Transvaal and the South African Republic, c. 1836–1896," M.A. dissertation, University of Bophuthatswana (1993).

wealth but, more importantly for the African communities, extracting the ever elusive labor.[86] In the Pilansberg during the 1860s, for example, because of their need for labor, Boer leaders accelerated their efforts to obtain more of it.[87] It was during this period that Paul Kruger, then commandant in the Rustenburg District, began to build a dam for a wheat irrigation project in Saulspoort. Kgatla men were inspanned to wagons and carts containing stone boulders and forced to pull them to the dam-construction site. One afternoon in April 1870, after the Bakgatla had refused to continue to work, their chief, Kgamanyane, was tied to a wagon and, in front of a large gathering, Paul Kruger himself publicly flogged the chief. Angered and humiliated by this incident, Kgamanyane and about half of his people emigrated to Mochudi in Kwena country in what was later to become Botswana, where their descendants have lived to this day.[88] But there were in fact precedents of other African chiefs in the Transvaal who were in similar conflict with Boer leaders. Breutz, for example has recorded that as early as the 1840s, "owing to trouble with the Boers," presumably over labor demands, the Tlhokwa chief, Matlapeng, and his people fled their home in the Matlapengsberg area of the Pilansberg "and sought refuge with the Kwena chief Sechele"[89] in today's Botswana. In about 1860, still in the Pilansberg, Chief Mabe of the Batlhako "got into trouble with the Boers who gave him a flogging. He then left with his tribe for Molepolole [i.e., in modern Botswana] and settled at Magagarape."[90] For the Marico (Madikwe) District, Andrew Manson has recorded that the Boers' "persistent demands for labour . . . eventually forced [Chief] Mangope to lead the rest of his community out of the Transvaal in 1858."[91]

African chiefs were in fact routinely punished by the Boer authorities if they were held to have transgressed the law or flouted authority. In 1851, Mahura, the chief of the Batlhaping, was summoned before the *Volksraad*

---

[86] See Trapido, "Aspects in the transition"; Delius, *The Land*, Chapter 6; "Abel Erasmus: power and profit in the eastern Transvaal," in W. Beinart et al. (Eds.), *Putting a Plough to the Ground* (Johannesburg: Ravan Press, 1986), p. 181.

[87] National Archives of South Africa (NASA), Pretoria, CAD, GOV/756/Ps 50, "Purchase of land by Natives after the Retrocession, 1884 to 1899," p. 83.

[88] B. Mbenga, "Forced labour in the Pilanesberg: The flogging of Chief Kgamanyane by Commandant Paul Kruger, Saulspoort, April 1870," *Journal of Southern African Studies*, 23(1) (March 1997), pp. 127–40.

[89] See Breutz, *The Tribes of the Rustenburg and Pilanesberg Districts* (Pretoria: Native Affairs Department, 1953), pp. 365, 380. The quotations are from the two pages, respectively.

[90] Breutz, *The Tribes*, p. 291. Our emphasis. Breutz does not state why Mabe was flogged, but it was presumably due to his inability to supply the required numbers of laborers. For details of two other Tswana groups who fled from the Pilansberg because of "trouble with the Boers," see Breutz, *The Tribes*, pp. 431, 439.

[91] Manson, "The Hurutshe," p. 92.

and forced to pay a fine of 2,070 head of cattle for allegedly attacking one of his Tswana neighbors and "shedding blood on lands belonging to the Republic."[92] During one of the Boer expeditions of conquest against black groups in the western Transvaal in the early 1850s, Commandant P. Scholtz, then based at the Klein Marico Camp in the Zeerust area, commanded Montshiwa, the chief of the Barolong "to send immediately two hundred armed men on horseback... with victuals for a fortnight to assist us in punishing Sechele."[93] When Montshiwa defied that order, Scholtz summoned him "before the Council of War to appear within five days to answer for your disobedience to my orders."[94] Sensing danger, Montshiwa and some of his followers abandoned their home, Lotlhakane, on September 15, 1852, and fled to Setlhagole, about 70 km to the west of present-day Mafikeng. A Boer commando pursued them but Montshiwa managed to escape and eventually fled to the relative safety of Ngwaketse country in what was to become the British Protectorate of Bechwanaland where he lived in exile from 1856 to 1870.[95]

MISSIONARIES, THE ZAR AUTHORITIES, AND AFRICANS

The foregoing kinds of relations between the Boer authorities and African chiefs became more conflictual over the matter of "bonded labor" about which we have already noted. "Bonded labor" was reportedly widely abused by the Boers and condemned as slavery by British missionaries and officials. African allies were also expected to return runaway captives. In 1848, for example, David Livingstone, of the London Missionary Society, reported meeting four Laka children at a Boer's farm in Rustenburg. Livingstone encouraged them to escape but "they said they had often run away but Mokhatla (*sic*) [chief of Bafokeng] caught them and returned them to their owners."[96] The missionary condemnation of the Boer practice of "bonded labor" originated from the 1850s when Livingstone, then working among the Bakwena of Chief Sechele, was accused by the Boers of influencing

---

[92] J. A. I. Agar-Hamilton, *The Native Policy of the Voortrekkers: An Essay in the History of the Interior of South Africa* (Cape Town: Maskew Miller, 1928), p. 78.

[93] Quoted in S. M. Molema, *Chief Moroka, His Life and Times* (Cape Town: Methodist Church, 1951), p. 91. Regarding details of the conflict between Chief Sechele and the Boers, see Ramsay, "The Rise and Fall of the Bakwena Dynasty," pp. 89–116.

[94] Molema, *Chief Moroka*, p. 92. See also T. V. Bulpin, *Lost Trails of the Transvaal* (Cape Town: Howard Timmins, 1965), pp. 83–4.

[95] P. L. Breutz, *The Tribes of Mafeking District* (Pretoria: Native Affairs Departartment, 1956), pp. 190–1.

[96] Cited in Morton, "Slave Raiding," from I. Schapera (Ed.), *David Livingstone's Family Letters, 1841–1856*, vol. I (1956) (London: Chatto and Windus, 1959), p. 236.

the Bakwena against them.[97] This resulted in the Boer dislike and distrust of missionaries, especially if they were of British origin, as they were suspected of inciting African communities against the Boer authorities. From then on, African chiefs under Boer authority were not allowed to accept missionaries, especially English-speaking ones, to work among their people without the permission of the Volksraad.[98] That was why in the Rustenburg area, the ZAR authorities invited, instead, German-speaking Hermannsburg missionaries, instead, to work among the Bakwena, because they felt that they were "not so dangerous to them in their foreign policy as the English missionaries."[99] The Rev. S. Hofmeyr, a Dutch Reformed Church missionary who worked among Africans in the Soutpansberg area during the early days of white settlement there, for example, was "practically boycotted" by the Boers in the area, "on account of his vocation,"[100] of doing missionary work among Africans.

From the late 1850s, when missionaries were seeking to work among African communities in the Transvaal, even if the Boer authorities had permitted them to do so, the next hurdle was getting the approval of the chief and his *lekgotla*. At first, the African groups simply had fear of the unknown. However, once the chief had agreed, missionary work proceeded fairly quickly. But sometimes a chief would expressly seek the services of a missionary. This often happened for security reasons. Chief Kgamanyane of the Bakgatla in the Pilansberg, for example, invited the Rev. Henri Gonin to his capital in 1865 because of conflict he had been experiencing with the Boer farmers around him for at least two decades. For the northern Transvaal, Isabel Hofmeyr has suggested that Chief Makopane of the amaNdebele invited the Berlin Mission Society missionaries to settle at his capital partly "for political and diplomatic ends, particularly because he had, for some time, been embroiled in a low level war with the Boers. Indeed, it was often as messenger and emissary that Makopane used the first missionary, W. Moschutz."[101] After having been permitted by the Boer authorities, the BMS missionaries first entered the ZAR in 1860

---

[97] Boer-missionary conflict is quite detailed in F. J. Ramsey, "The Rise and Fall of the Bakwena Dynasty of South-Central Botswana, 1820–1940," Ph.D. thesis, Boston University (1991), pp. 82–116. See also S. Glassman, "Livingstone confronts the Boer Commandants," *Midwest Quarterly*, 23(3) (1982), pp. 251–67.

[98] Eybers, *Select Constitutional Documents*, p. 414; Agar-Hamilton, *Native Policy*, p. 132.

[99] J. E. Carlyle, *South Africa and its Mission Fields* (London: Nisbet, 1878), p. 245.

[100] Agar-Hamilton, *The Native Policy*, p. 117.

[101] I. Hofmeyr, "Jonah and the swallowing monster: orality and literacy on a Berlin Mission Station in the Transvaal," *Journal of Southern African Studies*, 17(4) (December, 1991), p. 636.

and established mission stations among the Bapedi and Vhavenda in the Steelpoort and Soutpansberg areas. The BMS, the largest of the Lutheran societies operating in Southern Africa, had its most important station at Botshabelo, founded by Alexander Merensky, among the Bapedi with the permission of King Sekwati. As "the representative of the Z.A.R. among the Pedi," Merensky played a partisan role in support of the Boer authorities vis-à-vis the Bapedi on every issue, particularly in view of the fact that the Pedi polity was still independent and had not yet come under Boer rule. In the mid-1870s, French-speaking Swiss missionaries settled in the Spelonken foothills of the Soutpansberg where they worked among immigrants from the east whom they would later qualify as "Tsonga." As elsewhere in sub-Saharan Africa, the first Christian converts were initially harassed and shunned by chiefs until much later when the numbers of converts increased.[102]

Up to the 1880s, the missionary field in the Transvaal was dominated by four Christian denominations: the Dutch Reformed Church and the Hermmansburg Mission Society in the west and the Berlin Mission Society and Swiss Mission in the north. The first Christian missionaries to the Batswana were involved in spreading the Gospel and the rudiments of western education. In doing this they did not only impart their Christian beliefs but also their cultural, political, and commercial values. They introduced the use of agricultural aids such as, for example, plowing with oxen, irrigation, and wagons, while their wives taught domestic skills such as knitting, sewing, baking, nursing, and midwifery. They also produced religious and language texts in African languages, following the translation tradition first established by Robert Moffat at Kuruman in the 1820s. Each missionary society published materials for the people among whom they worked, the Dutch Reformed Church in Sekgatla, the Berlin Mission Society in Sepedi, and the Hermannsburg Mission Society in Sekwena. It was the disposition of an African chief that determined the success or failure of Christian missionary work. As Roger Beck has stated:

The rulers invited the missionaries in and determined where they could settle, what activities they could perform, what benefits they must provide, what members of society they could influence, and when they must leave. Missionary fortunes shifted with the political, social, and economic forces at work among the Sotho and Tswana, forces over which the missionaries had little control.[103]

---

[102] Delius, *The Land*, pp. 117–21.

[103] R. B. Beck, "Monarchs and Missionaries among the Tswana and Sotho," in R. Elphick and R. Davernport (Eds.), *Christianity in South Africa: A Political, Social and Cultural History* (Cape Town: David Philip, 1997), pp. 116–20. Quotation, pp. 119–20.

CONQUEST AND EARLY COLONIAL RULE IN NATAL

In the southeastern lowlands, disappointments befell Boer Trekkers who attempted to seize territory from the Zulu kingdom south of the Thukela River. Although they had killed 3,000 of King Dingane's soldiers in a battle at Ncome River (or Blood River) in December 1838, they were unable to compel his submission until the king's younger brother, Mpande, defected with 17,000 followers. It was Mpande's regiments rather than Boer commandos that brought about the final defeat of Dingane in January 1840. This left Mpande with a diminished Zulu kingdom north of the Thukela and a Boer "Republic of Natalia" south of the river. Even that state proved to be a flash in a pan. Officials at the Cape and humanitarian societies in Britain were so alarmed by the prospect that Boers might provoke a general flight toward their eastern frontier that an armed expeditionary force was despatched in 1842 to effect the annexation of Natal. After a spirited defense, the republicans relinquished their claims to sovereignty. And even though the British guaranteed land titles issued by Natalia, a large portion of the defeated Trekker families had grown fond of independence and preferred to join their compatriots on the Highveld.

One person's setback was usually another's opportunity. Just as the departure of Mzilikazi opened the way for chiefs and people to reclaim land in the northwest, the Zulu and Boer defeats in Natal left large tracts open to occupation by small- and middle-sized chieftaincies. Some of these groups were local people who had emerged from hiding, some were returning from exile to the lands of their ancestors and others were adventurers on the make. Zikhali ka Matiwane typified the movement. His father, Matiwane, had led a large body of his Ngwane followers away from the Zulu kingdom in the 1820s, first to glory in the Caledon Valley and then to catastrophic defeat by British and Xhosa forces at the battle of Mbholompo on the Umtata River in 1828. When Matiwane returned ignominiously to Zululand and was executed by Dingane, Zikhali sought refuge with Sobhuza in the nascent Swazi kingdom. Sensing an opportunity to rebuild the family fortunes when Mpande left the Zulu kingdom, Zikhali offered his services to the Boer–Zulu coalition that marched against Dingane in 1840. The Boer government of Natal showed no gratitude for Zikhali's contribution and actually threw him into jail for alleged misappropriation of captured cattle. With the Boers deposed, Zikhali established his headquarters on the slopes of the Drakensberg and sent messengers to the widely dispersed Ngwane, inviting them to live under his leadership. His experience was repeated by adventurous chiefs, so that within a few years the numbers of Africans settled in Natal grew from a few thousands to an estimated 100,000. This population movement dwarfed the great Boer Trek and created dilemmas for the newly established British authority, which did not get around to appointing a diplomatic agent to deal with the chiefs until 1845. Theophilus Shepstone, who filled that position (retitled secretary for native affairs in 1856), emerged as one of the most creative imperial administrators of his age. The system of government that evolved under his leadership was widely imitated as British colonization spread north to Kenya and laid the groundwork for the twentieth-century policy known as indirect rule.

Military, financial, and cultural considerations governed the development of Shepstone's system.[104] As an isiXhosa-speaking teenage son of a Methodist missionary, he had served as an interpreter on the staff of Major-General D'Urban during the war of 1834–35. Shepstone learned on the battlefield to respect the military capacities of his African adversaries. After the war he saw his own chief, D'Urban, dismissed for mishandling diplomacy, spending too much of taxpayers' money and pandering to the racial prejudices of settlers. Postwar employment as British resident agent among Xhosa groups on the eastern Cape frontier taught Shepstone something of the cultural forms and institutions of chieftaincy.[105] He put all these lessons into practice in Natal. The small British garrisons at Pietermaritzburg and D'Urban could not be expected to cope with an African uprising, even if they were reinforced by militia recruited from the tiny population of white settlers. Consequently, the first principle of Shepstone's military policy was to avoid actions that might provoke an uprising of chiefs or an invasion from the Zulu kingdom. That in turn required the provision of adequate land for the Natal chiefs – a task undertaken by a land commission in 1845. As European settlers were still thin on the ground, the commission had considerable scope for marking out large reserves even after endorsing the land titles granted by the Trekker government in a broad swath of territory from Ladysmith to Pietermaritzburg. Whereas settlers preferred farms on relatively flat land easily accessible by road, chiefs were accustomed to look for positions where cattle might be well defended. They did not mind "broken country" provided there was adequate rainfall and good pasturage. An additional factor bearing on the land commission's deliberations was missionary influence. Not only did his own background predispose Shepstone to favor missions, one of his fellow land commissioners was an American missionary. As originally envisaged, each reserve would have both a

[104] N. Etherington, "The 'Shepstone System' in the Colony of Natal and beyond the Borders," in A. Duminy and B. Guest (Eds.), *Natal and Zululand, a New History* (Pietermaritzburg: University of Natal Press, 1989), pp. 170–92.

[105] T. McClendon, "The Man Who Would Be *Inkosi*: Civilising Missions in Shepstone's Early Career," *Journal of Southern African Studies, 30* (2004), p. 346.

resident magistrate dispensing justice and resident missionaries, promoting "Christianity and civilization." Naturally, missionaries favored large reserves, hoping that their missions would gain a captive audience. The American missionaries were particularly favored by the provision of large reserves around their stations along the coast of Natal. The land commission could not have foreseen in 1846 that European growers of cane sugar would soon be demanding land in the coastal regions. On a map the distribution of "Native Reserves" suggests a grand design of social engineering – a wholesale relocation of chiefs and people to lands not required by settler farms. However, few if any people were moved in the first instance; the commission confirmed most chiefs in possession of land they already occupied. Moreover, large numbers of people continued to live outside the reserves on land theoretically held by settlers. A speculative commercial enterprise, the Natal Land and Colonization Company, took up large tracts of land earmarked for future settlement. While awaiting a boom in land values that would reap large profits, the company enjoyed a steady income by collecting rent from African "tenants."[106] Because tenants were exempt from the hut taxes, the rents were tolerable. So long as these tracts and the reserves provided adequate space for people and their cattle, Shepstone could feel reasonably confident that there would be no concerted rebellion against British rule.

Another imperative of Shepstone's system was financial: His administrative apparatus must pay for itself. In the early years he hoped for government grants large enough to pay for the direct government of the whole African population. When no such grants eventuated, Shepstone scaled down his plans. His principal source of revenue was the taxes paid annually by chiefs in cash on the basis of the number of huts inhabited by their followers. Also important were contributions made in kind through the forced labor demanded for roads and other public works. Reasoning that under the precolonial regime chiefs could command military and other services from young men, Shepstone insisted on his right to do the same. This not only gave him a labor force to build roads but a military force that could be mobilized to crush any threat of resistance. This aspect of the administration relied heavily on hand-picked men like Ngoza, who had no hereditary claims to chiefly status, but who was raised to an exalted position for his services to Shepstone and the government of Natal.[107]

The cultural aspects of Shepstone's system owed more to circumstances than to deliberate planning. In the early years, the government let chiefs

---

[106] H. Slater, "Land, Labour and Capital in Natal: The Natal Land and Colonisation Company 1860–1948," *Journal of African History, 16* (1975), pp. 257–84.

[107] N. Etherington, *Preachers, Peasants and Politics in Southeast Africa* (London: Royal Historical Society, 1978), p. 61.

rule their people pretty much as they wished, provided they paid their hut taxes and made no trouble. Given his limited resources, Shepstone could hardly do otherwise. However, in 1847 a difficult criminal case exposed the difficulties inherent in allowing two legal systems to flourish side by side.[108] Several men were brought to trial for killing an alleged witch. A senior Natal judge, Henry Cloete, insisted that this was a clear case of murder. Shepstone, in contrast, recommended clemency, arguing that customary practice had long sanctioned the execution of people convicted of witchcraft. Whereas British justice in the nineteenth century could not endorse witch trials, this case should not be treated as an ordinary homicide. Faced with the impossibility of reconciling the two positions, the colonial governor appealed to Britain's secretary of state for the colonies, Earl Grey, for a ruling. Although dual legal systems existed in Quebec, the Cape Colony, and certain parts of the British India Company's dominion, never before had the British Empire officially recognized the unwritten customary practices of indigenous people. Grey's masterly decision decreed that practices contrary to the principles of humanity must be suppressed, but that other customs could continue during the slow evolution toward "British civilization."[109] Thus, the killing of accused witches in Natal must cease, but other practices, such as polygamy and lobola could continue. Following Grey's decision, Shepstone set about gradually codifying the body of custom he called Native Law. This was not just law as understood by established chiefs. Natal's governor was formally constituted the supreme chief of all the African people. All magistrates on Native Reserves held concurrent commissions as administrators of Native Law and met with Shepstone from time to time to promote uniformity in the code. Discussions usually centered on matters of family law and inheritance, which differed dramatically from British practice.

A conspicuous feature of the new regime was that neither Shepstone nor his magistrates dealt with women. The oral annals of precolonial societies provide many examples of prestigious women wielding chiefly power. MaNthatisi, mother of Sekonyela, of the Batlokwa was only one of many well-known women who exercised such influence. On one occasion the impassioned speech of a matriarch in the councils of the amaHlubi stopped a threatened war with the amaNgwane.[110] However, women had no place in

---

[108] For an extensive discussion of parallel colonial legal systems, see M. Chanock, *Law, Custom and Social Order: The Colonial Experience in Malawi and Zambia* (Cambridge: Cambridge University Press, 1985).

[109] Earl Grey to H. Smith, December 10, 1847, based on James Stephen's Minute of September 17, 1847, CO 179/2, National Archives, Kew, Richmond, Surrey, UK.

[110] N. J. van Warmelo (Ed.), *History of Matiwane and the Amangwane Tribe, as told by Msebenzi to his kinsman Albert Hlongwane* (Pretoria: Native Affairs Depatment, 1938), pp. 124–6.

Shepstone's system. Thus, the laws he made to regulate family life reflected male opinions. It is for this reason that Jeff Guy has termed Shepstone's arrangements an "accommodation of patriarchs."[111] This should not be read as an accommodation of two equally patriarchal societies; it represented a European patriarchal conception of African social systems acquired through dealings with male chiefs.

As numbers of European settlers increased, Natal's government confronted a cultural problem of a different order. New settlers brought with them ideas about social class and color that predisposed them to view themselves as a master class born to rule the African majority, whom they termed "savages." Although the settler population was small before 1880 – mostly settled in Durban, Pietermaritzburg, and a few other small towns – their influence was out of all proportion to their numbers. They founded newspapers, formed town councils, held meetings, established armed militia, and, after a large measure of self-government was granted to Natal by the British parliament in 1856, elected a majority of the membership of the colony's Legislative Assembly. Very few accepted the dictum of Natal's constitution that the law would permit no distinction of color, religion, or social origin. On the contrary, they insisted on unequal treatment before the law. A Select Commission on Native Affairs in 1852 foreshadowed what might be expected from a settler-dominated government.

In the absence of any representative body to express African opinion, it fell to Shepstone as secretary for native affairs to speak for the majority of the population in the Legislative Assembly. The most frequent bone of contention was the settler demand that government do more to drive African men and women into wage labor as servants and manual workers. Their favored solutions to their labor problem were that the Native Reserves should be reduced in size, that taxes on huts and other aspects of African life be increased, and that the customs of lobola and polygamy be abolished so that African men could no longer live off the labor of their women folk. Shepstone answered these demands with the argument that wholesale interference with African land tenure and customs would provoke an armed rising that the colony was ill-equipped to quell. On questions of African law and custom, he worked to shore up the boundaries between the settlers' British legal system and his department's administrative structure of chiefly rule and Native Law. In the longer run, he hoped that British rule might be extended to neighboring territories which could provide a "safety valve" for Natal's growing African population.

[111] "An Accommodation of Patriarchs: Theophilus Shepstone and the Foundations of the System of Native Administration in Natal." Paper presented at Conference on Masculinities in Southern Africa, University of Natal, Durban (July 1997).

If the experience of Zikhali is any guide, most of Natal's chiefs appreciated Shepstone's administrative system until well into the late 1860s. The hut tax seemed a small price to pay for security from the threat of Zulu power across the Thukela and raiding parties from other Natal chiefs. He prospered in the midst of his reconstituted Ngwane chieftaincy. A German missionary who settled near his headquarters gave advice on how to deal with colonial authorities and dispensed lessons in reading, writing, and arithmetic. Zikhali's wealth and prestige caused even people from Zululand to join him saying, "it were far better for us to become subjects of the son of Matiwane."[112] The increase of his herds eventually won him a Swazi princess as his great wife. Not far away, the son of one of his father's determined enemies, Langalibalele ka Mthimkulu, also watched with satisfaction as his cattle and people multiplied on the slopes of the Drakensberg. After a falling out with Mpande, Langalibalele had led a large following out of Zululand. Shepstone welcomed them on the condition that they wage war on the "Bushmen raiders" who came down from the mountains to steal cattle from white farmers.[113] Natal's recognition of a form of customary law comforted people who had supposed the unsettling presence of Europeans would threaten the foundations of their existence. In particular, fathers who had feared a loss of control of their wives and daughters appreciated Shepstone's apparent understanding of their situation. Thus, a Victorian British social system that had yet to accord equal rights to women extended a helping hand to African men who worried that their control over the means of production and reproduction might be threatened by the new imperial order in Natal. Many chiefs welcomed the new order. A photograph taken in 1862, shortly before his death, shows Zikhali resplendent in a European military uniform surrounded by his most important subordinate chiefs.

Thus, the construction of the "Shepstone system" owed as much to Natal chiefs as colonial authority. It was an administrative and legal framework rather than a social order. Even its progenitors acknowledged that social and economic change must come. Shepstone frequently expressed the unrealistic hope that the whole population of Natal would move in the direction of enlightened progress. Whereas rapid changes occurred in very small sectors of society, they clearly indicated the course of future development. Settler demands for cheap labor required constant movement in and out of the designated reserves. To partially control those movements, colonial authorities resorted to an old Cape institution: the pass. Workers in villages and

---

[112] Van Warmelo, *History of Matiwane*, p. 126.

[113] J. Wright, *Bushman Raiders of the Drakensberg, 1840–1870* (Pietermaritzburg: University of Natal Press, 1971).

towns had to conform as well to dress codes, regulation of daily wages, and an unfamiliar criminal code. They learned new fashions, drank seriously alcoholic beverages, and caught new diseases. The few women who escaped control by husbands and fathers by moving to towns found themselves in demand as prostitutes; through sexual contact with settlers they acquired venereal diseases that gradually spread fear and loathing through the countryside. People who adopted the new faiths taught by foreign missionaries experienced even more startling change. As at the Cape, almost all missionaries insisted that Christianity came as part of a total cultural package. Conversion must be accompanied by outward and visible signs of inner change: European styles of dress; a new kind of family life based on radical changes in ideas about masculinity and femininity; novel notions of health and hygiene; and adaptation to an economy based on wage labor, and an aspiration to accumulate capital. The most challenging elements of the missionary cultural package were rules about marriage and kinship. Marriage was defined as the union of one man with one woman. Presentation of cattle to the father of one's bride was strongly discouraged, as was the widespread practicing of taking on the wife of one's dead brother. Resistance to the Christian cultural package was so widespread in the early days that missionaries gained very few followers. Those who did come to mission stations tended to be very young, very poor, or on the run. However, with the passage of time some converts to Christianity began to grow wealthy through growing cash crops, trade, and transport. Although Christians were not the only ones to prosper, their aspirations differed from people who clung to a more traditional lifestyle. Missionaries actively exhorted converts to be like them in all ways, including participation in the rights enjoyed by all the subjects of the British queen. By the early 1860s, converts to Christianity, known as the *kholwa* (believers), had begun to petition the government, demanding equality before the law.[114]

Shepstone's answer was to ask, equal before what law? Aside from missionaries, government officials, and a few brave individuals like David Dale Buchanan, editor of the *Natal Witness* newspaper, Europeans stubbornly resisted the extension of the vote beyond their own little circle. Torn between the settler's racial exclusivity and the constitution's insistence that there should be no legal distinctions based on color, Shepstone found a solution based on Earl Grey's recognition of Native Law. Legislation in 1865 decreed that no people subject to Native Law could vote unless they successfully applied for exemption on the basis of their property holdings, education, and commitment to conform to all British laws, including

---

[114]*Natal Witness*, 27 March 1863; Etherington, *Preachers, Peasants and Politics*, Chapter 5, pp. 87–114.

those on marriage.[115] The principle of this legislation outweighed any practical benefits because only a few dozen individuals ever succeeded in winning exemption from Native Law. Henceforth, Europeans inhabited a separate privileged world legally removed from the majority of the population. They used their privileges to ruthlessly minimize taxes on themselves while maximizing those paid by Africans. Though Britain's imperial government forbade them to occupy the Native Reserves, the settlers used every other means available to force labor into their service. These means included raising taxes and tariffs on imported goods primarily consumed by Africans, as well as government help in securing contract labor from neighboring territories and overseas. This brought Natal to a significant turning point in 1860 when the colony used taxes raised from Africans to finance the importation of laborers from Mozambique and indentured workers from British India. Unable to force local people into long-term contracts on their sugar estates, planters saw the imported workers as a stable, tractable labor force that would be available year round. The initial experiment with Indian indentured labor foundered during a recession and for a time Natal sought to build a stable labor supply for the plantations on the basis of migrants drawn from Mozambique. In 1874, Indian immigration resumed and, a decade later, as war in the Zulu kingdom and the lure of high wages at Kimberley made the importation of Mozambicans unprofitable, the plantations came to depend on these indentured workers.[116] For the next four decades, Indian men and women continued to come to Natal on the understanding that their rights would be looked after by Britain's India Office – a hope that was only partially fulfilled. Their presence complicated the question of social status in South Africa. From the settler point of view, they were another subordinated group to rule, as were the "shiftless amatongas." From Shepstone's point of view, the Indians' status was ambiguous; certainly they could not be brought under Native Law. So long as they were engaged in work contracts, their movements could be controlled by the colony's so-called Protector of Immigrants using the stringent provisions of the Masters and Servants Act. However, they had rights to legal representation and the free practice of their religion (there were Hindus, Muslims, and Christians among them). Many workers chose to return to India at the expiration of their contracts, but others exercised the right to stay on. Gradually, the independent Indian community expanded, a largely literate and commercially sophisticated society bent on exercising the full rights of citizenship.

---

[115] B. Guest and A. Duminy, *Natal and Zululand, A New History*, p. 147.
[116] P. Richardson, "The Natal Sugar Industry in the Nineteenth Century," in W. Beinart et al. (Eds.), *Putting a Plough to the Ground*, pp. 134–5.

From the beginning, the British colony of Natal was entangled in the affairs of all Southeastern Africa. Bonds of language, culture, kinship, and inheritance bound its people to neighbors on all sides. The complex laws governing ownership of cattle in particular caused Shepstone and his corps of resident magistrates to be constantly in contact with people from faraway places who came to claim the cattle they believed were owed them through lobola arrangements made years – sometimes decades – earlier. Because some important chiefs and their followers had moved from the Zulu kingdom to new residences as far afield as Mozambique, Malawi, and Zimbabwe, Shepstone had access to a network of information about southern Africa unprecedented in the annals of British administration. Communication, of course, worked both ways. Distant chiefs and kings knew a great deal about the affairs of Natal. They watched with interest as the results of this experiment in cooperation between semiautonomous chiefs and British colonialism unfolded. A great deal of attention focused on the comparative fortunes of the mixed government of Natal and the independent Zulu kingdom across the Thukela River.

Relations between the two regional powers were never entirely comfortable. Shepstone maintained a number of border agents whose job was to watch for signs of Zulu aggression. Mpande, likewise, constantly sent messengers and spies to Natal during his long reign (1840–72). The king seemed always to be in two minds about the wisdom of developing his state along western lines – an issue that in the early years centered on the missionary question. His predecessor, Dingane, had mixed experiences with missionaries. Allen Gardiner had proved an invaluable intermediary in dealing with the turbulent traders of Port Natal and the British Empire. Francis Owen, on the other hand, had proved worse than useless in the crisis sparked by the arrival of the Voortrekkers. After assuming power, Mpande allowed an American missionary, Aldin Grout, to establish a station in the southwest corner of the kingdom. When runaways, dissidents, and accused criminals gathered round the missionary, claiming independence of the king's authority, he closed the station down and would not admit other missionaries until 1851. When an intrepid Norwegian, Hans Schreuder, gained a foothold through an offer of secular medical and technological services, he shrewdly avoided challenging royal authority, accepting the king's policy of treating Christian converts as noncitizens while serving as Mpande's amanuensis in written communications with Natal. There the missionary influence might have ended but for a crisis that exposed the fragility of the Zulu constitution. Unlike his elder brothers, Shaka and Dingane, Mpande married many wives and acknowledged large numbers of children. As his eldest children grew to manhood, they began to jockey for the position of heir-apparent. Tensions between Cetshwayo and Mbuyazi came to a head in 1856. A dance competition provided the pretense for all-out war between their opposing factions that resulted in the death of Mbuyazi and the triumph of Cetshwayo's *Usutu* party.[117] Mpande grasped the danger that he might become the pawn – or perhaps the next victim – of his overbearing son and moved to counter Cetshwayo's influence through diplomacy. Suddenly the door was open to missionaries, although the policy of treating converts to Christianity as aliens remained in place. Unable to meet the demand with Norwegians, Hans Schreuder in 1858 invited fellow Lutherans attached to the Hermannsburg Missionary Society to take advantage of the new policy. These missionaries were active in trade and readily provided technical aid, as when the Hermannsburgers built wagons and carriages for the king. Cetshwayo's rivalry with his half-brothers did not end with the death of Mbuyazi. In the wake of the civil war some of Mpande's wives and sons had fled to Natal, where they posed an obvious future danger. One in particular, Mkungu, had settled with his mother on the mission station of Anglican Bishop John William Colenso, who had formed a close friendship with Shepstone.[118] Colenso spoke openly of Mkungu as a young prince who would be the future king of the Zulu. Fear that Zulu forces were about to invade Natal in 1861 (with the rumored intention of killing Mkungu) provided an opportunity for Shepstone and Colenso to visit Zululand in order to reach an understanding with Mpande and Cetshwayo. They reached an agreement that left Mpande in secure possession of the throne while officially acknowledging that Natal recognized Cetshwayo as his heir. Mpande also agreed that the door would be open to missionaries of all societies to establish stations in his kingdom. For a time, Colenso and Shepstone even toyed with the idea of going to the Zulu kingdom as spiritual and secular advisors, with the ultimate aim of bringing the kingdom under British protection. This demonstrated how far Shepstone's confidence in his system had advanced; it had become, in his own mind at least, a template for benevolent British rule of any region of Southeastern Africa.

DIPLOMACY AND CONFLICT BETWEEN THE ORANGE AND VAAL RIVERS

Whereas Natal remained far from a perfect illustration of the kind of future powerful chiefs desired, it certainly contrasted favorably with the war and

[117] C. de B. Webb and J. B. Wright (Eds.), *A Zulu King Speaks: Statements made by Cetshwayo KaMpande on the History and Customs of His People* (Pietermaritzburg: University of Natal Press, 1978), pp. 15–16.

[118] J. Guy, *The Heretic: A Study of the Life of John William Colenso, 1814–1883* (Johannesburg: Ravan Press, 1983), p. 222.

conquest inflicted on Xhosa chiefs over the last few decades. Shepstone was a man with whom chiefs could do business. Whereas earlier colonial officials had responded with derision to offers of marriage with any chief's daughter, Shepstone knew what to do when Mswati of Swaziland made such a proposal. He accepted with gratitude and married the princess to his military right-hand man, Ngoza. Like Mswati, Moshoeshoe, self-made king of the Basotho, realized the importance of Natal, especially after Shepstone sent two regiments to aid his enemies in 1851.[119] Moshoeshoe had actively pursued alliances with the Cape Colony since 1835, only to find his overtures rebuffed. A period of special danger began in 1845 when the British placed a resident at Bloemfontein to represent their interests on the Highveld. Hopes that a permanent alliance with the British might develop were crushed when Resident Henry Warden drew a boundary line that greatly diminished Moshoeshoe's claims to the Caledon Valley. Using his friendship with missionaries of the Paris Evangelical Missionary Society, the king sent vigorous protests to Cape Town. However, he soon discovered that the tide of missionary influence had greatly ebbed at the Cape, particularly with the return of Sir Harry Smith. Although the new governor had promised to reduce expenses and impose peace on the colony's troublesome frontiers, he soon revealed a very different personal agenda: to bring peace through a bold annexation of territory north of the Orange River.

British suzerainty to the north of the Orange River was limited to a treaty concluded in 1834 with the leader of the western Griqua community under Andries Waterboer and, two years later, the extension of the Cape of Good Hope Punishment Act to cover the area south of twenty-five degrees south latitude. In 1843, the British established similar treaties with Adam Kok at Philippolis and Moshoeshoe at Thaba Nchu. Moshoeshoe and other chiefs initially welcomed these attempts to bring order to the region as they secured their own land claims and curbed those of the Boers. Smith, however, actively sought friendship with the Boers – notwithstanding the armed resistance put up by Andries Pretorius at the Battle of Boomplaats in July 1848. After Pretorius and his diehards had retreated north of the Vaal River, Smith appointed surveyors to carve arable land into farms throughout the area he proclaimed as the Orange River Sovereignty. Smith endorsed Warden's policy of forming a coalition to oppose King Moshoeshoe's pretensions to dominance in the Caledon Valley. In 1851, Warden was ready to march against the king with a combined force contributed by Sekonyela, Moroka, Adam Kok, Andries Waterboer, and other minor chiefs. The ignominious

---

[119] Etherington, *Great Treks*, p. 318.

failure of this assault was part of the reason that Harry Smith was recalled as governor and his annexations on the Highveld were abandoned. A face-saving expedition led by Smith's replacement, Lt. Gen. George Cathcart, partially redeemed Warden's defeat and concluded a peace settlement with Moshoeshoe in December 1852.

Britain's withdrawal from the Highveld occurred in two stages. First, the Sand River Convention of January 1852 relinquished all land north of the Vaal River to the Krygsraad (war council) of scattered Boer communities. Second, by the Bloemfontein Convention of February 1854, the Orange River Sovereignty passed to a group representing British and Boer settlers and was renamed the Orange Free State. All treaties previously concluded between the Cape Colony and chiefs north of the Orange were declared null and void. This obliged many groups to fend for themselves. Moshoeshoe's kingdom was once more left to its own devices. The king's first act was to sweep the Caledon Valley of his old enemies, leaving only Boer farms undisturbed. Next, he resumed the program of economic development and armament that had been the foundation of his success in the 1830s. The principal sources of wealth were wages earned by Basotho men working in the Cape Colony and money earned from sales of grain. Though these were substantial, they could not compare with the revenue pouring into the coffers of the Orange Free State government, as farms multiplied and the wool boom spread prosperity. War for possession of farmland west of the Caledon River broke out in 1865, and once again Moshoeshoe put up surprisingly strong resistance against a combined mounted force of Transvaal and Free State troops. For a time, it seemed likely that Theophilus Shepstone would arrange a friendly occupation that would put Moshoeshoe under a system of indirect rule similar to that practiced in Natal. In the end, a treaty of 1869 laid down the modern borders of Lesotho and put the kingdom under British protection, but not under Shepstone.

Griqua communities took another course after the extinction of the Orange River Sovereignty. After a brief period of prosperity built on the expanding ivory frontier and a wool boom, they began to find that their Christian individualism put them at a disadvantage in dealings with immigrant farmers. Many succumbed to the temptation to sell or otherwise alienate land, a trend that the weak Griqua institutions of government proved unable to control. By 1861, about 2,000 Griqua decided to trek with Adam Kok across the mountains of Lesotho to a new home in an area popularly known as Nomansland, sandwiched between Faku's Mpondo kingdom and the colony of Natal. Although Natal had laid claim to the district, it had not yet been subjected to formal rule, so the Griquas established their position in "Griqualand East" through negotiation with Faku. The ironic result of their arduous trek was that they left their old homes just a few years before the discovery of diamonds made Griqualand West one of the most coveted regions on the face of the planet.[120]

EARLY DIAMOND DIGGING: THE DYNAMICS OF RACE, CLASS, CULTURE, AND MONOPOLY CAPITALISM

Although the first diamond find occurred in 1867, near the confluence of the Vaal and Hartz rivers, the decisive discovery occurred in 1870 when, for the first time in history, a motherlode of diamonds lodged in the core of an extinct volcano was found away from the river at Bultfontein. The following year a richer deposit was discovered at nearby Colesberg Kopje and this site, soon to be renamed the Kimberley mine, was "rushed" by prospective diggers. By the end of the year the area had been annexed by Britain as the colony of Griqualand West and fortune-seekers were streaming to the four Kimberley mines (Kimberley, De Beers, Bultfontein, and Dutoitspan) from many parts of Southern Africa and the world.

In the early days, few diggers could pay cash wages and they were obliged to engage men under a share-working system. The high cost of mining placed the small diggers under constant pressure to sell their claims to larger, better-capitalized companies. This pressure increased as the pits grew deeper and the cost of bringing blue ground to the surface rose proportionately. By 1873, the Kimberley mine was 200 feet deep and covered about ten acres. Steam engines powered the cars and buckets, drawn by a network of steel wires and pulleys, that gave access to the mine and that allowed excavated ground to be hauled to the surface. Steam pumped water out of the pits, drove the washing machines, and allowed men to add increasingly small diamonds to the stones they recovered at the sorting yards.

High wages added considerably to the cost of mining as employers had to attract workers to Kimberley from areas as far removed as Cornwall, England, and Mozambique; and frequently had to lodge and feed them in the "compounds" built next to the yards in which they washed and sorted through the excavated blue ground. Drawing men to the diggings was no simple matter, especially as the deepest and most profitable of the four pits became the most dangerous mine in the world. For migrant workers, going to Kimberley was very much a lottery. Traveling overland entailed enormous risks as men faced swollen rivers, severe cold, long distances without food, water, or fuel; and were assailed by wild animals and bandits. As the pits grew deeper they suffered from landslides and flooding, as well

---

[120] R. Ross, *Adam Kok's Griquas: a study in the development of stratification in South Africa* (Cambridge: Cambridge University Press, 1976), pp. 94–100.

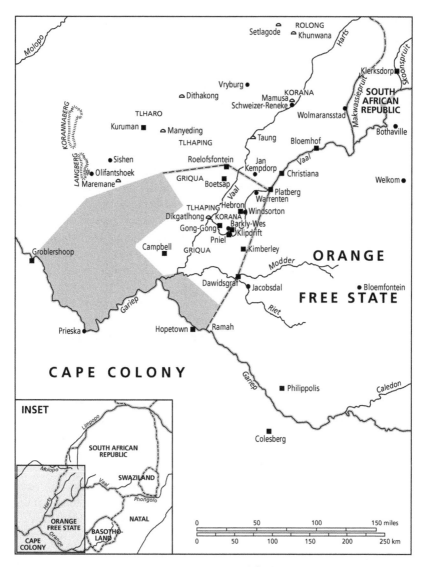

FIGURE 7.3. Diamond fields.

as numerous accidents caused by misfired charges or the unequal working of claims. The unhygienic conditions at the diggings bred diseases like dysentery, typhoid, and, especially, pneumonia. Epidemics of small pox and bubonic plague were never far off.

In these conditions, diggers found it difficult to discipline workers who sought to improve their conditions of work by stealing diamonds or by "deserting," to secure higher wages or simply escape a brutal situation.

Many workers attempted to break a foreign and inhuman rhythm of labor by turning to alcohol; but in the process they often injured themselves, broke their equipment or, most seriously, failed in large numbers to appear for work at the start of the week. The Saint Monday phenomenon, typical of the early stages of mining in many parts of the world, became a marker of life at Kimberley as men sought refuge in inebriation and, through the practice of commensality, tried to forge identities that were serviceable to life on the diggings.

Race and class became important issues. As individuals and companies started to buy out the small claim holders, the diggers attempted to exclude men of color from owning claims and to confine them to the role of manual labor. The confrontation between capitalists and claim-owners exploded in mid-1875 when the diggers attempted to ensure their position by seizing the government of Griqualand West. The crushing of the "Black Flag" revolt by the British army had two important consequences: On the one hand, it caused the government to accede to the diggers' demands to prohibit people of color from holding diggers' licenses, whereas on the other hand it was a major defeat for the small diggers as it brought in a government favorable to the amalgamation of claims in the hands of large-scale capitalists.[121] The hostility between African and white workers grew as whites came to depend on wages for their survival whereas most African workers retained a separate means of production in the rural areas. This meant that the interests of the working class were strictly divided by race; for although whites sought to protect their wages through organized labor combinations and the protection of individual rights, Africans found a more coherent defense of their working conditions in their ability to return home, a strategy that employers saw as "desertion."

African mine workers brought a rural culture to the mines and ordered their lives in ways that were often very different from those of European proletarians. Many came from societies with little or no experience of individual rights. In the rural areas, authoritarian chiefs and elders tended to dominate the lives of young men and shape their views on labor and how it should be performed. This had different consequences: in the Zulu kingdom the freedom with which young men moved onto the labor market was restricted by their obligation to provide the king with labor and military service. However, in most areas chiefs encouraged the emigration of labor, either by sending parties to the mines, by "selling" men to recruiters, or by taxing them on their return. In a few instances these men were servile laborers, sometimes even slaves. This frequently caused the

[121] R. Turrell, *Capital and Labour on the Kimberley Diamond Fields, 1871–1890* (Cambridge: Cambridge University Press, 1987), Chapter 3.

chief to determine the freedom with which men sold their labor, as well as the expected conditions under which they would work at Kimberley. The notion of work carried to the mines by these men was also shaped by an agricultural economy that demanded seasonal bursts of communal labor that, in turn, were dependent on sociability and leisure. On the Kimberly diggings, this concept of work frequently contradicted the employers' idea that costly machines should determine the rhythm and pace of labor. Nor was the length of time migrants were willing to stay at the diggings, and acquire mining skills, determined by Europeans' sense of the need to accumulate capital. Few African workers were driven to work, as was the case with many Europeans, by a dependence on a range of expensive commodities. Mostly, they worked a few weeks or months to earn the money needed to buy familiar products, such as clothing and imported liquor or perhaps beads and knives. Many bought guns at Kimberley with which they defended their independence and hunted game. The consumer needs of black workers grew as they came into contact with the Kimberley High Street-in-Africa; and their requirements spread into the rural areas when they returned to their villages laden with goods. Traders quickly gauged this new opportunity for wealth and moved into remote rural areas where they traded from their wagons or established stores and canteens. In some areas, men were pushed to the mines by the need to acquire a commodity with a special, local value. The Bapedi and Basotho particularly valued guns as a means of defending themselves against Boer aggression, whereas men in southern Mozambique used their wages to buy iron hoes with which they could acquire wives and the munificence needed to draw a following. But these demands could change suddenly. In the mid-1870s, French traders sought to benefit from the market for iron hoes at Lourenço Marques (Maputo) by manufacturing huge numbers of these items in Marseilles. The unimpeded importation of hoes caused a severe inflation in the brideprice and, eventually, to the adoption of gold coins as a more stable medium of bridewealth. By the early 1880s, Tsonga-speaking workers from southern Mozambique started to replace Sotho and Pedi workers at Kimberley who, recently conquered, were prohibited from acquiring guns. Almost everywhere, cyclical droughts and famines pushed men to the mines where they worked for as long as it took to earn the wages that would ensure the survival of their families back home.[122]

The process of amalgamation on the mines, whereby companies absorbed small claims into their holdings, sped up in the early 1880s as the price of diamonds collapsed just as working tunnels were driven under the

---

[122] P. Harries, *Work, Culture and Identity: Migrant Labourers in Mozambique and South Africa, c. 1860–1910* (London: Heinemann, 1994), pp. 86–90, 98–9.

Kimberley "big hole" and the cost of mining operations soared. This resulted in a spate of bankruptcies and takeovers; and the process of amalgamation grew as it became clear that, if one company could exercise a monopoly over the sale of diamonds, it would be able to determine the price of the stones worldwide. The mine owners also attempted to curtail the theft of diamonds by introducing strip searching, a practice almost entirely restricted to black miners, and by establishing special IDB (illicit diamond buying) courts. They also attempted to enclose black workers' living quarters within compounds in such a way as to isolate men from their sources of liquor, prevent them from deserting, and stop them from smuggling diamonds to illicit buyers. The first closed compound was erected in 1885 and, four years later, when C. J. Rhodes succeeded in placing all four mines under his De Beers Consolidated Mines, there were seventeen of these structures at Kimberley.[123] This greatly expanded the impact of migrant labor on family life, as men in the compounds lived entirely away from the company of women for long periods. Conversely, women in areas of high labor recruitment had to adapt to life with fewer young men. Yet at the same time, many rural families benefited from the growing market for their goods, largely maize and cattle, presented by growing towns and other centers of employment.[124]

This new form of monopoly capitalism would exercise a strong influence on labor relations in South Africa. It produced a class of industrialists, like Rhodes, J. B. Robinson, Abe Bailey, and Max Michaelis, who would invest heavily in the public institutions and politics of white South Africa.[125] Their influence, as distinctly South African capitalists, would soon impress itself on life on the Witwatersrand. The militancy of white workers at Kimberley was curbed as employers drew them into racially defined positions as supervisors of black labor. In this way, white workers were separated, both spatially and in terms of their interests and culture, from migrant black workers in the compounds. De Beers further domesticated white workers and separated them from their potential black class

---

[123] W. Worger, *South Africa's City of Diamonds: Mine Workers and Monopoly Capitalism in Kimberley, 1867–1895* (New Haven: Yale University Press and Johannesburg: Ravan Press, 1987), Chapters 5 and 6.

[124] C. Bundy, *The Rise and Fall of the South African Peasantry* (London: Heinemann, 1979), Chapter 3; K. Shillington, *The Colonisation of the Southern Tswana, 1870–1900* (Johannesburg: Ravan Press, 1985), pp. 62–70; W. Beinart, *The Political Economy of Pondoland 1860 to 1930* (Cambridge: Cambridge University Press, 1982), pp. 22–30. See also note 142 following.

[125] R. Rotberg, *The Founder: Cecil John Rhodes and the Pursuit of Power* (Johannesburg: Southern Book Publishers, 1988).

allies through an active policy of industrial paternalism.[126] A small black middle class started to emerge in parts of Kimberley in the early 1880s. Men who had acquired a degree of education in mission schools at the diggings or elsewhere found work as clerks, supervisors, or translators for mining companies, trading establishments, and, especially, the telegraph office. Some would establish families at Kimberley and contribute to the broad, British imperial culture of the town.[127]

Black workers continued to be drawn to Kimberley by competitive working conditions. Even as the compounds closed in the mid-to-late 1880s, few companies had to buy labor from recruiters as was the practice in other parts of South Africa. Instead, they kept wages sufficiently high to draw men away from other major employers of labor, such as the sugar plantations in Natal, the railways, harbors in the Cape, and gold mines of the eastern Transvaal. They initially allowed men in the compounds to consume strictly controlled amounts of alcohol and sometimes allowed them to spend weekends in town. Employers also encouraged black miners to engage in an extensive penny capitalism in the compounds and, through the initiation of work tickets and task work, as well as short work contracts, allowed men to influence the pace at which they labored as well as the duration of their contracts. However, although miners were still able to influence both the pace and rhythm of labor, and the general conditions of their work, the prison-like compounds introduced a new and frightening level of control over their working lives. This new discipline contributed to a sharp rise in productivity as, during the period 1882–92, the output of Kimberley mine workers doubled.

Mine workers returned home with wages, ideas, and experiences that introduced a new turbulence into rural society. Many came into contact with Christianity on the diggings; either directly, through evangelizing ministers, or through the written and sung texts that circulated in their living quarters and public spaces. Missionaries viewed the diggings as a prime position for evangelical work. This was partly because miners were in need of spiritual support, but mainly because they carried the Christian message into distant rural areas where, following religious texts or simply inspired by hymns, they could await the coming of a missionary. Kimberley was not simply a center for the accumulation of capital; it was also a space in

---

[126] A. Mabin, "Labour, capital, class struggle, and the origins of residential segregation in Kimberley, 1880–1920," *Journal of Historical Geography*, *12*, 1 (1986).

[127] R. Turrell, *Capital and Labour on the Kimberley Diamond Fields* (Cambridge: Cambridge University Press, 1987), pp. 184–94; B. Willan, *Sol Plaate: a Biography* (Johannesburg: Ravan Press, 1984), pp. 29–30.

which men learned new skills, such as reading, and acquired new identities, such as those associated with ethnicity, Christianity, and class.

DIAMONDS: THE SHORT- AND LONG-TERM IMPACT

At the structural level, development of the diamond fields accelerated some forces for change that were already present and launched other entirely new forces that permanently altered the course of South African history. In the short run, the demand for labor pushed up wages and expanded markets for African agricultural production. This in turn enabled the more powerful independent kingdoms and chieftaincies to push ahead with programs of military modernization designed to strengthen their defensive and offensive capabilities. Labor recruiters and gunrunners flourished in the independent kingdoms. British authorities reacted to the challenge with measures designed to disarm the most formidable of those states and to bring them under imperial control. Important streams of migrant labor passed through the independent republics of the Transvaal and the Orange Free State, Basotholand, and the colony of Natal, showing that a single regional economy had emerged.[128] As a result there was a renewed imperial interest to bring those states into a general federation under British sovereignty. The diamond fields also provided opportunities for small-scale African entrepreneurs already involved in the capitalist economy. Peasant producers prospered in many areas, especially those associated with Christian missions. Others built up preexisting operations as traders and transport riders. Groups of peasants banded together to buy land outside the reserves. Growth in paid employment was not limited to the mines themselves. Dockyards, roads, railways, and other infrastructure expanded to meet the needs of the mining industry as a whole. In some segments of the economy, workers for the first time discovered the power to better themselves through strikes and other forms of industrial action. The specter of worker power frightened many large- and small-scale employers who pushed for legislation to provide more control over the workforce. The development of closed compounds at the diamond fields provided the most extreme example of a captive labor force and set an example that other industries would attempt to imitate. Structural change was, of course, accompanied by social and cultural change. Settler communities showed unmistakable signs of unease, which manifested itself in moral panics over an alleged increase in crime, especially in relation to white

---

[128] Delius, *The Land Belongs to Us*, Chapter 3; A. Kirkaldy, *Capturing the Soul: The Vhavenda and the Missionaries, 1870–1900* (Pretoria: Protea Book House, 2005), pp. 38–43.

females. As young African men gained experience of migrant labor, they found opportunities to escape control by older men and chiefs. Cash in hand gave some young men unprecedented independence in contracting marriages. A few young women also found ways of circumventing parental authority, leading to a general feeling among older men that they were losing control over production and reproduction – an anxiety that frequently expressed itself in laments that young people had abandoned all morality.

These interlinked structural and cultural shifts underlay – but did not determine – the unfolding of events in the 1870s. These depended, as always, on contingent factors of people, ideas, and politics. Britain's annexation of the diamond fields in August 1871 and the Cape's incorporation of Basotholand a few months later had provoked Boer opposition to the idea of federation. Although Natal was too far from the action to join the unseemly struggles to lay claim to the diamond fields, the mining revolution nonetheless profoundly affected the colony. Individuals closed their businesses and went to seek their fortune, including the editor of the *Natal Witness* newspaper, and the brothers Herbert and Cecil Rhodes, who had been experimenting with cotton farming. Promoters of trade and transport hoped to make Durban the preferred point of entry to the Highveld and looked for ways to extend railways beyond the Drakensberg. Farmers, on the other hand, looked on with dismay as they saw their workforces walk away in search of higher wages. In the early days of the diamond rush, diggers had no time for the cheap labor policies practiced on settler farms. They needed workers immediately and paid whatever was asked. This not only caused men from Natal to trek off to the mines, it also threatened to divert established streams of migrant labor away from Natal. The unsettling effects of these developments may have underpinned South Africa's first "black peril" scare, which gripped white settlers in Natal from about 1869–73. Although no statistical evidence pointed to an upsurge of sexual assaults on white women, newspapers and politicians demanded action in the form of harsher penalties for black males guilty of actual or attempted rape. In line with the prevailing double standard, nothing whatever was said about white males assaulting black women – a much more common phenomenon.

Signs of increasing unease and internal tensions also appeared in the Zulu kingdom, even though it sent few workers to the diamond fields. Although the amaZulu lacked the resources necessary to arm themselves on the scale of other regional powers, observers noted a buildup of both guns and horses. Boer farmers from the southeastern Transvaal had been encroaching on the western borders of the kingdom since the late 1850s and it was quite conceivable that a war like that fought between the Boers and Basotho could break out at any time. It was obvious that old king Mpande had not long to live; Cetshwayo still felt some insecurity about the succession and worried that potential rivals may have been strengthening their capacity for independent action. All the amaZulu knew very well that chiefs such as Moshoeshoe, Soshangane, Sekhukhune, and Swazi king Ludvonga had been arming themselves with modern weapons. Rumors of war circulated constantly. What none of the independent kingdoms could know was that the British Empire was about to embark on a path that would reduce them all to a state of dependence.

The unexpected spark that set the process in motion was struck on the slopes of the Drakensberg in Natal where Langalibalele's amaHlubi people had been enjoying twenty-five years of uninterrupted peace and prosperity.[129] By 1873, the venerable chief had fifty-four sons, sixty-eight daughters, and vast herds of cattle. Some of the Hlubi young men had also traveled to the diamond fields and, like young Sotho and Pedi workers, had returned home with money to spend and guns to show off. Whereas Shepstone had made no serious effort to disarm the populations of the reserves, he had attempted to monitor gun ownership by requiring chiefs to register all firearms in their territories. John Macfarlane, the magistrate charged with oversight of Langalibalele, reported that many firearms had not been registered (including those brought back by Hlubi men who had accompanied Shepstone's son, George, on a fortune-seeking expedition to the diamond fields). In the edgy atmosphere of 1873 what might have been treated as an insignificant misdemeanor escalated into an armed confrontation. Soon after Macfarlane issued his first order that chief bring in his guns, the annual manuevers of the Natal volunteer militia was held nearby, an event that Langalibalele wrongly interpreted as preparation for an attack on his people. Natal settlers were themselves nervous about the state of Zululand following the death of Mpande. Having accepted an invitation to witness the installation of Cetshwayo as king, Shepstone decided the time was ripe for a display of colonial power and marched into Zululand at the head of a large armed column in August. Many feared that the troops might be heading into a trap, Shepstone returned safely, having announced that he had given laws to the new king. In mid-October he sent one of his right-hand men, Mahoiza, to demand that Langalibalele come immediately to Pietermaritzburg. Seeing that white farmers in the district had started moving their cattle out of harm's way, the chief decided he was about to be killed and tried to flee over the mountains to Lesotho. On Shepstone's

[129] N. Etherington, "Why Langalibalele Ran Away," *Journal of Natal and Zulu History* (1978), 1, pp. 1–25.

advice, Natal's governor, Benjamin Pine, sent an expeditionary force to punish the chief for the "crime" of attempting to leave the colony without permission. In a skirmish at the top of Bushmen's River Pass, four of the Natal troopers died, a misfortune that turned the expedition into a ferocious campaign of revenge marked by hideous atrocities such as the dynamiting of caves where Hlubi people had taken refuge. Following his capture on December 11, a forlorn Langalibalele was bound and taken for trial to the capital along roads lined by jeering settlers. Instead of trying the chief by British law with a jury, Shepstone invoked his version of Native Law and had Langalibalele condemned by a panel of chiefs headed by Governor Pine as titular supreme chief of the African people of Natal.

Because it epitomized all the currents of change swirling through the subcontinent and exposed central contradictions and anomalies in Britain's colonial policy, the misnamed rebellion became the occasion for agonized reappraisals in many quarters. Even before the crisis, the chiefs of Natal had begun to grumble about increased taxes. Now as they watched Hlubi herds and women led away in triumph by Shepstone's henchmen, the chiefs of Natal understood as never before the fragility of their own position. At the same time, the merits of Shepstone's system itself were being called into question at the heart of the British Empire. Appalled by the punitive expedition and the trial, Bishop Colenso abruptly terminated his long-standing friendship with the secretary for native affairs and set out to enlist what remained of the humanitarian/missionary lobby in a campaign to quash Langalibalele's sentence. Britain's House of Lords burst into amused guffaws when told that the governor of Natal, who was supposed to be conveying the blessings of European civilization to Africa, had taken up a position as a supreme chief. Benjamin Disraeli, who had led his Conservative Party to triumph at the general election of 1874, now faced the problem of putting into practice the high-flown rhetoric about the glories of empire he had lauded in a famous speech at the Crystal Palace in 1872. The task of balancing the needs of imperial defense, economic development, support for white settlers, and humane administration fell to Lord Carnarvon, the secretary of state for colonies. Taking up a policy of grouping small colonies into larger, self-sufficient states that had begun with the Confederation of Canada in 1867 and had already been discussed in relation to South Africa, Carnarvon set out to bring the Cape Colony, Natal, and the independent Boer Republics under a single government. But first he had to do something about Bishop Colenso's grave allegations. To gain an independent source of advice, Carnarvon commissioned historian James Anthony Froude to go on a fact-finding tour of South Africa. Not long after, Shepstone and Colenso arrived in London to give their own versions of the Langalibalele affair and recommendations for the future of South Africa.

As a result, Carnarvon had the benefit of three very different points of view. Froude articulated the most advanced views on racial science. Like his mentor, Thomas Carlyle, Froude dismissed Africans as people only fit for servitude and lauded white settlers – especially those descended from the Dutch – as a progressive force. Colenso, in contrast, argued on the base of abstract jurisprudence and tedious examination of evidence that nothing less than full restoration of Langalibalele to his chieftainship and the complete overthrow of the Shepstone system would vindicate Britain's claim to be the trustee of African welfare. Shepstone employed more subtle reasoning. Experience had taught him that Froude's trust in white settlers was misplaced. Certainly, a settler-dominated government in Natal could not be trusted to look after African interests. Only a firm but fair administration – such as his own – that understood African ways of life and thought could keep the peace and steer South Africa toward federation and a better life for all. Carnarvon drew something from each of these points of view. He was inclined to agree with Froude that Afrikaans-speaking people must be conciliated. He agreed with Colenso that Natal's administration of the African population was in urgent need of reform. But most of all, Shepstone bewitched Carnarvon with his apparent knowledge, wisdom, and broad view of South African affairs. Carnarvon's first move was to announce his intention to bring the colonies and republics into a confederation. Second, he dispatched the empire's most successful young general, Sir Garnet Wolseley, to deal with the unreliable colonists of Natal by persuading them to give up their limited powers of self-government. Third, as a signal of Britain's humanitarian intentions, he appointed Sir Bartle Frere, a noted champion of antislavery agitation and missions, to be high commissioner of South Africa. Finally, Carnarvon bestowed a knighthood on Theophilus Shepstone and sent him to the Transvaal, charged with a secret commission to annex the nearly bankrupt republic should circumstances appear propitious. Important as these agents would prove in their individual capacities, they must not be allowed to obscure the central importance of Carvarvon himself, a man too often dismissed by his political contemporaries and underestimated by historians. No one in Britain in the 1870s took a more ambitious approach to African affairs. Disraeli talked grandly about an imperial mission, but Carnarvon laid out the road map for achieving an empire stretching from Cape to Cairo. For strategic reasons Britain must safeguard the Suez Canal, in East Africa it must support measures designed to suppress the slave trade and close the door to potential European colonial rivals, and the emerging regional economy of mining, trade, and labor migration must be brought under a single British government. In a most revealing statement on Britain's destiny in Central Africa made in 1876 he told Bartle Frere:

I should not like anyone to come too near to us either on the south towards the Transvaal, which must be ours; or on the north too near Egypt and the country which belongs to Egypt. In fact when I speak of geographical limits I am not expressing my real opinion. We cannot admit rivals in the east or even the central part of Africa: and I do not see why, looking to the experience we now have of English life within the tropics – the Zambezi should be considered to be without the range of our colonisation. To a considerable extent, if not entirely, we must be prepared to apply a sort of Munro [sic] doctrine to much of Africa.[130]

A comparably frank statement of his policy for the control of labor in Southern Africa expressed Carnarvon's intention to implement in every territory "a common system of treatment which shall be clear of the reproach of a system of servitude, and yet shall put that moral screw on the native which is desirable for the safety and interest of all parties."[131]

Of all the pieces in his confederation puzzle, Natal's settlers proved easiest to fit in place. Privately contemptuous of Natal's settlers but gracious and charming in public, Garnet Wolseley soon convinced the Legislative Assembly to adopt a "Jamaican" constitution that gave appointed officials a decisive say in government. At the same time, he drew on his military knowledge to make recommendations on defense. In his opinion the Zulu kingdom posed a menace that could hardly be challenged by the forces currently stationed in Natal. Shepstone went to the Transvaal in 1877 with the Zulu threat as the trump card that he hoped would persuade the Boers to seek the shelter of British administration. At a time when the South African Republic teetered on the brink of bankruptcy and seemed to be losing a war against Sekhukhune's Pedi kingdom, Shepstone had good reasons to hope for success. Instead of following Wolseley's example and securing a formal agreement to a British takeover, Shepstone simply raised the Union Jack and annexed the Transvaal in April 1877 – just nine days before Bartle Frere arrived in Cape Town to assume the post of high commissioner. Frere faced grave problems from the moment he stepped ashore. The Cape legislature was torn by internal divisions and in no mood to rubber stamp his plans for confederation. A petty squabble on the eastern frontier in 1877 provoked the Ninth Frontier War with the amaXhosa. This led the Cape government to introduce a form of indirect rule in the recently conquered areas of the Transkei and, at the same time, to bring Griqualand West under its control. Meanwhile, the Cape's administration of Basotholand had proved a dismal failure and a crisis was coming to a head over the same issue that had undone

---

[130] Carnarvon to Frere, December 12, 1876, Carnarvon Papers, PRO 30/6/4.

[131] Carnarvon to Froude September 2, 1875, quoted in R. Cope. *Ploughshare of War: The Origins of the Anglo-Zulu War of 1879* (Pietermaritzburg: University of Natal Press, 1999), p. 83.

Langalibalele: guns. According to Shepstone, the "Zulu menace" identified by Wolseley was only one part of a larger, darker picture. He told Frere that his extensive intelligence network had uncovered a plot by all the large African kingdoms to combine in a general war on the Europeans. The key to winning the hearts of farmers and burghers in the Transvaal was to remove this threat before it exploded. Frere extended Shepstone's reasoning, linking the success of Carnarvon's confederation policy to a general disarmament of the independent kingdoms.

The kingdoms themselves had little or no idea of the workings of British officialdom. Although in touch with each other on a certain formal level, the kings had no plot for a combined rising in a general war. On the contrary, they saw themselves as engaged in desperate individual races to build up their own defensive strength to counter European aggression. Good social histories of life within the kingdoms in this period have yet to be written, probably because the common people of South Africa had little or no opportunity to influence the overall course of events. Most historical writing on the causes of the wave of war and conquest that swept across South Africa between 1876 and 1882 has emphasized the local factors that precipitated conflict. Undeniably local circumstances shaped local outcomes, but the overwhelming factor at work was the determination of Britain's Conservative government to bring about confederation through a process that involved neutering or destroying the military power of African kingdoms. Frere and the generals accomplished the military objective – though with far more difficulty than they had anticipated. However, the grand design itself was clearly unraveling by 1879. It fell apart completely when William Gladstone won the British general election of 1880 on an anti-imperialist platform promising to terminate ill-conceived overseas adventures.

The ruin of the confederation scheme commenced in the Transvaal. Within months of the annexation, dissidents were scheming to undo it. Though their petitions fell on deaf ears, they influenced Shepstone to make conciliation of the Boers the keystone of his administration. As a result, he neglected to implement the combination of indirect rule and hut tax collection that had been the foundation of his success in Natal. Instead of saving the Transvaal from bankruptcy, he piled up debts. Shepstone had never been very good at cultivating settlers in Natal; he did much worse in the Transvaal.[132] He promised to bring peace and security on the eastern frontier without explaining his program. Lacking the resources to strike a decisive blow against Sekhukhune, he let the Pedi war smoulder while he devoted his attentions to scoring a triumph in the Zulu kingdom that

---

[132] I. R. Smith, *The Origins of the South African War 1899–1902* (London: Longman, 1996), pp. 25–30.

would demonstrate the blessings of British rule. In Natal he had taken the side of Mpande against the Transvaal settlers squatting on Zulu territory. As administrator of the Transvaal he reversed his opinion, claiming to have seen documents in Pretoria that confirmed the Boer claims. He opened secret lines of communication to missionaries and other opponents of Cetshwayo's rule, promising that sometime soon soldiers would come to overthrow the king.

Dissatisfied with the independent line taken on the war and confederation by Cape Colony Prime Minister John Molteno, Frere peremptorily dismissed him and brought in a more tractable ministry led by Gordon Sprigg. It had become evident that Frere would pursue confederation at any cost. The scale of warfare conducted all over Southeastern Africa during his high commissionership dwarfed all previous conflicts in the region. Only the colonial habit of blaming all wars on African aggression and later historians' tendency to treat the history of Southern Africa on a region-by-region basis have prevented these conflicts from getting the label they deserve: the First British War for South African Unification (1877–82).

In February 1878, Sekhukhune signaled his intention to resist Transvaal demands for land, the admission of mineral prospectors and taxes with a renewal of armed struggle. Across the Highveld, Griqua and Tlhaping protests against the annexation of their territories along with the diamond fields led to another outbreak of fighting that continued through most of the year. For Frere, however, the main event on the schedule remained the Zulu kingdom. A boundary commission set up to pronounce on the respective claims of Cetshwayo and the Boers on the Transvaal frontier delivered an unexpected decision in favor of the Zulu king in June 1878. Frere reversed the practical effect of the ruling by extending British protection over all settler farms in the district, even those technically in the Zulu kingdom.[133] In December of the same year, Frere issued an ultimatum to Cetshwayo demanding nothing less than the destruction of the entire Zulu military organization – the cement that had bound the kingdom together since its foundation. Such proceedings in the 1830s would have been likely to provoke strong protests from humanitarian and missionary societies. On this occasion, divisions within the philanthropic camp rendered them largely ineffective. With the exception of Lesotho, the independent kingdoms had responded to Christian missionaries with a mixture of indifference and hostility. Many missionaries had arrived at

---

[133] Colin Webb, "The Origins of the Anglo-Zulu War," in A. Duminy and C. Ballard (Eds.), *The Anglo-Zulu War: New Perspectives* (Pietermaritzburg: University of Natal Press, 1981), pp. 4–5; C. Hamilton, *Terrific Majesty: The Powers of Shaka Zulu and the Limits of Historical Invention* (Cape Town: David Philip, 1998), pp. 104–06.

the conclusion that only conquest would open the door for conversions. Like many of his colleagues on the eastern frontier, the Anglican Bishop of St. John's, Kaffraria, Henry Callaway hailed war as "the God-sent power" effecting change, and predicted that whites would soon govern all of Southern Africa "not only with kindness and justice, but with the firm hand of the law."[134] All the Hermannsburg Lutheran missionaries made an ostentatious departure from the Zulu kingdom in 1877, loudly complaining of persecution. Anglican priest Robert Robertson wrote anonymous despatches to a Natal paper describing Cetshwayo's "tyranny and injustice."[135] Only a few missionaries stood out against the tide. Norwegian Hans Schreuder stayed in the Zulu kingdom pleading on Cetshwayo's behalf for peace even as British troops approached. Bishop Colenso also sought a diplomatic solution, though his intervention came much too late. Frere ignored all Cetshwayo's messages, refusing to accept anything short of full compliance with his impossible ultimatum. On its expiry, January 11, 1879, Frere put the fate of his grand design in the hands of the generals, as three columns of British soldiers moved across the Thukela. Contrary to the expectations of those who believed in the myth of a general South African rising, the Zulu forces made no move toward Natal, taking up a purely defensive posture.

No one knew how well the amaZulu would perform, as they had not engaged in serious campaigns since the civil war of 1856; even the oldest of them were too young to remember facing the Boers at Ncome River. They lacked experience with the guns and horses they possessed, so the fortunes of battle would depend on fitness gained through dance competitions, the force of their numbers, and blind luck.[136] On January 22, on the slopes of Isandhlwana hill, luck favored the amaZulu when their estimated force of 20,000 overran a British encampment, annihilating in less than two hours one-third of the column under commander-in-chief, Lord Chelmsford. That one engagement shook the military self-confidence of the world's largest empire and ensured the Zulu warrior a permanent place in the annals of military glory. More books and articles have been written on the war than any other aspect of Zulu history, most of them focusing on battles, tactics, and strategy. Few of them address at all the central question posed by the Zulu defense. Why were so many willing to fight and die when the chances of victory were so slight? Tradition is sufficient answer

---

[134] M. Benham, *Henry Callaway* (London: Macmillan, 1896), pp. 309–10, 322–4. D. Chidester, *Religions of South Africa* (London: Routledge, 1992), p. 41.

[135] Etherington, *Preachers, Peasants and Politics in Southeast Africa*, pp. 44–5.

[136] J. Laband, *Kingdom in Crisis: The Zulu Response to the British Invasion of 1879* (Pietermaritzburg: University of Natal Press, 1992), Chapter 3.

for military historians but in the broader context of South African history another hypothesis worth considering is that the sad experience of British campaigns against Xhosa chiefs and people taught others what they might expect. Since the 1830s, the most devastating tactic employed by British and colonial forces had been the burning of crops and capture of cattle. Every Zulu family knew that a similar campaign in their country would destroy not only their livelihoods but the basis of all family life, prestige, and prosperity. Fortunately, victory at Isandhwana largely spared them that catastrophe. Public opinion in Britain sought scapegoats, and the Conservative government moved to distance itself from Frere's grand design. A shrewdly calculated release of documents falsely suggested that the Colonial Office tried to head off an invasion of Zululand. Garnet Wolseley was sent back to South Africa as commander-in-chief and high commissioner for Southeastern Africa, effectively superseding both Lord Chelmsford and Bartle Frere. Chelmsford, instead of employing the slash and burn tactics the amaZulu feared, rushed to score a face-saving victory before his replacement could arrive. This he claimed to have achieved in the battle of Ulundi at Cetshwayo's headquarters. The engagement lasted less than an hour, resulting in Zulu losses of something between 1,000 and 1,500 men. It was thus hardly decisive in real terms, but it laid the basis for Wolseley to make peace with many of the leading chiefs while dropping many of the conditions specified in Frere's original ultimatum.[137] Wolseley's private journal entry for August 4, 1879, disclosed the real attitude he took to South African affairs, even as he bowed to current political imperatives.

Up to now beyond shooting and wounding some 10,000 men, we have not nearly punished the people as a nation, and our leniency in now allowing all the people to return to their kraals, retaining all their cattle may possibly be mistaken for fear. I should therefore like to let loose the Swazis upon these northern tribes at once, But I have to think of the howling societies at home who have sympathy with all black men whilst they care nothing for the miseries and cruelties inflicted upon their own kith & kin who have the misfortune to be located near these interesting niggers.[138]

Wolseley no doubt exaggerated the influence of the humanitarian movement but understood that his job was to get Britain out of the Zulu kingdom. With Cetshwayo captured on August 28, Wolseley set out to achieve a missionary-free settlement for Zululand. With the advice of John Dunn, a white man who had previously served as one of Cetshwayo's chiefs, Wolseley dismembered the kingdom into thirteen small chieftainships – the

---

[137] J. Guy, *The Destruction of the Zulu Kingdom* (London: Longman, 1979), pp. 58–9.
[138] A. Preston (Ed.), *The South African Journal of Sir Garnet Wolseley 1879–1880* (Cape Town: A. A. Balkema, 1973).

largest of which fell to Dunn himself. For neither the first nor the last time in history, the imperial authorities responsible for an unpopular and messy war concealed their failures under the guise of restoring self-government. The consequence was that whereas Bishop Colenso launched a campaign to free Cetshwayo from exile and Robben Island, a powerful struggle in the Zulu kingdom laid the groundwork for a disastrous civil war that would end in the annexation of the territory to Natal in 1887. Meanwhile, another sector of Frere's far flung battle line needed attention – one on which Wolseley could "let loose the Swazis."

Transvaal military operations against Sekhukhune had been suspended during the Zulu campaign. The Pedi kingdom took advantage of lull by shoring up their defenses and plainly stating their determination to resist any attempt to impose the Shepstone system. Sekhukhune's envoys declared:

> . . . they will never be subject to the English who compel their subjects to build forts and work for them; that the English are liars, that rather than be in the position of the subject tribes they will fight, that they won't pay taxes before they had a good fight for it.[139]

They correctly surmised that the Zulu kingdom had not been truly defeated, asking "how it was that cattle were not to be seen in the towns for sale, and how was it that prisoners were not sent to work on the road." For decades, the Swazi kingdom had sought to neutralize the threat of the Pedi kingdom to the north and the amaZulu to the east by allying themselves to the Transvaal. When Wolseley determined to attack the Bapedi, King Mampuru brought 8,000 Swazi men to the battlefield. Their attack from the rear made all the difference to Wolseley's successful assault on November 26, 1879. After the loss of perhaps a thousand dead, Sekhukhune surrendered and was taken off to join Langalibalele and Cetshwayo on Robben Island.[140] According to the blueprint devised by Shepstone and Frere, that ought to have been enough to demonstrate to white farmers in the Transvaal the "blessings" of British rule. To their considerable astonishment, it put the final nail in the coffin of confederation. Since the second occupation of the Cape in 1805, British policy in South Africa had been grounded on the premise that winning the allegiance of the settler population of Dutch and Huguenot descent was essential to the peace and prosperity of the colony. Even when all the evidence pointed to the futility of the policy, officials in the Cape and in London clung to the ideal. Under Harry

---

[139] Delius, *The Land Belongs to Us*, pp. 242–3. At this time the threat of the Shepstone system was present in the form of the chief diplomatic agents, both of whom came from Natal, Marshall Clarke, and Shepstone's son Henrique.

[140] *Ibid.*, 245.

Smith in the 1840s, the interests of all African kings and chiefs had been subordinated to that objective. Frere and Shepstone went down the same road, given added scholarly encouragement from Froude who assured them that their policy was grounded in scientific facts about race. Unfortunately, the leaders of the Orange Free State and the South African Republic had a different dream. Forty years' experience with independence had bred a self-confidence that was already blossoming into a sense of national identity and destiny.[141] Already people resented the label Boer and some had begun to speak of themselves as Afrikaners (or Afrikanders). The removal of threats from African kingdoms did not lead to faith in British leadership, but rather a sense that independence might now be reclaimed. Shepstone was not revered as a savior; he was reviled as a tax collector. In December 1879, 6,000 Transvaal farmers and burghers gathered at Wonderfontein and hoisted the Vierkleur, the flag of independence.

Elsewhere, the last of the wars launched on behalf of confederation and African disarmament had already begun in Lesotho, a territory theoretically under the protection of the Cape Colony, where the sons of Moshoeshoe were divided among themselves. Following the terms of the misnamed Peace Preservation Bill of 1878, the Cape Colony demanded that all Africans hand in their arms. An initial campaign in November 1879 was followed by a doubling of hut taxes and a general declaration of war in April 1880. By that time, the doom of Frere's grand design had been sealed by Gladstone's triumph in the British general election. Committed to a retreat from imperial adventures, he sent Bartle Frere home and instructed the new high commissioner, Hercules Robinson, to bring an end to the wars. At the end of the decade the Basotho were holding their own in the war and the Transvaal rebels had taken the field against British forces. In the changed political climate each would score a triumph: the Basotho by freeing themselves from rule by Cape settlers and gaining a Shepstonian administrator in the person of Marshall Clarke; the Transvaal Boers by demanding an independence that Gladstone, with his unbounded faith in the wisdom of settler colonial government, would readily grant.

CONCLUSION

On the eve of the mineral revolution in South Africa, the region had adopted most of the political borders that it would take into the twentieth century. The Transvaal's frontier with Mozambique was defined in 1869 and its western border in 1885. A decade earlier, the British had finally

---

[141] See, for example, H. Giliomee, *The Afrikaners: Biography of a People* (Cape Town: Tafelberg, 2003), Chapters 6–7.

relinquished their claims to the southern shore of Delagoa Bay.[142] In the north, Venda chiefs cooperated with Boer hunters and welcomed traders; but they discouraged the movement of white settlers into the Soutpansberg as effectively as did, in the low-lying areas to the east, the anopheles mosquito and tsetse fly. Although most of South Africa was mapped by 1880, much of this work was sketchy and inaccurate, and it left large areas unsurveyed. But cartographers had succeeded in condensing an otherwise engulfing landscape into the manageable proportions of a simple representation on paper; and they had filled empty spaces with names that were reassuringly familiar to white settlers.[143]

The economic growth initiated by the diamond discoveries brought a new wave of settlers to the subcontinent. Whites increasingly lived in a world defined by racial experiences and understandings. The racial divide grew firmer as the frontier closed and the discoveries of science described the indigenous peoples as "primitives," occupying an early stage of evolution, to be protected or annihilated. This view was contradicted by industrious African Christians who farmed and prospered on mission estates such as Edendale in Natal, Bethany in the Orange Free State, Botshabelo, and Welgeval in the eastern and western Transvaal, respectively.[144] In some areas, peasants in the reserves, or tenants living on white-owned farms, were able to benefit from the market opportunities that accompanied economic growth.[145] Many of these men increased their wealth by migrating to farms, plantations, railway works, and mines, where they sold their labor for limited amounts of time before returning home.[146] A few settled permanently in the towns and, like their rural kinsmen, invested in the education offered by mission schools. But black people were mainly confined

---

[142] Shillington, *Colonisation of the Southern Tswana, 1870–1900*, Chapter 6; Harries, *Work, Culture and Identity*, pp. 24, 84, 105.

[143] J. Carruthers, "Friedrich Jeppe: Mapping the Transvaal c. 1850–1899," *Journal of Southern African Studies,* 29(4) (2003).

[144] S. Meintjes, "Family and Gender in the Christian community at Edendale, Natal, in colonial times," in C. Walker (Ed.), *Women and Gender in Southern Africa to 1945* (Cape Town: David Philip, 1990); A. Schultz, "In Gottes Namen Hütten Bauen. Kirchlicher Landbesitz in Südafrika – die Berliner Mission und die Evangelisch-Lutherische Kirche Südafrikas zwischen 1834 und 2002," (unpublished Ph.D. thesis, Humboldt University, 2002).

[145] N. Etherington, "African Economic Experiments in Colonial Natal, 1845–80," *African Economic History* 5 (1978) pp. 1–15. Duminy and Guest (Eds.), *Natal and Zululand, A New History*, pp. 136, 288–9; E. Eldredge, *A South African Kingdom: The pursuit of security in nineteenth-century Lesotho* (Cambridge: Cambridge University Press, 1993), pp. 150–61. See also note 121 previously.

[146] K. E. Atkins, *The Moon is dead! Give us our Money! The Cultural Origins of an African Work Ethic, Natal, South Africa, 1843–1900* (London: Heinemann, 1993), Chapter 5.

to reserves segregated from both the settlers and the modern economy, or to menial roles as farm tenants or impermanent wage workers. In areas particularly affected by land alienation and overcrowding, such as the former British Kafraria, the lineaments of rural slums could be discerned.

People of mixed race increasingly took on a broad identity as coloreds or, like the San of the Drakensberg and the servile hunter–gatherers in the northern Transvaal, called "Vaalpens," headed for extinction. Bantu-speakers found new, ethnic identities as the missionaries and their African assistants determined the borders and content of standard, written languages. In 1865, a Zulu New Testament was added to the Xhosa, Tswana and South Sotho translations of the Bible. Swiss missionaries produced a Bible reader in Gwamba (xiTsonga) in 1883 whereas Berlin missionaries started to delineate standard North Sotho and Venda languages. Churchmen, traders, and travelers spread this new "vernacular" print culture, much of it coming from centers of Christianity like Kuruman, Lovedale, Morija, and Ekukanyeni, throughout the subcontinent. Readers of the seven standard South African "Bantu" languages had the means, along with their listeners, to escape the small communities bound by oral linguistic forms; and they found a shared recognition, common set of values, and a purposive unity in the images, symbols, and stories conveyed by these vehicular languages.[147] With the help of African community patriarchs, colonial officials in Natal and the Cape fixed the customs and habits of desultory communities into common "tribes" or peoples such as the amaXhosa and the amaZulu.[148] In the towns, these imagined communities became communities of action and experience as men shaped new forms of material and social culture, and new strategies of survival and advancement, into constructed ethnic identities. This new consciousness of self and others was strengthened when migrants returned home to the patchwork of "tribes" delineated by linguists and ethnographers.

A hesitant class consciousness emerged out of the social relations developed in areas of production as far removed as Cape Town and Kimberley,

[147] A. Ricard, "Introduction" to Thomas Arbousset, *Excursion missionnaire dans les Montagnes bleues* (Morija: Morija Archives, 1991), pp. 22–39; K. Mathieson, "Learning South African Languages: the historical origins of standard Xhosa" (M.A. thesis, University of Caoe Town, 2000); Harries, "The roots of ethnicity: Discourse and the Politics of language construction in South Africa," *African Affairs, 346* (1988). Translations of *The Pilgrims Progress* appeared in Tswana in 1848, Xhosa (1868), Zulu (1868), South Sotho (1872). I. Hofmeyr, *The Portable Bunyan: A Transnational History of The Pilgrim's Progress* (Johannesburg: Witwaterrsand University Press, 2004), pp. 116–7, 122, 242.

[148] N. Erlank, "Gendering Commonality: African men and the 1883 Commission on Native Law and custom," *Journal of Southern African Studies,* 29(4) (2003); Etherington, *Great Treks*, pp. 6–7.

Bloemfontein, and Botshabelo; and this new identity was reinforced as a slow retail revolution allowing wage-earners and peasants to express themselves in new ways as consumers of mass-produced goods. The practices and beliefs of Christianity particularly cut across the old divisions of kin and community. In many corners of what was soon to be South Africa, missionaries raised the fruit of Christianity from the seed first planted by migrant laborers. Once a mission was established, its influence often spread little further than the walls of its compound; and missionary Christianity tended to reinforce the racial divide in South Africa. But by the 1880s, most of the population in the region had been touched by Christianity. Some congregations had become financially self-supporting and, in turn, demanded more control over their affairs, even the right to elect elders and pastors. An indigenous clergy emerged, consisting of "Native Agents," "Evangelists," and a few ordained ministers, whereas men like Johannes Dinkwanyane in the eastern Transvaal and Nehemiah Tile in the eastern Cape established their own churches.[149] On the eastern frontier, some Christians traced the legitimacy for armed rebellion to their readings of the Holy Scriptures whereas, in the western Transvaal, others used the new religion to legitimize their claims to power.[150]

The settlers in the British colonies celebrated their membership of the British Empire by participating in pageants, festivals, town illuminations, regattas to mark the Queen's birthday, and royal ceremonies, such as the opening of the Cape Town breakwater by Prince Alfred in 1860.[151] Colonial soldiers quickly formed their own regiments and served on the eastern frontier, where they were initially appalled by the brutal discipline and ineptitude of the British army. Several Cape regiments fought in the Ninth Frontier War but, much to the displeasure of the newly responsible Molteno government, under a British commander.[152] The separate interests of the

---

[149] K. Rüther, *The Power Beyond: Mission Strategies, African conversion and the development of a Christian Culture in the Transvaal* (Munster: Lit. 2002), Chapter 6; C.C. Saunders, "Tile and the Thembu Church," *Journal of African History,* 11 (1970).

[150] Mostert, *Frontiers,* pp. 874, 1120; D. Attwell, "The Transculturation of Enlightenment" in P. Denis (Ed.), *The Making of an Indigenous Clergy in Southern Africa* (Pietermaritzburg: University of Natal Press, 1995), pp. 41–3; Elbourne, *Blood Ground,* pp. 363–7; P. Landau, *The Realm of the Word: Language, Gender and Christianity in Southern Africa* (Portsmouth and London: Heinemann, 1995).

[151] L. Witz, *Apartheid's Festival: Contesting South Africa's National pasts* (Bloomington: Indiana University Press, 2003), pp. 40–1.

[152] Cf. the Cape Town Rifles (1855), Cape Volunteer Artillery (1856), Port Elizabeth Rifle Corps (1856), the Queenstown Rifle Volunteers (1860), the Buffalo Volunteer Rifles (1876, renamed the Kaffrarian Rifles in 1883), and the First City Regiment (1875). Several participated in the Basotholand War of 1880–81. The Natal Carbineers (1855) fought in the Langalibalele campaign and in the Anglo-Zulu war.

colonists found expression in a thriving print culture that coalesced around local issues, such as eastern Cape separatism, the importation of convicts, or the Shepstonian system in Natal. In contrast to the Cape, the colonists in the Boer republics developed a system of democracy restricted to men of European descent. Even on the farms, bonds that had once been mutually accommodating often quickly skewed into exploitative relationships based on race. Boers found a common unity in opposition to the British, although this was more acute in the occupied Transvaal than in the Orange Free State. In 1881, the Transvaal Boers rose up against British rule and, after the victory at Majuba, regained their independence. All hope of federation seemed gone forever. However, a new threat to the independence of the Transvaal emerged at this time. For over a decade, considerable numbers of British and other foreign miners had made their way to the gold producing regions around Sabie and Barberton in the east. But these sources of gold would soon be dwarfed by the discovery in 1886 of outcrop reefs on the Witwatersrand. As a new wave of miners descended on the Transvaal, a new struggle for the soul of the republic was about to begin.

8

TRANSFORMATIONS IN CONSCIOUSNESS

PAUL S. LANDAU

This chapter considers changes in the way South Africans understood themselves, the world and their places in it, over almost the whole of the nineteenth century. As the rest of this volume shows, this was the formative century for South African society, entailing its bloodiest wars, its profoundest heterogeneity, the extension of colonial rule, and the reduction of most people to semiproletarian subjection. People's sense of who they were and what they were about changed during this time, giving rise to identities and affiliations in forms that are still recognizable today.[1]

That South Africans' consciousness changed may be so, but what can usefully be said about the process is a more confounding question. For instance, although Marx and Freud both put great stock in the idea of "making conscious," both also saw consciousness as an ephemera. Neither man thought a useful history could be written about ideology seen apart from the material apparatuses that give rise to it. Nietzsche depicted consciousness as a kind of side effect of life, with no agency; it was "the last and weakest of the senses." There are also philosophers who view consciousness as an yet-undiscovered physicochemical system in the brain.[2] In this chapter, habits are also of interest, what Pierre Bourdieu called praxis, the acting-through of ordinary life. Clearly, praxis is mostly not conscious. Wittgenstein pointed out that living always comes before rules: that, as he puts it, one learns to calculate by calculating. Social science rules are second-order principles, formed from descriptions of people who just "know their way around." The aim

[1] Thanks for encouragement or criticism go to Diana Jeater, David Gordon, Julie Livingston, John Wright, Robert Ross, Carolyn Hamilton, and Shula Marks, the responsibility for errors of fact or interpretation being mine.
[2] Karl Marx, *The German Ideology* (New York: Prometheus, 1998); Sigmund Freud's *Introductory Lectures* and *The Interpretation of Dreams* (trans. James Strachey), published by Norton/Liveright and Harcourt; Pierre Bourdieu, *The Logic of Practice* (Cambridge: Cambridge University Press, 1980), 30 ff.; John Searle, *The Mystery of Consciousness* (New York: New York Review of Books, 1997).

here is to show how, as the nineteenth century unfolded, people knew their way around – without reducing that knowledge to rules or principles.[3]

The working assumption throughout is that what they mean lies in what they do. In other words, speech-acts in the past only signified in terms of their usual (expected) preconditions, procedures, personal contexts, and consequences – which (ideally) should all be known.[4] Here my colleagues have done most of the work for me. At the center of this chapter, however, an attempt has been made to listen again to what ordinary people were saying, to figure out to what or whom they felt they belonged, what their boundaries were, and how they thought they could affect the world. For much of this information, especially for the first part of the century, missionaries' papers are crucial. Missionaries can supply vivid instances of important words used in lost contexts, so long as it is borne in mind that they were interested players in the game of making meaning themselves. Indeed, as translators they installed their biases in academic lexicons still in use today.[5] Other published primary sources came from travelers and officials. My excavation of all these sources has been shaped by readings in European

---

[3] Frederic Nietzsche, *Beyond Good and Evil* (trans. R.J. Hollingdale) (New York: Penguin, 1973), p. 30; c.f. Stuart Hall, "Cultural Identity and Diaspora," in Patrick Williams and Laura Chrisman (Eds.), *Colonial Discourse and Post-Colonial Theory, A Reader* (London: Harvester, 1993), p. 394; Louis Althusser, "Ideology and Ideological State Apparatuses," *Lenin and Philosophy and Other Essays* (New York: Monthly Review Press, 2001), and Antonio Gramsci, *Selections from the Prison Notebooks* (New York: International Publishers Co., 1971), esp. pp. 5–43, and 123 ff; c.f. Michel Foucault, *Discipline and Punish: the Birth of the Prison* (New York: Vintage, 1979) and *The Archaeology of Knowledge and the Discourse on Language* (New York: Tavistock, 1971); and Michel de Certeau, *The Practice of Everyday Life* (Berkeley: University of California Press, 2002).

[4] My reasoning stems from Wittgenstein's thinking about "the language game," which is also followed by Rodney Needham, Stanley Cavell, Umberto Eco, Richard Rorty, Paul Feyerabend, W.V.O. Quine, Stanley Fish, William Cantwell Smith, and Malcolm Ruel. Wittgenstein: see "Remarks on Frazer's *Golden Bough*," I, 1931 (MS 110), and II, ca. 1948 (MS 143), and 3.3.36, Rush Rhees' lec. notes, p. 290, in Ludwig Wittgenstein, *Philosophical Occasions, 1912–1951* (Indianapolis: Hackett, 1993); and Wittgenstein, *On Certainty* (London: Blackwell, 1969), §410, 20.3.51, p. 52e; and "The meaning of a word is not the experience one has in hearing or saying it, and the sense of a sentence is not a complex of such experiences. [. . .]," Wittgenstein, *Philosophical Investigations, II*, 3rd ed. (New York: Macmillan, 1969) vi., p. 181e. Lexicographers define the meaning of words by the same logic, building files of citations of their ordinary uses: Sidney Landau, *Dictionaries: the Art and Craft of Lexicography*, 2nd ed. (Cambridge: Cambridge University Press, 2002).

[5] I draw on books and papers of many missionaries and a few travelers and observers, including Robert Jacob Gordon, Hendrik Wikar, Eugene Casalis, Prosper Lemue, Samuel Rolland, John Campbell, Thomas Arbousset, D. F. Ellenberger, William Shaw, T. L. Hodgson, Samuel Broadbent, Robert Moffat, Robert Hully, John Cameron, W. J. Burchell, John Shrewsbury, William Colenso, William C. Willoughby, E. W. Smith,

and African social history, which are also dependent on records generated at the interface of popular culture and state or religious authority.[6]

Pathbreaking insights into the "colonization of consciousness" can be found in Jean and John Comaroff's work.[7] Elements of the approach taken here have been formulated in dialogue with their arguments, sometimes antithetically, and I note specific contributions of theirs in the following; broadly, my view is that one can no longer credibly discuss the beliefs of a tribe, and show them to have changed into today's views, at least if one is interested in the creation of "belief" and "tribe" themselves. The interrogation of these and other structuring concepts, as hegemonic they were, may be thought of as extending the Comaroffs' methods. The result, however, is to reject the vision of South Africa's early history as a meeting between pristine Africans and missionaries-as-harbingers of modernity. This will be clear from what follows. Finally, the narrative structure plotted by the Comaroffs recuperates the basic story of Christian evangelists: Custom and superstition fitfully give way before modernity, even as (in their hands) the result is a transformation rather than a giving-way. My argument does not conceptualize "modernity" at all, and in compensation, foregrounds the rationality and functionality – they are held to be the same thing – of Africans' perspectives, changeful as they were.[8]

The chapter begins by considering the house-polity structure and other attendant ideas basic to community consciousness in its early form in

Roger Price, John Mackenzie, Henry Callaway, and others. Citations to these and other primary sources have been minimized.

[6] E. Leroy Ladurie, *Montaillou* (New York: Vintage, 1979); Carlo Ginzburg, *The Cheese and the Worms* (New York: Viking Penguin, 1982); Robert Darnton, *The Great Cat Massacre* (New York: Vintage, 1984), and David W. Sabean, *Power in the Blood* (New York: Vintage, 1990); Michel Foucault, *History of Sexuality, Vol. 1* (London: Routledge, 1990); George L. Mosse, *Toward the Final Solution: A History of European Racism* (New York: Howard Fertig, 1978); Saul Dubow, *Scientific Racism in Modern South Africa* (Cambridge: Cambridge University Press, 1995); Jack Miles, *A History of God* (New York: Vintage, 1996); Jaroslav Pelikan, *Jesus through the Centuries* (New York: Vintage, 1982); Carolyn Walker Bynum, *Fragments* (New York: Vintage, 1990); J. R. S. Phillips, *The Medieval Expansion of Europe* (Oxford: Oxford University Press, 1988); John Bossy, *Christianity in the West, 1400–1700* (Oxford: Oxford University Press, 1985); and see Rodney Needham, *Belief, Language, and Experience* (Oxford: Blackwell, 1972), p. 188; Talal Asad, *Genealogies of Religion: Discipline and Reasons of Power in Christianity and Islam* (Baltimore: Hopkins, 1994), 28 ff., and Byron Good's useful summary of Wilfred Cantwell Smith's relevance for anthropology, *Medicine, Rationality, and Experience* (Cambridge: Cambridge University Press,1994), 15 ff.

[7] Notably, Jean and John Comaroff, *Of Revelation and Revolution, Vol. 1: Christianity, Colonialism, and Consciousness in South Africa* (Chicago: University of Chicago Press, 1991).

[8] A "Durkheimization" of society, after Emile Durkheim, *Elementary Forms of Religious Life* (trans. and with an intro. by Karen Fields) (New York: Free Press, 1995); ms., *The Samuelites of South Africa*, forthcoming.

Southern Africa. Heterogeneity and hybridity are shown in their central role in the fermenting of ideas and identities in South Africa. This same story, however, must explain the first stirrings of those racial, political, and religious distinctions that were later naturalized in political and public discourse. Given the extraordinary growth of Christianity in South Africa, much of the chapter is suitably about that, too; the innovation is to think about these trends altogether, and in the terms that were spoken by ordinary South Africans. In the context of midcentury shifts in relations of production, the growing reach of the colonial state, and diminishing access to land, it is argued that fertility and health were depoliticized in public speech throughout South Africa. The underclass was asked to deny the manifest incitement of Christian words, and to extrude its own agency to an untouchable plane. The reform of the boundaries around the resulting, newly weakened self, cut off from commonsensical connections, then further facilitated the extraction of labor from farming populations.

In the most trying circumstances, however, there arose people with new and tenuous allegiences, often literate or semiliterate, some whom the state labeled frauds and rabble-rousers, some whom it tolerated. Making no claim to universal coverage, I end the chapter with one such person, an obscure midcentury African evangelist in Natal, whose story both recapitulates some of the transformations already interrogated, and plots a recognizable path to the present day.

FLEXIBILITY IN BANTU ORGANIZING PRINCIPLES

The political history of early South Africa can be understood as a group of variations on what Jan Vansina calls "the house."[9] The flexible and tough nature of the house-form helps account for the success of Bantu-speakers in many different ecosystems, including the foundation of settlements involving non–Bantu-speaking clients (including the ancestors of pygmies and Khoekhoe). In general, "big men competed with each other to increase the size, the labor force, and the security of their houses," so houses could agglomerate into villages, kingdoms, and more. Out of the house tradition, a "luxurience of political formations" developed in Central and Southern Africa. The concept appears as *ntlo/-ndlu* (the maternal segment) or

---

[9] Drawing on Elgash, *African Fractals*, p. 29; Jan Vansina, *Paths in the Rainforest: Towards a History of Political Tradition in Equatorial Africa* (Madison: University of Wisconsin Press, 1990), conclusion; and (quotes) Vansina, "Pathways of Political Development in equatorial Africa and neo-evolutionary theory," in Susan Keech McIntosh (Ed.), *Beyond Chiefdoms: Pathways to Complexity in Africa* (Cambridge: Cambridge University Press, 1999), pp. 166–72.

motse/-muzi (household, village). As is done here, morphemes in the two major southern Bantu linguistic groups, Tswana and Nguni, often will be presented together, separated by a backslash, in order to emphasize the unities behind the innumerable ethnonyms in South African studies.[10]

The typical settlement pattern repeated a similar arrangement at several levels. Around the patrilineal residences were mother's huts, called by the same word as womb, *ntlo/ndlu,* arrayed like cattle posts around the patriarchal kraal. Each level, sometimes even the hut interior, contained recursive or "fractal" patterns separating statuses, genders, and productive activities. Ila people in Zambia built tiny huts in their central courtyard, calling them "ancestors' huts," *manda a mizhimo,* an inward turn of the same idea. In the high grasslands, Bantu-speakers used a variety of this pattern to engage Khoe pastoralists over a history of "1,500 years," in which the "Central Cattle Pattern" discussed by Simon Hall in this volume appeared. The elasticity in turn of this pattern can be seen in the difference between the massed populations in the Highveld (Tswana) towns, and the dispersed homesteads united through ideological ties in the eastern grasslands. Bantu culture flowered in its encounter with difference.[11]

Beyond any permutation of the house, other institutions and traditions also bound people to one another over long distances. Generational initiations instilled lateral ties among sex-segregated men and women. The so-called "traditional schools" culminated for boys with a group-circumcision, which made them into fully masculine, public, marriageable persons. Chiefs assigned them as age-set regiments to the field, to conduct hunts and fight enemies. The varied origins of the boys registered, like a snapshot, the contemporary extent of the nation. And nations were joined to one another through complex patrilineal rankings in putative kinship, some branches of which had fattened whereas others dwindled to nothing. Important brides, soldiers, merchants, and healers also traveled far afield. The "totem" as Europeans called it was a natural emblem (crocodile: *kwena,* for instance), a

---

[10] Norman Etherington, The *Great Treks: The Transformation of Southern Africa, 1815–1854* (London: Pearson, 2001) adheres to a similar grouping, of southern and northern Nguni people predominantly attached to the coastal grasslands as "Nguni," and northern and southern Sotho and Tswana peoples of the Highveld (shading into Kalanga-related people in the north) as Sotho-Tswana, herein abbreviated to "Tswana," because it is the earlier umbrella term.

[11] James Denbow, "Prehistoric Herders and Foragers of the Kalahari: The Evidence for 1,500 Years of Interaction," in Carmel Schrire (Ed.), *Past and Present in Hunter–Gatherer Societies* (Orlando: Academic, 1984), pp. 175–93; Ron Elgash, *African Fractals: Modern Computing and Indigenous Design* (New Brunswick: Rutgers, 1999); see Chapter 2.

coat-of-arms for chiefs, and a nonresidential affiliation by which strangers might assume mutual responsibilities.

Some healers, or more generically, specialists or "experts" (sing. *ngaka/ inyanga*), had transregional reputations to precede them. A few claimed affiliation with *mwali* (or *ngwali*), a cult based in Zimbabwe, although this is not certain until at least midcentury. Many more of them participated in a broader institution called *koma/ngoma*. This morpheme connoted drums and dance appearing in the performance of (re)incorporating unwell or disabled subjects into their communities. With no oversight or standardization, specific variants of the practices differed from place to place: there was call-and-response "divination" by an *isangoma* (diviner), communitywide rites supervised by *dikomana* (celebrants, petitioners), hostile *ngoma* dance competitions, and Christian *ngoma*, which was called "being smitten with the Spirit."[12]

An expert's knowledge was secret and could be somewhat uncanny. Specialists marked boundaries with substances and signs, and interpreted random arrangements of bones to produce wisdom about kin-relations and wealth and power. Sometimes in connection with wider movements, experts combatted harm-doers said to be operating like them in secrecy. Experts also treated people's bodily health. They differed in their media and emphasis by individual and region. A few worked only for top chiefs, plotting ecological strategies and managing resources. In Antonio Gramsci's terms, specialists were the organic intellectuals of landed African patriarchies, adjusting and mediating the inequalities around them.[13]

The "house" was a patriarchy, whether it took the form of a household, village, or nation-size grouping, as is registered in the primacy of the office usually glossed as "chief." This is a translation from southern Bantu languages of *kosi* (descending to *kgosi/inkosi*), alongside other terms such as *morena*. The chief was concerned with judgment, punishment, war, managing natural resources, human and agrarian fertility, propriety, and social

---

[12] John Janzen, *Ngoma: Discourses of Healing in South and Central Africa* (Berkeley: University of California Press, 1992); and Rijk van Dijk, Ria Reis, and Marja Spierenburg (Eds.), *The Quest for Fruition through Ngoma* (London: Currey, 2000); Eileen Krige, *The Realm of the Rain Queen* (Pietermaritzburg: University of Natal Press, 1943); Terence Ranger, *Voices from the Rocks: Nature, Culture, and History in the Matopos Hills of Zimbabwe* (Bloomington: Indiana University Press, 1999); and Louis Brenner, "'Religious' Discourses in and about Africa," in Karin Barber and P. F. de W. Farias (Eds.), *Discourse and Its Disguises* (Birmingham: Center for West African Studies, 1989), pp. 87–103. C.f. Steven Feierman, *Peasant Intellectuals: Anthropology and History in Tanzania* (Madison: University of Wisconsin Press, 1989).

[13] Thomas Mofolo, *Chaka*, trans. Daniel P. Kunene (Hanover: Heinemann, 1981) for such fear; Gramsci, "Modern Prince," *Selections*, p. 182, and Gramsci, "A Dialogue," quoted by Quintin Hoare in "General Introduction," xciii, for "intellectuals."

institutions. His (or occasionally her) physical person also symbolized the
landed nation, both ceremonially (in the "first-fruits" rite, for example),
and even more, in ordinary discourse, for "nations" were changeful associations of people named after a chief. There were chiefs well below the
level of the central court, too, of course. The missionaries Arbousset and
Daumas, touring South Africa in the 1830s, recorded the world *sechaba*
for "nation," their example of usage being, "They say in that sense, the
nation of Moshesh, of Sekaniela, of Makuana" (all chiefs).[14] The concept
was people (*ba-, aba-, va-, ama-*) of chief *X*, which suggests that the essence
of an ancestral chief lay among those who lived in his name. Especially if
the chief were long dead, as in Bapedi, Bakgatla, Mapulana, amaGcaleka,
and maShangaan, the identity was countenanced by colonial observers as
"tribe."

For centuries, southern Bantu-speakers have used words with the root,
-*dzim*, to mean great or terrifying things. With different prefixes -*dzim* in
the nineteenth century could indicate collective might, victory, success,
hurricanes, thunder, monstrous imaginations of the human form, cannibalism, and foundational chiefs. *Dzim* might be terrible, as in the turbulence
of raids and counterraids, in which Tswana people feared *madimo*, and
Nguni people saw *amazimuzimu*, cannibals. Cannibals or "ravenous eaters,"
marauders (*faqane* or *fetcani*) shorn of land and leadership, appeared and van-
ished in fragmentary accounts from the 1820s.[15] Moletsane, a chief from
the Sand River region with a changeful following, bemoaned his fortunes
thus: "I was once a great man [*golo/-khulu*], but I have now only about thirty
men . . . [my people] are scattered all over the country . . . the mothers eat
their own children." Such was *dzim* in a bad way.[16] Ancestors were made
from the root *dzim*, as *badimo, merimo*, and *melemo* derive from it, although
imidlozi, amathongo, and *abaphantsi* do not, but also meant ancestors. People
addressed their ancestors in formal recitations, "telling them everything,"
seeking transparency in their gaze, whereas publicly they spoke about them
very selectively.

---

[14] Thomas Arbousset and Francois Daumas, *Narrative of an Exploratory Tour to the Northeast
of the Colony of the Cape of Good Hope . . . In the Months of March, April and May, 1836*,
trans. John Brown (Cape Town: Struik, 1968 [1846]), and Henry Lichtenstein, *Travels in
South Africa in the Years 1803, 1804, 1805, and 1806*. 2 vols. (Cape Town: Van Riebeeck
Society, 1930 [1812–15]), 72 ff.

[15] Arbousset and Daumas, *Narrative*, 89 (majabatho bafokeng). There were also folktales of
madimo who swallow glowing iron and become trees. *Ubuzimuzimu*: Carolyn Hamilton,
Terrific Majesty: The Powers of Shaka Zulu and the Limits of Historical Invention (Cambridge:
Harvard University Press, 1998), p. 227, n104.

[16] Robert Moffat, *Apprenticeship at Kuruman: Being the Journals and Letters of Robert and
Mary Moffat, 1820–1828* (Ed. I. Schapera) (London: Chatto and Windus, 1951), p. 56;
Etherington, *Great Treks*, 136 ff.

The reason was that supposedly common forebears personified the agreements binding together senior men who were perhaps only recently affiliated, but who now conferred together under one chief. Maintaining a sizable community was not easy in Southern Africa even in peacetime; on the Highveld the inheritance of property and status came through the father, making matrikin exclusively supportive, but a man married his cross-cousins as a ideal preference, with the result that a wide net of people bore multiple and contradictory ties. One could interpret many kinship relations according to one's circumstance.[17] From around 1790 to 1828 (and again periodically in the 1840s), South African agrarian societies were rent by turmoil that historians associate with Nguni state-building, guns, and more tentatively, with slave-raiding (see John Wright, Chapter 5). People came together under small agnatic alliances supporting a chief or captain and raided one another for cattle, sometimes for women and children. In such circumstances, "forgetfulness," as Benedict Anderson puts it, soon became a condition for group identity. Facing "the Zulu" or the "Matabele" or the "Fetcani hordes," whoever these people were, relied on muting antagonisms of the past; naming an umbrella ancestor served to backdate the relationships between households sufficiently to overcome differences between them. As befit their station, specialists who claimed direct access to the *uber*-desires of deceased "great chiefs" usually reported that people must try to get along better, that petitioners should cast off their animosities, that an ox must be killed and shared in the honor of common forebears.[18]

It was in seeking a cognate, a suitable verbal vehicle, for "God" that early western travelers asked questions about (the or a) "greatest ancestor." "What did ancestor used to mean, long ago?" "Who is the father who

---

[17] See the discussion in Jean Comaroff, *Body of Power, Spirit of Resistance* (Chicago: University of Chicago Press, 1985), 54 ff., and Jean and John Comaroff, *Of Revelation and Revolution*, 132 ff. and 138; but also, e.g., Isaac Schapera *Bogwera: Kgatla Initiation* (19 pp.) (Mochudi: Phuthadikobo Museum, 1978), for cosmological detail, and Adam Kuper, *Wives for Cattle* (Oxford: Oxford University Press, 1982), for an attempt to link preferred marriage-types, at different levels of agnatic remove, to Nguni and Tswana social structure. C.f. Eileen Jensen Krige, *The Social System of the Zulus* (Pietermaritzburg: Shuter, 1965), and Adam Kuper, "The 'House' and Zulu Political Structure in the Nineteenth Century," *Journal of African History, 34* (1993), pp. 469–87.

[18] Benedict Anderson, *Imagined Communities: Reflections on the Origin and Spread of Nationalism* (London: Verso, 1983); Vansina, "Pathways"; and William Worger, "Parsing God: Conversations about the Meaning of Words in Nineteenth Century South Africa," *Journal Of African History, 42* (2001), pp. 417–47 (438–40 esp. offers examples here). Others: Moffat, *Apprenticeship, 48*, (March 24, 1822); and (fictionalized) A. C. Jordan, *The Wrath of the Ancestors* (trans. of *Ingqumbo Yeminyana*, Xhosa) (Cape Town: Lovedale Press, 1980), p. 5.

made everything?" "Who is the master up above?" they asked. But for most South Africans "to mean" was "to want to say." Men were born, not made, and the world just grew, like plants and animals. No master dwelt above them, and there was no easy gloss for "long ago," either. What people actually heard was more like: "What does an ancestor do? In what contexts does one speak about an ancestor?" Rarely, was the second answered. Or "I know nothing." The information was private. "An ancestor troubles people," was a response; "ancestors are underground" was another.[19] The subject elicited talk about death and funerals. Yet when the naturalist and spy Sir Andrew Smith asked Tswana people about "greatest" ancestor(s) in 1841, a man told him, "We swear by Machush. Ca moshush. What is by Moshush." Moshush (Moshoeshoe) "swears by himself" or by "his own father, Ca Mokachanee."[20] If this was a reasonable answer, as Smith's notes suggest, the question must have been heard as something like, "Who is the most powerful chief?" and Moshoeshoe, a chief, could "be" ancestor (*molimo* in Sotho orthography) in such a usage.[21]

In an aphorism about the meaning of "picture," Wittgenstein remarks that the body is the best possible picture of the soul. This perhaps echoes what southern Bantu-speakers meant when they used words that appear to have spanned picture, image, and soul. *Moya* (sometimes *mowa*), "spirit," "breath," etymologically linked to "throat" and "chest" or "heart," also presented itself to missionaries as potential glosses for soul. In isiZulu *isithunzi* and in Sesotho *seriti* mean reflexive self, double, or image, both often given as "shadow."[22] The London Mission director Campbell "was told there was

---

[19] Malcolm Guthrie glosses the dzim-root as "spirit" and Schoenbrun as "ancestral spirit," but Vansina sees "fade away" as earliest: Vansina, *Paths*, 95, p. 297; c.f. Malcolm Guthrie, *Comparative Bantu*, 4 vols. (Farnham: Gregg Press, 1967–71), p. 3: 168 (root 278); other arguments derive dzim- more tenuously as "digging" (as in farming) but no related activities have the root (David Schoenbrun, pers. comm. November 1999); Axel-Ivar Berglund, *Zulu Thought Patterns and Symbolism* (Uppsala: Swedish Mission Institute, 1976); Malcolm J. Ruel, *Belief, Ritual and the Securing of Life: Reflective Essays on a Bantu Religion* (Netherlands: Brill, 1997), p. 93; "telling them," S. M. Molema, *The Bantu, Past and Present* (Cape Town: Struik, 1963 [1920]). C.f. Andrew Apter, *Black Critics and Kings: The Hermeneutics of Power in Yoruba Society* (Chicago: University of Chicago Press, 1992), 149 ff.

[20] *Sic.* Andrew Smith folios, South African Museum (Library), vol. 12, "Memoranda A." "Swear by" is *go ikana ka*, to tell one's self by, and the root, *-ana-*, is to tell as a formal act, to "show honor" or revere, but another word may have been used.

[21] Moffat, *Missionary Labours and Scenes in Southern Africa* (London: Snow, 1842 [New York: New York Reprint Corp., 1969]), p. 263; Samuel Broadbent, *A Narrative of the First Introduction of Christianity amongst the Barolong* (London: Wesleyan Mission House, 1865), pp. 81–4 (January 1823). Moshoeshoe himself commented on this at Harriet Colenso's funeral, in John Gay, *A History of Lesotho* (Roma: University of Lesotho, 1993), p. 17.

[22] Ruel, *Belief*, p. 108, and Luke 23:45.

no Bootshuana word for soul or spirit, but heart or breath," and the Anglican catechism asserted that there were three *mewa* (plural of *mowa*, breaths) in God. The sense is indicated by the practice of handling the "chyme" from the first stomach of a killed bull or cow. Mediating between the grasses and the milk and flesh of cattle, the chyme marked the moment at which the stuff of the world becomes the stuff of the self, and it was sometimes touched to one's *umoyo* (throat, breath, chest, voice) during the slaughter.[23]

Under the subject of cattle, one must reference a number of matters similarly resistant to the reductions of English translation. Cows were, to begin with, what the anthropologist Claude Meillasoux describes as "elite goods," items exchanged solely by senior men, for instance, for wives to marry their dependent young men. Homestead heads knew their cattle as individuals and wrote songs to them. One way to say, "Don't ask me, I'm not party to it," was "I only know how to drink milk."[24] People grudgingly sold a few cattle, but in plush times when herds expanded, chiefs loaned out whole herds to distant subjects. Cattle indexed the estates of the past and so shaped the duties of the living; as a remedy for an exceptional crisis, the chief would kill a prized bull at the grave of a foundational chief. A few portions of innards were set aside for ancestors, the elderly ate next, then married people, all in order, reenforcing their social stations. Men risked death to capture herds for their chiefs. Hoyt Alverson points out that a Tswana praise-song (*ukubina/go bina*) sung to a favorite bull went: "modimo o nko e metse," or "ancestor with a wet nose!" which he translates as "God with the wet nose." I would argue that not God but rather "ancestor" found its perfect instantiation in a healthy bovine.[25]

In early discourse, one frequently encounters the root-word -*golo* [Sotho: -*holo*]/-*khulu*, an old root. In Kaguru in East Africa, for example, it is *koro*,

[23] Ruel, *Belief*, pp. 93, 106; and witnessed by P. L. in rural Lesotho and Botswana. Quote: John Campbell, *Travels in South Africa Undertaken at the Request of the London Missionary Society, Vol. 2* (Cape Town: Struik, 1874 [1st ed. 1822]), p. 79 (1816); and "Station de Motito: Lettres de Mes. Lemue et Rolland, 1833," *Journal des Missions Evangeliques*, 9 (1834), pp. 257–76.

[24] Claude Meillassoux, "'The Economy' in Agricultural Self-Sustaining Societies: A Preliminary Analysis," in David Seddon (Ed.), *Relations of Production: Marxist Approaches to Economic Anthropology* (London: Frank Cass, 1978), pp. 127–69; and Robert Moffat, *Missionary Labours*, p. 261; Liz Gunner and Mafika Gwala, translators and editors, *Musho! Zulu Popular Praises* (East Lansing: Michigan State University Press, 1991); Isaac Schapera, *Praise Poems of Tswana Chiefs* (Oxford: Oxford University Press, 1965).

[25] Hoyt Alverson, *Mind in the Heart of Darkness: Value and Self-Identity Among the Tswana of Southern Africa* (New Haven: Yale University Press, 1978), pp. 125–6, in a generally sensitive reading of northern Tswana praise poetry, citing D. F. van der Merwe, in *Bantu Studies*, 1941. Jean and John Comaroff, *Of Revelation and Revolution*, vol. 2 (2000), p. 175, discuss this praise as a "patent instance of fetishism in bovine shape."

forming "elder," *mokoro* and "ancestor" *omokoro*. Among northern Nguni-speakers remote from European settlements, the earliest use of the reiterative from, (*u*)*nkulu-nkulu*, was to denote a lineage's foundational ancestor (as was true for the southern Nguni *uhlanga* as well). As an Ngwane man explained, "All nations have their own Unkulunkulu [greatest ancestor]." In Thaba Nchu the head of the polity was *mogolo* of the men's assembly, and an ancestor proper might be a *mogolo* as well. Related to *go gola/ukukhula*, to grow (c.f. Tswana *goditse*, matured or senior), a *mogolo* meant a powerful person. In Thaba Bosiu, *baholo* meant elders, *morena moholo* "paramount chief," and in Natal, *isikhulu* meant a chief or notable. The "Great Being," one of the elliptical formulations Robert Moffat tried out for God, was some rendering of -*golo* now lost. To express "greatly more" in any dimension – time, emotion, or space – one exclaimed, *Bogolo bogolo!* or *Kakhulu kakhulu!* If power was manifest over a great distance (or from the past), it was mighty. A "very first" chief was therefore both "far" and "long ago" and "great," closely affiliated usages as was seen with "Moshush" previously. In twentieth-century dictionaries, the Tswana derivation *bogologolo* was standardized to mean "ancient times" or "long ago." In isiZulu, by contrast, *ubunkulunkulu*, the same word in the same noun-class, was deflected from antiquity and greatness to become "divinity," because John William Colenso made *unkulunkulu* indicate God after touring Natal in the 1850s looking for "the impressions of natural religion which [people] still retain."[26]

Real greatness was also the power to hurt. When Andrew Smith asked about ancestors in the early 1840s, he was told: "In early times they had an idea of something evil buried in the ground." That was his answer. "In early times" was again *bogologolo*, greatness. Yet what was "evil"? Campbell learned that *modimo* "kills men," and Moffat was told it was "evil only, always doing evil," and Ellenberger that an ancestor was "a pitiless master."[27] The German naturalist Lichtenstein thought it was good and evil both. This should not surprise, because in the nineteenth century, the striving for greatness brought death and destruction for many. Ngqika boasted to the Rev. Shaw he was "a very great man," although "God was greater," and

[26] Clement Doke, *Zulu-English Dictionary* (Johannesburg: University of Witswatersrand Press 1958); Andrew Smith, *The Diary of Sir Andrew Smith, 1834–1836*, 2 vols. P. R. Kirby (Ed.) (Cape Town: Van Riebeeck, 1939), p. 93; Thomas Arbousset, *Missionary Excursion into the Blue Mountains* (David Ambrose & A. Brutsch, eds. and trans.) (Morija: Museum and Archives, 1991), p. 90; and Berglund, *Zulu Thought*, 34 ff; Moffat, *Missionary Labours*, pp. 257–8, Xhosa "uhlanga," WMMS, Journal of the Rev. Shrewsbury, 1829, fiche 69, box 301; and Ruel, *Belief*, p. 150. In general, see David Chidester, *Savage Systems: Colonialism and Comparative Religion in Southern Africa* (Cape Town: University of Cape Town Press, 1996), p. 132, and *passim*.

[27] Moffat, *Missionary Labours*, pp. 263–5; D.F. Ellenberger, *History of the Basuto, Ancient and Modern*, trans. J. C. Macgregor (London: Caxton, 1912), p. 239; Campbell, *Travels*, *11*, March–June 1820, pp. 2–5, 110–11.

fearing to offend the senior chief Hintsa, that Hintsa was also "a very great [*khulu*] man." The term *thixo*, which missionaries adopted as "God" among southern Nguni, meant "one who induces pain" in Khoe. One chief told a missionary he would "kill his ancestor" if he met up with him. Collective action trampled individuals' interests in the name of a single house.[28]

The missionaries' evocation of "evil" is nonetheless suspect. The term chosen by Moffat (and his teacher, a Tswana chief named Bogachu) was *boikepo*. If "to separate oneself from the group or herd," *go ikepa*, was "wickedness," it was also exactly what converting to Christianity demanded.[29] The more common word for sin in both Nguni and Tswana languages was and is the same as that for "dirt." For evangelists among Bantu-speakers, the "dirtiness" of heathens was embodied and metaphorical at once. For example, the Tswana root *shula* signified a dangerous or physically dirty state: a man's thoughts were *shula* (Genesis 6:5), an evil act *leshwe* of a related root (Revelations 22:11), an unclean spirit *moyo o o mashwe*. *Boshula* was pollution, innate to "the world," as some Methodists said, dangerous and corrupting. In Genesis, the tree of "the knowledge of good and evil" concerned *molemo le boshula*, even though one would not have thought "filth" could be an object of knowledge. The term for "good," *molemo*, derived from the earthly harvest, as *go lema* meant "to work the soil." Dirt and sin had to be removed in order for wellness to ensue, but neither concept was very stable.[30]

RELIGIOUS REVERBERATIONS OF CHIEF, NATION, AND ANCESTOR

... [Y]ou tell us of a rich and benevolent chief who can increase our flocks, satisfy our mouths with fat things, and fill our dwellings with peace and prosperity; – these news [*sic*] are delightful: I, for my part, wish to settle near you, ... if I came, will you give me a heifer?[31]

---

[28] Janet Hodgson, "Christian Beginnings," in Richard Elphick and Rodney Davenport (Eds.), *Christianity in South Africa* (Johannesburg: University of Witswatersrand Press, 1996), p. 74; William Shaw, *The Journal of William Shaw* (W. D. Hammond-Tooke, Ed.) (Cape Town: Balkema, 1972), p. 72 (1827); Elizabeth Elbourne, *Blood Ground: Colonialism, Missions, and the Contest for Christianity in the Cape Colony and Britain, 1799–1853* (Montreal: McGill-Queens University Press, 2002), ms. p. 304 on van der Kemp; Lichtenstein, *Travels*, 72.

[29] I am drawing various dictionaries and on recited material I collected. C.f. Edward LiPuma, "Modernity and Forms of Personhood in Melanesia," in Michael Lambek and Andrew Strathern (Eds.), *Bodies and Persons: Comparative Perspectives from Africa and Melanesia*, (Cambridge: Cambridge University Press, 1998), pp. 53–79. My spelling of Bogachu reflects the early (1850s) family spelling.

[30] Landau, "Explaining Surgical Evangelism in Southern Africa: Teeth, Pain, and Faith," *Journal of African History*, 37(2) (1996), pp. 261–81.

[31] Arbousset and Daumas, *Narrative*, interlocutor in "Sotho" village, p. 169.

So said an inquirer to a Christian. From the beginning missionaries saw, quite correctly, that there had been no religion among South Africans, no separate domain for religious activity, and that one would have to be constructed out of available vocabularies, no matter how crudely. "No word to express the Deity by," said van der Kemp of the Xhosa; no knowledge "of *any* God true or false," wrote William Shaw. "They have no religion," said Robert Moffat, no degraded beliefs that might be rectified and restored; "they were neither theists nor idolators," wrote another.[32] Some people wondered to whom the Rev. John Campbell prayed, and were told "a Great Being" (*mogolo/(u)nkulu*); the problem with such an answer for his interlocutors was that "they did not know him, for they had never seen him." Africans were thought to be extremely pragmatic folk in the early century.[33]

By and large, however, Christians succeeded in making "ancestor" mean "God." Among evangelist Tswana-speakers, ancestor (*modimo*) and chief (*kgosi*) became the primary ways to say God. According to the Wesleyan James Allison, Nguni Christians themselves took to using ancestor (the non-*dzim* based term, *ithongo*) to mean God. They eventually settled on the reiterative *un<u>kulun<u>kulu</u></u>* meaning "greatest ancestor" instead. All uses of a singular-case "ancestor" were to be construed as necessarily referring to the same, universal being. The Tswana plural, ancestors (*badimo*), was glossed as "devils" by Thomas Hodgson and "demons" in Moffat's 1828 *Mark* (but as "fathers" by the French Protestants).

Why did Christianity spread, nonetheless, as it undoubtedly did, even in the nineteenth century? Christianity cheerfully embraced profound contradictions, variant ideas, and implausible stories, as truth. Contradiction was its strength, accommodating divergent interpretations in an apparently doctrinal language.[34] Christian evangelists relied on ambiguity, and directing people's fealty to an absent Chief Above or *inkosi phezulu* was but one instance of it. On a pragmatic level, evangelists, white and black, followed one of two basic strategies. They focused their attentions on chiefs

---

[32] Van der Kemp: Hodgson in Elphick and Davenport, *Christianity*, p. 70. The Rev. W. Shaw quoted in Clifton Crais, *White Supremacy and Black Resistance in Pre-Industrial South Africa: The Making of the Colonial Order in the Eastern Cape, 1770–1865* (Cambridge: Cambridge University Press, 1992), p. 101; Moffat, *Apprenticeship*, p. 264; and Nathaniel Matebule's amanuensis: see below.

[33] Eugene Casalis, *Etudes Sur La Langue Sechuana* (Paris: Comité. de la Societé des Missions. Evangeliques de Paris, 1841), xxix; Campbell, *Travels, 173* (1816). Ancestors might also become manifest in natural signs.

[34] Henry Staten, "How the Spirit (Almost) Became Flesh: Gospel of John," *Representations, 41* (Winter, 1993), pp. 34–57; and David Chidester, *Religions of South Africa* (London: Routledge, 1992), 157 ff.

and their households when they were forced (by circumstance) to ensconce themselves in African polities, or they built mission stations, with a main house and a school and land, to which dispossessed people fled. Where Africans retained a measure of political independence, men tended to keep women away from the foreign teachers. Where their political authority was wounded early and badly, such as in the eastern Cape and southern Highveld, women and then even men embraced the "teaching." Looking ahead for a moment, Khoekhoen and then a few refugees, Tswana and Nguni, configured their Christianities in the early years of the century, whereas Christianity on the central Highveld spread only after 1830, among Xhosa chiefdoms after 1858, and at the end of the century or later (or never) in the far north and northeast.

Mission stations in South Africa were essentially modeled after the Moravians' eighteenth-century community at Baviaans' Kloof, in the Cape, later called Genadendal. Stations attracted ex-slaves, divorced women with children, ambitious exiles, and misfits, all of whom had to exhibit conformities favored by the resident clerisy. The Genadendal exemplar was duplicated and transformed through circumstance, with Kuruman (Kudumane) under Moffat becoming a secondary model. Mission stations accrued a decent portion of South Africa's farmland. Most of them were autocracies, and prohibited practices that preceded the redemptive message of the New Testament such as polygamy, brideprice, circumcision, and the levirate – in other words, many of Africans' fundamental modes of social integration – along with dancing, liquor, and marijuana. Missionaries were themselves often anachronistic figures, hoping to keep their people from the *boshula* of advertising, popular literature, secular music, alcohol, prostitution, and class stratification. Much of missionaries' "modernity" was not in fact very modern.

In early settings, missionaries inevitably struggled to make themselves understood. When Robert Moffat first spoke "of God," he encountered "ridicule" or "violent bursts of laughter. The cross was the subject of loud laughter." In the 1820s, young Moffat preached, "Of his own choice, he brought us to birth by the word of truth to be a kind of firstfruits of creation" (James 1:18). In his vernacular attempt, this was: "O re tsetse kaha go ratan ga ga gagwe ka lehoko ya boamarure, gore re nne ekete re mabucwa pele a dibopiwa tsa gagwe." One can parse his words as follows: "He gave birth to us / because of his love by the accurate decision, /so we might become first-fruits of the harvest / of the things he made." This was incomprehensible. Moffat thus found "indifference and stupidity" and that generally "they laugh at what is urged, or reply *Maka haila*" ("Just lies"). "What do you announce?" Daumas and Arbousset were asked a decade later. "The words of the chief of heaven [*morena wa legorimo*]," was the reply. People howled with laughter: There was no master in the sky! Many people gestured to the ground when they were asked about ancestors, or said "ancestor is under the ground" to specify. The Rev. Casalis, when he learned that his father had died, said in broken Setswana, *Ntate o magolimong*, "My father is (now) up above." This exclamation "confounded them [his listeners], for according to their ideas it was into the bowels of the earth that people passed after death." Certainly, they buried them. The Tlhaping queen asked, "Will people who are dead rise up again? Is God under the earth or where is he?"[35] "Progress" was slow; the "truth" of the realm of the sacred could not be easily conveyed.

Those missionaries incompetent in the local language tried to convey their meaning with "our attitude, our gestures, our tone of voice," but such were and are the most culture-bound of signs. In 1830, Batswana north of the Vaal told the Rev. Thomas Hodgson to leave off preaching in Setswana and stick to Dutch. People engaged in craft labor during his sermons, or slept, or talked among themselves.[36] James Brownlee somehow preached that sin and sorcery were equivalents. Samuel Broadbent's assistant was an *oorlam* who suggested beating inquirers while African evangelists risked beatings and worse at the hands of their listeners.[37] In such circumstances, quite often, missionaries were dejected or otherwise unable to function.[38] People begged and stole from them. When Hodgson was starting out in the 1820s, he cherished rainy days so he could hole up in his wagon, safe from the grasping crowds. In 1841, James Cameron noted that his audience was sometimes drunk by the time they had collected to hear him, perhaps the better to be entertained. "In reading a part of the baptismal service I became so confused that I could scarcely proceed," Cameron confided to his journal. "The perspiration burst from every pore of my body . . . sometimes I am so discouraged as to fly from the work of the Lord, and bury myself in oblivion." The long-serving Methodist William Shaw began a stock sermon in the Transkei about God's sacrifice through

---

[35] Moffat, *Apprenticeship at Kuruman*, pp. 243, 244, 250; and pp. 43ff. 51, 63, and (long quote) 82; my translation based on "lehoko" meaning "expression or pronouncement" rather than a conventionally divided "word," and "ya boamarure" indicates claimed verifiability and accuracy. "Chief of heaven," e.g., Arbousset and Daumas, *Narrative*, 139; "legorimo" also means lightning, "izulu" in Nguni languages. Campbell, *Travels*, 173, in his gloss, "Is God under the earth, or where is he?" Casalis, *Etudes Sur La Langue Sechuana*, xxix. Ancestors also could become manifest in natural signs.

[36] Diary of James Cameron, ms., April 5, 1841, Rhodes University Library, Grahamstown; Journal of the Rev. Hodgson, June 7, 1830, CWM/MMS Personal Papers, Box 300.

[37] Brownlee: December 26, 1827, n52, cited in Crais, *Politics*, 257; Arboussett, *Missionary Excursion*, 65.

[38] Among many examples: Moffat, *Apprenticeship*, 83 (May 25, 1823); Eugene Casalis, *My Life in Basutoland* (Cape Town: Struik, facsimile reprint, 1971), p. 209.

Christ. "I had not spoken long when I felt the rays of the sun, together with a strong hot wind, greatly to affect me, [and I was] again relieved by vomitting. The people sat still as death."[39]

The central message missionaries brought to South Africa was "[Nonsense word] died for your sins so you may live." They heralded this first, and most basic, of their stories with the phrase "good news" because anyone who "agreed" or "accepted" it could join the "kingdom." As we have seen however, the news asked listeners to intuit in a way that was, to say the least, improbable. Unlike *unkulunkulu* or *modimo* or *inkosi*, "Jesus Christ" did not have any ordinary meaning; normally, proper names were intelligible phrases or exclamations. The idea that "he died for you" was, further, an opaque sentiment, a textual relationship between a signified entity (you) and an event that was a sign (Christ's death by crucifixion) that required one's personal commitment in order for it to become true for one's self. Christ was problematical, as the figure of a son equal to his father was repugnant. Further metaphors like "his blood washing away men's sins" and so on required many contexts of usage to assume any meaning at all.[40] I would argue that it was this very ambiguity that gave Christianity its early success, and which made it a threat to chiefly power. Where it was not opaque, it only looked more or less like other indigenous forms of authority. We will return to Christianity's successes shortly.

CULTURE BROKERS AND GROUP CONSCIOUSNESS: SERVANTS AND MASTERS

Evangelists were not the only brokers of new forms of consciousness. There were other adaptable types who did this job as well, most without leaving a paper trail: *metis* gunrunners, the educated sons of chiefs, teachers, ivory hunters, and traders passed back and forth over the frontier(s), and also subalterns, *oorlams*, imported slaves, and day-laborers. All such people pioneered new forms of habitus. If we consider the Western Cape as a point from which shifts in thought emanated, Khoekhoen were surely critical. The survivors of the destruction of Khoekhoe polities were subordinated in the Cape as unskilled laborers, "Hottentots." Some of them went to mission stations and converted to Christianity and hoped to remain free. Others of

---

[39] Cameron, "Journal," May 8, 1841; Hodgson: bk. 7, Pers. Papers, *op. cit.*; C. Germond (Ed.), *Chronicles of Basutoland: A Running Commentary on the Events of the Years 1830–1902, by the French Protestant Mission in South Africa* (Morija: Government Press, 1967), quoting Rolland, 1832; Shaw, Journal, May 24, 1830. C.f. Johannes Fabian, *Out of Our Minds: Reason and Madness in the Exploration of Central Africa* (Berkeley: University of California Press, 2000).

[40] Worger, "Parsing God," pp. 426–9.

their number on the Orange River took the offensive and became rustlers-cum-herders, called with other Khoe-speakers Korana (sing. Kora). Initially there was little overlap between such statuses, though one could convert from one to the next. Individuals among them traveled with better-known Europeans, hunters like Gordon Cumming, "transfrontiersmen" such as (notably) Conraad de Buys and the convict Jan Bloem. Their parties traveled far afield, as did *metis* pioneers like Jan Hendrick and Barend Barends and Danster ("Dancer"), a Dutch-speaking Nguni-descended interpreter for Lichtenstein and other travelers. Some representatives from the colony even established trade-based "mateships" (*maats*) on equal grounds with Tswana-speakers in Dithakong, which was the biggest upcountry African town in the 1810s. Such arrangements may have involved the "sharing" of wives (with or without women's permission).[41]

European men's liaisons with Khoekhoe, Bushman, and slave women produced the first home-grown *metis* people in South Africa, pithily called "Bastards." They found it difficult to secure loan farms because of their mixed ancestry, and some of them went inland, becoming "binnelanders" and bringing the culture of the Cape underclass with them. Some of them raided and mingled with the Korana, whereas others adopted the more proper, indigenous-sounding name, Griqua, following a suggestion by the missionary John Campbell in 1813, and settled in a "permanent" town. Some leaders, like Adam Kok, Piet Witvoet, and Abraham Kruger, first raided and then settled down, leaving their progeny scattered across the interior. Andries Pretorius was a deacon and yet described himself as a "Bushman"; some members of the Kok clan dressed in leathers and painted their faces with clay, whereas others essentially became landowning Boers. Trekkers captured women and children, and sold them in the so-called black ivory trade. Many captives were indentured, and grew up as *oorlams*, some of Tswana descent, sharing Boers' language and culture. Generally, on the Eastern Cape frontier, one historian argues, it was difficult to find much difference in the fabric of life between Khoekhoe servants and their self-conscious masters.[42]

[41] Martin Legassick, "The Northern Frontier to c. 1840: The Rise and Decline of the Griqua People," in Richard Elphick and Hermann Giliomee (Eds.), *The Shaping of South African Society, 1652 1840* (Middletown: Wesleyan University Press, 1989); Legassick, "The Griqua, the Sotho-Tswana, and the Missionaries," Ph.D. dissertation, UCLA, History, 1969.

[42] Schoeman, *Griqua Captaincy*, pp. 110, 115; Elizabeth Eldredge, *A South African Kingdom: The Pursuit of Security in 19th Century Lesotho* (Cambridge: Cambridge University Press, 1993), p. 44; and Nigel Penn, "The Orange River Frontier Zone, c. 1700–1805," pp. 21–109 in Andrew B. Smith (Ed.), *Einiqualand: Studies of the Orange River Frontier* (Cape Town: University of Cape Town Press, 1995); Penn, "The Northern Cape Frontier Zone, 1700–1815," Ph.D. dissertation, University of Cape Town, 1995, esp. p. 164; and

Although some servants were clearly slaves, then, the status of others was less clear. South Africanists disagree on whether servants who were slaves had a typical kind of experience and, by implication, group "consciousness," either before emancipation on December 1, 1838 – perhaps rooted in the Cape's big wine and wheat farms – or after that, as a section of the larger *metis* population commemorating the date with a carnival. But it is clear many of them were cosmopolitans and culture-brokers. The literature shows that chattel slaves lived under a variety of regimes, some suffering in the fields, but some "holding cockfights and . . . barbeque[ing] beef on the beaches of Table Bay," or prostituted to sailors, or even virtual members of the master's household.[43] As Robert Ross puts it, "a mild slave regime is a contradiction in terms." Nonetheless, Rob Shell has suggested that Cape slaves must have internalized most of the parameters for their own behavior, and surely he is also correct. The rebeled slave, Galant, said at his trial that he acted first of all because his master refused to feed and clothe him adequately. Yet Cape slaves, even after their effective creolization, seem not to have built an autonomous culture behind a façade of acquiescence, as Genovese tells us slaves did in the United States' South. Relations of servitude were not as nicely discerned in the Cape. The commonality of language and culture between masters and servants after all was such that the Dutch lingua franca, "Afrikaans," originated as a form of slave kitchen-talk. The multiple overlap of enserfed and enslaved people; the small number of slaves in an average farm; the existence of nested hierarchies such as the 200 urban free blacks who owned slaves in the early years of the century – this suggests a model of intersecting associations in an underclass subculture, rather than a unified slave or servant consciousness.[44] Whereas, as Rob

Natasha Erlank, "Christian Missionaries and the Xhosa, 1820–1850: The Scottish Case," *Kleio*, XXXI (1999), pp. 6–32; "one historian" is Susan Newton-King, *Masters and Servants on the Cape Eastern Frontier, 1760–1803* (Oxford: Oxford University Press, 1999).

[43] Hermann Giliomee, *The Afrikaners: Biography of a People* (Charlottesville: University of Virginia Press, 2003), pp. 171, 184 ff.; quote: Robert Ross, *Cape of Torments, Slavery and Resistance in South Africa* (London: Routledge, Kegan Paul, 1983), p. 22; cited by Andrew Banks, *The Decline of Urban Slavery and Emancipation in the Cape Colony in South Africa, 1806–1834* (Cape Town: Center for African Studies, 1995), 98 ff., in critique of Ross. See Robert C.-H. Shell, *Children of Bondage: A Social History at the Cape of Good Hope, 1652–1838* (Johannesburg: University of Witswatersrand Press, 1994); and "Paternalism Under Siege," Chapter 2 in Nigel Worden and Clifton Crais, *Breaking the Chains* (Johannesburg: University of Witswatersrand Press, 1994), by John Mason. See also John Edwin Mason, *Social Death and Resurrection: Slavery and Emancipation in South Africa* (Charlottesville and London: University of Virginia Press, 2003).

[44] Eugene Genovese, *Roll, Jordan, Roll: The World the Slaves Made* (New York: Vintage, 1976); George Frederickson, *White Supremacy: A Comparative Study in American and South African History* (Oxford: Oxford University Press, 1981), which was carefully read before

Turrell argues, the punishment for raping a woman of color judged to be sober in character was quite harsh, women of color per se clearly suffered from an overlap of legal debilities. As Pam Scully shows, this made them especially vulnerable to gendered forms of violence in the Cape. Upcountry in the ruinous aftermath of the Tlokwa chieftainess MmaNthatisi's aggressive state-building, elderly women were often abandoned or subjected to accusations of witchcraft. What dimension of oppression hinged not on a registered form of bondage but on a form of gender common to households in crisis? The borderline cases are often the most illustrative. Steyntjie, a Cape woman slave investigated by Fiona Vernal, is one such. Supported by abolitionists, Steyntjie brought a legal case against her third master, Anderson, and argued that her prior master, Weeber, had freed her. He had done this not only by his testament (perhaps forged), but by living with her like "man and wife," and indeed having children with her in the same house. In her statement, Steyntjie allowed that her first master, Stadler, had also fathered children by her, but not with her personal consent. From her point of view her "slave concubinage" with Weeber was of a different kind, and he let her dress like a citizen and claim the status of wife. (The lawyers on both sides called him a man of "the lowest sort.")[45]

This is also to say that inequalities created different forms of consciousness in the same milieu. In pastoralist climes, after a shared childhood, some youths were made masters, whereas others, often their half-siblings, were re-enserfed to the master. Thus, there is no question that Steyntjie's self-understanding was inflected by the nexus of "family" relations. But it follows that many "families" tolerated sexual abuse and brutality as a norm in their households. Listen to Christoffel Brand at a meeting of slaveholders in 1832.

Why may we not punish our subordinates when they misbehave? . . . Our children are beaten and punished when they deserve it. Yes, we chastise our own blood, and are the slaves better than that? . . . [Why may we] not privately punish our slaves, who are our children in our households, when they make false complaint?

publication by Leonard Thompson; Nigel Worden, *Slavery in Dutch South Africa* (Cambridge: Cambridge University Press, 1985), 86 ff.; Robert Ross, *Beyond the Pale: Essays in the History of Colonial South Africa* (Hanover: Wesleyan, 1993), Chapters 8 and 9.

[45] Pam Scully, *Liberating the Family? Gender and British Slave Emancipation on the Rural Western Cape, South Africa, 1823–1853* (Portsmouth: Heinemann, 1997); Robert Turrell, *White Mercy*, forthcoming; Fiona Vernal, "Concubinage and Manumission in the Cape Colony, 1777–1822," unpublished paper, Yale, 1998; c.f. Eugene Gevovese, "'Our Family, White and Black': Family and Household in the Southern Slaveholders' World View," in Carol Bleser (Ed.), *In Joy and In Sorrow* (Oxford: Oxford University Press 1991). As the astute anonymous reader suggested should be emphasized, inequalities stratified people's sense of self, depending on their social position within one system.

Opposing the eruption of the public sphere in slavery, Brand argued that his right to beat and wed his own children was at risk.[46] Historians have not yet asked how such domestic(ated) violence shaped the culture of adolescence in South Africa, but perhaps they ought.

Out of the same contexts came the status called Cape Colored. In Cape Town, many slaves retained a limited sort of autonomy in their lives and associations and built local networks of support. A Portuguese-based maritime creole briefly vied with Afrikaans among them. Many of them were further connected through Islam. Muslims made up a fifth of all slaves by 1830 and increasing numbers of free. Islam sometimes drew converts through dangerous liminal rituals, in which people signaled their removal from the hypocrisy of the Euro-Christian ethics that subjected them. Kin and family remained of paramount importance. After 1838, thousands of freed people of color followed kin and confessional brethren to new lives in Cape Town and missionary societies' land. The same year, for perhaps the very first time, a missionary was specifically (by white Methodists) to be assigned to coloreds on the Highveld, as opposed to this or that chiefdom or town.[47]

Elizabeth Elbourne argues that as Christianity was appropriated and adapted in Khoekhoe practice, it came unmoored from whiteness, and being white was in turn infused with new and different connotations. Respectable status was always more easily granted to whites, and brown people struggled over their lifetimes for it. Distinctions developed among freedmen, especially between Christians and Muslims, with the latter called "Malay," even though most were not Malayu speakers and it is not clear how many embraced the designation. A more pertinent fact united Muslim and Christian free people, their emerging status as "brown people," synonymous with "work people" in Cape Town. Such an equivalence meant, for example, that an impoverished laborer was likely to be known as a brown person and that Andries Stockenström, the frontier official of part slave descent,

---

[46] Christoffel Brand, "Why may we not punish our subordinates when they misbehave?" a speech by Brand published as a brochure in Cape Town, 1832, in Andre du Toit (Ed.), *Afrikaner Political Thought, Vol. 1* (Berkeley: University of California Press, 1983), sec. 3.10; Kirsten McKenzie, *The Making of an English Slave-owner: Samuel Eusebuis Hudson at the Cape of Good Hope, 1796–1807* (Cape Town: University of Cape Town Press, 1993), 60 ff; and see issues raised by Helen Bradford, "Women, Gender and Colonialism: Rethinking the History of the British Cape Colony and its Frontier Zones, ca. 1806–70," *Journal of African History,* 37 (1996), pp. 351–70; and Linzi Manicom, "Ruling Relations: Rethinking State and Gender in South African History," *Journal of African History,* 33(3) (1992), pp. 446–65.

[47] Banks, *Decline,* Chapter 4; Giliomee, *Afrikaners,* 189 ff.; Archbell to WMMS, January 1, 1839, in *The Wesleyan Mission in the O.F.S. 1833–1854,* Karel Schoeman (Ed.) (Cape Town: Human & Rousseau, 1991), p. 41.

was unlikely to be so known. Even in the 1850s, one finds colored used in official correspondence to indicate all nonwhite people in the Orange Free State. Eventually, administrators broadened its coverage from freedmen and the patrilineal descendants of *metis* people (or simply, non-Europeans who had Dutch surnames) to include all Hottentots and Bushmen who were, of course, natives.[48]

Afrikaner traced a long and winding path to whiteness. The genealogical meaning of the word – African – is not often remarked, perhaps because it is too obvious. Long before Afrikaners claimed racial fellowship with Englishman, the term indicated persons claiming Africa as their permanent home, but who did not say so as natives, *naturelles*. Thus the term covered the Dutch-speaking *metis* "Africanders," a clan of bandits of Khoekhoe ancestry; Estienne Barbier, the rebel against the Dutch East India Company; and the anglicizing urban population of Cape Town.[49] In contrast to Afrikanerness, Englishness emerged fairly quickly, in the Eastern Cape, because of the 1820 immigrants. Within two years nearly all the original 5,000 British settlers abandoned agriculture and moved to towns, and by the 1840s they assumed a kind Britishness unavailable to them back home, marked not only by shared language, but sentimental patterns of consumption, class obfuscations, and vigorous jingoism.

It was to an extent behind closed doors, in houses and cities, that whiteness, being a white person, subsequently took shape. Well *avant la lettre*, a universe of new built spaces (board rooms, restaurants, dens), were reserved essentially for whites and nonwhite servants only.[50] In contrast to those

---

[48] Elbourne, *Blood Ground*; Shamil Jeppie, "I.D. du Plessis and the 'Re-Invention' of the "Malay," c. 1935–1952," unpublished paper, University of Cape Town, September 1988; "Helen Ludlow, "Groenekloof after the Emancipation of Slaves, 1838–52," in Henry Bredekamp and Robert Ross (Eds.), *Missions and Christianity in South African History* (Johannesburg: University of Witswatersrand Press, 1995); Yusuf da Costa and Achmat Davids, *Pages from Cape Muslim History* (Pietermaritzburg: Shuter, 1994); Frank Bradlow and Margaret Cairns, *The Early Cape Muslims* (Cape Town: Balkema, 1978).

[49] Robert Ross, *Status and Respectability in the Cape Colony, 1750–1870: A Tragedy of Manners* (Cambridge: Cambridge University Press 1999); V.C. Malherbe, "Indentures and Unfree Labour in SA: Towards an Understanding," *South African Historical Journal*, 24 (1991), pp. 3–30; two contrary implications here, see Jonathan Gerstner, *The Thousand Generation Covenant: Dutch Reformed Covenant Theology and Group Identity in Colonial South Africa, 1652–1814* (Leiden: Brill, 1910); and Andre Du Toit, "No Chosen People: The Myth of the Calvinist Origins of Afrikaner Nationalism and Racial Ideology," *American Historical Review*, 88(4) (1983), pp. 920–52; Giliomee, *Afrikaners*, pp. 52–3.

[50] Nigel Worden, Elizabeth van Heyningen, and Vivian Bickford-Smith, *Cape Town: The Making of a City* (Cape Town: David Philip, 1998), pp. 127, 151 ff; Vivian Bickford-Smith, *Ethnic Pride and Racial Prejudice in Victorian Cape Town* (Cambridge: Cambridge University Press, 1995); David Cannadine, "The Context, Performance, and Meaning of Ritual: The British Monarchy and the 'Invention of Tradition,' c. 1820–1977," from

Boers who trekked, those who remained in urban environments took the lead in acculturating to whiteness and creating a Europeanist network of cultural ties from Grahamstown to Paarl. Unself-conscious whiteness in turn permitted a faction of liberals to emerge and even attack some of its underpinnings, as Dr. John Philip and his son-in-law John Fairbairn tried to do.

In the early years of the century, however, the great majority of rural communities in South Africa still lived in the shadow of the Bantu house through the propagation of fealty to an umbrella authority, whether chief, church, or historical figure. They did not cleave to long-term ethnic iden-tities. Rather, real greatness continued to be sought, chiefs who could gather and name people, and this very process often reamalgated the fitfully diverging designations colored and native. If some *metis* people managed to live as Boers, *metis* people and Batswana and southern amaNguni often lived side by side. Moffat thought the "Fetcani Hordes" were both dark and light-complected. At Philippolis in 1827, fifty "Bechuana" households outnumbered the twenty or twenty-five "Griqua" ones, so that Setswana was (according to Gottlob Schreiner) required for serious missionary work there. Most women at Philippolis "smeared and painted their bodies" in 1827, and "differ nothing from the Corannas." The most prominent sub-Griqua settlement on the Orange River at the time was that of Piet Sahba, a "former teacher of the LMS at Ramah," described as "a native" by Andrew Smith and as a "Griqua-Hottentot" by the Germans; according to John Melvill's journal, Sahba's "werf" consisted of "12 Griqua and 17 Bechuana families," apparently melded into Griquaness through their attendance to Sahba's Dutch-language sermons. Similarly, *metis* households lived under the authority of the Tlhaping chiefship in Dithakong, which was itself largely Korana by blood. Its people were locally distinguished not by eth-nicity but by production: they were called *Briqua* (*biri-qua*), goat-herding men and thus farmers. Refugees were welcome among them.[51]

Out of this situation came a new mode of homegrown governance, which increasingly claimed Christianity as integral to its expansion. "Griqua" Christians and their allies marginalized older mission subgroups and by the end of the 1830s laid claim to the entire Highveld. They effectively ban-ished refractory London Missionary Society missionaries, and even warded off Robert Moffat. The Cape Town executive John Philip's suzerainty over

The Invention of Tradition, in Eric Hobsbawm and Terence Ranger (Eds.) (New York: Cambridge University Press, 1983); Crais, *Making*; c.f. Homi K. Bhabha, "Signs Taken for Wonders: Questions of Ambivalence and Authority Under a Tree Outside Delhi, May 1817," *Critical Inquiry*, 12(1) (1985), pp. 144–65.

[51] Karel Schoeman, *The Griqua Captaincy of Philippolism, 1826–1861* (Pretoria: Protea, 2002), pp. 122, 119, citing the Journal of the Berlin Missionary Society for 1836.

Philippolis proved elusive. His planned brick homes with attached gardens never quite emerged, and most residents were transient, building werfs. Griquatown's Captain Andries Waterboer was an evangelist even though the LMS at one point excommunicated him, and he delivered many Sunday sermons himself. In Dithakong, the church's elders required no literacy from their catechumens. They banned the eating of meats killed in the hunt, taught that illness was punishment for sin, and determined among themselves whether a soul was going to Hell or Heaven. Such formations of power surmounted both ethnic and institutional connections. On the basis of the Griqua Church's successful evangelism, connected to Dithakong and even Thaba Nchu, Waterboer claimed to possess *bongaka* (he used the Tswana word), that is, to be a "specialist," eliminating the need for white missionaries in Griquatown and by extension over much of the central Highveld, where he proclaimed himself paramount.[52]

The amaZulu offer another example of human beings using fealty to an ambiguous umbrella authority. Although with their stabbing spears and shields "the Zulu" came to embody tribal difference in South Africa, the kingdom at its height entailed various degrees of common citizenship. Much like the Ndebele state in the Transvaal and later Zimbabwe, it was typified at its core by (contested) kin ties amid wider identities that had been submerged. The sense of being iZulu coalesced against a kind of in-group "other" called "the vulgarians," roughly (*amalala*); by emulation of royal culture; by comilitarized initiation groups; and at its widest, on the margins, by tribute and conflict. The word Zulu itself, although it perhaps denoted a chief in Shaka's father's past, more surely meant "of the heavens," and was thunderously expanded by chiefs extolled as *phezulu*, meaning up above, and *izulu*, like the firmament.

Sir Theophilus Shepstone entered Zulu political ceremony in the 1870s understanding the plurality of the kingdom's population under this designation. He ornamented his functions with chiefly regalia and a praise-singer and supported the pomp and circumstance of the throne. King Cetshwayo found Shepstone useful for underwriting his own legitimacy (as surely Shepstone knew), combating the also Shaka-descended royal faction that opposed his ascendency. When Shepstone coronated Cetshwayo in 1873, he acted "as Shaka," turning the *golo/khulu* tyrant into a useful symbolic unifier for Nguni under British hegemony, a "living ancestor" (ipso facto through Shepstone) — an authority-symbol of a decidedly non-Christian kind. Their collaboration informed the very meaning of

[52] Schoeman, *The Griqua Captaincy*, p. 170; Ross, *Adam Kok's Griquas*; Legassick, The Griqua, the Sotho-Tswana, and the Missionaries, esp. Chapter XI and p. 541; Elbourne, *Blood Ground*, esp. Chapters 6 and p. 320.

"Zulu." South Africa's policymakers drew on the same legacy in formulating apartheid.[53]

SOCIALIZATION AND GROUP CONSCIOUSNESS AMONG AFRICANS AND BOERS

Whereas the constructed nature of Afrikaner nationalism is accepted, much of the social history of Africans in South Africa still relies on the tribal model for early nineteenth-century indigenes, epitomized by the historiography of A. T. Bryant. It obscures the truth that the entire hierarchy of racial identities in South Africa was sorted out through gendered mechanisms. Men whose Dutch-patronymic fathers had impregnated women of color might be known as "Christian," or Bastard, or Griqua, and (if they were not too dark) even Boers; likewise, racial "native"-ness and national affiliation were inherited almost wholly through the father; slave status came from one's mother. Tribe is a poor vehicle for grasping such gendered collectivities. And, if we are to treat ethnicity as it is in other parts of colonial Africa, then it must be seen primarily a textual identity, a section of the scope of imperial surveillance, rather than a modality of social organization or descent.[54] It was a kingdom (Kongo), an artistic tradition (Baule), a status (Bamana), a predatory movement (Chokwe), a male pastoralist with a spear (Maasai), or "those people over there" – in other words, almost any sociality that managed to situate itself in the interface of colonial-African contact.

The ethnic model should therefore be reserved for the end of the century, when it came to describe an incipient form of mobilization and administration. The prior situation was more fluid, even if tribal appellations were used. Henry Francis Fynn led a settlement, the refugee "Fynn's People," on the Mzimkulu River. There was a mobile, raiding people in the 1820s outside Delagoa bay called "Olontone," which merely means "those of the London Missionary Society." Sefunela's following ("BaSeleka") suffered repeated attacks from Moletsane's men ("BaTaung"), but they were ethnically indistinguishable. Moletsane chased Sefunela from Platberg to Makwassie, and back again, capturing people and cattle until Sefunela allied himself to Kora, Bastard, and Bushman leaders – and two Methodist missionaries – to find some peace at Thaba Nchu as a "Barolong" chief.

[53] Hamilton, *Terrific Majesty*, 27, pp. 94–6, 128–9; David Welsh, *The Roots of Segregation: Native Policy in Natal, 1845–1910* (Cape Town: Oxford University Press, 1971).

[54] Robert Thornton, "Narrative Ethnography in Africa, 1850–1920: The Capture of an Appropriate Domain for Anthropology," *Man*, n.s., 8, 3 (September 1983), pp. 502–19. For Bryant, see John Wright, Chapter V.

Elsewhere, Sekhukhune brought together various Fokeng, Mfengu, "Northern Sotho," and Nguni people under the name Pedi, admitting some escaped slaves to become Bapedi, too. The kingdom of Lesotho is a further example of the elevation of political authority above race in nineteenth-century nation-making. Moshoeshoe (Moshesh) collected fragments of polities from all over South Africa, including some Korana and others of mixed descent, and he chose "Sotho" because the name meant almost nothing to his diverse people. Consider that Danster, Lichtenstein's "Xhosa" *oorlamsch* interpreter who had raided with de Buys, could not in Lesotho have become a Mokwena – the blood-linked clan of Moshoeshoe's father – but could and did become a Mosotho, in other words, one of Moshoeshoe's subjects in the 1840s.[55]

From the same perspective, it becomes possible to see the similarities between African and Afrikaner polities in a clearer light. African and settler pastoralists eschewed for the most part wells and irrigation and used seasonal pasturage to graze their stock year round; they relied on Khoe expertise for handling cattle, adopted the Khoe sheepskin kaross (as their "coverlet"), and wore straw hats like Khoe servants (clothing is discussed again later on in this chapter). Boers cooked sheep's entrails in tailfat and hung their meat to dry like local people, but they curried it like their colored relations living in the Cape. Politically, Boers' all-male republicanisms looked much like the stratified men-only advisory democracies of African chiefdoms. In both cases, patriarchs with substantial herds dominated the circle, free to speak their minds. The Republic of Natal's *volksraad* was "essentially an occasional and informal body," and in the Transvaal Hendrik Potgeiter "resembled more an African chief" than a European statesman. (When Piet Potgieter died, his successor Stephanus Schoeman even married the widow.)[56] It bears reminding that the Boer republics and most African polities were fragile structures: the South African Republic (ZAR) driven to bankruptcy by internal rifts and Sekhukhune's resistance; the Zulu Kingdom, so often termed the strongest state in nineteenth-century South Africa, a "rope of sand," which halved in 1843 and fragmented into

[55] See Carolyn Hamilton (Ed.), *The Mfecane Aftermath* (Johannesburg: University of Witswatersrand Press, 1995), esp. chapters by Elizabeth Eldredge, Norman Etherington, and Andrew Manson, and esp. Marjorie Kinsman, "'Hungry Wolves': The Impact of Violence on Rolong Life, 1823–1835," pp. 363–94; and Etherington, *Great Treks*, p. 138 (the translation of Olontone is mine). Moffat: *South African Commercial Advertiser*, January 7, 1824, as cited in G.M. Theal, *Records of the Cape Colony*, 1903, Vol. XVI, pp. 503–4.

[56] Peter Delius, *This Land Belongs to Us: The Pedi Polity, the Boers, and the British in the Nineteenth Century Transvaal* (London: Heinemann, 1982), pp. 171 ff., 192, 237 (quote); Tim Keegan, *Colonial South Africa and the Origins of the Racial Order* (Cape Town: David Philip, 2000), p. 204 (quote), pp. 252, 254; Fred Morton, "The Hurutshe and the Formation of the Transvaal State, 1835–1875," *International Journal of African Historical Studies*, 25(1) (1992), pp. 85–98; Burchell, *Travels*, p. 175.

principalities after 1880. Not only Waterboer and Moshoeshoe and Moroka (in Thaba Nchu) cultivated the legitimization of state churches, only to see sectarian and political schisms defeat them; so did the Boers of the ZAR and even the Orange Free State, which offered no other resolved identity to its citizens until the 1860s. Smaller communities, extended families, were more important, and regional factions in the Transvaal broke away like African subchiefs. Among all peoples in South Africa, women diffused conflicts that threatened the neighborhood peace, not least by relocating from village to village, and among Afrikaners and Africans both, they prodded menfolk to stiffen their spines in war.[57]

As Boers were regionalists, they were, as might be expected, unenthusiastic about cooperating in military adventures. The republics in their war efforts tended to employ regimented African men circumcised as a cohort, or rebellious sections of a polity under a pretender. In the time of the Great Trek, the leaders Louise Tregardt and Andries Pretorius relied on African chiefs for aid and provisions. Africans did much of the skirmishing for the Boers. Mediating further were "Fingoes," Bushmen hunters, and other cosmopolitans. João Albasini was a Portuguese appointed to administer the ZAR's northern flank. Abel Erasmus was a "Tsonga messenger" who performed diplomatic and commercial transactions for the ZAR. Authority did not always follow race. In the upper Caledon Valley, many Boers saw themselves as Moshoeshoe's subjects and staked their very sense of community, of *maatskappij*, to the chief. In 1848, after British troops under Major Warden had punished the Winberg Boers on the battlefield, a few families nonetheless joined the British and attacked Moletsane, Moshoeshoe's man on the spot. They were soon sorry, as Sotho men, along with the Korana, van der Kolf, and Gert Lynx, torched their homesteads and stole their cattle – shown to the proper houses by other Boers. Field commander Wessels stood amid the wreckage and warned that if Moshoeshoe were again provoked, the settlers would "reproach me, and laugh at me," saying "the Kafirs are masters, and I may go and fight them if I like."[58]

[57] Alan Lester, *Imperial Networks: Creating Identities in Nineteenth Century South Africa and Britain* (London: Routledge, 2001), pp. 74–5; Giliomee, *Afrikaners*, p. 170; John Laband, *Rope of Sand: The Rise and Fall of the Zulu Nation in the Nineteenth Century* (Johannesburg: Jonathan Ball, 1997); Jeff Butler, "Afrikaner Women and the Creation of Ethnicity in a Small South African Town, 1902–1950," in Leroy Vail (Ed.), *The Creation of Tribalism in Southern Africa* (London: James Currey, 1989); and Herman Giliomee and Heribert Adam, *Ethnic Power Mobilized* (New Haven: Yale University Press, 1979), esp. Chapter 4; and Deborah Gaitskell, e.g., "Wailing for Purity: Prayer Unions, African Mothers and Adolescent Daughters, 1912–1940," in Shula Marks and Richard Rathbone (Eds.), *Industrialization and Social Change in South Africa* (London: Longmann, 1982).

[58] British Parliamentary Paper 66 (1852–3), Asst. Com. Green to Gov. Cathcart, encl. 3 in No. 10, 49; and Asst. Com. Green to Major Warden, 12/6/52, 15; Wessels to Warden,

Similar alliances could be found in a minor key. There were farmowners as well as less reputable *bywoners*, van der Merwes and Ferreiras all, who not only sold weapons and ammunition to Africans, but even disguised themselves and rode as mercenaries with them against their rivals. Such men did not act out of kindness, but for booty, and it would be they who, in a bad drought, might offer to buy Africans' children.[59] In areas of more intensive agriculture, increasingly from the 1860s on, white and black farmers lived in close proximity. Sunday church was also useful for promulgating and enforcing local codes of propriety across racial divides. Surely something of the rich variety of relationships Charles van Onselen brilliantly recounts for rural people in the southern Transvaal might have been found earlier in the farms between Bloemfontein and Maseru, or Herschel, or Spelonken, or the pasturage around Oliphant's Hoek. In such places people negotiated a "modus vivendi embracing health, justice, language, production, recreation, and religious life."[60] Kas Maine, van Onselen's sharecropping biographer, born in the 1890s, was a product of such cultural hybridity, his very name a cross of Boer and "Sotho" culture: Kasianyane met by Caspar.

POLITICAL INTERVENTIONS AND THE DEPOLITICIZATION OF FERTILITY AND HEALTH

Jan van Rooij and Cornelius Goieman were perhaps early examples of another kind of entrepreneur in the hinterland of the Cape. Part-time Christians and part-time brandy-drinking traders, they willingly guided Europeans inland, for a price. Similarly, the colored Richard Miles led German

---

Bloemfontein, 13/12/51, 18. Other information in this paragraph comes from Elphick and Giliomee (Eds.), *Shaping*, Keegan, *Colonial*, and Adams and Giliomee, *Ethnic*.

[59] Peter Delius and Stanley Trapido, "Inboekselings and Oorlams: the creation and transformation of a servile class," in Belinda Bozzoli (Ed.), *Town and Countryside in the Transvaal: Capitalist Penetration and Popular Response* (Johannesburg: Ravan Press, 1983), pp. 53–88; Keegan, *Colonial*, p. 204; c.f. Gordon, *Bushman*, 169 ff.

[60] Charles van Onselen, *The Seed is Mine: The Autobiography of Kas Maine* (Johannesburg and Athens: Ohio University Press, 1996), 7 (quote), pp. 22, 234; Kasianyane also refers to a Taaibosch (Korana) stronghold wiped out by the ZAR around the time Kas was born. Colin Bundy's *The Rise and Fall of the South African Peasantry* (London: Heinemann, 1979) focuses on Herschel; Tim Keegan, *Rural Transformations in Industrializing South Africa: the Southern Highveldt to 1914* (London: Macmillan, 1982); William Beinart, *The Political Economy of Pondoland, 1860–1930* (Cambridge: Cambridge University Press, 1982); William Beinart, Peter Delius, and Stanley Trapido (Eds.), *Putting a Plough to the Ground: Accumulation and Dispossession in Rural South Africa, 1850–1930* (Johannesburg: Curry, 1986); c.f. Jean-Loupe Amselle, *Mestizo Logics* (Stanford: Stanford University Press, 1998).

missionaries inland before becoming a Korana agent. Jan Tzatzoe was such an intermediary on the eastern frontier. Up north, transport drivers, seamstresses, and "swart skuts" (trusted African gunmen) all brokered ideas along with Cape manufactures. The Englebrechts guided wagons out of Griquatown. Their predecessors were traveling specialists and rainmakers. They worked as free agents far from home, inadvertently supervising the creation over long distances of religious, ethnic, and national points of dissemination.[61]

The growth of Christianity involved a transfer of authority to churches and the depoliticization of powerful speech (ancestor, greatness, chief) in public contexts. A handful of chiefs' sons (and daughters) graduated from European institutions, Zonnebloem in the Cape, even British universities. Even so the last to give up the vocabulary of agency to discourse about God were the active nation-builders themselves. Chiefs Faku, Mothibi, Moletsane, even Moshoeshoe eventually rejected Christianity, not because it was strange but because it was familiar to them. Nguni monarchs never took it up. The Zulu king Dingane quizzed the Rev. Francis Owen about faith, listened to the responses, and then said, "I and my people believe there is only one God – I am that God."[62] Dingane was *inkosi enkulu*, the most *khulu* chief in Natal. Sir Harry Smith called himself "inkosi enkulu." According to an English diary, Mzilikazi said he was "bigger than God," and that he "was God," meaning that he spoke the same Nguni words that Smith used.[63] As the power-brokers of the era tried to bring diverse people together, with only the loosest regard for blood seniority, under one "great ancestor" or "great chief," the distinctions between them were not always apparent. Christian or not, the successful leader had access to weapons, ammunition, oxen, and wagons.[64] Gradually of course these usages began to diverge, and people came to recognize (*bokal-bonga*) authority in a way that made "everlasting life" assume a new kind of sense. This was not one process in one place, but from the 1830s through the 1870s, at different

---

[61] Miles: Schoeman, *Griqua Captaincy*, p. 102; Tzatzoe: Roger S. Levine, "Sable Son of Africa: the many worlds of an African cultural intermediary on the Eastern Cape frontier of South Africa, 1800–1848," Ph.D. thesis, Yale, 2004.

[62] R. Hully, *Zululand under Dingaan: An Account of the Rev. Mr. Owen's Visit . . .* in *South African Bound Pamphlets,* 140(6), reprinted from *Cape Monthly Magazine,* n.s. 2 (1880), pp. 321–32, as cited in Jennifer Weir, "Ideology and Religion: the Zulu State," Ph.D. dissertation, History, University of Western Australia, 2001.

[63] Mostert, *Frontiers,* p. 937; Andrew Smith, diary, October 4, 1835, in Kirby (Ed.), vol. 2, p. 253.

[64] Tim Stapleton, *Faku: Kingship and Colonialism in the Mpondo Kingdom (c. 1780–1867)* (Waterloo.: Laurier University Press, 2001), pp. 28, 128; and Janet Hodgson, "History of Zonnebloem," M.A. thesis, University of Witwatersrand, 1975, 2 vols., 403 ff.

places and times, people experienced the invention of belief with all its accompanying theatrical discourses.

As with the trend toward racial categorization, it follows that people did not experience a break in their consciousness of the world at any one point, even those who converted. Two examples are offered as illustrations: "squash" and "rain." The word for "squash" or "gourd," *sego*, was adopted to mean "to be holy" by Tswana Christians, because chiefs used gourds to anoint their bodies and initiate the community harvest in the mimetic and socially constitutive "first fruits" ceremony.[65] After that, the notion "to make *sego*" appeared in the Beatitudes and other parts of the Bible and catechisms that were concerned with what the missionaries saw as "sacralization" ("blessed are the meek"), the elevation of someone or something to an exalted status. At the same time, "to make *sego*" meant "treat as if it were the squash symbolically used by the chief in the harvest ceremony." Some of the functions of African leaders that had to do with human and agricultural fertility were placed under the care of Christians, who thereby aligned their practices with formal aspects of chiefly power. The authority of Africans in the countryside would be limited to custom, which denied politics in theory and often amounted to petty absolutism.[66] And yet no abrupt break can be recorded; for instance, well-watered people on the Mogalakwena River exported their good fortune to their neighbors in a *segwana*, the diminutive of *sego*, which also meant scrotum. Inside the *segwana* was tobacco, which a customary gesture connected to virile power: like the Turks, elders would pinch a boy toddlers' genitals and snort at their fingers. The word *goga* was the Highveld term not just for this act, but also in speaking about "pulling down rain" or rainmaking. These sorts of interaction barely surfaced in the written record, where "make *sego*" was supposed to mean "bless."[67]

---

[65] Krige, *Social System*, 249 ff.

[66] Martin Chanock, *Law, Custom and the Social Order: The Colonial Experience in Malawi and Zambia* (Cambridge: Cambridge University Press, 1985); Diana Jeater, *Marriage, Perversion and Power* (Oxford: Clarendon, 1993); and Mahmood Mamdani, *Citizen and Subject: Contemporary Africa and the Legacy of Late Colonialism* (Princeton: Princeton University Press, 1996), esp Chapter 3.

[67] Part of the source material here is in oral traditions I collected, and refers to Nguni-inflected Highveld chiefdoms (e.g., *Lete, Gananwa*); Isaac Schapera, *Rainmaking Rites of Tswana Tribes* (Cambridge: Cambridge University Press, 1971); Colin Murray, "Sex, Smoking and the Shades: A Sotho Symbolic Idiom," in M. G. Whisson and M. West (Eds.), *Religion and Social Change in South Africa* (Cape Town: Juta, 1975), pp. 58–81; J. D. Lewis-Williams and Thomas Dowson, *Images of Power: Understanding San Rock Art* (Cape Town: Struik, 1989); and Pippa Skotnes, *Heaven's Things: a Story of the /Xam* (Cape Town: University of Cape Town Press, 1999). *Sego* persists in the South African national anthem.

People on the Highveld shouted "Pula" as an acclamation for chiefs: "Rain!" Rain was also critical in the sloping grasslands of Nguni peoples; the words for God adopted for use among Xhosa, *qamata* and *thixo*, had rain-and-sky connotations, like *zulu*. In Tswana languages, lightning was based on the old power root, *dzim*, the same as in "ancestor." The most important expert in a nineteenth-century Highveld state was often the *moroka*, or rain-specialist, of the chief. Especially as missionaries lay claim to the heavens, Africans everywhere imputed this function to them, and beseeched them for rain, or accused them of blocking it. Clearly, the word "rain" is only an approximate translation, as precipitation was only part of this language-game. In the dry Kalahari, *pula* implied sharing, female fertility, and predictability, all features associated with good health. Nuances are lost to us. It was translation that turned practical associations into rules, so that Africans were said to "believe" unlikely propositions: "the smoke of the rainmaker's fire attracts the clouds," for instance. The production of such beliefs about rain marked a decline in Africans' access to land, in which investments in sharing, femininity, growth, and relative predictability were undermined.

Subsequently, Christians, and then others, countenanced ideas about rainmaking as beliefs. At St. Johns in the Eastern Cape, the local magistrate imprisoned six rainmakers, "because they were unable to make rain within the days appointed" by him, and had them flogged in the market center of Ladysmith, subscribing to their praxis with unmatched ferocity. The Rev. Shrewsbury reported that the Xhosa *inkosi* Hintsa had kicked out his rainmakers and that many said he, the missionary, claimed this authority. Worse, they wished to pray to him, saying he "was their God," and they coruscated him for not cooperating. Why, if it were not Shrewsbury's doing, would God withhold rain? His response was to reach for the simile of chief (*kgosi/inkosi*): in the same way, he said, that Hintsa did not always choose to loan out his cattle. At Thaba Nchu, the missionary led people in what he called prayer. "The heavens gathered . . . [and] rain commenced," and the traditional rainmakers were "ashamed and confounded" – and began themselves to "pray to God," an activity that in their same whispered words only days before might have been catalogued as ancestor veneration.[68]

David Livingstone argued with a "Kwena rainmaker" that "only God can make it rain" (perhaps, *modimo o le nosi o kgona go nesa pula*), not men, who can just pray for rain (*rapela pula*). A good deal of weight was thereby placed on the brand new distinction between *go rapela*, on the one hand,

[68] WMMS, Box 301, Fiche 69, Journal of J. Shrewsbury, Nov. 1829; and Anglican Missionary Archives, Rhodes House Library, Oxford University, E 25: 1869–70 W.T. Illing, St. Johns 30/9/1870.

and *go bina* (dance) on the other, for people already sang or danced their desires for rain:

> Pina ea morimo, u ee hae!
> Ki lema ka lefe?
> U ee gae, u ee gae![69]

In contrast, Livingstone recommended prayer, because men could not do the work of God, could not take credit for the weather, could not "pull down" (*go goga*) rain. Such conversations suggested new definitions for rain, God, "doctor," and perhaps even "credit," and one wonders if Livingstone used the term *sego* (gourd, blessed) in his discourse, with its inevitable connections to human agency. Typically, Europeans found themselves on alien epistemological terrain in such engagements, and Livingstone in this case contradicted himself, blaming the "rain-doctor" for the drought.[70] Part of the reason missionaries were asked for rain is that they were, correctly enough, reckoned as a kind of expert (*ngaka/inyanga*), land- and cattle-less, possessed of esoteric knowledge. They were thus asked for medicines that would allow a person to know how to read (Livingstone at least twice, in 1842 and 1868), and called "experts" (or "doctors") until they objected, everywhere in Southern and Central Africa. Some European shopkeepers also were pressed to act as surgeons. Western therapeutic practices usefully diverged from those of local experts: They aimed at interior spaces, the balance of humors, and parts of bodies. The enumeration of parts to be manipulated changed people's consciousness of their bodies. As it became possible to deal with mouth pain by removing a bad tooth, for instance, the pain itself shifted to become a toothache. The birth attendant, the eye-wash dispensary, and the amputation theater constructed new forms of care, and redefined illness and wellness in their ambits. On the other hand, even some Boers continued to patronize herbalists and other local experts well into the twentieth century, as people pursued their "quests for therapy" wherever they felt they might find relief.[71]

CONSCIOUSNESS AND THE CATTLE-KILLING OF 1857

In 1856–57, numbers of southern Nguni chiefdoms destroyed their stores of grain and killed their livestock, in "the Xhosa Cattle Killing," an act of

---

[69] Arbousset and Daumas, *Narrative*, p. 259: "Song of our forefather, come home to us! How shall I farm? Come home, come home!"

[70] Comaroffs, in *Of Revelation*, vol. 1, pp. 210–12; also analyze Livingstone's dialogue, which appears in different forms in Livingstone's books and journals.

[71] John Janzen, with Louis Arkinstall, *The Quest for Therapy: Medical Pluralism in Lower Zaire* (Berkeley: University of California Press, 1978).

inadvertent community suicide that has become quite well known. People recently slaughtered in battle were expected to rise when the wealth of this world was destroyed.

The wars of the Eastern Cape were the traumatic background to the crisis. Settlers' strategies ruptured the habitus of the westernmost Xhosa, culminating in the horrific War of the Axe. Death was supposed to commence ritual, even when a person perished far from home. Corpses were scrupulously avoided and occasioned mandatory washings. Married women supervised births and funerals and they developed their own philosophies in dealing with them, some of which survive today. Descriptions from both Nguni and Tswana areas hold that ideally, in a chief's funeral, the grave was dug at the rear of a fresh central kraal. In wartime all these practices lapsed, and Xhosa men buried their fallen lightly, near prominent trees or rocks. Settlers dug up some of those graves and desecrated the corpses. In turn, they left their fallen soldiers deep beneath hewn stones, sometimes engraved with family names. By digging them up, the Ngqika chiefdom of Xhosa recovered the land into their spoken ancestries again. The sepulchral violence of the wartime eastern frontier was itself a kind of conversation both about the land and about the infinite.[72]

Two early prophets, Nxele and Ntsikana, acted out paradigmatic responses to the promise of salvation in such circumstances: Ntsikana preached in conformation with political and ecclesiastic authority, whereas Nxele in 1818 led an Ngqika–Xhosa attack on Grahamstown. Further prophetic activities fell between them. Not all had to do with the imminent enfleshment of the dead. In 1850, an 18-year-old named Mlanjeni stirred people to battle by asking them to rid their communities of maleficient persons, to kill all their light-colored cattle (cattle being the earthly picture of ancestors, or community authority, consider the message here), and arise to "fight for our country," their own ancestors, and their chiefship. Colony servants, trusted domestics, and indeed whole congregations of Christians left to join him, until they were brutally routed. In 1856–57, several young prophets, the most famous of whom was an adolescent girl named Nongqawuse, said that "the dead would arise" if people killed their cattle (many of which was ill with lungsickness) and destroyed their grain. The girl was vouchsafed by a respected patriarch, Mhlakaza, and great

[72] David Bunn, "The Sleep of the Brave: Graves as Sites and Signs in the Colonial Eastern Cape," in Paul Landau and Deborah Kaspin (Eds.), *Images & Empires: Visuality in Colonial and Postcolonial Africa* (Berkeley: University of California Press, 2002), pp. 56–90; Jean and John L. Comaroff, *op cit*, p. 154; Leonard Thompson, *Survival in Two Worlds, Moshoeshoe of Lesotho* (Oxford: Oxford University Press, 1970), p. 92. Monica Hunter Wilson, *Reaction to Conquest: The Effects of Contact with Europeans on the Pondo of South Africa* (London: Oxford University Press, 1961), p. 228; Elgash, *African Fractals, 29*.

numbers of his peers, perhaps goaded by commoners, did as they were told. Possibly 50,000 people starved to death as a result.[73]

Makana, Nxele, Mlanjeni, and other bricoleur "prophets" before Nongqawuse relied on visions that demanded actions in the waking world. The concept of the dream and private vision was joined to the authorless authority of writtenness, which it was said required a leap of faith. Ordinary evangelists for decades proclaimed the apocalyptic unworthiness of the world and yet spoke about ancestor as if a fallen father or uncle were actually present. There was a mobile gray area of singulars and plurals, in which evangelists said "the living God" and "living ancestor" in the same words, at the same time (a unity chiefs wished to maintain); analagously, "everlasting life" meant "still alive." Which was which? The phrase *modimo o o sa tshelang* / *unkulunkulu usaphilayo*, "the ancestor who still lives," asserted immediacy and presentness. From 1824, missionaries preached in the imminent second coming of Christ and the end of the world. Khoekhoe, too, had been told by van der Kemp that the dead would arise, and there was a cattle-killing prophecy among them. The question of when created a second gray area. Moffat reported that his discussion of the resurrection made listeners look "as if they expected the latter to take place while I was speaking." Brownlee found that Xhosa wanted to know "where Christ was." In the decades before 1857, apocalyptic predictions faded but individuals were still told to expect a real meeting with their ancestors at the day of reckoning or after their death (*-fa/-swa*). Most important to grasp is that every pulpit proclaimed a truth independent of the senses, of the kind found in text and in believing a 17-year-old prophetess.[74]

Ntsikana is still recalled by some Xhosa as having received the Gospel in a revelation. And for many, the Gospels became the truest kind of truth, taking precendence over all others. That said, in the decades before 1856, some Christians had already begun taking the position that a story in the Bible was just that, whose importance was its usefulness as a piece of pedagogy. The Anglican Bishop John William Colenso in the 1850s came to doubt the doctrines he was forced to state so baldly to Nguni confidants. First, he questioned the eternal nature of damnation for an unintentional sin; then he recognized that he could not honestly say he believed Noah's flood. In

---

[73] Jeffrey Peires, *The Dead Will Arise: Nongqawuse and the Great Xhosa Cattle-Killing Movement of 1856–7* (Bloomington: Indiana University Press, 1989).

[74] Moffat, *Missionary*, p. 579; Crais, *Politics*, p. 127, citing Joseph Williams, CWM, LMS 6 (3) D, 1816–17. For an influential treatment of rumor, see Luise White, *Speaking with Vampires: Rumor and History in Colonial Africa* (Berkeley: University of California Press, 2000); and Helen Bradford, "Women, gender and colonialism: rethinking the history of the British Cape Colony and its frontier zones, c. 1806–70," *Journal of African History* (XXXVII) (1996), pp. 351–57. I owe some of the following analysis to listening to Elizabeth Elbourne in conferences and panel discussions.

the end he found himself rejecting the idea that the Bible was the "literal word of God." Other modernizing Nguni Christians, some stemming from Ntsikana's circle, were unconvinced by the imminence of the resurrection. For men such as Tiyo Soga (in 1856 the first ordained African in South Africa), the eschatological realm, *bogologolo/ubunkulunkulu*, was postponed to an indefinite future.[75] In contrast, those who killed cattle in 1856–57 – the "softs" – continued to believe that *bogologolo/ubunkulunkulu* lived in the politics of their lives. Chiefdom-by-chiefdom embraced and decreed the truth of what Christians had long preached. Their aim was to restore the fullness of their autonomy, of chief, nation, and land under ancestor. After the tragedy and the resulting famine, survivors took the message seriously a second time: Xhosa people after 1858 converted in large numbers. It so happens that the apocalyptic Book of Revelations grew in influence after the turn of the century, its phantasmagoric imagery informing the visions and dreams of novices in the growing "Spirit" church movement. But the apocalypse had already come.

LITERACY, ICONICITY, AND RECIPROCITY

Arguably, the most important broader shift in consciousness in South Africa concerned the onset of literacy and widespread iconicity in representations. Textual truth, surnames, projections of the self into narrative, and visual pictures were all part of this transformation. Early in the century, in 1828, Moffat and his African assistants translated a whole book of the New Testament into a version they called "Sechuana." The earliest uses of the root term, written *moetjuanna* or *booshuanas*, suggest the word (today, "Tswana") had meant "they are the same as us"; now it was a language. Other Biblical translations soon followed: a complete New Testament, then a southern Nguni (Xhosa) New Testament in 1846, a complete "Sotho" Bible in 1857 (like the Sepedi and Serolong ones that followed, taken from within Setswana), a northern Nguni (Zulu) New Testament in 1867, and lastly, aimed at the coloreds, an Afrikaans Bible in 1872. Except for Afrikaans, they marked the veritable initiation of literacy in their vernaculars; Afrikaans first appeared in Arabic script among Muslim slaves and became the medium of instruction in in Cape Town's Muslim classrooms. Early literacy in South Africa was valorized around the content of what was read, instilling the idea that forms of the written word had special claims to truth, for Christians and Muslims both. Literacy was an avenue to power.

[75] Jeff Guy, *The Heretic: A Study of the Life of John William Colenso, 1814–1883* (Pietermaritzburg: University of Natal Press, 1983), pp. 72, 142, 185 ff; Les Switzer, *Power and Resistance in an African Society: The Ciskei Xhosa and the Making of South Africa* (Madison: University of Wisconsin Press, 1993), pp. 74, 120 ff.

Beginning with rural passes in the Cape and the Free State, one had to be written down in person in order to travel and work. First, the ledger, the signed note, and then the photograph all made unassailable claims to tell the truth and arbitrate identities. Even the nonliterate began vouching for facts as being written down in a book or preserved in a photograph, as the bureaucratic use of those mimetic techniques expanded.[76]

Discussing the various exchanges by which Africans and Europeans came to readjust their perceptions of the world, Jean and John Comaroff have usefully focused on literacy in South Africa. They argue that there was a long conversation in nineteenth-century colonialism, through which a text-based epistemology penetrated and reorganized the mentalities of Africans. The process of accommodating or resisting and so transforming colonialism unfolded in an alternation between the acceptance into habit and the formation of ideology or consciousness. Literacy in their view facilitated self-alienation, helping to condition Africans to "spontaneously consent" to the demands of capital, yet the same alienation also offered them the means to self-representational and advocative clarity.[77] The Comaroffs suggest that the Tswana notion of "good work," *tiro*, which pertained to social as well as material labor, came to be counterposed to the European understanding of alienable work, *go bereka*. The dialectic brought to mind more clearly what *tiro* was about, and by extension, that *tiro* was something particularly Tswana, informing the meaning of Tswana itself.[78]

How might the introduction of actual mirrors, or pictures in books for that matter, have had something like the same effect? The Comaroffs consider the gifting of looking glasses to African leaders by missionaries as indicative of the process whereby South Africans came to recognize their social selves.[79] Chiefs also posed for studio photographs and were presented

---

[76] Achmat Davids' work, e.g., "Words the Cape Slave Made: A Socio-Historical Linguistic Study," *South African Journal of Linguistics,* 8(1) (1990), pp. 1–24; Worden et al. (Eds.), *Cape Town, Vol. 1*, pp. 123–8. John Tagg, *The Burden of Representation: Essays on Photographs and Histories* (London: Macmillan Education, 1989).

[77] Comaroff, *Of Revelation and Revolution,* 2 vols. (1991 and 2000); Gramsci, "Modern Prince," p. 182; and see Shula Marks and Dagmar Engels (Eds.), *Contesting Colonial Hegemony: State and Society in Africa and India* (London: Routledge, 1994).

[78] Comaroffs, *Revelation, Vol. 1:* pp. 141, 260, and Jean Comaroff, *Body of Power,* p. 71. The adoption of "tradition" became a mode for opposing colonial depredations: see Christopher Lowe, "Swaziland's Colonial Politics: The Decline of Progressive South African Nationalism and the Emergence of Swazi Political Traditionalism, 1910–1939," Ph.D. dissertation, Yale University, 1998.

[79] See Frederick Barthes, "Introduction," in Barthes (Ed.), *Ethnic Groups and Boundaries: The Social Organization of Cultural Difference* (Boston: Little, Brown, 1969); and Michael Taussig, *Mimesis and Alterity: A Particular History of the Senses* (New York: Routledge, 1993).

with portraits of the Queen, all of which made a new kind of sense. Iconic signs were not new in nineteenth-century South Africa, as rock art and figurines, notably the Lydenberg statues, testify.[80] Yet it is so that the mimetic representation of the face had lapsed. Burchell described the first time Tswana people at Dithakong saw a drawing of a man in 1824: They crowded around and pronounced it well done, astonished even to the point of fear at "seeing Mollemui in a book." But Burchell also tells us that a less artful portrait was pronounced *mashwe*, ugly or dirty, and that the chief refused to sit for his portrait. Others saw a painting of Mr. and Mrs. Moffat, and were taken aback, "glad that the originals of the pictures were both present else they should have concluded that these were their ghosts, or their skins stuffed." By the 1870s, however, some people were so jaded that they doubted the existence of the Queen of England, feeling that she was only an image on money.[81]

Literacy allowed various elements of South African society to redeploy memory and intellect, but oral modes remained just as important. In the domain of jurisprudence, for instance, surely the oral continued to reign over the written. Depositions, testimonies, confessions, prayers, and swearings-in were all oral, a signature proving the hand of the subject. Both customary and Roman Dutch forms of law were in practice, negotiated and then backdated as traditions. Magistrates might invoke Sir Henry Maine and Justinian's Code in locating precedents for dealing with *ukutwala*, the custom of kidnapping African women before marriage, but it was an ad hoc sort of thing, a response to the need to see *ukutwala* as timeless and so as written.[82] Converting nonliterate practice into written law changed both.

Writing may have preceded reading. At Klaarwater in 1812, Burchell's Tswana-speaking servant had heard of *schryvende* but not books. Campbell supplied a sealed letter as Exhibit A in his advertisement for missionaries among Tswana-speakers in 1813. Chiefs right away demanded amanuenses. It is no surprise that Mzilikazi described Moffat's penning a letter as being "at God's writing."[83] At the mundane level, people interacted with writing officially and semivoluntarily. First, transitional moments in life came

---

[80] See Chapter 2 in this volume.

[81] W.J. Burchell, *Travels in the Interior of South Africa* (London: Longman, 1824), pp. 463, 480, 493; Paul Landau, "Photography and Colonial Administration," Chapter 5 in Landau and Kaspin (Eds.); the "Lydenberg Heads" excavated in South Africa date from over 1,000 years ago; and Henry Methuen, *Life in the Wilderness; or, Wandering in South Africa* (London: R. Bentley, 1846), p. 31, re: the 1840s.

[82] The burden of Martin Chanock, *The Making of South African Legal Culture, 1902–1936* (Cambridge: Cambridge University Press, 2001).

[83] Burchell, *Travels*, p. 338; R. Wallis, *The Matabele Journals of Robert Moffat, Vol. 1* (London: Chatto, 1945), p. 302.

to be represented in fixed entries in calendars. Posted banns legitimized marriages, and old people signed their grandchildren's registers with an "X." Rural couples carried signed passes from their home congregations to distant pastors who could marry them. Masters-and-servants laws confined travelers to preestablished signing stations. But farm laborers also wrote. With very little schooling, they drafted and circulated petitions in opposition to the alienation of their land. Gradually, South Africans came to be marked and masculinized through tax books, court documents, police reports, and church ledgers. Surnames grew out of parish registers and tax rolls. Tswana women's renaming upon bearing their firstborn (X), as "Mma-X," remained "oral," without leaving any mark. Consider that Selogilwe, a sharecropping "Rolong" man living in Philippolis, was first called *plaatje* by his Griqua landlord because of the flat or plate shape of his head. "Rolong" was thereafter left out, of private interest only in the places where Plaatjes thereafter held sway, and left their signatures in consequence.

Toward the end of the nineteenth century, all varieties of South Africans wrote letters, read books, and edited newspapers. Even then, however, common people relied on oral interactions to supplement texts. Oral meant the subject received personal acknowledgment. Agreements between landowners and *bywoners* included much that was mutually understood, just as did the annual *akkoord* (contract) between farmers and black tenants. Moshoeshoe used as messengers illiterate men with excellent memories. European administrators were forced to maintain personal contact through announcements, which might permit voiced objections on the spot. Correspondence with Native Commissioners usually involved personal contact, which makes many of them hard to decipher. The borders of text also opened up to rhetorical forms that properly may be considered "oral."[84] School lessons absorbed "histories" – the word in Tswana languages also means "tribes" – and grandfathers' tales vouched for authenticity. Oral history about Shaka affected Nathaniel Isaacs's 1836 farrago and Thomas Mofolo's 1907 epic. Schoolbook accounts fed back into popular lore. The Bible led the way as a genre-busting set of paradigms, but Bunyan's *Pilgrim's Progress* achieved a similar apotheosis at the edge of literacy, in themes and tropes, alternately oral, textual, and both at once.[85]

---

[84] Notwithstanding Vail and White's points in *Power and the Praise Poem* (Charlottesville: University of Virginia Press, 1991), Intro; and, "the subject" refers to Barthes' argument that writing destroys the point of origin of text, in "The Death of the Author," in *Image, Music, Text* (New York: Routledge, 1978).

[85] Isabel Hofmeyr, *"We Spend out Years as a Tale that is Told": Oral Historical Narrative in a South African Chiefdom* (Johannesburg: University of Witswatersrand Press, 1993), p. 14; Chanock, *Making*, pp. 175–6; Ted Matsetela, "The Life Story of Nkgono

Christianity delivered a kind of flexibility as it made itself more at home in its new vocabularies. Its stories about the travails of a colonized people, the ungodliness of injustice, the surety that their struggle would end in freedom, found more and more eager inquirers toward the end of the century. Bunyan and the Bible were texts inviting the projection and emancipation of the self. "Text is a machine conceived for eliciting interpretations," Eco remarks; reading is a kind of stationary journey with its own sort of vistas.[86] Colonial authorities did not always like the view. Christians deployed Revelations, Joseph, Noah, and Genesis to claim a moral equality that could plausibly be turned against colonialism itself. Not only African peasants but trekkers invoked the narrative of Exodus, themselves becoming Israelites in the desert in search of land and nationhood. This meant that the state was Pharaoh. In Nguni languages the word for nation is *isizwe*, and land is *(il)izwe*, the same root in two noun-classes, very close ideas. By the 1880s, changes in production and the use of armed force pushed representatives of every community off their land, and one finds Afrikaners, farm laborers in the Orange Free State, and later even a revived Griqua movement imagining themselves in the framework of the Exile of the Chosen.[87]

For governance in South Africa, the value of literacy was manifest. Political power moved around in currency, duplicated orders, collected reports, posted regulations, signed passes, correspondence, registeries of land, and so forth. In 1890, even with property illiterates were denied the Cape franchise.[88] The usages and vocabularies found in texts have been overemphasized because they are what historians have to rely on. But, just as most people's daily routine scarcely came to the notice of any text, South Africans' orality more generally was not switched off or quickly disabled by texts, either.

Mma-Pooe: Aspects of Sharecropping and Proletarianisation in the Northern Orange Free State, 1890–1930," in Marks and Rathbone (Eds.), *Industrialisation and Social Change*, pp. 221–35; Thompson, *Survival*, p. 234; Dan Wylie, *Savage Delight: White Myths of Shaka* (Pietermaritzburg: University of Natal Press, 2001); Hamilton, *Terrific Majesty;* and Hofmeyr, *The Portable Bunyan: A Transnational History of The Pilgrim's Progress* (Johannesburg: Witwatersrand University, 2004). Mofolo wrote Shaka almost twenty years before it was put to press: Mofolo, *Shaka* (Portsmouth: Heinemann, 1984), trans. and ed. by Daniel Kunene; Introduction. *Ditso* is from *go tswa* to come out from.

[86] Umberto Eco, *Experiences in Translation* (Toronto: University of Toronto Press, 2001), p. 6; Roger Chartier, "Texts, Printing, Readings," in *The New Cultural History*, Lynn Hunt (Ed.) (Berkeley: University of California Press, 1989), pp. 154–75.

[87] Leonard Thompson, *The Political Mythology of Apartheid* (New Haven: Yale University Press, 1985), 35 ff.

[88] Keith Breckenridge, *Archival State: Documentary Government and the Biometric Function in the Making of Apartheid*, forthcoming (esp Chapters 2 and 3).

DANCE AND SONG

There has already been occasion to mention dance (*-bina* in both Tswana and Nguni languages) several times in this chapter. Dance performed the political and social position of a person by abbreviating and exaggerating its form. "I find it impossible to give by means of mere description," wrote Burchell in 1812, "a correct idea . . . of the kind of effect [the dance] produced upon my mind and feelings." Dance performances were political events charged with power and potential violence. Gradually dance moved into new domains and somatized new forms of consciousness, even as it was marginalized from politics.

In Tswana languages, *seboko* meant both praise and totem, but neither English word quite captures the sense. "To praise," *boka/-bonga*, involved the adoption of specified poses and the invocation of the names and exploits of ancestors. The noun form of the same root is often given as "totem," the nature-linked institution of nonresidential alliances among households. Yet the question, "what totem do you respect?" was, word-wise, "what do you dance?" Recall that in honoring ancestors, people recognized the heritage, putative or real, of an agnatic core of men ("brothers," kin, etc.), with the chief first among them. These men were ranked in spatial displays in the central courtyard in villages and towns, as they were at funerals, initiations, and other important convocations, in most of which dance played a part. The activity of praising or uttering narratives about specific ancestors or living chiefs in public similarly directed attention to aspects of the community's power, its stamp, and its legitimacy. Existing collections of chiefly praise-poetry display a highly impacted form of language, and are strewn with half-recalled references and mnemonic devices from the past. They included tropes for power (*-dzim-, zulu, golo/khulu*), similitudes (elephants, lions, droughts, storms), descriptions of stratagems, widely found narrative clichés, and they reminded listeners of their totems.[89] Praises occupied a central place in the self-celebration of most African polities, and later attempts to write histories of tribes drew on them.

Leroy Vail and Landeg White in their studies of this poetry suggest that Southern African societies have always granted a special status to oral performances, licensing them to criticize power in ways that ordinary speech was prohibited from doing – and that such freedom continued under colonial labor regimes. Songs were designated using the root *-bina*, and also inflected relationships to authority. *Bina* had a useful ambiguity about it.

---

[89] Burchell, prev. para: *Travels*, 66; and, e.g., Isaac Schapera, *Melaô ya BaTswana*. (Collection of texts by native informants, Kgatla, Ngwato, Ngwaketse, and Kwena) (Alice: Lovedale Press, 1940); Schapera, *Praise Poems*; Gunner, *Poetry*; and Bourdieu, *Logic of Practice*, p. 35.

Thus, Mzilikazi's people "chanted, danced, and seemed to congratulate themselves" in self-praise when an Ndebele miscreant was executed, or captured cattle were herded into the central kraal; but Chief Mzilikazi's people also imitated him in *bina* (dance) moves, and *bina'*d complaints ("sang their grievances") to him. Chief Ngqika said he would "dance and praise (*bina*) my [cattle] as much as I please and shall let all who see who is Lord of this land." *Bina* was tied up with warfare and the hunt (killing), and *ngoma* and San trances (healing). Some San dances were somehow mimetic of large game animals and swept slowly through the Kalahari in waves, the "Giraffe," the "Gemsbok," and so on. In the context of war, "skill in dancing ranked with skill in song-making and recitation as a mark of cultural attainment." One is told "Moshoeshoe killed five men with a club of rhinoceros horn, which his father used in dancing."[90] Days of practice preceded competitions, which might last for hours. In Shaka's danced confrontation with the Qwabe polity, his amaZulu were shamed as inferior. Shortly afterwards he assassinated the Qwabe chief. Perhaps the missionary Casalis gives the best example of dance as an act of state. *Les guerriers ont passé en chantant*, dancing before the homes of brave men, recalling the acts that made them so, inviting and challenging each to join the war party. At the climax the leader of the dance thrusted his lance into a *cercle bruyant*, shouting; then silence followed, the line reforming, gravely and with "melancholy."[91]

Over the course of the century, with the transformations in chiefly authority already outlined, this concept was taken into different registers, and so the word *bina* came to mean veneration and affiliation, or dance and song. The particularization of the notion followed the logic of Christians' placement of prayer in opposition to dance. Prayer, that "highly tensed condition of inactivity," in Nietzsche's words, was foundational to Christianity, and evangelists repudiated its propinquity to dance as physicalizations of submission and exaltation. In private letters, however, churchmen were less certain and remarked that new Christians often "stayed up praying all night," signaling an acceptance of dance and praise in shaping the meaning of prayer. Of *oorlams* of Khoe descent, in Ohrigstad in the late 1840s, Stanley Trapido tells us, "when their master slept, they came together to dance and sing."[92] Perhaps they were praying. Hymns became the single most effective means of evangelism for Africans, but missionaries also

---

[90] Vail and White, "Ndebele Praises," in *Power*; Germond, quoting Lemue, in Mosega, March 1832; Robert Gordon, "Captured on Film: Bushmen and the Claptrap of Performative Primitives," Chapter 8 in Landau and Kaspin (Eds.), *Images*.

[91] Casalis, *Etudes*, 74 ff; Etherington, *Great Treks*, pp. 83, 163, 92.

[92] "Conditions" (plural) in the original, Nietzsche, *Will to Power* (New York: Vintage, 1968 [1887]), p. 114; Delius and Trapido, "Inboekselings," p. 70; Comaroff and Comaroff, *Of Revelation, Vol. 1*, pp. 239, 244.

found people singing church hymns over pots of beer on Sunday, bending Sankey's verses to carry alternative messages.[93] There were yet other sorts of Sunday *-bina*: drunken dancing in Kimberley in the 1870s, "grand displays" attracting the nonwhite population of Cape Town consisting of music played by Mozambique and Malagasy slaves, and "rainbow balls," which like the famous Octoroon Balls of New Orleans, introduced white men to women of color. Generally, dance was individuated as it became indecorous. Proper Muslims disliked the *Khalifa* body-piercings and dervish-like moves facilitated by trance, just like orthodox Christian evangelists discouraged "emotionalism."[94] The textualism of modernizing African elites, Malay *ulama*, and churchgoing coloreds, all opposed dancing. Mzilikazi's warriors, after raiding a pious rival polity, danced with stolen Bibles affixed to their headdresses.[95]

Bushmen and Khoikhoi people danced themselves into states of altered consciousness. People used tobacco and marijuana (*dagga*) to do this as well, but smoking does not account for their depictions in rock paintings with noses streaming blood. In /Xam thought, rain lived in the shape of heavenly game animals and came down to healers in the altered state of trance-dances. The prominence of dance in their lives reminds us that their destruction was itself an erasure of thought, as the Swy ei and /Xam (Bushmen) formations nourished unique forms of consciousness with few textual anchors. Moving from the Northwest Cape up into to the eastern interior, they were extirpated. Bushmen were chased into the Thirstland, reduced to starvation, and then when they "stole" settler cattle, hunted, and shot like vermin; settlers continued to target those who sheltered with the *metis-*, Kora-, or Tswana-centered polities of the Orange River. Others enserfed themselves to colonists, and as their descendants became coloreds, dance fragmented into children's games and brief celebratory displays.

A little bit of the consciousness that has gone missing from South Africa may be glimpsed in the archive made with jailed /Xam by Wilhelm Bleek and Lucy Lloyd in the 1850s. They recorded *kukummi* or performative recitations, each of which varied the components of a thematically stable story or cliché. Many of the texts look like they are supposed to be sung, so

---

[93] Tshidiso Maloka, "Women, Labour, and Migrancy in Lesotho," Ph.D. dissertation, History, 1999, p. 257; and Gabriel Setiloane, *The Image of God among the Sotho-Tswana* (Rotterdam: A.A. Balkema, 1976).

[94] Marc Epprecht, *'This Matter of Women is Getting Very Bad': Gender, Development and Politics in Colonial Lesotho* (Pietermaritzburg: University of Natal Press, 2002), p. 169; David Coplan, *In the Time of Cannibals: the Word Music of South Africa's Sotho Migrants* (Chicago: University of Chicago Press, 1994); and Chidester, *Religions, op. cit.*

[95] Paul Landau, *The Realm of the Word: Language, Gender and Christianity in a Southern African Kingdom* (Portsmouth: Heinemann, 1995), p. 144.

that among /Xam people, dance and historiography may have overlapped. *Kukummi* made no distinction between plausible and dreamlike motifs, wove commentaries into narrative, and were, because they were *kukummi*, true. Even given grammar and syntax, most of the texts are opaque today. Readers require forms of lived interactions with which to make sense of signs, but Cape San culture is defunct.[96]

It must be noted that alcohol transformed dance – and many other expressions of consciousness, besides. The common-calabash beer party had invited talking more than dancing and celebrated women's distribution of ordinary food, and men's (and some grandmothers') consumption of it. It had the sensibility of the hearth. On the farms that taxed and restricted Africans' food production, the *dop* system of alcohol payments appeared as early as 1830, and calabash beer (*boj{y}alwa/utshwala*) shrank in significance. This trend only accelerated when farmers (white or black) acted to limit the number of unproductive kin living on the land. The meaning of alcohol then was signaled in 1847 by Chief Sandile, who requested a regimen of daily tots in prison. Why, he was asked, as he had never drunk. "I am now the white man's child," he replied.[97] Toward the end of the century, bottled brandy and then municipal canteens appeared in the towns, and (to look ahead for a moment) -*bina* became "Marabi" and "dance hall." This music was infused with American jazz, in the consciousness – or semiconsciousness – of drinkers of "Skokiaan" and "kilimikwik," which were sometimes fortified with battery acid and benzene. Town women or *matekatse* danced in flowing dresses, and *famo* dancers hotly tormented drunken miners the night after payday. Perhaps most intriguing was the remaking of the tradition of self-praise (*bonga/boka*) in the same torrid environment, drawing also on the *ngoma* initiation form, in "songs of experience" or *dihela* (the word also means hymns). Lesotho's migrant miners composed and sung these narratives about their own journeys into the world of industrial work-cannibalism, opening up a new men's deliberative space in rural shebeens.[98] On the

[96] David Bunn, "The Brown Serpent of the Rocks: Bushmen arrow toxins in the Dutch and British imagination, 1735–1850," in Brenda Cooper and Andrew Steyn (Eds.), *Transgressing Boundaries: New Directions in the Study of Culture in Africa* (Cape Town: University of Cape Town Press, 1996), pp. 58–85; Pippa Skotnes (Ed.), *Miscast: Negotiating the Presence of Bushmen* (Cape Town: University of Cape Town Press, 1996); Nigel Penn, "The Northern Cape Frontier," p. 182; Robert J. Gordon, *The Bushman Myth: The Making of a Namibian Underclass* (Boulder: Westview, 1992). J.D. Lewis-Williams (Ed.), *Stories that Float from Afar: Ancestral Folklore of the San of Southern Africa* (Cape Town: David Philip, 2002), is the most accessible translation of some Bleek and Lloyd texts.

[97] Elbourne, *Blood Ground*, p. 266; quote in Mostert, p. 928.

[98] Coplan, *Cannibals*; and see Pamela Scully, "Liquor and labour in the Western Cape, 1870–1900," in Jonathan Crush and Charles Ambler (Eds.), *Liquor and Labour in South Africa* (Pietermaritzburg: University of Natal Press, 1992).

reef, choirs based in mine compounds evolved "a distinctive church–music culture . . . using body gestures to illustrate moods, meanings, and certain phrases," and "tribal dancing" competitions increasingly replaced barracks' faction-fights.[99] In the end, dance continued to tie individual effort to authority and power. Certainly, the *toyi-toyi* restored its political meaning near the end of the twentieth century.

SPATIAL BOUNDARIES AND CONSCIOUSNESS

The section following considers the shifts in South Africa of notions of correctness in clothing, home, and work. In the same context, there follows a consideration of repositioning of the self in space and in time. The refashioning of everyday boundaries favored the intrusion of surveillance and force in subordinate communities. Time peeled off from human intervals and curves straightened into lines, and individuals found themselves moving to rhythms set by international markets and industrial timetables.

Some of the first culture-brokers eschewed the signs of difference in their clothing and homes. The working-class background of missionaries in the early days of Baptist and Congregational missions encouraged such radicalism. A special LMS "synod" in Cape Town effectively aborted this policy for missionaries in 1817, however, and thereafter Christians in South Africa promoted their own forms of bourgeois morality and lifestyle, dress foremost among them. Especially in the eastern Cape in the 1840s, after a century of war, in the development of a bitter racism among whites, one finds an association of African "traditional" dress with notions of savagery, darkness, and promiscuity, reflecting all that urban whiteness wanted to keep outside itself. Africans bodies were dirty, their kinfolk crowded together, the women slatterns – this was part of the attack on independent Xhosa authority.[100]

---

[99] Maloka, pp. 208, 257; T. Dunbar Moodie, "Mine Culture and Miners' Identity on the South African Gold Mines," in Bozzoli (Ed.), *Town and Countryside*; Patrick Harries, *Work, Culture and Identity: Migrant Labourers in Mozambique and South Africa, ca. 1860–1910* (Hanover: Heinemann, 1994), p. 122; and Veit Erlmann, *Africa Stars: Studies in Black South African Performance* (Chicago: University of Chicago Press, 1991).

[100] Ann Laura Stoler, *Race and the Education of Desire* (Durham: Duke University Press, 1995); Comaroffs, *Of Revelation, Vol. 1*, esp. Chapter 3; Nancy Rose Hunt, *A Colonial Lexicon*, Chapter 4; Tim Burke, *Lifebuoy Men, Lux Women: Commodification, Consumption and Cleanliness in Modern Zimbabwe* (Durham: Duke University Press, 1996); Nicolas Thomas, *Colonialism's Culture: Anthropology, Travel, and Government* (Princeton: Princeton University Press, 1994); Catherine Gallagher and Thomas Laqueur, *The Making of the Modern Body: Sexuality and Society in the Nineteenth Century* (Berkeley: University of California Press, 1987); C.f. Ifi Amadiume, *Male Daughters, Female Husbands: Gender and Sex in an African Society* (London: Zed, 1987).

With the coming of home rule in the Cape, it became even more important to replace local, situational knowledge, which is largely closed to inspection, with standardized behavior and predictable spatial and temporal orders. For Xhosa chiefdoms, the land outside the homestead was threaded by pastoralist routes, dotted with runoff-conserving trees and the stone cairns known as *isivivane*; in contrast, "the Zuurveld" (sour-veld: re cattle grazing utility) was gridded with reservations and controls. The Crystal Palace exhibitions of 1851 exhibited the same principle in arraying African tools and weapons in visual fans and simple morphologies, as did colonial anthropometry (body-measuring) when it put photography on ruled paper in an effort to make it more precise.[101] By the end of the 1850s, the progressive evangelical imperative was waning. If "blacks" or "niggers" (for such occurs in corporate correspondence to the colonial office in the 1880s and 1890s) could not be civilized, they could at least be made to "fall into line."

Europeans insisted that their own manners were linear and clear; this was itself a kind of ideology. The "straight path" was a controlling trope in Christianity, Islam, and Judaism. Africans also held straightness and clarity to be virtues and agreed that Europeans were straightforward if that meant "free from invisible local entanglements." As others have shown, rectilinearity structured classroom seating, pews, buildings, fencing, lines of print, hemlines, erect bearing, reasoning, morals, sexuality, even one's gaze was supposed to be straight. The "Central Cattle Pattern" had placed sleeping quarters in maternal segments; the new propriety suggested that the patriarchal enclave (emptied of adult married men and their families) was to reside behind squared walls. Indeed, male wage earners transformed feminine, domestic spaces into extensions of the public sphere by adopting right-angles. Settlers enclosed the land when they could, and the indeterminate area between private and public narrowed to become a length of barbed wire. As Lewis Mumford points out, the ancient and medieval town laid out its roads like a spider web, slowing traffic to tax it; the provincial towns favored the open grid pattern. In 1843, Grahamstown decreed that its broad streets should flow in parallels (intersecting only at 90 degrees if possible), and legislated to prevent the "promiscuous settling" of land outside the grand plan. Only African locations were exempted, and they were exiled toward refuse dumps.[102]

---

[101] Hofmeyr, *"We Spend . . . ,"* Chapter 3, Annie E. Coombes, *Reinventing Africa: Museums, Material Culture and Popular Imagination in Late Victorian and Edwardian England* (New Haven: Yale University Press, 1997).

[102] Comaroff and Comaroff, vol. 1, Chapters 3 and 4; Chanock, *Making*, p. 401; Maynard Swanson, "The Sanitation Syndrome: Bubonic Plague and Urban Native Policy in the Cape Colony, 1900–09," in William Beinart and Saul Dubow (Eds.), *Segregation and Apartheid in Twentieth-Century South Africa* (London: Routledge, 1995), pp. 25–42;

At the same time, looking back, African housing styles also influenced European practices. Pioneer Boers favored housing that permitted mobility, just like Korana. Even in their more solid farmhouses, they hybridized indigenous modes, incorporating low mud or clay walls "of rectangular shape" with thatched roofs bound up with thongs. "The [Boers'] so-called cookhouse is a separate hut [with a] fire on the floor in the middle of the room," a floor itself smeared with dung, of which even Mary Moffat came to approve, saying "the fine clear green" liquid on her floors worked like an insecticide.[103] The effort to reform Africans' housing encountered difficulties as already noted. Tax collection by hut as opposed to head packed more persons in each hut. Khoekhoe at the station of Theopolis built square houses with internal partitions and then retired to live in their rondavels behind them. Some progressive chiefs did the same.[104] The Kat River settlement, just like the Glen Grey plan five decades later, preferred square houses for their residents but could not mandate every particular in them. Families might divide an interior with a clay wall and still go outside to bathe in the iron tub. In the end, the effort to inculcate new spatial separations succeeded mainly where employers or the state provided housing, in mining compounds, barracks, maids' rooms, and warehouses. In the twentieth century, the introduction of tarmac streets, cinder block and brick housing, and numberless alleyways of crates and corrugated metal sheet, would confine the old ways to the diminishing countryside.

How did people's self-presentations actually change? People spoke in many body sign systems, using beads, perfumes, body oils, coiffures, and so forth, but Europeans demanded Africans cover their bodies and this they learned to do.[105] In fact, Africans quickly learnt new clothing codes referencing status, pretensions, decency, background, and sexuality. Thus, Moshoeshoe "dressed like a Boer" to receive Andrew Smith, sitting on horseback, and selected other items for other kinds of foreign visitor, trying

Lewis Mumford, *Technics and Civilization* (New York: Harcourt, 1943); Thomas, *Colonialism's Culture*; Simon Hall, forthcoming; and see Paul Virilio, *Vitesse et Politique* (Paris: Editions Galilee, 1977).

[103] Mary, the elder. Petrus J. van der Merwe, *The Migrant Farmer in the History of the Cape Colony, 1657–1842* (trans. Roger Beck)(Athens, Ohio: Ohio University Press, 1994), 176 ff, and (first quote) p. 167; Leonard Guelke, "Freehold," in Elphick and Giliomee (Eds.), *Shaping;* Leon de Kock, *Civilising Barbarians* (Johannesburg: Witwatersrand University Press and Lovedale Press, 1996), p. 157, quoting Cecil Northcott, *Robert Moffat* (London: Lutterworth, 1961), p. 83.

[104] Elbourne, *Blood Ground*, ms. p. 465; Claude-Helen Perrot, *Les Sotho et les Missionaires Européens au XIXe Siècle* (Abidjan: Annales de l'Univ., 1970), p. 36.

[105] Ann Hollander, *Seeing Through Clothes* (New York: Viking, 1978), quote p. 85; and pp. 83, 381; Hilda Kuper, "Costume and Identity," *Comparative Studies in Society and History, 15* (1973), p. 356.

for particular presentations in each case. Other chiefs did the same, entering and leaving Khoe, Sotho, "Pedi," "Tebele," and further styles. Then in 1848, a movement among Lesotho's population rejected their European clothing in protesting Moshoeshoe's concessions to Christianity, such as divorcing all but one of his wives. Some of Lesotho's subchiefs forbade their men to wear trousers. Xhosa traditionalists also preferred blankets and "red ochre" on the skin, even thought Sir Harry Smith tried to suppress those signs. That said, most photographs of rural patriarchs – even in those in the quasi-independent hinterlands of South Africa that became Basutoland and Bechuanaland – show a preference for shirts, trousers, and (deteriorating) hats, the women in blankets in the background. Imported blankets and three-legged iron pots entered people's lives for the same reason: economy. By the same logic men led the way in novel forms of self-presentation because they and not women came to control a disposible income. Midcentury, Sekhukhune's subjects returned home from the Cape, "each . . . wrapped in a long sheep skin cloak" got with their wages, and with "various forms of headgear, some had red woolen tasseled caps, others felt and straw hats abundantly decorated with ostriche feathers." New signs for new statuses. Even deep in the Transvaal, Christians by the 1860s adopted at least the shapes of shirts and pants in skins and cloth fabrics when they could get them, the men doing the tailoring (an inheritance from the high-status skill of the skin-dresser).

All good Christians wore cuffs and collars on Sunday, whether made of linen or "wipe-clean xylonite," test-sheets designed to reveal errors in the care of the body. By 1870, most African men had some store-bought clothes for formal use. This did not prevent their being insulted as "dandies," and they learned quickly to dress modestly before whites, careful to reject any sign of class superiority. European observers were irked by what appeared to them to be mix-and-match African dress, of "half-dressed" natives, because it dealt them a blow of unwanted self-knowledge. It pointed out the arbitrary nature of the sign-systems in their own clothing, much of which borrowed from the class above theirs; the lapels and split tail-coats favored by the English in Cape Town, for instance, came from riding and hunting gear.[106] Thus, the way "immodest women" were dressing in Pretoria provoked the stern Lutheran missionary Bruenberger to make a public bonfire out of their hooped petticoats, even as, contrarily, the Rhenish introduced huge petticoats to congregations of Namibian

---

[106] Delius, *This Land*, p. 65; Christopher Breward, "Sartorial Spectacle: Clothing and Mass Identities in the Imperial City, 1860–1914," Chapter 13 in Felix Driver and David Gilbert (Eds.), *Imperial Cities: Landscape, Display and Identity* (Manchester: Manchester University Press and St. Martins, 1999), p. 245.

Herero women, whose daughters continued to wear them the following century.[107]

We cannot leave the matter of boundaries without considering people's consciousness of time, which seemingly rules the world today. Social historians have drawn attention to the way time was reconstructed in early modern Europe. Similar work is in its infancy in South African historiography, but some observations may be made. The word *lebaka* (or *lobaka*) in Setswana can signify a span in space or in time. This single notion was conceived as an interval of human activity by farmers, not as an abstract continuum punctuated by marks with no earthly significance. There were no fixed intervals shy of the day, nor were there Mondays and Sundays. Time was (and perhaps among a very few rural South Africans still is) a matter of experiential duration and predicted cycles. Scattering and gathering opened and closed communities, whereas transhumant cycles and plantings and harvests (and hunger) structured experience. From the perspective of the many, the recurrence of daybreak was the constant, and the 8:00 A.M. church bell pealed at ever-different moments. Similarly, the call to prayer for Muslims in Cape Town always came at sunrise, but foremen whistled when they chose. It is no that surprise schoolteachers and shopkeepers complained that pupils and staff arrived at unsynchronized moments. Europeans perceived a lack of respect for the worth of labor power. "For on their time, these people set no value," Burchell wrote way back in 1812. The truth was that new modes of time-keeping emerged when contexts for time-keeping expanded.[108]

The very distant past was perhaps always another country. By definition, men were not men, and societies had not come. Directions of origin were recorded in oral traditions: "we came from the north," true in a sense, or from a wetlands or rock, true in another sense.[109] A typical beginning of a spoken history in nineteenth-century South Africa went like this: "First, we were Hurutshe, long, long ago" (or " . . . , in great, greatness"). Understood as a statement about history, the feminized ancestor Mohurutshe (possibly

---

[107] Kristen Reuther, "Heated Debates over Crinolines: European Clothing on 19th century Mission Stations in the Transvaal," *Journal of South African Studies,* 28(2) (2002), pp. 360–78; van Onselen, *Seed,* p. 38; and see especially Patricia Hayes, Wolfram Hartmann, and Jeremy Sylvester (Eds.), *The Colonising Camera: Photographys in the Making of Namibian History* (Athens, Ohio: Ohio University Press, 1998).

[108] Dipesh Chakrabarty, *Provincializing Europe* (Princeton: Princeton University Press, 2003), p. 75; Frederick Cooper, "Urban Space," Chapter 8 in Cooper (Ed.), *The Struggle for the City: Migrant Labor, Capital, and the State in Urban Africa* (Beverly Hills: Sage Publications, 1983); BNA, PP 2/1/2, Isaac Schapera archive, "Histories, vernacular texts by various authors," collected in the 1940s.

[109] I.E. Ellenberger, *History* 1.

mo-ha-rotse, related to "place of the Rozvi"), or male ancestor Hoja or Moatshe or Rapulana ("First, we were people of Rapulana"), is identified as the beginning of collective consciousness. The kernel of the historical past, one might say, curled up on itself "in greatness" like a spiral of DNA. This was entirely alien to what Dipesh Chakrabarty identifies as "continuous, empty time." As the memory of a deceased chief faded away (one inflection of *-dzim*, as in *go dimelela*), or alternatively, was invented, his name was assumed as one's own – Moatshe, Rapulana, Mpondo, Morolong, etc. Two or three layers of names in this mode was not uncommon. Can we speak of an embodied past, a sense of cyclical timeliness? We have already seen that the "distant past" or "greatness" slipped into meaning "the divine realm" in isiZulu. A northern Tswana chief, talking to a Victorian missionary, drew a straight line on the ground to represent the western way of thinking, and looped circles to represent his own. "Now, suppose a black man tells a story," he said, tracing the curves in the dirt. The recurring aspect of time and history was uncoiled to the degree that people's lives changed.[110]

Still one must be careful, if only because time has long been a tool used to subordinate colonized people, and historians know little about the reorganization of time in the contested farmlands of nineteenth-century South Africa. Keletso Atkins has shown how the culture of work in mid-century Natal was conditioned not just by clocks but by the assumptions and requirements of Nguni men still enmeshed in the life of the countryside. They demanded to be paid according to their understanding of "months," shouting, "the moon is dead! give us our money!" and fled cane fields and farmlands to plant or harvest their own crops regardless of the needs of their employers. However, migrants to the towns of the Cape or Natal experienced real changes living in "a complex fabric of merchant time, church time, leisure time controls," having to get used to the timed A.M. cannon-shot in Pietermaritzburg, for example, instead of rising at "first visible silhouette of oxen on the horizon." They brought continuities in their consciousness of work and time with them.[111]

NATHANIEL MATEBULA, TEACHER

Because of the continued relevance of indigenous experts in the lives of rural people, as practitioners and theorists, Christians had to fight to replace them. They called them "witch-doctors," and pastors copied their duties,

---

[110] Bruce Bennet, "Suppose a Black Man Tells a Story," *Pula* (Special Issue in Honor of Leonard Ngcongco), 11(1) (1997), pp. 43–53.

[111] Atkins, *"Moon is Dead,"* and Daniel P. Kunene, pers. comm. 1988. The quoted term was a single word.

and took over their social station. The semantic register of this contest is now blurred, no longer fully translatable. A man "named Kotlane . . . who is esteemed as a prophet," intimidated people at the Tsantsabane church in 1835. "MaNtsopa," a woman in Lesotho, gained favor with Moshoeshoe as a "prophetess," but was only baptized much later, in the 1860s. "Sabrina" was a woman in the 1830s who expanded the use of baptisms and divined using bits of fragmented text, and she had a following. David Mokgatle Modibane, a Methodist in Thaba Nchu in 1839, the heartland for the "Tswana *oorlams*" who dispersed into Bloemfontein and its hinterland, had no institutional backing at all (until he acquired the patronage of Dutch missionaries). And so on.

In the following, I consider the biography of a minor Christian preacher named Nathaniel (born [u]Mbotshane) Matebula, of the Pongola River region on the Swazi border. The Rev. Matebula was an evangelistic "culture broker." His story appears to have been written and revised by a missionary, but it bears the recognizable marks of having originated in the Rev. Matebula's own recitation.[112] In his story we will also recapitulate some of the central themes of the chapter.

Mbotshane was born in 1824 during the accelerating conflicts historians still call the *mfecane*. The usual way of depicting African polities in its grasp is with vector lines, ethnonyms, and clash points. Instead, let us imagine the Zulu and Swazi social groupings as two amoeboid political forms, trading streams of cattle and sometimes women hijacked and tithed and swapped back and forth, pocked with violence and spasms of property destruction from time to time as they swell and deflate. He was a junior son of the headman of Mhlangampisi, a district of Nguni-speaking homesteads in the mountains between these forms. In his story, his own people had no worship,

---

[112] All the block quotes pertaining to Matebula are from "The late Rev. Nathaniel Matebule, Native Minister, Sketch of his Life, Labours and Death, Copied 23/11/85 (d. 21–12-83)," from the Synod Minutes of the South African Methodist Missionary Society, 1885. Other figures mentioned are in Nicolas Cope, *To Bind the Nation: Solomon kaDinuzulu and Zulu Nationalism* (Pietermaritzburg: University of Natal Press, 1993); Norman Etherington, *Preachers, Peasants, and Politics: South East Africa: African Christian Communities in Natal, Pondoland, and Zululand* (London: Royal Historical Society, 1978); James T. Campbell, *Songs of Zion: The African Methodist Episcopal Church in the United States and South Africa* (Athens: Ohio University Press, 1998); and see Janet Hodgson, "Soga and Dukwana: The Christian Struggle for Liberation in Mid-19th Century South Africa," *Journal of Religion in Africa*, 60 (1986), pp. 187–208; Robert Edgar and Hilary Sapire, *African Apocalypse: The Story of Nontetha Nkwenkwe, a Twentieth-Century South African Prophet* (Athens and Johannesburg: Ohio University Press and University of Witswatersrand Press, 2000); Paul Landau, "The Spirit of God, Pigs and Demons: the 'Samuelites' of Southern Africa," *Journal of Religion in Africa*, 29(3) (1999), pp. 313–40.

There were indeed some absurd legends about fabulous beings who, though credited with some sort of creative power, were not objects of worship. The only belief they held in the Supernatural was on that of the spirits of the departed [. . .].

Ideas about ancestors and political unity are here removed to the domain of legend and the supernatural. Although the mind of Mbotshane, or Nathaniel as he would be baptized,

was impregnated with these notions it yet had other thoughts which at times worked within him, and he was often heard to relate in later [years that] these crude beliefs did not satisfy the enquiries which increasingly would force themseves upon [him. Nearby] were some high pieces of rock near his father's kraal shaped and heaped one upon the other in a manner that suggested design, and in them Nathaniel was faced by a silent suggestion of the Almighty. While his youthful companions were away hunting or dancing [*bina*], Nathanial was often seen lying upon the ground intently gazing upon these miracles of stones wondering whose hand could have shaped and placed them thus. He tells that the conclusion in his own mind was that there must be some being whom his nation had not heard of. He had nothing [?] to help him beyond that conclusion so there it rested for the time.

Note that Mbotshane is named Nathaniel even though he had not yet taken the name. Internally, he has already been baptized. It is likely that Nathaniel as a pastor included this story in sermons. In it he intuitively grasps the existence of "the Almighty" on his own. Other traditions tell how Dingiswayo, Shaka, Sobhuza, or Ntsikana predicted the coming of change; sometimes a white man was visualized, riding a horse, holding a gun, the Bible, or some coins. Such tales put foreknowledge of the present in the past, a kind of prolepsis.[113]

In 1844, Chief Mswati settled the Rev. James Allison and his Wesleyan Methodist Missionary "Native Assistants" in five stations as a southwestern buffer against Mpande's Zulu kingdom, so as to protect his (Mswati's) control of the countryside around the Pongola River. This was a common thing to do. Mothibi of Dithakong, Moshoeshoe of Lesotho, and Andries Waterboer of Griquatown all sought to reinforce strategic parts of their borders in the same way. Northern Nguni polities were in flux throughout the 1840s, and one frayed edge of Swazi suzerainty lay in the hilly region of Mahamba and Mhlangampisi. The Rev. Allison, who obliging settled his assistants in a line of homesteads along the Swazi border, did not grasp how he was being used.

---

[113] Philip Bonner, *Kings, Commoners and Concessionaires: The Evolution and Dissolution of the Swazi State* (Oxford: Oxford University Press, 1982), pp. 41–57; and Hodgson in Elphick and Davenport (Eds.), p. 73; Elbourne, *Blood Ground*, ms., p. 300.

Thus, Johanne Kumalo began to teach in the confederation of homesteads in which Mbotshane was a ranked son. Mbotshane/Nathaniel at age 17 had "already passed through early heathen rites in preparation for marriage," and wore the woven-in *isicoco* ring on his head, the visible marker of regional Nguni manhood. New Christians sometimes objectified the Natal culture as libidinous, undisciplined, lazy. In a similar fashion, initiate experts passed through a period of rejecting the most common foods and other comforts of human sociality. Had Mbotshane behaved as he did before Kumalo's arrival, he might have entered a period of preparation for training at the foot of a local herbalist or divination expert.

Nathaniel [Mbotshane] became one of his [Johanne Kumalo's] smartest and most interested students. . . .

Better things however were in store for him than a course of life conformed to heathen customs. The Spirit of God laid hold of him as if it were already said in the Divine Counsel. Nathaniel soon became singled out from the rest of his confreres by deep seriousness and thoughtfulness.

Whilst the chief delight of the other people in having a missionary among them was the belief that it would lead to the termination of the loss of the land, Nathaniel's greatest concern was to learn from him how to how to end a worse warfare than the strife of [battle] – To find peace with God and bring a brotherhood about to rest in the Saviour.

The emphasis here is on the trope of internal struggle, which missionaries applied to what they saw as honest conversions, directly contrasted with political struggle. Christians' sermons and biomedical therapies appeared to work directly on the forces they termed good and evil (*bi* in this milieu), the evil of sicknesses, witchcraft, and misfortune, in the body. Countervailing forces fought for his soul (or image, or shadow, or throat/breath). It was in his body that good would prevail, with no appeal to the various constellations of kinfolk, relationships that were anyhow strained to breaking by warfare. A "worse warfare" than battle would resolve within him.

Teachers were esteemed, sometimes more than ordained men, who were often less charismatic individuals. If resident missionaries did not ordain black pastors because they feared losing control over their words, how much more did ordinary teachers plot their own course? Teachers-in-the-making could arrogate authority in turn by adducing the invisibility and interiority of the "internal battle" in turn.

On a Sunday morning in the early part of 1845, while attending Divine Service in the chapel, [Mbotshane] became overwhelmingly convinced that he must then and there surrender himself to God. He rose from his seat, threaded his way quickly through the crowded mass of nude and staring people crouched upon the floor, and made for the usual praying place in the neighboring mountains.

The "usual praying place!" What could that be, aside from the location of some half-forgotten element of the landscape, a grave or a point in history to be reoccupied. Others spoke of the moment of conversion as being "smitten" or rather, "broken through," "pierced," or "ruptured." An initiate "specialist" of the old order (*ngaka/inyanga*) was, at the same time, often "stabbed" by illness and moved to retreat to a mountain for more possession or "penetration." Speaking of punctured subjectivity was to deny culpability; the initiate does not seek gnostic knowledge, she has it thrust upon her. Here Mbotshane succumbed to a force that bade him eschew Johanne's oversight, let alone the Rev. Allison's, to retreat into the mountains that divided Chief (*kgosi/ inkosi*) Mpande's aggressive Zulu nation from Swaziland.[114]

There above without food or shelter [Mbotshane] spent the rest of the day and night and the whole of the day following, pleading and wrestling with God for a personal and conscious Salvation. Early on Tuesday morning he returned to Johanne with the joyful announcement that he had found the Saviour and knew himself to be the Child of God.

Needless to say this was not the approved practice among Methodists. If the account is taken literally, Mbotshane declared he himself was an *umntwana wenkosi enkulu*, which would have meant: I am the child of great chief *and* I am a child of God (as has been shown with "muleemo" [*modimo*] and Moshoeshoe). The statement would only resolve into one or the other meaning as people like Mbotshane in his actions created Christianity. He was claiming himself a place in a foreign hierarchy which he knew little about. Had he recognized Mpande or Mswazi as his *inkosi enkulu* he would have been pledging himself to the Zulu or Swazi nations instead of Christianity. These choices were mutually exclusive analogues of one another around the Pongola headwaters. As a Norwegian missionary said, after he makes some progress in preaching to Zulu listeners, "they always object, 'But then we should have to abandon Umpande.'"[115] Over the course of the following decades, the differences between modes, or contexts for being an *umntwana wenkosi enkulu*, were worked through. *Amakholwa* (Christians) in Natal had shirts, whereas maSwazi and amaZulu living north of the Thukela wore the *ibesha*. One involved -*bina* and -*khonza* (honoring, dancing, pledging to), the other involved -*khuleka* (Nguni, praying).

---

[114] Callaway, "The Initiation of a Zulu Diviner," in *Religious System.*

[115] Wettergreen, in *Norske Missionstidende, 19* (1864), p. 197, quoted in Torstein Jørgensen, "Zulu Responses to Norwegian Missionaries," in Twaddle and Hanson (Eds.), *Christian Missionaries and the State*, p. 91.

Women's groups and schoolhouses gave Christianity more of its quotidian meaning. By the 1910s, Christianity lay beside Zuluness, which was therefore redefined as an ethnicity or heritable fact in individuals. Z. K. Matthews recalled of his youth when his parents embraced traditions and Christian identity with no apparent division between them: "in their minds the values common to both had blended and become a whole."[116]

But the politics of the midcentury frontier were different. Mpande, the *inkosi enkulu* of the Zulu polity, wanted to make one more push to settle in Swaziland and to get away from his distrusted allies, the Boers. His unmarried regiments of men were to take Swazi wives and populate the new location. Chief Mswati's elder brother, Malambule, had assembled a regiment under his own authority and put his men in Mbotshane's home area in preparation for such an incursion. Then for some reason Mswati turned against Malambule, and sent men to attack him, and the Christians fled what would have been an unpleasant occupation. At some point, Mbotshane convinced a single unmarried sister, a woman with an ailment, to join him in his new adherence. For Mbotshane's senior half-brothers, the insult to their authority was clear. A sibling was claiming a status in a hierarchy that trumped the order in their family, connected to a new but somehow more ancient and greater (*khulu: unkulunkulu*) patriarch than theirs. They beat him senseless.

A murderous party, including some of his own brothers, were soon upon his back and before he had recovered from the exhaustion of the flight, he was assailed by his pursuers. They dragged him out of a hut in which he had taken refuge, stripped and beat him fiercely, over the head and body and then pitched what in they supposed to be the lifeless corpse into the grass.

Nathaniel however was not quite a corpse. The members of the mission party who witnessed the scene finding that there was still life in the body tenderly removed it back to the hut and washed the wounds. Contrary to all expectations the poor boy revived in a few days. All the native breathren [*sic*] having now assembled, the young sufferer was placed in the wagon and a start made for Natal.

This is a narrative cliché, not only in the invocation of the iconic pioneer "wagon," but also in the recovery "near death," which again draws on the framework of the passage to expertise. The theme would be replayed, for instance, in the prophet and leader Isaiah Shembe's 1906 autobiography. In that case too there is the echo of Christ's death on the cross, in which

[116] Z. K. Matthews, *Freedom for My People: The Autobiography of Z.K. Matthews: Southern Africa 1901–1968* (London: R. Collings, 1981), pp. 15–16, quoted by Richard Elphick, "Writing Religion into History," in Henry Bredekamp and Robert Ross (Eds.), *Missions and Christianity in South African History* (Johannesburg: University of Witswaterand Press, 1995), p. 20, n34.

"Ancestor" is recuperated fully as the bereft Father. Of course, the elderly Nathaniel had a deep familiarity with the Bible. In his recollection his brothers tore off his clothing, denying him his primary way of signaling his different status. The verb *go swa/ukufa* was less "to die" than to suffer major trauma, whatever happened next.[117] Nathaniel relocated to the farmland around Pietermaritzburg and was baptised eighteen months later. Women most likely supervised the rebirth. He became a teacher, reading and talking before Nguni Christians, who would mainly have been married women, probably low-status or noninheriting wives.

Nathaniel's textual presence is owed to the Wesleyan missionaries, to their "writing down" of him, fitting his unique odyssey into an acceptable Christianity. At the same time, however, home-grown culture brokers like Nathaniel were the people who gave content to the projects of orthodox Protestant churches. The congregations of "native agents" of various backgrounds, Paris Evangelical Society, Wesleyans, or as in Waterboer's state, ostensibly, the LMS, held loyalties that were often more ambiguous and closer to home than these Society designations suggest. Officials and missionaries at the turn of the century were often surprised to find fully functioning congregations in the Cape interior, in Namibia, and in the northern Transvaal; parishes organized locally and never formally affiliated to the confession they claimed. Nathaniel led an orthodox Methodist congregation seldom seen by European Christians or institutional representatives of Methodism.[118] Probably, he was formally ordained only near the end of his career, and it is only by chance that his story was recorded. He reminds us of the divorce between the world of texts and the lives of most South Africans, and so of how partial our perspective remains. Indeed, Christianity returned to Swaziland not with a European missionary, but with the Methodist *unzondelelo* movement of Daniel Msimang in 1881. The uses of such men always threatened to overspill the allotted frame, "in the sight of God."[119]

---

[117] See Peter Geschiere, *The Modernity of Witchcraft: Politics and the Occult in Post-colonial Africa* (Charlottesville: Univeristy of Virginia Press, 1997); W. D. Hammond-Tooke, *Boundaries and Belief: The Structure of a Sotho Worldview* (Johannesburg: University of Witswatersrand Press, 1981); and Isak Niehaus, "Witchcraft, Power and Politics: an Ethnographic Study of the South African Lowveld," Ph.D. dissertation, Anthropology, University of Witswatersrand, 1997, p. 23.

[118] J. Stuart, unpublished paper, "Zulu Contact with Civilized Races," cited in Jorgenson, "Zulu Responses," in Hansen and Twaddle (Eds.), *Christian Missionaries and the State*, p. 97, and James Stewart of Lovedale, cited in Gaitskell, "Girls' Education in South Africa," Chapter 9.

[119] Campbell, *Zion*, p. 107.

CONCLUSIONS AND QUESTIONS

I began with the concept that meaning resides in usage, seeing that praxis, or the embodied disposition to certain usages, must accommodate the changing world. The subsequent overview traced a genealogy of organizing concepts in transition, beginning with autonomy itself, and running parallel to the gradual proletarianization of most South Africans. However improbable an effort to comprehend changes of this sort, it is worse to treat concepts as absolutes, universal, and immobile, understood either well or badly from era to era and place to place. As Umberto Eco reminds us, no perfect language lies behind individual acts of translation.[120]

The consciousness of South Africans changed by engaging the world. The prognoses of experts dwindled in scope and relevance, their injunctions relating the body to the social body diverging from experience, as the relationships they mediated fragmented. Men exerted authority over nations, women, and juniors, in contexts that were themselves transformed by colonialism. Greatness and ancestry once offered ways of backdating political alliances to a stopping point of useful mutual identity; now both components were isolated and nominalized as God. Text-based fact replaced eloquence and collective judgment as a final appeal, the appeal to the state as recordkeeper. South Africans created innovative forms of dress, housing and speech, embracing some demands, rejecting others, while in general moving toward western conformity. Dance shifted from expressing, in concentrated form, the habitus of political interaction, to become a personal form of expression. Time and space tended to disengage from seasonal cycles. The notion that precolonial Africans believed unlikely things emerged, deriving from situations where settlers restated Africans' praxis as rules, rules that were clearly untrue in their world.

By the latter years of the nineteenth century, with the exploitation of diamonds and gold, people's consciousness of hierarchy and community had already been transformed. Conquered farmers nursed the hope of reconstituting themselves as a landed community and struggled to that end when they could. But new understandings of ethnicity also emerged among them: "Sotho" and "Zulu" and "Tsonga" linked people across national borders and past antagonisms, taking advantage of parochial orthographies, stereotypes, and the fields of influence touched by chiefs, clerks, and evangelists.[121] Indentured servants from the Indian subcontinent first came

[120] Eco, *Experiences*, p. 10.

[121] Shamil Jeppie, "Reclassifications: Coloured, Malay, Muslim," Chapter 4 in Zimitri Erasmus, *Coloured by History, Shaped by Place: New Perspectives on Coloured Identities in Cape Town* (Cape Town: Kwela, 2001); and chapters by Cheryl Hendricks, Pumla Dineo Gqola, and Thiven Reddy; Patrick Harries, "Field Sciences in Scientific Fields," in Saul Dubow (Ed.), *Science and Society in Southern Africa* (Manchester: Manchester University

to South Africa in 1860 and they too forged an ethnic consciousness. The Muharram festival, memorializing the death of Imam Husain, brought together not only different languages and castes, but Muslims with Hindus, so that whites called it "Coolie Christmas" – the common identity having no parallel in India itself. At the same time, Christianity unsettled colonial authorities, foreshadowing populist struggles to come. In 1884, Nehemiah Tile briefly reunited church and state (under the Thembu chief Ngangelizwe), much as some of the Bechuanaland Protectorate chiefs in the north were doing. Around the same time the African Methodist Episcopal Church began its dramatic expansion in South Africa, it and its daughter churches galvanizing thousands of semiliterate Africans. All these associations aimed for "the day when the black man shall have his freedom," in the fullest sense.[122]

Many questions remain for us to ponder. This chapter has dealt sparingly with the gendering and regendering of praxis. It has mostly bypassed the thoughts and self-presentations of elites, both white and black, in deference to others' efforts.[123] More might have been said about the changing culture of misfortune, disease, and witchcraft; about shifts in consumption and leisure activities; about sexual practices. Such topics are at present still difficult to trace in existing literatures. No rigorous linguistic analysis has been attempted, nor a real survey of indigenous literatures, music, grammar, or mindset.[124]

Press, 2001), Chapter 2; Mohammed Adhikari (Ed.), *Straatpraatjes: Language, Politics and Popular Culture in Cape Town, 1909–1922* (Pretoria: Schaik, 1996).

[122] Bill Freund, *Insiders and Outsiders: The Indian Working Class of Natal, 1910–1990* (Portsmouth: Heinemann, 1990); S. Bhana (Ed.), *Essays on Indentured Indians in Natal* (Leeds: Peepal tree, 1990), pp. 89–115; and Goolam Vahed, "Constructions of Community and Identity among Indians in Colonial Natal, 1860–1910: The Role of the *Muharram* Festival," *Journal of African History, 43* (2002), pp. 77–93; Christopher Bayly, *Indian Society and the Making of the British Empire* (Cambridge: Cambridge University Press, 1988); Switzer, *Ciskei,* 182 ff.; Christopher Saunders, "Tile and the Thembu Church: Politics and Independency on the Eastern Cape Frontier in the late 19th Century," *Journal of African History, 11*(4) (1970), pp. 553–70. "Freedom": quoting the judge at the trial of Enoch Mgijima after the Bullhoek massacre in 1921, cited in Chanock, *Making*, p. 34; Campbell, *Song, passim.*

[123] Manicom, "Ruling Relations"; de Kock, *Civilizing Barbarians*; and Catherine Higgs, *The Ghost of Equality: The Public Lives of D.D.T. Jabavu, 1885–1959* (Cape Town: David Philip, 1996); Tiyo Soga, *The Journal and Selected Writings of the Revererd Tiyo Soga* (Cape Town: Balkema, 1983); and Solomon T. Plaatje's writings, for example, Brian Willan (Ed.), Solomon T. Plaatje, *Native Life in South Africa: Before and Since the European War and the Boer Rebellion* (Oxford: Oxford University Press, 1991).

[124] But see Randall Packard, *White Plague, Black Labor: Tuberculosis and the Political Economy of Health and Disease in Southern Africa* (Berkeley: University of California Press, 1989); Landau, "Teeth"; Comaroff, *Body*; Isak A. Niehaus, Eliazaar Mohlala, Kally Shokane, *Witchcraft, Power and Politics: Exploring the Occult in the South African Lowveld* (Cape Town: Pluto Press, 2001); and Julie Livingston, "Long ago we were all still walking when we

In return for such silences, however, the chapter has, especially by situating South Africa as part of the subcontinent, considered a few trends in greater depth. One such was the elaboration of the stranger-absorbing motifs in indigenous South African community-formations, into apparently unbidden multiethnic, semi-Christian, Highveld-based political forms. From the 1840s, however, the power of the colony and its legal reach grew, and its power to name. Racial and ethnic categories depoliticized African organization, and religion redirected their political language – with, it was argued, unintended consequences in 1856–57. The patrilineal ancestor, in whose name citizens assembled polities, became on the one hand an inscrutable authority over individuals, and on the other, one's ethnic heritage. South Africa was once a place in which Africans attained power, produced their food, waged war, and migrated; over the century, it became a place where they did not. By 1900, Robert Ross has argued, most black South Africans were a "harshly exploited black labor force" living on white-owned farms. Their political language beneath the level of the state had also been curtailed to religion and custom, to vetted ritual forums. At the same time, as later populist movements would demonstrate, such a curtailment was never total, and perhaps cannot be.

died: Disability, Aging, and the Moral Imagination in Southeastern Botswana, c. 1930–1999," Ph.D. dissertation, History, Emory, 2001. C.f. Megan Vaughan, *Curing their Ills: Colonial Power and African Illness* (Stanford: Stanford University Press, 1991); and Jonathan Sadowsky, *Imperial Bedlam: Institutions of Madness in Colonial Southwest Nigeria* (Berkeley: University of California Press, 1999).

INDEX

Africa, debate on history of prior to colonialism, 4–5. *See also* Africans; Mozambique; South Africa; Zambia

African Methodist Episcopal Church, 447

African National Congress (ANC), 38

Africans: and acquisition of land in Transvaal, 350–2; black intellectuals and production of history in early twentieth century, 36–43; Boer relations with in 1840–1880 period, 340–50; concepts of chief, nation, and ancestor in consciousness of, 403–407; dance and song in consciousness of, 430–34; Great Trek and appropriation of African-occupied land, 338–40; group consciousness and depoliticization of fertility and health, 418–22; native administration and production of history in early twentieth century, 33–7; population of in Natal in 1840s, 358–9; servants as culture brokers and group consciousness of, 407–15; socialization and group consciousness among, 415–18; spatial boundaries and consciousness of, 434–9. *See also* Bantu and Bantu-speakers; chiefdoms and chiefs; Khoekhoen; San; South Africa; Tswana; Xhosa; Zulu kingdom

Afrikaans language, 31, 425

Afrikaners: and early forms of nationalism, 31–3; Great Trek and nationalism of, 288–93; and nationalism in twentieth century, 46; race and group consciousness of, 412–13. *See also* Afrikaans language; Boers; Zuid Afrikaansche Republiek (ZAR)

agriculture: and appearance of farming in eastern South Africa, 69–75; and Cape Colony in eighteenth century, 189–90; and interactions between early agriculturalists and foragers, 91–9. *See also* farming communities; food production; land tenure and land policy; livestock; maize; pastoralists

Ajayi, Jacob, 5n2

Albasini, Joao, 343, 417

Allison, James, 404, 441

Almeida, Francesco d', 170

Alverson, Hoyt, 401

amabutho (age sets of young men), 221–3, 229, 230, 238, 242, 250

amakholwa (Christian, educated Africans), 27

Amalinde, battle of, 267

ancestors: and organization of Bantu society, 398–400, 402–403; religious reverberations of in African consciousness, 403–407

Anderson, Benedict, 399

anthropology: emergence of historical in 1990s, 57–9; and liberal version of South African history, 47–8; and new departments in South African universities in 1920s, 36–7; and precolonial history of African societies, 51. *See also* ethnography

Lightning Source UK Ltd.
Milton Keynes UK
UKHW041437211118
332665UK00001B/27/P

9 780521 517942